Conceptions of Giftedness

Second Edition

What does it really mean to be gifted and how can schools or other institutions identify, teach, and evaluate the performance of gifted children? Gifted education is a crucial aspect of schooling in the United States and abroad. Most countries around the world have at least some form of gifted education. With the first edition becoming a major work in the field of giftedness, this second edition of *Conceptions of Giftedness* aims to describe the major conceptions of what it means to be gifted and how these conceptions apply to the identification, instruction, and assessment of the gifted. It will provide specialists with a critical evaluation of various theories of giftedness, give practical advice to teachers and administrators on how to put theories of gifted education into practice, and enable the major researchers in the field to compare and contrast the strengths of their theoretical models.

Robert J. Sternberg, PhD, is IBM Professor of Psychology and Education at Yale University and Director of the PACE Center at Yale. He was the 2003 President of the American Psychological Association. He is the author of more than 1,000 publications on topics related to cognition and intelligence. He has won numerous awards from professional associations and holds five honorary doctorates.

Janet E. Davidson is Associate Professor of Psychology at Lewis & Clark College, where she won the Professor of the Year award in 1997. She does research on several aspects of giftedness, including the roles that insight and metacognitive skills play in gifted problem-solving performance. In 1988, she won a Mensa Education and Research Foundation Award for Excellence.

Conceptions of Giftedness

Second Edition

Edited by

ROBERT J. STERNBERG
Yale University PACE Center

JANET E. DAVIDSON
Lewis & Clark College

UNIVERSITY PRESS

CAMBRIDGE UNIVERSITY PRESS
Cambridge, New York, Melbourne, Madrid, Cape Town, Singapore, São Paulo

Cambridge University Press
40 West 20th Street, New York, NY 10011-4211, USA

www.cambridge.org
Information on this title: www.cambridge.org/9780521838412

First edition published 1986
Second edition published 2005

Printed in the United States of America

A catalog record for this publication is available from the British Library.

Library of Congress Cataloging in Publication Data
Conceptions of giftedness / edited by Robert J. Sternberg, Janet E.
Davidson. – 2nd ed.
    p.   cm.
Includes bibliographical references.
ISBN 0-521-83841-x – ISBN 0-521-54730-x (pbk.)
1. Genius.   2. Gifted children – Psychology.   I. Sternberg, Robert J.
II. Davidson, Janet E.   III. Title.
BF412.C66   2005
153.9'8 – dc22   2004023791

ISBN-13   978-0-521-83841-2 hardback
ISBN-10   0-521-83841-x hardback

ISBN-13   978-0-521-54730-7 paperback
ISBN-10   0-521-54730-x paperback

Contents

Preface

Emanuel Feuermann was hired to the faculty of the University of Cologne at the age of 16 to teach the cello to students, all of whom were older than he was. He was a child prodigy who made good and became a superstar as an adult. In contrast, his brother, Sigmund Feuermann, was an even more amazing child prodigy than was Emanuel. But by the age of 31, Sigmund returned to his parents' home in Vienna in semiretirement. His career as a mature violinist had been, to a large extent, a bust. What is it that distinguishes gifted children who later go on to become gifted adults from those who do not? Indeed, what does it even mean to be gifted, and how can schools or other institutions identify, teach, and evaluate the performance of gifted children?

Gifted education is a crucial aspect of schooling in the United States and abroad. Most countries around the world have at least some form of gifted education. To help those with an interest in the field of gifted education, we edited a volume that was published in 1986 by Cambridge University Press, *Conceptions of Giftedness*. However, that book has been out of print for several years. Since the book went out of print, the senior editor of this volume has received many requests for permission to copy material from that book and also for a new edition of the book. This book is that new, second edition.

This book describes the major conceptions of what it means to be gifted and how these conceptions apply to the identification, instruction, and assessment of the gifted.

There are several reasons, we believe, for a book on conceptions of giftedness:

1. *Need for theoretical guidance.* Although there are many gifted programs, the large majority of them continue to be based on no theory in particular. Rather, they use off-the-shelf measures, such as tests of intelligence, creativity, or achievement, without any clear motivation

in the choice of tests. A book such as this one would help specialists in the field of giftedness choose a model with which to work.

2. *Need for translation of conceptions of giftedness into practice.* In retrospect, the first edition of the book probably overemphasized theory at the expense of information regarding how theory can be put into practice. Because the large majority of readers of the book are likely to be teachers, it is important that the book emphasize application in addition to theory. Translation into practice needs to deal with identification procedures, instructional methods, and instruments for assessment of achievement in gifted individuals.

3. *Need for comparison of conceptions.* Theorists often present their own work without giving full consideration to how their work compares with that of others. Yet, in order to evaluate competing conceptions, teachers of the gifted need to know the similarities and differences among the conceptions. They cannot be expected to figure out these similarities and differences on their own.

WHY PUBLISH A SECOND EDITION?

Since 1986, the field has changed, as have some of the major contributors to it. We therefore believe that the time is ripe for this second edition of *Conceptions of Giftedness*, which reflects the current state of the field.

Each author was asked to address the following five questions in his or her chapter, as well as any other questions he or she might wish to entertain:

1. What is giftedness?
2. How does your conception of giftedness compare with other conceptions?
3. How should gifted individuals be identified?
4. How should gifted individuals be instructed in school and elsewhere?
5. How should the achievement of gifted individuals be assessed?

You will find in this volume a wide range of views, from Borland's suggestion that we do not need a conception of giftedness, to Callahan and Miller's view that we need enhanced and more powerful conceptions. You, the reader, may choose, or come up with your own conception!

We have designed this book to be relevant to several potential audiences: students, teachers of the gifted, professors in gifted-education programs, parents of gifted children, and people who themselves have been labeled as gifted or believe they should have been. We hope you all enjoy and learn from our volume.

RJS

JED

Contributors

Sasha A. Barab
Indiana University
Bloomington, IN

James H. Borland
Teachers College
Columbia University
New York, NY

Beatrice L. Bridglall
Teachers College
Columbia University
New York, NY

Linda E. Brody
Johns Hopkins University
Baltimore, MD

Carolyn M. Callahan
University of Virginia
Charlottesville, VA

Laurence J. Coleman
University of Toledo
Toledo, OH

Tracy L. Cross
Ball State University
Muncie, IN

John F. Feldhusen
Purdue University
West Lafayette, IN

Joan Freeman
Middlesex University
London, England

Francoys Gagné
Université du Québec à Montréal
Montréal, Canada

Edmund W. Gordon
Teachers College
Columbia University
New York, NY

Elena L. Grigorenko
Yale University
New Haven, CT

Kurt A. Heller
University of Munich
Munich, Germany

Linda Jarvin
Yale University
New Haven, CT

Ida Jeltova
Fairleigh Dickinson University
Teaneck, NJ

Michael W. Katzko
Radboud University Nijmegen
Nijmegen, Netherlands

Tock Keng Lim
PsychMetrics International
Singapore

Richard E. Mayer
University of California,
  Santa Barbara
Santa Barbara, CA

Erin M. Miller
University of Virginia
Charlottesville, VA

Franz J. Mönks
Radboud University Nijmegen
Nijmegen, Netherlands

Susan J. Paik
Claremont Graduate University
  School of Educational Studies
Claremont, CA

Christoph Perleth
University of Rostock
Rostock, Germany

Jonathan A. Plucker
Indiana University
Bloomington, IN

Sally M. Reis
University of Connecticut
Storrs, CT

Joseph S. Renzulli
University of Connecticut
Storrs, CT

Nancy M. Robinson
University of Washington
Seattle, WA

Mark A. Runco
California State University,
  Fullerton
Fullerton, CA

The Norwegian School
  of Economics and
  Business Administration
Bergen, Norway

Dean Keith Simonton
University of California, Davis
Davis, CA

Julian C. Stanley
Johns Hopkins University
Baltimore, MD

Robert J. Sternberg
Yale University
New Haven, CT

Rena F. Subotnik
American Psychological
  Association
Washington, DC

Joyce VanTassel-Baska
The College of William
  and Mary
Williamsburg, VA

Catya von Károlyi
University of Wisconsin,
  Eau Claire
Eau Claire, WI

Herbert J. Walberg
Hoover Institution
Stanford University
Palo Alto, CA

Ellen Winner
Boston College
Boston, MA
Harvard's Project Zero
Cambridge, MA

Albert Ziegler
University of Ulm
Ulm, Germany

Gifted Education Without Gifted Children

The Case for No Conception of Giftedness

James H. Borland

I am quite confident that the conception of giftedness set forth in this chapter differs significantly from those found in the other chapters of this book in that the conception I advance is no conception at all. By that, I do not mean that I have chosen not to advance a conception of giftedness. Rather, I am actively advancing the idea of no conception of giftedness as a positive development for the field of gifted education.

To be clear about what I am advocating, let me state my position unequivocally. I believe that the concept of the gifted child is logically, pragmatically, and – with respect to the consequences of its application in American education – morally untenable and that the aims of the field of gifted education would have a greater likelihood of being realized if we were to dispense with it altogether.

Because I realize that this is a radical position for a contributor to this book to take, I want to clarify my motivation and my positionality before advancing my argument. I write as one who considers himself to be a scholar in and of the field of gifted education. I have taught in programs for gifted students, and my doctorate is in this field. I believe that there are individual differences in elementary and secondary students' school performance that probably derive from a complex of ability and motivational, social, cultural, sociopolitical, and other factors and that these have important educational implications. In other words, although I believe that all students are equal in their right to and need for an appropriate education, I do not believe that what constitutes an appropriate education is the same for all students born in a given calendar year. Educators must, to be effective and ethical, provide educational experiences that reflect the inescapable fact of individual differences in how and how well school students learn at a given time in a given subject. A one-size-fits-all curriculum makes no more sense to me than would a one-size-fits-all shoe.

Moreover, along with my colleagues in the gifted-education field, I believe that high-achieving or high-ability students are among those who are the most ill-served when curriculum and instruction are not differentiated. The basic beliefs that undergird the field, such as the conviction that it is wrong to think that bright students can succeed on their own if treated with a policy of benign neglect, are ones that I share. In other words, insofar as advocating for the educational needs of students who have historically been the recipients of services in this field, I think I differ from those who subscribe to the admittedly foundational belief that we cannot have gifted education without gifted children only with respect to means, not ends. That is, whereas we agree that it is essential to provide an appropriate education for students who have traditionally been labeled *gifted*, we disagree as to whether this requires gifted programs or even the concept of gifted children.

I also want to make it clear that my interest in gifted education is focused on educational programs intended to provide differentiated curriculum and instruction, not the development of precocious talent. I concede that there are gifted people, even gifted children, whose abilities in various pursuits clearly merit that label. A 10-year-old violinist who performs Beethoven's *Violin Concerto* with a major orchestra is indisputably a gifted child, as is a child who demonstrates prodigious accomplishment in chess or basketball or any demanding domain. However, these are not the people to whom the term "gifted child" is typically applied. That term is usually used to designate an appreciable number of students in a school with a "gifted program" who have been chosen to fill that program's annual quota. It is in that context, the context of educational policy and practice, that I believe that the concept of giftedness has outlived whatever usefulness it once may have had.

Each contributor to this volume was asked to address a series of five questions. The first, "What is giftedness?" is most central to my thesis, and I devote most of my space to it.

WHAT IS GIFTEDNESS?

My short answer to this question is that giftedness, in the context of the schools, is a chimera. But, because I am an academic, there is a predictably longer answer. I believe that the concept of the gifted student is incoherent and untenable on a number of grounds. The first of these is that the concept of the gifted child in American education is a social construct of questionable validity. The second is that educational practice predicated on the existence of the gifted child has been largely ineffective. The third is that this practice has exacerbated the inequitable allocation of educational resources in this country. I elaborate on each of these assertions in this section of the chapter.

The fourth component of my thesis is that the construct of the gifted child is not necessary for, and perhaps is a barrier to, achieving the goals that brought this field into existence in the first place. In other words, I argue that we can, and should, have gifted education without gifted children. I discuss this in the following section in responding to another of the questions we were asked to address, "How should gifted individuals be instructed in school and elsewhere?"[1]

THE QUESTIONABLE VALIDITY OF THE CONSTRUCT
OF THE GIFTED CHILD

There were no "gifted" children in the 19th century, simply because the construct of the gifted child had not yet been dreamed up. Gifted children began to exist, as far as I can tell, in the second decade of the 20th century as a result of a confluence of sociocultural and sociopolitical factors that made the creation of the construct useful. With the publication of *Classroom Problems in the Education of Gifted Children. The Nineteenth Yearbook of the National Society for the Study of Education* (Henry, 1920) at the end of that decade, the educational establishment signaled that it had acceded to the belief that there were, indeed, gifted children in our schools.

By situating the construction of giftedness in a particular place and time, I mean to suggest its historical contingency. That is, giftedness did not happen to be discovered in the second decade of the 20th century and to become progressively better understood in the third decade. Rather, the construct that emerged from that period reflects specific forces that served sociopolitical interests as they played out in the educational system. If the construction of the notion of gifted children was necessary, it was as a result of historical, not empirical, necessity. Giftedness emerged in the manner that it did, and has more or less remained, because it served, and continues to serve, the interests of those in control of the schools and the disciplines that informed and guided American education at that time.

Of the factors that I believe led to the invention of the construct of the gifted child, one, the mental testing movement, which began in the early 20th century, is frequently acknowledged. It is no coincidence that the person regarded as being the "father" of gifted education in this country, Lewis M. Terman, was also the developer of the Stanford–Binet Intelligence Scale and one of those most responsible for the widespread use of mental testing in American schools. The enthusiasm for the use of mental tests, especially IQ tests, at this time is not difficult to understand. These instruments were

---

[1] Although we were asked to address five questions, I will implicitly respond to three of them in addressing the two I have identified here. The question "How does your conception of giftedness compare with other conceptions?" has been discussed earlier and will be obvious to all but the most somnolent readers. "How should gifted individuals be identified?" and "How should the achievement of gifted individuals be assessed?" should also be obvious from the discussion that follows.

seen as being "scientific" at a time when that term was unambiguously one of approbation. Intelligence, another recently constructed concept, was widely believed to be general and quantitative; it was the same thing for everyone, and everyone had a certain amount of it, as Spearman (e.g., 1927), among others, argued. Mental tests were seen as modern tools that allowed professionals to assess the amount of this universal intelligence a person possessed, regardless of his or her life circumstances.

This modernist view of mental tests may seem quaint and naïve to us today, as so many things do through the lens of history, but the acceptance of these tests as valuable tools of objective science led to their extensive use in the schools to classify, guide, group, and, as some have argued, control children. And control was seen as a desideratum, owing to the increasing diversity of the school population, the second of the major factors that I see as creating the circumstances leading to the construction of the concept of the gifted child.

In the decade before World War I and again in the early 1920s, what is usually described as a "wave" of immigrants came to this country, not from the Western European nations from which most previous new arrivals had hailed, but from countries such as Austria, Hungary, Italy, and Russia. There were many children among these newcomers and many more born after the immigrants settled into their new homes. With respect to language, dress, religious beliefs, and a number of other cultural factors, these children were unlike the children with whom educators were used to dealing. This created a new set of challenges for public school authorities, who responded by making the "Americanization" of these children – that is, the homogenization of the school-age population through a set of common school experiences designed in large part to inculcate cultural norms derived from the Western European heritage of those in power – an explicit goal of American public education.

The diversity of the school population was increasing as a result of other factors as well. For example, greater differences in classroom performance were noted as compulsory education laws were enacted and enforced. One result of such laws was that students who would previously have eschewed school for the factory or the farm remained in school longer, despite having little interest in or apparent aptitude for formal schooling. There was also considerable variance in performance on the aforementioned mental tests, which is not surprising in retrospect, in light of the cultural, linguistic, and socioeconomic heterogeneity of the school population being tested. As testing became more common after the use of the Army Alpha and Army Beta tests in World War I, and as IQs were arrayed on the normal distribution, appreciable and predictable numbers of children fell one, two, three, or more standard deviations above and below the mean of 100.

The advent of widespread mental testing in the schools and a much more diverse student population were factors that nourished each other in a symbiotic fashion. The more diverse the population, the greater was the need for tools, such as tests, to quantify and control students. And the more students were tested and quantified, the more their linguistic, cultural, and socioeconomic diversity was reflected in variance in test scores, that is, in greater diversity in the school population.

One way to understand how this led to the construction of such concepts as giftedness is by referring to the work of Foucault (e.g., 1995; Gallagher, 1999). Foucault believed that control in modern society is not exerted through raw displays of state power (public executions, regal processions, and so forth) but through knowledge-producing disciplines. For Foucault, knowledge and power are inseparable. He wrote that "power and knowledge directly imply one another; . . . there is no power relation without the correlative constitution of a field of knowledge, nor any knowledge that does not presuppose and constitute at the same time power relations" (1995, p. 27).

Foucault believed that power develops through a number of processes, "small acts of cunning endowed with a great power of diffusion," that satisfy the need for knowledge on which discipline depends: "the success of disciplinary power derives no doubt from the use of simple instruments; hierarchical observation, normalizing judgment and their combination in a procedure that is specific to it, the examination" (1995, p. 170). These are his well-known "technologies of power."

Coming back to our discussion of testing and the growing diversity in the school population in the early 20th century, one can relate Foucault's first technology of power, *hierarchical observation*, to mental testing. Foucault discussed hierarchical observation in reference to the *panopticon*, Jeremy Bentham's plan for an ideal prison, in which each inmate lives, and is aware that he lives, under the ceaseless gaze of an anonymous guard "to induce in the inmate a state of conscious and permanent visibility that assures the automatic functioning of power" (1995, p. 201). By testing students, Foucault would argue, educators do essentially the same thing, reminding students that they are subordinate to adults who have the power to observe them from a position of power. Moreover, students internalize the knowledge that they are constantly being observed, that is, tested, and that the consequences of being observed are quite serious. This awareness is a powerful means of control.

Foucault's second technology of power, *normalizing judgment*, is, I believe, evident in the way educators responded to the growing heterogeneity of the school-age population in the early 20th century, specifically to the heterogeneity in test scores. Normalizing judgment is the process that "measures in quantitative terms and hierarchizes in terms of value the abilities, the level, the 'nature' of individuals . . . [and] traces the limit that will define difference in relation to all other differences, the external frontier of the abnormal" (Foucault, 1995, p. 183).

Normalizing judgment was manifested, first, in the reduction of multi-dimensional human diversity to a bipolar continuum and, second, in the labeling of certain regions of this continuum as the "normal" range and the rest as the "abnormal." Thus did students whose IQs fell below a certain score become "the subnormal" (Goddard's infamous "idiots," "imbeciles," and "morons," 1919), whereas students whose IQs exceeded a certain threshold (e.g., 140 in Terman's study, 1925/1959) became, in the original terminology, the "supernormal" and then, by the time of the publication of the *Classroom Problems in the Education of Gifted Children* (Henry, 1920), the "gifted."

It is important to stress that the central concept in this process, the *normal*, is, as Foucault demonstrates, an invention, not a discovery. It is imposed as an exercise of disciplinary (in both senses) power, as a way to control, even, to cite Foucault's most influential work, to discipline and punish. Foucault writes of the examination (the third technology of power, hierarchical observation combined with normalizing judgment) that "with it are ritualized those disciplines that may be characterized in a word by saying that they are a modality of power for which *individual difference* is relevant" (1995, p. 192, emphasis added). In other words, the disciplines of psychometrics and education made certain students "normal," "subnormal," and "supernormal" (or gifted).

It is useful to think about the genesis of the concept of giftedness and whether its advent in the field of education was inevitable or necessary (in an educational, psychological, or philosophical sense; a critical theorist might well argue that the creation of giftedness was a historical necessity arising from power relations playing out in an inequitable society). The concept did not arise *ex nihilo*. Clearly there was, and is, a situation in public education that could not be ignored. Children develop at different rates and in different ways, and this affects how and how well they deal with the traditional formal curriculum. To the extent that we are concerned with educational effectiveness and fairness, we need to make appropriate instructional and curricular modifications to respond to individual needs. The question is how to do this.

One possible response is to make curriculum and instruction flexible enough to accommodate the needs of all children, foregoing classification, labeling, and the examination in the Foucaultian sense that incorporates the normalizing gaze. This assumes that human variation is multifaceted, multidimensional – indeed, "normal" – and that the "average child" is different in many ways, some of them educationally significant, from other "average" children. However, the social and political conditions at the time the field of gifted education was created and the ascendant social efficiency movement in American public education (Kliebard, 1995) ensured that technologies of power, rather than more democratic forces, would shape the field.

Thus, the profession's response to the fact that children differ in the ways in which they interact with the school curriculum (or curricula, including the informal curriculum) was to believe that at least some of this difference is the result of the existence of distinct groups of children, including gifted children, who possess characteristics that separate them from the average. Once one accepts that there exist separate, qualitatively different groups, the inevitable next steps are to try to fashion a workable definition of the populations whose existence has been posited, to develop and implement identification procedures to locate these populations, and then to develop and implement separate educational provisions to meet their needs. This is the course of action that was adopted and, I would argue, why we have gifted children today.

There is an inescapable circularity in the reasoning here, especially with respect to giftedness. Sapon-Shevin writes, "Participants agree – sometimes explicitly and sometimes tacitly – to a common definition and then act as though that definition represents an objectifiably identifiable category. In this way, the category assumes a life of its own, and members of the school organization learn common definitions and rules" (1994, p. 121). The category was created in advance of the identification of its members, and the identification of the members of the category both is predicated on the belief that the category exists and serves, tautologically, to confirm the category's existence.

This simplistic dichotomization of humanity into two distinct, mutually exclusive groups, the gifted and the rest (the ungifted?), is so contrary to our experience in a variety of other spheres of human endeavor as to cause one to wonder how it has survived so long in this one. Is anything in human life that simple, that easily dichotomized? And are these two groups – the gifted and the rest – the discrete, discontinuous, structured wholes this crude taxonomy implies? That is, is giftedness really its own thing, qualitatively different from normality, making those who possess it markedly different, different in kind, from the rest of humanity? Can such a notion, expressed in those terms at least, really ring true for many people?

However implausible, these beliefs are implicit in the manner in which the word *gifted* is employed in both professional and everyday discourse. We glibly talk about "identifying *the* gifted"; about so-and-so being "truly gifted"; about the "mildly," "moderately," even "severely." In other words, we treat giftedness as a thing, a reality, something people, especially children, either have or do not have, something with an existence of its own, independent of our conceiving or naming of it.

Even a casual examination of the field of gifted education illustrates how difficult this dichotomy is to put into consistent and ultimately defensible practice. I frequently talk to my students about something I facetiously call "geographical giftedness," the not-uncommon phenomenon whereby a gifted child, so labeled by his or her school district, finds himself or herself no longer gifted after moving to another school system. If we hold on to the notion of two discrete classes of humans, defined by measurable traits into which children can be placed through correct educational assessment, we can explain this child's existential crisis only in terms of measurement error or one school system's adherence to an "incorrect" definition of giftedness.

But what is a "correct" definition of giftedness? Our failure, as a field, to answer that question is reflected in the multiplicity of definitions that have been proposed over the years. No one, to my knowledge, has as yet counted how many there are, but they are not few in number, nor are the differences between them insignificant. Take, for example, traditional psychometric definitions of academic giftedness that result in students with high IQs and reading and mathematics achievement being identified as gifted. Contrast this with Renzulli's (e.g., 1978) highly influential three-ring definition, in which only "above average" ability is required, combined with creativity and task commitment. Were a school district that had relied on a traditional IQ/achievement-test definition to change to Renzulli's definition, and if both old and new identification practices were based faithfully on the different definitions, there would be a pronounced change in the composition of the group of children labeled gifted. Some "gifted students" would stop being gifted, and some "nongifted students" would suddenly find themselves in the gifted category.

Not only do these two definitions of giftedness vary considerably from each other, but there is no empirical basis for choosing one over the other, or over any of the scores of others that have been proposed, because, I maintain, defining giftedness is a matter of values and policy, not empirical research. And in many, if not most, states, definitions are not mandated. The result is that local educators are free, indeed required, to choose, or write, a definition of giftedness for their program for gifted students, one that, to a large extent, determines who will and who will not be gifted. In other words, giftedness in the schools is something we confer, not something we discover. It is a matter of educational policy, not a matter of scientific diagnosis. It is a social construction, not a fact of nature.

All of this strongly suggests that "the gifted" and "the average," rather than being preexisting human genera, are labels for socially constructed groups that are constituted, in both theory and practice, in ways that are far from consistent and, in many cases, anything but logical, systematic, or scientific. Giftedness has become, and probably always was, what Stuart Hall (e.g., 1997), writing about race, calls a "floating signifier," a semiotic term "variously defined as a signifier with a vague, highly variable, unspecifiable or nonexistent signified. Such signifiers mean different things to different people: they may stand for many or even *any* signifieds; they may mean whatever their interpreters want them to mean" (Chandler, 2001, p. 33). Thinking about gifted children in the schools is, therefore, not a mirroring of nature but an invented way of categorizing children who must be judged on a utilitarian or pragmatic basis. Thus, the basic question to ask about giftedness is not whether giftedness exists but whether the outcomes of the application of the construct, especially in the field of education, are beneficial, innocuous, or harmful.

THE QUESTIONABLE VALUE AND EFFICACY OF GIFTED EDUCATION

Some have responded to the assertion that giftedness is a social construct by arguing that most things can be accurately so designated. James Gallagher (1996) writes,

We should admit that "gifted" is a constructed concept... But "opera singer" is a constructed concept, "shortstop" is a constructed concept, "boss" is a constructed concept; every concept that we use to describe human beings is a constructed concept. Is giftedness an educationally useful construct? That is the important question. (p. 235)

I think Gallagher is right to argue that we should apply utilitarian and pragmatic criteria to the construct rather than ontological ones, but I would argue that the application of these criteria to the constructs he equates with giftedness reveals that, unlike giftedness, they are functional categories of demonstrable necessity. Opera exists; without opera singers, there is no opera. Baseball, thankfully, exists as well, and without a shortstop, there is no baseball team. Schools also exist, but can one reasonably argue that without gifted children there would be no schools?

One central question regarding the utility of the construct of the gifted child concerns the efficacy of gifted programs. I believe there is little evidence that such programs are effective. Most programs for gifted students in this country take the form of part-time "pull-out" programs, in which students spend most of their time in regular heterogeneous classrooms that they leave for a period of time each week to meet with a special teacher and other students identified as gifted to receive some form of enrichment (Shore, Cornell, Robinson, & Ward, 1991). However, according to Slavin (1990), "well-designed studies of programs for the gifted generally find few effects of separate programs for high achievers unless the programs include acceleration" (p. 486). In other words, there is ample evidence that acceleration, as a means of differentiating the curriculum for high-ability students, does what it is intended to do: match content to the instructional needs of advanced students. Similar evidence that enrichment is an effective means of meeting goals, other than the goal of providing enrichment, is exiguous at best (Horowitz & O'Brien, 1986).

Over a decade ago, Shore et al., in their landmark *Recommended Practices in Gifted Education* (1991), wrote that since "Passow (1958) remarked on the dearth of research on enrichment three decades ago, . . . the situation has changed little" (p. 82). In the absence of empirical data, they concluded that the frequently recommended practice, "Enrichment should be a program component," was not among those supported, wholly or in part, by research but was instead among the practices "applicable to all children" (p. 286).

Not only is evidence supporting the efficacy of pull-out enrichment programs scanty, but what does exist is not very convincing. Two studies stand out as worthy of serious consideration. In a meta-analysis focusing on the effects of pull-out programs, Vaughn, Feldhusen, and Asher (1991) conclude that "pull-out models in gifted education have significant positive effects" (p. 92). However, this meta-analysis drew on only nine studies and examined outcomes related to four dependent variables. Because a maximum of three studies was used to compute effect sizes, there is reason to question the validity, robustness, and replicability of this conclusion.

An admirable attempt to address the problem of lack of efficacy studies was the Learning Outcomes Study (Delcourt, Loyd, Cornell, & Goldberg, 1994). The subjects of this study were 1,010 students from 10 states who were either in gifted programs, including pull-out programs, or in no program at all. Students in the latter group included students identified as gifted, formally and informally, and others nominated by teachers as comparison subjects. The authors concluded that the students in their sample who were in gifted programs academically outperformed both students given special provisions within heterogeneous classrooms and students receiving no provisions at all.

The problem with this conclusion is that the students whose academic performance was superior were formally identified as gifted and placed in special programs. The students with whom they were compared were either students identified as gifted but not placed in programs or students not identified as gifted at all (and thus not in programs). What Campbell and Stanley (1963) call "selection" is, unfortunately, as good an explanation for achievement differences as is program type or presence of a program. That is, there is reason to suspect that the groups were not comparable, that students formally identified and placed in gifted programs were different in nontrivial ways from students who were not in programs and those who were not identified as gifted, and that these differences, as much as anything else, might have affected the outcomes.

In short, there is remarkably little evidence that the most common type of programming for gifted students is effective. However, as Slavin (1990) argues, and as Shore et al. (1991) agree, the efficacy of one approach advocated for gifted students, acceleration, has research support. Does this not suggest that some gifted programs are effective? I believe not. Few programs identified as gifted programs use acceleration as their primary means of meeting the needs of gifted students because, although it is strongly supported by research data, acceleration is controversial, misunderstood, and even feared (e.g., Coleman & Cross, 2001; Southern & Jones, 1991).

Moreover, schools can, and do, employ acceleration without having gifted programs per se. Acceleration does not require identifying students as "gifted," special teachers, pull-outs, or any of the ordinary trappings of traditional gifted programs. If a student can work ahead of his or her age peers in, say, mathematics, he or she can simply be allowed to do so; there is no reason to identify the student as gifted. To sound a theme to which I return later, acceleration is one example of how gifted education can be effected without either gifted programs or gifted students.

GIFTED EDUCATION AND SOCIAL AND EDUCATIONAL INEQUITY

From the beginning, gifted education has been criticized for being at odds with education in a democracy and for violating principles of equity that are, or ought to be, paramount in our society. Gifted programs and their proponents have been called "elitist" and worse; advocates of gifted education have been seen as the last-ditch defenders of tracking and other damaging educational practices (Oakes, 1985). Educators in this field have vigorously countered these charges, denying that their goals are anti-egalitarian and that gifted programs are necessarily antidemocratic.

Defenders of the field, of whom I have been one (e.g., Borland, 1989), are, I believe, sincere in advocating gifted programs as a means of helping to realize the goal of an appropriate education for all children. They see gifted education as redressing a wrong, as a way of making the educational system meet the legitimate needs of an underserved minority. Moreover, professionals in gifted education believe that appropriate educational programs for students identified as gifted can be implemented without being elitist, racist, sexist, or blighted by socioeconomic inequities.

If, as I believe, the intentions of educators in the field of gifted education are unexceptionable, I also think that the results of our efforts too often betray the purity of our intentions. Sufficient evidence exists to suggest that the practice of gifted education is rife with inequities that have been extremely difficult to eliminate. Racial inequalities in the identification of gifted students have been a constant throughout our history (see, for example, Borland & Wright, 1994; Ford, 1996; Ford & Harris 1999; Passow, 1989), and they persist today.

With regard to socioeconomic inequity, which, in our society is not unrelated to racial and ethnic inequity, The National Educational Longitudinal Study of eighth-grade programs for gifted students by the U.S. Department of Education (1991) dramatically reveals the extent of the problem. Data from this study indicate that students whose families' socioeconomic status places them in the top quartile of the population are about five times more likely to be in programs for gifted students than are students from families in the bottom quartile. Despite decades of efforts to eliminate racial and socioeconomic imbalances in how gifted students are identified and educated, gifted programs have continued to serve White middle-class and upper-middle-class children to a degree disproportionate to their numbers in the population while underserving poor children and children of color. It is worth repeating that this has nearly always been seen, within the field, as wrong and remediable. However, the persistence of the problem tempts one to question just how tractable the problem is within the field as it is currently established (see Borland & Wright, 2001, for a pessimistic speculation).

Moreover, there have been instances in which gifted programs have served purposes that few, if any, within the gifted education field could countenance. According to Sapon-Shevin,

Within large urban districts, particularly those characterized by impoverished, struggling schools and large, ethnically diverse populations, gifted programs (including gifted magnet programs) have served (and sometimes been promoted) as a way of stemming *white flight*; by providing segregated programming for "gifted students," some white parents – whose children are in the gifted program – will remain within the district . . . (1994, p.35)

I think that two things are indisputably true. The first is that professionals in the field of gifted education, no less than any other group of educators, are opposed to racial and other forms of inequity and are committed to fairness in access to education. Indeed, most would argue that educational equity is what brought them to the field in the first place. The second is that, despite the best of intentions, gifted education, as historically and currently practiced, mirrors, and perhaps perpetuates, vicious inequities in our society.

HOW SHOULD GIFTED INDIVIDUALS BE INSTRUCTED?

Gifted Education Without Gifted Children

If, as I have argued above, (a) the construct of the gifted child, as it is widely understood in American education, is neither required nor supported empirically or logically, (b) the acceptance of this construct has led to practice that fails to satisfy both utilitarian and pragmatic criteria, and (c) the practice of gifted education, contrary to the goals and values of the overwhelming majority of its advocates, has too often had unfortunate social and moral consequences, this should force us to consider alternatives, both to our practice and to our field's foundational axiomatic base.

The alternative I propose is that we try to conceive of gifted education without gifted children. In other words, I am suggesting that we dispense with the concept of giftedness – and such attendant things as definitions, identification procedures, and pull-out programs – and focus instead on the goal of differentiating curricula and instruction for all of the diverse students in our schools. Curriculum, after all, is the field of gifted education's *raison d'être*. The only justification for gifted programs is a special educational one, grounded in a belief that the regular curriculum designed to meet the needs of most students is inappropriate for some students who, by virtue of disability or ability, are exceptional and will not receive the education to which they are entitled unless the curriculum is modified. Gifted education has as its major goal and justification curriculum differentiation as a way of making education fairer and more effective. If differentiating the curriculum for students traditionally labeled "gifted" is the justification and the goal of the field of gifted education, then such things as defining giftedness, identifying "the gifted," and preparing teachers to work in gifted programs are merely means to this greater end. As such, professionals in the field are subject to questions as to whether they further the end they serve.

So, how best to achieve our goal of providing not only a differentiated curriculum but a *defensible* differentiated curriculum for the students whose needs are our particular focus in this field? Does it make sense to start by positing the existence of a class of individuals called *gifted children* and then to wrestle with the problem of defining giftedness, something on which we have not agreed, and then move to the process of identification, whereby we endeavor to separate "the gifted" from the rest, and finally to proceed to the development of differentiated curricula, reserved exclusively for those identified as gifted? Or does it make more sense to start with the curriculum itself, which, after all, is the goal of our efforts? In suggesting that we consider gifted education without gifted children, I am urging that we direct our efforts toward curriculum differentiation, bypassing the divisive, perhaps intractable, problems of defining and identifying giftedness. Were we to set as our goal the creation of schools in which curricula and instruction mirrored the diversity of the students found in classrooms, and were we to achieve this goal, the only legitimate aim of gifted education would be achieved.

In such schools, the idea of "normal" and "exceptional" children would, for the most part, be abandoned, as would the procrustean core curriculum into which students have to fit or be labeled "exceptional." Curricula and instruction would be predicated on students' current educational needs. For example, our expectations for students' learning in, say, mathematics would be determined by what they now know and what instruction they demonstrably need in that subject, not on whether their ages mark them for the third-grade curriculum, the fourth-grade curriculum, or whatever. For students who are mathematically precocious, the differentiated curriculum would not be what Stanley (see Benbow, 1986) calls "busy work," "cultural enrichment," or "irrelevant academic enrichment," but a mathematics curriculum that is appropriate for these students with respect to its pace and its level of challenge.

Moreover, we would not be in the illogical position in which we now find ourselves, with an educational system predicated on the following beliefs: (a) the majority of students in our schools are unexceptional or normal, and their curricular and instructional needs at any given time are determined by their year of birth; (b) some students have disabilities, and their curricular and instructional needs are determined by the nature of their disabilities; (c) some students are gifted, and their curricular and instructional needs are determined by any one of a number of diverse conceptual rationales and any one of a number of diverse educational models and schemes; and (d) the existence and constitution of the aforementioned groups are determined, in no small part, by race, ethnicity, and socioeconomic status. Thus, not only would making differentiated curricula and instruction the norm for all students go a long way toward meeting the needs of students traditionally labeled "gifted," it would make schooling more effective and humane for many students labeled "disabled" as well as all of those students thrown together in that agglomeration known as the "normal" or "average," a group that, in practice, is largely educationally undifferentiated but that, in reality, is remarkably diverse.

The idea of inclusive schools with heterogeneous classes, no labeling of students, and differentiated, responsive curricula and instruction has been advanced before by, among others, advocates of inclusion in the field of special education (e.g., Stainback & Stainback, 1990) and critics of gifted education (e.g., Sapon-Shevin, 1994, 1996). However, among those within the field of gifted education, this notion has been met either with hostility and suspicion or assertions that it is too idealistic and impractical, given the realities of contemporary American education. Too many, including myself not very long ago (see, for example, Borland, 1996b), react to criticisms of gifted programs as if they were attacks on the idea that high-achieving students require appropriately differentiated curricula, defending the means, not the end, of gifted education and wasting energy trying to preserve gifted programs instead of considering whether there is a better way to achieve our goals (Borland, 1996a). Not only do I think we can remain true to our commitment to capable students by considering, and ultimately adopting, alternatives to gifted programs, but in light of the exiguous evidence for the effectiveness of our traditional practice in this field, I think we can become even more effective advocates for these students by doing so.

With those who argue that it is easier to advocate than it is to create inclusive schools with curricula and instruction that are responsive to the diverse needs of individual students – schools in which the labels "normal," "disabled," and "gifted" not only are eschewed but make no sense – I can only agree. However, if one believes that such a state of affairs would make for a system of education that is not only more effective but more just, one is compelled at least to try to envision what would be required to make it a reality (see Borland, 2003, for some suggestions).

It is important to stress the direct and reciprocal linkage between heterogeneous classes in which diverse groups of children without labels learn together happily and effectively and the practice of differentiating curricula and instruction. Educationally inclusive diversity demands differentiation. The alternative is not to respect the difference and uniqueness of each child and to force individual children to conform to a one-size-fits-all curriculum, which inevitably, I believe, leads us to such concepts as "the normal" and "the abnormal," and subjects the inescapable and delightful variegation that is humanity to Foucault's normalizing judgment.

A Paradigm Shift in Gifted Education

Changing practice within a well-established field is difficult. Convincing professionals in that field to abandon what most of them would view as its defining construct is more difficult yet. I have suggested that we try conceiving of gifted education without gifted children. I hope the foregoing discussion has helped some readers view conceiving of the field in that way as a possibility, and perhaps this could be a prelude to real change. As Susan Gallagher writes, for change to take place, "we need to recognize how our taken-for-granted way of thinking from within the discipline's meaning-making system impacts the educational process in perhaps unintended ways" (1999, p. 69).

Actually to abandon the construct of the gifted child and to proceed accordingly would truly constitute a paradigm shift, to borrow an overused and frequently misused term from Thomas Kuhn's *The Structure of Scientific Revolutions* (1962/1996). In this landmark work of intellectual history, Kuhn attempts to explain how "normal science," which he defines as "research firmly based on one or more past scientific achievements, achievements that some particular scientific community acknowledges for a time as supplying the foundation for its further practice" (p. 10), changes over time. Why, Kuhn asks, do scientists working today believe different things, ask different questions, proceed in methodologically different ways from their colleagues in, say, the early 19th century?

Kuhn's explanation relies on the concept of the "paradigm," which Phillips defines as "a theoretical framework . . . that determines the problems that are regarded as crucial, the ways these problems are to be conceptualized, the appropriate methods of inquiry, the relevant standards of judgment, etc." (1987, p. 205). A paradigm is the complex of theories and practices that constitutes the prevailing world view and the accepted *modus operandi* of scientists, and, as such, it is often what is distilled in textbooks as scientific truth and scientific method. A paradigm allows normal science to proceed; indeed, Kuhn argues, a paradigm is necessary for scientific inquiry. Inevitably, however, inquiry yields empirical data that are inconsistent with the prevailing paradigm. Often this leads to modifications of principles and theories that alter, but do not undermine, the paradigm. However, sooner or later, the reigning paradigm cannot accommodate the increasing accumulation of data unpredicted by and contrary to its fundamental bases. At that point, the paradigm has to give way to a new one that can account for and explain new knowledge.

If what I am proposing, gifted education without gifted children, is ever to evolve beyond the level of a thought experiment, something equivalent to a paradigm shift in gifted education will be required. I do not underestimate either the difficulty that would entail or the resistance it would engender. Our equivalent to normal science, which one could call *normal practice*, is, to quote Kuhn with multiple elisions, "firmly based upon...past...achievements...that...supply...the foundation for...further practice" (1962/1996, p. 10). These are the achievements of such pioneers as Terman (1925/1959) and Hollingworth, who gave the field its start and its professional respectability in the first half of the 20th century, and those of a host of leaders who reestablished gifted education as an integral aspect of American education during the last quarter of that century.

If something as radical as a paradigm shift in gifted education appears unlikely, the same might be said of maintaining the status quo. Normal practice in the field of gifted education – sorting students on the basis of being identified, or not identified, as gifted and then temporarily removing those identified from their heterogeneous classes to receive curricular enrichment and then return to join their nonidentified peers – has held sway in this field since the publication of the landmark Marland Report (Marland, 1972) almost 30 years ago. The model has come under criticism from many outside the field (e.g., Margolin, 1994, 1996; Oakes, 1985; Sapon-Shevin, 1994, 1996) and, increasingly, from some within. Moreover, it has produced very little with respect to demonstrable positive educational results.

There appear to be three possible courses of action for the field of gifted education with respect to the traditional paradigm. One is to cling to it steadfastly, ignoring or deflecting criticism and hoping for a return of more congenial *zeitgeist*. I think this is unrealistic and ignores substantive changes in how educators think about diversity, grouping, exceptionality, and related issues. For example, the notion of exceptionalities, such as giftedness, being rooted in medical or psychometric necessity instead of reflecting historical and sociocultural forces, is increasingly under attack (see, for example, Franklin, 1987; Sleeter, 1987). It would require an unusually struthious stance on our part to believe that all of this will simply go away and we can return to the halcyon days of proliferating pull-out programs.

A second possibility when a paradigm is threatened by discrepant findings is to modify, but not to abandon, the paradigm to accommodate the data that do not fit it. This strategy can be seen in some recent writing in the field, including some of mine (e.g., Borland & Wright, 1994), in which proposals to remedy some of the field's more egregious failings, such as the chronic underrepresentation of poor children and children of color in gifted programs, have been advanced. However, the problems persist, and in a recent paper (Borland & Wright, 2001), we contemplate the possibility, rooted in Isaiah Berlin's notion of *value pluralism* (see Berlin, 1990; Gray, 1996), that there is no attainable reality in which we can effect the reconciliation of such indisputable goods as educational equity and such putative goods as differentiated programs for students labeled gifted. In other words, there may be no way to tinker with the paradigm, and its derivative normal practice, so that such things as effective education and equitable education can coexist with gifted education.

The third possibility is the fundamental change whose consideration I have been urging throughout this chapter. As radical as this may seem to some, it may be the only choice facing the field if, as I suspect, the prevailing paradigm comes to be seen either as something held on to by a progressively smaller band of retrograde gifted education stalwarts or as a framework in which indispensable educational, social, and moral goods cannot coexist. If that were to become the case, we might be faced with the paradox of viewing the gifted education without gifted children as the only way to ensure the field's viability.

References

Benbow, C. P. (1986). SMPY's model for teaching mathematically precocious students. In J. S. Renzulli (Ed.), *Systems and models for developing programs for the gifted and talented* (pp. 1–26). Mansfield Center, CT: Creative Learning Press.

Berlin, I. (1990). *The crooked timber of humanity: Chapters in the history of ideas* (H. Hardy, Ed.). Princeton, NJ: Princeton University Press.

Borland, J. H. (1989). *Planning and implementing programs for the gifted.* New York: Teachers College Press.

Borland, J. H. (1996a). Gifted education and the threat of irrelevance. *Journal for the Education of the Gifted, 19,* 129–147.

Borland, J. H. (1996b). [Review of *Playing Favorites* by Mara Sapon-Shevin]. *Roeper Review, 18,* 309–311.

Borland, J. H. (2003). The death of giftedness. In J. H. Borland (Ed.), *Rethinking gifted education* (pp. 105–124). New York: Teachers College Press.

Borland, J. H., & Wright, L. (1994). Identifying young, potentially gifted, economically disadvantaged students. *Gifted Child Quarterly, 38,* 164–171.

Borland, J. H., & Wright, L. (2001). Identifying and educating poor and underrepresented gifted students. In K. A. Heller, F. J. Mönks, R. J. Sternberg, & R. F. Subotnik (Eds.). *International handbook of research and development of giftedness and talent* (pp. 587–594). London: Pergamon Press.

Campbell, D. T., & Stanley, J. C. (1963). *Experimental and quasi-experimental designs for research.* Chicago: Rand McNally.

Chandler, D. (2001). *Semiotics for beginners.* Retrieved from http://www.aber. ac.uk/media/ Documents/S4B/semo2a.html

Coleman, L. J., & Cross, T. L. (2001). *Being gifted in school: An introduction to development, guidance, and teaching.* Waco, TX: Prufrock Press.

Delcourt, M. A. B., Loyd, B. H., Cornell, D. G., & Goldberg, M. D. (1994). *Evaluation of the effects of programming arrangements on student learning outcomes.* Charlottesville, VA: The National Research Center on the Gifted and Talented.

Ford, D. Y. (1996). *Reversing underachievement among gifted Black students.* New York: Teachers College Press.

Ford, D. Y., & Harris, J. J. (1999). *Multicultural gifted education.* New York: Teachers College Press.

Foucault, M. (1995). *Discipline and punish: The birth of the prison* (A. Sheridan, Trans.). New York: Vintage. (Original work published 1975.)

Franklin, B. M. (1987). The first crusade for learning disabilities. In T. Popkewitz (Ed.), *The formation of school subjects: The struggle for creating an American institution* (pp. 190–209). London: Falmer.

Gallagher, J. J. (1996). A critique of critiques of gifted education. *Journal for the Education of the Gifted, 19,* 234–249.

Gallagher, S. (1999). An exchange of gazes. In J. L. Kinchloe, S. R. Steinberg, & L. E. Villeverde (Eds.), *Rethinking intelligence* (pp. 69–84). New York: Routledge.

Goddard, H. H. (1919). *Psychology of the normal and the subnormal.* New York: Dodd Mead.

Gray, J. (1996). *Isaiah Berlin.* Princeton, NJ: Princeton University Press.

Hall, S. (Ed.). (1997). *Representation: Cultural representations and signifying practices:*Vol. 2. *Culture, media and identities.* Beverly Hills, CA: Sage.

Henry, T. S. (1920). *Classroom problems in the education of gifted children. The nineteenth yearbook of the National Society for the Study of Education (Part II).* Chicago: University of Chicago Press.

Hollingworth, L. S. (1929). *Gifted children: Their nature and nurture.* New York: Macmillan.

Horowitz, F. D., & O'Brien, M. (Eds.) (1986). *The gifted and talented: Developmental perspectives* (pp. 99–123). Washington, DC: American Psychological Association.

Kliebard, H. M. (1995). *The struggle for the American curriculum.* New York: Routledge.

Kuhn, T. S. (1962/1996). *The structure of scientific revolutions.* Chicago: University of Chicago Press.

Margolin, L. (1994). *Goodness personified: The emergence of gifted children.* New York: Aldine de Gruyter.

Margolin, L. (1996). A pedagogy of privilege. *Journal for the Education of the Gifted, 19,* 164–180.

Marland, S. P. (1972). *Education of the gifted and talented. Report to Congress.* Washington, DC: U.S. Government Printing Office.

Oakes, J. (1985). *Keeping track: How schools structure inequality.* New Haven, CT: Yale University Press.

Passow, A. H. (1989). Needed research and development in educating high ability children. *Roeper Review, 11,* 223–229.

Phillips, D. C. (1987). *Philosophy, science, and social inquiry.* Oxford, England: Pergamon.

Renzulli, J. S. (1978). What makes giftedness? *Phi Delta Kappan, 60,* 180–184, 261.

Sapon-Shevin, M. (1994). *Playing favorites: Gifted education and the disruption of community.* Albany, NY: State University of New York Press.

Sapon-Shevin, M. (1996). Beyond gifted education: Building a shared agenda for school reform. *Journal for the Education of the Gifted, 19,* 194–214.

Shore, B. M., Cornell, D. G., Robinson, A., & Ward, V. S. (1991). *Recommended practices in gifted education: A critical analysis.* New York: Teachers College Press.

Slavin, R. E. (1990). Achievement effects of ability grouping in secondary schools: A best-evidence synthesis. *Review of Educational Research, 60,* 471–499.

Sleeter, C. E. (1987). Why is there learning disabilities? In T. Popkewitz (Ed.), *The formation of school subjects: The struggle for creating an American institution* (pp. 210–237). London: Falmer.

Southern, W. T., & Jones, E. D. (Eds.) (1991). *The academic acceleration of gifted children.* New York: Teachers College Press.

Spearman, C. (1927). *The abilities of man.* New York: Macmillan.

Stainback, W., & Stainback, S. (1990). *Support networks for inclusive schooling: Interdependent integrated education.* Baltimore: Brookes.

Terman, L. M. (1925/1959). *Genetic studies of genius.* Stanford, CA: Stanford University Press.

United States Department of Education. (1991). *National educational longitudinal study 88. Final report: Gifted and talented education programs for eighth grade public school students.* Washington, D.C.: United States Department of Education, Office of Planning, Budget, and Evaluation.

Vaughn, V. L., Feldhusen, J. F., & Asher, W. J. (1991). Meta-analyses and review of research on pull-out programs in gifted education. *Gifted Child Quarterly, 35,* 92–98.

2

Youths Who Reason Exceptionally Well Mathematically and/or Verbally

Using the MVT:D⁴ Model to Develop Their Talents

Linda E. Brody and Julian C. Stanley

The Study of Mathematically Precocious Youth (SMPY) was established at Johns Hopkins University in 1971 by Professor Julian Stanley to help youths who reason extremely well mathematically find the educational resources they need to achieve their full potential (Benbow & Stanley, 1983; Keating, 1976; Stanley, 1977; Stanley, Keating, & Fox, 1974). After administering above-grade-level tests to identify students with advanced mathematical reasoning abilities, SMPY provided counseling and created programs to meet their academic needs. Eventually, university-based talent centers were established around the country to continue the practices SMPY pioneered. Because SMPY's methods for developing talent evolved over time in a very pragmatic way, that is, in response to the needs of individual students, the psychological and conceptual bases for this approach have not been especially emphasized in the literature.

In the first edition of this book, for example, Stanley and Benbow (1986) suggested that SMPY was "not concerned much with conceptualizing giftedness" and had "not spent much time contemplating the psychological underpinnings of giftedness" (p. 361). However, Duke University psychologist Michael Wallach, in a review of one of SMPY's early books (Stanley, George, & Solano, 1977), observed that:

What is particularly striking here is how little that is distinctly psychological seems involved in SMPY, and yet how very fruitful SMPY appears to be. It is as if trying to be psychological throws us off the course and into a mire of abstract dispositions that help little in facilitating students' demonstrable talents. What seems most successful for helping students is what stays closest to the competencies one directly cares about: in the case of SMPY, for example, finding students who are very good at math and arranging the environment to help them learn it as well as possible. One would expect analogous prescriptions to be of benefit for fostering talent at writing, music, art, and any other competencies that can be specified in product or performance terms. But all this in fact is not unpsychological; it is simply different psychology (Wallach, 1978, p. 617).

There was always a strong rationale behind the choices and decisions that were made by SMPY (Stanley, 1977). Three principles from developmental psychology, in particular, have contributed to the programmatic recommendations that were adopted. These principles are that learning is sequential and developmental (Hilgard & Bower, 1974), that children learn at different rates (Bayley, 1955, 1970; George, Cohn, & Stanley, 1979; Keating, 1976; Keating & Stanley, 1972; Robinson & Robinson, 1982), and that effective teaching involves a "match" between the child's readiness to learn and the level of content presented (Hunt, 1961; Robinson & Robinson, 1982). The implication of these principles, as delineated by Robinson (1983), Robinson & Robinson (1982), (Stanley, 1997), and Stanley and Benbow (1986), is that the level and pace of educational programs must be adapted to the capacities and knowledge of individual children. The pioneering work of Hollingworth (1942), who used above-grade-level tests to measure students' precocity (see Stanley, 1990), and of Terman (1925), who was among the first to systematically identify and study gifted students, also profoundly influenced the direction of SMPY.

All of SMPY's work was very much research-based, as the principal investigators sought validation of their hypotheses and evaluated the effectiveness of various intervention strategies. Today, longitudinal studies of early SMPY participants are still being conducted by David Lubinski and Camilla Benbow at Vanderbilt University (e.g., Benbow, Lubinski, Shea, & Eftekhari-Sanjani, 2000; Lubinski, Benbow, Shea, Eftekhari-Sanjani, & Halvorson, 2001; Lubinski, Webb, Morelock, & Benbow, 2001), and the university-based talent search programs that have adopted SMPY's principles and practices also engage in ongoing research related to the students they serve. Consequently, there exists a large body of published empirical evidence in support of this approach to talent identification and development, something many theories lack.

In this chapter, the conceptual and operational components of this model are summarized. It is meant to help youths who reason extremely well mathematically and/or verbally develop their talents. We begin with the history of SMPY.

BACKGROUND AND HISTORY OF SMPY

It was in the summer of 1968 that Julian Stanley was told about Joe, a 12-year-old who was doing some amazing work in a computer science course for middle school students at Johns Hopkins University. Eager to know more about the extent of Joe's abilities, Stanley arranged that fall to have this eighth-grader (unfortunately, without practicing beforehand) take the College Board Scholastic Aptitude Test (SAT), a test designed for college-bound high school seniors. Joe scored 669 on SAT-Mathematical Reasoning (SAT-M), higher than the average student entering Johns

Hopkins as a freshman. He also scored 590 on SAT-Verbal Reasoning (SAT-V), 772 on SAT-II (achievement test) Math, and 752 on SAT-II Physics, all exceptional scores for college-bound students and especially for a 13-year-old student who had not yet entered high school.

When local high schools, both public and private, proved unwilling to adjust their programs to accommodate his advanced educational needs, this 13-year-old entered Johns Hopkins University as a regular, full-time freshman. He did well, earning good grades and obtaining both his undergraduate and master's degrees in computer science by age 17. Then, a year after Joe was tested, another 13-year-old eighth-grader emerged, who also scored exceptionally well on SAT aptitude and high school achievement tests and who, with Stanley's help, also entered Johns Hopkins in lieu of going to high school. Finally, within a short time, a third accelerant enrolled at Hopkins after the 10th grade under Stanley's guidance. (For more information about these early radical accelerants, see Stanley, 1974.)

SMPY's experience with these exceptional youths suggested that the SAT-M, administered above grade level, was an effective means of identifying students who reasoned extremely well mathematically at a young age and who were capable of learning advanced subject matter in mathematics and science. The SAT offered many advantages over other assessment measures. Most importantly, it provided adequate ceiling to discriminate among students, all of whom might score well on in-grade-level tests. It also offered national above-grade-level norms for comparison purposes, and the test was secure, in that students could not get access to the questions in advance.

Because few seventh- and eighth-graders have formally studied the mathematical content that high school students have, the SAT appeared to be more of a reasoning test for seventh- and eighth-graders than for high school juniors and seniors. Presumably, students who score well on this difficult test without exposure to its content do so by using extraordinary reasoning abilities at the "analysis" level of Bloom's (1956) taxonomy. The predictive validity of the SAT for later high achievement among talent search participants has been documented (Benbow, 1992; Benbow & Stanley, 1983). SMPY also found that further assessment of a student's verbal reasoning and achievement levels, as well as other attributes, was valuable and important for guiding educational decisions.

SMPY began to launch systematic talent searches in an effort to find other students who exhibited advanced mathematical reasoning abilities similar to Joe and the other accelerants. It was expected that only a few such students would be found and that accommodations to meet their needs could be made on an individual basis. The first SMPY talent search took place in March 1972 on the Johns Hopkins campus for 450 seventh-, eighth-, and accelerated ninth-graders. They took advanced tests in math and/or science. Many more of the participants scored at higher levels than the researchers expected; for example, of the 396 who took the SAT-M, 13 percent scored 600 or more. Achievement levels were also surprisingly high among these students, who had had little formal exposure to the subject matter tested. The number of students found with exceptional abilities documented the need to search for such students on a regular basis and to find ways to meet their academic needs (Stanley et al., 1974).

Other talent searches and extensive experimentation with accelerated courses for the high scorers followed in 1973, 1974, 1976, 1978, and 1979 (Benbow & Stanley, 1983; Keating, 1976; Stanley, 1996). Finally, in late 1979, the entity that is now the Center for Talented Youth (CTY) at Johns Hopkins was established to expand the talent searches greatly, including emphasis on SAT-V scores, and to provide residential academic programs, while SMPY continued under Stanley's direction to focus on research and counseling extremely mathematically precocious students.

People often ask why SMPY itself chose to focus exclusively on mathematical reasoning ability. With a small staff and little funding to pursue the initial work, limited resources are part of the answer as to why not all talent areas were pursued. However, scientific knowledge was also a focus in the first (1972) talent search, and for a short time the project was called the Study of Mathematically and Scientifically Precocious Youth. Because quite a few of the high scorers on the college-level test of scientific knowledge did not score exceptionally well on SAT-M, it was decided early to drop the science test from the talent search and, instead, administer it later only to those examinees scoring well on SAT-M.

Because the purpose was to help gifted youths supplement their school-based education, it seemed sensible to focus on an ability closely related to several major subjects in the academic curricula of schools in the United States. Moreover, to capitalize on the precocious development of this ability by greatly accelerating students' progress in the subject matter concerned, it was necessary to choose school subjects more highly dependent on manifest intellectual talent for their mastery than on chronological age and associated life experiences. The published literature supported the choice of mathematics in that such writers as Cox (1926), Bell (1937), Gustin (1985a, 1985b), Roe (1951), Lehman (1953), Kramer (1974), Weiner (1953), and Zuckerman (1977) have documented the existence of great precocity in mathematics and the physical sciences. Concern about meeting the needs of verbally talented students in the talent searches did lead quickly to the establishment of a separate Study of Verbally Gifted Youth (SVGY) (McGinn, 1976). Coexisting with SMPY at Johns Hopkins from 1972–1977, it was the predecessor of CTY's dual emphasis on mathematical and verbal reasoning. Its writing instructor is still a member of the CTY staff.

From the beginning, SMPY's goal was not just to identify precocious students but also to help them develop their exceptional abilities.
The researchers assumed not only that many students with advanced
mathematical reasoning abilities can learn precalculus mathematics and
related subjects far more quickly than schools ordinarily permit, but also
that motivation to learn may suffer appreciably when the pace of instruction is too slow and unchallenging (Stanley & Benbow, 1986). With few
alternative programs available in those days, SMPY emphasized acceleration but, never intending that radical early entrance to college should be the
only or the main option even for the most gifted students, the researchers
identified and developed numerous forms of acceleration and curricular
flexibility. In an effort to match the level and pace of instruction to the abilities and needs of the students, Stanley and colleagues experimented with
a variety of strategies to speed up the learning of math, biology, chemistry,
and physics (Benbow & Stanley, 1983; Fox, 1974; George et al., 1979; George
& Denham, 1976; Stanley, 1976, 1993; Stanley & Benbow, 1986; Stanley &
Stanley, 1986).

Evaluation of these strategies was ongoing, and research results supported the value of accelerated instruction for mathematically precocious
students (see Benbow & Stanley, 1983). In addition to ability, motivation
and interest were found to be crucial components to successful learning
in accelerated environments. Thus, the researchers preferred to work directly with the youths themselves, rather than their parents, to ensure that
they were eager to embark on any accelerative path they chose (Stanley &
Benbow, 1986). Consideration of a broad "smorgasbord of educationally
accelerative options" (Stanley, 1979, p. 174) came to be recommended when
counseling gifted students about their educational needs, from which students could pick those that best served them as individuals.

EXPANDING THE SEARCH

The decision in 1979 to create CTY at Johns Hopkins to run the talent search
was intended to allow for its expansion. Until then, all of the testing and
scoring and many of the programs (all commuting, none residential) had
been held on the Hopkins campus. The success of SMPY's efforts was creating a huge demand from parents to have their children participate. Many
were driving long distances for testing and programmatic opportunities.
The time had come to expand the search geographically, establish residential summer programs so that students would not have to commute such
a long way, and address the needs of students with high verbal scores
because SVGY was no longer in existence. Once CTY was established,
SAT testing was offered to seventh-graders (and later expanded to serve
other age groups) through regular Educational Testing Service testing nationwide. The first residential program was held in southern Maryland in

the summer of 1980, featuring courses in the humanities as well as math and science. Since then, some courses in the social sciences have also been added.

CTY's talent search and programmatic offerings have grown rapidly from 1980 to the present. Today, approximately 85,000 second- through eighth-grade students from any of 19 states, the District of Columbia, and countries throughout the world participate in the annual talent search (Barnett & Juhasz, 2001). In recognition of the increasing importance of spatial reasoning in today's world, CTY developed a Spatial Test Battery to supplement assessment of mathematical and verbal reasoning (Stumpf & Mills, 1997). The summer program has also expanded, with approximately 10,000 students currently taking courses each year at 23 sites throughout the United States, and distance education courses help meet students' academic needs throughout the year (Brody, 2001). In addition, CTY's international efforts have led to the establishment of programs in Ireland, England, Spain, and elsewhere (e.g., see Gilheany, 2001; Touron, 2001). A strong research department, diagnostic and counseling center, and family academic conferences supplement CTY's many programmatic offerings. CTY's Study of Exceptional Talent (SET) continues SMPY's emphasis on serving the highest scorers by providing them with individualized counseling and other resources.

Soon after CTY was created, regional talent searches based on the Johns Hopkins model were established at Duke University, Northwestern University, and the University of Denver. Programs utilizing SMPY's talent search approach were also established at California State University-Sacramento, Arizona State University, Iowa State University, the University of Iowa, Carnegie Mellon University, and elsewhere. Collectively, these programs identify and serve several hundred thousand students each year who score well on above-grade-level mathematical or verbal aptitude tests (Lupkowski-Shoplik, Benbow, Assouline, & Brody, 2003; Olszewski-Kubilius, 2004; Stanley & Brody, 2001).

Numerous other initiatives across the country have also been influenced by research disseminated by SMPY, especially with regard to utilizing accelerative strategies and providing special supplemental opportunities to serve students with advanced cognitive abilities. For example, when SMPY began in 1971, very few academic summer programs for precollege students existed, whereas today many colleges and universities offer accelerative or enriching courses for gifted middle and high school students. Early college entrance programs have also been established at selected colleges and universities, many with Stanley's help, to allow young college entrants to enroll as a cohort and receive more academic and emotional support than is typically provided to regular-age college students (Brody, Muratori, & Stanley, 2004; Muratori, Colangelo, & Assouline, 2003; Sethna, Wickstrom, Boothe, & Stanley, 2001; Stanley, 1991).

The MVT:D⁴ Model

The first book-length report of SMPY's initial work was titled *Mathematical Talent: Discovery, Description, and Development* (Stanley et al., 1974). The three "D" words indicate the steps utilized by SMPY to find and serve talented youths. As a way to emphasize these steps, as well as the mathematical reasoning ability that the early talent searches involved, the book's title and this model of talent development was sometimes abbreviated to MT:D³. Later, a fourth D was added in acknowledgment of an increasingly important dimension: *Dissemination* of its principles, practices, and procedures (Benbow, Lubinski, & Suchy, 1996; Stanley, 1980).

These four steps continue today as the model utilized by the talent searches and other programs that have adopted these principles. Because programs have also been established for students who exhibit exceptional verbal abilities, it is appropriate to add a "V," for verbal talent, to the acronym. The MVT:D⁴ Model, therefore, stands for building on Mathematical and/or Verbal Talent through Discovery, Description, Development, and Dissemination.

The first step, *discovery*, refers to the systematic identification of talent. Through annual talent searches, large numbers of students are found whose exceptional mathematical and/or verbal reasoning abilities may have been largely unnoticed prior to this testing. Even among students who may have been labeled "gifted and talented" by their schools, parents and educators are often surprised to discover the level of their precocity after they take above-level tests through the talent searches. Other examinees who score very high wonder why they are not in their school's gifted-child program. Multiple criteria, some of them not related to ability, may have excluded them. Thus, relying on parents, teachers, or in-grade assessments to recognize giftedness is inadequate. Systematic talent identification programs utilizing above-grade-level assessments are sorely needed. The talent searches provide this.

Description refers to the assessment of students' characteristics in addition to the primary talent area, as well as to the research that helps evaluate various programmatic interventions. Individual differences in students' cognitive strengths and weaknesses, personality characteristics, motivation, learning styles, and content knowledge need to be considered when determining the strategies that will help maximize talent development. In addition, both short-term and longitudinal research studies are important to program evaluation. Through many years of research, SMPY and the talent searches have made consistent and important contributions to what is known about the characteristics and needs of gifted students and have validated numerous intervention strategies.

Development refers to providing gifted students with the challenging educational programs they need to develop their talents as fully as possible.

Through a variety of accelerative strategies, the pace and level of content can be adjusted to meet their needs. Special programs designed for advanced students serve to augment the typical school curriculum in important ways. SMPY and the talent searches have developed numerous programs that they offer directly to academically advanced students, often via summer courses or distance learning via computer, in addition to working to enhance the level of challenge available to academically talented students in their schools.

Finally, *dissemination* refers to sharing these principles, practices, and research results with educators, policy-makers, parents, and other researchers. Books, articles, and other publications; presentations at conferences; consultations with schools; and e-mail correspondence are all intended to further this goal. Over the last three decades, Stanley and colleagues have worked hard to disseminate their ideas.

Conceptualizing Giftedness

This volume depicts a variety of conceptions of giftedness, each distinguishable in some way. Although other theorists are likely to identify with the four steps of discovery, description, development, and dissemination previously described as they seek to identify and serve gifted students, the focus on precocity within specific areas of aptitude and the accompanying need to serve these students through accelerating the learning of subject matter make the SMPY and talent search model nearly unique within the field of gifted education (e.g., see Renzulli & Reis, 2004, for a somewhat different approach).

What Is Giftedness? The strategies embraced by SMPY and the talent searches are very much grounded in a belief in the psychology of individual differences. Although this view strongly endorses the importance of quality education for all, it is not assumed that everyone in society will achieve equally in all areas, even if they are given equal opportunities. Some individuals do have special talents, and recognizing and nurturing these talents is crucial not only for the individual but also for the future of society, as these individuals have the potential to be our future problem solvers. This view does not require students to be advanced in all areas to be considered "gifted." Rather, individuals vary considerably in their cognitive profiles, in their specific strengths and weaknesses. A given individual can be strong in one area but not in another (e.g., strong in math reasoning but weak in verbal, such as the student who, at age 12, recently scored 800 on the SAT-M but 340 on the SAT-V).

In defining giftedness, we are concerned therefore with those who exhibit exceptional reasoning ability in a specific area of aptitude, primarily math or verbal reasoning, but also spatial, mechanical, and other specific abilities (e.g., see Shea, Lubinski, & Benbow, 2001; Stanley, 1994). An important component of this view is the concept of precocity (e.g., gifted students are those who, because they learn at a faster rate and can comprehend more advanced ideas at younger ages, can reason much like older students). This equates giftedness with advanced mental age in specific areas, not just with being a good learner among age peers.

Talent development is important to achieving one's full potential, however. Although the talent searches identify advanced reasoning abilities that are already evident rather than potential that might be hidden at that point, the assumption is that ongoing educational support will be crucial to developing that gift. Thus, the talent search programs stress the development of challenging programmatic options to foster the development of talent.

How Does this Conception Compare with Other Conceptions of Giftedness? Although the emphasis that Terman (1925), Hollingworth (1942), and others placed on general IQ has diminished somewhat over time, there are still many educators who equate giftedness with high general ability. Sometimes this means it can be difficult to comprehend that a highly gifted student with exceptional mathematical reasoning ability can also be average in some content areas or even have a learning disability (Brody & Mills, 1997). Although the SMPY view does not deny the existence of a general intelligence factor (g) as some do, the measurement of specific aptitude has been found to be much more useful educationally than general IQ for identifying precocity. We have found boys and girls with *extremely* high IQs, even 212, who were asymmetrical with respect to V versus M, that is, far better on M than V, or on V than M.

Because the focus described here is on specific areas of aptitude, some may conclude that this view overlaps with those who propose multiple intelligences as a conception of giftedness, and to some extent it does. However, we would hesitate to use the word "intelligence" to describe mathematical or verbal reasoning ability and would also hesitate to apply equal weight to some of the areas that have been labeled intelligences. In addition, some schools that have adopted the multiple intelligence model fail to address students' primary talent areas to the extent we would recommend (Kornhaber, 2004; Stanley, 1997).

Some theorists include such affective traits as motivation and self-concept in their definitions of giftedness. SMPY's research on values, interests, and aspirations clearly shows the importance of these characteristics in predicting achievement (e.g., see Achter, Lubinski, Benbow, & Eftekhari-Sanjani, 1999). However, many affective characteristics can be altered by interventions; therefore, it seems unwise to include them as defining characteristics of giftedness.

Other gifted-child specialists stress creativity either as a separate area of giftedness or as a key component to identifying gifted individuals. SMPY's philosophy is that creativity needs to be embedded in content areas. True creative production can come only once a significant amount of content has been mastered (an argument for acceleration of subject-matter acquisition and allowing gifted individuals to enter into a creative phase at a younger age).

Finally, some theorists suggest that giftedness can be recognized only in adult achievement. This seems valid, which may be one reason the early writings of SMPY avoided using the word "gifted" in favor of descriptors like "precocious" and "exceptional." High-scoring young students have the potential to excel, but the true test of excellence must come after content has been mastered and original work or activities can be pursued. Early identification of this potential, however, is important so that students receive the educational opportunities that will allow this potential to be fulfilled.

How Should Gifted Individuals Be Identified? Identification strategies should match the program. Thus, one might use general IQ for a general enrichment program, but exceptional mathematical reasoning ability is crucial for an accelerated mathematics program in which the outcome knowledge is evaluated carefully. Because our concern has been with students who are unchallenged by age-in-grade instructional programs, finding those whose abilities are far above grade level is important. The SAT administered above grade level has proven valid and useful for the purpose of identifying students with exceptional mathematical or verbal reasoning abilities.

Whichever test is used for identifying talented students should have adequate ceiling to determine the full extent of the student's abilities. In CTY's talent search, for example, participants, all of whom have scored at or above the 97th percentile on the mathematics, verbal, or total score of an in-grade achievement test, can (and some do) score anywhere between 200 and 800 on the above-their-level SAT. This distinguishes the students who are bright and learn well but are not ready for more advanced work from those who are truly exceptional and need a differentiated educational program.

We also recommend using aptitude tests in specific academic areas to identify students in need of advancement in those areas. Although tests of general IQ can be useful for many purposes, IQ is a global composite of different cognitive abilities. As previously noted, we have not found IQ to be very useful for identifying students who are brilliant in a specific academic area (e.g., mathematics or science).

SMPY followed up their testing on the SAT with assessment of numerous other traits, for example, achievement in math and science, spatial and mechanical aptitude, values, and career interests (Stanley et al., 1974; Stanley, 1979; Keating, 1976). A full assessment of a variety of factors can be important in determining appropriate intervention strategies to meet a student's needs.

How Should Gifted Individuals Be Instructed in School and Elsewhere? The typical school program is designed for students with average abilities. Students whose abilities are advanced in particular areas need advanced work in those fields, and the more talented the student, the greater the need for a differentiated curriculum. Typically, this means accessing content designed for older students, or acceleration. Unfortunately, many people think of acceleration only in terms of skipping grades. In fact, there is an educational "smorgasbord" of at least 20 ways to accelerate a student in subject matter or grade placement (Southern, Jones, & Stanley, 1993).

When designing a program for a gifted student, the goal is to achieve an "optimal match" (Robinson & Robinson, 1982; see also Durden & Tangherlini, 1993; Lubinski & Benbow, 2000) between a student's cognitive and other characteristics and his or her educational program. An individualized program utilizing curricular flexibility is needed (Brody, 2004). This requires willingness, when appropriate, to adjust the level and pace of instruction, to place advanced students in classes with older students, and/or to allow them to do independent work (Benbow & Stanley, 1996). Effective articulation at the next stage to assure continuation of the advanced curriculum is also a key component of interventions recommended by SMPY (Stanley, 2000).

A "bridging" strategy developed by SMPY is the Diagnostic Testing – Prescriptive Instruction model (Stanley, 2000). Basically, this refers to pretesting, diagnosing specific content that has not been mastered, and structuring an academic program to teach only the new content. Long used in special education for students with academic deficits, this approach is too rarely used with students with advanced academic skills and knowledge. SMPY's application of it was to mathematics, but it can be adjusted for other subjects, such as English grammar.

Supplemental educational programs are also important and valuable. Although schools can attempt to address the needs of advanced students through curricular flexibility, the fact that they may have few truly exceptional students in the school population limits programmatic options. Today, there is an abundance of academic summer programs, dual enrollment programs in cooperation with universities, and distance education that can provide access to a broad array of subjects not offered in school. Extracurricular activities can also enhance learning and develop leadership in a field. Academic competitions such as the Intel (formerly Westinghouse) Science Talent Search and the International Mathematical Olympiad can be particularly challenging for even the most advanced high school students.

SMPY's counseling efforts encouraged students to develop challenging individualized programs. This approach is now used in CTY's SET program, which helps students who score at least 700 on SAT-I M or SAT-I V before age 13 find opportunities to accelerate and/or supplement their school programs (Brody, 2004; Brody & Blackburn, 1996). SET encourages students to consider a variety of options to supplement and/or accelerate school programs. Academic summer programs, distance education, and challenging extracurricular options are considered important components of most students' programs. Attention is also given to helping students find ways to interact with intellectual peers. Whether through school-based classes, out-of-school programs, or participation in activities or competitions, the opportunity for advanced students to interact with peers who share their abilities and interests can be critical to social and emotional development, areas of growth often overlooked by educators in favor of only academic development.

How Should the Achievement of Gifted Individuals Be Assessed? Assessing students' content knowledge is critical to meeting their educational needs. In particular, students with advanced cognitive abilities tend to pick up much information from their environment, so pretesting before offering instruction will help define what they already know so they can be taught only what they don't yet know (Stanley, 2000). Additional assessment after instruction is completed will also affirm mastery of content at that level and help students gain credit (or, at least, appropriate placement) for accelerated work.

Both criterion-referenced measures and standardized tests with norms are important in assessing gifted students' performance. Because in-grade standardized tests often do not measure the advanced content that is appropriate for students with exceptionally high cognitive abilities, content-specific criterion-referenced measures are needed. At the same time, the normative comparisons provided by standardized tests can be useful when evaluating learning compared with age-mates. When learning is accelerated, above-grade-level achievement tests should be used in lieu of in-grade tests, which usually lack adequate ceiling.

In some areas, a portfolio of products and accomplishments, such as written reports, artwork, science projects, and performance in academic competitions, can be valuable measures of student achievement. Certainly, winning a top prize ($100,000 for the top contestant) in the Intel Science Talent Search or qualifying to represent the United States in an international competition is a clear testimony to a student's learning and stellar achievement.

CONCLUSION

Many persons seem hostile toward intellectually talented youths, though perhaps a little less so toward those splendid in mathematics than toward the verbally precocious. This attitude contrasts sharply with the American public's generally favorable feelings about prodigies in music and athletics. Friedenberg (1966) and Stanley (1974), among others, have discussed how deep-seated this prejudice is. Expressions such as the following abound in literature back to Shakespeare's time: "Early ripe, early rot," "So wise so young, they say, do never live long," "For precocity some great price is always demanded sooner or later in life," and "Their productions ... bear the marks of precocity and premature delay" (Stanley, 1974, pp. 1–2).

There is also a prevailing assumption that intellectually talented students do not need any special help, that they will make it on their own. In fact, some seemingly do well, earning top grades in grade-level courses and entering selective colleges, but their goals and aspirations may be less than they might have been with greater challenge. Of more concern are the ones who become underachievers. Never having had to study to learn something, they fail to develop the study habits necessary even to achieve well compared with their age-mates. These students are at great risk of being "turned off" to anything academic and to developing social and emotional difficulties as well.

Another misconception is that gifted students, to be truly exceptional, must be achieving at the level of the great thinkers of the world, such as Gauss, Euler, Fermat, Bertrand Russell, Mozart, Galois, Pascal, Newton, Sweitzer, or (especially) Einstein. Terman encountered a great deal of this, with critics noting that among the 1,528 boys and girls to whom he administered an individual intelligence test in California in the early 1920s, he did not discover anyone who became a worthy successor to the greatest musicians, artists, and writers of all time. It was not enough that, for example, he found a youth who became a great, highly cited psychometrician and president of at least three very important national professional societies. Some insight into problems of defining and predicting genius may be obtained from Albert (1975), Bell (1937), and Simonton (1994).

In describing the work of SMPY, Stanley has often paraphrased Browning's "A man's reach should exceed his grasp, or what's a heaven for?" as "A mathematically precocious youth's reach should exceed his or her grasp, or what's an educational system for?" The goal is to extend the reach and the grasp of students with exceptional gifts, so that they dream bigger dreams, aspire to greater accomplishments, learn more at younger ages, and ultimately achieve higher levels. We do not guarantee identifying future Nobel laureates, Pulitzer Prize winners, U.S. poet laureates, or Fields Medalists through our talent searches, much less Einsteins!

But we are finding youths with exceptional reasoning abilities and helping them achieve far beyond what they would probably have done without intervention. And, as they become future scientists and mathematicians, physicians and entrepreneurs, politicians and teachers, and humanists, our society will benefit from their enhanced abilities to solve problems and contribute to progress.

References

Achter, J. A., Lubinski, D., Benbow, C. P., & Eftekhari-Sanjani, H. (1999). Assessing vocational preferences among gifted adolescents adds incremental validity to abilities: A discriminant analysis of educational outcomes over a 10-year interval. *Journal of Educational Psychology, 91,* 777–789.

Albert, R. S. (1975). Toward a behavioral definition of genius. *American Psychologist, 30* (2), 140–151.

Barnett, L. B., & Juhasz, S. E. (2001). The Johns Hopkins University talent searches today. *Gifted and Talented International, 16,* 96–99.

Bayley, N. (1955). On the growth of intelligence. *American Psychologist, 10,* 805–818.

Bayley, N. (1970). Development of mental abilities. In P. H. Mussen (Ed.), *Carmichael's manual of child psychology* (3rd ed., Vol. 1, pp. 1163–2109). New York: Wiley.

Bell, E. T. (1937). *Men of mathematics.* New York: Simon & Schuster.

Benbow, C. P. (1992). Academic achievement in mathematics and science of students between ages 13 and 23: Are there differences among students in the top one percent of mathematical ability? *Journal of Educational Psychology, 84,* 51–61.

Benbow, C. P., Lubinski, D., Shea, D. L., & Eftekhari-Sanjani, H. (2000). Sex differences in mathematical reasoning ability: Their status 20 years later. *Psychological Science, 11,* 474–480.

Benbow, C. P., Lubinski, D., & Suchy, B. (1996). Impact of the SMPY model and programs from the perspective of the participant. In C. P. Benbow & D. Lubinski (Eds.), *Intellectual talent: Psychometric and social issues* (pp. 266–300). Baltimore, MD: Johns Hopkins University Press.

Benbow, C. P., & Stanley, J. C. (Eds.) (1983). *Academic precocity: Aspects of its development.* Baltimore: Johns Hopkins University Press.

Benbow, C. P., & Stanley, J. C. (1996). Inequity in equity: How "equity" can lead to inequity for high-potential students. *Psychology, Public Policy, and Law, 2,* 249–292.

Bloom, B. S. (Ed.) (1956). *Taxonomy of educational objectives: Handbook I. The cognitive domain.* New York: McKay.

Brody, L. E. (2001). The talent search model for meeting the academic needs of gifted and talented students. *Gifted and Talented International, 16,* 99–102.

Brody, L. E. (2004). Meeting the diverse needs of gifted students through individualized educational plans. In D. Boothe & J. C. Stanley (Eds.), *In the eyes of the beholder: Critical issues for diversity in gifted education* (pp. 129–138). Waco, TX: Prufrock Press.

Brody, L. E., & Blackburn, C. C. (1996). Nurturing exceptional talent: SET as a legacy of SMPY. In C. P. Benbow & D. Lubinski (Eds.), *Intellectual talent: Psychometric and social issues* (pp. 246–265). Baltimore: Johns Hopkins University Press.

Brody, L. E. & Mills, C. J. (1997). Gifted children with learning disabilities: A review of the issues. *Journal of Learning Disabilities, 30* (3), 282–296.

Brody, L. E., Muratori, M. C., & Stanley, J. C. (2004). Early college entrance: Academic, social, and emotional considerations. In N. Colangelo, S. G. Assouline, & M. U. M. Gross (Eds.), *The Templeton National Report on Acceleration*, Vol. II. Philadelphia: Templeton Foundation.

Cox, C. M. (1926). *Genetic studies of genius: Vol. 2. The early mental traits of three hundred geniuses.* Stanford, CA: Stanford University Press.

Durden, W. G., & Tangherlini, A. E. (1993). *Smart kids.* Seattle: Hogrefe & Huber.

Fox, L. H. (1974). A mathematics program for fostering precocious achievement. In J. C. Stanley, D. P. Keating, & L. H. Fox (Eds.), *Mathematical talent: Discovery, description, and development* (pp. 101–125). Baltimore: Johns Hopkins University Press.

Friedenberg, E. Z. (1966). *The dignity of youth and other atavisms* (pp. 119–135). Boston: Beacon.

George, W. C., Cohn, S. J., & Stanley, J. C. (Eds.) (1979). *Educating the gifted: Acceleration and enrichment.* Baltimore: Johns Hopkins University Press.

George, W. C., & Denham, S. A. (1976). Curriculum experimentation for the mathematically gifted. In D. P. Keating (Ed.), *Intellectual talent: Research and development* (pp. 103–131). Baltimore: Johns Hopkins University Press.

Gilheany, S. (2001). The Irish Centre for Talented Youth – An adaptation of the Johns Hopkins talent search model. *Gifted and Talented International, 16,* 102–104.

Gustin, W. C. (1985a). The development of exceptional research mathematicians. In B. S. Bloom (Ed.), *Developing talent in young people* (pp. 270–331). New York: Ballantine.

Gustin, W. C. (1985b). One mathematician: "Hal Foster." In B. S. Bloom (Ed.), *Developing talent in young people* (pp. 332–347). New York: Ballantine.

Hilgard, E. R., & Bower, G. H. (1974). *Theories of learning* (4th ed.). Englewood Cliffs, NJ: Prentice Hall.

Hollingworth, L. S. (1942). *Children above 180 IQ Stanford-Binet: Origin and development.* Yonkers, NY: World Book.

Hunt, J. M. (1961). *Intelligence and experience.* New York: Ronald Press.

Keating, D. P. (Ed.) (1976). *Intellectual talent: Research and development.* Baltimore: Johns Hopkins University Press.

Keating, D. P., & Stanley, J. C. (1972). Extreme measures for the exceptionally gifted in mathematics and science. *Educational Researcher, 1*(9), 3–7.

Kornhaber, M. L. (2004). Using multiple intelligences to overcome cultural barriers to identification for gifted education. In D. Boothe & J. C. Stanley (Eds.), *In the eyes of the beholder: Critical issues for diversity in gifted education* (pp. 215–225). Waco, TX: Prufrock Press.

Kramer, E. A. (1974). *Nature and growth of modern mathematics.* New York: Fawcett World Library.

Lehman, H. C. (1953). *Age and achievement.* Princeton, NJ: Princeton University Press.

Lubinski, D., & Benbow, C. P. (2000). States of excellence. *American Psychologist, 55,* 137–150.

Lubinski, D., Benbow, C. P., Shea, D. L., Eftekhari-Sanjani, H., & Halvorson, M. B. J. (2001). Men and women at promise for scientific excellence: Similarity not dissimilarity. *Psychological Science, 12,* 309–317.

Lubinski, D., Webb, R. M., Morelock, M. J., & Benbow, C. P. (2001). Top 1 in 10,000: A 10-year follow-up of the profoundly gifted. *Journal of Applied Psychology, 86,* 718–729.

Lupkowski-Shoplik, A., Benbow, C. P., Assouline, S. G., & Brody, L. E. (2003). Talent searches: Meeting the needs of academically talented youth. In N. Colangelo & G. A. Davis (Eds.), *Handbook of gifted education,* 3rd edition (pp. 204–218). Boston: Allyn & Bacon.

McGinn, P. V. (1976). Verbally gifted youth. In D. P. Keating (Ed.), *Intellectual talent: Research and development* (pp. 160–182). Baltimore: Johns Hopkins University Press.

Muratori, M., Colangelo, N., & Assouline, S. (2003). Early-entrance students: Impressions of their first semester of college. *Gifted Child Quarterly, 47,* 219–238.

Olszewski-Kubilius, P. (2004). Talent search: Purposes, rationale, and role in gifted education. In D. Boothe & J. C. Stanley (Eds.), *In the eyes of the beholder: Critical issues for diversity in gifted education* (pp. 251–262). Waco, TX: Prufrock Press.

Renzulli, J. S., & Reis, S. M. (2004). Curriculum compacting: A research-based differentiation strategy for culturally diverse talented students. In D. Boothe & J. C. Stanley (Eds.), *In the eyes of the beholder: Critical issues for diversity in gifted education* (pp. 87–100). Waco, TX: Prufrock Press.

Robinson, H. B. (1983). A case for radical acceleration: Programs of the Johns Hopkins University and the University of Washington. In C. P. Benbow & J. C. Stanley (Eds.), *Academic promise: Aspects of its development* (pp. 139–159). Baltimore: Johns Hopkins University Press.

Robinson, N. M., & Robinson, H. B. (1982). The optimal match: Devising the best compromise for the highly gifted student. In D. Feldman (Ed.), *New directions for child development: Developmental approaches to giftedness and creativity* (pp. 79–94). San Francisco: Jossey-Bass.

Roe, A. (1951). A psychological study of eminent physical scientists. *Genetic Psychology Monographs, 43,* 121–239.

Sethna, B. N., Wickstrom, C. D., Boothe, D., & Stanley, J. C. (2001). The Advanced Academy of Georgia: Four years as a residential early-college-entrance program. *Journal of Secondary Gifted Education, 13,* 11–21.

Shea, D. L., Lubinski, D., & Benbow, C. P. (2001). Importance of assessing spatial ability in intellectually talented young adolescents: A 20-year longitudinal study. *Journal of Educational Psychology, 93,* 604–614.

Simonton, D. K. (1994). *Greatness: Who makes history and why.* New York: Guilford.

Southern, W. T., Jones, E. D., & Stanley, J. C. (1993). Acceleration and enrichment: The content and development of program options. In E. A. Keller, F. K. Monks, & A. H. Passow (Eds.), *International handbook of research and development of giftedness and talent* (pp. 387–409). Elmsford, NY: Pergamon.

Stanley, J. C. (1974). Intellectual precocity. In J. C. Stanley, D. P. Keating, & L. H. Fox (Eds.), *Mathematical talent: Discovery, description, and development* (pp. 1–22). Baltimore: Johns Hopkins University Press.

Stanley, J. C. (1976). Special fast-math classes taught by college professors to fourth-through twelfth-graders. In D. P. Keating (Ed.), *Intellectual talent: Research and development* (pp. 132–159). Baltimore: Johns Hopkins University Press.

Stanley, J. C. (1977). Rationale of the Study of Mathematically Precocious Youth (SMPY) during its first five years of promoting educational acceleration. In J. C. Stanley, W. C. George, & C. H. Solano (Eds.), *The gifted and the creative: A fifty-year perspective* (pp. 75–112). Baltimore: Johns Hopkins University Press.

Stanley, J. C. (1979). The study and facilitation of talent for mathematics. In A. H. Passow (Ed.), *The gifted and the talented: Their education and development. The seventy-eighth yearbook of the National Society for the Study of Education* (pp. 169–185). Chicago: University of Chicago Press.

Stanley, J. C. (1980). Manipulate important educational variables. *Educational Psychologist, 15*(3), 164–171.

Stanley, J. C. (1990). Leta Hollingworth's contributions to above-level testing of the gifted. *Roeper Review, 12*(3), 166–171.

Stanley, J. C. (1991). A better model for residential high schools for talented youths. *Phi Delta Kappan, 72*(6), 471–473.

Stanley, J. C. (1993). Boys and girls who reason well mathematically. In G. Bock & K. Ackrill (Eds.), *The origins and development of high ability* (pp. 119–138). New York: Wiley.

Stanley, J. C. (1994). Mechanical aptitude: Neglected undergirding of technological expertise. *The Journal Portfolio* (Article 7). Evanston, IL: Illinois Association for Gifted Children.

Stanley, J. C. (1996). In the beginning: The Study of Mathematically Precocious Youth. In C. P. Benbow & D. Lubinski (Eds.), *Intellectual talent: Psychometric and social issues* (pp. 225–235). Baltimore: Johns Hopkins University Press.

Stanley, J. C. (1997). Varieties of intellectual talent. *Journal of Creative Behavior, 31*(2), 93–119. Commentaries by Howard Gardner and Joyce VanTassel-Baska, 120–130.

Stanley, J. C. (2000). Helping students learn only what they don't already know. *Psychology, Public Policy, and Law, 6*(1), 216–222.

Stanley, J. C., & Benbow, C. P. (1986). Youths who reason extremely well mathematically. In R. J. Sternberg & J. E. Davidson (Eds.), *Conceptions of giftedness* (pp. 361–387). New York: Cambridge University Press.

Stanley, J. C., & Brody, L. E. (2001). History and philosophy of the talent search model. *Gifted and Talented International, 16*, 94–96.

Stanley, J. C., George, W. C., & Solano, C. H. (1977). *The gifted and the creative.* Baltimore: Johns Hopkins University Press.

Stanley, J. C., Keating, D., & Fox, L. H. (Eds.) (1974). *Mathematical talent: Discovery, description, and development.* Baltimore: Johns Hopkins University Press.

Stanley, J. C., & Stanley, B. S. K. (1986). High school biology, chemistry, or physics learned well in three weeks. *Journal of Research in Science Teaching, 23*, 237–250.

Stumpf, H., & Mills, C. J. (1997). *The computerized CTY Spatial Test Battery (STB): Findings from the first two test administrations.* (Technical Report 16). Baltimore: Johns Hopkins University Center for Talented Youth.

Terman, L. M. (1925). *Genetic studies of genius: Vol. I. Mental and physical traits of a thousand gifted children.* Stanford, CA: Stanford University Press.

Touron, J. (2001). School and College Ability Test (SCAT) validation in Spain: Overview of the process and some results. *Gifted and Talented International, 16*, 104–107.

Wallach, M. A. (1978). Care and feeding of the gifted. *Contemporary Psychology, 23,* 616–617.

Weiner, N. (1953). *Ex-prodigy: My childhood and youth.* Cambridge, MA: MIT Press.

Zuckerman, H. (1977). *Scientific elite: Nobel Laureates in the United States.* New York: Free Press.

3

A Child-Responsive Model of Giftedness

Carolyn M. Callahan and Erin M. Miller

There are two paths that gifted children can follow that can be facilitated by educators within the context of the public school system, and that subsequently will lead to productive lives. These paths reflect educational responses to two unique, although partially overlapping, domains of giftedness. The proposed overall construct of giftedness is not a totally new construct, but rather is a reflection of an attempt to resolve an artificial dichotomy that seems to have evolved in the gifted literature.

The conception of giftedness proposed is one based on student learning and performance needs, hence the label *child-responsive model*. The model accepts, while adapting, some basic premises of two existing paradigms of giftedness that have competed for attention in the schools. It is predicated on the belief that the school environment should recognize the behaviors and characteristics of the exceptional learner from these two realms and respond to the concomitant learner needs in each group by creating learning environments that will maximize the opportunities for exceptional learners to extend their achieved and potential expertise in areas of high performance. The response involves creating the most challenging learning tasks – requiring students to utilize the knowledge, skill, and understanding they bring to the situation at the highest level possible, but also challenging them to extend those achievements beyond their current stage of accomplishment. In other words, learning experiences should be based on Vygotsky's (1978) notion of zone of proximal development across the domains of performance excellence that the gifted learner brings to the learning situation. However, as the subsequent discussion illustrates, the teacher (whether the classroom teacher, the specialist in gifted education, special tutor, instructor, or mentor in domains outside of school such as musical performance or gymnastics) must extend the gifted student's thinking to define the goal of expertise for the particular child. The goal, as with any successful learning program, is to engage the gifted learner in the learning process in a fashion that is most conducive to development.

The two clusters of gifted students are designated the *academic activists* and the *problem-solving innovators*. The division of the gifted population into these two categories is similar in many ways to the conception of giftedness provided by Tannenbaum (1986), who described two aspects of giftedness: one involving innovation and invention and the other referring to highly developed proficiency in highly demanding tasks. However, the model is distinct from Tannenbaum's in the recognition that students can engage in highly demanding and productive tasks at a young age. The child-responsive definition of giftedness also incorporates the notions of Winner (1997) and Renzulli (1978, 1986), who also recognize the differences among kinds of academically talented students.

Within this model, we attend specifically to the groups of students within each of those categories who can be reasonably served by the current school structure. We acknowledge that there may be a need to identify and respond to other groups of children whose talents may reflect valued expertise that cannot be served within the school structure because of the natural limitations that evolve from financial constraints or political forces in schools. These groups may include students with particular expertise in dance, musical performance, gymnastics, and so forth.

THE ACADEMIC ACTIVIST

The first group of students who present extraordinary learner characteristics, the academic activists, reflect the traditional conceptions of giftedness in school that are widely accepted by most educators and the lay public. They are characterized by quickness in attaining the basic curriculum goals, a wide range of knowledge in either general or specific areas, and a passion for absorbing new understandings of the world and how it works. They also reflect exceptional performance in the analytic realm described by Sternberg (1981) in his tripartite description of intellectual abilities. These children may exhibit the exceptional ability to rapidly engage in application of accumulated knowledge, in the performance of advanced skills, or in the display and application of understanding of the concepts, principles, and generalizations across any or all of the domains that have been identified by Gardner (1983; 1991). That is, these children may be very advanced in verbal/linguistic knowledge, skills, and understanding; in logical/mathematical knowledge, skills, and understanding; and so on. And they are likely to be very capable of engaging in analytical and critical thinking in each of those domains. This group of students is closely akin to those described by Winner (2000) as notationally gifted (able to master rapidly the two kinds of notational symbol systems valued in school: language and numbers), but also includes those with more uneven profiles, perhaps focusing on just language arts, or just mathematical knowledge and skills, or even just science within the traditional disciplines. In schools, we have traditionally focused on the traditional disciplines in academics (language arts, mathematics, science, social studies, and foreign languages) for identification and placement of these students in appropriate services.

The academic activist is an exceptional learner and synthesizer of knowledge. This type of student has the ability to amass a large amount of knowledge without necessarily being interested in creating a novel product. The immersion in a domain and the accumulation of the skills and knowledge of that domain is an end in itself. These students pursue their studies for the satisfaction that intellectual stimulation brings. This drive for intellectual stimulation is present in the child regardless of the situation or learning environment. Much of the research on the learning characteristics of gifted students of this type has been based on students with high IQ scores and high achievement performance. Research on these students indicates that they possess wider and deeper knowledge bases than their age and grade peers, learn more rapidly, are goal driven, have greater automaticity of thought processes, have greater metacognitive skills, are more flexible in their problem solving, are better strategy planners, prefer complexity and challenge, are better able to take another's perspective, and possess a hierarchical and extensive webbing of knowledge about both facts and procedures that differentiates them from other students (Butterfield & Ferretti, 1987; Coleman & Shore, 1991; Hoover, 1994; Kanevsky, 1990; Porath, 1991; Shavinina & Kholodnaja, 1996; Sternberg & Horvath, 1998; Shore, 2000). These students possess a sophisticated mental toolbox that is available to them regardless of the current context of their lives. However, cultural forces often influence the domain in which they choose to apply their abilities (Sternberg, 1985).

The learner characteristics and requisite characteristics of appropriate learning environments for these children have been widely discussed, if not acknowledged and attended to in traditional classrooms. For example, Clark (1992) created a very extensive list of the cognitive characteristics of the gifted child that create educational needs and suggests the types of curricular modifications necessary to address the child who would easily be frustrated by the inability to pursue the passion for learning within the traditional curriculum. The learner characteristics range from extraordinary quantity of information, to unusual capacity for processing information, to advanced or accelerated thought processes, to early and sophisticated conceptual frameworks, to persistent goal-directed behavior and persistence. Renzulli has labeled these students as "school-house" gifted, and his recommendations for compacting the curriculum address the challenges and problems presented by the students' advanced content knowledge by providing opportunities for students to eliminate or quickly master the standard or general curriculum of the given school year (Renzulli & Smith, 1978). But the only options offered for these children in the compacting model are acceleration or undefined enrichment of curriculum. Unfortunately, the term has come to have pejorative associations, whereas observation of these students reveals that they are indeed students who will achieve great mastery of a domain if given opportunities for in-depth study.

PROBLEM-SOLVING INNOVATORS

The second group, the problem-solving innovators, are students who bring both a capability and desire to engage in the identification of problems, challenges, and questions in a discipline and who have a drive to participate in the creation of new and unusual solutions to problems. The problem-solving innovative group subsumes those identified by Renzulli as gifted by virtue of having a coalescence of above-average ability, creativity, and task commitment in a given domain of performance and are labeled creative producers (Renzulli, 1978). But it also includes students who bring creative orientations to the learning environment without a particular product that has been self-determined and whose talents are best served by engaging in extending and learning new problem-solving skills in the disciplines they study. They may or may not be ready to focus on real-life problems of a creative, productive sort identified by Renzulli. The category includes those identified by Sternberg (1982) as excelling in synthetic abilities and also those identified as having practical intelligence. Thus, their ultimate performances may be in realms that will be regarded by the public as making extraordinary breakthroughs in their disciplines. Or their ultimate products may result from bringing their talents to bear on practical issues and problems using knowledge, skills, and understandings that have been the result of creative productivity of the synthetic producers. They may be either the scientist with the conceptions of a new cure for cancer or the collaborator/proposal writer who can translate those ideas into a successful means of attaining the money to test the hypotheses.

CAVEATS

Although we have described the two groups as if they were distinct and fixed, we may find a student who is an academic activist and at some point becomes a problem-solving innovator. The in-depth study of the complex world of a given discipline may spark a creative response, a drive to address an unknown realm within the discipline, to restructure the discipline, or to challenge existing paradigms. The student identified as a problem-solving innovator may find himself or herself unable to identify new questions or to unlock new solutions because of a need to gain a further in-depth understanding of the disciplines that will lead to the capacity to engage in meaningful problem solving. Hence, the identification procedures and the interventions proposed should be considered fluid guidelines, and educators should be alert for the changing focus of a given student and provide the necessary child-responsive adjustments in programming.

Programming/Curriculum Options for the Gifted

The two paths that gifted students may follow in this model are the academic–accelerative path and the creative–productive path. Each path is of equal importance and deserves equal attention in the planning for addressing the needs of gifted students in our schools.

ACADEMIC–ACCELERATIVE PATH

The ability and desire to take in and synthesize a great deal of information is the hallmark of the group of academic activist students best served by the academic–accelerative path. Facility with the content and manipulation of knowledge bases allows these students to excel on traditional tests of intelligence, aptitude, and/or achievement[1] and to exhibit extraordinary displays of knowledge and understanding in one or more content domains. Regardless of the domain that the student chooses to pursue, students who are best served by an academic–accelerative path seek immersion in a domain or sometimes several domains. These students have an intrinsic drive to immerse themselves in their domain(s) that has been described by Winner (1997) as a "rage to master." They demonstrate an eagerness for moving ahead rapidly, which Stanley and Benbow (1986) identify as a characteristic of students who are successful in programs that allow students to progress at their own pace and learn at the level that they are currently able. These students desire a path toward expertise in one or more disciplines, and the curriculum offered to these students should offer ever-increasing opportunity for them to study increased levels of depth and complexity in the domain as exemplified by experts.

Conceptualizations of giftedness as developing expertise arose from research from the field of cognitive psychology on the difference between novices and adults who, through study and work, have become experts in their fields (Sternberg & Horvath, 1998; Shore, 2000). The performance of gifted children has been compared with the performance of adults to ascertain whether expert adults and gifted children use similar cognitive processes. Sternberg (2000b) describes academically gifted children as those who have and are currently developing expertise in the requirements and structure of formal school as well as expertise in taking tests.

---

[1] Gifted underachievers who are academic may exhibit patterns of underachievement that reflect low performance on traditional assessments because their intense interest in a learning domain may have been thwarted by the lack of stimulating engagement in the traditional classroom.

However, the ultimate goal of students who are best served by an academic–accelerative path is not to become expert lesson-learners or test-takers. Rather, these students want to pursue a path toward expertise in a domain. Thus, students are following a path toward becoming expert performers and producers in their domain (Tannenbaum, 1997, 2000).

Essential to understanding why a student with high abilities would desire to follow an academic–accelerative path is an understanding of these students' intrinsic motivation for learning. Intrinsic motivation is often noted as a characteristic of gifted children (Csikszentmihalyi, Rathunde, & Walen, 1993; Kanevsky, 1992). What seems to be less discussed is having an intrinsic motivation for learning for learning's sake. Gifted students are often stimulated and motivated by the workings of their own minds (Winner, 1997). Csikszentmihalyi (1990) describes this experience as the "flow of thought." The concept of "flow" was coined by Csikszentmihalyi to describe optimal experiences in which time passes quickly, and one is enjoyably immersed in a task that is challenging without being overwhelming. The task does not necessarily need to be focused toward production. In fact, Csikszentmihalyi (p. 117) indicates "some of the most exhilarating experiences we undergo are generated inside the mind, triggered by information that challenges our ability to think, rather than from the use of sensory skills." Although flow of thought is an opportunity open to all, because flow of thought requires memory ability and knowledge of abstract symbol systems (Csikszentmihalyi, 1990), those with intellectual gifts seem especially suited to finding flow in this way. Students who are best served by an academic–accelerative path are able to achieve flow by setting challenges for themselves (Kanevsky, 1992). For these students, learning is in itself a pleasurable activity that is self-motivating. The more one learns, the more one is motivated to pursue knowledge and skills.

A similar concept to flow is the theory of work adjustment (Dawis & Lofquist, 1984), which serves as one aspect of the conceptual basis for the Johns Hopkins/Study of Mathematically Precocious Youth model (Benbow & Lubinski, 1997; Lubinski & Benbow, 2000). According to this model, optimal educational environments are those that maximize satisfactoriness and satisfaction. Satisfactoriness is a measure of the correspondence between one's ability and the requirements of the task. Contexts that provide a match between ability and the demands of successful performance would have high satisfactoriness. Satisfaction is the correspondence between personal needs and the rewards provided by the environment. Satisfaction is a measure of personal fulfillment. Flow, satisfactoriness, and satisfaction are all highly desirable conditions. Students with advanced abilities are seeking these conditions, and the appropriate response is to allow them to pursue an academic–accelerative path in school.

To achieve satisfaction, the curriculum for the students would be structured to allow for more advanced, more rapid presentation of advanced knowledge, but would also be structured to allow for both depth and complexity of learning that would demand sophisticated levels of analysis, the opportunity to create and develop individualized plans of study (alone or with similar peers) along with the opportunity to engage in advanced research and critical productivity (e.g., Kaplan, 1986, 2001; Tomlinson et al., 2002), and the opportunity to work with experts in the domain of study through mentorships.

ACADEMIC-FOCUSED CREATIVE–PRODUCTIVE PATH

The student who is best served by an academic-focused creative–productive path is a child who, given the opportunity and right environment, can apply his or her gifts in open-ended contexts to create products and/or solve authentic and/or real-world problems. These students pursue their problem solving through tackling projects for the satisfaction that comes from creating something new. According to Renzulli, these students do not always feel this drive to create new and real-life solutions to a problem. In his conception of the creative producer, giftedness is a behavior that emerges under the right circumstances. The students described by Renzulli (1978, 1986) in his three-ring conception of giftedness possess above-average ability, creativity, and task commitment and would be served by the creative–productive path, as would the students Sternberg (1986; 1995) describes as those gifted in creative and practical intelligences and those described by Gardner (1993) in *Creating Minds*. In addition, other students who are driven to identify new questions, new possibilities for explanation, and new solutions to problems would be served by this path. The creative–productive path is the path toward the development of original products – whether driven by authentic, composed problems embedded in the curriculum, or student-identified real-life problems or, at the most sophisticated level, at reconstructing of thought systems.

The hallmark of students who are best served by an academic-focused creative–productive path is their differential response to the environmental context in which they find themselves. Context is essential to these students because their performance is dependent on the topic and situation – particularly the degree to which they have the drive to attempt a solution to the problems posed externally or internally.

Creative–productive individuals seem to have the ability to take advantage of the entire spectrum of personality, depending on the demands of the task or environment (Csikszentmihalyi & Wolfe, 2000). For example, they are independent workers when solitude is needed and then social when the task requires cooperation. Thus, the learning characteristics of these students are more difficult to describe. Further, because of the central role that contextual factors play in their lives, it is much more difficult to predict how, when, or in what domain they will manifest their talent.

Nevertheless, like the student on the academic–accelerative path, creative–productive students will likely become immersed in their domain of interest and will need the supportive structure within the gifted programming options to pursue that immersion. Like the academic activist, the problem-solving innovator is committed to the domain, but rather than seeking immersion and mastery of learning in a domain as an end in itself, the problem-solving innovator is initially drawn into the domain through interest, curiosity, or an orientation toward discovery (Csikszentmihalyi & Wolfe, 2000; Getzels & Csikszentmihalyi, 1976). The immersion in the domain is fueled by a desire to introduce novelty into that domain, engage in novel solutions to problems, or devise new questions to solve (Csikszentmihalyi & Wolfe, 2000; Gardner, 1993) rather than a rage to master the domain.

Students who are best served by the creative–productive path have a desire to generate change. Although creative individuals are a diverse group, creators are often rebellious, impatient, intrinsically motivated, resistant to convention, and dissatisfied with the status quo (Csikszentmihalyi, 1996; Gardner 1993; Runco, 2004; Winner, 2000). Sternberg (2000a) describes creative individuals as making the choice to redefine problems, to be skeptical about established ideas, to have a flexible view of knowledge, to be open to sensible risks, and to constantly look for new problems and new solutions. The creative–productive path is a match for students who are currently making the choice to embrace those characteristics because of the pleasure that comes from productivity. It is this intrinsic pleasure in creating that is motivating, not the possibility of extrinsic rewards (Amabile, 1996). The subjective experience of pleasure is the same as that pursued by the student on the academic–accelerative path; the creative–productive person is also seeking flow. However the creative–productive person is not seeking "flow of thought," but rather, flow arising from engaging creative–productive endeavors in situations that are intellectually challenging (Csikszentmihalyi & Wolfe, 2000).

The difference in the achievement of flow experiences between students following the academic–accelerative path and students following the creative–productive path lies in the effect of the context and domain. Students who are best served by the academic–accelerative path are able to achieve flow through the workings of their own minds. Thus, they are less affected by the outside context; their only requirement is an unfettered access to higher knowledge. Students who are best served by the creative–productive path need to find their area of passion. Once they are immersed in this area, they are able to find flow. Thus, they need repeated and varied exposure to different intellectual domains so that they may explore their interests. The best way to facilitate creativity is to allow students to do something they love, to allow choice, and to focus on student interests (Collins & Amabile, 1999; Csikszentmihalyi, 1996). However, as Gardner

(1993) and Csikszentmihalyi (1996) have noted, the student in this domain will require continually more and more knowledge, skill, and understanding in the domain of problem focus to raise the likelihood of success in finding creative solutions to identified problems. Even the identification of important problems requires increased sophistication in the discipline. Hence, the curriculum for this student must be one that capitalizes on both the ability of the student to engage in the kind of thinking that leads to creative and productive thinking, but it must also accommodate complexity and depth of discipline learning to support that thinking.

Identification

The two groups of students whom we have described share some common characteristics, but are distinguished by uniquenesses that should be taken into account in the identification process. Looking first to identify the academic activists, educators should look at instruments that identify both general and specific aptitudes and academic achievement. However, the key is looking for specific aptitudes and achievements. Although these students may be characterized as academic activists in more than one discipline, it is quite possible that students will be gifted in only one domain. An identification plan should comprise several separate strands that would allow for a student with only one talent area to emerge. We need to accommodate the Thomas Jeffersons of our schools, but we also need to accommodate the Albert Einsteins. Further, we should not only be accommodating those who are extreme in their display of talents; we should be doing close and careful study of an array and range of talents and developing a continuum of services that allows for fluid movement from differentiation in the regular classroom, to special resource services, to special schools, to out-of-school mentorships, as the specific needs of the students dictate.

Second, the identification plan should have a nomination process that allows for students who may not test well on traditional achievement or aptitude tests to enter into consideration. These may be students who are in any one of the following categories:

1. Students from minority or traditionally underserved groups who do not have the skills in test taking or the traditional knowledge or skills measured by those traditional standardized tests but who have clearly used their passion for learning in ways that have led to demonstration of extraordinary knowledge or skills in a domain.
2. Underachieving students who have demonstrated extraordinary knowledge outside the areas measured by traditional domains: a student, for example, who can wax eloquent on the events of World War II, but does not score well on a social studies achievement test.

3. Handicapped students whose knowledge and abilities may be underestimated by traditional tests.

The school nomination process should comprise both teacher nominations and the collection of portfolio and self-report information that would allow for the gathering of a pool of students to be considered. The second stage would be a "curricular assessment" process. The teacher would create learning environments where these students are aided in identifying, specifying, and pursuing the interests and passions indicated by the tests and/or nomination processes. These opportunities would be structured to allow for more rapid learning, depth and complexity of learning, and sophistication of tasks, and would be monitored with specific guidelines for interpreting the degree to which the modification in the curriculum results in the pursuit of greater commitment to and benefit from the learning situation. Like the "action information" orientation of Renzulli or many of the talent development models that have evolved, "identification" would be tied to the curricular modification to be pursued.

Like nomination of the academic activists, nomination of the problem-solving innovators would require the use of multiple strategies for gathering information on students who would benefit from the path of study offered: first, the screening of performance on traditional assessments for students who have above-average specific academic aptitude based on the assumption that creative production requires advanced knowledge of a discipline. However, the second area for consideration for nomination should focus on creativity as defined by skills in and the motivation to engage in the identification of new questions in a discipline and the ability to generate new and unique solutions to a problem, to evaluate solutions, and to pursue solutions to their logical end. At the point where initial nominations occur, the use of tests such as the Torrance Tests of Creativity, carefully structured teacher nominations, and portfolios would be appropriate. As in the first identification scheme, the second stage would be a curricular focus using inquiry-based learning, creative problem solving, and/or Type III Enrichment (Renzulli, 1977; Renzulli & Reis, 1985) models of instruction. These learning tasks would also be accompanied by carefully developed strategies for documenting and evaluating the response of students to the tasks.

Each of these plans for identification of the gifted deliberately contains a major component based on curricular response. Because the measurement of potential presumes the ability to predict, it seems most appropriate to present clear opportunities for students to perform directly in the educational tasks that would be the core of the curricular response. This approach is based on an assumption that the best predictor of future behavior is past behavior.

Assessing the Achievement of Gifted Students

The evaluation of the achievement of these students would be based on the assumption that there would be two valued outcomes. The evaluation of the model and student success would be based on assessment of two valued outcomes. The first dimension to consider would be whether the curriculum and activities are child-centered, whether those students identified and served assess the curriculum and school as challenging, whether students and teachers attribute learning and growth in the identified areas of talent to the interventions of the school, and whether students deem their educational experience to be one of engagement and productive learning, regardless of the path(s) they take. The second level of assessment would relate to the degree to which students were engaged in learning and/or productivity at a level higher than one might expect if they had not been provided the opportunities for engaging in the learning tasks. This would require that the academic activists be assessed on the degree of achieved expertise in the discipline. For some students, this might involve the measurement of such mundane outcomes as earlier and greater success on Advanced Placement or International Baccalaureate exams. However, more important would be the development of portfolio review forms that would engage experts in the disciplines in defining ascending levels of expertise in the achievement of understanding of complex concepts and structures of the disciplines, research skills, critical analysis skills, moral and ethical dilemmas of the discipline as appropriate, and achievement of expertise in the presentation of advanced levels of performance (e.g., the critical analysis of literature).

For the problem-solving innovators, portfolios of work would be evaluated that took into account ascending levels of productivity and application of inquiry, creative problem solving, and analytic and synthetic productivity. These evaluation methods would again require consultation with experts to explicate how we would imagine students ascending through the levels of productivity in a discipline.

CONCLUSION

Both the accelerative and creative paths have equal value in the world. There seems to be an artificial dichotomy or tension between the two paths that is unnecessary and unproductive. Although we have identified two groups of gifted students, the key lies in the availability of both of the academic–accelerative and creative–productive paths and not the academic or creative student, because students may follow different paths at different times in their intellectual lives. Often, individuals must master the domain first before creativity can emerge (Gardner, 1993, Csikszentmihalyi, 1996). A student may begin in the academic–accelerative path and then, at a later time, the services of the creative–productive path may be a better match. At other times, a curiosity and inclination for problem solving may lead to the need to pursue great in-depth study of a domain. The key lies in flexibility so that students are facilitated in their individual journeys to adult career paths.

Tannenbaum (1997; 2000) has described the range of adult paths, including those he calls quota, scarcity, and surplus talents. Quota talents include professions such as physicians, engineers, lawyers, business executives, and pharmacists. Scarcity talents describe the necessary contributions of the creative scientist or social leader. Surplus talents describe those persons whose life works have enhanced human life, such as Bach or Picasso. There is a sense that people who go on to demonstrate scarcity and surplus talents are more valuable than those who demonstrate quota talents. Scarcity and surplus talents are important; however, expertise is a valued life goal as well. Society needs experts, and we should not expect that all gifted children will grow up to change the world (Winner, 2000). Renzulli (1986, p. 59) writes that the "first purpose of gifted education is to provide young people with maximum opportunities for self-fulfillment through the development and expression of one or a combination of performance areas where superior potential may be present." The goal in our model is to recognize the critical need to identify all children for whom the traditional curriculum falls short of challenging the abilities they have and who are mired in situations in which they cannot pursue the passion for learning through curricular options that maximize their potential to grow up to be happy and self-fulfilled – whether as experts in their fields, creative producers, or creative implementers.

References

Amabile, T. (1996). *Creativity in context.* Boulder, CO: Westview Press.

Benbow, C. P., & Lubinski, D. (1997). Intellectually talented children: How can we best meet their needs? In N. Colangelo and G. A. Davis (Eds.), *Handbook of gifted education* (2nd ed., pp. 155–169). Needham Heights, MA: Allyn & Bacon.

Butterfield, E. C., & Ferretti, R. P. (1987). Toward a theoretical integration of cognitive hypotheses about intellectual differences among children. In J. G. Borkowski & J. D. Day (Eds.), *Cognition in special children: Comparative approaches to retardation, learning disabilities, and giftedness* (pp. 195–233). Norwood, NJ: Ablex.

Clark, B. (1992). *Growing up gifted* (4th ed.). New York: Macmillan.

Coleman, E. B., & Shore, B. (1991). Problem-solving processes of high and average performers in physics. *Journal for the Education of the Gifted, 14,* 366–379.

Collins, M. A., & Amabile, T. M. (1999). Motivation and creativity. In R. Sternberg (Ed.), *Handbook of creativity* (pp. 297–312). New York: Cambridge University Press.

Csikszentmihalyi, M. (1990). *Flow: The psychology of optimal experience.* New York: HarperCollins.

Csikszentmihalyi, M. (1996). *Creativity: Flow and the psychology of discovery and invention.* New York: HarperCollins.

Csikszentmihalyi, M., Rathunde, K., & Whalen, S. (1993). *Talented teenagers: The roots of success and failure.* New York: Cambridge University Press.

Csikszentmihalyi, M., & Wolfe, R. (2000). New conceptions and research approaches to creativity: Implications of a systems perspective for creativity in education. In K. Heller, F. Monks, R. Sternberg, & R. Subotnik (Eds.), *International handbook of giftedness and talent* (2nd ed., pp. 81–93). New York: Elsevier.

Dawis, R. V., & Lofquist, L. H. (1984). *A psychological theory of work adjustment.* Minneapolis: University of Minnesota Press.

Gardner, H. (1983). *Frames of mind: The theory of multiple intelligences.* New York: Basic Books.

Gardner, H. (1991). *The unschooled mind: How children think, how schools should teach.* New York: Basic Books.

Gardner, H. (1993). *Creating Minds: An anatomy of creativity seen through the lives of Freud, Einstein, Picasso, Stravinsky, Eliot, Graham, and Gandhi.* New York: Basic Books.

Getzels, J. W., & Csikszentmihalyi, M. (1976). *The creative vision: A longitudinal study of problem finding in art.* New York: Wiley.

Hoover, S. M. (1994). Scientific problem finding in gifted fifth-grade students. *Roeper Review, 16,* 156–159.

Kanevsky, L. (1990). Pursuing qualitative difference in the flexible use of problem-solving strategy by young children. *Journal for the Education of the Gifted, 13,* 115–140.

Kanevsky, L. S. (1992). The learning game. In P. Klein & A. J. Tannenbaum, *To be young and gifted* (pp. 204–241). Norwood, NJ: Ablex.

Kaplan, S. N. (1986). The grid: A model to construct differentiated curriculum for the gifted. In J. S. Renzulli (Ed.), *Systems and models for developing programs for the gifted and talented* (pp. 182–193). Mansfield Center, CT: Creative Learning Press.

Kaplan, S. N. (2001). Layering differentiated curriculum for the gifted and talented. In F. A. Karnes & S. M. Bean (Eds.), *Methods and materials for teaching the gifted* (pp. 133–158). Waco, TX: Prufrock.

Lubinski, D., & Benbow, C. P. (2000). States of excellence. *American Psychologist, 55,* 137–150.

Porath, M. (1991). Stage and structure in the development of children with various types of "giftedness." In R. Case (Ed.), *The mind's staircase: Exploring the conceptual underpinnings of children's thought and knowledge* (pp. 303–317). Hillsdale, NJ: Lawrence Erlbaum Associates.

Renzulli, J. S. (1977). *The enrichment triad model: A guide for developing defensible programs for the gifted and talented.* Mansfield Center, CT: Creative Learning Press.

Renzulli, J. S. (1978). What makes giftedness: Reexamining a definition. *Phi Delta Kappan, 60,* 180–184, 261.

Renzulli, J. S. (1986). The three-ring conception of giftedness: A developmental model for creative productivity. In R. J. Sternberg & J. Davidson (Eds.), *Conceptions of giftedness* (pp. 53–92). Cambridge, UK: Cambridge University Press.

Renzulli, J. S., & Reis, S. N. (1985). *The schoolwide enrichment model: A comprehensive plan for educational excellence.* Mansfield Center, CT: Creative Learning Press.

Renzulli, J. S., & Smith, L. H. (1978). *The compactor.* Mansfield Center, CT: Creative Learning Press.

Runco, M. A. (2004). Creativity. *Annual Review of Psychology, 55,* 657–687.

Shavinina, L. V., & Kholodnaja, M. A. (1996). The cognitive experience as a psychological basis of intellectual giftedness. *Journal for the Education of the Gifted, 20*(1), 3–35.

Shore, B. M. (2000). Metacognition and flexibility: Qualitative difference in how gifted children think. In R. C. Friedman & B. M. Shore (Eds.), *Talents unfolding: Cognition and development.* Washington, DC: American Psychological Association.

Stanley, J. C., & Benbow, C. P. (1986). Youths who reason exceptionally well mathematically. In R. J. Sternberg & J. E. Davidson (Eds.), *Conceptions of giftedness* (pp. 361–387). New York: Cambridge University Press.

Sternberg, R. J. (1981). A componential theory of intelligence. *Gifted Child Quarterly, 25*, 86–93.

Sternberg, R. J. (1985). *Beyond IQ: A triarchic theory of human intelligence.* Cambridge, England: Cambridge University Press.

Sternberg, R. J. (1986). A triarchic theory of intellectual giftedness. In R. J. Sternberg & J. Davidson (Eds.), *Conceptions of giftedness* (pp. 223–243). Cambridge, England: Cambridge University Press.

Sternberg, R. J. (1995). *A triarchic approach to giftedness.* Storrs, CT: National Research Center on the Gifted and Talented.

Sternberg, R. J. (2000a). Identifying and developing creative giftedness. *Roeper Review, 23*, 60–64.

Sternberg, R. J. (2000b). Giftedness as developing expertise. In K. A. Heller, F. J. Monks, R. J. Sternberg, & R. F. Subotnik (Eds.), *International handbook of giftedness and talent* (2nd ed., pp. 55–66). Oxford, England: Elsevier.

Sternberg, R. J., & Horvath, J. A. (1998). Cognitive conceptions of expertise and their relations to giftedness. In R. C. Friedman & K. B. Rogers (Eds.), *Talent in context: Historical and social perspectives on giftedness* (pp. 177–191). Washington, DC: American Psychological Association.

Tannenbaum, A. J. (1986). Giftedness: A psychosocial approach. In R. J. Sternberg & J. Davidson (Eds.), *Conceptions of giftedness* (pp. 21–52). Cambridge, England: Cambridge University Press.

Tannenbaum, A. J. (1997). The meaning and making of giftedness. In N. Colangelo & G. A. Davis (Eds.) *Handbook of gifted education* (2nd ed., pp. 27–42). Needham Heights, MA: Allyn & Bacon.

Tannenbaum, A. J. (2000). Giftedness: The ultimate instrument for good and evil. In K. A. Heller, F. J. Monks, R. J. Sternberg, & R. F. Subotnik (Eds.), *International handbook of giftedness and talent* (2nd ed.). New York: Elsevier.

Tomlinson, C. A., Kaplan, S. N., Renzulli, J. S., Purcel, J., Lappein, J., & Burns, D. (2002). *The parallel curriculum: A design to develop high potential and challenge high-ability learners.* Thousand Oaks, CA: Corwin.

Vygotsky, L. S. (1978). Mind in society. Cambridge, MA: Harvard University.

Winner, E. (1997). Exceptionally high intelligence and schooling. *American Psychologist, 52*, 1070–1081.

Winner, E. (2000). The origins and ends of giftedness. *American Psychologist, 55*, 159–169.

4

School-Based Conception of Giftedness

Tracy L. Cross and Laurence J. Coleman

The development of human potential occurs in a vast array of settings across the world. In the United States, in addition to the options of both public and private schools, parents homeschool their children and send them to academic summer programs, often resulting in able students developing to a point of extraordinary accomplishment. Some talents are typically developed early in life (e.g., piano playing), whereas others manifest much later (e.g., architecture). Some talents are developed entirely outside of school, whereas others are developed in schools to a considerable extent. Some talents are in domains that schools have key roles in developing, others may have no direct relationship to a school's curriculum. Given the limited resources and dominion of schools, we set out to create a conception of giftedness that is situated in schools. It is our belief that a school-based conception of giftedness (SCG) will clarify what talents schools can and cannot be expected to develop. The SCG will allow for clearer communication among educators, administrators, and school boards about the role and responsibilities of our schools in developing talent.

ADVANCED DEVELOPMENT AND SCHOOL-BASED GIFTEDNESS

In this chapter, advanced development and giftedness within the context of the school are discussed. Our contention is that advanced development is the fundamental concept for understanding giftedness, and we attempt to explain our position by offering a definition, describing the roots of the definition – explaining the changes in our thinking – that have led to a deeper understanding of giftedness and schooling, and proposing a modified definition. We also discuss some implications of the ideas we have proposed.

Origins of the SCG

The foundation of the definition we propose in this chapter originally appeared in the definition by Coleman (1985) and later by Coleman and Cross (2001):

The definition in this text differs from others by proposing a change in the criteria that describe giftedness, accounting for changes in abilities with advancing age in school. The criteria became narrower with increased age. This means that in the early grades, giftedness would appear more in the areas of general ability or specific skills, but as a child moves through the grades, evidence of ability and achievement would manifest within a specific area of study. This is a developmental model that has its roots in the writings of Fliegler (1961), Newland (1976), Renzulli (1977), Feldman (1997), and Simonton (1997).

Preadolescent gifted children have the potential or demonstrated ability in two areas: general cognitive ability and creative ability. Adolescent children have demonstrated ability in abstract thinking, have produced creative works in some worthwhile area, and have demonstrated consistent involvement in activities of either type. (pp. 19–20)

The writing of that definition was based on a particular understanding of giftedness in 1985. The most significant idea was that giftedness does not exist solely within an individual (Feldman, 1997). Individuals in a particular context express giftedness in an area of human endeavor. The context sets the opportunities that are necessary for development to occur. Advanced development occurs when opportunities for learning are available in the environment and are seized by the person. High cognitive ability and creativity are the sources of advanced development in young children as reflected in the many definitions of giftedness. Having ability and creativity may predispose one to develop in an area, but it is insufficient to explain advanced development. Some children who possess both do not perform in a way that demonstrates giftedness in secondary school. If a child is not behaving as if she or he is gifted, does it make sense to continue the designation? In secondary school, giftedness is manifested by consistent interest, creative production, and achievement in an area of the curriculum. Being gifted means moving beyond potential to actual performance. Thus, one might shed the label of giftedness as one ages and does not manifest potential. Furthermore, children who were not considered gifted and begin to perform in secondary school as if they were gifted, should be accorded the label. These thoughts were largely responsible for the earlier definition.

School Focus

While the original conception was continued by Coleman and Cross (2001), a body of new evidence was accumulating that began to change the philosophical underpinnings of that definition, but not the definition itself. This evidence was not reflected in the 2001 definition. Overall, our basic concern was how to produce a workable definition that made sense within the context of the school, where a significant proportion of the development of giftedness takes place, and to be consistent with what we understood about the development of persons who are gifted. We argue that the school organization and the curriculum should be modified along the lines of talent development to foster advanced development. We would like to see children have opportunities for growing as fast as they want and are able. Our present definition of giftedness is similar to the early definition, but is held together by different conceptual glue. In recent years, rudimentary ideas about giftedness, advanced development, and schooling have become more explicit and the relationship between the concepts better articulated. We begin by defining some terms to lay out the territory.

Giftedness is an age-specific term that refers to the potential of young persons who are judged to have demonstrated rapid learning compared with their peers. The judgment is made on the basis of some normative standard. Giftedness is normally distributed in the population so that relatively few are very rapid learners.

Development is the change in a person that occurs over time, manifesting itself in movement from concrete behavior and thought to abstract, complex behavior and thought. Human development is conceptualized as proceeding through periods that summarize significant changes in that person in myriad areas, such as the social, intellectual, and physical. Development is generated by biological forces and by learning. The latter leads to development, as suggested by Vygotsky (1978). Development is continuous, unconscious at early stages, and volitional at the most advanced stages.

Context is a broad term referring to the environment surrounding a person. The environment may be thought of in various ways (e.g., Bronfenbrenner, 1994). Environments can be categorized by terms such as *cultural, familial,* and *school-related.* School-related conditions are the focus of this chapter. Environments are not randomly distributed. Some environments are more conducive to some forms of advanced development than others. Impoverished environments generally depress advanced development.

Creativity is a term that denotes the production of an original idea or behavior that changes the way others think about or behave in an area of worthwhile human endeavor. The standards for judging creativity extend from the personal to the societal. In our view, the appropriate standard is beyond the personal.

Domain refers to areas of human endeavor that are often referred to as talents, fields, or disciplines. A domain is defined by persons who work in that area, by their recognition of others' work as belonging to that area, and by their ability to distinguish among varying levels of accomplishment. Each domain has its own meanings or rules of operation that are shared by members who possess that talent. The place where giftedness, development, context, and creativity converge is in the domain. Compared with the general population, a relatively small proportion of persons are members of a domain, and within the domain an even smaller number develop to the most advanced levels. Gifted persons are those who learn rapidly in a domain; talented persons are the most advanced in that domain. The change from giftedness to talent is a mark of development within the domain, rather than a chronological point. This difference is promoted by commitment, opportunity, and needs. The most advanced forms of talent are when the person redefines or reconceptualizes the domain and is what we mean by creative.

WHAT IS THE ROLE OF SCHOOL IN PROMOTING ADVANCED DEVELOPMENT?

The common school is a societally created context where many domains may be promoted, but typically only a few are. The domains, or talents within domains, that are developed are valued by the parental society and are necessarily restricted because of values and availability of limited resources. The common school gets into peculiar difficulties when dealing with giftedness as advanced development in two ways: the assignment of children to the gifted category and the meaning of creativity.

Who is Gifted?

In schools, we find instances of children being assigned to the gifted category based on ability scores and not assigned membership based on performance. At first glance, this may seem a trivial difference, but actually two problems appear. We find members of the gifted group who have not shown their ability, except that they have scored well on an ability measure, sitting beside peers who are performing as well as or better than the gifted group. Does assignment of the label make sense in this situation? What message is being sent? Is potential more important than performance?

The second problem that becomes evident is that membership in the gifted group earns placement in special programs whether gifted students perform well or not. Those who perform as well as or better, but had lower ability scores, are not assigned to the special program. Thus, another message is sent: High performance does not get you special programming. In effect, this practice denies appropriate instruction for low-performing gifted children and high-performing children. Neither is being taught at their instructional level. Inappropriate instruction benefits no one unless you count being excused from regular class a benefit. Based on what is known about advanced development, this situation is contradictory and paradoxical.

What Is Creative?

A parallel situation to the question of who is really gifted is the problem of using creativity as a criterion for being gifted and/or as a criterion of advanced development. In schools, we find instances of children being considered creative who have done nothing but score well on some measure of creative potential. This designation seems workable in the early grades where novelty in terms of one's own development is the evidence for creativity. At this point in school, there is no conflict between measures of ability and behavior. It is in secondary school that this means of identifying creativity becomes unstable because the standard for judging creativity changes from that of the individual to that of performance in a particular domain, which is the same standard as in the adult world. The discontinuity between measures of creative potential and creativity in a domain produces the odd circumstances we have just shown. What is the message being communicated about the meaning of creativity? We can certainly use different means for identification at different ages, but we need to be able to show a strong connection between child and adult creativity. Such evidence is lacking.

In both of our examples about giftedness and creativity, the situation is similar. Signs of potential are used for purposes of identification, and those signs have limited connection to later behavior. Having a group with unrealized potential is unacceptable because students are supposed to perform near their potential. The typical reply to this situation is to assert that the child has some problem that is inhibiting his or her development or the context is the source of the limiting factors. Hence, the school needs to fix the problem.

We find this reply unsettling on several fronts. It presumes that the ability measure has high predictive power in terms of later advanced development, and unrealized potential is a consequence of malevolent uncontrollable forces, inside or outside the child. Both views are unhelpful in terms of fostering advanced development. Further, a false connection is established between identification based on ability and outcomes based on performance in domains. We believe these explanations are inadequate and irrelevant to advanced development and miss key points about advanced development and the context of school. Unrealized potential makes no sense as we move to the higher levels of development because the highest levels of development require commitment to the domain.

This incorrect notion about the match between ability and performance gets educators into strange arguments and illustrates the confusion about giftedness and advanced development. Furthermore, it ignores what we know about advanced development. The entire situation is exacerbated by the fact that the school personnel who work in one context for advanced development misunderstand domains and are wedded to a model of schooling that is antithetical to the encouragement of advanced development.

MISUNDERSTANDING DOMAINS

The subjects that are most promoted in schools are domains in themselves. For example, mathematics, reading, writing, music, and art are both subjects and domains. Most significantly, they also serve as foundations for other domains that operate outside the common school. For example, math is related to architecture as a domain, reading to law, and art to sculpture. Other school-based domains are also fostered, such as football, auto mechanics, and civics, but these domains are self-contained and do not spread readily to advanced development in other domains. The former we will call foundational domains and the latter, performance domains.

Foundational domains and performance domains are typically identified differently in schools, although it does not have to be that way. The foundational domains are determined by a test of ability and/or achievement. The performance domain is based usually on achievement and/or performance. We find a mismatch between ability and performance within the foundational domains, but rarely in the performance domains. Significantly, for the foundational domains, the mismatch is less likely to happen when achievement rather than ability is the basis of the identification.

The present assessment situation between the domain types does not mean that foundational domains must be assessed differently from performance domains. When achievement measures are used with foundational domains, assessment issues in terms of identification and outcomes become the same; that is, performance is the key. The transfer power of foundational domains remains the same, even when the assessment changes. When foundational domains are treated as performance domains, advanced development can be placed in a more sensible manner in the context of the school. Dropping the use of ability measures would be an antidote to the present situation. Advanced behavior in terms of identification and outcomes would be more closely associated. In this manner, we would solve the ability, creativity, and performance discontinuity by keeping advanced development under the mantle of domains.

MODELS OF SCHOOLING

The problem created by lack of recognition about the difference between the two types of domains is fed by the conflict between two models of schooling and their relationship to advanced development. The talent/multiple abilities model of schooling competes with the whole child model of schooling for resources and the promotion of giftedness (Coleman, 1985; Coleman & Cross, 2001). The models conceive of goals, the role of the student, and schooling in opposite ways. These differences have profound effects on advanced development.

The dominant model of schooling, the whole child model, promotes ideas that do not match what we know about advanced development in a domain. In the whole child model, advanced development is honored in the mission statements of schools, but demonstration of advanced development by students is met with uneasiness, suspicion, even hostility in some cases. A contrary situation occurs in the talent/multiple abilities model, in which advanced development is welcomed and nurtured. The whole child model presumes that children should be relatively well balanced in their achievement and interests. The standard for advanced development is derived from averaging estimates of peers' performance at particular age/grade levels. A peer-based standard is preferred over a domain-based standard. The whole child model is concerned more about remediating holes and deficiencies in development than worrying about missed opportunities for advanced development. The fear is that leaving imbalances alone will end in serious future problems for the learner.

The talent/multiple abilities model presumes that the goal of education is to maximize advanced development. For those talents that are identifiable during the school years, students are encouraged to learn rapidly, and being highly motivated in the strength area is expected. Lack of development is traced to ineffective teaching rather than learner deficiencies. The standard for development is gauged against the growth in the domain or talent area itself. The norm in this instance is the pattern of development of the domain. Lack of opportunity in areas not related to the domain is viewed as minor; learners will deal with that later by themselves. Balanced development is not actively pursued because it is presumed to be irrelevant to advanced development.

The influence of the whole child model distorts the school-based context and promotes contradictory policies and practices that work against advanced development. One example of the manifestation of this is the disconnection between ability and performance discussed earlier. That detachment raises the issue of whether there is a point at which claims of high potential ability make little sense. We believe there is. In our view, by secondary school, one should be demonstrating an engagement in a domain. Without that commitment, advanced development is unlikely because deliberate engagement is necessary. Holding on to potential as the precursor for advanced development is no longer viable because the individual must take a role in his or her own development.

So, to summarize our position, our assertion about advanced development and school-based giftedness begins with the recognition that giftedness does not exist solely within an individual. Individual actors in a domain in a particular context express giftedness. The context sets the conditions needed for advanced development to occur. The individual's growth has a trajectory and associated antecedent conditions. Development occurs when opportunities for learning are available in the environment and the person seizes on those opportunities. Having ability may predispose one to develop in an area, but ability is insufficient to explain advanced development. Being gifted means moving beyond potential to long-term activity within the domain. As one advances to the edge of a domain, creativity becomes a driving force in the birth of the highest levels of a domain. The student moves into more circumscribed contexts where others who share a commitment to the domain are located. The interactions in those more specialized contexts propel development to the highest levels. However, advanced development is fragile, and many forces may subvert reaching the highest levels.

Our thinking leads us to propose a reworked definition. Giftedness in school is an age-related phenomenon. Young children and preadolescent children who are gifted show high general cognitive ability, either through potential (ability), actions (performance), or rapid learning in school-related domains. By secondary school, gifted children should be demonstrating advanced development in a foundational domain or have produced creative works in some societally valued area and have demonstrated consistent engagement in activities associated with either type. If these attributes are not evident, then the child is no longer gifted in terms of the school's curriculum.

IMPLICATIONS

The Distribution of Advanced Development

Our new thinking means a reinterpretation of other ideas associated with giftedness and school. Much of advanced development, if not all, is learned. Limited evidence suggests this might not be so for all domains (Winner, 1996), but for many domains the evidence suggests that inborn ability is not necessary. Although potential to be gifted may be normally distributed, advanced development is not. Opportunity and commitment are the keys. Both are contextually linked. The environment presents the former; the latter is personal. Environments that are unresponsive to rapid learning, have inadequate resources relevant to a domain, and provide no models for development inhibit advanced development. Impoverished environments have the most pervasive negative effect. These contextual features of the environment are out of the control of young persons. Interest across domains is not normally distributed. Some contexts promote the development of the individual more than others. Unless an interest becomes a passionate activity, the most advanced development is unlikely to happen because of the energy that must be directed to mastering and creating new levels of the domain.

The Meaning of Advanced Development

Advanced development is quite ordinary in the sense that most people are capable of it. Development advances in all domains. What is less common is that some persons continue to develop beyond where most people slow down or stop. Recognizing that some actions or thoughts are out of the ordinary means the person does something that either happens earlier than is expected or is original in terms of its related domain. As one attains or creates the upper levels of a domain, fewer persons may be able to recognize it. Knowledge at the highest level of development requires deep understanding of the domain.

The Power of the Context

An ongoing concern of the field of gifted education has been underachieving gifted students. The philosophical underpinning of this concern originally was giftedness as an entity. Gifted people are born that way, so if they do not rise to the expectations of ability measures, they are determined to be underachievers. Our school-based conception of giftedness changes the issues surrounding underachievers. Because of the change in criteria from potential to achievement within domains, over time, the likelihood of a gifted student demonstrating rapid learning and/or expertise in a domain greatly diminishes. In many domains, the student's once-demonstrated potential would be akin to missing one's ship. And, as we stated earlier, "unrealized potential makes no sense as we move to the higher levels of development because the highest levels of development require commitment to the domain" (Cross & Coleman, in press). Given this situation, it means the qualities of the context, or environment, become more and more important as one moves deeper into a domain. Rapid learners in a domain need to find themselves in a responsive environment. The characteristics of these environments change as one progresses through a domain. How they should change is not yet clear, but one piece is certain. Being in an environment with like-minded peers promotes advanced development. It may serve to help persons define themselves as members of that domain. This aspect of context should be exploited in schools.

The Congruence of Acceleration to Advanced Development

Authors in the field have argued about the efficacy of different grouping types for years. For example, Vaughn, Feldhusen, & Asher (1991) showed evidence of enrichment being effective, whereas Stanley (1973) has long touted the effectiveness of acceleration. In their meta-analytic study, Kulik & Kulik (1991) determined that acceleration was a stronger intervention for advanced development than was enrichment, despite repeated efforts to show the effectiveness of the latter. One reason for this recurring finding is because acceleration more closely parallels the natural progression of learning in a domain, that is, the movement from simple to complex, from concrete to abstract, from unfocused creativity to focused creativity. Enrichment, on the other hand, disperses the drive for advanced development and short circuits the thrill of learning. Another reason is that, in an accelerated educational environment, a means of assessment becomes readily detectable. When an individual continues to participate in one domain for a sustained period, the prerequisites to later development are evident. This visibility means that focused feedback can be given to the person, either by self-observation or by the teacher or coach. In an accelerated context, growth and advancement in the domain are apparent to the person as well as to outsiders. The mystery of how it happens is not revealed, but the progression is. The teacher and the students see the results of their efforts. Recognition of advanced development and success comes from that and in turn clarifies what one can do and be in that domain. In other words, a process of self-definition begins and continues as development advances. These are powerful determinants of advanced development.

Ability Measures for Nonmodal Gifted

In general, we would abandon the widespread use of ability measures in the identification of children who are gifted because the practice leads to policies that are antithetical to advanced development, as we have noted in this chapter. On the other hand, we advocate the use of ability measures with nonmodal children, the children who are typically missed in our identification systems. Our view may seem perverse because the conventional wisdom is that ability measures are heavily biased. In our view, the ability measure provides an imprecise but useful indicator of general development for those children who are growing rapidly in the face of less than maximal contexts for advanced development.

SUMMARY

Giftedness is a combination of advanced development and creativity. It is developmental in nature in that it begins as potential (generally in young people), evolves into achievement within recognizable domains during the school years, and becomes increasingly advanced (compared with peers) through the nonuniversal development of the individual. Although the authors recognize that development continues across the life span, the

School-Based Conception of Giftedness was created to emphasize the development of talents from the early years through late adolescence. Moreover, innumerable talent domains exist; only some manifestations are within the charge of our nation's schools. The domains in which giftedness are recognized are reflective of society's values and are subject to historical influences. Giftedness, therefore, represents a complex series of interactions that include the coordination of many traits of the individual student, such as motivation and perseverance, with context variables, such as teacher expertise and opportunities for practice, along with the general ability levels of the individual in terms of academic domains, and levels of creativity. Consequently, although the potential to be gifted *may* be normally distributed, giftedness is not.

Ultimately, giftedness is a consequence of development of the individual over time. Although people generally follow certain forms of universal development, such as those described in developmental psychology, the pattern of those developing extraordinary talent is necessarily nonuniversal by its very nature (Feldman, 1997). It may represent common patterns within specific disciplines and, therefore, will be both idiosyncratic and normal. Hence, people may be born with the potential to be gifted but many do not actually become gifted because to be gifted means to be gifted at something.

References

Bronfenbrenner, U. (1994). Ecological models of human development. In T. Husen & T. N. Postlethwaite (Eds.), *International encyclopedia of education* (Vol. 3, 2nd ed., pp. 1643–1647). Oxford, England: Pergamon/Elsevier.

Coleman, L. J. (1985). *Schooling the gifted*. Reading, MA: Addison-Wesley.

Coleman, L. J., & Cross, T. L. (2001). *Being gifted in school: An introduction to development, guidance, and teaching*. Waco, TX: Prufrock Press.

Feldman, D. H. (1997, August). *Developmental theory and the expression of talent*. Paper presented at the 12th World Conference of the World Council for Gifted and Talented Children, Seattle, WA.

Fliegler, L. A. (1961). *Curriculum planning for the gifted*. Englewood Cliffs, NJ: Prentice-Hall.

Kulik, C., & Kulik, J. (1991). Ability grouping and gifted students. In N. Colangenlo & A. G. Davis (Eds.), *Handbook of gifted education* (2nd ed., pp. 230–242). Boston: Allyn & Bacon.

Newland, T. E. (1976). *The gifted in socio-educational perspective*. Englewood Cliffs, NJ: Prentice Hall.

Renzulli, J. S. (1977). *The enrichment triad model: A guide for developing defensible programs for the gifted and talented*. Wethersfield, CT: Creative Learning Press.

Simonton, D. (1997). When giftedness becomes genius: How does talent achieve eminence? In N. Colangelo & G. Davis, *Handbook of gifted education* (2nd ed., pp. 335–349). Boston: Allyn & Bacon.

Stanley, J. C. (1973). Accelerating the educational progress of intellectually gifted youth. *Educational Psychologist, 10*, 133–146.

Vaughn, V., Feldhusen, J., & Asher, W. (1991). Meta-analysis and review of research on pullout programs in gifted education. *Gifted Child Quarterly, 35*(2), 92–98.

Vygotsky, L. S. (1978). *Mind and society: The development of higher mental processes.* Cambridge, MA: Harvard University Press.

Winner, E. (1996). *Gifted children: Myths and realities.* New York: Basic Books.

5

Giftedness, Talent, Expertise, and Creative Achievement

John F. Feldhusen

Giftedness, talent, expertise, and creative achievement are inextricably linked concepts. As we seek to understand the development of abilities in youth and the rise to high-level achievement in adulthood, these concepts may guide our efforts to nurture and establish conditions for their full fruition. The purpose of this chapter, then, is to examine the basic nature of giftedness, talent, expertise, and creative achievement and their interrelationships as they affect and guide the education of gifted and talented youth and to delineate guidelines for the development of high-level and creative achievement in adulthood.

What genetic potentials and facilitative conditions combine and interact to produce expertise and/or high-level creative achievement? From exhaustive study of the lives of creative achievers, Gardner (1993) and Simonton (1997) offer some insights based on in-depth analysis of the lives of high-level, creative achievers. At first one is struck by the diversity among very high achievers: staid Albert Einstein, flamboyant Picasso, isolated Georgia O'Keefe, scholarly Darwin, and adventurous Ernest Hemingway! Are there common characteristics that might account for their genius or serve as predictors of creative achievement? Or are they too unique as examples of high-level achievement? Insights derived from research on the lives of great achievers are examined later in this chapter.

GIFTED AND PRECOCIOUS

Gifts come from people. Nature gives no gifts, but it does transmit some genetic potentials (Bouchard, 1997; Plomin, 1997; Scarr, 1997). Genetic potentials unfold in interaction with stimulating experiences structured by parents, family, home, schools, teachers, and curricula. Some children have genetic potential to learn more easily, earlier, and faster than others, to learn more complex and more abstract schemas than others, and to remember and retrieve information better than others. Given opportunities to engage in advanced cognitive and learning activities earlier than typical age-grade experiences, the genetic potential of these precocious children interacts with the stimulating experiences, producing learning and school achievements at above-average or extremely high levels (Wachs, 1992). There is abundant evidence that children who are gifted, as evidenced by their high IQs, and who enjoy their parents' and teachers' rich nurturance, develop superior abilities and achieve at much higher levels than do those who are not gifted (Ericsson, 1996; Benbow, Lubinski, & Buchy, 1996; Terman & Oden, 1959; Bloom, 1985; Holahan & Sears, 1995; Simonton, 1997). They learn rapidly and get far ahead of age-mates and thus may be seen as precocious.

Precocious children and their parents often have abundant resources and opportunities to advance and enhance their development and education in the United States and in many other cultures, particularly if their parents are affluent professionals or artists, but children from poverty-stricken homes may be denied many stimulating and excellent educational experiences, and thus suffer lifelong deficits in achievement and the development of cognitive abilities. The book *New York Families Can't Live Without It: The Essential Guide for New York City Parents; Family Resource Guide* (Vol. 8, 1999–2000) lists more than 500 resources for the education, enrichment, and enhancement of experiences for children such as after-school classes, language learning, museums, dance lessons, gymnastics, and so on; all, or nearly all, however, include fees that would often be a burden for needy families.

FROM GIFTS TO FACTORS TO TALENTS

The term "gifted" was originally used chiefly to refer to children who exhibited unusual precocity or, after the development of intelligence tests, to children with high IQs. In several fields of art, the term was, and still is, also often used to refer to people with extraordinary talent. School programs for intellectually precocious children are also often referred to as "gifted education" and the children who qualify for the programs as "gifted children." All uses of the term "gifted" naturally emphasize genetic or inherited endowment of the special abilities that are thought to constitute "giftedness."

Pioneering research on gifted children began with the work of Lewis Terman at Stanford University in 1920 (Terman, 1925). Using the Stanford–Binet Intelligence Scale that he had developed and published in 1916, he went on to identify 1,528 children (average age: 12) with IQs above 135 (most had IQs above 140) and to study their lives in great detail. The first major finding of the study, published in 1925, was that the children overall were not, as commonly thought, a group of social misfits characterized by eccentric behavior, but rather they were generally quite normal except for their academic superiority and very good health. Although the sample was quite biased in favor of White middle-class families, the findings were widely accepted in educational settings and came to focus educators' attention on the children's special need for more high-level and challenging instruction.

The understanding of intelligence and its role in giftedness was enhanced a great deal by Thurstone's (1936) discovery of factors of intelligence and the fact that people have differentiated and unique patterns of cognitive capabilities – numerical, verbal, spatial, and fluency, all of which are really components of general intelligence. Later, the same analytical tools of factor analysis would be used (Cattell, 1971) to show that some aspects of intelligence are predominantly genetically determined (fluid) and others are acquired through the interaction of genetic disposition with learning opportunities (crystallized). Thus, reasoning is more closely a fluid aspect of intelligence, whereas mathematical ability may be a learned capacity that in turn manifests itself in intelligent behavior.

The componential approach to understanding intelligence and giftedness in a sense ran wild when Guilford (1959), using new methods of factor analysis, seemingly found hundreds of factors or facets of intelligence. Guilford and Hoepfner (1971) went on to propose a "structure of intellect" (p. 19) in which there were three dimensions: content or input on which thinking operates, operations or thinking processes and skills, and products or outcomes of the operations. The model was widely embraced, especially because of its inclusion of divergent or creative thinking as an operation.

Comprehensive reviews of the factor analytic literature and their own research via factor analysis of test measures of ability led Carroll (1993), Jensen (1997), Scarr (1997) and a host of other researchers to multifactor conceptions of the structure of human cognitive abilities as well as a general, or g, factor. All of them recognized both a strong genetic determination of abilities as well as a substantial influence of the cultural, parental, and school environments on the development of these abilities. It is an interactive process operating probably in all animals and, especially as Hebb (1949) showed us a long time ago, in the realm of intelligence of rats, dogs, and, as a host of researchers demonstrated, human organisms. The nature of the structure continues to be uncertain, as represented by the highly speculative structure proposed by Gardner (1983), and perhaps much more well defined, if we are conservative and limit ourselves to the fluid and declarative processes first proposed by Cattell (1963) and confirmed much later by Carroll (1993) with much more subfactor specificity. The major issues that continue to be debated are the possibility of g, the heritability of abilities, and whether pencil-and-paper test scores represent the true nature of human abilities. Thus, Scarr's (1997) argument in favor of rating scale assessment of observed human abilities and Gardner's (1983) support of teachers' classroom evaluation by observation of children's intelligences are supports for the validity of current conceptions of cognitive abilities.

In the 1980s and 1990s, our conceptions of intelligence and giftedness were strongly influenced by the research and theorizing of Sternberg and Gardner. Both were highly influential in educational practice and in education of the gifted and talented. Sternberg's work was based solidly in psychology, whereas Gardner drew insights for his speculation from a wide diversity of fields.

Drawing on the work of the factor analysts and other sources of theoretical and empirical support, Gardner (1983; 1999) proposed that there are possibly nine potential intellectual strengths: logical–mathematical, verbal–linguistic, visual–spatial, musical, bodily–kinesthetic, intrapersonal, interpersonal, naturalist, and existential. The first seven are well established in his theoretical framework, whereas the latter two are more tentative. Many schools have embraced the concept of multiple intelligences and are using them to identify individual student strengths in both regular and gifted programs (Gardner, Walter, & Hatch, 1992). The Key School (K–12) in Indianapolis, Indiana, has a well-established model program based on the multiple intelligences.

Sternberg's (1997) triarchic theory of intelligence proposes three major information-processing components of intelligence, or subtheories. The first is the higher-order executive processes of planning, monitoring, evaluating, and problem solving; the second is performance components that execute and evaluate the operations; and the third is knowledge acquisition, which refers to learning how to solve problems.

The second aspect of the triarchic theory is experiential in moving to smooth, automatic processing of the componential functions. Finally, the third, contextual aspect, refers to applications of the components in relatively new situations and environments. Sternberg (1997) has gone on beyond theory development to application of the theory in instructional programs for youth and gifted youth in particular, working with the National Center for Gifted and Talented Youth.

Finally there is a transition to talent orientation, particularly with the publication in 1985 of Gagné's new delineation and theoretical formulation of the relationship between giftedness and talent. In subsequent research and publications, Gagné (1993, 1995, 1999) refined the model and increasingly influenced the field of gifted education to move beyond perfunctory and meaningless use of the term "gifted and talented" to a true delineation of talents as specific abilities that emerge out of general giftedness.

Feldhusen continued the effort to focus gifted educators on talent recognition and development with his Talent Identification and Development in Education (TIDE) model (1992, 1994, 1995, 1998, 1999). Along with Gagné, Feldhusen's research delineated basic categories of talent such as mathematical, musical, personal–social, technological, artistic, athletic, and vocational.

Many of these analytical approaches to human abilities have been used to identify youths' special abilities in gifted programs and as models for educational programs for gifted youth. In each approach there is emphasis not just on enhancing general giftedness or on the traditional enrichment curricula offered in gifted programs, but rather on the curriculum and instruction focus on developing special abilities. In Gardner-oriented programs the focus is on developing the intelligences; in Sternberg-oriented programs, it is on developing the special cognitive processes delineated in the model; and in talent-oriented programs, it is on developing the special talents the researchers have delineated. If the identification process moves beyond the traditional model based on intelligence, achievement tests and rating scales, the process of identification may become more informal, be based on observation of performance, and become a more long-term process.

EXPERTISE AND CREATIVE ACHIEVEMENT

Expertise is high-level mastery of the declarative and procedural knowledge of a field. The declarative knowledge base has been estimated to be 100,000 or more units of information and well-honed convergent and creative cognitive skills (Glaser, 1984). Further, it is estimated that on average it takes about 10 years of study and/or practice to achieve such an immense knowledge base. Once it is acquired, the expert solves problems and creates new designs, products, or inventions with fluency, ease, and confidence (Ericsson, 1996).

Ericsson (1993) postulated that expertise depends very little on intellectual ability but mainly on instruction and practice. Study, study, study, and learn, learn, learn is the advice given to neophytes. Although transmission of knowledge is often seen as mere rote memory learning, fluent and useable retention of knowledge that is intellectually well organized and highly retrievable is a fundamental ability of the expert and also a basic component of fluent functioning (Pollert, Feldhusen, Von Monfrans, & Treffinger, 1969). Schools often place excess curricular emphasis on cognitive skills and assume that students can apply those skills to the solution of real-world problems even though they may have a weak knowledge base. Indeed, it seems more likely that a well-organized knowledge base is essential in all higher-level cognitive processing operations. The expert's knowledge base is not only large but also well organized in categories and interrelationship that facilitate retrieval for use in higher-level, creative cognitive operations.

Pioneers in the study of expertise and problem solving (Newell & Simon, 1972; Glaser, 1984) established the fundamental characteristics of expert problem solvers and the processes they use, and later researchers (Ericsson & Smith, 1991; Bereiter & Scardamalia, 1993) clarified the relationship between expertise and creative achievement. Gardner (1993) summarized that relationship and the basic nature of each component in his model of high-level creative production: There must be some special talents that have emerged in the creatively productive individual beyond the initial generally high-level intelligence; there must be a large knowledge base that the individual has acquired over a period of years; and finally there must be technical skills or procedural knowledge.

Expertise is high-level technical proficiency in a field; it is mastery of procedural operations and problem-solving skills of a discipline; it is the prelude to creative production. The creative individual:

solves problems, fashions products, poses new questions in a domain in a way that is initially considered to be unusual but eventually accepted within at least one cultural group (Gardner, 1993, p. 35).

Gardner (1993) and Simonton (1994) are most explicit in their delineation of the developmental components and experiences for very high-level creative achievers. Based on intensive study of the lives of seven exemplars (Freud, Einstein, Picasso, Stravinsky, Eliot, Graham, and Ghandi), Gardner found that the creative achievement must be in a particular domain. Creative achievers strive to be creative across their life spans. They create a new product or solution to a problem; their product is recognized as creative in a culture. Furthermore, creative individuals' families value learning, achievement, and hard work; the individuals' talent strengths are recognized early; and a decade of study and work brings the talent to potential fruition. They will gravitate toward a city and people working in that talent domain but will work alone or in isolation a great deal. After much hard work, their creative production is transmitted to judges, critics, and evaluators who are competent to make the judgment that the work is innovative, creative, and of value to society.

Simonton (1997), analyzing creative genius from a Darwinian perspective, concluded that most creative achievers are highly productive: many publications, many pieces of music, many inventions, many works of art, many scientific breakthroughs. Creative genius also requires a modicum of intelligence and knowledge as well as a capacity to make associations and see disparate relationships between ideas. From a personality point of view, creative geniuses are open to diverse experience, tolerate ambiguity well, and have a wide range of interests. They love their work, are introverted, and may be extremely independent. In sum, Simonton says the creative achiever is intelligent, enthusiastic, persistent, committed, and able to work long and hard.

Boden (1991) stressed the idea that creative production always follows a long period of preparatory work in a field and another long period of development after the initial crude solution, discovery, or invention. During the latter period, the creators present their production to the appropriate world and await the judgment of the leading individuals in that world. Application or use in the world at large may follow if the judgment is positive and the time is right. Often the discoverer is lucky enough to generate a group of followers who embrace the new ideas and also fight for their acceptance.

Creative producers who get their production in some way into the consumers' world are loaded with energy and stick-to-it-iveness and are able to commit themselves to a long-range developmental effort. They are metacognitively aware of their efforts and thinking processes (Gardner, 1993). Eysenck (1993) proposed that the major accompanying personality strengths are strong internal motivation, confidence, nonconformity, and openness. He also summarized other research that found the following personality characteristics of creative producers: (1) independence, (2) introversion, (3) openness, (4) wide interests, (5) self-acceptance, (6) flexibility, (7) asocial attitudes, (8) radicalism, and (9) rejection of external constraints. Although the pattern of personal characteristics would obviously vary widely from creative producer to producer, it is likely that a combination of these factors would often characterize the creatively productive individual.

Educating Gifted and Talented Youth for Expertise and Creative Achievement

Talented youth should have educational experiences and planning activities that help them set long-range goals and strive for mastery, expertise, and creative achievement (Bereiter & Scardamalia, 1993; Simonton, 1997). Their goals should be in fields that are outgrowths of their aptitudes and talents. In setting goals, talented youth can profit from the guidance of teachers, counselors, and parents.

Kay (1999) has developed a system to help precocious youth identify their talent strengths by recording from year to year the awards, honors, prizes, and other forms of recognition they have received, thereby helping them to envision their potential long-range achievements. Feldhusen and Wood (1997) have also developed a system in which youth inventory their achievements from year to year, plan ideal school activities, and set long-range career achievement goals. These planning activities should involve counselors and parents.

For meaningful career planning, talented youth need models and mentors (Bandura, 1993; Pleiss & Feldhusen, 1995; Schunk, 1987). Models are people who illustrate high-level expertise and creative achievements and who can be observed closely by gifted and talented youth. Mentors are people who illustrate high-level achievement, who help gifted and talented youth experience activities in their fields, and who offer insights, guidance, and encouragement about entering the field. Haeger and Feldhusen (1989) reported on their experience in developing a mentor program for gifted students in grades 4 to 12. University professors and graduate students at Purdue University and community professionals and artists served as mentors. The students were all required to take a basic course in the Purdue Super Saturday program for one semester before doing the mentor experience the next semester. Mentors received training in the skills of mentoring and then worked with the students after school and on Saturdays for 10 weeks. Evaluations of the program showed it to be successful in getting youth to think about and clarify their career goals. Moore, Feldhusen, and Owings (1978) also developed a mentor program especially for minority youth. Positive results were also reported for this program in getting youth to think about and clarify their career goals. Both programs also reported that mentor training was essential to clarify the career education goals of the programs.

Expertise and creative achievements begin to emerge with high school and college/university experiences. High-level and challenging peers, expert instructors, models, mentors, and excellent curricula in high school and at still higher levels in college/university are the basics of eventual creative achievement. Throughout the several stages of education, gifted and talented youth should be setting goals that are commensurate with their emerging talents and abilities. Correspondingly, the learning challenges and successes at each level help them understand their abilities and potential for high-level achievement.

Principles of Appropriate Curriculum and Instruction for Precocious Youth

Some professionals in gifted education assert that the methods used with gifted youth often turn out to be useful with youth at all levels of ability. In truth, they may be admitting failure to provide differentiated instruction for precocious youth.

Programs for gifted and/or talented youth often consist of bland, superficial enrichment activities involving projects and thinking-skills activities at a level, pace, depth, and complexity far beneath the ability of precocious youth. High-level achievements for highly able youth come from curricula and instruction that are at the upper level of youths' current capabilities (Feldhusen, Check, & Klausmeier, 1961), or zone of proximal development (Vygotsky, 1978). Research by Belcastro (1987) and Cox, Daniel, and Boston (1985) revealed that instructional activities for gifted youth rarely meet such criteria. The "diagnostic–prescriptive" approach developed by Stanley (1978) for teaching precocious youth and Reis and Renzulli's (1992) "compacting" are approaches to appropriate instruction. They stress initial assessment of current achievement levels and the provision of new instruction at advanced levels. Archambault et al. (1993) conducted research for the National Research Center on the Gifted and Talented and found that appropriate instruction for precocious youth is a rarity in American classrooms. More commonly, they are bored and unmotivated (Feldhusen & Kroll, 1991) by low-level curricula and teaching (Gallagher, 2000).

Giftedness and superior talent are evidenced by precocity. Children have genetically different abilities (Plomin, 1994; Bouchard, 1994) and they also need differential nurturance for the development of those capabilities throughout their school and learning experience. They need to learn and achieve:

1. Self-understanding and integration of talents, motivations, and learning styles with personal, social, academic, and career goals (Csikszentmihalyi, 1993; Betts, 1995).
2. Competence goals as reflected in striving for excellence, expertise, and mastery (Bloom, 1985; White, 1959).
3. High academic, artistic, technical, or personal–social achievements (VanTassel-Baska, 1994) and broad declarative knowledge in their areas of talent and emerging expertise.
4. The procedural knowledges of problem solving, reasoning, and coping skills (Treffinger, Feldhusen, & Isaksen, 1990; Treffinger & Feldhusen, 2000).
5. Self-regulatory and metacognitive skills (Schunk & Zimmerman, 1994).
6. Positive relationships with peers and social adaptability (Steinberg, 1996).
7. Creative productivity as an outgrowth of expertise (Bereiter & Scardomalia, 1993; Torrance, 1987).

These are ideal goals for all youth, but for highly talented and precocious youth, lofty and appropriate levels should be pursued. In childhood, their abilities are just emerging. In adolescence, they become more explicit, and in late adolescence and young adulthood, they may emerge or develop fully. Some parents and teachers will try to get children to avoid such goals because the stress, pressure, and risk is worrisome. Many youth will also elect instead to strive for less demanding, less risky, less high-level goals and go instead for education and career goals at a modest professional level of performance in which community status, a good income, and lower risks are outcomes.

Maker and Nielson (1995) suggested that curricula for the gifted follow four principles, each represented by one or two words: person, process, product, and learning environment. "Person" is a need for the curriculum to be adjusted to characteristics of the gifted such as their speed of learning, their high ability in memory and fluency tasks, their large knowledge bases, and their ability to construct and/or understand complex ideas and schema. "Process" is a need for curricula to adapt to their high capacity in cognitive and thinking skills. "Product" is a need to engage gifted youth in producing papers, designs, musical composition, complex models, graphic art, inventions, reports, and so on, that reflect both the complex and creative products that are appropriate for the gifted. Finally, "learning environment" refers to the general conditions of the learning environment, such as openness, learner centeredness, grouping conditions, flexibility, opportunities to work independently, and abundance of resources. Major guides and principles for curricula and curriculum products have been developed by VanTassel-Baska (1994). Her guides provide the curricula structure to implement the principles set forth in the model.

Viewing Education: The Talent Development of Gifted Youth as Integration Toward Creative Functioning

Csikszentmihalyi, Rathunde, & Whalen (1993) conducted research on talent development among adolescents and concluded that teens whose talents are emerging in positive ways are involved in both analytical and integrative processes regarding their abilities and personal characteristics. The analytical processes are all the efforts to come to know and understand oneself, and one's strengths and weaknesses. Students can be guided in the processes of self-analysis by counselors who administer self-rating instruments, get teacher ratings of the youth, administer ability tests, help students create a self-profile or self-portrait, and help students interpret and understand the information (Feldhusen & Jarwan, 2000; Feldhusen et al., 1993; Stanley, 1984). Students can then be engaged in goal setting and planning for future educational experiences. In a sense, it is a constructive process of using all the information to create a vision and goals for one's ideal future. The vision will be influenced by the culture and the zeitgeist (Feldhusen, 1994), significant people (Pleiss & Feldhusen, 1995), crystallizing experiences (Walters & Gardner, 1986), and chance (Tannenbaum, 1983). Hopefully, the vision embodies achievement of expertise and/or high-level creative achievement.

Counselors, parents, and other significant people can open doors to information, experiences, and people, and guide youth in self-evaluation or analysis and integrative goal setting, and planning of how to attain their goals. With good models of high-level creative achievement, the goals set by talented youth will include careers in fields in which creative achievement is possible and encouraged.

Gifts Are from People; Nature Transmits Potential for Expertise and Creative Achievement

To be born with high talent potential and later possibly be talented in some career-oriented field means that nature endowed a child with aptitudes, talents, or intelligences above or far above the average child. It also means that, given nurturance at home and school, learning will be easy and faster than it is for most children. The general measure of nature's potential is intelligence, as usually indicated by an IQ test score. The specific measures of potential are talents or aptitudes. The family's gifts are good health care, love, attention, abundant resources such as books and computers, enrollment in summer and Saturday classes, and modeling of high-level and/or creative achievement. The school offers didactic instruction, socializing peer interactions, opportunities to learn how to think and solve problems, and models (some students and teachers) of academic excellence.

With minimum or medium effort (no sweat) gifted and talented children can achieve comfortable lives with an abundance of life's amenities. Herrnstein and Murray (1994) presented good evidence in their book *The Bell Curve* that high IQ pays off in higher-level occupations and thus more of the luxuries of life. Therefore, the "gifted" child is truly an "advantaged" child. He or she will not have to struggle to learn, will often learn to read and do numbers earlier than other children, will usually be a high achiever throughout the school years, and will end up in a relatively high-level professional position. The few who are willing to work very hard, who strive for expertise or for creative achievement, may go on to regional, national, or international recognition and make major contributions in the arts, sciences, and other fields.

Many schools make no effort to differentiate the curriculum for gifted children. Sometimes gifted students are bored in school or try to learn from whatever resources they can find (libraries, computers, books, television) and continue to do well on achievement and aptitude tests. However, some gifted children, because of their extreme precocity, have problems in peer relations and personal and social adjustment (Hollingworth, 1942; Moon, Kelly, & Feldhusen, 1997). Their problems may lead to misbehavior, isolation, or arrogance. However, they usually get along well when they are placed in educational experiences with intellectual peers (Kennedy, 1989). Special schools and classes provide the academic challenge, the advanced curriculum, faster pace and depth of instruction, and teachers who are models of academic excellence.

Giftedness is a result of nature and nurture. To be gifted is to have potential to learn rapidly, to deal well with complex and abstract ideas, and to have a large knowledge base. Gifted and talented youth should be very much concerned about their futures. They need better and better recognition and understanding of their talents and of how they must guide their own talent development. Schools, teachers, counselors, and parents play major roles in talent development processes and in advancing gifted youth toward expertise and high-level creative achievement.

SUMMARY

Development of Gifts and Talents to High-Level Expertise and Creative Achievement

The nurturance of gifts and talents begins with efforts to help youth come to know and understand their special aptitudes and talents and to seek educational services and opportunities to develop those special abilities. This should include opportunities to engage in challenging learning experiences in potential areas of talent and to get feedback that confirms or questions the suspected talents.

The nurturance of gifts and talents also calls for opportunities at all grade levels to be engaged in higher-order thinking activities: planning, monitoring, evaluating, and problem solving. It is also essential for talented youth to be able to develop a large base of declarative and procedural knowledge. This means extensive reading, attending high-level lectures, studying and examining natural phenomena, and testing their ability to identify and solve problems in their areas of special talent. Above all, it means getting the knowledge basis well organized to facilitate fluent retrieval of conceptual information and skills when they are needed.

Ideally, youths' talents are recognized early at home and at school, and they are encouraged to engage in experiences that foster those talents. Parents, teachers, counselors, and models/mentors encourage openness, diversity of experiences, stick-to-it-iveness, and independence. Ideally they are engaged in experiences that help them recognize their emerging talent strengths, set short- and long-range educational and career goals, and are enrolled in educational experiences and curricula that are at the edge of their learning capabilities.

References

Archambault, F. X., Westberg, K. L., Brown, S. W., Hallmark, B. W., Zhang, W., & Emmons, C. L. (1993). Classroom practices used with gifted third and fourth grade students. *Journal for the Education of the Gifted, 16*(2), 103–119.

Bandura, A. (1993). Perceived self-efficacy in cognitive development and functioning. *Educational Psychologist, 28*(2), 117–148.

Belcastro, F. P. (1987). Elementary pullout program for the intellectually gifted: Boon or bane? *Roeper Review, 9*(4), 17–21.

Benbow, C. P., Lubinski, D., & Suchy, E. (1996). The impact of SMPY's educational programs from the perspective of the participant. In C. P. Benbow & D. Lubinski

(Eds.), *Intellectual, talent: Psychometrical and social issues* (pp. 266–300). Baltimore: Johns Hopkins University Press.

Bereiter, C., & Scardamalia, M. (1993). *Surpassing ourselves: An inquiry into the nature and implications of expertise*. Chicago: Open Court.

Bloom, B. S. (1985). *Developing talent in young people*. New York: Ballantine.

Boden, M. A. (1991). *The creative mind*. New York: Basic Books.

Bouchard, T. J. (1994). Genes, environment and personality. *Science, 264,* 1700–1701.

Bouchard, T. J. (1997). IQ similarity in twins reared apart: Findings and responses to critics. In R. J. Sternberg & E. Grigorenko (Eds.), *Intelligence, heredity, and environment* (pp. 126–160). New York: Cambridge University Press.

Carroll, J. B. (1993). *Human cognitive abilities*. New York: Cambridge University Press.

Cattell, R. B. (1971). *Abilities: Their structure, growth and action*. Boston: Houghton-Mifflin.

Cox, J., Daniel, N., & Boston, B. O. (1985). *Educating able learners: Programs promising practices*. Austin, TX: University of Texas Press.

Csikszentmihalyi, M. (1993). *The evolving self: A psychology for the third millennium*. New York: Harper Collins.

Csikszentmihalyi, M., Rathunde, K., & Whalen, S. (1993). *Talented teenagers*. New York: Cambridge University Press.

Ericsson, K. A. (1996). *The road to excellence*. Mahwah, NJ: Lawrence Erlbaum Associates.

Ericsson, K. A., & Smith, J. (1991). *Toward a general theory of expertise*. New York: Cambridge University Press.

Eysenck, H. J. (1979). *The structure and measurement of intelligence*. Berlin: Springer-Verlag.

Eysenck, H. J. (1993). Creativity and personality: Suggestions for a theory. *Psychological Inquiry 4,* 147–148.

Feldhusen, J. F. (1994). A case for developing America's talent and where we go from here. *Roeper Review, 16*(4), 231–233.

Feldhusen, J. F. (1995). Talent development vs. gifted education. *The Educational Forum, 59*(4), 346–349.

Feldhusen, J. F. (1998). A conception of talent and talent development. In R. C. Friedman & K. B. Rogers (Eds.), *Talent in context: Historical and social perspectives* (pp. 193–209). Washington, DC: American Psychological Association.

Feldhusen, J. F. (1999). Talent identification and development in education: The basic tenets. In S. Kline & K. T. Hegeman (Eds.), *Gifted education in the twenty-first century* (pp. 89–100). New York: Winslow Press.

Feldhusen, J. F., & Jarwan, F. A. (2000). Identification of gifted and talented youth for educational programs. In K. A. Heller, F. J. Mönks, R. J. Sternberg, & R. F. Subotnik (Eds.), *International handbook of giftedness and talent* (pp. 271–282). New York: Elsevier.

Feldhusen, J. F., & Kroll, M. D. (1991). Boredom or challenge for the academically talented. *Gifted Education International, 7*(2), 80–81.

Feldhusen, J. F., & Wood, B. K. (1997). Developing growth plans for gifted students. *Gifted Child Today, 20*(6), 24–26, 48–49.

Feldhusen, J. F., Check, J., & Klausmeier, H. J. (1961). Achievement in subtraction. *The Elementary School Journal, 61*, 322–327.

Feldhusen, J. F., Jarwan, F. A., & Holt, D. (1993). Assessment tools for counselors. In L. K. Silverman (Ed.), *Counseling the gifted and talented* (pp. 239–259). Denver: Love.

Gagné, F. (1993). Constructs and models pertaining to exceptional human abilities. In K. A. Heller, F. J. Mönks, & A. H. Passow (Eds.), *International handbook of research and development of giftedness and talent* (pp. 69–87). New York: Pergamon Press.

Gagné, F. (1995). From giftedness to talent: A developmental model and its impact on the language of the field. *Roeper Review, 18*(2), 103–111.

Gagné, F. (1999). *Tracking talents: Identifying multiple talents through peer, teacher, and self-nomination.* Waco, TX: Prufrock Press.

Gallagher, J. J. (2000). Changing paradigms for gifted education in the United States. In K. A. Heller, F. J. Mönks, R. J. Sternberg, & R. F. Subotnik (Eds.), *International handbook of giftedness and talent* (pp. 681–694). New York: Elsevier.

Gardner, H. (1983). *Frames of mind: The theory of multiple intelligences.* New York: Basic Books.

Gardner, H. (1993) *Creating minds.* New York: Basic Books.

Gardner, H. (1999). *Intelligence reframed: Multiple intelligences for the 21st century.* New York: Basic Books.

Gardner, H., Walter, J., & Hatch, T. (1992). If teaching had looked beyond the classroom: The development and education of intelligences. *Innotech Journal, 16*(1), 18–35.

Glaser, R. (1984). Education and thinking: The role of knowledge. *American Psychologist, 39*(2), 93–104.

Guilford, J. P. (1959). Three faces of intellect. *American Psychologist, 14*, 469–479.

Guilford, J. P., & Hoepfner, R. (1971). *The analysis of intelligence.* New York: McGraw-Hill.

Haeger, W. W., & Feldhusen, J. F. (1989). *Developing a mentor program.* East Aurora, NY: DOK Publishers.

Hebb, D. O. (1942). The effect of early and late brain injury upon test scores, and the nature of normal adult intelligence. *Proceedings of the American Philosophical Society, 85*, 275–292.

Herrnstein, R. J., & Murray, C. (1994). *The bell curve: Intelligence and class structure in American life.* New York: Free Press.

Holahan, C. K., & Sears, R. R. (1995). *The gifted group in later maturity.* Stanford, CA: Stanford University Press.

Hollingworth, L. (1942). *Children above 180 IQ.* Yonkers, NY: World Book.

Jensen, A. R. (1998). *The g factor.* New York: Praeger.

Kay, S. I. (1999). The talent profile as a curricular tool for academics, the arts, and athletics. In S. Cline and K. T. Hegeman (Eds.), *Gifted education in the twenty-first century* (pp. 47–59). New York: Winslow.

Kennedy, D. M. (1989). Classroom interaction of gifted and nongifted fifth graders. Unpublished doctoral dissertation. West Lafayette, IN: Purdue University.

Maker, C. J., & Nielson, A. B. (1995). *Teaching models in education of the gifted.* Austin, TX: PRO-ED.

Moon, S. M., Kelly, K. R., & Feldhusen, J. F. (1997). Specialized counseling services for gifted youth and their families: A needs assessment. *Gifted Child Quarterly, 41*(1), 16–25.

Moore, B. A., Feldhusen, J. F., & Owings, J. (1978). *The professional career exploration program for minority and/or low income gifted and talented high school students.* (Tech. Ref. GO 7710103–15821). West Lafayette, IN: Purdue University, Department of Education.

Newell, A., & Simon, H. A. (1972). *Human problem solving.* Englewood Cliffs, NJ: Prentice-Hall.

Pleiss, M. K., & Feldhusen, J. F. (1995). Mentors, role models, and heroes in the lives of gifted children. *Educational Psychologist, 30*(3), 159–169.

Plomin, R. (1994). *Genetics and experience: The interplay between nature and nurture.* Beverly Hills, CA: Sage.

Plomin, R. (1997). Identifying genes for cognitive abilities and disabilities. In R. J. Sternberg & E. Grigorenko (Eds.), *Intelligence, heredity, and environment* (pp. 89–104). New York: Cambridge University Press.

Pollert, L. H., Feldhusen, J. F., Van Monfrans, AP. P., & Treffinger, D. (1969). Role of memory in divergent thinking. *Psychological Reports, 25*, 151–156.

Reis, S. M., & Renzulli, J. S. (1992). Using curriculum compacting to challenge the above average. *Educational Leadership, 50*(2), 51–57.

Scarr, S. (1997). Behavior–genetic and socialization theories of intelligence: Truce and reconciliation. In R. J. Sternberg & I. Grigorenko (Eds.), *Intelligence, heredity, and environment* (pp. 3–41). New York: Cambridge University Press.

Schunk, D. H. (1987) Peer models and children's behavioral changes. *Review of Educational Research, 57*(2), 149–174.

Schunk, D. H., & Zimmerman, B. J. (1994). *Self-regulation of learning and performance.* Hillsdale, NJ: Lawrence Erlbaum Associates.

Simonton, D. K. (1994). *Greatness.* New York: Guilford Press.

Simonton, D. K. (1997). When giftedness becomes genius: How does talent achieve eminence? In N. Colangelo & G. A. Davis (Eds.), *Handbook of gifted education* (pp. 335–352). Boston: Allyn & Bacon.

Snow, R. E. (1996). Abilities as aptitudes and achievements in learning situations. In J. J. McArdle & R. W. Woodcock (Eds.), *Human cognitive abilities in theory in and practice.* Mahwah, NJ: Lawrence Erlbaum Associates.

Stanley, J. C. (1978). Educational non-acceleration: An international tragedy. *G/C/T/, 3*, 2–5, 53–57, 60–64.

Stanley, J. C. (1984). Use of general and specific aptitude measures in identification: Some principles and certain cautions. *Gifted Child Quarterly, 28*, 177–180.

Steinberg, L. (1996). *Beyond the classroom.* New York: Simon & Schuster.

Sternberg, R. J. (1997). The concept of intelligence and its role in lifelong learning and success. *American Psychologist, 52*, 1030–1037.

Tannenbaum, A. J. (1983). *Gifted children: Psychological and educational perspectives.* New York: Macmillan.

Terman, L. M., & Oden, M. H. (1959). *The gifted group at mid-life.* Stanford, CA: Stanford University Press.

Thurstone, C. L. (1936). A new concept of intelligence and a new method of measuring primary abilities. *Educational Record, 17* (Suppl. 10), 124–138.

Torrance, E. P. (1987). Teaching for creativity. In S. G. Isaksen (Ed.), *Frontiers of creativity research* (pp. 189–215). Buffalo, NY: Bearly Ltd.

Treffinger, D. J., & Feldhusen, J. F. (2000). *Planning for productive thinking and learning*. Waco, TX: Prufrock Press.

Treffinger, D. J., Feldhusen, J. F., & Isaksen, S. G. (1990). Organization and structure of productive thinking. *Creative Learning Today, 4*(2), 6–8.

VanTassel-Baska, J. (1994). A synthesis of perspectives: Another view. In J. B. Hansen & S. M. Hoover (Eds.), *Talent development: Theories & practice* (pp. 299–307). Dubuque, IA: Kendall/Hunt.

Vygotsky, L. S. (1978). *Mind in society: The development of higher psychological processes*. Cambridge, MA: Harvard University Press.

Wachs, T. D. (1992). *The nature and nurturance*. Newbury Park, CA: Sage.

Walters, J., & Gardner, H. (1986). The crystallizing experience: Discovering an intellectual gift. In R. J. Sternberg & J. E. Davidson (Eds.), *Conceptions of giftedness* (pp. 306–331). New York: Cambridge University Press.

White, R. W. (1959). Motivation reconsidered: The concept of competence. *Psychological Review, 66*(5), 297–333.

6

Permission to Be Gifted

How Conceptions of Giftedness Can Change Lives

Joan Freeman

No conception of giftedness or talent works in a cultural vacuum, which is why an international overview in this area of human development can cut across many assumptions (Freeman, 1998). A cross-cultural view picks up a wide variety of international templates for the identification and education of the gifted and talented, which are sometimes entirely opposing. The wider view can demonstrate unrecognized stereotyping and expectations, and illustrate the often serious effects of social influences on opportunities for the development of high-level potential and its promotion throughout life. Although cultural nuances are complex and their dynamics difficult to define, it is clear that excellence can come from widely differing special educational provision or from no special educational provision at all. Whatever the cultural conceptions of giftedness, they are influential in their actualization, in the acceptability of both the individual and the abilities, that is, who may be gifted and who may not, and in which abilities may be considered as gifts and which may not.

Context is all in the identification of giftedness because "gifted" is an adjective, a description, so the recognition of individuals who are seen as meriting that term depends on comparisons. Even in the same town, for instance, a child in a competitive-entry school may be seen as of only modest ability, although he or she could be admired as gifted in a nonselective school. How individuals react to their classification as gifted is also dependent on personality and home support. This was highlighted by a 37-year-old woman in Freeman's (2001) British 30-year study of gifted and nongifted children, who told of the distress the label "gifted" had caused her, largely because of her unsupporting low socioeconomic background. She felt she could never live up to the expectations of the image as she saw it, and had felt herself a failure until she had children: They did not know about the label, she said, and loved her for herself.

HOW CONCEPTS AFFECT CHOICE OF THE GIFTED AND TALENTED

The choice of children as gifted depends neither on their high-level potential nor their manifest excellence in any field of endeavor. Selecting for giftedness depends on what is being looked for in the first place, whether it is tested academic excellence for formal education, innovation for business, solving paper-and-pencil puzzles for an IQ club, gaining entry to a summer program for the gifted and talented, or competitive athletics for one's country. Selection as gifted without testing could be affected by, for example, the interaction between the personalities of everyone concerned, what the children look and behave like, the agreed definition of giftedness, or even the percentages of ethnic representation demanded by educational authorities. Parental choice is beset by cultural stereotypes, usually meaning that two boys are chosen for every girl, a strangely stable gender proportion found all over the world, from Britain to China (Freeman, 2003). Choice by age-peers is affected by fashion, stereotypes, and popularity (Gagné, 1995).

There are perhaps 100 definitions of giftedness around, almost all of which refer to children's precocity, either in psychological constructs, such as intelligence and creativity, but more usually in terms of high marks in school subjects (Hany, 1993), although in formal school education, social or business talents are rarely considered. How teachers perceive and thus identify the gifted has been seen to vary considerably between different cultures. For example, estimations of the percentages of gifted children taken from more than 400 secondary teachers in Germany along with 400 in the United States were compared with those of 159 teachers in Indonesia (Dahme, 1996). The German teachers recognized 3.5 percent of children as gifted, the Americans 6.4 percent, and the Indonesians 17.4 percent. Even within the United States, percentages of the child population identified as gifted by teachers varied between 5 percent and 10 percent across the states (Office of Educational Research and Improvement, 1993). It is to be expected that the definitions and special facilities provided by educational authorities would have some effect on teachers' estimations of how many children are gifted.

There can also be wide variation between teacher judgments and objective measures. Individually, teachers' attitudes toward the very able vary greatly; some feel resentment, whereas others overestimate bright youngsters' all-around abilities, as was found in a Finnish–British survey (Ojanen & Freeman, 1994). But teachers have been found to judge the highly able reliably in that they will continue to pick the same kind of children (Hany, 1993). In Germany, Hany (1995) found teachers biased in their judgments in that they would choose pupils who were most like their expectations and did not fully consider the basis of comparisons or nonobvious characteristics. Creativity was not usually seen as an aspect of giftedness, and emotionally, the gifted were often expected to be play-ful, arrogant, uncontrolled, and even disturbed. The teachers often kept a mental image of a gifted pupil who would have exceptionally good logical reasoning, quick comprehension, and intellectual curiosity – in combina-tion with good school grades. Individual gifted pupils were often vividly remembered by teachers, who would use those characteristics to identify others.

Children selected by high grades in school will be different in many ways from others who have gymnastic potential, and the creatively gifted are often less comfortable and less conforming in conventional school set-tings than scholarly youngsters who are more likely to be seen as gifted (Freeman, 1995; Sternberg & Lubart, 1995). If children are chosen subjec-tively by teachers and parents, even if the choices are further refined by tests, the selection will be different from those chosen entirely by tests.

Cultural conceptions set up barriers to the development of high-level potential, especially if that potential is not in the curricular mainstream. The barriers are potently effective by undermining children's developing sense of self-worth and thus their courage to devote themselves to an outcome that may not be acceptable (Dweck, 1999). Subotnik (2003) put it succinctly, "In order to be gifted, that is, to be exceptional, as one matures, one needs to be increasingly active in one's own development" (p. 15). An unacceptable goal need not only be to become, for example, a criminal, but it could also be to become an artist for a boy with fine-art aspirations in a rough family. Satisfaction with a moderate performance, apparently suitable for one's perceived place in life, does not bring excellence. The major obstructions to the realization of gifted potential are socioeducational, and they exist everywhere in the world in different forms. They can be summed up in just three powerful and overlapping aspects: (1) morality, (2) gender, and (3) emotion.

Recognized Giftedness Depends on Accepted Morality

There is a tangled thread of morality that winds through concepts of gift-edness. Cognitive-developmental morality measures, such as the stages promoted by Piaget (1948) or Kohlberg (1984) in his tests of moral devel-opment, correlate positively with high IQ scores and high-level educational achievement (Freeman, 2004). Yet an overview of international research by Italians Pagnin & Adreani (2000) could not find any recognizable relation-ship between high cognitive ability and *actual* behavior, but stated rather that it is a basis for "coming to a justified agreement . . . shared by those concerned" (p. 481). American author Rothman (1992) pointed out that "IQ explains but little in the development of moral reasoning" (p. 330). It is as though the intellectually gifted know what is expected as answers on the tests and are able to perform the necessary intellectual acrobatics to score highly, but may not choose to abide by the answers they write down. Yet, in some societies, such as those that are strong adherents to Islam, received morality is itself a form of giftedness, and gifted cognitive ability may be seen as largely irrelevant. In Muslim Malaysia, for example, success in education is specifically outlined in government policy as "a belief in God and high moral standards" (Adimin, 2002, p. 26) and, in many such countries, unquestioning submissiveness to the Koran and priestly edicts is seen as the true gift. As there are an estimated 1.3 billion Muslims, one sixth of the world's population, conceptions of giftedness are clearly varied and must be recognized.

The West is not exempt from its assumed relationship between received morality and giftedness. The basic idea is that the higher the IQ, the more moral the scorer, which also influences who may be recognized as gifted (as presented by, e.g., Galton, 1869; Jensen, 1998; Herrnstein & Murray, 1994). Yet many top-ranking Nazis were intellectually gifted and beautifully cultured, which did not stop them from behaving immorally (Zilmer, Harrower, Rizler, & Archer, 1995). Because of this implicit association, youngsters with high IQ scores can anticipate entry to leadership courses (at least in the United States). From earliest childhood, the gifted leader is supposed to show enthusiasm, easy communication, problem-solving skills, humor, self-control, and conscientiousness, as well as very high intelligence (Sisk, 2001). Of course, the students are not being offered leadership tutoring per se, but leadership within the received moral structure.

On the other hand, some claim the gifted are morally more fragile, so that educational frustration will direct them to crime more than less able youngsters (George, 1992) or that they have "nothing in common" with other children to the extent that if forced to mix they may become ill or socially misbehave (Gross, 1992). In spite of some strong beliefs of a relationship between morality and giftedness – positive or negative – the only evidence lies in paper-and-pencil morality tests, an association based on the shared Western, largely Protestant, morality the tests tap. Although in real life there is no measured evidence of a relationship between morality and gifts in either children or adults, those who are able to respond in the way of the dominant morality are more likely to be chosen as gifted. There are often special allowances, though, for highly creative people, such as Pablo Picasso or Ernest Hemmingway, who fit the model of the wild "Bohemian" artist.

Gender Affects Gifted Development

Internationally, concepts of gender provide a clear and relatively easy measure example of socioeducational permission to be gifted. Most obviously, gender achievements in countries where girls are not allowed any education beyond puberty, if at all, will grossly exaggerate the apparent differences in native ability between the sexes. Heller and Ziegler (1996), in an international review of research on gender differences in mathematics and natural sciences, failed to find any reliable evidence that girls are inherently less able than boys. Consequently, they suggested that girls and boys can act as experimental controls for each other to gauge the power of social effects, eventually best seen in career outcomes. They pointed out, for example, that even on present tests of spatial abilities at which boys do better, one would expect only twice as many male engineering graduates as females, whereas there are 30 times as many. In the United States, Wilson, Stocking, and Goldstein (1994) reported that female and male adolescents generally selected courses that followed traditional gender stereotypes, males generally preferring mathematics and science.

Comparing gifted gender achievements, even between the cousinly relationship of the United States and Britain, highlights some highly statistically significant differences between which gender may be permitted to be seen as gifted and in what subject areas (Freeman, 2003). In Britain, the academic achievements of gifted girls at school are now surpassing those of gifted boys in virtually all areas of study and at all school ages, including mathematics and the hard sciences, although excluding physical education (Arnot, Gray, & Rudduck, 1998; Department for Education and Skills, 2000). This phenomenon, the reversal of conventional notions of gender achievement, is also growing in other parts of Europe and Australia, although not in Germany or Italy. The reasons for the British changes are probably twofold:

- greater female confidence in their abilities, that is, changing concepts of who may be seen as gifted and in what subject areas, and
- changes in the style and content of school curriculum and assessment methods, that is, fewer short-term memory examinations, such as multiple choice, and greater reliance on long-term, dedicated, project-based work.

In the United States, however, the gifted gender picture is quite different. For example, in mathematics, science, and vocational (male-type) aptitude scales, "talented" 17-year-old boys scored 8 to 10 times more frequently within the top 10 percent (Hedges & Nowell, 1995). For several tests, no female managed to score at all in the top 3 percent. However, the researchers found the talented boys to be at a profound disadvantage in literacy skills, by as much as a year and a half. They concluded that there are innate, unalterable gender differences. Other American work, notably by Benbow and her team (e.g., Lubinski, Benbow, & Morelock, 2000), found the same "robust gender differences" in mathematical reasoning ability in favor of boys, which they have found to be longitudinally stable. Winner (1996) writes that when girls start school in the United States, they are identified in the same proportions as boys for gifted programs but, as they get older, there is a striking fall in the proportion of girls. Although girls make up half the gifted population in kindergarten, this proportion, she writes, shrinks to less than 30 percent at junior high school and even lower at high school. Thus, it seems that, in the United States, conceptions of giftedness and gender are more specifically associated with subject areas than in Britain. These concepts of who may be gifted, and in what areas, patently affect the individual careers of men and women, and their achievements and earning power across the life span.

Expected Emotional Development Affects the Choice of Children as Gifted

Around the world, lists of the supposed characteristics of gifted children are given to teachers to help them in selection of special educational provision. As these lists are based on local conceptions, the characteristics vary widely. Many are concerned with the presentation of the child's self, such as manners, articulacy, and appearance. They can be entirely negative, as in this *complete* list (Northamptonshire County Council, 1994, p. 15):

Prefers friendship with older pupils or adults.
Excessively self-critical.
Unable to make good relations with peer groups and teachers.
Emotionally unstable.
Low self-esteem, withdrawn and sometimes aggressive.

Indeed, this negativity is widespread. Plucker & Levy (2001) describe the life of the gifted and talented in the United States as beset with emotional problems, such as "depression and feelings of isolation" (pp. 75–76), and they suggest that the appearance of contentment is false, recommending preventative therapy. American gifted girls especially have been found to be more depressed than equally able boys, often underestimating their abilities because of conflicts between of success and "femininity" (Luthar, Zigler, & Goldstein, 1992). At least as much evidence provides the entirely opposite picture, the gifted being at least as emotionally well-balanced as any others. For example, a recent study of more than 220 gifted and nongifted American children in their first year of high school concluded that the gifted saw themselves as being more intimate with friends, took more sports-related and danger-related risks, and felt that they were at least as good in social skills as their nongifted peers: Their teachers agreed (Field et al., 1998). Freeman's (2001) 30-year study in Britain found that it was the labeled gifted who had more emotional problems than the identically able but unlabeled gifted.

It seems as though emotional development as part of the concept of giftedness rather depends on the cultural stereotype and the research methodology. And if emotional development forms part of the conceptual guide for selection, there will be wide variation in who is seen as gifted along the spectrum of what is seen as emotionally normal to emotionally disturbed. American work has shown that teachers trained to see through the myths are better at finding the gifted (Hansen & Feldhusen, 1994). Fortunately, many teachers can be very perceptive, spotting and nurturing talent that others or tests may miss. Such intuitive, inspiring teachers are lauded in creative literature, if not recognized in statistical tables.

INTERNATIONAL DIFFERENCES IN CONCEPTIONS OF GIFTEDNESS

Although Sweden hosts the Nobel Prize for world-class excellence, gifted children at school are barely recognized either there or in any of the other Scandinavian countries. The standard of basic education in those countries, however, is extremely high in world terms, such that not only are Scandinavian youngsters usually at the top in international surveys but, in proportion to their size, the countries produce as many world-class creatively gifted adults as anywhere. Yet, across their northern borders, Russian culture is associated with a passion for the promotion of talent and national pride in its high achievers (Persson, Joswig, & Balogh, 2000). Indeed, long before the Communist Revolution in 1917, gifted and talented children from all over the country were sent to Moscow and Saint Petersburg to high-level specialist schools, rich in tradition, in fields such as painting, ballet, and music. In the United States, millions of dollars from educational authorities and parents support a multitude of gifted programs for children, and although there is no proportional shortage of world-beaters there either, it is far from sure how much of their success is a result of any of those programs.

But where giftedness is recognized, there is a major split in its conception between Eastern and Western philosophy (Stevenson, 1998; Freeman, 2002b). The balance is between the relative effects of genetics and environment, and according concern and practical provision made for individuals according to those concepts. Understanding the two major approaches at either end of the spectrum throws a fresh light on what is normally regarded in the Western world as universal understanding about gifts.

The two ends of the spectrum of approaches to giftedness can be summarized roughly as follows:

- In the Far East, environmental influences are generally accepted as dominant. Every baby is seen as being born with similar potential; the main difference in children is in the rate of development, which to a large extent is in the power of each individual to fulfill through hard work. However, some Far Eastern countries practice the Western idea of selecting children by high measured ability for special education (e.g., Taiwan, Singapore, and Hong Kong).

- In the Western world, genetic influences are generally seen as dominant. Consequently, Western children are assessed and tested to discover their aptitudes – the vast majority being seen as incapable of high-level learning and achievement, other than in egalitarian countries, such as Scandinavia, or less interested ones, such as Italy.

The Concept of Widespread Potential

Confucian views, first aired more than 2,000 years ago, continue to exert an influence on how achievement is regarded today in East Asian cultures. Although innate factors are recognized, the keys to progress in all aspects of life are seen as diligence, persistence, and practice, along with the belief by both teacher and pupil that the latter is capable of the learning. The teacher's efforts, therefore, are seen as critical to the pupil's success rather than only the child's innate ability. Acceleration and special schooling in China are tiny in terms of its population of around 2.2 billion people; almost all extra education for the gifted and talented is by self-selection. There is no elite group whose status or privileges are defined in terms of inborn superiority; each one has to earn his or her place. In Japan, all primary-age children are regarded as similar in potential so that differences in their achievement are due both to their hard work as well as the teacher's competence. The potential long-term rewards for the diligence these small children must shoulder are in their choice of secondary school, providing access to university, followed by a good career – and a good pension. It is possible that this style of learning is even enhancing the IQ scores of Japanese children, which are rising along with their improving academic work (Flynn, 1991).

In almost all international comparisons of children's achievements, those of East Asian elementary and secondary school pupils have been outstanding, even among the top performers. In the Third International Mathematics and Science Study (TIMSS; Mullis et al., 1999), for example, "the top four of the 41 participating countries in mathematics, and three of the top four countries in science were from East Asia" (Stevenson, Lee, & Mu, 2000, p. 167). Chinese children show no special precocity in mathematics during their preschool years; differentiation in their accomplishments starts at school. Nor is this excellence limited to a few star performers, as in the Western model.

The Concept of Limited Gifts

Internationally, the most frequently used concept of giftedness is that resulting from an appropriately nurtured base of high-level potential. The United States took the lead in this view in the early 1900s, putting energy, research, and government commitment into the scientific study of giftedness a century earlier than anywhere else. Those foundation concepts from the 1920s still affect practice in the sense that abilities are seen as sufficiently measurable to use precise cut-off points for the selection of children. For example, the widespread talent searches in the United States select a band of students for gifted programs based on the top-scoring 1 to 5 percent on tests, the students often being first chosen for these tests by teacher selection (Freeman, 2002b).

A further surge in the final quarter of the 20th century was encouraged by reports such as the *Nation at Risk* (National Commission on Excellence in Education, 1983), alerting the nation to an educational slide into mediocrity, as well as the TIMSS study (1999), which showed that in mathematics in eighth grade, American students were rated 19th of the 21 countries studied. This worryingly low standard, compared with other developed countries, provides some understanding of U.S. concern and industry in special education for the gifted and talented. By 1990, all American states had enacted legislation and had policies for gifted students in place and, although these policies are mostly mandatory, more than a decade later, provision is far from even. Where the basic standard of education is lower, there seems to be a greater need to provide extra help for those with the most promise, to "rescue" the brightest children.

Across the centuries, however, Western Europe has always recognized some individuals as capable of a higher level of functioning than most others – from the philosophers of ancient Greece to the present day – influencing world history. But unlike the United States, there has never been a concerted effort across large areas to promote gifts and talents until the European Council (a body for intergovernmental cooperation among 25 European states) recommended special educational provision for gifted children (Council of Europe, 1994). It did, however, bow to political correctness by insisting that this should "in no way privilege one group of children to the detriment of the others" (p. 1). There is still a fierce political struggle in Western European education between the ideals of elitism and egalitarianism.

The United Kingdom and the United States provide the closest comparison of ideas of giftedness. Until 1998, when the U.K. government announced that "gifted" and "talented" were the terms of choice, there had been a strong aversion to those terms among teachers, with their implications of fixed abilities and unearned privilege. This produced a thesaurus of circumlocutions, such as "more able" or "very able," or quite simply "able." In line, although the American Marland Report was published in 1972, the U.K. equivalent by Freeman was not published until a quarter of a century later (Freeman, 1998). Perhaps there is general agreement on either side of the Atlantic that provision is inconsistent, geographically biased, and associated with both the reality and the fear of elitism.

These different concepts of giftedness, whether limited in the Western view to a tiny proportion of the population or spread more widely in terms of potential in the Confucian view, inevitably make a difference as to who is given access to opportunities to develop excellence.

CONCEPTIONS AND PRACTICE

Unfortunately, scientific evidence as a basis for any educational action is not usual in any part of the world. Typically, published research reflects the culture and language of the population on which it was done. In many edited books (e.g., from Spain, France, Italy, Russia, and the United States), every paper reflects that culture without mention of the world outside, other than perhaps referring to a well-known international star. It is important, however, to know the approach taken in any study because this "grounds" the work in a specific epistemological stance in which data are perceived and analyzed, and from which general conclusions are drawn.

In spite of considerable searching of the literature and questioning of practitioners, this writer has not yet found a single scientific comparison between specific gifted programs, either cross-culturally or within one country. Nor has there even been a comparison between one aspect of such a program and any other, whether in school or out. As a result, it is hard to be precise as to what type of provision would be the most appropriate and effective in any given cultural situation. International comparisons are generally made between varied approaches in terms of competitions (e.g., the Mathematics Olympiad) or surveys such as TIMMS (1999) and Fox, Engle, and Paek (2001). National advances and economic success can be surveyed and compared in terms of education, such as was done by Lynn and Vanhanen (2002) of 60 countries, who identified a positive correlation between assessments of national mental ability and real gross domestic product. The countries of the Pacific Rim, they found, had a notably rising high IQ and a commensurate economic growth.

In whatever manner the gifted are selected for special provision, the outcome is most likely to be positive. It is not, after all, surprising that those carefully selected, bright, keen children will learn more than those who have not experienced extra programs of any kind, whether because of the extra education and/or the "Hawthorn Effect." Indeed, it would be strange if there was no positive change. This means that raw comparisons between the achievements of potentially equally able youngsters who have attended a particular scheme and of those who have not do not provide reliable evidence of which aspects of that scheme are the most efficient.

The growing trend around the world is to offer nonselective open access to very high-level learning opportunities, so that no keen youngster is turned away without even a chance of attempting it. This is seen in the Children's Palaces of China, which provide nonselective, inexpensive, high-level, out-of-school education for youngsters who are prepared to put in the effort. Children's Palaces are essentially learning centers of a very high standard, with accommodations varying from a converted house to a purpose-built skyscraper. They are a thriving and integral part of the Chinese education scene, working across the arts, sciences, and technology. The clustering of resources across different disciplines also enables children to discover activities they did not know existed (J. Shi, personal communication, March 2002).

A very different, but equally open, approach is taken by the American Renaissance Quest Camps, which are designed for the whole family, offering the educational means and support to take interests to any height. In Israel, The Technological Centre for the Galilee offers extremely high-level self-selected science education (Brumbaugh, Marchaim, & Litto, 1994). The center works with the local comprehensive school, from which teenagers have been invited for more than 18 years to work on their own projects under supervision. Youngsters design and conduct work on original problems for which there are neither existing answers nor (often) methods, continuing to work with the data back at school. The youngsters' work can reach master's-degree standard. The cost is low and largely supported by the state.

In these previous examples, the concept of giftedness is neither fixed nor are the children preselected, allowing the possibility of unrecognized gifts and talents to emerge and grow with provision and encouragement, fueled by the motivation of all concerned.

The Western model of diagnose-and-treat for educating the gifted and talented is in direct opposition to the Eastern model of open access, although both concepts operate across the world. Each reflects a social construction of identity and developmental potential. It is not always easy for educational practitioners to see the effects of unrecognized assumptions about gifts and talents, and it would not seem wise to copy any educational action directly from one culture to another without recognizing and adapting to the inevitable differences in background and outlook. Not only does a wider view challenge the unrecognized dominant conceptions and educational effects, but it can offer support to educational providers who aim to make changes. Each individual life and its opportunities are unique, and so the most pertinent approach must remain holistic and long-ranging, seeing gifts and talents in terms of individual patterns within a culture (Baltes, Staudinger, & Lindberger, 1999).

FREEMAN'S 30-YEAR STUDY

In 1974, this writer took a sample of 72 children identified as gifted by their parents (with minimal testing), who had joined the National Association for Gifted Children (United Kingdom) on their behalf (Freeman, 2001). Each of these children was matched for age and gender with two comparison children – the first was a nonrecognized but identically able child, and the second was taken at random, each trio from the same school class, varying from a music school to a nonselective school. They were originally aged between 5 and 14 years, two boys to every girl. The sample contained 210 children, 210 sets of parents, 61 head teachers, and 61 class teachers.

The children were tested in their schools and homes on a wide variety of measures, including Stanford–Binet IQ, personality, musical ability, and general creativity, and they and their parents were interviewed with open-ended newly designed questionnaires in their homes. The class teachers completed a standardized questionnaire on the children's behavior in class, and they and the head teachers were interviewed in the schools. The children's environmental circumstances were rated. At all stages, the interview data were rated for statistical analysis, as well as being audiotaped and transcribed for further interpretation. The home- and school-based information proved to be much richer than that which can ever be obtained from a ticked mailed questionnaire, a telephone interview, or an entirely school-based project. Stanford–Binet IQs for the whole sample were as follows:

- 65 students had IQs between 97 and 120;
- 63 students had IQs between 121 and 140; and
- 82 students had IQs between 141 and 170 (of whom 16 scored IQ 170).

This is an ongoing investigation, in which the sample is still being traced and contacted for the 30-year follow-up. Following is an overview of how the study looks now with regard to most of the labeled and unlabeled gifted.

Early Bases Affect the Life Path

This research has shown that strong pressure to conform to expectations – positive or negative – has affected the participants' life paths for decades. The greater the individual inclination to accept that pressure, the less likely he or she is to stand out in terms of excellence and gifts into adulthood. In general (but not always), those with exceptionally high IQs, say within the top 1 percent, did much better than those with merely a very high score, say within the top 10 percent. The least successful had remained with less mature and effective shorter-term cognitive techniques, such as rote-memorizing their lesson-notes at school and rarely looking things up or using other resources.

The idea that the recognized gifted should be more advanced in school achievements than their age-peers was current among teachers. Youngsters who were identically able but not labeled as gifted were under much less pressure and benefited in their growing up both socially and in the breadth of their learning and activities. Some children (especially boys) appeared to subdue their personalities in their striving for high grades, so their healthy emotional development, including the freedom to play and be creative, had been severely curtailed (as Sternberg & Lubart have also described, 1995). In fact, such pressure sometimes had the opposite effect from what was intended, the worst affected being the accelerated boys specializing in science. They missed out on the healthy development of social skills and relationships, and their self-images were poor. All work and no play not only makes Jack a dull boy, but a sad and lonely one, too. Today, in their late thirties, many regret the way their childhood was spent in heavy study. The respect of others is important to the developing young person; when the gifted received it, allowing them enough responsibility to make many of their own discoveries and decisions, they were able to lead more satisfying lives.

In terms of conventional success in life, such as high examination marks, climbing the corporate ladder, or making money, the primary building blocks were always keenness and hard work, allied with sufficient ability, educational opportunity, and an emotionally supportive home. For the high achievers in adulthood, there was usually a mutually rewarding situation both at home and school and a feeling of comfort with their desire to learn, based on their parents' early pride in them as individuals. The most successful as adults were also more robust and sociable as children and had an external support system of responsive schools, sometimes sincerely felt religion, and a high IQ (rather in line with Sternberg's idea of "successful intelligence," 1997). High-level creativity, though, as seen in adult careers, demanded a particular type of personality that enabled the individual to act independently of others' opinions. Whether youngsters were modest, conventional, and rule-abiding or constantly straining to change the world, they usually carried their personal style through to adulthood. The boy who gained his PhD at 21, for example, is now a professor. The artistic boy who simply removed himself from school from time to time to write poetry and think has become a very successful and sensitive international architect.

Poor emotional home circumstances, such as a constant change of "uncles," did nothing but harm to the possibility of adult excellence; no member of this sample proved to be a tortured genius in the 19th-century mold. Although some early emotional problems, sometimes attributed to giftedness, proved to be those of childhood and simply vanished with maturity, early poor self-concept often took its toll in low ambition and continued low feelings of self-worth. In general, it was true that poverty disables and wealth enables. The boy born into poverty suffered in his cold house from ear, nose, and throat infections and therefore missed a lot of school. In spite of his IQ of 170, he did not seem to have enough physical and mental strength to enjoy it. He became clinically depressed and is now living with his wife in modest circumstances. The identically able but rich gifted girl, however, took a year after her English boarding school to sample Harvard University (United States), seen as her rightful and natural progression, before entering Cambridge University (England). She is now a high-ranking civil servant.

Negative social pressures virtually always had negative effects. Unfortunately, too many had learned from their circumstances and parental outlook that some of the good things in life, such as a professional career, were not for them, even though they had the ability to do almost anything. They barely attempted to fulfill the early dreams they had described and opted for secure, modestly paid occupations. Unfortunately, too, teachers sometimes seemed to feel a need to put the liveliest and more creative youngsters in their "place." But there are, of course, many nonscholastic routes to satisfaction in achievement, such as the boy born to poverty who did not see white-collar work as being for "the likes of me," went to work for the local electricity company, and is now in charge of electricity for the southwest region of the country at the age of 34.

As William Shakespeare wrote in *Twelfth Night*, "Wherefore have these gifts a curtain before 'em?" The nagging question throughout this long study was why so many bright, eager children had been obliged to struggle so hard to even partly realize their gifts. Far too much of their energy went into fighting their school regimens (and their teachers, who were supposedly there to help them). Some gifts were more encouraged in schools than others, particularly science and mathematics, possibly because easily recognizable outstanding results could be more easily achieved in those subjects. Too many youngsters wasted time and energy following wrong channels because of poor educational guidance. At times, subjects told the writer that they had known exactly what they had wanted to do but were thwarted by school time-tabling or strong teacher opinion. One quiet girl at a high-powered school, for example, was told that biology was not for her; the teachers appeared to support those with stronger personalities. But she defied them by secretly entering a competition with her own biological research and won. The school then recognized her potential and permitted her to study in the subject area of her choice. Her own initiative and hard work enabled her to be the success she is today as a (still determined) research pharmacist.

The social pressures that can diminish a growing child's feelings of worth were not helped much by the schools and universities they attended. For example, there was neither adequate preparation from her school nor support from Oxford University for the gentle, sensitive girl of IQ 170 who had made a mighty intellectual jump to get there from the wrong side of the tracks. Totally unprepared by her school and by her single mother, she found that the social hurdles of this upper-class institution among people with far more money and experience than she could have imagined shocked her deeply. She left in tears after just a few months for a much more modest future than had been anticipated. Although educational institutions cannot be responsible for the infinite interactions of individual personality and ability, there is a great deal that hers could have done to help her and, indeed, improve the care of their brightest students.

Being labeled as gifted was associated with sometimes complicated outcomes, depending on the concepts underlying the labels. These could affect progress positively or negatively. Some young people rose to the challenge and thrived on it, whereas others, who felt they could never live up to the image, had chosen a career below their capabilities in order to shine. Others simply ignored their potential, fitting in with the local culture, which did not have a place for giftedness. The participants' memories were not always reliable, and many had retained very different impressions of their younger lives from what had been audiotaped and transcribed years earlier.

It was crystal clear that high-level school grades were not a passport to adult success. But it also seems that many influences on happiness and excellence are like love – it is possible to describe how it feels and what happens because of it, but there is no sure recipe. What we do have is very clear information about what the gifted and talented need by way of support for excellence – a challenging education, high-level opportunities, and someone who believes in them.

References

Adimin, J. (2002). *Predictive validity of a selection test for accelerated learning in Malaysian primary schools*. Unpublished doctoral dissertation, Manchester University, Manchester, England.

Arnot, M., Gray, J., & Rudduck, J. (with Duveen, G.) (1998). *Recent research on gender and educational performance*. London: Stationery Office.

Baltes, P. B., Staudinger, U. M., & Lindberger, U. (1999). Lifespan psychology: Theory and application to intellectual functioning. *Annual Review of Psychology, 50*, 471–507.

Brumbaugh, K., Marchaim, U., & Litto, F. M. (1994, March). *How should developing countries plan for and implement educational technology: One example*. Paper presented at the 11th International Conference on Technology and Education, London, March 27–30.

Council of Europe. (1994). Recommendation no. 1248 on education for gifted children. Strasbourg, France.

Dahme, G. (1996, September). *Teachers' conceptions of gifted students in Indonesia (Java), Germany and USA*. Paper presented at the 5th conference of the European Council for High Ability, Vienna, Austria.

Department for Education and Skills. (2000). *The Standards Site: Gender and achievement*. Retrieved December 20, 2002, from http://www.standards.dfee.gov.uk

Dweck, C. S. (1999). *Self theories: Their role in motivation, personality, and development*. Washington, DC: Taylor & Francis.

Field, T., Harding, J., Yando, R., Gonzales, K., Lasko, D., Bendell, D., et al. (1988). Feelings and attitudes of gifted students, *Adolescence, 33,* 331–342.

Flynn, J. R. (1991). *Asian Americans: Achievement beyond IQ.* Hillsdale, NJ: Lawrence Erlbaum Associates.

Fox, L. H., Engle, J. L., & Paek, P. (2001). An exploratory study of social factors and mathematics achievement among high-scoring students: Cross-cultural perspectives from TIMSS. *Gifted and Talented International, XVI,* 7–15.

Freeman, J. (1995). Conflicts in creativity. *European Journal for High Ability, 6,* 188–200.

Freeman, J. (1998). *Educating the very able: Current international research.* London: Stationery Office. (www.joanfreeman.com)

Freeman, J. (2001). *Gifted children grown up.* London: David Fulton.

Freeman, J. (2002). Out of school educational provision for the gifted and talented around the world: Report for the Department for Education and Skills (U.K. Government). (www.joanfreeman.com).

Freeman, J. (2003). Gender differences in gifted achievement in Britain and the USA, *Gifted Child Quarterly, 47,* 202–211.

Freeman, J. (2004, September). The gifted and moral values. Paper presented at the Conference of the European Council for High Ability, Pamplona, Spain.

Gagné, F. (1995). Learning about the nature of gifts and talents through peer and teacher nominations. In M. W. Katzko & F. J. Mönks (Eds.), *Nurturing talent: Individual needs and social ability.* Assen, The Netherlands: Van Gorcum.

Galton, F. (1869). *Hereditary genius.* London: Macmillan.

George, D. (1992). *The challenge of the able child.* London: David Fulton.

Gross, M. U. M. (1992). The early development of three profoundly gifted children of IQ 200. In P. S. Klein & A. J. Tannenbaum (Eds.), *To be young and gifted.* Norwood, NJ: Ablex.

Hansen, J. B., & Feldhusen, J. F. (1994). Comparison of trained and untrained teachers of gifted students. *Gifted Child Quarterly, 38,* 115–121.

Hany, E. A. (1993). How teachers identify gifted students: Feature processing or concept based classification. *European Journal for High Ability, 4,* 196–211.

Hany, E. A. (1995). Teachers' cognitive processes of identifying gifted students. In M. W. Katzko & F. J. Mönks (Eds.), *Nurturing talent: Individual needs and social ability.* Assen, The Netherlands: Van Gorcum.

Hedges, L. V., & Nowell, A. (1995). Sex differences in mental test scores, variability, and numbers of high-scoring individuals. *Science, 269,* 41–45.

Heller, K. A., & Ziegler, A. (1996). Gender differences in mathematics and natural sciences: Can attributional retraining improve the performance of gifted females? *Gifted Child Quarterly, 41,* 200–210.

Herrnstein, R. J. & Murray, C. (1994). *The bell curve.* New York: Free Press.

Jensen, A. R. (1998). *The g factor: The science of mental ability.* London: Praeger.

Kohlberg, L. (1984). *The psychology of moral development. Vol 2. Essays on moral development.* New York: Harper and Row.

Lubinski, D., Benbow, C. P., & Morelock, M. J. (2000). Gender differences in engineering and the physical sciences among the gifted: An inorganic-organic distinction. In K. A. Heller, F. J. Mönks, R. Sternberg, & R. Subotnik (Eds.), *International handbook of giftedness and talent* (pp. 203–212). Oxford, England: Pergamon.

Luthar, S. S., Zigler, E., & Goldstein, D. (1992). Psychosocial adjustment among intellectually gifted adolescents: The role of cognitive-developmental and experiential factors. *Journal of Child Psychology and Psychiatry, 33*, 361–373.

Lynn, R., & Vanhanen, T. (2002). *IQ and the wealth of nations.* Westport, CT: Greenwood.

Mullis, I. V. S., Martin, O., Gonzales, E. J., Gregory, K. D., Garden, R. A., O'Connor, K. M., et al. (1999). *Third International Mathematics and Science Study. International Mathematics Report. Findings from the IEA's repeat of the Third International Mathematics and Science Study at the eighth grade.* Retrieved July 14, 2002, from http://isc.bc.edu/tmss1999i/math_achievement_report.html

National Commission on Excellence in Education. (1983). *A nation at risk. The imperative for educational reform. A report to the nation and the Secretary of Education; United States Department of Education.* Washington, DC: April, 1983. http://www.ed.gov/pubs/NatAtRisk

Northamptonshire County Council. (1994). *The more able child.* Northampton, England: NIAS.

Office of Educational Research and Improvement. (1993). *National excellence: A case for developing America's talent.* Washington, DC: U.S. Department of Education.

Ojanen, S., & Freeman, J. (1994). *The attitudes and experiences of headteachers, classteachers, and highly able pupils towards the education of the highly able in Finland and Britain.* Savonlinna, Finland: University of Joensuu.

Pagnin, A., & Adreani, O. D. (2000). New trends in research on moral development in the gifted. In K. A. Heller, F. J. Mönks, R. Sternberg, & R. Subotnik (Eds.), *International handbook of giftedness and talent* (pp. 467–484). Oxford, England: Pergamon.

Persson, R. S., Joswig, H., & Balogh, L. (2000). Gifted education in Europe: Programs, practices, and current research. In K. A. Heller, F. J. Mönks, R. Sternberg, & R. Subotnik (Eds.), *International handbook of giftedness and talent* (pp. 203–212). Oxford, England: Pergamon.

Piaget, J. (1948). *Moral judgement of the child.* Glencoe, IL: Free Press.

Plucker, J. A., & Levy, J. J. (2001). The downside of being talented. *American Psychologist, 56*(1), 75–76.

Rothman, G. R. (1992). Moral reasoning, moral behavior, and moral giftedness: A developmental perspective. In Pnina S. Klein & A. J. Tannenbaum (Eds.), *To be young and gifted.* Norwood, NJ: Ablex.

Sisk, D. A. (2001). Creative leadership: A study of middle managers, senior level managers and CEOs. *Gifted Education International, 15*, 281–290.

Sternberg, R. J., & Lubart, T. I. (1995). *Defying the crowd: Cultivating creativity in a culture of conformity.* New York: Free Press.

Sternberg, R. J. (1997). *Successful intelligence.* New York: Plume.

Stevenson, H. W. (1998). Cultural interpretations of giftedness: The case of East Asia. In Friedman, R., & Rogers, K. B. (Eds.), *Talent in context: Historical and social perspectives on giftedness* (pp. 61–77). Washington, DC: American Psychological Association.

Stevenson, H. W., Lee, S., & Mu, X. (2000). Successful achievement in mathematics: China and the United States. In C. F. M. Lieshout & P. G. Heymans (Eds.), *Developing talent across the life span* (pp. 167–183). Hove, England: Psychology Press.

Subotnik, R. (2003). A developmental view of giftedness: From being to doing. *Roeper Review, 26,* 14–15.

Wilson, J. S., Stocking, V. B., & Goldstein, D. (1994). Gender differences in motivations for course selection: Academically talented students in an intensive summer program. *Sex Roles, 3,* 349–367.

Winner, E. (1996). *Gifted children: Myths and realities.* New York: Basic Books.

Zilmer, E. A., Harrower, M., Rizler, B. A., & Archer, R. P. (1995). *The quest for the Nazi personality:* A psychological investigation of Nazi war criminals. Hillsdale, NJ: Lawrence Erlbaum Associates.

7

From Gifts to Talents

The DMGT as a Developmental Model

Francoys Gagné

The field of gifted education defines its special population around two key concepts: giftedness and talent. Using the entries for these two terms in the Subject Index of the first edition of this book (Sternberg & Davidson, 1986) – or, for that matter, the present edition or any handbook in the field (e.g., Colangelo & Davis, 2003; Heller, Mönks, Sternberg, & Subotnik, 2000) – the curious browser will soon discover the fascinating creativity of scholars in their attempts to circumscribe the nature of giftedness and talent. In some cases, the concept of talent does not appear or is not defined (e.g., Davidson, 1986; Renzulli, 1986; Sternberg, 1986); in other cases, which is the dominant position in the literature, both terms are used as synonyms, as in Marland's (1972) well-known definition ("Gifted and talented children are. . . ." p. 4). Csikszentmihalyi and Robinson explicitly announce that nondifferentiation, stating: *"talent, giftedness, and prodigious performance* [italics in text] will be used interchangeably" (1986, p. 264). Occasionally, talent becomes a subcategory of giftedness: "The second component of giftedness is talent," affirms Feldhusen (1986, p. 113); or "giftedness encompasses a wide variety of abilities, talents, or propensities" (Haensly, Reynolds, & Nash, 1986, p. 131). For his part, Feldman (1986) associates talent with potential and giftedness with achievement. He affirms: "Talent from a cognitive-developmental perspective is the potential for constructive interaction with various aspects of the world of experience. . . . If these processes of interaction lead to high level performance, then it is appropriate to speak of giftedness" (p. 287). On the other hand, Tannenbaum does the opposite when he defines giftedness as follows: "Keeping in mind that developed talent exists only in adults, a proposed definition of giftedness in children is that it denotes their potential for becoming critically acclaimed performers or exemplary producers of ideas" (1986, p. 33). These examples do not exhaust the diversity of the conceptions and definitions proposed in the 17 chapters of this book's initial edition.

If conceptions abound and often contradict one another, scholars keep mentioning one particular idea in almost every discussion of the giftedness construct: they acknowledge, implicitly or explicitly, a distinction between early, emerging forms of giftedness, to some extent innate and usually manifested in childhood, and fully developed adult forms of giftedness. The distinction is expressed with terms such as potential versus achievement, aptitude versus realization, or promise versus fulfillment, but it rarely, if ever, is systematically operationalized. I believe it can be done. As I recently argued (Gagné, 1999a, 1999c), aptitudes can be described as natural abilities in a particular domain and achievement as systematically developed skills in a particular talent field. Since its first presentation (Gagné, 1985), the Differentiated Model of Giftedness and Talent (DMGT) has used that distinction to anchor its definitions of the two concepts:

Giftedness designates the possession and use of outstanding natural abilities (called aptitudes or gifts), in at least one ability domain, to a degree that places an individual at least among the top 10 percent of age peers.

Talent designates the outstanding mastery of systematically developed abilities (or skills) and knowledge in at least one field of human activity to a degree that places an individual at least among the top 10 percent of age peers who are or have been active in that field or fields.

These definitions reveal that the two concepts share three characteristics: (a) both refer to human abilities; (b) both are normative, in the sense that they target individuals who differ from the norm or average; and (c) both refer to individuals who are "non-normal" because of outstanding behaviors. These commonalities help clarify why professionals, as well as people in the street, so often confound them.

The DMGT introduces four other components (see Figure 7.1) that help represent more accurately the complexity of the talent development process: intrapersonal catalysts (IC), environmental catalysts (EC), learning and practicing (LP), and chance (C). Moreover, as stated in the formal definitions previously mentioned, precise thresholds quantify the meaning of "outstanding." Finally, the DMGT discusses the long-term process of talent development, proposing various dynamic interactions among the six components. The present overview is structured around the three themes previously identified: (a) the six components, (b) the prevalence issue, and (c) the dynamics of talent development. In the final section, I briefly highlight the main differences between the DMGT and other well-known conceptions of giftedness.

A COMPONENTIAL OVERVIEW

The six components of the DMGT can be subdivided into two trios. The first describes the core of the talent development process, namely, the

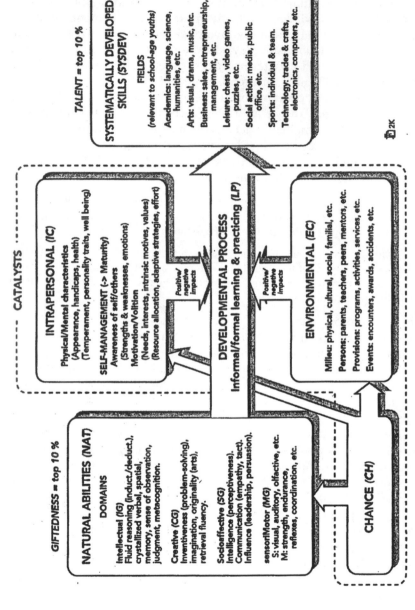

FIGURE 7.1. Gagné's Differentiated Model of Giftedness and Talent (2003 update).

progressive transformation, through a long learning and training process, of outstanding natural abilities into the high-level skills typical of a particular occupational field. The members of the second trio have in common the concept of *catalyst* because they facilitate or inhibit the talent development process. Because I consider prevalence estimates to be an essential part of a complete definition of giftedness and talent, they are discussed at the end of this overview.

The Talent Development Trio

The DMGT's differentiation of gifts from talents is a particular case of the general distinction between aptitude (or potential) and achievement. Some prominent scholars (e.g., Anastasi, 1980) have questioned the relevance and validity of the concept of aptitude. In counterpoint, Angoff (1988) built a strong defense for such a distinction, using the following differentiating characteristics: (a) slow growth for aptitudes versus rapid growth for achievement; (b) informal learning versus formal; (c) resistance to stimulation versus susceptibility to it; (d) major genetic substratum versus major practice component; (e) more general content versus more circumscribed; (f) "old formal" learning versus recent acquisitions; (g) more generalizable skills and knowledge versus narrower transfer; (h) prospective use (predicting future learning) versus retrospective use (assessing amount learned); and (i) applicable to general population evaluation versus limited to systematically exposed individuals. These characteristics apply perfectly to the DMGT's differentiation of gifts from talents.

Gifts (G). The DMGT proposes four aptitude *domains* (see Figure 7.1): intellectual, creative, socioaffective, and sensorimotor. Each can be divided into any number of categories. Figure 7.1 shows exemplars borrowed from various sources. These subdivisions should *not* be considered essential subcomponents of the model; within each of the four domains, many competing classification systems exist. Just with regard to cognitive abilities, some of the better-known taxonomies include Carroll's (1993) three-level system of abilities, Gardner's (1983/1994) multiple intelligences, and Sternberg's (1986) triarchic theory. As knowledge progresses within each ability domain, no doubt, new taxonomies will be proposed. For instance, recent work related to the concept of emotional intelligence (Matthews, Zeidner, & Roberts, 2002) could help structure internally the socioaffective domain.

Natural abilities can be observed through the various tasks confronting children in the course of their development. These include the intellectual abilities needed when learning to read, speak a foreign language, or understand new mathematical concepts and the creative abilities applied to solving various technical problems or producing original work in science, literature, and art. Physical abilities are involved in sports, music, or carpentry, whereas social abilities manifest themselves in children's daily interactions with peers and adults. These natural abilities are present in all children to a variable degree; the gifted label will be used only when the level of expression becomes outstanding. High aptitudes or gifts can be observed more easily and directly in young children because environmental influences and systematic learning have exerted their moderating influences in a limited way. However, gifts still manifest themselves in older children, even in adults, through the facility and speed with which some individuals acquire new skills in any given field of human activity; the DMGT assumes a substantial relationship between the level of natural abilities and learning ease and speed.

Two domains, the intellectual and the psychomotor, have developed psychometrically valid measures of natural abilities. IQ tests, group or individually administered, are generally recognized as the most reliable and valid assessments of general cognitive functioning, often labeled the "g" factor (Jensen, 1998). In the psychomotor domain, one finds complex batteries of tests to assess the physical fitness of children in elementary or junior high schools (Australian Sports Commission, 1994; President's Council on Physical Fitness and Sports, 2001). The creative domain also has tests, but their psychometric qualities remain well below those of IQ tests, especially in terms of predictive validity (Plucker & Renzulli, 1999). The socioaffective domain lags behind in terms of psychometrically sound measures; but recent efforts appear promising (Matthews et al., 2002).

Is there still any need to defend the genetic basis of natural abilities? Nowadays, few researchers in the social sciences deny the significant contribution of genetic factors to human characteristics, including physical and mental abilities, interests, or temperament. The two domains with the best measures of natural abilities are also those with the most extensive analyses of the nature–nurture question. Especially during the last two decades, dozens of studies have examined the contribution of genes to individual differences in general cognitive functioning, comparing identical twins reared together or apart (Bouchard, 1997), identical twins with fraternal ones, or adopted siblings (Rowe, 1994). If any degree of contention remains, it concerns essentially the relative contributions of nature and nurture. Similar proof has been accumulating with regard to psychomotor abilities (Bouchard, Malina, & Pérusse, 1997).

Talents (T). Talents progressively emerge from the transformation of high aptitudes into the well-trained skills characteristic of a particular field of human activity. These fields cover a wide spectrum; indeed, *any* occupational field in which a series of skills needs to be mastered generates large individual differences in performance, ranging from minimum competence to high-level expertise. All individuals whose outstanding skills place them among the top 10 percent within their occupational field are recognized as talented within the DMGT framework.

Measuring talent is a straightforward enterprise: It simply corresponds to outstanding mastery of the specific skills of *any* occupational field. During the developmental phase of most talents, many occasions for normative assessment present themselves: teacher examinations, achievement tests, competitions, scholarships, and so forth. After individuals have completed their training, performance rankings usually disappear. How will you know if the plumber you have called is below or above average compared with peers? How about the mechanic working on your car, the dentist repairing a filling, or the coach managing your child's hockey team? Most of the time, the only guideline will be word of mouth. Only professional athletes have to deal with constant normative comparisons of their performances!

No direct bilateral relationship exists between giftedness domains and talent fields. Manual dexterity can be modeled into the particular skills of a pianist, a painter, or a video-game player; similarly, intelligence can be modeled into the scientific reasoning of a chemist, the game analysis of a chess player, or the strategic planning of an athlete. Yet, some occupational fields are associated more directly with specific ability domains. For instance, sports skills are built on the foundations of motor abilities; wine tasting develops from outstanding taste acuity; knowledge-dependent fields (e.g., traditional professions, technical occupations, mental sports such as chess or bridge) build their expertise from natural cognitive abilities; and talent in social-interaction occupations (e.g., sales, teaching, health services) naturally depends on high socioaffective abilities.

Talent is a developmental construct, which means that soon after youngsters have begun learning a new set of skills, it becomes possible to assess their performances normatively, comparing them with others who have been learning for an approximately equal amount of time. In schools, such assessments begin as early as kindergarten. Assessments also exist for beginners in music, dance, visual arts, or sports. Note that the level of achievement can change as learning progresses. During her first years in school, a student can obtain grades within the top 10 percent of her class and, consequently, be labeled academically talented. Then, for whatever reason, her progress may slow, justifying a decision to remove her from the talented group. The reverse is equally possible. However, high correlations between yearly achievements indicate that most academically talented students maintain their label through their formal schooling.

Learning and Practicing (LP). The talent development process consists of transforming specific natural abilities into the skills that define competence or expertise in a given occupational field. Competence corresponds to levels of mastery ranging from minimally acceptable to well above average, yet below the defined threshold for talented or expert behavior. Thus, academic talent is to gifted education what competence is to general education. As usually defined (see Ericsson, 1996), the concept of expertise largely overlaps the DMGT's concept of talent.

Developmental processes can take four different forms: (a) maturation, (b) informal learning, (c) formal noninstitutional learning, and (d) formal institutional learning. *Maturation* is a process almost totally controlled by the genome; it ensures the growth and transformation of all biological structures: bones, internal organs, brain, and so on. That developmental process in turn impacts other functions at the phenotypic level. For instance, research has shown that major changes in brain physiology directly coincide with parallel changes in cognitive achievements (Gazzaniga, Ivry, & Mangun, 1998; Lawson, 2003). *Informal learning* corresponds to knowledge and skills acquired during daily activities. Much of what is called "practical intelligence" (see Sternberg & Wagner, 1986) results from such informal or unstructured learning activities. The general knowledge, language skills, social skills, or manual skills mastered by young children before they enter the school system also emerge through such unstructured activities.

The last two developmental or learning processes are formal or systematic in the sense that there is a conscious intention to attain specific learning goals, and there is a systematically planned sequence of learning steps to reach these goals. The first case, *noninstitutionalized formal learning*, corresponds to autodidactic or self-taught learning. Many individuals, young and old, decide to develop competencies in a particular occupational field, most of the time as a leisure activity. Few will achieve performances that would compare with the best in these fields. But, sometimes, a self-taught pianist may outperform a majority of music students who have trained for five or six years. In the DMGT framework, these outstanding autodidacts would be labeled talented (Gagné, 1993). Still, most learning activities are institutionally based and lead to some form of official recognition: attending school, joining a sports team, a music school, a cooking academy, or a public-speaking program.

Theoretically, both gifts and talents can grow through all four types of developmental processes described previously. In practice, some types appear much more appropriate to gifts than talents, and vice versa. For instance, maturation affects the growth of talents only indirectly, that is, through its action on natural abilities, the building blocks of talents. On the other hand, early stimulation programs such as Head Start (Haskins, 1989) represent formal institutional attempts to develop general cognitive abilities (intellectual giftedness); unfortunately, such systematic interventions are very uncommon. As a general rule, the four processes contribute to the development of gifts in inverse proportion to their degree of formality. In other words, the major developmental agent for gifts is maturation, closely followed by informal learning. In the case of talents, it is the opposite, with institutional (or autodidactic) systematic learning accounting for most of the developmental impact.

The Trio of Catalysts

In chemistry, the term *catalyst* designates substances introduced into a chemical reaction, usually to accelerate it. At the end, these contributors regain their initial state. In other words, catalysts contribute to a reaction without being constituents of the final product. The DMGT posits that the *constituent* elements of talents are the natural abilities, which are slowly transformed into specific skills. Talent is strictly measured through the level of skill mastery; neither the type of contributing catalysts nor the strength of their contribution has relevance for talent assessment. The DMGT comprises three types of catalysts: intrapersonal, environmental, and chance factors. Each of them may be examined with regard to two dimensions: *direction* – facilitating versus hindering – and *strength* of causal impact on the developmental process.

Intrapersonal Catalysts. Until recently (see Gagné, 2003b), the intrapersonal catalysts were subdivided into five parallel subcomponents: physical characteristics, motivation, volition, self-management, and personality; self-management was the most recent addition to that group. Its introduction as a distinct category results from recent personal research on multitalented individuals (Gagné, 1999b), in which high-level self-management was perceived by virtually all parent interviewees to be one of the most typical characteristics of their multitalented adolescent. From these parent interviews, the concept was defined as covering behaviors such as initiative, time management, autonomy, concentration, and good work habits. Its definition overlaps a large group of terms commonly found in the scientific literature (e.g., self control, dependability, self-efficacy, mental self-governance, enterprise, self-regulation, and many others).

Based on a conception of self-management proposed by De Waele, Morval, & Sheitoyan (1993), this catalyst was recently redefined (Gagné, 2003a) and given a much broader and central role. De Waele et al. view self-management as "a practical philosophy of life" (p. 5). More concretely, it means "working toward the optimal integration of one's emotional, spiritual, intellectual, and physical life, at every stage of one's life. It also means recognizing opportunities for using appropriations [self-knowledge, knowledge of others and the environment], relation [mostly interpersonal], decision, and action as resources, to respond to one's needs and develop one's potential" (p. 8). This redefinition produced a new dichotomy among intrapersonal catalysts: physical and mental *characteristics* on one side and *processes* on the other. *Physical* characteristics may take many forms. For instance, when dance schools select young candidates for training, they often use physical parameters (e.g., height, slenderness, leg length) to determine the chances that a young student may attain high performance levels. In music, hand span directly affects the repertoire of a young musician. The same applies to sports, where physical templates have been defined for many sports.

Mental characteristics cluster around two major constructs: temperament and personality, which represent the nature and nurture poles, respectively, or basic tendencies as opposed to behavioral styles (McCrea et al., 2000). Most personality researchers recognize the existence of five basic bipolar personality dimensions, called "The Big Five" (Digman, 1990) or the Five-Factor Model (FFM). They are commonly labeled: Extraversion (E), Agreeableness (A), Conscientiousness (C), Neuroticism (N), and Intellect/Openness (O). McCrea and Costa (1999) affirm: "Much of what psychologists mean by the term *personality* [italics in text] is summarized by the FFM, and the model has been of great utility to the field by integrating and systematizing diverse conceptions and measures" (p. 139). There is growing evidence for a close relationship between temperament dimensions and adult personality traits (Rothbart, Ahadi, & Evans, 2000); that relationship probably explains why all FFM dimensions have significant genetic underpinnings (Rowe, 1997).

Self-management, as redefined along the lines of De Waele et al.'s (1993) work, becomes the overarching governing process of a person's self-development. Its goal is to foster the highest possible level of personal maturity and self-actualization. As shown in Figure 7.1, it comprises two major dimensions. The first one, labeled awareness, includes both of Gardner's (1983/1994) personal intelligences (*intra* and *inter*), as well as any process having an influence on the development of the self-concept and self-esteem. The second dimension, labeled motivation/volition, proposes a clear distinction between goal-setting behaviors and goal-attainment behaviors. This distinction is borrowed from Kuhl and Heckhausen's Action Control theory (see Kuhl & Beckmann, 1985); Corno (1993) adapted it to school learning. The term *motivation* is reserved for goal-setting processes (e.g., identifying and selecting interests, needs, motives, passions, values), whereas the term *volition* covers all goal-attainment activities (e.g., resource and time allocation, delay of gratification, effort, perseverance, self-regulation). Both constructs play a significant role in initiating the process of talent development, guiding it, and sustaining it through obstacles, boredom, and occasional failure.

Environmental Catalysts. In the DMGT, four distinct environmental inputs are distinguished (see Figure 7.1). The *milieu*, or surroundings, can be examined both at macroscopic (e.g., geographic, demographic, sociological) and microscopic levels (e.g., size of family, socioeconomic status, neighborhood services). For example, young gifted persons who live far from large urban centers do not have easy access to appropriate learning resources (e.g., sports training centers, music conservatories, magnet schools). Within the child's home environment, the parents' financial comfort, the absence of one of the caregivers, the number and age distribution of siblings within the family, as well as many other elements of the immediate environment, can impact the child's access to talent development opportunities. Psychological factors, for instance, the parents' value of educational pursuits or their personal psychological health, belong to the "persons" category, which follows.

The concept of environmental input usually brings to mind significant *persons*: parents, siblings, the extended family, friends, educators, mentors, idols, and so forth. The significant impact of persons on other persons is probably easier to imagine than that of any other source of influence within the environment. Moreover, the traditional environmentalist beliefs of most professionals in the social sciences, what Tooby and Cosmides (1992) label the Standard Social Science Model (SSSM), stress the primary importance of humans as significant agents in the lives of fellow humans. Thus, it is not surprising that a good percentage of the professional literature on talent development, not only in academics, but also in arts, business, or sports, focuses on the potential influence of significant individuals in the immediate environment of gifted or talented youngsters (Bloom, 1985; Cox, Daniel, & Boston, 1985; Hemery, 1986; Simonton, 1994).

The *provisions* subcomponent includes a large diversity of individual or group interventions specifically targeted at talent development. Provisions have been traditionally subdivided into three groups: enrichment (often labeled "differentiation"), grouping, and acceleration. This trilogy suffers from two major logical flaws. First, it unduly opposes enrichment and acceleration, encouraging the stereotypic image that acceleration practices are not enriching. Second, the categories are not mutually exclusive because many accelerative practices require ability grouping, for instance, Advanced Placement courses (College Board, 2001). Massé and Gagné (1983) proposed instead that enrichment be considered the general goal of *all* provisions offered to gifted or talented youngsters. Common administrative formats would then be categorized according to two main criteria: (a) the presence or absence of ability grouping, or (b) the presence or absence of acceleration. In this way, four major types of formats are distinguished, all of them potentially enriching. Finally, significant *events* (e.g., the death of a parent, winning a scholarship, suffering a major accident or illness) can markedly influence the course of talent development.

Chance. Tannenbaum (1983) first introduced chance as a contributing factor to talent development. Borrowed from that model, chance first appeared in the DMGT as a fifth element among the environmental catalysts. It soon became clear, however, that chance influences all the environmental catalysts. For example, children have no control over the socioeconomic status of the family in which they are raised, the quality of the parenting they receive, or the availability of talent development programs in the neighborhood school. Moreover, chance manifests itself in one other major event, namely, the transmission of hereditary characteristics. Few human phenomena are more dependent on chance than the specific mix of genes resulting from the random meeting of a particular ovum and one among millions of spermatozoids. Tannenbaum cites Atkinson's belief that all human accomplishments can be ascribed to "two crucial rolls of the dice over which no individual exerts any personal control. These are the accidents of birth and background" (1983, p. 221). Atkinson's "accidents of birth" stress the role of chance outside the EC zone, especially through the action of the genetic endowment in the G and IC components. In brief, as shown in Figure 7.1, some degree of chance affects all the causal components of the model, except the LP process.

The Prevalence Issue

This section briefly explains why a complete definition of giftedness or talent should include a prevalence estimate and how the DMGT deals concretely with that fundamental issue (see Gagné, 1993, 1998, for detailed discussions).

Background. The term *prevalence* refers to the percentage of a subgroup within a larger population. Concepts representing subgroups (e.g., poverty, obesity, mental deficiency, genius, deafness) base their definition on normative judgments. Galton (1892/1962) was among the first to argue that a complete definition of a normative concept requires its quantitative operationalization. He applied that principle in his study of eminent Englishmen, defining eminence as high enough renown to be among the top 1 in 4,000 within the general population. When they introduce a percentage estimate or a threshold value, scholars specify the "extension" of a normative concept, in other words, the boundary separating those who belong to that special category from those who do not. In turn, knowledge about the size of the special population further clarifies the meaning of a normative concept. For instance, if we define the gifted as the top 1 percent of the population, it conveys a totally different image about their exceptionality than if we define them as the top 20 percent of the population.

Identifying appropriate thresholds is a difficult task because no objective markers on a measurement scale indicate the passage from one category (e.g., average ability, normal weight) to the next (e.g., gifted, overweight). Any proposed threshold is localized somewhere within a grey zone, with some experts showing more openness and others defending stricter positions. Because there is no "correct" answer, specialists within a

TABLE 7.1. *Gagné's Metric-Based (MB) System of Levels within the Gifted/Talented Population*

Level	Label	Ratio in Population	IQ Equivalents	Standard Deviation
5	Extremely	1:100,000	165	+ 4.3
4	Exceptionally	1:10,000	155	+ 3.7
3	Highly	1:1,000	145	+ 3.0
2	Moderately	1:100	135	+ 2.3
1	Mildly	1:10	120	+ 1.3

field will have to eventually agree on a "best" choice, one that will become generalized. This is what happened when nutritionists agreed on specific values of the body-mass index to quantify the concepts of overweight and obesity; it greatly facilitates prevalence assessments, as well as comparisons between age groups, nations, or sexes. Alas, such agreement does not exist in the field of gifted education. In fact, the authors of major handbooks very rarely discuss the subject of prevalence, and only one (Marland, 1972) of the more popular definitions of the last three or four decades includes a prevalence estimate. The fact that the prevalence question is not discussed does not mean that estimates have not been regularly proposed. In fact, they abound, and the result of that "creativity" is huge variability. Scholars' proposals can easily range from the 1 percent adopted by Terman (1925), with his threshold of a 135 IQ, or the 3 to 5 percent in the previously mentioned Marland definition, to the 20 percent advanced by Renzulli (1986) to create the talent pools in his Revolving Door model.

The Metric-Based (MB) System. The DMGT proposes a five-level system of cutoffs based on the metric system, hence its MB acronym and the choice of 10 percent as the initial threshold. Although that minimum leans slightly toward the generous pole of the range observed in the literature, it is counterbalanced by the introduction of five degrees of giftedness or talent, labeled *mildly, moderately, highly, exceptionally,* and *extremely,* respectively. Following the metric system rules, each group represents the top 10 percent of the previous group. Table 7.1 shows these five groups with their corresponding ratios in the general population; z scores, as well as approximate IQ equivalents, complete the table. Note that the 10 percent estimate applies to each natural ability domain and each talent field. Because there is only partial overlap between domains and fields, it follows that the *total* percentage of gifted and talented individuals far exceeds 10 percent.

A Note of Caution. Most keynote speakers and writers have the unfortunate habit of illustrating their statements with examples taken from children who show exceptional precocity either in verbal, mathematical, scientific, moral, or social development. As effective as such examples may be to impress an audience, they describe behaviors that the vast majority of gifted students identified in school districts – the mildly gifted or talented between the 90th and 99th percentiles – will rarely exhibit. Think about it. Individuals with *exceptional* intellectual gifts, those with IQs of 155 or more, account for approximately 1 in 10,000 within the general population. Even *within the gifted population*, the prevalence of these exceptionally gifted individuals equals 1 in 1,000, approximately 1 in 30 to 40 homogeneous *groups* of intellectually gifted students. Even full-time teachers of the gifted would, in the course of their whole career, encounter at best just a few of them. In short, exceptional giftedness is a very rare phenomenon. Consequently, when we present extreme examples of behavior to groups of parents or teachers, we risk conveying a distorted image of who really is the "garden variety" of mildly gifted and talented individuals. And if we present giftedness and talent as very exceptional phenomena, school administrators might argue that such a rare population does not require large investments of time and money to cater to their very special needs.

TOWARD A TALENT DEVELOPMENT THEORY

The second part of this chapter succinctly covers two major questions (see Gagné, 2003b, for an extended discussion). First, what relationships do the six components of the DMGT entertain among themselves? Second, is it possible to create a hierarchy of the five factors in terms of their relative causal power? In other words, where lies the difference between those who become talented and those who do not?

A Complex Pattern of Interactions

The most fundamental relationship involves the first trio. As described earlier, talent development corresponds to the transformation of outstanding natural abilities or gifts into the skills characteristic of a particular occupational field. In the DMGT, natural abilities are treated as the "raw materials" or the constituent elements of talents. For instance, the skills of a young pianist derive from general perceptual and motor abilities, among them hand coordination, finger dexterity, auditory discrimination, visual memory, and rhythm. Because of that basic relationship, the presence of talent necessarily implies the possession of well-above-average natural abilities; one cannot become talented without first being gifted, or almost so. However, the reverse is not true; outstanding gifts can remain potentialities, as witnessed by the phenomenon of academic underachievement. The arrows in Figure 7.1 indicate that I and E catalysts typically act through the LP process. That moderator role is quite normal; it confirms that talent does not manifest itself overnight. The skills have to be built, even when, thanks to very high natural abilities, the first achievements appear almost instantaneous and effortless. Sometimes, environmental influences do not act directly on the learning process, but through an intrapersonal catalyst. For instance, when coaches help their athletes develop visualization abilities, they are trying to improve a specific IC component that will in turn improve the training process.

Interactions can take many forms. Without having yet covered in depth the literature on talent development, I believe that empirical evidence exists to support bidirectional interactions between *any* pairing of the five causal components, excluding only those that target the chance factor. We have already mentioned examples of EC → IC influences; the reverse is also common. For example, if a child expresses a strong interest in astronomy, the parents will probably be more willing to invest in a high-quality telescope. The impact, positive or negative, on one's self-concept of becoming aware of gifted abilities is a typical case of G → IC interaction. Conversely, ICs may exert an impact on the development of natural abilities; individuals with little motivation to take care of their health will avoid physical activities. Talent usually plays the role of dependent variable in most predictive validity studies. But it can become an independent variable, for instance, when it enters into a feedback loop and influences the performers and/or influential persons in their environment. No doubt that the early successes of young students, young artists, or young athletes serve to heighten their motivation to pursue their training, even increase its intensity. Similarly, parents will become more motivated to maintain or increase their support, coaches will feel more eager to supervise young athletes whose early outstanding performances reveal high talent promise and even sponsors will open their purses wider! As the saying goes, "success breeds success."

In summary, no causal component stands alone. They all interact with each other and with the learning process in very complex ways, and these interactions will differ significantly from one person to the next. As I argued elsewhere after analyzing with the DMGT the life story of a young exceptionally talented Vietnamese classical guitarist (Gagné, 2000), individual talent emerges from complex and unique choreographies between the five groups of causal influences.

What Makes a Difference?

Even though individual choreographies are unique, what can we say about averages? Are some factors generally recognized as more powerful predictors of outstanding performance? For all those involved in the study of talent development, this is *the* question. Yet, in spite of its theoretical and practical importance, the causal hierarchy question has rarely been asked, let alone answered. Just within the field of education, thousands of empirical studies have compared achieving students with less performing ones, hoping to unravel the network of causal factors leading to academic success. Dozens of variables, covering every component and subcomponent of the DMGT, have been measured. Unfortunately, individual studies include too few independent variables to bring even a semblance of an answer to this complex question. Literature reviews, meta-analytic (Walberg, 1984) or anecdotal (Simonton, 1994), have shed little light on the question, especially because their authors refused to commit themselves to a ranking of causal factors.

My current answer (Gagné, 2003b) to the hierarchy question could be summarized by the acronym *C.GIPE*; it describes a decreasing order of causal impact, from chance at the top to environmental catalysts at the bottom. Why is chance given such a predominant role? The answer lies in Atkinson's two rolls of the dice mentioned earlier: the genetic and parental rolls. Note that the genetic endowment affects not only the G component, but also the IC component, as shown by the arrows in Figure 7.1. The second rank given to gifts rests essentially on data from two giftedness domains: cognitive and physical abilities. In the first case, research has shown that IQ measures are, by far, the best predictor of academic achievement (Jensen, 1998). In the case of physical abilities, there is also growing evidence that natural "talent" (giftedness) is a major differentiator between those who can attain excellence in sports and those who cannot. For instance, the Australian Institute of Sport (AIS), in collaboration with state institutes and academies of sport, identifies potential Olympians as follows. Using the secondary schools' approach to fitness assessment, a general fitness test is offered to students mostly in grades eight and nine. Only those in the top 2 percent of national norms are invited to pass a second battery of more advanced physiological and performance tests. Again, only those who achieve among the top 10 percent on subgroups of these tests, depending on the competitive sport chosen, will be invited for further testing and potential inclusion in an advanced training program (J. Gulbin, personal communication, January 5, 2004). Such a selection procedure leaves aside at least 99.5 percent of all adolescents, an eloquent testimony of the AIS' belief that very high natural abilities are required for athletes to develop their talent to national standards.

The placement of intrapersonal catalysts in third position brings up two questions: (a) why do they follow gifts, and (b) why do they precede learning and practice? With regard to the first question, the research literature on academic excellence suggests that the best "contenders" to prominence among IC factors would be motivation-related constructs. What does research say about them? Virtually every comparative study of the relative explanatory power of motivational constructs over IQ measures has shown a clear superiority of the latter. After reviewing the literature, Gagné and St Père (2002) concluded that IQ scores "explain" *five times* more achievement variance on average when compared directly with *any* measure of motivation or volition. As for other constructs included in the IC component, there is little literature on their *unique* contribution to talent development. The second question concerns the priority of intrapersonal catalysts over the LP component. Some scholars (see Ericsson, 1996) would strongly oppose such a low ranking, accumulating evidence for a strong causal relationship between level of talent and amount – and quality – of practice. But others have strongly contested their interpretations (Schneider, 2000). Two additional arguments support the placement of the LP component below that of IC factors. First, the IC group comprises a large number of variables that have been linked to achievement, whereas the LP process offers just a few measures, both quantitative and qualitative. Second, to use a common metaphor, the LP "motor" needs fuel to run, and that fuel comes directly from the intrapersonal and environmental catalysts. It is passion, competitiveness, parental support, coach admonitions, or any other IC or EC element that helps maintain a steady regimen of learning and practice, especially when learners encounter obstacles.

Relegating the environmental catalysts to the bottom of the causal hierarchy contradicts common sense, as well as much of the social sciences literature. Yet, over the last two decades, researchers in behavioral genetics have strongly questioned the causal importance of environmental inputs, thus triggering a heated debate (see Collins, Maccoby, Steinberg, Hetherington, & Bornstein, 2000). Four major arguments are advanced. The first one, commonly labeled "the nature of nurture," states that most environmental measures are partly influenced by the genotype, which artificially inflates their contribution (Rowe, 1994; Scarr & Carter-Saltzman, 1982). The second argument is based on the recurring observation in twin and adoption studies that *shared* family influences – the aspects of the family environment that affect all siblings similarly – account for a very small percentage of individual differences in cognitive abilities and personality (Rowe, 1997; Scarr, 1992). In other words, the parents' rearing behaviors have little to do with what makes their children similar and, at the same time, different from those of other families. A third argument invokes the phenomenological perspective, according to which EC influences are continuously filtered through the eyes of the persons who are targeted by them. That perceptual filtering gives more importance to ICs, strengthening the argument in favor of their placement immediately after the G component. Finally, the growing interest in the study of resilience (O'Connell Higgins, 1994), the ability of some individuals to achieve high personal maturity in spite of having suffered exceptionally negative environmental influences, suggests that detrimental environmental obstacles can be surmounted.

COMPARING THE DMGT WITH OTHER CONCEPTIONS

Space does not allow a detailed comparison of the DMGT with other leading conceptions. To do that process justice would require examining each
of them individually. As a shortcut approach, I have summarized four
characteristics of the DMGT that appear to me very specific and, in conjunc-
tion, make the DMGT a very distinct and unique conception of giftedness
and talent.

First, the DMGT stands alone in its clearly differentiated definitions
of the field's two key concepts. The separation of potentialities/aptitudes
from realizations/achievements is well operationalized through a distinction between natural abilities and systematically developed skills, both
concepts associated with the labels giftedness and talent, respectively. This
distinction leads to another clear definition, that of talent development,
which becomes the transformation of natural abilities into the systematically developed skills typical of an occupational field. Only in the DMGT
does the concept of talent become as important as that of giftedness to
understanding the development of outstanding skills and knowledge. Finally, this differentiation between potentialities and realizations permits
a much clearer definition of underachievement among gifted individuals. It becomes simply the *non*transformation of high natural abilities into
systematically developed skills in any occupational field. This definition
applies to any pairing of one – or more – giftedness domain(s) with any
given field of talent.

Second, the introduction within the giftedness and talent definitions of
prevalence estimates (top 10 percent) also constitutes a unique facet of the
DMGT among existing conceptions of giftedness. Because it confronts the
prevalence issue and proposes a metric-based system of five levels that
applies to any giftedness domain or talent field, the DMGT helps maintain
a constant awareness of levels of giftedness and talent. The availability of
clear thresholds and labels could facilitate not only the selection and description of study samples, but also the comparison of results from different
studies. Moreover, the MB system of levels should remind educators in the
field that the vast majority of gifted or talented individuals (90 percent)
belong to the lowest (mild) category and that only a tiny fraction of those
identified as gifted or talented in their youth will ever achieve eminence
in their chosen field.

Third, the DMGT's complex structure clearly identifies every significant
etiological factor of talent emergence, especially those located within the intrapersonal and environmental catalysts. But that comprehensive outlook
maintains the individuality of each component, clearly specifying their precise nature and role within this talent development theory. The giftedness
construct remains well circumscribed, thus more easily operationalized.

The catalysts are clearly situated outside the giftedness and talent concepts themselves. This sets the DMGT apart from many rival conceptions where disparate elements are lumped together in the giftedness definition itself. For instance, Feldhusen defines giftedness as follows: "Our composite conception of giftedness then includes (a) general intellectual ability, (b) positive self-concept, (c) achievement motivation, and (d) talent" (1986, p. 112). And Renzulli presents the following definition: "Gifted behavior consists of behaviors that reflect an interaction among three clusters of human traits – these clusters being above average general and/or specific abilities, high levels of task commitment, and high levels of creativity. Gifted and talented children are those possessing or capable of developing this composite set of traits and applying them to any potentially valuable area of human performance" (1986, p. 73).

Finally, most published conceptions focus almost exclusively on intellectual giftedness (IG) and academic talent (AT), as well as academically based professions (e.g., scientists, lawyers, doctors, and so forth). That tendency led me to label "IGAT" the target population of most enrichment programs (Gagné, 1995). The DMGT follows an orientation adopted explicitly by only a few past scholars (e.g., De Haan & Havighurst, 1961; Gardner, 1983; Marland, 1972), namely, to broaden the concept of giftedness and acknowledge its various manifestations. In that respect, the DMGT stands almost alone in bringing physical giftedness within the fold of the giftedness construct, defining that domain much more broadly than Gardner's bodily–kinesthetic intelligence. This openness should foster closer ties between professionals focusing on academic talent development and those who devote their energies to athletic talent development.

CONCLUSION

So much more would need to be said to faithfully convey the complexity of the DMGT as it now exists in published (and unpublished!) documents. Now that its basic contents and structure are well stabilized, future efforts will focus on the developmental theory itself, with two major directions pursued. The first will consist of a search for additional empirical evidence to support the present developmental hypotheses and for additional hypotheses and corollaries. The second research effort will examine possible interactions between the C.GIPE causal hierarchy and (a) stages of talent development, (b) fields of talent, (c) levels of excellence, (d) gender differences, or (e) cultural differences. The past decades of slow progress to clearly identify "what makes a difference" should be a humbling reminder that this goal is not within easy reach. But what an exciting challenge it offers to all scholars who dream of unearthing the roots of excellence!

ACKNOWLEDGMENT

This chapter is adapted from Gagné, F. (2003). Transforming gifts into talents: The DMGT as a developmental theory. In N. Colangelo & G. A. Davis (Eds.), *Handbook of gifted education* (3rd ed., pp. 60–74). Boston: Allyn & Bacon.

References

Anastasi, A. (1980). Abilities and the measurement of achievement. In W. B. Schrader (Ed.), *Measuring achievement: Progress over a decade* (pp. 1–10). San Francisco: Jossey-Bass.

Angoff, W. H. (1988). The nature-nurture debate, aptitudes, and group differences. *American Psychologist, 41*, 713–720.

Australian Sports Commission. (1994). *The search is over: Norms for sport related fitness tests in Australian students aged 12–17 years.* Canberra, Australia: Author.

Bloom, B. S. (1985). *Developing talent in young people.* New York: Ballantine.

Bouchard, C., Malina, R. M., & Pérusse, L. (1997). *Genetics of fitness and physical performance.* Champaign, IL: Human Kinetics.

Bouchard, T. J. (1997). IQ similarity in twins reared apart: Findings and responses to critics. In R. J. Sternberg & E. Grigorenko (Eds.), *Intelligence, heredity, and environment* (pp. 126–160). New York: Cambridge University Press.

Carroll, J. B. (1993). *Human cognitive abilities: A survey of factor-analytic studies.* Cambridge, England: Cambridge University Press.

Colangelo, N., & Davis, G. A. (Eds.) (2003). *Handbook of gifted education* (3rd ed.). Needham Heights, MA: Allyn & Bacon.

College Board. (2001). *Advanced placement program.* Retrieved August 17, 2002, from www.collegeboard.org/ap/

Collins, W. A., Maccoby, E. E., Steinberg, L., Hetherington, E. M., & Bornstein, M. H. (2000). Contemporary research on parenting: The case for nature and nurture. *American Psychologist, 55*, 218–232.

Corno, L. (1993). The best-laid plans: Modern conceptions of volition and educational research. *Educational Researcher, 22*, 14–22.

Cox, J., Daniel, N., & Boston, B. O. (1985). *Educating able learners: Programs and promising practices.* Austin: University of Texas Press.

Csikszentmihalyi, M., & Robinson, R. E. (1986). Culture, time, and the development of talent. In R. J. Sternberg & J. E. Davidson (Eds.), *Conceptions of giftedness* (pp. 264–284). New York: Cambridge University Press.

Davidson, J. E. (1986). The role of insight in giftedness. In R. J. Sternberg & J. E. Davidson (Eds.), *Conceptions of giftedness* (pp. 201–222). New York: Cambridge University Press.

DeHann, R. F., & Havighurst, R. J. (1961). *Educating gifted children* (rev. ed.). Chicago: University of Chicago Press.

De Waele, M., Morval, J., & Sheitoyan, R. (1993). *Self-management in organizations: The dynamics of interaction.* Seattle, WA: Hogrefe & Huber.

Digman, J. M. (1990). Personality structure: Emergence of the five-factor model. In M. R. Rosenzweig & L. W. Porter (Eds.), *Annual Review of Psychology* (Vol. 41, pp. 417–440). Palo Alto, CA: Annual Reviews.

Ericsson, K. A. (Ed.). (1996). *The road to excellence: The acquisition of expert performance in the arts and sciences, sports, and games.* Mahwah, NJ: Lawrence Erlbaum Associates.

Feldhusen, J. F. (1986). A conception of giftedness. In R. J. Sternberg & J. E. Davidson (Eds.), *Conceptions of giftedness* (pp. 112–127). New York: Cambridge University Press.

Feldman, D. H. (1986). Giftedness as a developmentalist sees it. In R. J. Sternberg & J. E. Davidson (Eds.), *Conceptions of giftedness* (pp. 285–305). New York: Cambridge University Press.

Gagné, F. (1985). Giftedness and talent: Reexamining a reexamination of the definitions. *Gifted Child Quarterly, 29*, 103–112.

Gagné, F. (1993). Constructs and models pertaining to exceptional human abilities. In K. A. Heller, F. J. Mönks, & A. H. Passow (Eds.), *International handbook of research and development of giftedness and talent* (pp. 63–85). Oxford, England: Pergamon.

Gagné, F. (1995). From giftedness to talent: A developmental model and its impact on the language of the field. *Roeper Review, 18*, 103–111.

Gagné, F. (1998). A proposal for subcategories within the gifted or talented populations. *Gifted Child Quarterly, 42*, 87–95.

Gagné, F. (1999a). Is there any light at the end of the tunnel? *Journal for the Education of the Gifted, 22*, 191–234.

Gagné, F. (1999b). The multigifts of multitalented individuals. In S. Cline & K. T. Hegeman (Eds.), *Gifted education in the twenty-first century: Issues and concerns* (pp. 17–45). Delray Beach, FL: Winslow Press.

Gagné, F. (1999c). My convictions about the nature of human abilities, gifts and talents. *Journal for the Education of the Gifted, 22*, 109–136.

Gagné, F. (2000). Understanding the complex choreography of talent development through DMGT-based analysis. In K. A. Heller, F. J. Mönks, R. J. Sternberg, & R. Subotnik (Eds.), *International Handbook for Research on Giftedness and Talent* (2nd ed., pp. 67–79). Oxford, England: Pergamon.

Gagné, F. (2003a, November). *Self-management: A crucial catalyst.* Paper presented at the 50th annual conference of the National Association for Gifted Children, held in Indianapolis, IN.

Gagné, F. (2003b). Transforming gifts into talents: The DMGT as a developmental theory. In N. Colangelo & G. A. Davis (Eds.), *Handbook of gifted education* (3rd ed., pp. 60–74). Needham Heights, MA: Allyn & Bacon.

Gagné, F., & St Père, F. (2002). When IQ is controlled, does motivation still predict achievement? *Intelligence, 30*, 71–100.

Galton, F. (1892/1962). *Hereditary genius: An inquiry into its laws and consequences.* New York: Meridian Books.

Gardner, H. (1983/1994). *Frames of mind: The theory of multiple intelligences.* New York: Basic Books.

Gazzaniga, M. S., Ivry, R. B., & Mangun, G. R. (1998). *Cognitive neuroscience: The biology of mind.* New York: Norton.

Haensly, P., Reynolds, C. R., & Nash, W. R. (1986). Giftedness: Coalescence, context, conflict, and commitment. In R. J. Sternberg & J. E. Davidson (Eds.), *Conceptions of giftedness* (pp. 128–148). New York: Cambridge University Press.

Haskins, R. (1989). Beyond metaphor: The efficacy of early childhood education. *American Psychologist, 44*, 274–282.

Heller, K. A., Mönks, F. J., Sternberg, R. J., & Subotnik, R. (Eds.). (2000). *International handbook for research on giftedness and talent* (2nd ed). Oxford, England: Pergamon.

Hemery, D. (1986). *The pursuit of sporting excellence; A study of sport's highest achievers.* London: Willow Books.

Jensen, A. R. (1998). *The "g" factor: The science of mental ability.* New York: Praeger.

Kuhl, J., & Beckmann, J. (Eds.). (1985). *Action control: From cognition to behavior.* New York: Springer-Verlag.

Lawson, A. E. (2003). *The neurological basis of learning, development and discovery.* Dordrecht, The Netherlands: Kluwer.

Marland, S. P. (1972). *Education of the gifted and talented: Report to the Congress of the United States by the U.S. Commissioner of Education.* Washington, DC: U.S. Government Printing Office.

Massé, P., & Gagné, F. (1983). Observations on enrichment and acceleration. In B. M. Shore, F. Gagné, S. Larivée, R. H. Tali, & R. E. Tremblay (Eds.), *Face to face with giftedness* (pp. 395–413). Monroe, NY: Trillium Press.

Matthews, G., Zeidner, M., & Roberts, R. D. (2002). *Emotional intelligence: Science and myths.* Cambridge, MA: MIT Press.

McCrae, R. R., & Costa, P. T., Jr. (1999). A five-factor theory of personality. In L. A. Pervin, & O. P. John (Eds.), *Handbook of personality: Theory and research* (2nd ed., pp. 139–153). New York: Guilford.

McCrae, R. R., Costa, P. T., Jr., Ostendorf, F., Angleitner, A., Hrebickova, M., Avia, M. D., et al. (2000). Nature over nurture: Temperament, personality, and life span development. *Journal of Personality and Social Psychology, 78*, 173–186.

O'Connell Higgins, G. (1994). *Resilient adults: Overcoming a cruel past.* San Francisco: Jossey-Bass.

Plucker, J. A., & Renzulli, J. S. (1999). Psychometric approaches to the study of human creativity. In R. J. Sternberg (Ed.), *Handbook of creativity* (pp. 35–61). New York: Cambridge University Press.

President's Council on Physical Fitness and Sports. (2001). *President's challenge: Physical fitness program packet.* Retrieved August 17, 2002 from www.fitness. gov/challenge/challenge.html

Renzulli, J. S. (1986). The three-ring conception of giftedness: A developmental model for creative productivity. In R. J. Sternberg & J. E. Davidson (Eds.), *Conceptions of giftedness* (pp. 53–92). New York: Cambridge University Press.

Rothbart, M. K., Ahadi, S. A., & Evans, D. E. (2000). Temperament and personality: Origins and outcomes. *Journal of Personality and Social Psychology, 78*, 122–135.

Rowe, D. C. (1994). *The limits of family influence: Genes, experience, and behavior.* New York: Guilford.

Rowe, D. C. (1997). Genetics, temperament, and personality. In R. Hogan, J. Johnson, & S. Briggs (Eds.), *Handbook of personality psychology* (pp. 367–386). New York: Academic.

Scarr, S. (1992). Developmental theories for the 1990s: Development and individual differences. *Developmental Psychology, 63*, 1–19.

Scarr, S., & Carter-Saltzman, L. (1982). Genetics and intelligence. In R. J. Sternberg (Ed.), *Handbook of human intelligence* (pp. 792–896). Cambridge, England: Cambridge University Press.

Schneider, W. (2000). Giftedness, expertise, and (exceptional) performance: A developmental perspective. In K. A. Heller, F. J. Mönks, R. J. Sternberg, & R. Subotnik (Eds.), *International handbook for research on giftedness and talent* (2nd ed., pp. 165–177). Oxford, England: Pergamon.

Simonton, D. K. (1994). *Greatness: Who makes history and why.* New York: Guilford.

Sternberg, R. J. (1986). A triarchic theory of intellectual giftedness. In R. J. Sternberg & J. E. Davidson (Eds.), *Conceptions of giftedness* (pp. 223–243). New York: Cambridge University Press.

Sternberg, R. J., & Davidson, J. E. (Eds.). (1986). *Conceptions of giftedness.* New York: Cambridge University Press.

Sternberg, R. J., & Wagner, R. K. (Eds.). (1986). *Practical intelligence: Nature and origins of competence in the everyday world.* New York: Cambridge University Press.

Tannenbaum, A. J. (1983). *Gifted children: Psychological and educational perspectives.* New York: Macmillan.

Tannenbaum, A. J. (1986). Giftedness: A psychosocial approach. In R. J. Sternberg & J. E. Davidson (Eds.), *Conceptions of giftedness* (pp. 21–52). New York: Cambridge University Press.

Terman, L. M. (1925). *Genetic studies of genius: Vol. 1. Mental and physical traits of a thousand gifted children.* Stanford, CA: Stanford University Press.

Tooby, J., & Cosmides, L. (1992). The psychological foundations of culture. In J. M. Barkow, L. Cosmides, & J. Tooby (Eds.), *The adapted mind: Evolutionary psychology and the generation of culture* (pp. 19–136). New York: Oxford University Press.

Walberg, H. J. (1984). Improving the productivity of America's schools. *Educational Leadership, 41*(8), 19–27.

8

Nurturing Talent in Gifted Students of Color

Edmund W. Gordon and Beatrice L. Bridglall

> Gifted Black students are a minority within a minority – an anomaly in gifted programs. As a gifted Black student, I walked in two worlds. Teachers had a difficult time understanding me, for I was gifted *and* Black – it was an oxymoron, just as gifted underachievement appears paradoxical. . . . As a gifted Black student who *learned* to underachieve, I needed several things to ensure a healthy school experience.
>
> Donna Y. Ford (1996, p. xi)

For many students of color in the United States, the identification, assessment and nurturance of giftedness are complicated by limited opportunities to learn, psychological and social pressures, and racial and ethnic discrimination. One of the most pernicious expressions of these complicating factors is the persistent though unacknowledged notion of intellectual inferiority. Unlike most of their European American and Asian American peers, Black and other ethnic minority gifted youth are confronted with the potential for academic failure that defies predictions based on demonstrated ability and even trumps expectations of high achievement. To the extent that a significant number of students of color in college, particularly Black males, perform well below their tested abilities, as research on the predictive value of the Scholastic Achievement Test (SAT) attests (Bridgeman, McCamley-Jenkins, & Ervin, 2000; Young, 2001), it is incumbent on researchers and practitioners to find effective means to nurture the intellective development of students of color with exceptional academic ability. Further, our traditional indicators of academic giftedness have been drawn so narrowly as to result in the exclusion of many persons in whom the capacity to perform at high academic levels is not recognized, nor is it developed (Borland & Wright, 1994; Donovan & Cross, 2002). Giftedness is generally used to refer to highly developed and specialized abilities and the capability to demonstrate these abilities in academic performance. Perhaps the most widely recognized and acclaimed expressions are in artistic and intellective prowess. In some circles, high levels of general adaptive ability, creativity, efficiency, speed, and/or relational skills may be recognized as gifted. Gardner (1999) has identified more than seven dimensions along which one may be said to demonstrate giftedness.

In determining the various ways in which giftedness may be conceptualized and identified, it may be useful to consider taking a second look at a category of persons who show potential for being identified as academically gifted, but who tend not to perform at levels of academic achievement that are sufficiently high to be included in the gifted population. Without changing the criteria by which academic giftedness is judged, we may be able to increase the pool of persons who perform above the 85th percentile by efforts directed at reversing the tendency of some achievement indicators to overpredict the academic performance of some students of color. To that end, this chapter reinforces the importance of nurturing academic ability in gifted students of color by describing the structural supports of an exemplary student academic development program, the Meyerhoff Scholars Program (MSP), at the University of Maryland, Baltimore County. Over a span of 15 years, the MSP has become one of the nation's leading producers of undergraduate students of color, particularly Blacks, who go on to graduate study and research careers in the sciences, mathematics, and engineering.

In this context, we briefly review several conceptualizations of giftedness; review the scope of the underrepresentation and overprediction phenomenon for gifted students of color; elaborate on some of the causes of this national crisis; provide evidence of how the MSP nurtures the academic excellence of gifted and talented students of color; discuss those theoretical constructs from the social sciences that we believe inform practices having to do with academic attitudinal and behavioral changes; and conclude with a discussion of those aspects of the program that can be transferred in efforts to reduce the overprediction phenomenon and increase the persistence and academic excellence of gifted and talented students of color.

CONCEPTUALIZATIONS OF GIFTEDNESS

In traditional conceptualizations of giftedness, high intelligence was believed to be reflected in high scores on tests of intelligence or academic achievement (Terman, 1925). The association between giftedness and high IQ scores was established at the beginning of the 20th century when tests were developed to measure intelligence and eventually were depended on to identify gifted children. The idea of giftedness as above-average cognitive and academic ability seems to have dictated both the design of these assessment instruments and the characteristics that teachers and counselors use as indicators of giftedness. This conceptualization of giftedness may have prevented the identification of some gifted students who underachieve on standardized tests or who do not impress their teachers as being smart.

Contemporary theories of giftedness have begun to move beyond a unidimensional view of giftedness to incorporate a complex understanding of abilities and behaviors. Robert Sternberg's (1985) triarchic theory of human intelligence, for example, consists of the following interacting subtheories: (1) the componential subtheory, which argues for the importance of mechanisms that enable the acquisition of information and knowledge and the performance of metacognitive tasks; (2) the experiential subtheory, which views intelligence as vying with known and unknown phenomen a with varying degrees of success; and (3) the contextual subtheory, which proposes that intelligence occurs in sociocultural contexts and necessarily involves adaptation to novel and quotidian circumstances and situations.

Renzulli's (1986) theory of giftedness makes a distinction between "schoolhouse" giftedness and "creative–productive" giftedness, two types of intelligence that may coexist and interact within the same person. The former is most prevalent in highly able learners who do well on standardized and cognitive ability tests. Programs for the gifted are generally modeled on this type of intelligence and are best suited to serve this type of student. Renzulli suggests, however, that giftedness also includes the ability to develop new products from acquired knowledge and to use and apply "information (content) and thinking processes in an integrated, inductive, and real-problem-oriented manner" (1986, p. 58). Accordingly, this type of giftedness is harder to measure and presents more programming challenges than schoolhouse giftedness. Creative–productive intelligence involves the interaction among three key qualities (Renzulli's "three-ring conception"): above-average ability, creativity, and commitment to task. These qualities combine to generate inventions, art, scientific discovery, and cultural innovation, all of which depend on "... productive people of the world, the producers rather than the consumers of knowledge" (1986, p. 59). Renzulli suggests that, although above-average ability is associated with this type of giftedness, it is not a necessary trait.

What is interesting about Renzulli's theory, particularly in relation to the philosophical underpinnings of the MSP, is the equal placement of task commitment, a noncognitive factor, within the three-ring conception of giftedness. Task commitment, from Renzulli's perspective, is as important as the ability to process information, reason analytically, understand spatial relations, and think conceptually. Task commitment is characterized by perseverance, dedicated practice, endurance, self-confidence, trust, and effort that is guided by concrete, problem-oriented, and creatively guided goals. It can be argued that programs for gifted students, such as the MSP and others, must (1) support and hone rigorous academic discipline; and (2) train students to increase their motivation, persistence, and goal-orientation.

Both Renzulli's (1986) and Sternberg's (1985) perspectives on giftedness incorporate nonacademic and noncognitive components and point to the interaction of extraordinary character traits and the sociocultural adaptive skills that appear to be essential to giftedness. Gordon's (2001) idea of intellective competence also conceptualizes human intellect along a spectrum of social, psychological, behavioral, and cultural abilities and adaptive competencies. Gordon argues that "it may be more appropriate that we think of developed intellective abilities or intellective competencies as the meta-expressions of a wide range of human learning achievements, some of which are related to what happens in schools. These developed abilities are not so much reflected in the specific discipline-based knowledge a student may have, but in the student's ability and disposition to adaptively and efficiently use knowledge, technique, and values in mental processes to engage and solve both common and novel problems" (2001, p. 3). For all intents and purposes, the referenced perspectives on giftedness seem not to have influenced the identification and assessment of not only the traditional notions of cognitive knowledge, skills, and dispositions, but also the social, cultural, and motivational dimensions of high levels of human learning and intellect.

We contend that this misalignment between narrow conceptions of giftedness and its identification, assessment, and development may have a role in perpetuating the long-standing gap in academic achievement between Black, Hispanic, and Native American students and their European American and Asian American peers. Although the gap exists at all levels, the serious underrepresentation of students of color among those who perform in the top quartile has received relatively little attention in elementary, secondary, or postsecondary education. Where attention is directed to the academic achievement gap, special efforts are more likely to be seen directed at the generic problems of academic underachievement of students who cluster in the left and middle of the academic achievement distribution. The failure to recognize a broader range of expressions of giftedness and the failure especially to nurture latent expressions of intellective potential in these populations may be contributing to the achievement gap.

UNDERREPRESENTATION AND OVERPREDICTION

The chronic underrepresentation of Blacks, Hispanics, and Native Americans among gifted and talented high-achieving students in the United States led to the formation in 1997 of the College Board's National Task Force on Minority High Achievement, co-chaired by Professors Edmund W. Gordon and Eugene Cota-Robles. The College Board's (1999) Task Force Report, "Reaching the Top," details the fact that, in 1995, these ethnic minority students constituted about 30 percent of the under-18 population, yet received only 13 percent of the bachelor's degrees, 11 percent of the professional degrees, and 6 percent of the doctoral degrees presented by colleges and universities in the United States. It further observed that "Until many more underrepresented minority students from disadvantaged, middle-class, and upper middle-class circumstances are very successful educationally, it will be virtually impossible to integrate our society's institutions completely, especially at the leadership levels" (p. 2). This observation is reflected in DuBois' (1940) warning almost 65 years ago against the neglect of gifted and talented minority students.

Current attention, however, is primarily focused on the overrepresentation of minorities on the left end of the academic achievement distribution to the neglect of those problems able and gifted students encounter on the right end. Specifically, the gap in academic achievement is greater between students of high socioeconomic status (SES) students than it is between low-income Black and European American students. The achievement gap is also larger between groups of students whose parents have earned baccalaureate degrees than it is between students whose parents have completed less than 12 years of schooling. Additionally, traditional indicators of academic achievement, such as high scores on standardized achievement tests and strong high school grade-point averages (GPAs), tend to overpredict the subsequent academic achievement of many minority students. This often-ignored finding was first reported by Coleman et al. (1966) in *Equality of Educational Opportunity* and was emphasized again in the 1980s (Durán, 1983; Willingham, 1985), 1990s (Camara & Schmidt, 1999; Ramist, Lewis, & McCamley-Jenkins, 1994), and the early 2000s (Bridgeman et al., 2000; Young, 2001). Ramist et al. (1994) suggest that the overprediction phenomenon is particularly acute in minority students' freshman year and in gateway courses in the sciences, engineering, and mathematics. This discrepancy between the tested academic ability and college performance of students of color also affects their rate of degree completion (Bowen & Bok, 1998).

Bowen and Bok (1998) discuss the overprediction phenomenon at some length in their book *The Shape of the River*. In their examination of 28 elite colleges and universities, they found the class ranking for Black graduates with mean SAT-I scores of 1,300 and above (the highest category) to be four percentiles lower than White graduates whose mean SAT scores were less than 1,000 (the lowest category). These findings suggest that elite institutions have not succeeded in eliminating the performance gap between Blacks and Whites, even though they may recruit, enroll, and graduate some of the most able and gifted Black students at higher rates than other colleges and universities.

An extensive examination of achievement gaps at all levels of education has resulted in the development of divergent theories. Bowen and Bok (1998) suggest that the achievement gap can be partially explained by inadequacies in high school preparation. Yet, others conclude that the underrepresentation in the top quartile of students of color is solely due to the behavior and characteristics of the students. The seemingly intractable gap, however, cannot be completely explained by student characteristics or lack of academic preparation. There is evidence of more plausible causal variables. Maton, Hrabowski, and Schmitt (2000) suggest that this persistent underperformance may be attributable to students' academic and social isolation; lack of exposure to support, motivation, monitoring, and advisement; and, for those who perform below the norm, weaknesses in their knowledge and skill development (Treisman, 1990, 1992).

CAUSES OF UNDERREPRESENTATION FOR GIFTED STUDENTS OF COLOR

We have understood for some time now that the sources of disparities in academic achievement affecting racial and ethnic minority groups include low socioeconomic status; a high percentage of parents with little or poor quality formal education; racial and ethnic prejudice and discrimination; cultural attributes of the home, community, and school; and the quality, amount, and uses of school-related resources (College Board, 1999).

Although these institutional, ecological, and personal sources of academic disparities continue to have an impact on the chronic underrepresentation of gifted students of color among high-achieving students, we limit our discussion to an examination of the academic and social isolation of these students and the relationship of such isolation to their mastery of academic knowledge and skills. Academic isolation seems to negatively affect student access to academic support, monitoring, and advisement structures. It also appears that academic and social isolation influence and are influenced by student attitudes and motivation. According to Nettles (1988) and Seymour and Hewitt (1997), students of color who major in the sciences, engineering, and mathematics have a greater likelihood of becoming academically and socially isolated on majority White campuses than do European American or Asian American students. Redmond (1990), Allen (1992), and McHenry (1997) also posit that academic and social isolation occur because students of color are not a critical mass on majority-White campuses, do not have contact with faculty outside of the classroom, nor develop mentoring relationships with faculty (including with minority faculty).

Treisman's (1990) research explores the relationship of such isolation to students' mastery of academic knowledge and skills. In this context, Treisman examined why Black and other students of color were not doing as well as their Asian American and European American counterparts in calculus courses. During 1975–76, he examined the academic and social lives of selected Black and Chinese American student populations at the University of California, Berkeley. The Chinese American students were chosen because faculty members and graduate student instructors had often observed that large numbers of Chinese American students do extremely well in calculus.

One of Treisman's (1990) findings suggested that the source of Black students' poor grades in calculus was not the result of the absence of family support, poor motivation, or poor academic preparation (as widely assumed). Rather, the crux of the problem was the social and academic isolation Black students experienced on a predominantly White campus. In comparison with the integration of Chinese American students' social and academic lives, the Black students' isolation was striking. Specifically, Treisman (1990) found that Black students studied alone and socialized with a different group of friends from those at college. On the other hand, the Chinese American students studied first by themselves before gathering in groups to collectively review their work. These group meetings often included food, music, and at times, students' brothers, sisters, cousins, and friends. Steinberg, Dornbusch, and Brown (1992) also observed this tendency in Asian cultures for groups to work and study collaboratively.

Further, "prejudicial beliefs on the part of faculty and other students, exclusionary social practices on the campus, and other factors that make up a 'chilly' campus climate" seem to result in underachievement (Gándara, 1999, p. 52). Other variables include motivational and performance vulnerability in the face of negative stereotypes and perceived and actual discrimination (Allen, 1992; Maton et al., 2000; Seymour & Hewitt, 1997; Steele & Aronson, 1995). With respect to the idea of stereotype threat, Steele and Aronson (1995) suggest that when students find themselves in situations (e.g., classes or exams) in which they perceive an external expectation based on their minority status, their anxiety that they may confirm the stereotype can lead to diminished performance. Other explanations include:

- fear of disapproval or rejection by peers, including fears of acting White (Fordham & Ogbu, 1986);
- hostile or unsupportive environments associated with residual racism (Aronson et al., 1999);
- absence of adequate socialization to the attitudinal and behavioral demands of the academy (Ogbu, 2003); and
- limited contact with and exposure to models of academic excellence and exemplars of scholarly practice (Gordon, 2001).

The absence of adequate access to financial aid and other forms of education-related capital (Bourdieu, 1986; Coleman, 1988) and low motivation for academic achievement are also associated with low levels of academic success. The lack of financial capital is one of the barriers Black, Hispanic, and Native American students cite as a barrier in the achievement of their educational and career goals (Miller, 1995). Many of these students also do not have access to the cultural, health, human, institutional, social, and political capital (Bourdieu, 1986) that are known to facilitate successful movement through educational experiences.

Attitudes and affective states are also involved. These include low faculty and peer expectations for ethnic minority student success, lack of access to academically supportive peer networks, and unawareness of the need for strong study habits and tutoring. These attitudes and affective states are among the variables affecting student agency, motivation, self-regulation, self-efficacy, and collective efficacy. Uneven and inadequate monitoring and advisement may also result in misinformation concerning coursework, students' preparedness regarding the next level of study, and unawareness of how to prevent or regulate the influence of emerging academic or personal problems (Glennen, Baxley, & Farren, 1985).

Taken together, the referenced theories and empirical research seem to suggest that the structural domains and associated individual correlates (student attitudes and behaviors as evidenced in their sense of agency, self-efficacy, motivation, self-regulation, and collective efficacy) are not inconsistent with the forms of education-relevant capital that Bourdieu (1986) and Coleman (1988) advocate and that Gordon (2001) emphasizes are necessary for gifted students of color to achieve in education. These forms of education-relevant capital include:

- health capital: mental and physical developmental integrity, health, and nutrition (Lee & Lockheed, 1990);
- human capital: intellective and social competence (Gordon, 2001), tacit knowledge, and other education-derived abilities as personal or family assets;
- personal capital: dispositions, attitudes, aspirations, efficacy, and sense of power (Bandura, 1986; Bourdieu, 1986); and
- social capital: social networks and relationships, social norms, cultural styles, and values (Bourdieu, 1986; Coleman, 1988).

Clearly, there seems to be wastage in the supply line with respect to the flow of students of color through systems of education. It is logical to assume that some of this loss is at the high end of the academic achievement distribution. To engage this issue, however, at least three problems must be overcome. There is the obvious problem of better conceptualizing the giftedness phenomenon so as to expand the categories of abilities and behaviors that can be used as indicators. Several of the chapters in this book address that problem. Once we have achieved a more inclusive conceptualization of giftedness and established its relevance for high levels of academic performance, we have the problem of developing the measurable indicators of these dormant, emerging, or developed abilities. At a third level, we face the problem of nurturing these atypical latent or developing characteristics for expression in traditional or emerging academic conditions. Although we would commend successful efforts at solving any one or all of these three problems, we propose that greater and more targeted effort be directed at salvaging giftedness in persons who show high levels of ability on traditional indicators of academic ability, but for whom these indicators have traditionally overpredicted their subsequent academic performance.

In this salvage mode, attention is given to identification through the use of traditional indicators, with some possible effort directed at accommodations informed by concern for Steele and Aronson's (1995) idea of stereotype confirmation. In this mode, emphasis is given to (1) prescriptive assessment and placement; (2) targeted knowledge and skill development to correct for specific challenges and to ensure foundational mastery; (3) academic, cultural, and social integration to reduce the experience of isolation and marginalization; (4) the deliberate shaping of proacademic attitudes, dispositions, and self-regulatory behavior to better support engagement in and effort at relevant learning behaviors; (5) the design and management of cooperative learning situations to take advantage of distributed knowledge; and (6) encouragement of trust in the learning situation, trust of others in the learning community, and trust in oneself as an academic learner (Bryk, 2003; Mendoza-Denton, 2003). The combination of these factors is thought to contribute to the achievement of collective and self-efficacy (Bandura, 1986; Bridglall, 2004).

Although some of the possible solutions to these chronic problems include changing student attitudes and behaviors, they also require changes in institutional interventions. Various programs on the elementary and secondary level that combine rigorous selection criteria with learning environments that are demanding and supportive have been identified. It is in institutions of higher education, however, that we find a few comprehensive efforts designed to develop, nurture, and accelerate the intellective competencies (Gordon, 2001; Bridglall, 2004) of able and gifted ethnic minority students. These include:

- the Emerging Scholars Program;
- the Biomedical Honor Corps at Xavier University;
- the Challenge Program at Georgia Institute of Technology;
- the Minority Access to Research Careers program; and
- Spend a Summer with a Scientist at Rice University.

The best exemplar of programs that strive to reduce the underdevelopment of gifted students of color and the overprediction phenomenon they often face may be the MSP at the University of Maryland, Baltimore County (UMBC). This program was begun by Dr. Freeman Hrabowski in 1988 with the following goals: (1) increasing the number of gifted students of color who could successfully complete a course of study in the science, engineering, and mathematics fields in which they were historically underrepresented; (2) academically and socially preparing these students to pursue PhDs and or MD/PhDs in these fields; (3) reducing the overprediction phenomenon between majority and underrepresented students of color at the right end of the achievement distribution; and (4) increasing the number of ethnic minority professionals in these fields and in the university professorate (thus creating much needed role models for students of color of later generations).

With a focus on academic excellence rather than remediation, Hrabowski and colleagues designed the MSP's infrastructure to support and foster intellective competencies (Gordon, 2001; Bridglall, 2004) and social responsibility. The conceptual underpinnings of the MSP are thus reflective of the idea that giftedness in students of color is not a guarantee of academic success; rather, achievement ability and motivation must be strengthened by a deliberate and purposeful system of academic, social, and personal support. Although all gifted students may face similar psychological pressures, including isolation, low self-esteem, and low sense of adequacy, gifted students of color are further hindered by racial and identity issues that the MSP appears to successfully anticipate.

THE MSP AT THE UNIVERSITY OF MARYLAND, BALTIMORE COUNTY

The MSP achieves its goals through a deceptively simple group of integrated program components that emphasize (1) the careful selection of students; (2) the provision of merit financial support to reduce concerns about finances; (3) a mandatory summer bridge program to acclimate students to the rigors of freshman year; (4) peer study groups for academic and social support; (5) the responsibility of each Meyerhoff student to each other and to community service; (6) the importance of taking advice; (7) meaningful and sustained interaction with faculty and mentors; (8) the importance of continued family involvement; (9) the centrality of academic excellence and scholarship; and (10) the significance of rigorously and systematically documenting and evaluating program outcomes. The MSP operates on the assumption that every student selected has the ability to excel in engineering and the sciences if they are provided with appropriate challenges, resources, and opportunities.

Several theoretical notions that are associated with the social sciences and have relevance for education were used as lenses through which to better understand the MSP. These notions include (1) structural supports for the nurturance of giftedness; (2) integration into a high-performance learning community; (3) access to development-related capital; and (4) attitudinal and motivational attributes of students.

Structural Supports for the Nurturance of Giftedness

In designing the MSP, Hrabowski's observation that even gifted students needed a stronger foundation in mathematics and science influenced his establishment of a first-year algebra minicourse designed to strengthen students' mathematics skills. He also collaborated with faculty to reconceptualize the content and relevancy of physics, chemistry, biology, and engineering courses, for example. In chemistry, for instance, students are introduced to the faculty's research interests. In an engineering course, students' participation in a project for the homeless enables them to gain a realistic perspective concerning how engineers conceptualize and work toward solving certain social problems. This approach relates theoretical concepts to real-world concerns. Students' courses also include a lesson in which the standards and requirements are made explicit, and students are required to plot the number of hours needed for study in order to get an A in a class.

The expectation that students participate in faculty research and the requirement that they study in groups are other strategies used to increase students' internalization and understanding of conceptual material. In peer study groups, for example, gaps in students' mathematical preparation are addressed in situ; that is, the fundamental concepts in algebra or trigonometry are reviewed and mastered within the context of working on demanding calculus problems. This strategy has proved more effective mathematically and psychologically than the alternative strategy of routing students to remedial programs. Given Hrabowski's emphasis on succeeding at the highest levels, he has integrated exemplary upperclassmen to function as teaching assistants and to counsel new students on what is required for academic excellence. On yet another level, the Meyerhoff scholars have set up a test bank, where they share prior exams and notes to help each other succeed. This emphasis on addressing students' gaps in ongoing work with faculty is a robust characteristic of the MSP model.

Integration into a High-Performance Learning Community

Over the course of the program's implementation, it has become evident that peer study groups serve more than the purpose of helping students master the concepts in their fields; they also enable students to regard themselves as part of a high-performance learning community. Peer study groups promote conversations in which participants have to articulate their own ideas and listen to the ideas of others. Peer study group interactions also ensure that students make their work and thinking public and become more aware of the different perspectives and the knowledge fund of their peers. As a result, students are disabused of the notion that their ability is based on sheer talent. The peer study group setting exposes students to peers who also struggle with various ideas and subject content. The result is that students learn quickly that excelling in a subject does not mean being able to solve problems quickly and easily but rather it means working very hard and persevering.

This shared process of working in peer study groups seems to also reduce what social psychologist Claude Steele (1997) described as "stereotype threat." Steele and Aronson's (1995) work demonstrates that Black students' scores in mathematics can decline when they are aware that others may judge their performance in terms of their racial background, rather than in terms of their individual background. MSP student participation in peer study groups (where it is expected that everyone must work hard to succeed) may reduce potential threats of stereotyping.

Access to Development-Related Capital

The MSP promotes student academic and social integration through a committed and involved program staff whom we have observed to be remarkably supportive in every aspect of program implementation. As the Meyerhoff scholars adjust to their new environment during the summer bridge orientation process, for example, program staff work tirelessly to help students become academically focused and socially and emotionally comfortable. This strategy is particularly significant given the importance of academic confidence and identification with the university for student persistence, retention, and graduation (White & Sedlacek, 1986).

This orientation process and continuous interaction between program staff and students seems to be essential as minority students manage the social and academic challenges that may emerge in daily interactions with faculty and students of other races. In the process, students learn how to take responsibility for their own behavior, exercise self-regulation, manage their time effectively, and cope with change and related stresses (Ting & Robinson, 1998). In both formal and informal interactions with students, program staff emphasize their expectations concerning respectful behaviors that honor the different ways in which UMBC celebrates student diversity. Program staffs' effectiveness in helping students to develop a sense of belonging, bond with students from different ethnic groups, and perceive themselves as valuable members of the campus community is reflected in the MSP's retention rate of 95 percent.

Attitudinal and Motivational Attributes of Students

In support of a high-performance learning community, the MSP provides a family-like social and academic support system for its students. This structure includes opportunities for older students to be supportive of first-year students and for each student to have a designated mentor (who may be a faculty or staff member and who may or may not be different from the student's academic advisor). The MSP also fully expects that its students will (1) support each other both academically and personally; (2) seek support from a variety of sources; (3) set clear and attainable academic goals; and (4) examine possible careers related to their intended major. These expectations are made explicit and emphasized as early as selections weekend (a recruitment activity) and are usually internalized by the time students are sophomores and juniors (L. Toliver, personal communication, July 11, 2003). One of the outcomes of the MSP's sense of community and collective efficacy is reflected in the return of its graduates to assist and inspire freshman students.

RELEVANT THEORIES FROM THE SOCIAL SCIENCES

Understanding of the MSP may be informed by systems of thought advanced by Bandura's (2001) agentic behavioral perspective. These theoretical constructs are examined for their capacity to contribute to our understanding of the structural and student characteristics that may be necessary to reduce the overprediction phenomenon for gifted and talented students of color. On examination of this exemplary program, it is clear that, in addition to the structural components that are designed to provide support for students' development, the core of the initiative rests on the attitudes and behaviors of the students served. Bandura's notion of human agency provides useful leverage.

Bandura (2001) suggests that the core features of human agency include intentionality, forethought, self-reactiveness, and self-reflectiveness. Accordingly, to be an agent is to intentionally make things happen by one's actions. Agency thus characterizes the "endowments, belief systems, self-regulatory capabilities, and distributed structures and functions through which personal influence is exercised" (Bandura, 2001, p. 2) and through which people can play a role in their own development, adaptation, and renewal. These states of mind or being can be achieved through deliberately accessing information for the purpose of selecting, creating, regulating, or evaluating various courses of action.

Intentionality is not only an expectation of future action but also a representation of a future course of action and a realistic commitment to bringing it about. Bandura (2001) suggests that intentions and actions are different elements of a functional relationship divided in time. Intentions can therefore be thought of as anchored in self-motivators that influence the probability of actions at a later point in time.

Forethought is defined as the setting of goals, the anticipation of the probable consequences of potential actions, and the selection and implementation of courses of action that are likely to produce the preferred outcomes (Bandura, 1991). On a practical level, the exercise of forethought enables people to motivate themselves and to channel their actions in anticipation of future results. This cognitive representation in the present of anticipated events enables behaviors that are both self-motivated and self-regulated (by possible goals and expected outcomes). Bandura (2001) further suggests that when this practice occurs over an extended period of time on matters of value, "a forethoughtful perspective provides direction, coherence, and meaning to one's life" (p. 7).

Self-reactiveness is the intentional motivation and regulation of goal implementation. This interdependent web of self-direction functions through self-regulatory processes that relate thought to action. The self-regulation of motivation, affect, and action is managed through self-monitoring of performance, self-guidance through personal standards, and corrective self-reactions (Bandura, 1986, 1991).

The self-monitoring of certain behavior and the associated cognitive and environmental conditions under which it occurs appears to be one of the first steps toward influencing behavior. Personal monitoring also enables the comparison of one's performance with personal goals and standards that, when anchored in a value system and a sense of personal identity, can give meaning and purpose to activities. The result is that people give direction to their pursuits and maintain their efforts for goal attainment by developing appropriate self-incentives.

General goals such as "do my best" do not increase motivation. Bandura (1986) suggests that it is proximal goals rather than distant goals that result in greater motivation. (Students are motivated by goals that they perceive as challenging but attainable, not by goals that they perceive as too easy or excessively difficult.) Similarly, students who perceive their goal progression as acceptable and anticipate satisfaction from accomplishing their goals feel both efficacious about continuing to improve and motivated to complete the task (Bandura, 1986). Goal properties, such as specificity, proximity, and difficulty level (Bandura, 1988; Locke & Latham, 1990), influence self-efficacy because progress toward a specific goal is measurable. Students' negative evaluations of their progress do not necessarily decrease their motivation if they believe they are capable of improving by working harder. Alternatively, motivation may not increase if students believe they lack the ability to improve or to succeed (Locke & Latham, 1990).

Self-regulation, within the context of agency and social cognitive learning theory (Bandura, 1986; 2001), includes the cognitive and behavioral processes that are concerned with initiating, adapting, modifying, or changing a person's physiological responses, emotions, thoughts, behaviors, or environment (Carver & Scheier, 1998; Compas, Connor, Saltzman, Thomsen, & Wadsworth, 1999; Eisenberg, Fabes, & Guthrie, 1997). These cognitive and behavioral self-regulatory processes have implications for the interaction between personal, social, and environmental factors during the teaching and learning process.

In an effort to implement the idea of self-regulation, Zimmerman (1998) adapted Bandura's notions of agency to create a three-phase self-regulation model: (1) forethought, (2) performance (volitional) control, and (3) self-reflection. Zimmerman and Schunk (2001) suggest that self-regulation refers to the self-directive processes through which students translate their intentions into task-related academic competencies. As a proactive activity, self-regulated learning does not occur in isolation from the social forms of learning (i.e., modeling, guidance, and feedback from peers, staff, and faculty). Self-regulated learning is evidenced by students' personal initiative, perseverance, and adaptive abilities within a social context. Students' use of various processes to regulate their learning and their perceptions of themselves as learners seem to significantly influence their levels of academic achievement (Zimmerman, 1986).

Zimmerman's (1986) perspective regarding self-regulated learning has instructional and structural implications, respectively, for how teachers teach and how schools are organized. In the social cognitive theoretical framework, self-regulation is not a general trait or a particular level of development but considered to be largely context dependent. Although some self-regulatory processes such as goal-setting may generalize across situations, students need to learn how to adapt to certain contexts and feel efficacious about doing so. Zimmerman (1986) suggests that self-regulation becomes possible when students have some options in their academic and social environments and in how they manage their time, for example.

Self-regulated learning and motivation. Self-regulated learners are considered to be autonomous, reflective, and efficient learners who use certain cognitive strategies; act on certain motivational beliefs and attitudes; and engage in metacognition to understand, monitor, and direct their own learning (Boekaerts, Pintrich, & Zeidner, 2000; Schunk & Zimmerman, 1994). Self-regulated learners also seem to be motivated by certain adaptive beliefs and attitudes that influence their willingness to engage in and persist at academic tasks. These students appear to be highly self-efficacious in their efforts at increasing their level of mastery. They are found to perceive the material they are learning in school as valuable, interesting, and useful to know (Pintrich, 2000; Schunk & Ertmer, 2000; Wigfield, 1994).

Self-reflectiveness includes the self-assessment of behaviors and attitudes. In the context of motivation, self-regulated students use self-assessments of their behaviors and attitudes to influence their motivation and actual progress. Self-evaluation seems to be most valuable when it focuses on the particular conditions under which a behavior occurs and on whether change is needed. For example, students who observe that their time is used less effectively when they study with a friend than when they are alone may increasingly study by themselves. Students who monitor how they actually spend their time are surprised to learn how much time they waste on nonacademic activities. For these students to alter their study habits, they need to believe that changing their habits will enable them to accomplish more (outcome expectation) and that they actually will be able to change those habits (self-efficacy) (Bandura, 1986; Wolters, 2003). Thus, behavior change may be influenced through self-reflectiveness.

Social Cognitive Theory: Self-Efficacy

Within the framework of social cognitive learning theory, Bandura (1986) suggests that human functioning involves reciprocal interactions between cognitions, behaviors, and environmental factors. This reciprocity is illustrated with an important construct in Bandura's theory: perceived self-efficacy, or beliefs about one's capacity to learn particular behaviors and perform them at certain levels. A growing body of research demonstrates that students' self-efficacy beliefs influence their choice of tasks, effort, persistence, and achievement (Schunk, 1995). Students' sense of efficacy is validated as they engage in tasks, observe and monitor their progress, and are appropriately rewarded. When rewards are not linked to performance, students may conclude that they do not have the necessary ability and are not expected to excel.

Enactive Learning. Learning is defined as a change in behavior or behavioral potential (Schunk, 2001) produced by progressively rigorous formal courses (Gordon, 2001) and supplementary education experiences (Gordon, Bridglall, & Mcroe, 2004). From the perspective of cognitive social learning theory, learning by doing, or enactive learning, seems to rely on successfully reinforced activities and tasks (Bandura, 2001). The mastery of complex skills typically involves some form of enactive learning. In many cases, however, students learn some components of a complex skill and not others. The challenge for teachers is to provide corrective feedback and instruction that is systematic.

What differentiates social cognitive theory from earlier reinforcement theories is not the belief that students learn by doing but rather its explanation for why this is so. Skinner (1953) suggested that (1) competent performances are gradually achieved through reinforcement of successive approximations to the target behavior, a process known as shaping; and (2) that cognitions may accompany behavioral change, but they do not influence it. Alternatively, social cognitive theory argues that behavioral outcomes serve as sources of information and motivation rather than as response strengtheners (Bandura, 1986). For example, students selectively engage in cognitive activities that assist learning and are motivated to persist in those tasks they believe are significant and rewarding.

Vicarious learning, in addition to learning by doing, occurs by observing others, by reading, and by exposure to the media, for example. Academic knowledge and skill development often combine enactive and vicarious learning. In mathematics, for example, students (1) learn operations by observing how teachers apply them; and (2) improve their skills through targeted feedback and practice. This form of modeling may motivate students to believe that learning mathematical operations is worthwhile.

The concepts of learning, performance, and modeling are distinguished in social cognitive theory. For example, students can acquire declarative knowledge (facts), procedural knowledge (concepts, rules, algorithms), and conditional knowledge (when and why it is important to use declarative and procedural knowledge) (Paris, Lipson, & Wixson, 1983) by monitoring and observing models (Schunk, 1987). They may not demonstrate this knowledge at the time of learning.

Collective Efficacy: Community, Social Cohesion, and Social Capital

Kawachi and Kennedy (1997) suggest that social integration can be perceived as both an individual and a societal characteristic. A socially integrated individual has social connections in the form of intimate social contacts (i.e., spouse, relatives, and friends) and more extended connections (i.e., membership in religious groups, various professional and social institutions, and other voluntary associations). At the group level, a socially cohesive high-performance learning community has what Bourdieu (1999) and Coleman (1988) call social capital, which includes moral resources such as trust among students, faculty, and staff and norms of reciprocity.

There are several ways in which social cohesion influences academic achievement (Kawachi & Berkman, 2000). At the interpersonal level, the engagement in academically related behaviors is a function of the access to and participation in the social supports that is characteristic of socially cohesive communities of high achievers. Students in these communities take responsibility for themselves as well as their peers (Hrabowski, 2002). There are, however, successful academic communities that are not cohesive or supportive but competitive and cutthroat. Both communities and individuals perform successfully. Somehow, in both types of learning communities, self- and collective efficacy are enabled. At the environmental level, differences in available community resources may explain the counterintuitive finding that students with few social ties but access to socially cohesive communities do not appear to perform less well academically when compared with socially isolated students in less cohesive communities (Sampson, Raudenbush, & Earls, 1997; Kawachi & Berkman, 2000).

Although the referenced theoretical constructs (agency, social capital, self-efficacy, and collective efficacy) were discussed in a relatively discrete and uncomplicated manner, the reality is that they are deeply complex in how, why, and under what conditions they interact and influence each other.

TOWARD THE NURTURANCE OF TALENT AND THE DEVELOPMENT OF ACADEMIC ABILITY FOR GIFTED STUDENTS OF COLOR

The persistent problem of underachievement of gifted students of color can be examined from several perspectives, including (1) the underdevelopment of academic ability of students who cluster on the low end of the achievement distribution; and (2) the underdevelopment of talent and the tendency of standardized tests scores and strong high school GPAs to over-predict subsequent academic achievement for high-achieving students of color. The MSP is a good illustration of an integrated approach that emphasizes the nurturance of giftedness and the reduction of the overprediction phenomenon. The MSP's inputs, processes, and contexts seem to produce high-achieving students who (1) are academically and socially integrated; and (2) have developed appropriate knowledge and skills at very high levels as a result of targeted support, motivation, monitoring, and student advisement.

As a strengths-based, theoretically driven model for the nurturance of giftedness, the developers of the MSP have culled from the research literature (Allen, 1981, 1992; Fullilove & Treisman, 1990; Treisman, 1990, 1992; Tinto, 1993) to create the following practices to deliberately and systematically craft a student academic development model that privileges:

- the creation of a critical mass of academically able and motivated students of color;
- the use of a summer bridge pre-freshman program to provide academic socialization, diagnostic assessment, and community building;
- making explicit the conceptual, procedural, and tacit demands of a rigorous curriculum;
- ensuring solid mastery of foundational subject matter through the assignment of the most effective faculty members to teach freshman courses, and through the requirement that this coursework be passed with a grade of B or higher;
- providing institutional structural support for cumulative knowledge and skill development;
- constructing supportive groups at varying levels for students' academic and social lives;
- providing comprehensive financial support;
- providing culturally relevant experiences; and
- comprehensively monitoring, mentoring, and advising students throughout their undergraduate careers rather than emphasizing only the freshman year.

1. Creating a critical mass of academically motivated students of color

The research suggests that being one of a few students of color on a campus or in a program can be psychologically, academically, and socially isolating (Allen, 1981; Gándara, 1999; Gordon, 1986). The absence of academically and socially supportive peers with whom a student can (1) share his or her self-doubts and/or (2) seek academic help without fear of reinforcing extant stereotypes about ethnic inferiority places students at risk of marginalization. Extant evidence suggests that these students are much more likely to underachieve academically or leave the university system (Allen, 1981, 1992; Miller, 1995). The systematic and deliberate creation of a critical mass of academically motivated ethnic minority students who have (1) access to and substantive contact with faculty outside of the classroom; and (2) mentoring relationships with faculty (including with minority faculty) seems to increase the likelihood of persistence, retention, and academic excellence (Maton et al., 2000).

2. Requiring a pre-freshman summer bridge program

Attending a required pre-freshman summer bridge program is one of the venues for socializing students to the explicit and tacit academic and social expectations of the university (Matonet al., 2000). In addition to some emphasis on content mastery, the summer bridge component gives special attention to the development of teamwork and the cultivation of trust between and among peers. This component also enables students to forge positive relationships with faculty and program staff and seems to encourage students to develop attitudes and behaviors (such as agency, motivation, self-regulation, self-reflectiveness, self-efficacy, and collective efficacy) that appear to influence increasing levels of academic excellence.

3. Making the rigor of the curriculum explicit

The curriculum to which MSP students are exposed is quite rigorous. The curriculum's specific requirements are made clear to students early and constantly. Faculty and more advanced students share examples of exemplary work – a test bank of former exams and essays are available to students, for example. Additionally, students who earn a grade of C or below in any foundation course are required to retake the course and earn at least a grade of B. The MSP has and continues to be engaged in internal evaluation of its science, mathematics, and engineering curricula in focused attempts to identify (1) any weaknesses; (2) whether and how it should be taught differentially; and (3) what aspects require more time and concentrated study to internalize. Additionally, the teaching and learning of the curriculum is supplemented with peer study groups and tutoring to ensure that difficult concepts are conceptually mastered and practically applied. A recent report, *Parsing the Achievement Gap* by the Educational Testing Service (2003), found that the rigor of the curriculum and its implementation is one of the correlates of academic achievement for ethnic minority students.

4. Assigning the best faculty to teach freshman courses

The attrition of underrepresented minority students between the freshman and sophomore years suggested to the MSP's developers that these students are more sensitive to teaching quality than majority students from more advantaged backgrounds. As a result, freshman students (both

Meyerhoff and non-Meyerhoff) at UMBC are taught by tenure-track faculty who are considered effective; who interact substantively with students; and who can play vitally important roles in engaging, encouraging, and guiding students in identifying and making use of supportive resources on the university and department level.

5. Providing institutional structural support for cumulative knowledge and skill development

The MSP operates on the assumption that its students are intellectively competent (Gordon, 2001); motivated, and self-confident. However, the MSP also recognizes that some of these high-achieving students may not have adequate or the requisite preparation for success in technical courses. Correcting for these gaps in knowledge or understanding becomes the focus of both peer and tutorial interventions, for instance. Bridglall's (2001) qualitative analysis of the MSP suggests that the program is systematic in its approach to helping students to identify where they have knowledge gaps, providing faculty who can reinforce fundamental concepts, and exposing students to rigorous, challenging material.

6. Constructing supportive groups at varying levels for students' academic and social lives

Peer study groups and tutors provide academic and social support that is integrated into students' entire undergraduate lives in the MSP. It appears that the institutionalization of rigorous courses and faculty, mentors, upperclassmen, and peers as consistent structural supports has contributed to the MSP's effectiveness in increasing the pool of high-achieving minority students in the sciences, engineering, and mathematics.

7. Providing comprehensive financial support

In a deliberate attempt to increase student persistence and to reduce the negative impact that inadequate finances have on underrepresented students' academic achievement and completion of rigorous study in the sciences and engineering, MSP students are provided with full or partial scholarships that are contingent on consistently high GPAs.

8. Providing culturally relevant experiences

Given the MSP's emphasis on minority high achievement in the sciences, mathematics, and engineering, various aspects of these students' cultures are incorporated into the program. For example, students attend church with the president and are active in church choirs. Our conversations with program staff suggest that this approach also serves to socially and academically integrate students. Additionally, regular meetings with the president in which students discuss issues such as racism, for instance, seems to help students to put these issues into perspective and persist (L. Toliver, personal communication, July 11, 2003).

9. Comprehensively monitoring, mentoring, and advising students throughout their undergraduate career rather than emphasizing only the freshman year

The MSP does not focus exclusively on freshman students, but rather, provides continuous and institutionalized monitoring and other services to students throughout their undergraduate careers in the program. The overarching assumption is that given the referenced support and resources, competitively selected underrepresented minority students are capable of succeeding in the sciences, engineering and mathematics.

CONCLUSION

At this point in the 21st century, we seem to know a great deal concerning the nurturance of giftedness and intellective talent in able and gifted minority students. This is evidenced by the commitment and success of the talent development programs at UMBC, Georgia Institute of Technology, California Institute of Technology, Washington University at St. Louis, and Xavier University in Louisiana. It may be worth developing a consortium among these institutions to share lessons learned, further refine practical knowledge, and codify best practices for others to emulate. The unwavering commitment of UMBC's leadership, faculty, and staff to minority student academic excellence and achievement prompts them to consistently consider how they can enable their students to (1) become more competitive on traditional academic measures (i.e., grades, standardized test scores, and represented in gifted and talented classes); (2) compete successfully for admission to college; (3) prepare for productive careers; and (4) develop and implement strategies to increase the presence of minorities as research scientists and university professors. This commitment is especially significant and relevant given the moderate success of various programs at increasing minority science, engineering, and mathematics achievement at the undergraduate level and relatively little success at the graduate level. Hrabowski (2002) believes that only by creating and supporting a larger pool of high-achieving minority students can we ultimately increase the number of faculty of color in the nation's colleges and universities and the number who become leading professionals.

It seems that a research agenda that is committed to the bidirectional nature of theory and praxis is in order. Such an effort would involve the serious examination and application of relevant theoretical constructs and the systematic mining of practices utilized in these exemplars. Gordon (1976) believes that we have developed sufficient models and practices to begin controlled comparative studies to determine empirically those practices that produce specifiable results. Such studies could help us to identify patterns of intervention as the treatments of choice for specific developmental ends. The range of achievements in these high-achieving minority students is quite broad. The study of outliers in this population, that is, highly successful persons, could contribute to our understanding of personal, process, and situational correlates of success and failure for minorities in the sciences, engineering, and mathematics.

The MSP is one of a few isolated efforts at bridging curriculum and teaching, social science, and cognitive science to more effectively apply this knowledge to the problems of nurturing talent in underrepresented students. Such work should be encouraged and could contribute to the scientific basis for pedagogy, just as comparable expansions in our knowledge of the biological and social sciences, the physical sciences, and public health were integrated to form the scientific basis for medicine. Conceptual studies that build on the exciting empirical findings from neuroscience and cognitive science may inform the next generation of interventions in the educational development of populations at risk of underdevelopment. There is a host of smaller ideas and practical studies that should be undertaken. Examples to consider include differential approaches to tutoring; application of instrumental intellectual enhancement strategies; peer tutoring and team learning; instruction through computer simulation; and computer-managed adaptive and interactive instruction. The list is almost endless, but an experimental approach to work at increasing the pool of gifted students will require that we draw on the expertise of scholars from other disciplines.

Collectively, educators, policymakers, parents, and students can begin to make progress in reducing the loss to our society that is reflected in the underachievement of certain populations and the schools that serve them. Tests of academic ability certainly can underpredict achievement, but it is with the complicity of educators and educational institutions that these tests overpredict. If students can demonstrate high levels of academic ability on our tests, we have a moral responsibility to nurture their potential and enable the realization of academic excellence and achievement.

References

Allen, W. R. (1981). *Summary findings from a preliminary study of Black student adjustment, achievement and aspirations at the University of Michigan (Ann Arbor), Winter, 1980. Pretest of a national study.* (ERIC Document Reproduction Service No. ED 224 373)

Allen, W. R. (1992). The color of success: African-American college student outcomes at predominantly White and historically Black public colleges and universities. *Harvard Educational Review, 62*(1), 26–44.

Aronson, J., Lustina, M. J., Good, C., Keough, K., Steele, C. M., & Brown, J. (1999). When White men can't do math: Necessary and sufficient factors in stereotype threat. *Journal of Experimental Social Psychology, 35*(1), 29–46.

Bandura, A. (1986). *Social foundations of thought and action: A social cognitive theory.* Englewood Cliffs, NJ: Prentice Hall.

Bandura, A. (1988). Self-efficacy conception of anxiety. *Anxiety Research, 1,* 77–98.

Bandura, A. (1991). Human agency: The rhetoric and the reality. *American Psychologist, 46*(2), 157–162.

Bandura, A. (2001). Social cognitive theory: An agentic perspective. *Annual Review of Psychology, 52,* 1–26.

Boekaerts, M., Pintrich, P., & Zeidner, M. (2000). *Handbook of self-regulation.* New York: Academic Press.

Borland, J. H., & Wright, L. (1994). Identifying young, potentially gifted, economically disadvantaged students. *Gifted Child Quarterly, 38*(4), 164–171.

Bourdieu, P. (1986). The forms of capital. In J. Richardson (Ed.), *Handbook of theory and research for the sociology of education* (pp. 241–258). Westport, CT: Greenwood.

Bourdieu, P. (1999). *The weight of the world: Social suffering in contemporary society.* Cambridge, England: Polity Press.

Bowen, W. G., & Bok, D. (1998). *The shape of the river: Long-term consequences of considering race in college and university admissions.* Princeton, NJ: Princeton University Press.

Bridgeman, B., McCamley-Jenkins, L., & Ervin, N. (2000). *Predictions of freshman grade-point average from the revised and recentered SAT I: Reasoning Test* (College Board Report No. 2000–1). New York: College Board.

Bridglall, B. L. (2004). *Structural and individual characteristics that enable high academic achievement for underrepresented students of color.* Unpublished doctoral dissertation. Teachers College, Columbia University, New York.

Bryk, A. S. (2003). Trust in schools: A core resource for school reform. *Educational Leadership, 60*(6), 40.

Camara, W. J., & Schmidt, A. E. (1999). *Group differences in standardized testing and social stratification.* New York: College Entrance Examination Board.

Carver, C. S., & Scheier, M. F. (1998). *On the self-regulation of behavior.* New York: Cambridge University Press.

Coleman, J. S. (1988). Social capital in the creation of human capital. *American Journal of Sociology, 94,* s95–s120.

Coleman, J. S., Campbell, E. Q., Hobson, C. J., McPartland, J., Mood, A. M., Weinfeld, F. D., et al. (1966). *Equality of educational opportunity.* Washington, DC: U.S. Government Printing Office.

College Board. (1999). *Reaching the top: A report of the National Task Force on Minority High Achievement.* New York: The College Entrance Examination Board.

Compas, B. E., Connor, J. K., Saltzman, H., Thomsen, A. H., & Wadsworth, M. (1999). Getting specific about coping: Effortful and involuntary responses to stress in development. In M. Lewis & D. Ramsay (Eds.), *Soothing and stress* (pp. 229–256). Mahwah, NJ: Lawrence Erlbaum Associates.

Donovan, M. S., & Cross, C. T. (Eds.) (2002). Minority students in special and gifted education. Washington, DC: National Academy Press.

DuBois, W. E. B. (1940). *Dusk of dawn: An essay toward an autobiography of a race concept.* New York: Harcourt Brace.

Durán, R. (1983). Prediction of Hispanics' college achievements. In M. Olivas (Ed.), *Latino college students* (pp. 241–245). New York: Teachers College Press.

Educational Testing Service. (2003). *Parsing the achievement gap.* Princeton, NJ: Policy Information Center, Educational Testing Service.

Eisenberg, N., Fabes, R. A., & Guthrie, I. K. (1997). Coping with stress: The roles of regulation and development. In S. A. Wolchik & I. N. Sandler (Eds.), *Handbook of children's coping: Linking theory and intervention* (pp. 41–70). New York: Plenum.

Eisner, E. W. (1967). Educational objective: Help or hindrance? *School Review, 75,* 250–266.

Ford, D. Y. (1996). Reversing underachievement among gifted Black students: Promising practices and programs. New York: Teachers College Press.

Fordham, S., & Ogbu, J. U. (1986). Black students' school success: Coping with the "burden of acting White." *Urban Review, 18*(3), 176–206.

Fullilove, R. E., & Treisman, P. U. (1990). Mathematics achievement among African American undergraduates at the University of California, Berkeley: An evaluation of the Mathematics Workshop Program. *Journal of Negro Education, 59*(3), 463–478.

Gándara, P. (with Maxwell-Jolly, J.). (1999). *Priming the pump: A review of programs that aim to increase the achievement of underrepresented minority undergraduates.* New York: College Board.

Gardner, H. (1999). *Intelligence reframed: Multiple intelligences for the 21st century.* New York: Basic Books.

Glennen, R. E., Baxley, D. M., & Farren, P. J. (1985). Impact of intrusive advising on minority student retention. *College Student Journal, 35*(4), 335–339.

Gordon, E. W. (1976). *Research in human development.* Princeton: Educational Testing Service.

Gordon, E. W. (1986). *Foundations for academic excellence: First report to the Chancellor from the Chancellor's Commission on Minimum Standards for the New York City Public Schools.* Brooklyn, NY: NYC Chancellor's Commission on Minimum Standards, NYC Board of Education. (ERIC Document Reproduction Service No. ED 270 529).

Gordon, E. W. (2001). *The affirmative development of academic ability* (Pedagogical Inquiry and Praxis, No. 2). New York: Institute for Urban and Minority Education, Teachers College, Columbia University.

Gordon, E. W., Bridgall, B. L., & Meroe, A. S. (Eds.). (2004). *Supplementary education.* Boulder, CO: Rowman and Littlefield.

Hrabowski, F. A., III. (2002). Postsecondary minority student achievement: How to raise performance and close the achievement gap. *College Board Review, 195,* 40–48.

Kawachi, I., & Berkman, L. (2000). Social cohesion, social capital and health. In L. Berkman & I. Kawachi (Eds.), *Social epidemiology* (pp. 180–184). New York: Oxford University Press.

Kawachi, I., & Kennedy, B. P. (1997). The relationship of income inequality to mortality: Does the choice of indicator matter? *Social Science and Medicine, 45*(7), 1121–1127.

Lee, V. E., & Lockheed, M. M. (1990). The effects of single-sex schooling on achievement and attitudes in Nigeria. *Comparative Educational Review, 34*(2), 209–231.

Locke, E. A., & Latham, G. P. (1990). *A theory of goal setting and task performance.* Englewood Cliffs, NJ: Prentice Hall.

Maton, K., Hrabowski, F. A., III, & Schmitt, C. (2000). African American college students excelling in the sciences: College and postcollege outcomes in the Meyerhoff Scholars Program. *Journal of Research in Science Teaching, 37*(7), 629–654.

McHenry, W. (1997). Mentoring as a tool for increasing minority student participation in science, mathematics, engineering, and technology undergraduate and graduate programs. *Diversity in Higher Education, 1,* 115–140.

Mendoza-Denton, R., & Aronson, J. (2003). *Making the pinnacle possible: Psychological processes associated with minority students' achievement.* Unpublished manuscript.

Miller, L. S. (1995). *An American imperative: Accelerating minority educational advancement.* New Haven, CT: Yale University Press.

Nettles, M. T. (1988). *Toward Black undergraduate student equality in American higher education.* Westport, CT: Greenwood.

Ogbu, J. U. (2003). *Black American students in an affluent suburb: A study of academic disengagement.* Mahwah, NJ: Lawrence Erlbaum Associates.

Paris, S. G., Lipson, M. Y., & Wixson, K. (1983). Becoming a strategic reader. *Contemporary Educational Psychology, 8,* 293–316.

Pintrich, P. R. (2000). The role of goal orientation in self-regulated learning. In M. Boekaerts, P. Pintrich, & M. Zeidner (Eds.), *Handbook of self-regulation* (pp. 451–502). New York: Academic.

Ramist, L., Lewis, C., & McCamley-Jenkins, L. (1994). *Student group differences in predicting college grades: Sex, language, and ethnic groups.* New York: College Entrance Examination Board.

Redmond, S. P. (1990). Mentoring and cultural diversity in academic settings. *American Behavioral Scientist, 34*(2), 188–200.

Renzulli, J. S. (1986). The three-ring conception of giftedness: A developmental model for creative productivity. In R. J. Sternberg & J. E. Davidson (Eds.), *Conceptions of giftedness* (pp. 53–92). New York: Cambridge University Press.

Sampson, R. J., Raudenbush, S. W., & Earls, F. (1997). Neighborhoods and violent crime: A multilevel study of collective efficacy. *Science, 277,* 918–924.

Schunk, D. H. (1987). Peer models and children's behavioral change. *Review of Educational Research, 57,* 149–174.

Schunk, D. H. (1995). Self-efficacy, motivation, and performance. *Journal of Applied Sport Psychology, 7*(2), 112–137.

Schunk, D. H. (2001). Social cognitive theory and self-regulated learning. In B. J. Zimmerman & D. H. Schunk (Eds.), *Self-regulated learning and academic achievement: Theoretical perspectives* (2nd ed., pp. 125–152). Mahwah, NJ: Lawrence Erlbaum Associates.

Schunk, D. H., & Ertmer, P. A. (2000). Self-regulation and academic learning: Self-efficacy–enhancing interventions. In M. Boekaerts, P. R. Pintrich, & M. Zeidner (Eds.), *Handbook of self-regulation* (pp. 631–649). New York: Academic Press.

Schunk, D. H., & Zimmerman, G. J. (Eds.). (1994). *Self-regulation of learning and performance: Issues and educational applications.* Hillsdale, NJ: Lawrence Erlbaum Associates.

Seymour, E., & Hewitt, N. M. (1997). *Talking about leaving: Why undergraduates leave the sciences.* Boulder, CO: Westview.

Skinner, B. F. (1953). *Science and human behavior.* New York: Macmillan.

Steele, C. M. (1997). A threat in the air: How stereotypes shape intellectual identity and performance. *American Psychologist, 52,* 613–629.

Steele, C. M., & Aronson, J. (1995). Stereotype threat and the intellectual performance of African Americans. *Journal of Personality and Social Psychology, 69,* 797–811.

Steinberg, L., Dornbusch, S. M., & Brown, B. B. (1992). Ethnic differences in adolescent achievement: An ecological perspective. *American Psychologist, 47*(6), 723–729.

Sternberg, R. J. (1985). *Beyond IQ: A triarchic theory of human intelligence.* New York: Cambridge University Press.

Terman, L. M. (1925). *Genetic studies of genius: Vol. 1. Mental and physical traits of a thousand gifted children.* Stanford, CA: Stanford University Press.

Ting, S. R., & Robinson, T. L. (1998). First-year academic success: A prediction combining cognitive and psychosocial variables for Caucasian and African American students. *Journal of College Student Development, 39*(6), 599–610.

Tinto, V. (1993). *Leaving college: Rethinking the causes and cures of student attrition* (2nd ed.). Chicago: University of Chicago Press.

Treisman, P. U. (1990, July). A study of the mathematics performance of Black students at the University of California, Berkeley. In H. B. Keynes, N. D. Fisher, & P. D. Wagreich (Eds.), *Mathematicians and education reform: Proceedings of the July 6–8, 1988 workshop, Issues in Mathematics Education, Conference Board of Mathematical Sciences* (pp. 33–56). Providence, RI: American Mathematical Society, Mathematical Association of America.

Treisman, P. U. (1992). Studying students studying calculus: A look at the lives of minority mathematics students in college. *College Mathematics Journal, 23*(5), 362–372.

White, T. J., & Sedlacek, W. E. (1986, Spring). Noncognitive predictors: Grades and retention of specially admitted students. *Journal of College Admissions, 3,* 20–23.

Wigfield, A. (1994). The role of children's achievement values in the self-regulation of their learning outcomes. In D. H. Schunk & B. J. Zimmerman (Eds.), *Self-regulation of learning and performance: Issues and educational applications* (pp. 101–124). Mahwah, NJ: Lawrence Erlbaum Associates.

Willingham, W. W. (1985). *Success in college: The role of personal qualities and academic ability.* New York: College Board.

Wolters, C. A. (2003). Regulation of motivation: Evaluating an underemphasized aspect of self-regulated learning. *Educational Psychologist, 38,* 189–205.

Young, J. W. (with Kobrin, J. L.). (2001). *Differential validity, differential prediction, and college admission testing: a comprehensive review and analysis.* New York: College Board.

Zimmerman, B. J. (1986). Becoming a self-regulated learner: Which are the key subprocesses? *Contemporary Educational Psychology, 11,* 307–313.

Zimmerman, B. J. (1994). Dimensions of academic self regulation: A conceptual framework for education. In D. H. Schunk & B. J. Zimmerman (Eds.),

Self-regulation of learning and performance: Issues and educational implications (pp. 3–21). Hillsdale, NJ: Lawrence Erlbaum Associates.

Zimmerman, B. J. (1998). Developing self-fulfilling cycles of academic regulation: An analysis of exemplary instructional models. In D. H. Schunk & B. J. Zimmerman (Eds.), *Self-regulated learning: From teaching to self-reflective practice* (pp. 1–19). New York: Guilford.

Zimmerman, B. J., & Schunk, D. H. (2001). Self-regulated learning and academic thought. Mahwah, NJ: Lawrence Erlbaum Associates.

9

The Munich Model of Giftedness Designed to Identify and Promote Gifted Students

Kurt A. Heller, Christoph Perleth, and Tock Keng Lim

A decisive factor in the determination of effective gifted education is the fit between the individual cognitive and noncognitive (e.g., motivational and other personality) factors of the developmental and learning processes on the one hand and the environmental influences that are mainly from the social settings of family, school, and peers on the other hand. This chapter is based on multidimensional conceptions of giftedness and talent, such as the Munich Model of Giftedness (MMG), as well as on interaction models, such as the Aptitude–Treatment Interaction (ATI) by Cronbach and Snow (1977) and Corno and Snow (1986).

When considering the MMG as an example of a multifactorial conception of giftedness, along with the recently developed dynamic process approach to this model (Munich Dynamic Ability–Achievement Model of Giftedness [MDAAM]), the following questions arise: How should gifted individuals be identified and instructed? And how should their learning outcomes or excellent performance be assessed? These and other questions will be answered according to the MMG and the MDAAM, respectively.

GIFTEDNESS AND TALENT FROM A THEORETICAL POINT OF VIEW

Our knowledge regarding giftedness and talent is supplied by different sources of information and research paradigms. Approaches that are particularly relevant to conceptualizing giftedness or talent are the psychometric approach, the expert–novice paradigm, explanatory approaches from the field of cognitive science or cognitive psychology, and social psychology, as well as retrospective and prospective (longitudinal) studies. Giftedness models developed in the 1980s and 1990s are characterized, almost without exception, by multidimensional or typological ability constructs, for example, Renzulli (1978), Mönks (1985), Gardner (1983, 1993), Gagné (1985, 1993, 2000), Heller and Hany (1986), Heller (1989, 1991/1996), or

Sternberg (1985, 1997, 2000, 2003). For conceptions of giftedness from a metatheoretical perspective, please refer to Ziegler and Heller (2000).

The Psychometric Approach

The Munich longitudinal study of giftedness – one of the most enlarged European studies in the last two decades (Heller, 1991, 2001; Heller & Hany, 1986; Perleth & Heller, 1994) – is based on a psychometric classification approach with several types of giftedness or talent factors. This multidimensional model consists of seven relatively independent ability factor groups (predictors), and various performance domains (criterion variables), as well as personality (e.g., motivational) and social environmental factors that serve as moderators for the transition of individual potentials into excellent performances in various domains (see Figure 9.1).

According to this nationally and internationally validated model (see Heller 1992, 2001; Perleth, Sierwald & Heller, 1993), giftedness is conceptualized as a multifactorized ability construct within a network of noncognitive (e.g., motivation, control expectations, self-concept) and social moderators, as well as performance-related variables. For diagnostic purposes, the differentiation between predictor, criterion, and moderator variables is of particular interest.

The Expert–Novice Paradigm

Explanatory concepts regarding giftedness are hardly less problematic. These concepts differ from one another in terms of the significance they attach to personality and/or sociocultural determinants within the structure of giftedness versus their manifestations in exceptional aptitude. Although the psychometric paradigm of research on individual ability potential (predictors) under specific motivational and social conditions (moderators) focuses *prospectively* on expected performance excellence (criteria) in scholastic, university, or career matters, expertise research tries another approach. In the expert–novice paradigm – consider, for example, the comparison of experts (e.g. physics teachers or professors) and beginners (e.g., students in an introductory physics course) – the central conditions surrounding knowledge and expertise acquisition are *respectively* recorded, providing an important supplemental contribution to the prospective approach of the psychometric research. It is only recently that theoretical and empirical attempts have been made to combine both research paradigms to optimize the amount of insight to be obtained from research (cf. Perleth, 2001; Schneider, 2000).

Synthetic Approaches

In recent years, *synthetic approaches* have been favored in the field of giftedness research. Thus, introducing findings from the expertise and

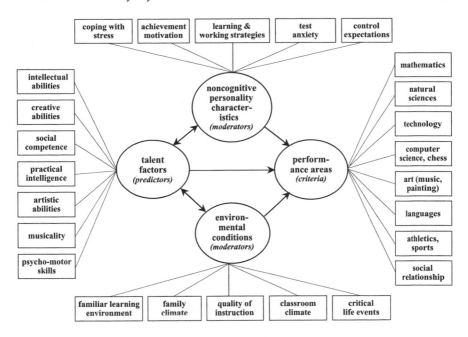

FIGURE 9.1. The Munich Model of Giftedness (MMG) as an example of multi-dimensional, typological conceptions (according to Heller et al., 1992, 2001).

Legend:

Talent factors (predictors)
– intelligence (language, mathematical, technical abilities, etc.)
– creativity (language, mathematical, technical, artistic, etc.)
– social competence
– musicality
– artistic abilities
– psycho-motor skills
– practical intelligence

(Noncognitive) personality characteristics (moderators)
– achievement motivation
– hope for success vs. fear of failure
– control expectations
– thirst for knowledge
– ability to deal well with stress (coping with stress)
– self-concept (general, scholastic, of talent, etc.)

Environmental conditions (moderators)
– home environmental stimulation ("creative" environment)
– educational style
– parental educational level
– demands on performance made at home
– social reactions to success and failure
– number of siblings and sibling position
– family climate
– quality of instruction
– school climate
– critical life events
– differentiated learning and instruction

Performance areas (criteria variables)
– mathematics, computer science, etc.
– natural sciences
– technology, handicraft, trade, etc.
– languages
– music (musical-artistic area)
– social activities, leadership, etc.
– athletics/sports

cognitive functioning approaches, as well as evidence from the research of connections between cognitive abilities and professional achievement, Perleth and Ziegler (1997; also see Ziegler & Perleth, 1997) extended the original Munich Giftedness Model from Figure 9.1 to the Munich Process Model depicted in Figure 9.2. The triangle symbolizes the formation of

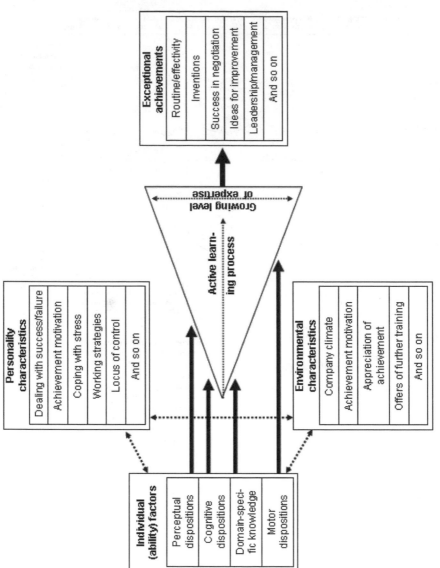

FIGURE 9.2. The Munich Process Model of Giftedness by Ziegler and Perleth (1997).

expert knowledge and routines in the course of a long and intense learning process (see *deliberate practice* by Ericsson, Krampe, & Tesch-Römer, 1993). Referring to Ackerman (1988) in the Ziegler and Perleth (1997) model, cognitive, perceptual, motor, and knowledge variables play the role of predictors or prerequisites for exceptional achievement instead of global ability factors as in the original MMG. According to this, it becomes clear that with an increasing degree of expertise, active learning processes influence expansions of knowledge and the acquisition of domain-specific competencies.

Conceptions referring to the expertise research imply that noncognitive personality characteristics, such as interests, task commitment (according to Renzulli), or achievement motivation are to be accorded increased significance regarding achievement development. It is questionable whether the time spent in active learning is exclusively responsible for achievement excellence in a specific domain, as implied by Ericsson's construct of *deliberate practice*. In any case, convincing proof has yet to be forthcoming from Ericsson and colleagues (e.g., Ericsson, 1996, 1998; Ericsson, Krampe, & Tesch-Römer, 1993) that adolescents or young adults are capable of reaching the same degree of expertise as the gifted in randomly chosen domains – independent of individual talent prerequisites. The formulation of threshold hypotheses (e.g., Schneider, 1993) is an attempt to rescue research findings accumulated with the expertise paradigm, without having to relinquish any significance of the cognitive learning and achievement potential for the development of expertise with a high standard (excellence) confirmed in psychometric giftedness research. This concern is actually more important than the insights gained from expertise research – not because of the realization of achievement excellence, but rather the information gained on how individual resources can be used for personal development.

Other synthetic approaches are Sternberg's conceptions of "giftedness as developing expertise" (Sternberg, 2000, p. 55) and his recent WICS model of giftedness (Sternberg, 2003), which is an acronym for Wisdom, Intelligence, Creativity, Synthesized. In the mentioned articles, Sternberg explains not only the relationship between giftedness and expertise, but he also argues "that giftedness is, ultimately, expertise in development" (p. 101). Intelligence, creativity, and wisdom are considered as the salient elements of giftedness.

The Munich Dynamic Ability–Achievement Model (MDAAM) – An Extended Version of MMG

Perleth (1997, 2000, 2001) made an attempt to bridge the gap between the research into giftedness and the more process-oriented field of cognitive and expertise research in the development of excellence. As he explains, an integrative model of giftedness has to fulfill the following requirements:

- conceptualize abilities and skills in a differentiated manner;
- take into account findings of genetic psychology and cognitive information processing research;
- consider the domain-specific character of achievements;
- make clear how cognitive abilities are transformed into achievements (e.g., by learning processes, amount of time spent learning, and the quality of experiences);
- consider acquisition of knowledge processes and the role of knowledge as prerequisites of achievement;
- include personality traits (e.g., interests, task commitment, stress resistance);
- pay attention to characteristics of variables such as family and school environment, as well as the role of peers and the professional community;
- be presented at an appropriate level of complexity so that it is convincing to teachers as well as parents of gifted children and youth (fulfilling one of Sternberg's [1990] criteria for a *good definition of giftedness*).

The model presented in Figure 9.3 attempts to integrate important perspectives of giftedness and expertise research and put them into a common and consistent frame. Even if Figure 9.3 might produce an opposite impression, Occam's razor was used for the conception of the model – *Entia non sunt multiplicanda sine necessitate*. The seeming complexity is due to the examples that were chosen for the illustration of the different groups of variables. Of course, no examples for the expertise domain were given because no selection seems adequate in the face of nearly unlimited possibilities.

Individual characteristics, such as aspects of attention and attention control, habituation, memory efficiency (speed of information processing) and working memory aspects, level of activation, and aspects of perception or motor skills can all be seen as innate dispositions or prerequisites of learning and achievement. Indeed, these characteristics represent the basic cognitive equipment of an individual (see Perleth, Schatz, & Mönks, 2000).

The model distinguishes between three or four stages of achievement or expertise development, which are related to the main phases of school and vocational training: preschool, high school, and university or vocational training. These stages can be roughly characterized by Plomin's classification (1994), which distinguished passive (preschool age), reactive (primary-school age) and active (adolescence and older) genotype–environment relations. It is to be expected that deviations from the "normal" development, especially with gifted individuals, are bound to occur. The fourth phase of professional activities is only indicated in

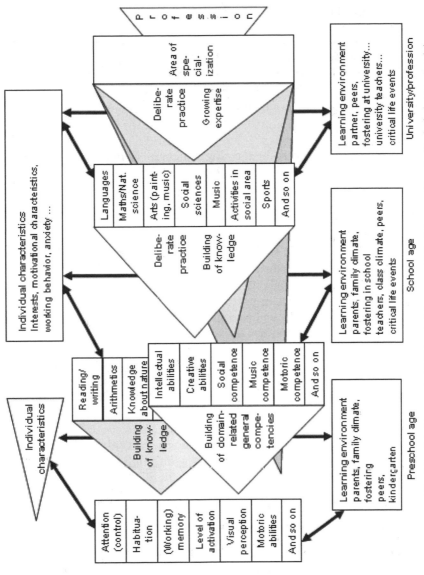

FIGURE 9.3. The Munich Dynamic Ability–Achievement Model according to Perleth (2001, p. 367).

the model and has to be completed by conception, as in the model by Ackerman (1988).

Certain learning processes belong to each of these stages. They serve the building up of competencies and are symbolized by the grey triangles. These triangles open to the right, indicating growth in abilities, knowledge, or competencies. The left corner of the triangles indicates when the respective learning process begins (the different tones of grey are just to make the figure clearer):

- During preschool years, the forming of general domain-related competencies is assumed. These are abilities or talents, such as intellectual or creative abilities, social competencies, and musical or motor abilities, which are depicted in the MMG as giftedness factors.
- The development of these competencies is contrasted by the accumulation of knowledge (nature, reading, writing, calculation).
- During school years, the formation of knowledge in different areas predominates (languages, natural and social sciences, arts, music, social behavior), and this knowledge has to be acquired in active, goal-specific learning processes (deliberate practice).
- The stage of university or vocational training serves the increasing specialization and development of expertise in a respective domain. Depending on the domain, this specialization can also start considerably earlier: Professional musicians or high-performance athletes often begin to occupy themselves with their domains as early as preschool or primary school (symbolized by the respective long triangles in Figure 9.3).

The MDAAM not only identifies ability factors and knowledge domains, as well as the respective learning processes, but it also highlights personality characteristics that are important for the development of achievement and expertise. As shown in the model, these traits develop during preschool and the first years of primary school (see Helmke, 1997), and they are conceptualized as being relatively stable during high school, university, or vocational training.

Finally, aspects of the learning environment are emphasized in the model for the development of achievement and expertise. Different factors for the three main stages of development are specified (see Figure 9.3 for more details). All in all, the influence of the family dominates in the first years, and then the characteristics of the school's learning environment (e.g., extra courses for the fostering of the gifted, school and class climate, extracurricular activities) gain more and more influence. At the same time, the importance of friends and like-minded individuals increases. Refer to Perleth (1997, 2001) for a more detailed description of the MDAAM.

IDENTIFYING AND PROGRAMMING

Methodological Problems of Talent Search and Identification of Gifted Individuals

The talent search for particular support programs is legitimized (a) through the right of every individual to receive optimal nurturance of talents and development; and (b) through the social demands on each individual, including the gifted, to make an appropriate contribution to the society (i.e., the gifted also have a duty to achieve special accomplishments that result from the needs of society).

Regarding the *function of talent searches*, it is necessary to be aware that the individual prerequisites and the demands of the new learning content in the advancement program for individual candidates "fit" together. Unfortunately, pure success criteria are often in the foreground of the selection process without consideration of moderators in the assessment (see following discussion). A comprehensive and differential evaluation of supportive measurements should, therefore, be an indispensable component of every talent search (cf. Feldhusen & Jarwan, 2000; Hany, 1993).

From a methodological standpoint, there must be differentiation between three groups of variables (see also Figure 9.1): (1) person-related talent indicators or *predictors*, (2) achievement *criteria* variables, and (3) person-related noncognitive traits of gifted individuals and sociocultural condition variables – both of these often serve as systematic *moderators* of the relationship (correlation) between predictors and criteria. Figure 9.4 illustrates the relationships based on the diagnosis-prognosis approach (according to Heller, 1989, p. 147).

The following skill concepts are psychometrically relevant as *cognitive personality characteristics* of gifted individuals:

- intelligence in the sense of differential abilities (e.g., verbal, quantitative, nonverbal, technical) or convergent thought processes (according to Guilford, 1959);
- creativity in the sense of divergent thought processes (according to Guilford, 1959) or divergent–convergent problem-solving styles (according to Facaoaru, 1985);
- self-concept, locus of control, and so on.

In contrast, the following process variables (in the sense of *metacomponents of cognitive control*) are appropriate for cognitive psychological approaches:

- problem sensitivity;
- planning and selection criterion for goal-oriented solution and action steps (during the solution of demanding, complex thought problems);
- attention, action control, and so on.

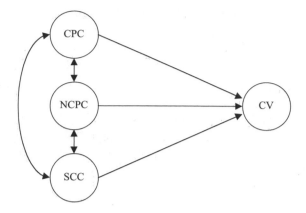

Legend: CPC = cognitive personality characteristics or traits of gifted individuals (predictors); NCPC = Non-cognitive personality characteristics or traits of gifted individuals (moderators); SCC = Socio-cultural condition variables (moderators); CV = Criterion variables (of achievement behavior in gifted individuals).

FIGURE 9.4. Causal model of performance behavior in the gifted.

As *noncognitive personality traits*, the following concepts need to be mentioned:

- interests, task commitment, and so on;
- drive for knowledge and achievement motivation (hope for success versus fear of failure);
- strategies for coping with stress, study, and work strategies;
- learning style, strategies of working memory, and so on.

The following items should be considered in the procedure of assessing *sociocultural conditions of the learning environment* or ecopsychological determinants of the development of talent, and the achievement behavior of gifted children and adolescents:

- quality of stimulation and expectation pressure of the social environment;
- reaction of peers, as well as teachers, parents, and siblings, to successes or failures of gifted students;
- socioemotional climate in the family and at school;
- sociometric peer status, teaching and instructional style;
- incidental factors, critical life events, and so on.

Finally, depending on the goals and/or purposes of the concerned gifted program, the following variables come into question as *criteria* of the talent search:

- school grades or other achievement indicators (e.g., test results, teacher ratings, grade-point average [GPA])

- success criteria related to a specific program for especially capable students (e.g., achievement variables in math or science courses);
- indicators of subjective personal gains, satisfaction with the support program, and so on.

If at all possible, life data, questionnaire data, and test data (according to Cattell, 1971) should be employed in the talent search. However, the different scale qualities must be considered in the data analysis.

The identification of gifted children and adolescents generally occurs in a procedure involving several steps. First, there usually is a *screening* process, which may be performed on the basis of teacher checklists or parent nominations for preschoolers, whereas older students are occasionally requested to nominate themselves. The most common method is probably the use of teacher or parent checklists (with or without rating scales), which are based on the operationalism of behavioral characteristics of domain-specific talents. In this way, a range as broad as possible of cognitive and motivational behavior traits is determined, which provides information about the presumed talent and assessed performances. Because ratings and other "soft" data can be assumed to be less accurate than test data, the screening should attempt to "lose" as few gifted candidates as possible (for a gifted program). This can be prevented through the conscious inclusion of none-too-small "false hits," It will not be until the second or third selection step – with the aid of more accurate diagnosis instruments that are, however, more limited in breadth – that a final selection can be made. As examples of *multidimensional* conceptualized measurement instruments, Sternberg's Triarchic Abilities Test (Sternberg, 1993; Sternberg, Castejón, Prieto, Hautamäki, & Grigorenko, 2005) and the Munich High Ability Test Battery, by Heller and Perleth (1999) are mentioned here.

Using the strategy described previously, the bandwidth–fidelity dilemma inevitably becomes a problem, as it is constantly encountered in personnel decisions (Cronbach & Gleser, 1965). Furthermore, the question of which type of error is more tolerable must also be addressed. It is well known that all selection decisions are fallible, so all that is left is to choose the lesser evil in the concrete decision situation. The risk of *type I errors* (alpha errors) exists in identifying someone as gifted when they are not. The risk of *type II errors* (beta errors) exists in failing to identify someone as gifted when indeed they are. The first type of error can be reduced by making the criteria more rigid; the second, by making them less strict. Simultaneous reduction of both types, however, is not possible. To maximize *individual* usefulness in a gifted program, for example, one decides to minimize the beta error. Occasionally, it is justifiable and sensible to reduce the alpha error, for example, in determining a sample for a study (of course, with voluntary participation). It should carefully be considered whether or not the research questions could be served just as well by using a *classification strategy* instead of a *selection strategy*. More discussion of the decision paradigms mentioned here, and elsewhere, is given in Cronbach and Gleser (1965), Wiggins (1973), Heller (1989), Hany (1993), or Sternberg and Subotnik (2000). Finally, one should be alerted to the regression effect of retesting when conducting successive identification procedures.

The quality of such an identification strategy can be evaluated on the basis of Pegnato and Birch's (1959) suggested criteria of effectivity and economy. The *effectivity* is considered to be the percentage of those students who are correctly identified as gifted during the screening. The *efficiency* or economy can be considered as a measure of the effort necessary for the total identification process. When trying to find all gifted persons, priority would be given to the first criterion (effectivity).

Instructional Strategies and Favorable Social (Learning) Environments Needed for Gifted Education

The transformation of ability potential into adequate scholastic or academic performance necessitates motivational learning and performance prerequisites on the part of the individual, as well as a supportive learning environment. What does *learning environment* mean?

A supportive or "effective" learning environment is to be understood as the customary *comprehensive stimulating social* (family, school, extracurricular) environments in which children and adolescents grow up. What are the distinguishing characteristics of effective or "creative" learning environments compared with less creative social environments? An empirical effort to answer this question can be made by comparing especially successful teachers with those who are less successful. One finds a high level of flexibility in the instructional practices of the successful teachers and a more accepting approach to the individual differences among their students. Compared with less successful colleagues, the effective teachers demonstrate a more positive attitude toward especially capable children and adolescents. This finding, made by researchers working in the United States (cf. Baldwin, 1993; Gallagher, 2000; Gallagher & Gallagher, 1994; Peterson & Fennema, 1985), has been replicated in scientific gifted program evaluation studies conducted in Germany (e.g., Heller, 2002; Heller & Reimann, 2002; Neber & Heller, 2002).

The postulation of a fit between individual learning needs and learning opportunities with instructional and support conditions provides us with a double objective: to transform individual learning potentials into corresponding scholastic or academic achievements (essentially a function of personality development) and just as importantly to maximize this learning potential by enabling independent and lifelong learning. These tasks correspond to the goals of adaptive instruction, which strive to hamper students' inabilities and increase their individual ability potentials (Corno & Snow, 1986). By stimulating and optimizing the learning processes through individually appropriate performance demands (e.g., task difficulty), the underchallenging of gifted students and the overtaxing of weaker students can be avoided. This can only be accomplished through sufficient "internal" (instructionally integrated) and/or "external" (scholastic/educational) *differentiation measures*. As a result, students with gaps in their knowledge, or so-called previous knowledge deficits caused by the inadequate utilization of learning opportunities, can be better encouraged to become more successful (e.g., through remedial learning) than those students with weaker talents. Among the latter, the treatment efficacy, according to investigative findings by Helmke (1992), is substantially less favorable (Helmke & Weinert, 1997).

Internal differentiation stipulates that learning tasks become the most important components in the promotion of talent and giftedness. The transformation of an individual's ability potentials into corresponding feats of excellent achievement necessitates tasks that offer a grade of difficulty lying on the boundaries of the individual's capabilities in order to make them sufficiently challenging. This need does not only correspond to common experiences found among highly talented adolescents, but it has also been confirmed by scientific investigations (Benbow & Arjmand, 1990; Gruber & Mandl, 2000).

To guarantee the quality of educational learning environments with respect to instructional differentiation measures, the following learning conditions are of substantial importance:

- Encouragement of an *active* role for the student through self-selected learning material and/or student-selected designs of their learning processes. This involves a selection of learning and problem-solving strategies emphasizing the objective to attempt new solution methods and find original solutions.
- A continuous *diagnostic evaluation of individual learning progress* to determine the level of knowledge attained and the requirements for further learning progress. In this case, achievement assessment in the form of report cards is less suitable.
- Securing an *explorative variety* of learning sources and materials to encourage self-initiated discoveries and conclusions.
- *Individualization of learning processes*, that is, making individual learning courses and paces possible, freedom to base the subject matter of activities on one's interests. These learning goals are achieved through the lucidity of learning courses and learning progress, as well as through individualized (teacher) feedback.

In attempting to formulate effective or creative (scholastic) learning environments, the fact that students are not only influenced by their respective instruction and its characteristic qualities must be taken into account – despite the salient importance of the teacher being primarily responsible for the instructional process. Students are also influenced by the direction that the instruction follows and how individual characteristics affect their learning behavior. Each form of instruction is more or less a product of interaction. Regarding the promotion of the gifted and talented, it is not only the interactive patterns of cognitive and noncognitive student characteristics (i.e., motivation and self-related concepts) that are to be considered, but also person–environment interactions.

PROGRAMMING AND ASSESSMENT

How do we translate the theoretical MMG or its extended version MDAAM into practice and ensure that gifted programs have the necessary educational and social learning environment? How do we modify the different types of educational and enrichment programs offered to gifted students (both in schools and elsewhere) in terms of content, process, product, and a conducive and stimulating learning environment to promote creativity, personality, and motivational traits? It is also necessary to have innovative modes of assessment in a gifted program to realize gifted potential, particularly in terms of excellent performance and creative products.

Currently, a variety of programming models, both part- and full-time, provide gifted children with instruction to fulfill their needs and potential. They present strategies and curricula of all types, many claiming to be "ideal" for highly gifted and talented students. The part-time programs in Europe, the United States, or East Asia include pull-out programs offering educational enrichment, honors classes, after-school programs, specialized camps, and summer schools featuring special coursework. The better known programs, such as the Center for Talented Youth (Institute for the Academic Advancement of Youth at The Johns Hopkins University; see Campbell, Wagner, & Walberg, 2000), focus on acceleration. Summer courses also include science and technology programs similar to those offered by many American universities (iD Tech Camp), Weizmann Institute of Science in Rehovot Israel (cf. Maoz, 1993; Subhi & Maoz, 2000), or the German Pupils Academy (Neber & Heller, 2002; Wagner, Neber, & Heller, 1995). Passow (1993) provides an international perspective on programming. For a greater overview, see Heller, Mönks, Sternberg, and Subotnik (2000, pp. 671–828).

Full-time programs could be specially designed gifted classes in regular schools, as seen in Singapore (Lim, 1996a) or Germany (Heller, 2002), or special high schools for the gifted, such as Bronx Science and Illinois Math and Science Academy in the United States (see Passow, 1993), and the Israel Arts and Science Academy (see Passow, 1993; Subhi & Maoz, 2000). These gifted classes and schools run an intensive curriculum of subjects with emphasis on sophisticated topics and enrichment activities. Such schools usually organize mentor programs in which students are matched with professionals in the community for special learning experiences (Lim, 1996b, 2002; Zorman, 1993).

The Curriculum of Gifted Programs

In a gifted program, a specially designed differentiated curriculum is needed to address and nurture gifted characteristics, such as abilities, motivations, and interests. Such a strategy transforms gifted potential into excellent scholastic performance and creative performance and products (cf. Sternberg, 1997; Sternberg & Grigorenko, 1995). This type of an optimized program has to be qualitatively (rather than quantitatively) different than the basic curriculum.

According to VanTassel-Baska (1988, 1992), differentiated curricula in terms of content, process, and products respond to diverse characteristics of gifted learners by accelerating the mastery of basic skills. This is done through testing-out procedures and reorganization of the curriculum according to higher-level skills and concepts. We can engage students in active problem-finding and problem-solving activities and research by providing opportunities for them to focus on issues, themes, ideas, and making connections within and across systems of knowledge.

Many successful gifted programs tend to modify content through acceleration in individual subjects, or thematic, broad-based, and integrative units. An entire content area arranged and structured around a conceptual framework can be mastered in much less time than is traditionally allotted (VanTassel-Baska, 1988, 2000). In an integrated curriculum, materials can provide a balance of content and process considerations, including an emphasis on original student investigations, concept development, and interdisciplinary applications. Current special schools and summer programs incorporate expertise very well by providing advanced knowledge. For a prominent German example, see the well-evaluated G8-model on the basis of MMG in Baden-Württemberg (Heller, 2002; Heller, Osterrieder, & Wystrychowski, 1995; Heller & Reimann, 2002). These programs, however, often do less well in terms of creativity, transforming gifted potential into excellent performance, and creative products with applications in real-life contexts.

Learning and Teaching Problems Within Gifted Programs

Acceleration is but one of the means used to stimulate gifted students to excel. Gifts can also be effectively actualized through independent research and projects (modification of product). Students with exceptional aptitude in a particular field or subject can be stimulated by activities to demonstrate their abilities and challenged to achieve peaks of excellence. Thus, we effectively support independence among the students in exploration, discovery learning, and creative problem solving.

In terms of modified process, the gifted as a group comprehend complex ideas more easily and learn more rapidly and in greater depth than their peers. Some may exhibit different interests from those of their peers, whereas others may prefer time for in-depth exploration to manipulate ideas and draw generalizations from seemingly unconnected concepts. Consequently, teachers of the gifted need to integrate traditional subject areas (math, science, reading, language, and social studies) in ways that support and extend their interests and development. The gifted can then look into real-life problems and consider issues with societal implications. Teachers also have to establish a climate that encourages the students to question openly, exercise independence, and use their creativity to be all that they can be. Changes in assessment will require the gifted to exhibit skills and not just content mastery.

Products are the "ends" of instruction. Encouraging the gifted to do projects and portfolios in thematic units of integrated curriculum and concept-based instruction emphasizes the scientific and research process within an integrated framework (e.g., exploring a topic, planning how to study it and carrying out a study, judging results, and reporting). These methods encourage students to take an active role in their own learning and emphasize using problem-solving strategies to attempt new solution methods and find original solutions (Heller, 1999). Projects also expand opportunities to address real problems, concerns, and audiences; to generalize, integrate, and apply ideas; and to synthesize rather than summarize information. Students acquire an integrated understanding of knowledge and the structure of the disciplines through this process. Projects and portfolios also promote intra- and interdisciplinary learning, as well as provoke divergent and complex reasoning (Stepien, Gallagher, & Workman, 1993; Wiggins, 1989). Research opportunities associated with Type III activities are also promoted through the use of projects and portfolios (Renzulli & Reis, 1985, 1994, 2000).

The modification of such content, process, and product requires a high level of flexibility in the instructional practices of the teachers. Instruction is inquiry-oriented, using strategies like problem-based learning and Socratic questioning. Students are thus able to construct their own understanding of the subject in such a way that encourages the application of appropriate processes to new situations. Through guided questions by the teacher, collaborative dialogue and discussion with peers, and individual exploration of key questions, the gifted can grow in the development of valuable habits of mind that are found among scientists and researchers – namely skepticism, objectivity, and curiosity (Sher, VanTassel-Baska, Gallagher, & Bailey, 1992). With these features firmly in place, a community of inquiry in the classroom can then be created.

Teachers play a vital role in a gifted program. The research of Csikszent-mihalyi (1999; Csikszentmihalyi, Rathunde, & Whalen, 1993; Csikszentmihalyi & Wolfe, 2000) on creative lives (e.g., gifted and creative people who have achieved their potential, won Nobel Prizes) has shown that some have considered particular high school and university teachers as a source of inspiration. These were the teachers who showed care and concern for their students. Teachers must be able to give their talented students intellectually demanding, rigorous, and challenging activities in such a way that they can be treated as fun rather than as chores. Such teachers are hard to come by – they have to be very interested in the gifted, and they must mutually share research passion with students. It is of utmost importance to have such teachers in a gifted program, both at the high school and at the university levels (cf. Arnold, 1994; Heller & Viek, 2000; Subotnik & Steiner, 1993, 1994).

As mentioned previously, to ensure the success of a differentiated curriculum involving content, process, and product, the support of a conducive and creative teaching–learning environment featuring innovative assessment modes is needed. The learning environment requires an interaction of cognitive and noncognitive student characteristics (i.e., motivation and self-related concepts), as well as interaction of person and environment (Gruber & Mandl, 2000; Heller, 2002). Creative and stimulating environments provide new insights for students, such as those available in universities, research centers, think tanks, and schools like Bronx Science (Csikszentmihalyi, 1996, 1999; Csikszentmihalyi & Wolfe, 2000). These environments have the ability to inspire and nurture creative ideas by providing freedom of action and conditions that arouse attitudes of creativity in the gifted, such as curiosity, risk taking, persistence, perseverance, and inner motivation.

Assessment Needed for Gifted Programs

Novel assessment modes suitable for a differentiated curriculum of content, process, product, and environment have to be authentic in nature, student-based, and portfolio-driven, rather than teacher-directed assignments and standardized tests. These novel performance assessment techniques and authentic assessments are better for evaluation, and they provide continuous diagnostic feedback to students, with greater emphasis on critical thinking and creativity. They can make use of real-world problems for gifted students to demonstrate understanding and transfer of key ideas and processes that mirror problem solving in real-life contexts. Assessment, therefore, reflects the interdisciplinary challenges of real-life situations and simultaneously recognizes and values the multiple abilities of gifted students. Assessment must also tolerate varied learning styles and diverse backgrounds. Gifted students can also collaborate in their own assessment, because many have high standards and expectations of themselves. It is possible to work out an optimum combination of self, peer, teacher, and mentor assessment. As pointed out by Tombari and Borich (1999), authentic learning and assessment enhance intrinsic academic motivation. Characteristics of gifted students that are nurtured through authentic assessment include intrinsic motivation, goal directedness, and persistence and preference for independent learning (Moltzen, 1996).

CONCLUSION

The present and future of identification/talent search and gifted education will primarily reflect the advances made in theoretical and empirical research with increased levels of quality. Through the examples set by expertise research and cognitive psychology, along with tried and tested psychometric models, it becomes clear that interdisciplinary approaches to the study of giftedness are mediators in tandem with new theoretical perspectives in related fields of giftedness research that are readily convertible into practice.

Furthermore, cross-cultural studies in gifted education (cf. Hernández De Hahn, 2000) offer the possibility to revise older theories and to gain a broader understanding of special needs concerning identification and programming. Increasing globalization demands international perspectives. When we are able to understand the chances being offered here, gifted education will not only help to secure our economic living conditions in the third millennium, but it will also provide a salient contribution to our understanding of other cultures and their needs, as well as the understanding and validation of giftedness models and empirical findings in the field.

References

Ackerman, P. L. (1988). Determinants of individual differences during skill acquisition: Cognitive abilities and information processing. *Journal of Experimental Psychology: General, 117*, 288–318.

Arnold, K. D. (1994). The Illinois Valedictorian Project: Early adult careers of academically talented male high school students. In R. F. Subotnik & K. D. Arnold (Eds.), *Beyond Terman: Contemporary longitudinal studies of giftedness and talent* (pp. 24–51). Norwood, NJ: Ablex.

Baldwin, A. Y. (1993). Teachers of the gifted. In K. A. Heller, F. J. Mönks, & A. H. Passow (Eds.), *International handbook of research and development of giftedness and talent* (pp. 621–629). Oxford, England: Pergamon.

Benbow, C. P., & Arjmand, O. (1990). Predictors of high academic achievement in mathematics and science by mathematically talented students: A longitudinal study. *Journal of Educational Psychology, 82*, 430–441.

Campbell, J. R., Wagner, H., & Walberg, H. J. (2000). Academic competitions and programs designed to challenge the exceptionally talented. In K. A. Heller,

F. J. Mönks, R. J. Sternberg, & R. F. Subotnik (Eds.), *International handbook of giftedness and talent* (2nd ed., pp. 523–535). Oxford, England: Pergamon.

Cattell, R. B. (1971). *Abilities, their structure, growth, and action*. Boston: Houghton Mifflin.

Corno, L., & Snow, R. E. (1986). Adapting teaching to individual differences among learners. In M.C. Witrock (Ed.), *Handbook for research on teaching* (3rd ed., pp. 605–629). New York: Macmillan.

Cronbach, L. J., & Gleser, G. C. (1965). *Psychological tests and personnel decisions* (2nd ed.). Urbana: University of Illinois Press.

Cronbach, L., & Snow, R. (1977). *Aptitudes and instructional methods: A handbook for research on interactions*. New York: Irvington.

Csikszentmihalyi, M. (1996). *Creativity: Flow and the psychology of discovery and invention*. New York: HarperCollins.

Csikszentmihalyi, M. (1999). Implications of a system's perspective for the study of creativity. In R. J. Sternberg (Ed.), *The handbook of human creativity* (pp. 313–338). New York: Cambridge University Press.

Csikszentmihalyi, M., Rathunde, K., & Whalen, S. (1993). *Talented teenagers: The roots of success and failure*. New York: Cambridge University Press.

Csikszentmihalyi, M., & Wolfe, R. (2000). New conceptions and research approaches to creativity: Implications of a systems perspective for creativity in education. In K. A. Heller, F. J. Mönks, R. J. Sternberg, & R. F. Subotnik (Eds.), *International handbook of giftedness and talent* (2nd ed., pp. 81–93). Oxford, England: Pergamon.

Ericsson, K. A. (Ed.). (1996). *The road to excellence. The acquisition of expert performance in the arts and sciences, sports and games*. Mahwah, NJ: Lawrence Erlbaum Associates.

Ericsson, K. A. (1998). The scientific study of expert levels of performance: General implications for optimal learning and creativity. *High Ability Studies, 9*, 75–100.

Ericsson, K. A., Krampe, R. T., & Tesch-Römer, C. (1993). The role of deliberate practice in the acquisition of expert performance. *Psychological Review, 100*, 363–406.

Facaoaru, C. (1985). *Kreativität in Wissenschaft und Technik [Creativity in science and technology]*. Bern, Switzerland: Huber.

Feldhusen, J. F., & Jarwan, F. A. (2000). Identification of gifted and talented youth for educational programs. In K. A. Heller, F. J. Mönks, R. J. Sternberg, & R. F. Subotnik (Eds.), *International handbook of giftedness and talent* (2nd ed., pp. 271–282). Oxford, England: Pergamon.

Gagné, F. (1985). Giftedness and talent: Reexamining a reexamination of the definitions. *Gifted Child Quarterly, 19*, 103–112.

Gagné, F. (1993). Constructs and models pertaining to exceptional human abilities. In K. A. Heller, F. J. Mönks, & A. H. Passow (Eds.), *International handbook of research and development of giftedness and talent* (pp. 69–87). Oxford, England: Pergamon.

Gagné, F. (2000). Understanding the complex choreography of talent development through DMGT-based analysis. In K. A. Heller, F. J. Mönks, R. J. Sternberg, & R. F. Subotnik (Eds.), *International handbook of giftedness and talent* (2nd ed., pp. 67–79). Oxford, England: Pergamon.

Gallagher, J. J. (2000). Changing paradigms for gifted education in the United States. In K. A. Heller, F. J. Mönks, R. J. Sternberg, & R. F. Subotnik (Eds.), *International handbook of giftedness and talent* (2nd ed., pp. 681–693). Oxford, England: Pergamon.

Gallagher, J. J., & Gallagher, S. A. (1994). *Teaching the gifted child* (4th ed.). Boston: Allyn & Bacon.

Gardner, H. (1983). *Frames of mind. The theory of multiple intelligences.* New York: Basic Books.

Gardner, H. (1993). *Multiple intelligences: The theory in practice.* New York: Basic Books.

Gruber, H., & Mandl, H. (2000). Instructional psychology and the gifted. In K. A. Heller, F. J. Mönks, R. J. Sternberg, & R. F. Subotnik (Eds.), *International handbook of giftedness and talent* (2nd ed., pp. 383–396). Oxford, England: Pergamon.

Guilford, J. P. (1959). *Personality.* New York, NY: McGraw Hill.

Hany, E. A. (1993). Methodological problems and issues concerning identification. In K. A. Heller, F. J. Mönks, & A. H. Passow (Eds.), *International handbook of research and development of giftedness and talent* (pp. 209–232). Oxford, England: Pergamon.

Heller, K. A. (1989). Perspectives on the diagnosis of giftedness. *German Journal of Psychology, 13,* 140–159.

Heller, K. A. (1991). The nature and development of giftedness: A longitudinal study. *European Journal for High Ability, 2,* 174–188. Reprinted in A. J. Cropley & D. Dehn (Eds.). (1996). *Fostering the growth of high ability: European perspectives* (pp. 41–56). Norwood, NJ: Ablex.

Heller, K. A. (Ed.). (2001). *Hochbegabung im Kindes- und Jugendalter [High ability in childhood and adolescence].* Göttingen, Germany: Hogrefe.

Heller, K. A. (1999). Individual (learning and motivational) needs versus instructional conditions of gifted education. *High Ability Studies, 10,* 9–21.

Heller, K. A. (Ed.). (2002). *Begabtenförderung im Gymnasium [Gifted education at the German gymnasium].* Opladen, Germany: Leske & Budrich.

Heller, K. A., & Hany, E. A. (1986). Identification, development, and achievement analysis of talented and gifted children in West Germany. In K. A. Heller & J. F. Feldhusen (Eds.), *Identifying and nurturing the gifted: An international perspective* (pp. 67–82). Bern, Switzerland: Huber.

Heller, K. A., Mönks, F. J., Sternberg, R. J., & Subotnik, R. F. (Eds.). (2000). *International handbook of giftedness and talent* (2nd ed.). Oxford, England: Pergamon.

Heller, K. A., Osterrieder, K., & Wystrychowski, W. (1995). A longitudinal follow-up evaluation study of a statewide acceleration program for highly gifted students at the German gymnasium. In M. Katzko & F. J. Mönks (Eds.), *Nurturing talent: Individual needs and social ability* (pp. 269–274). Assen, The Netherlands: Van Gorcum.

Heller, K. A., & Perleth, Ch. (1999). *The Munich High Ability Test Battery (MHBT).* Unpublished test.

Heller, K. A., & Reimann, R. (2002). Theoretical and methodological problems of a 10-year-follow-up program evaluation study. *European Journal of Psychological Assessment, 18,* 229–241.

Heller, K. A., & Viek, P. (2000). Support for university students: Individual and social factors. In C. F. M. van Lieshout & P. G. Heymans (Eds.), *Developing talent across the life span* (pp. 299–321). Hove, England: Psychology Press.

Helmke, A. (1992). *Selbstvertrauen und schulische Leistungen [Self-confidence and school performances]*. Göttingen, Germany: Hogrefe.

Helmke, A. (1997). Individuelle Bedingungsfaktoren der Schulleistung – Ergebnisse aus dem SCHOLASTIK-Projekt [Individual conditions of school achievement]. In F. E. Weinert & A. Helmke (Hrsg.), *Entwicklung im Grundschulalter* (S. 203–216). Weinheim, Germany: Beltz.

Helmke, A., & Weinert, F. E. (1997). Bedingungsfaktoren schulischer Leistungen [Conditions for school performance]. In F. E. Weinert (Ed.), *Psychologie des Unterrichts und der Schule, Bd. 3 der Pädagogischen Psychologie (Enzyklopädie der Psychologie)* (pp. 71–176). Göttingen, Germany: Hogrefe.

Hernández De Hahn, E. L. (2000). Cross cultural studies in gifted education. In K. A. Heller, F. J. Mönks, R. J. Sternberg, & R. F. Subotnik (Eds.), *International handbook of giftedness and talent* (2nd ed., pp. 549–561). Oxford, England: Pergamon.

Lim, T. K. (1996a). Formative evaluation of The Chinese High Gifted Education Program. *Roeper Review, 19*, 50–53.

Lim, T. K. (1996b). Nurturing giftedness through the Mentor-Link Program. *High Ability Studies, 7*, 169–177.

Lim, T. K. (2002). Utilizing mentorship to maximize gifted potential in science and technology. Presented at the International Conference on the Education for the Gifted in Science. In Korean Educational Development Institute (Ed.), *International Conference on Education for the Gifted in Science* (pp. 191–207). Seoul, South Korea: KEDI.

Maoz, N. (1993). Nurturing giftedness in non-school educative settings – Using the personnel and material resources of the community. In K. A. Heller, F. J. Mönks, & A. H. Passow (Eds.), *International handbook of research and development of giftedness and talent* (pp. 743–752). Oxford, England: Pergamon.

Moltzen, R. (1996). Characteristics of gifted children. In D. McAlpine & R. Moltzen (Eds.), *Gifted and talented: New Zealand perspectives* (pp. 43–62). Palmerston North, New Zealand: ERDC Press.

Mönks, F. J. (1985). Hoogbegaafden: een situatieschets. In F. J. Mönks & P. Span (Eds.), *Hoogbegaafden in de samenleving* (pp. 17–31). Nijmegen, The Netherlands: Dekker & van de Vegt.

Neber, H., & Heller, K. A. (2002). Evaluation of a summer-school program for highly gifted secondary school students: The German Pupils Academy. *European Journal of Psychological Assessment, 18*, 214–228.

Passow, A. H. (1993). National/state policies regarding education of the gifted. In K. A. Heller, F. J. Mönks, & A. H. Passow (Eds.), *International handbook of research and development of giftedness and talent* (pp. 29–46). Oxford, England: Pergamon.

Pegnato, C. W., & Birch, J. W. (1959). Locating gifted children in junior high schools – A comparison of methods. *Exceptional Children, 25*, 300–304.

Perleth, Ch. (1997). *Zur Rolle von Begabung und Erfahrung bei der Leistungsgenese. Ein Brückenschlag zwischen Begabungs- und Expertiseforschung* [The role of ability and experience in the development of school/vocational performance] (Habilitationsschrift). München, Germany: LMU.

Perleth, Ch. (2000). Neue Tendenzen und Ergebnisse in der Begabungs- und Intelligenzdiagnostik [New trends of measuring giftedness and intelligence]. In H. Joswig (Hrsg.), *Begabungen erkennen – Begabte fördern* (S. 35–64). Rostock, Germany: Univ. Rostock.

Perleth, Ch. (2001). Follow-up-Untersuchungen zur Münchner Hochbegabungsstudie [Follow-ups to the Munich Study of Giftedness]. In K. A. Heller (Ed.), *Hochbegabung im Kindes- und Jugendalter [High ability in children and adolescents]* (2nd ed., pp. 357–446). Göttingen, Germany: Hogrefe.

Perleth, Ch., & Heller, K. A. (1994). The Munich longitudinal study of giftedness. In R. F. Subotnik & K. D. Arnold (Eds.), *Beyond Terman: Contemporary longitudinal studies of giftedness and talent* (pp. 77–114). Norwood, NJ: Ablex.

Perleth, Ch., Schatz, T., & Mönks, F. J. (2000). Early indicators of high ability. In K. A. Heller, F. J. Mönks, R. J. Sternberg, & R. F. Subotnik (Hrsg.), *International handbook for giftedness and talent* (2nd ed., pp. 283–310). Oxford, England: Pergamon.

Perleth, Ch., Sierwald, W., & Heller, K. A. (1993). Selected results of the Munich longitudinal study of giftedness: The multidimensional/typological giftedness model. *Roeper Review, 15*, 149–155.

Perleth, Ch., & Ziegler, A. (1997). Überlegungen zur Begabungsdiagnose und Begabtenförderung in der Berufsaus- und -weiterbildung [Considerations about identification in vocational schools]. In U. Kittler & H. Metz-Göckel (Eds.), *Pädagogische Psychologie in Erziehung und Unterricht* (pp. 100–112). Essen, Germany: Die Blaue Eule.

Peterson, P. L., & Fennema, E. (1985). Effective teaching, student engagement in classroom activities, and sex-related differences in learning mathematics. *American Educational Research Journal, 22*, 309–335.

Plomin, R. (1994). *Genetics and experience. The interplay between nature and nurture.* Beverly Hills, CA: Sage.

Renzulli, J. S. (1978). What makes giftedness? Reexamining a definition. *Phi Delta Kappan, 60*, 180–184, 261.

Renzulli, J. S., & Reis, S. M. (1985). *The schoolwide enrichment model: A comprehensive plan for educational excellence.* Mansfield Center, CT: Creative Learning Press.

Renzulli, J. S., & Reis, S. M. (1994). Research related to the schoolwide enrichment triad model. *Gifted Child Quarterly, 38*, 7–19.

Renzulli, J. S., & Reis, S. M. (2000). The schoolwide enrichment model. In K. A. Heller, F. J. Mönks, R. J. Sternberg, & R. F. Subotnik (Eds.), *International handbook of giftedness and talent* (2nd ed., pp. 367–382). Oxford, England: Pergamon.

Schneider, W. (1993). Acquiring expertise: Determinants of exceptional performance. In K. A. Heller, F. J. Mönks, & A. H. Passow (Eds.), *International handbook of research and development of giftedness and talent* (pp. 311–324). Oxford, England: Pergamon.

Schneider, W. (2000). Giftedness, expertise, and (exceptional) performance: A developmental perspective. In K. A. Heller, F. J. Mönks, R. J. Sternberg, & R. F. Subotnik (Eds.), *International handbook of giftedness and talent* (2nd ed., pp. 165–177). Oxford, England: Pergamon.

Sher, B., VanTassel-Baska, J., Gallagher, S., & Bailey, J. (1992). *Developing a scope and sequence in science for high ability students K-8.* Williamsburg, VA: College of William and Mary, Center for Gifted Education.

Stepien, W. J., Gallagher, S. A., & Workman, D. (1993). Problem-based learning for traditional and interdisciplinary classrooms. *Journal for the Education of the Gifted, 16*, 338–357.

Sternberg, R. J. (1985). *Beyond IQ. A triarchic theory of human intelligence.* New York: Cambridge University Press.

Sternberg, R. J. (1990). What constitutes a "good" definition of giftedness. *Journal for the Education of the Gifted, 14*, 96–100.

Sternberg, R. J. (1993). *Sternberg Triarchic Abilities Test (Level H).* Unpublished test.

Sternberg, R. J. (Ed.). (1997). *Thinking styles.* New York. Cambridge University Press.

Sternberg, R. J. (2000). Giftedness as developing expertise. In K. A. Heller, F. J. Mönks, R. J. Sternberg, & R. F. Subotnik (Eds.), *International handbook of giftedness and talent* (2nd ed., pp. 55–66). Oxford, England: Pergamon.

Sternberg, R. J. (2003). WICS as a model of giftedness. *High Ability Studies, 14*, 101–126.

Sternberg, R. J., Castejón, J. L., Prieto, M. D., Hautamäki, J., & Grigorenko, E. L. (2001). Confirmatory factor analysis of the Sternberg Triarchic Abilities Test in three international samples. *European Journal of Psychological Assessment, 17*, 1–16.

Sternberg, R. J., & Grigorenko, E. L. (1995). Styles of thinking in school. *European Journal for High Ability, 6*, 201–219.

Sternberg, R. J., & Subotnik, R. F. (2000). A multidimensional framework for synthesizing disparate issues in identifying, selecting, and serving gifted children. In K. A. Heller, F. J. Mönks, R. J. Sternberg, & R. F. Subotnik (Eds.), *International handbook of giftedness and talent* (2nd ed., pp. 831–838). Oxford, England: Pergamon.

Subhi, T., & Maoz, N. (2000). Middle-East region: Efforts, policies, programs and issues. In K. A. Heller, F. J. Mönks, R. J. Sternberg, & R. F. Subotnik (Eds.), *International handbook of giftedness and talent* (2nd ed., pp. 743–756). Oxford, England: Pergamon.

Subotnik, R. F., & Steiner, C. L. (1993). Adult manifestations of adolescent talent in science. *Roeper Review, 15*, 164–169.

Subotnik, R. F., & Steiner, C. L. (1994). Adult manifestations of adolescent talent in science: A longitudinal study of 1983 Westinghouse Science Talent Search winners. In R. F. Subotnik & K. D. Arnold (Eds.), *Beyond Terman: Contemporary longitudinal studies of giftedness and talent* (pp. 52–76). Norwood, NJ: Ablex.

Tombari, M., & Borich, G. (1999). *Authentic assessment in the classroom: Applications and practice.* Columbus, OH: Merrill.

VanTassel-Baska, J. (1988). Developing a comprehensive approach to scope and sequence: Curriculum alignment. *Gifted Child Today*, September–October, 42–45.

VanTassel-Baska, J. (1992). *Planning effective curriculum for gifted learners.* Denver, CO: Love.

VanTassel-Baska, J. (2000). Theory and research on curriculum development for the gifted. In K. A. Heller, F. J. Mönks, R. J. Sternberg, & R. F. Subotnik (Eds.), *International handbook of giftedness and talent* (2nd ed., pp. 345–365). Oxford, England: Pergamon.

Wagner, H., Neber, H., & Heller, K. A. (1995). The BundesSchülerAkademie – A residential summer program for gifted adolescents in Germany. Part II: Evaluation of the program. In M. Katzko & F. J. Mönks (Eds.), *Nurturing talent: Individual needs and social ability* (pp. 281–291). Assen, The Netherlands: Van Gorcum.

Wiggins, G. (1989). A true test: Toward more authentic and equitable assessment. *Phi Delta Kappan, 70,* 9.

Wiggins, J. S. (1973). *Personality and prediction. Principles of personality assessment.* Reading, MA: Addison-Wesley.

Ziegler, A., & Heller, K. A. (2000). Conceptions of giftedness from a metatheoretical perspective. In K. A. Heller, F. J. Mönks, R. J. Sternberg, & R. F. Subotnik (Eds.), *International handbook of giftedness and talent* (2nd ed., pp. 3–21). Oxford, England: Pergamon.

Ziegler, A., & Perleth, Ch. (1997). Schafft es Sisyphos, den Stein den Berg hinaufzurollen? Eine kritische Bestandsaufnahme der Diagnose- und Förder-möglichkeiten von Begabten in der beruflichen Bildung vor dem Hintergrund des Münchner Begabungs-Prozeß-Modells [Will Sisyphus be able to roll the stone up the mountain? A critical examination of the status of diagnosis and promotion of the gifted in occupational education set against the Munich Talent Model]. *Psychologie in Erziehung und Unterricht, 44,* 152–163.

Zorman, R. (1993). Mentoring and role-modeling programs for the gifted. In K. A. Heller, F. J. Mönks, & A. H. Passow (Eds.), *International handbook of research and development of giftedness and talent* (pp. 727–741). Oxford, England: Pergamon.

10

Systemic Approaches to Giftedness

Contributions of Russian Psychology

Ida Jeltova and Elena L. Grigorenko

Since 1957, when the Soviet Union launched its satellite *Sputnik*, until the dissociation of the Soviet Union in 1991, the Russian tradition of educating gifted children had been world-renowned. However, with a restructuring of society's major domains of functioning in the early 1990s, the Soviet system of complete federal support for gifted education all but disappeared. In this chapter, we argue that the system, despite the challenges of the 1990s, has survived its toughest times. We illustrate that, by capitalizing both on past and current theories of giftedness and cognitive development, the field of gifted studies in Russia continues to develop and that it is in the process of re-creating itself in the changed social and cultural context of Russia.

Russian definitions and approaches to giftedness can be described as very different from Western approaches, particularly the American psychometric approach. For various social, political, cultural, and historical reasons, Soviet (Russian) psychological and pedagogical science developed its own unique theoretical and methodological paradigms. The Great October Socialist Revolution of 1917 resulted in a regime that tried (or claimed) to minimize individual differences and establish equity in all areas of human enterprise. Empirical research into individual differences was viewed unfavorably, because it would imply testing, quantification of variation between people, and, consequently, challenging the underlying ideological societal postulates.

Russian society, however, has always been interested in identifying and utilizing outstanding abilities of gifted and talented individuals for the societal "common good," especially in math and sciences. Given that the educational system in Russia was centralized and homogeneous (e.g., all schools but schools for gifted children had the same curriculum, textbooks, and examinations), it was easy to identify children who did better than others in specific subject areas. In the language of psychometrics, giftedness and talent were identified mainly via criterion-referenced, performance-based assessment. In the language of everyday life, children whose performance on written and oral examinations was consistently outstanding in one or more achievement domains were labeled "gifted and talented" (Grigorenko, 1997; Karp, 2003).

External and internal political changes brought about by Perestroika in the late 1980s effectively ended the reign of math and physics as the most important disciplines, thus facilitating redistribution of attention and resources across multiple domains in arts and sciences (Donoghue, Karp, & Vogeli, 2000). Perestroika also brought along fundamental political and economic changes that eventually resulted in the collapse of the Soviet regime and long-lasting crisis and economical instability in the country. In the late 1990s, the political situation stabilized but the economic insecurity and strain continues to be the leitmotif in public education and multiple areas of social services even now.

On the bright side, the crisis in the federal support of education resulted in a redistribution of power and priorities in the educational system as a whole and gifted education in particular. Parents and children themselves have become both far more involved and empowered than before with regard to issues of schooling (Y. Gatanov, personal communication, September 12, 2003). As the child's personal needs have taken center stage, parents, teachers, and the state are recognizing and gaining an appreciation for the professional roles that psychologists may and do play in children's psychoeducational development. Psychologists are often invited to consult with schools on reforming their curricula and optimizing their programs for gifted children. Consequently, psychological science faces a need to meet the demand and provide sound recommendations for identification and education of gifted children.

This chapter attempts to address questions of identifying, educating, and caring for gifted children by capitalizing on Russian psychological science and its past and present accomplishments in the field of gifted and talented research. First, based on works of multiple Russian psychologists, a systemic multidimensional model of giftedness is introduced. The model integrates extant Russian psychological research, extends available conceptualizations, and suggests directions for future research. Next, we describe current practices for the identification and education of the gifted and talented in Russia. Finally, the chapter introduces suggestions for best practices for assessment of achievement in gifted individuals and projections for future research in the field.

PROPOSED SYSTEMIC MULTIDIMENSIONAL MODEL OF GIFTEDNESS

To facilitate the discussion of defining, identifying, and developing giftedness in Russia, we propose an integrated model of giftedness. The model rests on two major notions: the notion of qualitative differences between processes and products involved in giftedness and the notion of congruence (internal and external).

Process-related variables include cognitive, physiological, genetic, emotional, and motivational factors that make up the potential of a given child. *Product-related* variables include performance or behaviors in any given domain. Whether a given process variable is translated into superior performance (i.e., the product-related variable) depends on the degree of *internal congruence* or compatibility between that variable and other variables (e.g., superior intellectual functioning may be offset by extreme anxiety), as well as on the degree of *external congruence* in terms of the environmental demand for the underlying process variables (i.e., person–environment fit) and environmental support when the potential is realized. The person–environment fit will determine if the executed performance is recognized as superior, the kind of feedback it generates, and/or the possibility of future opportunities for performance.

Internal and external congruence may be the necessary conditions contributing to the *resilience* of gifted individuals. It is possible that only resilient gifted children grow to become gifted adults. Whether the nature of resilience in gifted individuals is different from that in mainstream individuals is an empirical question, the answer to which may help us to develop programs for gifted children that will help them become gifted adults.

The present model defines giftedness in dialectical terms (i.e., appreciating the coexistence and tension between genetic and environmental factors contributing to the formation of a talent), thus viewing giftedness as a product of dynamic person–environment interactions. The personal, internal level consists of cognitive processes (e.g., memory, imagination), personality factors (e.g., motivation, self-regulation), and developmental characteristics. The environmental, external level consists of culture, societal expectations and standards, educational opportunities, and so on. The model, however general, permits contextualization of the work of Soviet/Russian psychologists. Specifically, within the framework of this model, we present the existing theoretical and empirical work of Soviet/Russian psychologists through a discussion of the following factors: (a) type and extent of manifestation (general and domain-specific giftedness; actual and potential giftedness; covert and overt giftedness); (b) creativity and giftedness; (c) the developmental dimension; (d) the personality dimension; and (e) the sociocultural dimension.

Presentation of each factor and dimension is followed by the discussion of its implications for the identification and education of gifted children in the context of the model presented here. Particular attention is paid to the roles of various subsystems involved in child development (e.g., family, schools, organizations providing options for after-school activities, and community).

INTERNAL PROCESS VARIABLES

General and Domain-Specific Giftedness

The concept of general giftedness encompasses several assumptions. First, many psychologists working in the field of giftedness considered an existence of a cluster of general mental abilities that could be applied to different domains; the existence of such a cluster was a "prerequisite" for giftedness (Teplov, 1985). Presence of such general giftedness is evidenced by the fact that gifted individuals are rarely gifted in only one area. History provides an abundance of examples when gifted and famous individuals displayed superior performance in multiple areas. For example, Alexander Borodin, a famous 19th-century Russian composer, was also a productive researcher in chemistry.

Teplov (1985) argued that contemporary societies have drifted in the direction of high fragmentation and specialization in terms of utilization of human intellect. As a result, many gifted individuals are never asked to use their abilities in more than one area (usually their strongest area). It would be a mistake, however, to expect every gifted student in a particular domain to be *globally gifted* or gifted in every other domain. Every gifted individual has a profile of abilities with unique patterns of relative and absolute strengths and weaknesses. Although it is reasonable to provide opportunities for advanced stimulation in multiple domains, it is unrealistic to expect equally superior performance in all domains. The idea that once an individual displays superior abilities in one domain this individual may also demonstrate superior abilities in other domains brings us to the notion of potential giftedness.

Actual and Potential Giftedness. Russian psychologists and educators distinguish between giftedness that is already evident through performance and giftedness that is present as potential (Babayeva & Voiskunovskiy, 2003; Leitis, 2000). Actual giftedness may be demonstrated through achievements in a given domain(s) that are extraordinary relative to one's peers and/or to the established experts in the domain(s). Potential giftedness, on the other hand, refers to one's potential and/or predisposition for extraordinary achievement (Leitis, 1996).

Various researchers and practitioners call for attention to the overall psychological maturity of an individual and his/her functioning in spheres other than the scholastic. There is qualitative evidence that superior performance in extracurricular activities (e.g., clubs for young scientists) often translates into superior performance in real-life tasks (e.g., on the job) (Kolgomogorov, 2001b; Yurkevitch, 1996). Thus, formal schooling may not always provide the stimulation and conditions for giftedness to mature and reveal itself.

Although it is hard to overestimate the significance of developing sensitive measures of assessing potential giftedness, it may be just as important to develop measures for recognizing gifted performance that takes on unusual forms. There is a difference between potential giftedness and giftedness that is expressed but not recognized. Often it is only in retrospect that we recognize that a given individual's performance was gifted or that a given child's seemingly peculiar ways of expressing himself or herself were in fact markers of upcoming brilliant achievement.

Overt and Covert Giftedness. Giftedness may often be masked by multiple external (e.g., social, economic) and internal factors (e.g., uneven development across psychoemotional domains). For example, Albert Einstein was not considered to be gifted as a child. He engaged in solitary, repetitive play, was uninterested in formal learning, and appeared to be immature for his age (Gardner, 1993). It is very possible that he was gifted as a child, but that his giftedness was masked by peculiar behaviors and thus went unrecognized.

Myths about gifted children often contribute to the manifestation, perception, and identification of a covert state of giftedness (e.g., Yurkevitch, 1996). One such myth claims that gifted individuals always display superior speed in mental operations. Consequently, "slow" gifted children are (a) rarely identified as gifted, or (b) presented with additional resources and challenging tasks. Covertly gifted individuals present atypical patterns of abilities and skills that the environment fails to recognize as outstanding. Consequently, the environment may attempt to "fix" the atypical pattern and, hence, may introduce additional stress and barriers.

Recognition of the concept of covert giftedness has significant implications for teacher education. Educational professionals must be trained to remain open-minded in their work with children so they do not "lose slowly developing great minds" (Kolmogorov, 2001a, p. 105). From this point of view, accelerated educational programs for gifted children may not necessarily advance their gifts. The exploration of and experimentation with the world by means of fantasy and creativity so typical of young children and so frequently observed in covertly gifted individuals may serve the critical function of preparing them for later tasks of assimilation and accommodation of formal information via formal means of schooling (Vygotsky, 2000).

Children's ability to engage their imagination and to create may serve multiple functions, one of which is self-regulation of affect and mental energy. Many Russian researchers and clinicians (e.g., Leitis, 2000; Scheblanova, 1998) firmly believe that creativity plays one of the central roles in the development of gifted individuals. To some extent, engagement in creative processes is an acceptable way to regress into childlike states, to blur the established rules and limits, and to go beyond "average" or "normal" (Kolmogorov, 2001a). We discuss the relationship between giftedness and creativity in more depth in the following section.

Giftedness and Creativity

The construct of creativity has attracted much attention in contemporary Russian psychological science. Although there is no clear consensus among Russian psychologists regarding specific roles of creativity in identifying and developing giftedness, there is unanimous recognition of its significance in the educational process of all children and in gifted children in particular (e.g., Bogoyavlenskaya, 1999; Matiyushkin, 1990).

It may be helpful to examine whether creativity is a necessary condition for superior intellectual functioning and whether gifted individuals engage in thinking that is "creative" from the point of view of a regular person. In other words, intellectually gifted individuals may not engage in creative thinking when they are thinking. Maybe when, by their own standards, they do engage in creative thinking, the process and products of gifted creative thinking are so far beyond a regular person's capacities for processing that such ideas or products may be considered bizarre.

In the next section, we introduce the developmental dimension of giftedness, which partly addresses why some gifted children do not grow up to be gifted adults and why some gifted adults were not gifted as children.

Developmental Dimension

Leitis (2000) addresses the construct of giftedness from a developmental perspective. He questions the utility of a unidimensional definition of giftedness as general cognitive ability and focuses on *sensitive periods* that predispose individuals to actualizing various abilities at different periods of the life span. According to Leitis, specific developmental characteristics may evoke otherwise dormant abilities. For example, many Russian teachers and parents encounter a so-called late bloomer phenomenon in teenagers. The phenomenon refers to a situation in which some students previously performing intellectually at average and even below-average levels begin demonstrating superior performance once they transition from one developmental period to the next. Leitis hypothesizes that the adolescent tendency to self-reflect, the need to define oneself, and the need to gain control over oneself might contribute to the restructuring of priorities and interests and leads to the elevation of abilities.

Leitis relies extensively on longitudinal observational methods and case studies as his mode of inquiry. His conclusions draw particular attention to the problem of assessing and making prognoses about one's level of abilities. Specifically, his work clearly delineates possible routes of under-identification and misalignment of educational goals with developmental tasks for gifted children in early schooling, when identification is typically carried out (Leitis, 2000).

Kholodnaya (1993) examines middle-age productivity and conceptualizes giftedness as intellectual maturity similar to wisdom. She, too, criticizes traditional approaches to intellectual assessment as inherently limited and deficit-oriented. Intellectual tests measure cognitive processes (e.g., memory) and do not measure one's level of maturity of interpretations of events (i.e., wisdom). Thus, traditional tests would not reflect the intellectual attainments made in middle age because many of the attainments are due to continuous accommodation and assimilation of life experiences – that is, wisdom.

Giftedness as a Personality Trait

More and more Russian psychologists (Bogoyavlenskaya & Schadrikov, 2000) recognize that giftedness and creativity cannot be separated from personality characteristics and viewed as purely cognitive characteristics. Particular attention is devoted to the dynamics between achievement motivation and intellect, and affect and intellect (e.g., Kholodnaya, 1993; Tikhomirov, 1984).

Motivational characteristics such as achievement motivation and attributional styles are believed to play critical roles in how one's giftedness unfolds and reveals itself. Yurkevitch (1996) postulates that *potrebnost' poznat'* ("the need to learn") is the vehicle that determines the level and the trajectory of development of intellectual giftedness. Among other personality characteristics believed to be associated with giftedness are: (a) intrinsically motivated elevated levels of selective attention to certain aspects of various activities (e.g., sounds, symbols) and/or certain aspects of one's own activities (e.g., physical, cognitive, artistic); (b) a pronounced need and desire to excel accompanied by great dedication, perseverance, and work ethics; (c) a great intellectual curiosity and ability to "think outside the box"; (d) a high tolerance of and preference for unknown, ambiguous, and contradictory evidence; and (e) high internal standards, a drive to excel, and a need for challenge (Bogoyavlenskaya & Shadrikov, 2000).

Synergy of these characteristics may culminate in a person's elevated performance level. Furthermore, these characteristics may help individuals reform their environment to create optimal conditions for self-actualization. Although some of these traits may be common to gifted individuals across different cultures, the actual behavioral expressions of these traits are likely to be culturally determined. The next dimension we discuss considers culture as one of the key determinants of giftedness.

EXTERNAL VARIABLES

Cultural Dimension

Cultural and societal environmental factors often play a critical role in what becomes recognized as giftedness and what opportunities are created for gifted individuals. Stetzenko (1997) has been expanding Vygotsky's socio-cultural approach to giftedness in that she recognizes that culture is not just an external factor that impacts individuals, but is also an internal factor. Individuals create culture as they live it. Culture is to a large extent internalized by its members across multiple generations (e.g., archetypes) and so it becomes part of psychological processes (cognitive and emotional). Culture also provides internal tools for development (e.g., thinking patterns). This line of inquiry implies a dynamic nature of reciprocity in culture–person–environment relationships and has been discussed and utilized by Talyzina (1975) and Gal'perin (1985) in their research. Socio-cultural approaches to giftedness may be one of the unique contributions of Russian psychological science to the conceptualization of giftedness. Further empirical research in this direction is needed to identify mechanisms by which gifted individuals utilize their culture and if and how culture shapes giftedness.

In sum, contemporary Russian psychological science recognizes the complexity of socioemotional as well as intellectual development in the gifted and strives to build up resilience throughout the pedagogical process. Traditionally, both culturally and societally, Russian educational and psychological sciences have distinguished and supported gifted individuals. This is true as well today. Timely identification and recognition of abilities is one of the many steps in creating a supportive environment for gifted individuals. The next step is to provide the individual with opportunities to mature, harness, and apply his gifts. In other words, environmental conditions need to be manipulated to enhance person–environment fit. In the next sections, we discuss diagnostic and educational practices for gifted youths used in Russia.

IDENTIFICATION OF GIFTED CHILDREN

Russian psychologists and educators distinguish between identifying gifted children and making a prognosis (prediction) for giftedness. The identification implies selection of gifted children from among children with very high levels of achievement (relative to the norm). The prognosis implies uncovering giftedness in children and providing them with optimal environmental conditions to elicit, nurture, and harness their gifts. There is recognition in the research and educational communities that the current, primary mode of operation is mere identification and selection based on already evident achievements (Bogoyavlenskaya & Schadrikov, 2000).

The 1990s were marked by an emergence of multiple trends in the assessment of giftedness and creativity in Russian psychology. In 1995, Scheblanova and Averina translated the figural form of the Torrance Tests (Torrance, 1974) of Creative Thinking from English into Russian (Dorfman, 2000). Russian versions of the Stanford–Binet, along with nonverbal measures of intelligence, such as the Cattell and the Raven Progressive Matrices, are widely used for screening and diagnostic purposes by clinicians and researchers (Y. Gatanov, personal communication, September 12, 2003). Despite prevalent use, it is not clear whether, when, and/or how these instruments were standardized in Russia and Russian norms were established.

Dorfman (2000) identified the following trends in Russia with regard to ability assessment: (a) critical evaluation and careful adaptation of existing Western instruments, and (b) the development of new instruments based on Russian theories (e.g., giftedness as wisdom, Kholodnaya, 1993; giftedness as personality structure, Merlin, 1986). According to parents, however, prestigious preschool and elementary school settings in Moscow and St. Petersburg are relying more and more on school psychologists and psychometric approaches (Western instruments that are not standardized to the current Russian population) in identifying potentially gifted students (Y. Gatanov, personal communication, September 12, 2003). Clearly, the idea here is to unify practices in the diagnosis and prognosis of giftedness by taking best from both worlds (i.e., Western and Russian psychological traditions) and training psychologists in the identification and development of giftedness.

Although aptitude testing and psychological assessment of giftedness and creativity are burgeoning innovations, criterion-referenced assessment of giftedness remains a tradition that continues to hold its ground. Olympiads are a time-honored tradition for showcasing giftedness.

Tradition: Olympiads and Performance-Based Assessment

Olympiads in various scholastic disciplines, festivals of children's art and creativity, young musicians' competitions, and other functions serve to reveal young talents. The selection procedure for such Olympiads is a statewide, multistep process that cuts across levels of school, district, and region. At each level, on the same day, cohorts of students take identical written assignments, which are then scored by a panel of judges. Finalists of the regional Olympiads participate in a nationwide round of the competition. Winners of the nationwide round usually compete for the national team and represent Russia in international Olympiads (Karp, 2003).

Since 1968, the Russian team has participated in 28 international physics Olympiads. During that time, the Russian team failed to make the top five only twice. Fifteen times, young Russian physicists took first place in individual competitions (Moscow Institute of Physics and Technology, 2003). In 2000, the Russian teams took second place in international Olympiads in physics and mathematics, losing to China by 3 and 2 points, respectively. Yet, Russian students took first places in individual competitions in both events (Moscow Institute of Physics and Technology, 2003).

Whereas the Soviet system was heavily invested in technocratic talents (Grigorenko, 1997), the post-Perestroika Russian system recognizes the need to support gifted and talented individuals in arts and humanitarian sciences and diversify its investment. For example, the festival *Isskustvo i Deti* ("Art and Children") is held annually. Young musicians, artists, poets, and other artistically talented children take part in this festival. Young people gifted in computer science, engineering, and architecture have their own annual convention where they present their work and meet leading specialists in their areas of interest (Presidential Program *Odarennye Deti* ["Gifted Children"], cited in Bogoyavlenskaya & Schadrikov, 2000). These functions allow gifted young people to share their achievements with others, meet interesting people, and network for future opportunities. What do these special opportunities entail? Following, we describe educational programs for the gifted that are currently in existence in Russia.

RUSSIAN EDUCATIONAL PROGRAMS FOR GIFTED

Specialized Secondary Schools

There are a few highly specialized boarding schools at the secondary level for gifted adolescents (12 years and up) in mathematics, science, and computer science. Students in specialized boarding schools for scholastic disciplines have very rigorous working schedules. For example, the school day at the Novosibirsk School for the mathematically gifted starts at 7:15 with breakfast. Classes begin at 8:30 a.m. and run until 9:25 p.m., with several short breaks for recreation and long breaks for meals in between (total recess time is 3 hours). Children retire to bed at 11:00 p.m. (Evered & Nayer, 2000).

Educational programs in boarding schools for the gifted follow enriched and/or accelerated models of regular education (Grigorenko, 1997). In addition to mandatory core courses, students are required to spend a significant number of hours in special seminars in their majors and additional hours in the humanities (Evered & Nayer, 2000). The students are expected to participate in Olympiads specific to their areas of giftedness and are oriented toward and prepared for receiving competitive prizes (see previous discussion). The graduates of these schools typically enter very prestigious universities in Russia (e.g., Moscow Physical-Technical Institute) and abroad because many of the schools have worldwide reputations (e.g., Donoghue, Karp, & Vogeli, 2000, report that more than 10 nations have now adopted the Russian system of specialized boarding schools for children with gifts in mathematics and physics).

Multidisciplinary Educational Programs for Gifted Children Aged 4–15

In this section, we discuss the model of the Moscow School *Sozvezdie* ("Constellation") to illustrate the methodological innovations for gifted education that are being examined in Russia (Shumakova, 1996).

Moscow School 1624, *Sozvezdie*, is a research site for a new educational methodology in gifted education. The experimental methodology, *Odarennyi Rebenok* ("Gifted Child"), is very different from traditional regular education and from accelerated enriched models for the gifted. It is an interdisciplinary and systemic program for children 4 through 15 years of age.

The proposed curriculum focuses on major philosophical themes. Each theme is defined in very general terms to allow for flexible adaptation of the materials to developmental and individual differences among pupils in any given class. The themes progress in a spiral rather than a linear order. The students are presented with interdisciplinary generalizations, for example: change can be beneficial and harmful; benefits and costs of changes are relative, so that one change can engender another change. The rationale for such an approach is that the interdisciplinary education for gifted children is believed to contribute to multidisciplinary application of their intellectual gifts.

The theoretical foundation for this educational model can be found in the theories of Vygotsky (2000), Elkonin (1989), and Davydov (1990) (typically referred to as the approach of developing education). The educational process in developing education is focused on enabling the learner to first develop conceptual understanding of a given subject matter (its blueprint) and then to teach the students the research skills so that they can independently work with various types of information within a given subject area outside of learning situations (Repkin & Repkina, 1997).

The instructional methodology used at *Sozvezdie* is similar to the Elkonin–Davydov model. However, *Sozvezdie* teaches the critical thinking skills and general constructs across various subject matters. Also, strategies for creative thinking are taught to the students, and they are expected to combine a high level of sophistication with high levels in creativity when they discuss interdisciplinary generalizations.

The first outcomes of *Sozvezdie* demonstrated that all children identified as gifted in this program increased their level of intellectual performance, whereas 30 percent of gifted children from programs that follow a traditional accelerated enrichment model showed a decrease in their intellectual performance. Overall, the proposed methodology was found to be superior to existing methodologies in terms of its impact on intellectual, motivational, creative, and academic functioning in students over a period of 8 years. Some of the significant results include increases in intrinsically motivated independent research activities among students.

Although *Sozvezdie* seems to produce encouraging results, it is still an experimental program, the long-term outcomes of which are yet to be evaluated. It is also a program that provides educational programming for gifted children from ages 4 to 15. There is no specific information as to how the graduates of this program will continue their education. The concern about continuing education and then employment for gifted individuals is shared by all the educational institutions for gifted children. Although the schools cannot change the realities of contemporary Russia, they can certainly integrate certain elements that prepare their graduates for transitions out of specialized settings into mainstream settings. For example, schools for gifted children intend to prepare their graduates for "real life" challenges by arranging for internships with research and consulting institutions where the students can apply their skills and test their readiness for the workplace. In addition, and particularly relevant to graduates of self-contained boarding schools, gifted students need to be empowered with knowledge and skills on how to transition from a "gifted" setting into the mainstream setting, how to cope with routine and mundane tasks at their future places of higher education and employment, and how to find application for their talents upon graduation. The latter is a challenging task for school psychologists, who need to receive specialized training for working with gifted children, adolescents, and adults.

CONCLUSIONS AND PROJECTIONS FOR FUTURE RESEARCH

Russian study of the gifted and talented has made significant unique theoretical contributions to the field. It conceptualizes giftedness as a multidimensional systemic phenomenon that may differ in form and nature across various developmental stages (e.g., heightened intellectual activity in early childhood as opposed to wise, meaningful, influential, and oriented toward the common good in middle age). Hence, Russian psychology does not commit to understanding giftedness as a gift provided to a given individual in a given domain; it states that gifts can manifest themselves at different developmental stages across individuals and in multiple domains within an individual.

Although descriptive and qualitative research into this conceptualization of giftedness has provided a wealth of information, the gap between research and practices in identifying and educating gifted children has been bridged only in a few instances (e.g., project *Sozvezdie*). With the growing emphasis on the personal growth of gifted children, psychologists and educators must be trained to meet the psychosocial needs of gifted children as well as their intellectual needs. Resilience of gifted individuals needs to be increased by means of psychosocial and educational interventions with children and their immediate environment. Furthermore, there is a particularly strong need for empirical research and for developing and validating measures for various dimensions of giftedness in Russian language with representative Russian standardization samples (e.g., Bogoyavlenskaya, 2000; Dorfman, 2000).

In a prior edition of this volume, Grigorenko (1997) identified four major challenges facing Russian programs for gifted and talented. First and foremost, there exists significant financial strain and lack of funds to support day-to-day operations of programs for the gifted. Second, there is a lack of specialized training for teachers of the gifted and talented. Third, there is a lack of a unified theoretical paradigm driving the education for gifted and talented. Fourth, there is Russia's lack of ability to engage and retain its gifted individuals. At present, we can report the changes that have taken place regarding retaining the brain power in the country. Specifically, institutions of higher education began to provide their students and graduates with employment opportunities by connecting them with various research and consulting employment opportunities in Russia and abroad (Moscow Institute of Physics and Technology, 2003). Even when graduates work abroad, they do so with a contract and do not immigrate.

The other two challenges (lack of specialized training and lack of a unified theoretical paradigm) remain strong despite the collective efforts of psychologists, educators, parents, and policy makers. There are still no (or a very limited number of) newly educated teachers prepared to work with gifted children. In addition, the number of newly developed programs and curricula for gifted and talented education is limited; and these innovations are not well tested or not tested at all. Russia sustained the collapse of an old political and economic system but is still in process of building a new system. Until the society at large stabilizes and develops a solid infrastructure of social policies, among which education should be (but currently is not) ranked as a No. 1 priority, it may be unrealistic to expect significant progress in creating a new public nationwide system for gifted education in Russia.

In sum, Russia's gifted children are living through interesting, challenging, and changing times. As a result, they may be presented with opportunities to develop their gifts and mature in educational settings that will address their intellectual, emotional, and personal needs with equal respect. The new generation of gifted Russian children can reflect the changed culture in how they display and apply their gifts but if, and only if, the state sets policies that facilitate the support of education and gifted education in particular.

ACKNOWLEDGMENT

Preparation of this essay was supported by Grant REC-9979843 from the National Science Foundation and by a grant under the Javits Act Program (Grant No. R206R00001) as administered by the Institute for Educational Sciences, U.S. Department of Education. Grantees undertaking such projects are encouraged to express freely their professional judgment. This chapter, therefore, does not necessarily represent the position or policies of the National Science Foundation, the Institute for Educational Sciences, or the U.S. Department of Education, and no official endorsement should be inferred. We express our gratitude to Ms. Robyn Rissman for her editorial assistance. The contact addresses for the authors are Dr. Ida Jeltova, Fairleigh Dickinson University, Metropolitan Campus, School of Psychology, School Psychology Program, 1000 River Road, WH-1, Teaneck, New Jersey 07666 (or via jeltova@fdu.edu), and Dr. Elena L. Grigorenko, Yale University, PACE Center, 340 Edwards Street, PO Box 208358, New Haven, CT 06520–8358 (or via elena.grigorenko@yale.edu).

References

Babayeva, Yu. D., & Voiskunovskiy, A. E. (2003). Odarennyi rebenok za komp'yuterom. [Gifted child behind the computer.] Ministry of Education of Russian Federation: Presidential program "Children of Russia."

Bogoyavlenskaya, D. B. (1999). "Sub'ekt" deyatel'nosti v problematike tvortchestva. [Subject and activity in creativity.] Voprosy Psikhologii, 2, 35–41.

Bogoyavlenskaya, D. B., & Shadrikov, V. D. (Eds.) (2000). Odarennost': Rabotchaya kontzeptziya. Ezhegodnyk Rossiiskogo psikhologitcheskogo obstchestva (Vol. 8, part 1) [Giftedness: Working definition]. Annual Report of Russian Psychological Society.

Davydov, V. V. (1990). Teoriya razvivayutchego obutcheniya. [Theory of developing education.] Moscow: Pedagogika.

Donoghue, E. F., Karp. A., & Vogeli, B. R. (2000). Russian schools for mathematically and scientifically talented: Can the vision survive unchanged? Roeper Review, 22, 121–128.

Dorfman, L. (2000). Research on gifted children and adolescents in Russia: A Chronicle of theoretical and empirical development. Roeper Review, 22, 123–152.

El'konin, D. B. (1989). Psykhologiya obutcheniya mladshikh shkol'nikov [Educational psychology of elementary school children]. Moscow: MGU.

Evered, L. J., & Nayer, S. (2000). Novosibirsk's school for the gifted – changing emphases in the new Russia. Roeper Review, 23, 22–27.

Gal'perin, P. Ya. (1985). *Metody obuchenia i umstvennoe razvitie rebenka* [Methods of learning and child intellectual development]. Moscow: MGU.

Gardner, H. (1993). Creating minds: An anatomy of creativity seen through lives of Freud, Einstein, Picasso, Stravinsky, Elliot, Graham, and Gandhi. New York: Basic Books.

Grigorenko, E. L. (1997). Russian gifted education in technical disciplines: Tradition and transformation. In K. A. Heller, F. J. Monks, R. J. Sternberg, & R. F. Subotnik (Eds.). *International handbook of research and development of giftedness and talent* (pp. 729–736) Amsterdam: Elsevier.

Karp, A. (2003). Thirty years after: The lives of former winners of Mathematical Olympiads. *Roeper Review, 25*, 83–92.

Kholodnaya, M. A. (1993). Psykhologitcheskie mechanismy intellektual'noi odarennosti. [Psychological mechanisms of intellectual giftedness.] *Voprosy Psikhologii, 1*, 32–39.

Kolmogorov, A. N. (2001a). O razvitii matematitcheskich sposobnostei (pis'mo Krutetzkomu) [Regarding development of abilities in Mathematics (letter to Krutetzskoi)]. *Voprosy Psikhologii, 3*, 103–107.

Kolmogorov, A. N. (2001b). Otvety A.V. Kolmogorova na voprosy ankety o problemach razvitiya mathematicheskikh sposobnostei [Kolmogrov's responses to "Phenomenon of mathematical abilities" survey]. *Voprosy Psikhologii, 3*, 101–103.

Kondrat'yev, M. Yu. (1995). Osobennosti mezhlitchnostnykh otnoshenyi v professional'nych spetzializirovannykh internatakh. [Defining features of interpersonal dynamics in self-contained specialized boarding schools.] *Voprosy Psikhologii, 6*, 33–37.

Leitis, N. S. (Ed.) (1996). *Psykhologiya odarennosti detei i podrostkov* [Psychology of gifted children and adolescents]. Moscow: Academic Press.

Leitis, N. S. (2000). *Vozrastnaya odarennost' shkol'nikov* [Developmental giftedness in school children]. Moscow: Academia.

Matiyushkin, A. M. (1990). A Soviet perspective on giftedness and creativity. *European Journal for High Ability, 1*, 72–75.

Merlin, V. S. (1986). Otcherk integral'nogo issledovaniya individual'nosti. [Essay on integral examination of personality.] Moscow: Pedagogika

Moscow Institute of Physics and Technology (2003). Information obtained from www.mipt.ru.

Phyztech's Educational Approach. Retrieved on September 10, 2003, from http://www.mipt.ru/eng/questions/approach.

Repkin, V. V., & Repkina, N. V. (1997). *Sistema razvivayutchego obutcheniya: Proekt i real'nost'.* [System of developing education: Project and reality.] Riga, Latvia: International Association for Developing Education.

Scheblanova, E. I. (1998). Dinamika kognitivnykh i nekognitivnykh litchnostnykh pokazatelei odarennosti u mladshikh shkol'nikov. [Characteristics of non-cognitive and motivational development of gifted elementary school students.] *Voporsy Psikhologii, 4*, 111–122.

Shumakova, N. B. (1996). Mezhditziplinarnyi podkhod k obutcheniyu odarennykh detei. [Interdisciplinary approach in gifted education.] *Voporsy Psikhologii, 7*, 34–43.

Stetzenko, A. P. (1997). Sociokul'turnaya paradigma v izutchenii odarennosti: nedostayutshie zven'ia. [Sociocultural paradigm of giftedness: Missing links.]

In D. B. Bogoyavlenskaya (Ed.). *Osnovnye sovremennye kontzeptzii tvortchestva i odarennosti.* [Contemporary conceptualizations of giftedness and creativity.] Moscow: Molodaya Gvardiya.

Talyzina, N. F. (1975). Upravlenie protsessom usvoenia znania [Management of learning]. Moscow: Pegagogika.

Teplov, B. M. (1985). Psykhophyziologiya individual'nykh razlitchiy. [Psychophysiology of individual differences.] In B. M. Teplov, Izbrannye trudy, tom 2. [Collected Works, 2nd volume.] Moscow: Pedagogika.

Tikhomirov, O. K. (1984). *Psikhologiya myshleniya* [Psychology of thinking]. Moscow: MGU.

Torrance, E. P. (1974). Torrance tests of creative thinking: Norms – technical manual. Princeton, NJ: Personnel Press.

Vygotsky, L. S. (2000). *Psikhologiya.* [Psychology]. Moscow: Exmo-Press.

Yurkevitch, V. S. (1996). *Odariennyi rebenok: illyuzii i real'nost'.* [Gifted child: Illusions and reality.] Moscow: Prosvetshenie.

11

Giftedness and Gifted Education

Franz J. Mönks and Michael W. Katzko

WHAT IS GIFTEDNESS?

Most disciplines of psychology have had difficulties with defining their technical terms, and the situation is no different with the term "giftedness." A definition should give a formal and concise description of the meaning of a concept or construct. Unfortunately, the scientific language of psychology is full of words inherited from everyday language and terms such as *giftedness* are not only linked to synonyms like "high ability," "aptitude," or "talent" but each term can assume different meanings. These meanings carry a long history of cultural use, "folk" wisdom, and/or misconception. Furthermore, a concise definition is almost impossible because the context within which the definition is made may refer to a process, key elements of giftedness, provisions for the gifted, or education of the gifted. In addition, it is not easy completely to separate theoretical and practical concepts because adherence to a theory of giftedness determines one's research and educational approaches.

If all this was not bad enough, the meanings are tainted by an emotionalism that seems to engulf the concept of giftedness. For example, in German the word for giftedness can be *begabung* or *hochbegabung*. The connotation with *hochbegabung* can be value laden, associating giftedness with elitism. A similar situation exists in French (*doués* or *surdoués*) and in Spanish (*dotado* or *superdotado*). Such a connotation evokes emotional reactions and negative feelings that have hampered worldwide progress in educating the gifted (Williams & Mitchel, 1989).

As a first step it is probably better to worry less about the words and focus more on the conceptual task of making important and meaningful distinctions. In general, four main groups of definitions of giftedness can be found in the literature (Hany, 1987). Two refer to psychological constructs (trait-oriented models and cognitive component models), a third focuses on achievement and performance, and the fourth takes an

environmental view. Each of these types of definitions can be closely interrelated as four strands of historical development that have been slowly
converging over the years. Within these strands three key ideas can be
seen to underlie the use of the term *giftedness*. These concern the *domain
specification*, the notion of *quantitative level*, and the notion of *potential* or
latency.

We can begin with the simplest approach. Representatives of the *trait-
oriented* approach consider giftedness to be a relatively stable personality
trait, not dependent on the environment, historical period, or socioeconomic condition. This approach reflects the "describe and classify" task of
science. Within the context of assessment, this is a logical course to take.
However, in this context, the term *giftedness* does not adequately separate the notion of domain from the notion of quantitative difference. Thus,
the meaning of giftedness has been more or less equivalent to high (i.e.,
quantitative level) intelligence (i.e., domain specification). For example,
the pioneer of psychological testing and of the study of giftedness, Lewis
Terman (1877–1956), saw intelligence as a unitary inherited trait and identified giftedness with an IQ score of 135 or higher. He was convinced that
intelligence and thus giftedness was biologically determined. This g-factor
theory goes back to the English scientist Spearman. Gardner calls this the
"hedgehog" position, compared with the "fox" position, in which multiple factors according to Thurstone determine our intellectual achievements
(Gardner, 1983).

It is interesting to note that, for his doctoral research, Terman followed
the Thorndike position, that is, there is not just one g factor but rather
multiple factors (Minton, 1988). But he later shifted to the one-factor or
the g-factor theory of intelligence. For good reasons, from his perspective:
(1) Intelligence, measured with an intelligence test, is genetically determined and therefore permits the possibility to predict later achievements,
and (2) the genetic or innate origin of one factor is easier to study thoroughly than more factors. As another example, the German psychologist
Rost (1991, 1993) picks up where Terman started. Rost focuses on intelligence as the main factor for the identification of giftedness. His longitudinal
study is guided by the overemphasis of intelligence and its stability over
time. We could say "history repeats itself."

Perhaps ironically, the empirical findings of Terman's own longitudinal
research, which he started in 1921–1922 and that is still ongoing, changed
his trait orientation. Two years before he died, he came to the conclusion
that personality strength and a supportive environment are irreplaceable
(see Terman, 1954).

The more recent historical advance is to distinguish more clearly between the domain issue and the quantitative difference. The term *gifted*
maintains the implication of quantitative difference but is now generalized
to a wider range of domains, with intelligence being only one special case.

This can be seen in several writers attempting to identify a wider range of ability domains. Gardner (1999), for example, describes eight types of intelligences. At the other extreme, Gagné (1995) has described 40 descriminable ability domains. The assumption in all these cases is that individuals may differ both in terms of the domain and the quantitative level within each domain.

But description and classification are only the first step in scientific advancement. Whatever the pragmatic value of the psychometric or assessment approach to giftedness is, it has lacked theoretical substance in providing meaning to the term *giftedness*. For example, Terman's assessment criterion of an IQ above 135 is about as useful as saying that "hot" means a temperature above 30 degrees Celsius: It begs the question regarding the meaning of the dimension along which the quantitative assessment has been made. The *cognitive component approach* is aimed at providing a correction to this theoretical shortcoming. This approach produces a more detailed analysis of the mental or information processing that presumably underlies assessment scores. Here, it is not the quantifiable results of testing that are important but the way in which they are the outcome of psychological processes. Rüppell, Hinnersmann, and Wiegand (1986), representatives of this orientation, propose to replace IQ with QI (Quality of Information) processing.

The cognitive component approach can be broadened to include models such as Renzulli's (1978) "ring" model or any other model that attempts to analyze giftedness into components that include at least intelligence, creativity, and motivation. We must remember that the issue here is not so much where one places concepts such as intelligence versus creativity. The important theoretical advance is that a more analytic approach is taken in analyzing a multicomponent processing approach. It will be noted that this approach is logically neutral with regard to the domain issue, even though, traditionally, the domain has been "intelligence."

This introduces the third major idea that underlies the use of the term *giftedness*: A distinction is made between potential and realized performance. Almost a century ago, William Stern (1916) concluded that giftedness is only a potential for good or outstanding performances. An *achievement-oriented model* explicitly distinguishes accomplishments and achievements as observable output of mental processes. It is clear that this distinction between potential versus performance is a logical correlate of the more analytic or cognitive approach in that it makes explicit the distinction between process and product. For the purpose of gifted programs, this distinction is helpful. For example, the underachiever is characterized by a discrepancy between potential and performance. He or she, for whatever reason, is not able to demonstrate what is in accordance with the individual abilities. Identification of the reasons behind the discrepancy provides the opportunity for intervention.

Once this distinction has been made, the *environmental or socio-cultural model* is the logical consequence. The potential versus performance distinction now allows the researcher to raise questions about inhibitors and facilitators of the process potential. Such models consider the "Zeitgeist" as a main steering component in performance quality.

In summary, the research and program provisions literature is currently dominated by descriptive and categorical approaches that fit the first type of definition, as well as an emphasis on the third definition fitting an applied approach in educational settings. However, we can expect that, as the analytic approaches become more advanced, reflected in cognitive information-processing models, they will subsume the approaches of the first type. Such types of definitions are logically consistent with definitions of the third type. The fourth type of definition, with its emphasis on socio-economic and political concerns, will increasingly affect the availability and planning of programs for the gifted rather than purely theoretical research on the gifted.

HOW DOES OUR CONCEPTION OF GIFTEDNESS COMPARE WITH OTHER CONCEPTIONS?

With these distinctions in mind, it should be clear that differences among researchers are, to a certain extent, a matter of relative emphasis on one or more of the three main ideas within a particular pure or applied research concern. Our own conception of giftedness has arisen out of a background in developmental psychology. Human development is regarded as the result of the interaction between individual characteristics and environmental conditions and is an ongoing and lifelong process.

The notion of development naturally is concerned with the idea of *potential*, that there are genetic factors that give initial shape to mental aptitudes, personality, and other behavioral characteristics. However, the further development of these factors is dependent on an environment that includes social, ecological, familial, social, political, and geographical aspects. These environmental conditions can facilitate or inhibit the development of individual potential. But only the manifest behavioral performance can show how able a person is. In the final analysis, our emphasis has been on optimizing the achievements of individual performance.

A definition that strongly emphasizes personality traits, neglecting the interactive nature of human development, does little justice to the dynamic interplay of developmental processes. A multidimensional approach, including personality and social components as determining factors, seems to be the appropriate framework. As our own developmental concerns have had an applied and educational emphasis, our theoretical interests have not emphasized the domain issue. Also, although not being concerned with a detailed cognitive analysis, we have still emphasized a multicomponent approach for diagnostic purposes. For this reason, Mönks (1992)

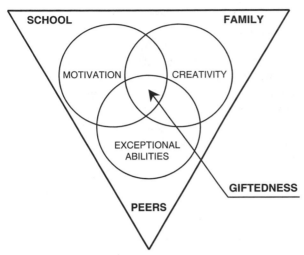

FIGURE 11.1. Multifactor model of giftedness (Mönks, 1986).

modified Renzulli's three-ring Model and included environmental components, resulting in the following Multifactor Model.

Figure 11.1 shows the Multifactor Model of Giftedness, with the three personality characteristics, *creativity, motivation,* and *outstanding/exceptional achievements,* and the three most significant social environments, *family, school,* and *peers.* Giftedness as expressed in outstanding accomplishments can only develop when there is a fruitful interaction among the various dimensions. Fruitful and positive interaction supposes *individual social competencies* (Mönks, 1992).

In summary, our working definition of giftedness can be summarized as follows: *Giftedness is an individual potential for exceptional or outstanding achievements in one or more domains.* This definition reflects our concern for practical, educational issues in a developmental context.

HOW SHOULD GIFTED INDIVIDUALS BE IDENTIFIED?

Some decades ago, a great deal of controversy surrounded the issue of identification. Bartenwerfer (1978) was a strict opponent of identification. He argued that if you do not know what giftedness is, you cannot identify it. Today, there is no doubt that identification is important. From an educational perspective, if we follow the principle that all individuals are to be given the opportunity to develop fully their potential and talent, then identification is essential. The main tasks are (1) the identification of gifted individuals for appropriate nurturing, and (2) individual diagnosis for specific individual programs. But identification is also important from a societal perspective because there is a growing public awareness that gifted people form a significant resource in society. Worldwide efforts to identify gifted children and to give them appropriate programs can be seen as an expression of this objective.

In 1988 the Center for the Study of Giftedness was established at Radboud University Nijmegen. The frame of reference for research and also for the advisory work was the Multifactor Model, that is, giftedness is not identical to high IQ; there are always several personal and environmental factors involved. In the reports for parents and schools, the IQ will never be mentioned. We are convinced that a pure figure does not reflect the real potential of an individual. Only a multifaceted identification can give direction to appropriate gifted education.

It should be noted that identification always depends on the objective to be achieved. For example, a general screening methodology is different from an in-depth individual diagnosis. However, once one abandons the simplest notions of giftedness as a trait-like character in a single-ability domain, the task of identification of giftedness becomes problematic and complex for several reasons. One has to include a variety of cognitive as well as noncognitive personality characteristics and also take the social learning environment into account to be able to make a reliable judgment of individual development potential. Another problem is related to gender differences and minorities. For example, even though females are generally regarded as less able in the MINT subjects (mathematics, informatics, natural sciences, and technical sciences), the literature implies that there are no innate differences between males and females regarding these subject areas (Lubinski, Benbow, Shea, Eftekhari-Sanjani, & Halvorson, 2001). Finally, when different identification procedures are based on different theoretical positions, it can well be the case that a child identified as gifted by a multifactor approach may not be considered gifted in the light of a different model, such as the one-factor approach.

These considerations imply that identification should fulfill the following requirements:

(1) follow a theoretically based model of giftedness;
(2) meet high methodological standards (which diagnostic instruments can be used?); and
(3) take into account identification difficulties related to social preconceptions, for example, of minorities and women.

Recently, Ziegler & Stöger (2003) described the ENTER model for the identification of giftedness, referring to the Multifactor Model (Mönks, 1992) mentioned previously. ENTER is an acronym for explore, narrow, test, evaluate, and review. These five steps of identification can overlap. The first three steps refer to what Cattell called L-, Q-, and T-data: Life, Questionnaire, and Test (Ziegler & Stöger, 2003). The collection and the quality of data are the basis for identification. During the exploration phase, all kinds of anamnestic data are collected. How are the family life, early development of the child, school experiences, leisure time activities, and friends?

Depending on the questions of the parents, the objectives are narrowed. If the parents want to know more about motivation and intelligence, one can focus more on these behavior areas. What is important is that all factors of the model are always included in the first three steps.

Identification provides a varied view on the child's motivation and his or her social and cognitive abilities. The collected information and test results give direction to the evaluation phase, when the needed and appropriate provisions are made. It is important that the recommended programs are realistic. It does not make sense if programs are proposed that cannot be realized because a school does not have the teachers and the necessary equipment. Recommendations based on the results but necessary for future developments have to include proposals for educational provisions that are not out of reach.

Finally, the review phase continuously monitors both the reasons for the initial identification and the model of giftedness used in that identification. It is necessary to continuously review both because there has to be a "fit" or correspondence between the model of giftedness and the practical recommendations made in the evaluation phase. Otherwise, the model is not or is only partly in accordance with the detected behavior patterns.

This sort of identification process can be illustrated with the case history of 9-year-old John. John was the oldest child in the family, with a sister two years his junior. The parents came to our center for consultation because John hated to go to school, was only interested in computers and watching TV, and was endlessly fighting with his sister. Two years previously, his parents had taken John to a psychologist to have his abilities assessed and his behavioral problems diagnosed. The psychologist concluded that John was a highly gifted boy but that he needed play therapy to correct his behavioral problems. So when he came to us, he had already been receiving therapy for two years. When his mother was asked whether his behavior had changed in a positive or negative sense, she answered that there had been no change at all.

John was not very enthusiastic during his visit to the center for testing and diagnosis, which, in his opinion, was just a lot of stupid questions. Nonetheless, his scores on the subtests of the Wechsler intelligence scale varied from average to extremely high. He scored very high on arithmetic and the maximum on digit span. It was clear that numbers were his passion, and here he showed some real intrinsic motivation. It was also evident that he was only partially motivated and that, for him, a supportive school program had to start from these "healthy parts" of his personality. Our philosophy is that we have to start from substantial ground, that is, the area with most intrinsic motivation. Our intention was to "repair" his personality, especially his social behavior, by using the healthy parts.

We needed a school where John could work under the supervision of a teacher with a computer and where he would be accepted. This last point was extremely important because John was on his way to becoming a drop-out. A young teacher, a computer enthusiast, was willing to work with John to establish a program for young students. The intention was to allow John to learn and experience that it is reinforcing and satisfying to help other students. It soon became clear that John was much more skillful in handling the computer than the teacher. Four weeks after entering this new school, his mother called the center to say that John, in spite of the fact that he had to travel for more than an hour by bus every morning, was happy and liked going to school. Three years later, John was enrolled in and enjoying secondary school. He was very good in arithmetic and other subjects, and his social skills were reasonable. John is now 22 years old and completed a master's degree in informatics within one year. He is currently studying pure mathematics and is planning to receive a doctoral degree.

We can conclude that John's intrinsic motivation for the field of numbers and math was manifest in elementary school. Unfortunately, the school was neither able nor willing to meet his special needs. On the contrary, the school staff was happy when he left the school as we advised. The essential part of our treatment involved taking advantage of the defining features of his high ability (i.e., motivation for math), which is what was ultimately beneficial for John. Such an approach is often the only way to help gifted/creative individuals.

HOW SHOULD GIFTED INDIVIDUALS BE INSTRUCTED IN SCHOOL AND ELSEWHERE?

The core principle of gifted education is individualization and differentiation. Primary schools continue to be organized as age-graded classes, even though homogeneous age groups are heterogeneous regarding developmental and learning needs. In 1985, the kindergarten (ages 4–6) and the elementary school (ages 6–12) were integrated in The Netherlands. The Dutch Department of Education encouraged schools "to change from whole classroom teaching (teacher in front of class) to grouping procedures that might pay more respect to differences between students" (Reezigt, 1993, p. 153). But how can the elementary school meet the individual learning needs of all students – including the gifted – as much as possible? What can the so-called New School Movement contribute to this issue?

The origins of the New School Movement, also called the School Reform Movement, go back to the beginning of the 20th century. In 1900, the Swedish teacher and writer Ellen Key (1849–1926) published the groundbreaking book *The Century of the Child*. It advocated for the rights of the child and against the Old School of the 19th century, which focused mainly on intellectual training. The personality – and socioemotional development – of the child was neglected.

It is striking to see that the changes of school philosophy emerged at a similar time in Europe and the United States. The Progressive Movement in the United States, with leaders like Dewey, Burk, Washburn, and Parkhurst (see Semel, 1992) had a great impact on school reform in favor of the individual child. The New School Movement had the same direction but different leaders and approaches. Three types of New Schools were established: Montessori, Dalton, and Jena Plan elementary schools. The main objective was and is to serve the intellectual as well as the social and emotional needs of the child. To illustrate how they serve the learning and developmental needs of gifted children, the Jena Plan schools are described in some detail.

Jena Plan Schools

The German educator and scientist Peter Petersen (1884–1952) was one of the central leaders of the Reform Movement in Europe. In 1916, he was the editor of the book *Der Aufstieg der Begabten (The Rise of the Gifted)*. One of the contributors to the book was William Stern, professor of psychology at the University of Hamburg. Stern stated in his chapter that elementary schools need extended programs for the top 2 percent of talented students and the top 10 percent of gifted students. Today, "extended programs" are referred to as provisions for enrichment and acceleration.

In 1923, Petersen, as professor of education at the University of Jena (Germany), founded a laboratory school of which he was director till 1950. In that year, the school was closed by the then-socialist government, using the argument "we don't need an island of capitalistic education." This laboratory school became a place for the realization of new educational concepts and an important institution for teacher training. Petersen had never had the intention to establish a school for gifted students only. On the contrary, he wanted to integrate all levels of ability in one school. A geneticist colleague argued, however, that a university experimental school should enroll only gifted students (Retter, 1996). In reality, Petersen's concept was brilliant for gifted education on the elementary level. The working principles are as follows:

1. According to Petersen, the school should not be an institute only interested in and concentrating on intellectual training and progress. The emphasis on intellectual training of the old school (19th and beginning 20th century) required isolation from the normal life situation. Schools should be integrated in the social environment.
2. The unnatural age-graded class was replaced by the home group (Stammgruppe). Petersen argued that the age structure in school should be family-like, namely, heterogeneous. Like Montessori, there are three different levels: lower-, middle-, and upper-level. Within each level, there are three different age levels. This heterogeneous age grouping facilitates the natural learning process among the children.

3. *Instruction groups* are pull-out groups based on ability and level. Students from different home groups, but with similar achievement levels, are instructed in subjects like arithmetic, grammar, reading, and language. This principle shows that the revolving-door system already existed in the early 20th century.

4. In *table groups*, the students in the classroom are grouped around tables. Four or six students form a table group. There can be many reasons for such a grouping, and it can be changed twice or more during the year. However, the main purpose of these small groups is to facilitate social as well as cooperative learning and teamwork. The children may choose themselves, or the teacher may bring together good and slow learners.

5. Petersen was convinced that schools should reflect as much as possible *natural learning situations* in everyday life. Human communication and learning have four basic forms: conversation, play, work, and celebration. The curriculum of a week is organized according to these basic communication forms. Realization of these forms stimulates the feeling of social togetherness.

6. *Social learning* is emphasized. Students work together, play together, and talk with each other. However, special events are also celebrated, for example, the beginning and closing of the week, birthdays of classmates, and significant events in the lives of students.

It is evident that Jena Plan Schools are not established for only gifted education but for all levels of ability. There are Jena Plan Schools in many European countries, but the majority are in The Netherlands, which has more than 300 elementary Jena Plan Schools. However, the principles of differentiation and individualization are core elements of gifted education. It is only during the last decades that schools involved in the New School Movement are rediscovering the potential of their systems. They are able to serve the learning and developmental needs of all levels. We can conclude that gifted education existed in Europe since the beginning of the 20th century, but it was a "hidden curriculum."

HOW SHOULD ACHIEVEMENT OF GIFTED INDIVIDUALS BE ASSESSED?

When we examine the question of the assessment of achievement, that is, of production rather than potential, we must consider the issue of domains. In fact, when one thinks about assessing achievement across a variety of ability domains, an interesting dilemma appears to emerge.

Consider first a relatively uncontroversial domain of high achievement, such as sports. In this case, the benchmark for high achievement is typically an easily defined external standard, such as head-to-head competitions with peers and listed world records based on past performance. A similar situation exists in domains such as the performing arts. But we begin to see the roots of the dilemma when we consider artistic products such as music or painting. Even when we control for popularity in contrast to quality, it is nonetheless the case that the high-quality products of artistic gifts are not always easily or quickly recognized. Such individuals may be appreciated by only a few and so are labeled "ahead of their time." This reveals the problem that assessing achievement may under some circumstances be an act of social comparison. Even the record books in sports can be seen as a very literal record of such social norms, but that happen to be broadly accepted.

When we consider intellectual gifts, the latent conflict between the gifted person and the social standards against which his or her performance is to be assessed is frequently revealed historically. We previously mentioned that there is an aura of emotional evaluation latent in the meaning of the term *gifted*, and the evaluation is not always positive. For example, as a professor at the University of Hamburg in Germany, William Stern had a strong impact on theoretical and practical approaches to giftedness. But he and his colleagues were not able to fulfill their mission because the Zeitgeist of 1916 was not ready for this particular area of research and education. It is evident that the economic situation, political climate, and public opinion determine, to a great extent, whether the study of gift-edness and gifted education is seen as a priority. Giftedness and provi-sions for the gifted are defined and determined in the context of openness and real concern for the learning and developmental needs of gifted individuals.

It seems, therefore, that society has a habit of viewing high *intellectual* ability, the traditional definition of giftedness, as being threatening, per-haps threatening to the stable conventions of society itself. For this reason, intellectual innovation and achievement are so difficult to evaluate. This concern is deeply rooted in the study of giftedness. For example, "Terman was a man with a mission. Through his work as a psychologist he believed that he could contribute to the shaping of an American Society based on the principle of *meritocracy* – that is, the establishment of a hierarchical di-vision of labor that would commensurate with the distribution of ability in the population" (Minton, 1988, p. 225). Is it possible that a democratically organized society can accept meritocracy?

Meritocracy has two (opposite) sides. From one point of view, it guar-antees "equal chances for everybody" because the focus is on the achieve-ments (merits) of individuals and not on their descent. What counts are the abilities and performances of an individual. But from another point of view, it is an unquestionable fact that, as a consequence of (inborn) talents and hard work, some will succeed and will have success and others will not. Terman focused heavily on intelligence and the mea-surement of intelligence because he thought that intelligence tests would be the best instruments to realize a meritocratic structure of society. His mission was to build a meritocratic society based on differences in intelligence.

But the question is whether a society based on differences in intelligence would be in accordance with democratic principles, for example, "political fairness." In reality, Terman defended *elitism*. What he saw as an ideal societal structure was not in agreement with *egalitarianism*, the perspective that all human beings to a certain extent are equal. The publication of the *Bell Curve* by Herrnstein and Murray in 1994 provoked many critical reactions, mainly in the United States. They argued that differences in IQ underlie social differences and class structure. Their pessimistic view of the future was that a small group of intellectual elitists will get and keep the best positions in society. According to them, "small town communities" could be a remedy to overcome these negative consequences of elitism.

Henry's (1994) *In Defense of Elitism* shed a different light on this issue. There has been an ideological struggle between the values of elitism and egalitarianism for several decades, with the latter currently having the upper hand. Henry argued that there is only one logic for all societies that wish to improve, and this logic is that they need the better performers, the better experts, the better thinkers. Thus, elitism is necessary. This book actually gives an explanation of why Terman never could realize his ideal. There has been for decades in the United States and Europe an opposition between elitism and egalitarianism. According to Henry, egalitarianism has been winning this struggle. One of the consequences has been the deterioration of standards of excellence. A ridiculous interpretation of equal chances is the following example: A deaf woman was accepted to participate in a public speaking competition, with the consequence that the competition never took place. Henry argues that we are different by nature, we all have different gifts, and some are better than others. What is in fact different cannot be made equal by decree. He gives an example of why, at present, there is a decrease of standards of excellence. When he went to school and it was said, "He is an exceptional child," the only meaning was "He is very gifted." Today, the same expression means, "He is a learning disabled child" and "He needs special education."

Thus, the problem of assessing high achievement may rest finally on adjusting social standards for what is acceptable and required in domains of far greater importance than, for example, sports. People differ in many ways, and it follows that some individuals may be better or more capable at certain tasks than others: Some are smarter, some invest more effort in their activities, some learn more, some are more productive, and some are more difficult to replace. Society needs excellent lawyers, teachers, and physicians. We make a choice for a good medical doctor because of his performance and his merits. The logical consequence is that high standards of excellence in all domains are required if we are to balance society and not create imbalance.

References

Bartenwerfer, H. (1978). Identifikation der Hochbegabten. In K. J. Klauer (Ed.), *Handbuch der Plädagogischen Diagnostik* (Vol. 4, pp. 1059–1069). Düsseldorf: Schwann.

Gagné, F. (1995). Learning about the nature of gifts and talents through peer and teacher nominations. In M. W. Katzko & F. J. Mönks (Eds.), *Nurturing talent – Individual needs and social ability* (pp. 20–31). Assen, The Netherlands: Van Gorcum.

Gardner, H. (1983). *Frames of mind: The theory of multiple intelligences.* New York: Basic Books.

Gardner, H. (1999). *Intelligence reframed: Multiple intelligences for the 21st century.* New York: Basic Books.

Hany, E. A. (1987). *Modelle und Strategien zur Identifikation hochbegabter Schüler.* Unpublished doctoral dissertation, University of Munich, Germany.

Henry, W. A., III (1994). *In defense of elitism.* New York: Doubleday.

Herrnstein, R. J., & Murray, C. (1994). *The bell curve: Intelligence and class structure in American life.* New York: Free Press.

Lubinski, D., Benbow, C. P., Shea, D. L., Eftekhari-Sanjani, H., & Halvorson, M. B. (2001). Men and women at Promise for Scientific Excellence: Similarity not dissimilarity. *Psychological Science, 12,* 309–317.

Minton, H. L. (1988). *Lewis M. Terman – Pioneer in psychological testing.* New York: University Press.

Mönks, F. J. (1992). Development of gifted children: The issue of identification and programming. In F. J. Mönks & W. A. M. Peters (Eds.), *Talent for the future* (pp. 191–202). *Proceedings of the Ninth World Conference on Gifted and Talented Children.* Assen, The Netherlands: Van Gorcum.

Petersen, P. (Ed.). (1916). *Der Aufstieg der Begabten.* Leipzig, Germany: Teubner.

Reezigt, G. J. (1993). *Effecten van differentiatie op de basisschool [Effects of differentiation in elementary schools].* Groningen, The Netherlands: RION.

Renzulli, J. S. (1978). What makes giftedness? Reexamining a definition. *Phi Delta Kappan, 60,* 180–184, 261.

Retter, H. (1996). *Peter Petersen und der Jenaplan: Von der Weimarer Republik bis zur Nachkriegszeit.* Weinheim, Germany: Deutscher Studien Verlag.

Rost, D. H. (1991). Identifizierung von "Hochbegabung." *Zeitschrift für Entwicklungspsychologie und Pädagogische Psychologie, 23,* 197–231.

Rost, D. H. (1993). *Lebensumweltanalyse hochbegabter Kinder.* Göttingen, Germany: Hogrefe.

Rüppell, H., Hinnersmann, H., & Wiegand, J. (1986). QI instead of IQ: New tests for the prediction of exceptional problem solving abilities in mathematical–scientific–technological areas. Paper presented at the 6th World Conference on Gifted and Talented Children, Hamburg, Germany.

Semel, S. F. (1992). *The Dalton School: The transformation of a progressive school.* New York: Lang.

Stern, W. (1916). Psychologische Begabungsforschung und Begabungsdiagnose. In P. Petersen (Ed.), *Der Aufstieg der Begabten* (pp. 105–120). Leipzig, Germany: Teubner.

Terman, L. M. (1954). The discovery and encouragement of exceptional talent. *American Psychologist, 9,* 221–230.

Vygotsky, L. S. (1978). *Mind in society: The development of higher mental processes.* Cambridge, MA: Harvard University Press.

Williams, W. G., & Mitchell, B.G. (1989). *From Afghanistan to Zimbabwe: Gifted education in the world community.* New York: Peter Lang.

Ziegler, A., & Stöger, H. (2003). ENTER – Ein Modell zur Identifikation von Hochbegabten. *Journal für Begabtenförderung, 3,* 8–21.

12

The Importance of Contexts in Theories of Giftedness

Learning to Embrace the Messy Joys of Subjectivity

Jonathan A. Plucker and Sasha A. Barab

At a recent conference, a clinical psychologist who works with gifted students engaged the first author in an exciting and challenging conversation. As we discussed specific research and case studies involving gifted children, we realized that we were talking almost exclusively about the importance of context in defining and addressing giftedness. During the rest of the conference, we noticed the role of context in talent development in every session we attended. On the first author's return home, one question kept leaping into his mind: If the need to consider context comes up in most research sessions and so many practical applications, why don't we spend more time exploring its role in theories of giftedness? In this chapter, we explore the role of context in some classic and contemporary theories and models of giftedness, propose an alternative view, and explore the practical implications of that perspective.

HOW SHOULD WE CONCEPTUALIZE GIFTEDNESS AND TALENT?

Defining terms is very important in conceptual discussions such as those included in this volume. The need for precise definitions is especially critical when dealing with constructs such as creativity, intelligence, and talent, given the wide range of commonly used definitions for these terms. The discussion in this chapter relies on a definition drawn from the following conceptualization of creativity:

Creativity is the interaction among aptitude, process, and environment by which an individual or group produces a perceptible product that is both novel and useful as defined within a social context.

Plucker, Beghetto, and Dow (in press) elaborate on this definition, noting that creativity emerges from an interaction among aptitudes, cognitive processes, and influences from the environment in which an individual or group exists. Although creativity involves latent, unobservable abilities and processes, Plucker et al. argue for the importance of generating and identifying documentable artifacts (e.g., behaviors, products, ideas) to serve as necessary evidence from which the presence of creativity can be determined and evaluated.

With respect to the construct of giftedness, it is also a construct shaped by multiple influences, and its existence is best determined in the presence of unambiguous evidence of extraordinary achievement (i.e., both novelty and usefulness) within a specific social context. With this definition in mind, the question is not, who is gifted? but rather, how can we match children to specific instructional contexts to help them realize their potential giftedness?

An example from the first author's work involves the experiences of a student during an intensive academic summer program for talented students and illuminates the role of context. The student took a course that required a great deal of group work, self-regulation, and creativity due to its constructivist, problem-based curriculum. Her performance throughout the first half of the course was very poor, and her social interactions with her peers were not constructive. The course instructors questioned how the student could have been admitted into the program, given her apparent lack of ability. But as the course intern began to work with the student, who was from an urban school district, the intern realized that the student was simply uncomfortable in an instructional setting where self-regulation was required and the social milieu was dominated by middle-class suburban students.

All definitions of giftedness imply the necessity of a social context because such a context is requisite for determining whether (and how) a person, action, or product will be defined or judged as gifted. For example, regarding creativity, Nuessel, Stewart, and Cedeño (2001) implicitly highlight social context by noting that creativity "fashions or defines new questions in a domain in a way that is initially considered novel but *ultimately becomes accepted in a particular cultural setting*" (p. 700, italics added). In this way, identifying giftedness in small children is problematic, primarily because they have not had time to exhibit giftedness yet and because giftedness does not solely exist *in* the child. There is certainly potential for giftedness in small children, but expecting real-world, gifted behaviors is a very high standard for these students to reach given the nature of the contexts that they participate in as children.

In other words, highly talented people certainly exist, but if they cannot provide evidence of that talent within one or more contexts, it does not really matter how talented they are. Put more abstractly, a tree in my region of the country is certainly falling in the ice storm that rages as this chapter is being written. However, we don't hear or see it, so we'll never know. Conceptions of giftedness place too much emphasis on the potential for giftedness, ignoring environmental–individual interactions that form the foundation of the argument in this chapter. Rather than restrict the study of giftedness, this view allows a much broader examination of talent than normally occurs.

For example, adapting an example from Plucker et al. (in press), consider the giftedness of a fourth-grade student participating in a science fair versus that of a Nobel Prize–winning scientist. Taking context into account allows the behaviors of fourth-grade science projects to be judged as valid as studies of Nobel Prize–winners (e.g., this particular fourth-grade science project is exemplary in the context of fourth-graders, science fairs, or for this particular student). At the same time, specifying context does not allow for relativistic claims that a fourth-grade science project is necessarily as significant as a Nobel Prize–winning discovery (e.g., this particular fourth-grade science project is viewed as quite pedestrian when considered within the context of the projects and discoveries of Nobel Prize–winning scientists, but the distinction matters little to the fourth-grader, the scientist, and those who work with each of them).

The addition of social context to the previously discussed facets of the definition (i.e., interaction among aptitude, process, and environment; criteria of tangibility; and the combination of uniqueness and utility) provides researchers with a broad framework from which they can begin to articulate what giftedness "looks like" in light of the various stakeholders who will be evaluating gifted behaviors. Further, it treats giftedness as an observable, manifest behavior and not simply as a latent construct potentially existing within the child.

Traditional Conceptions of Giftedness

Traditional conceptions of intelligence and giftedness, ranging from general factors and related approaches (Cattell, 1987; Jensen, 1998; Spearman, 1904) to more differentiated models (Carroll, 1993; Feldhusen, 1998; Guilford, 1967; Thurstone, 1938), view the constructs as residing within the individual. Although many of these theories acknowledge the role of the environment in the development of intelligence, the focus is firmly placed on the individual as the locus of control and unit of interest. Approaches to talent development based on these traditional conceptions of intelligence are common and popular. For example, the Talent Search model initiated at Johns Hopkins University now works with more than 250,000 children per year (at varying levels of service) at several university-based regional centers across the country (Stanley, 1980; Stanley & Benbow, 1986). Many school districts around the country base their gifted education and talent development programs on the identification of high-ability children using instruments focused primarily on each individual's capabilities (e.g., Hunsaker & Callahan, 1995).

A few contemporary approaches include reference to the environment when they discuss intellectual ability and talent. For example, Sternberg's (1985, 1986) triarchic theories of intelligence and giftedness include environmental interactions within their contextual subtheories, Ceci's (1990) bioecological approach to intelligence notes the role of context, Das, Naglieri, and Kirby's (1994) PASS theory describes specific cognitive processes that may be influenced by the environment, and Gardner (1983) emphasizes cultural context throughout various applications of his theory of multiple intelligences. These theorists discuss the role of the environment or context, yet none of them directly articulate explicit processes for how these interactions occur. When they do refer to intellectual talent, they describe a trait that exists in the individual's mind with allusions to context simply being about the application of talent – not its ontological existence. Renzulli's (1978) three-ring conception, perhaps the most well-known theory of giftedness, focuses on the interaction among above-average ability, creativity, and task commitment. Other conceptions of giftedness vary qualitatively from Renzulli's approach, but most still focus on the qualities of the gifted individual (see Sternberg & Davidson, 1986). Although these broader theories of intelligence and giftedness are much more comprehensive than earlier conceptions of ability regarding environmental factors, the focus remains on the individual during his or her interactions with the environment.

Educational approaches to talent development based on these broader theories (see Coleman & Cross, 2001; Karnes & Bean, 2001; Renzulli & Reis, 1985) are becoming more prevalent, but the traditional "find the gifted child" model remains a common approach across much of the world. These strategies, similar to the theoretical assumptions on which they are based, are predominantly focused on the individual as the unit of analysis or, more accurately, on identifying intellectually gifted children than providing environments in which they can thrive academically. In contrast, new areas of theory and research hold promise for the reconceptualization of talent development efforts.

An Alternative to Traditional Conceptions

The separation of mind and context at the heart of traditional conceptions of talent development polarizes learner and context, either implicitly or explicitly stating that, in the case of talent and giftedness, the individual impacts or influences the environment. Barab et al. (1999) have a strong reaction to this perspective, stating that "the history of such dualistic thinking reveals its inadequacies as a way of explaining thought and knowledge in that it sets up an incommensurability between knower and known, with one language to describe that which is known and another to describe the individual doing the knowing" (p. 355). Snow (1992) shared a similar perspective, decrying the "tendency to think of persons and situations as independent variables, rather than persons-in-situations as integrated systems" (p. 19). More to the point, Snow emphasized that a more fruitful analysis would examine "the processes that connect persons and situations – *the processes that operate in their interface*" (p. 19, italics added). Similar perspectives are offered by Lave (1993, 1997) in her analysis of mathematics ability within and out of context. These studies, in which people perform differently in different settings when attempting to solve similar problems, challenge the validity of official competence/performance distinctions in which talent is considered to be a possession of the individual and not an outcome of persons-in-situations (Lave, 1997).

From a motivational standpoint, recent research provides evidence that the perspective of giftedness residing solely within the individual has important limitations. For example, attribution theory suggests that internal, stable attributions (e.g., I am an intelligent and talented person) may be difficult to maintain in light of challenging assignments, whereas internal, unstable attributions (e.g., I succeeded or failed because of my effort) place a greater sense of responsibility on the person-in-situation and leads to "achievement motivation" (Weiner, 1992). Conversely, students who are not succeeding can quickly descend into learned helplessness if they believe that they are not talented and will not succeed, regardless of their level of effort (Diener & Dweck, 1978). The creation and maintenance of stable internal attributions for success and failure produce further complications when the label of "good student" or "bad student" is attached to a learner. Teachers treat students differently based on teacher expectancies of student ability, often resulting in increased or decreased student achievement (Jussim & Eccles, 1995).

Advances in research over the last 20 years have further illustrated the weakness of traditional approaches to ability and talent in light of learning and thinking styles, the importance of context, and other factors (Marsh, Byrne, & Shavelson, 1988; Plucker & McIntire, 1996; Simonton, 1999, 2001; Snow, 1997; Stanford Aptitude Seminar, 2001). We know much more about human achievement than we did only a generation earlier, yet educators often use instructional strategies that are based on conceptions of talent and ability that are decades old (Bransford, Brown, & Cocking, 2000). Returning to the earlier example of the student in the summer program who felt like a fish out of water, the instructors changed the instructional environment to scaffold self-regulating behaviors, and the student performed much more effectively during the remainder of the course. The issue was not the student or the environment, but the interaction of the two.

Central to all of these criticisms is the conviction that giftedness cannot be characterized in purely cognitive terms (as internal stable traits), nor does it have a purely environmental explanation. Instead, these perspectives imply that giftedness is the visible result of the *interaction* of individual and environment. In a similar vein, Pea (1993) believes that the ability to act intelligently is accomplished rather than possessed. This perspective draws heavily on the research in ecological psychology (Gibson, 1979/1986; Turvey, 1992; Turvey & Shaw, 1995), situated cognition (Bredo, 1992; Greeno, 1997; Lave, 1997), distributed cognition (Barab & Kirshner, 2001; Cobb & Yackel, 1996; Pea, 1993), apprenticeship learning (Lave & Wenger, 1991), and psychoanalytic theory (Stolorow, Atwood, & Orange, 2002).[1]

This conceptualization appears to be at odds with popular systems theories of creativity and related constructs, and it is. For example, Csikszentmihalyi (1988; see also Csikszentmihalyi & Robinson, 1986) provides a systems theory of creativity that emphasizes the roles of individuals and the domain and field in which they are attempting to create. Rather than consider how an individual operates within a domain and field, we believe a better perspective is to consider how operating within the domain and field fundamentally change how one thinks and acts. We see similar phenomena within education policy research.

For example, in debates on the effectiveness of full-day kindergarten versus traditional half-day programs, policy makers often say that "It's not full-day kindergarten that matters, it's what *happens* in full-day kindergarten that matters." That statement provides a great sound bite, but it fundamentally misinterprets the research on teacher behaviors within full- and half-day programs: Research provides evidence that teachers, given the additional time in full-day programs, not only do more of specific instructional strategies but also use different instructional strategies (e.g., Denton, West, & Walston, 2003; Elicker & Mathur, 1997). The changing environment changes everything, including the way teachers perceive the environments and interact with students. The person–environment interaction has a more pronounced influence on behavior than either individual or environmental factors can explain in isolation.

In an earlier, related analysis (Barab & Plucker, 2002), we briefly reviewed the potential contributions of this conceptualization of talent development, with an emphasis on design challenges faced by educators who seek to foster emerging excellence (i.e., giftedness). We summarized our perspective with the statement "nobody has talent, yet everybody has the opportunity to engage in talented transactions" (p. 179). Our hope was that educators would come to characterize entire contexts as gifted and develop educational innovations that support learners in functioning as part of, and creating, such contexts. We concluded by stating that educators

[1] The contributions of most of these theoretical perspectives are discussed in detail in Barab and Plucker (2002).

must support the development of smart contexts and not simply that of smart individuals.

Since that article was published and in ensuing conversations with colleagues, our view has moderated slightly. We would now say that *anyone can be talented, yet one needs the opportunity to engage in talented transactions to realize their giftedness.* Talent is potential, but – returning to the definition of giftedness – we need to see evidence of novel, useful accomplishment to determine the presence of gifted behaviors. In our schools, our goal should be to design those environments that provide students with opportunities to develop talents with the eventual goal of producing evidence of giftedness.

HOW DO WE DEVELOP TALENTS CONTEXTUALLY?

A major problem with situated theories is that they sound good in theory, but they are rarely (and ironically) applied to realities faced by teachers and students in classrooms.[2] In the remainder of this chapter, we attempt to show what an applied situated perspective for developing talent and achieving giftedness could look like, with attention to compromises that are necessary for this approach to succeed in our schools.

Identifying Talents

Standardized ability and achievement tests are very good at identifying certain types of (usually decontextualized) potential, but they tell us very little about giftedness, in large part because they examine behavior out of context. Context-laden conceptions of giftedness would tend to view gifted behavior as the best indicator of giftedness. If apparently talented children are not producing gifted behaviors, educators and parents should be examining which opportunities are necessary for students to interact in environments that foster gifted behaviors.

A common reaction to this position is, "Well, that works great in philosophy land, but I have a school of 500 children and can only provide gifted education services to a small percentage of those students." In general, we would argue that the limited resources would be better spent differentiating curriculum within each and every classroom, with special attention to the instructional techniques discussed in the next section.[3] But even within

---

[2] Most published examples describe short-term interventions or extracurricular applications. These are often excellent, provocative programs, but they have little impact on day-to-day activities in our schools.

[3] Or at least the use of flexible approaches to identification, such as those encouraged by the Schoolwide Enrichment Model.

the realities of formal identification procedures, the importance of context can be addressed.

For example, much has been written about the need for multidimensional assessments (e.g., Machek & Plucker, 2003), which consider multiple objective and subjective assessments of ability and achievement when identifying gifted students. A problem with these identification systems is that they often collect a range of interesting and relevant data, only to heavily weight standardized test scores, rendering the interpretation of the additional data moot. As a former enrichment program coordinator, the first author understands the reliance on tests scores: They are reliable, relatively easy to interpret (especially if drawn from norm-referenced tests), and provide an easy way to rank students. But we have become convinced that the messy nature of subjective measures, such as performance assessments and teacher, parent, peer, and self-nominations, is their greatest strength – acknowledging the subjectivity of such measures is an implicit acceptance of the role of context. For example, if 10 children in a specific school have high ability and high scores on achievement tests, and are consistently mentioned on teacher ratings and recommendations, educators will have little problem establishing the reliability and validity of their gifted identification process. However, if two or three students have decent scores, only occasionally score well on teacher rating scales, yet have exceptional samples of work in their portfolios, the conception of giftedness explored in this chapter suggests that second group of children are no less talented than the first group and would perhaps view the second group as providing evidence of giftedness, whereas the first group has not yet provided such evidence.

Instruction for Giftedness

Given the interactive framework proposed in this chapter, classrooms are not the location of talent development but rather the context for a specific cultural milieu through which students develop understandings of what constitutes a talented interaction – an interaction that is partly defined and validated in terms of the day-to-day practices and rituals of the school culture. As a result, educators need to select carefully the daily rituals and activities so that students learn skills and participate in practices that are consistent with those environmental and sociocultural structures and processes outside of schools. This idea is commonly associated with the work of Dewey (1925/1981, 1938), Whitehead (1929), and others, and remains as applicable today as it was roughly 100 years ago.

Barab and Plucker (2002) note that this approach has considerable potential for motivating students. Although some students are able to motivate themselves and regulate their intellectual behaviors regardless of context, most students are divorced from the curriculum because of a lack of applicability or challenge, which often manifests as appearances of boredom (Csikszentmihalyi, 2000; Plucker & McIntire, 1996). To address this problem, Barab and Plucker suggest that

Drawing on his expertise, the educator is responsible for initiating the learner into those practices and meaningful relations that are reflective of the types of relations occurring in the culture at large. This initiation cannot be handed to the learner or the student all at once. Rather, this coupling must emerge from individual–environment interactions. Student-owned – not textbook- or teacher-owned – interactions provide meaning and value to the subject matter, and build connections to the learner's life and activity more generally. (p. 175)

Barab and Plucker (2002) further stated that this learner–environment interaction is the avenue through which children produce evidence that they are gifted. But how do we accomplish this blending of child and instructional environment? One alternative is classroom-based, problem-based learning (PBL). One interesting approach is that of anchored instruction, instruction in which the material to be learned is presented in the context of a specific problem that serves to provide meaning to the material. Further, by immersing the material in a larger context, the instruction allows the material to be examined from multiple perspectives (Barab & Landa, 1997). The Cognition and Technology Group at Vanderbilt (CTGV; 1990, 1993) is given much of the credit for developing anchored instruction within the context of technology-delivered problem-solving opportunities. A similar example is the use of Web design tasks with college students (Lim, Plucker, & Bichelmeyer, 2003). By anchoring specific content within the task of designing a Web page, students gain a greater understanding of the material as they organize and modify the information to be presented on the Web site.

A specific example within gifted education involves high school students participating in a summer program on invention and design (Gorman & Plucker, 2003; Gorman, Plucker, & Callahan, 1998; Plucker & Gorman, 1999). Students in this context were told that the historical setting for the class was immediately before Alexander Graham Bell filed his telephone patent in 1876, and they were asked to work in groups to design a telephone, build a working prototype, write a patent application, and present and defend their design and prototype to a person acting the role of a patent examiner – a role undertaken by an inventor from AT&T. Students had access to a variety of materials, most of which would have been available to inventors around the time of the Bell patent, and they were also provided with access to various patents, notebooks, and paperwork from many of the inventors who worked on voice transmission technology in the late 1900s. Most of the students had little knowledge of circuit design, the physics of sound, and other important content. The instructor, an experienced physics teacher, circulated among the groups and delivered mini-lectures on these topics to students who appeared to need the information. The teacher occasionally stopped all the groups and delivered a 20- to 30-minute just-in-time lecture on content with which most of the class was having difficulty. These lectures were infrequent, and the teacher usually imbedded the content in a historical context, which added further to the real-life application of the creative skills and content.

Other approaches to PBL include Type III activities within the framework of the Schoolwide Enrichment Model (Renzulli & Reis, 1985) and less formal approaches recommended by Savery and Duffy (1996), Plucker and Nowak (2000), Grow and Plucker (2003), and many others. Renzulli (1994) has recently taken this model a step further, encouraging schools to use his contextual approach as a comprehensive school reform model, which is a promising development from our theoretical perspective. Barab and Duffy (2000) offer a very provocative approach to creating "communities of practice," arguing that such situated communities cannot be modeled – real-world contexts need to be situated in the real world. This position seems a bit extreme and, frankly, untenable in most of today's classrooms; a more realistic option, neither ideal nor utopian, is the classroom-based approach described previously. In general, research on PBL effectiveness is positive, although more research is needed on how applied, contextual approaches to teaching and learning impact student performance on standardized achievement tests, such as those used in every state's federally mandated educational accountability system.

Educational Assessment and Giftedness

Instruction and assessment, although traditionally discussed as separate techniques or areas of interest, are highly interdependent. Consequently, we should not be surprised to find the same learner-as-unit-of-interest emphasis in the history of educational assessment (see Brown, 1992; Schoenfeld, 1992; Snow, 1997; VanTassel-Baska, 1998). Using assessments that respect local context are essential if we are to have valid interpretations – both ethically and empirically – of what constitutes gifted transactions (Barab & Plucker, 2002). Furthermore, our assessment strategies need to be consistent with the nature of instruction in the context of interest (Nowak & Plucker, 2002). For example, assessing problem-based instruction with a context-free pencil-and-paper multiple-choice exam is hardly conceptually or instructionally consistent, nor is the use of problem-based, context-bound assessments to measure student progress during traditional, lecture–recitation instruction.[4]

---

[4] Refer to Nowak and Plucker (2002) for additional examples and guidelines for assessment in problem-based learning.

One other area of assessment, heavily context-dependent, is the importance of allowing students to present and defend their intellectual work. Few areas of human activity are as neglected in the classroom as constructive criticism, both in terms of providing such criticism and learning to use such criticism to improve one's work. Within the context of creative production, the first author thinks of this process as *creative articulation*. Before describing this concept, we would like to share the following anecdote about the power of criticism.

Within one section of our program's doctoral qualifying exams, students are required to critique one theoretical or conceptual article in 3 hours. The students often provide responses that read like book reviews, merely summarizing the authors' main points, or that are uniformly positive or negative, with little balance in the true sense of a critique. We meet with many of these students both before the exam, to emphasize the need to critique, and after the exam, to debrief our assessments of the students' work. During these meetings, it often worries us that the students do not understand what we mean by *critique* or even *criticize*. As a result, students may not be able to achieve the goal for this section of the exam, which is to provide evidence that they can take information from their courses and apply it in a common academic context: critiquing someone's ideas.

This situation strikes us as a failure on our part, as educators at every level of instruction, to pay sufficient attention to the criticism's importance in most areas of human activity.[5] Research on human creativity is replete with examples of eminent creators persuading critics and other stakeholders of the benefits of the creators' approaches to specific problems. For example, Gardner's (1993) profiles of several major creative figures, including Gandhi, Freud, and Martha Graham, contain several references to these individuals' ability to use criticism to their advantage and persuade their audiences that the creators' particular solutions were valuable (see also Latour, 1987).

Although the literature contains a few examples of classrooms with cultures of critique (e.g., Brown et al., 1999), how often do we allow students to persuade their classmates and teachers about the quality of their work? Unfortunately, the answer in most classrooms is that educators do not create this type of environment. By not doing so, we continue to rob learning of context, creating an instructional misalignment in which work results from person–environment interactions, yet assessment continues to exist under the guise of context-free objectivity. An alternative is, during assessment, to embrace context in all of its complex, messy, and challenging glory, engaging children in the activity of argumentation as they attempt

---

[5] This problem is obviously not restricted to graduate students. Indeed, researchers often complain that few journal reviewers know how to provide constructive criticism.

to ground their claims in credible and trustworthy arguments (Toulmin, 1958). When students learn in context-rich PBL environments, they are afforded the opportunity to present and defend their work to the class, help their peers learn to provide constructive criticism, and allow the presenters the opportunity to revise their work and present it back to the group (e.g., Barab, Hay, Barnett, & Hay, 2001; Gorman et al., 1998). The result will be students who seek out opportunities to receive criticism, articulate the value of their work, and engage in a dynamic social conversation about their achievements.

CONCLUSION

In this chapter, we have attempted to illustrate the power of situated person–environment interactions as models for talent development. The major advantage, in our view, is the acknowledgement that context is critically important both to understanding giftedness and to developing giftedness in young people. We also addressed a weakness of many situated approaches to learning and knowing by providing concrete suggestions for applying this perspective to everyday educational situations.

However, we have not addressed another weakness of using a lens of situated cognition to view talent development and giftedness: the lack of a major theory that explains how specific contexts interact with certain abilities and dispositions to produce specific outcomes. We believe several major theorists are headed in the right direction (e.g., Csikszentmihalyi, 1988; Renzulli, 2002; Sternberg, 1985), but these perspectives tend to be trait-focused rather than state-focused and lack testable outcomes that can be predicted from specific contextual variables. A theory with these characteristics may not be possible at this moment in time – admittedly, such a theory is largely absent from broader discussions in education and psychology – but a specific, testable theory of context in the development of gifted behaviors should be a goal of theorists and researchers.

In summary, we propose that adults view children with potential as being talented, with our goal as educators being to design social contexts in which these talents can emerge as gifted behaviors. Although it is tempting to identify specific individuals as "gifted" in the absence of exceptional real-world achievement, doing so ignores the situated and dynamic nature of human accomplishment. Exclusivity (i.e., these students are gifted, these others are not) is a logical extension of the individual-as-processor approach to giftedness, whereas the human–environment perspective is more inclusive due to the emphasis on finding optimal environments in which students can develop their talents into truly gifted behaviors.

References

Barab, S. A., & Duffy, T. (2000). From practice fields to communities of practice. In D. Jonassen & S. M. Land (Eds.), *Theoretical foundations of learning environments* (pp. 25–56). Mahwah, NJ: Lawrence Erlbaum Associates.

Barab, S. A., & Kirshner, D. (2001). Guest editors' introduction: Rethinking methodology in the learning sciences. *The Journal of the Learning Sciences, 10*(1&2), 5–15.

Barab, S. A., & Landa, A. (1997). Designing effective interdisciplinary anchors. *Educational Leadership, 54,* 52–55.

Barab, S. A., & Plucker, J. (2002). Smart people or smart contexts? Talent development in an age of situated approaches to learning and thinking. *Educational Psychologist, 37,* 165–182.

Bransford, J. D., Brown, A. L., & Cocking, R. (Eds.). (2000). *How people learn: Brain, mind, experience and school.* Washington, DC: National Academy Press.

Bredo, E. (1992). Reconstructing educational psychology: Situated cognition and Deweyian pragmatism. *Educational Psychologist, 29,* 23–35.

Brown, A. L. (1992). Design experiments: Theoretical and methodological challenges in creating complex interventions in classroom settings. *The Journal of the Learning Sciences, 2*(2), 141–178.

Brown, A., Ash, D., Rutherford, M., Nakagawa, K., Gordon, A., & Campione, J. (1994). Distributed expertise in the classroom. In M. D. Cohen & L. S. Sproull (Eds.), *Organizational learning* (pp. 188–228). Beverly Hills, CA: Sage.

Carroll, J. B. (1993). *Human cognitive abilities: A survey of factor-analytic studies.* New York: Cambridge University Press.

Cattell, R. B. (1987). *Intelligence: Its structure, growth and action.* Amsterdam, The Netherlands: Elsevier.

Ceci, S. J. (1990). *On intelligence – more or less: A bio-ecological treatise on intellectual development.* Englewood Cliffs, NJ: Prentice Hall.

Cobb, P., & Yackel, E. (1996). Constructivist, emergent, and sociocultural perspectives in the context of developmental research. *Educational Psychologist, 31,* 175–190.

Cognition and Technology Group at Vanderbilt. (1990). Anchored instruction and its relationship to situated cognition. *Educational Researcher, 19,* 2–10.

Cognition and Technology Group at Vanderbilt. (1993). Anchored instruction and situated cognition revisited. *Educational Technology, 33,* 52–70.

Coleman, L. J., & Cross, T. L. (2001). *Being gifted in school: An introduction to development, guidance, and teaching.* Waco, TX: Prufrock Press.

Csikszentmihalyi, M. (1988). Society, culture, and person: A systems view of creativity. In R. J. Sternberg (Ed.), *The nature of creativity: Contemporary psychological perspectives* (pp. 325–339). New York: Cambridge University Press.

Csikszentmihalyi, M. (2000). *Beyond boredom and anxiety.* San Francisco: Jossey-Bass.

Csikszentmihalyi, M., & Robinson, R. E. (1986). Culture, time, and the development of talent. In R. J. Sternberg & J. E. Davidson (Eds.), *Conceptions of giftedness* (pp. 264–284). New York: Cambridge University Press.

Das, J. P., Naglieri, J. A., & Kirby, J. R. (1994). *Assessment of cognitive processes: The PASS theory of intelligence.* Boston: Allyn & Bacon.

214 *Jonathan A. Plucker and Sasha A. Barab*

Denton, K., West, J., & Walston, J. (2003). *The condition of education special analysis: Reading – young children's achievement and classroom experiences* (U.S. Department of Education, Institute of Education Sciences, NCES 2003-070). Retrieved October 17, 2003, from http://nces.ed.gov/pubs2003/2003070.pdf

Dewey, J. (1938). *Experience & education.* New York: Collier MacMillan.

Dewey, J. (1981). Experience and nature. In J. A. Boydston (Ed.), *John Dewey: The later works: Vol. 1.* Carbondale, IL: Southern Illinois University Press. (Original work published 1925.)

Diener, C. I., & Dweck, C. S. (1978). An analysis of learned helplessness: Continuous changes in performance, strategy, and achievement cognitions following failure. *Journal of Personality and Social Psychology, 36,* 451–462.

Duschl, R., & Ellenbogen, K. (1999). Middle school science students' dialogic argumentation. In M. Komorek, H. Behrendt, H. Dahncke, R. Duit, W. Gräber, & A. Kross (Eds.), *Proceedings: Second international conference of ESERA: Research in science education. Past, present, and future: Vol. 2* (pp. 420–423). Kiel, Germany: IPN.

Elicker, J., & Mathur, S. (1997). What do they do all day? Comprehensive evaluation of full day kindergarten. *Early Childhood Research Quarterly, 12,* 459–480.

Feldhusen, J. F. (1998). Programs for the gifted few or talent development for the many? *Phi Delta Kappan, 79*(10), 735–738.

Gardner, H. (1983). *Frames of mind: The theory of multiple intelligences.* New York: Basic Books.

Gardner, H. (1993). *Creating minds: An anatomy of creativity seen through the lives of Freud, Einstein, Picasso, Stravinsky, Eliot, Graham, and Gandhi.* New York: Basic Books.

Gibson, J. J. (1979/1986). *The ecological approach to visual perception.* Hillsdale, NJ: Lawrence Erlbaum Associates.

Gorman, M. E., & Plucker, J. (2003). Teaching invention as critical creative processes: A course on technoscientific creativity. In M. A. Runco (Ed.), *Critical creative processes* (pp. 275–302). Cresskill, NJ: Hampton.

Gorman, M. E., Plucker, J., & Callahan, C. M. (1998). Turning students into inventors: Active learning modules for secondary students. *Phi Delta Kappan, 79*(7), 530–535.

Greeno, J. G. (1997). Response: On claims that answer the wrong questions. *Educational Researcher, 26,* 5–17.

Grow, P. L., & Plucker, J. (2003). Good problems to have: Implementing problem-based learning without redesigning a curriculum. *The Science Teacher, 70*(9), 31–35.

Guilford, J. P. (1967). *The nature of human intelligence.* New York: McGraw-Hill.

Hunsaker, S. L., & Callahan, C. M. (1995). Creativity and giftedness: Published instrument uses and abuses. *Gifted Child Quarterly, 39,* 110–114.

Jensen, A. R. (1998). *The g factor: The science of mental ability.* New York: Praeger.

Jussim, L., & Eccles, J. (1995). Naturally occurring interpersonal expectancies. In N. Eisenberg (Ed.), *Social development: Review of personality and social psychology, 15* (pp. 74–108). Beverly Hills, CA: Sage.

Karnes, F. A., & Bean, S. M. (Eds.). (2001). *Methods and materials for teaching the gifted.* Waco, TX: Prufrock Press.

Latour, B. (1987). *Science in action: How to follow scientists and engineers through society.* Milton Keynes, England: Open University Press.

Lave, J. (1993). Situating learning in communities of practice. In L. B. Resnick, J. M. Levine, & S. D. Teasley (Eds.), *Perspectives on socially shared cognition* (pp. 17–36). Washington, DC: American Psychological Association.

Lave, J. (1997). The culture of acquisition and the practice of understanding. In D. Kirshner & J. A. Whitson (Eds.), *Situated cognition: Social, semiotic, and psychological perspectives* (pp. 17–36). Mahwah, NJ: Lawrence Erlbaum Associates.

Lave, J., & Wenger, E. (1991). *Situated learning: Legitimate peripheral participation*. New York: Cambridge University Press.

Lim, B., Plucker, J., & Bichelmeyer, B. (2003). Learning by Web design: How it affects graduate student attitudes. *College Teaching, 51*(1), 13–19.

Machek, G. R., & Plucker, J. (2003, December). Individual intelligence testing and giftedness: A primer for parents. *Parenting for High Potential,* 10–15.

Marsh, H. W., Byrne, B. M., & Shavelson, R. J. (1988). A multifaceted academic self-concept: Its hierarchical structure and its relation to academic achievement. *Journal of Educational Psychology, 80,* 366–380.

Nowak, J. A., & Plucker, J. (2002). Do as I say, not as I do? Student assessment in problem-based learning. *Inquiry: Critical Thinking Across the Disciplines, 21*(2), 17–31.

Pea, R. (1993). Practices of distributed intelligence and designs for education. In G. Salomon (Ed.), *Distributed cognitions: Psychological and educational considerations* (pp. 47–87). Cambridge, England: Cambridge University Press.

Plucker, J., Beghetto, R. A., & Dow, G. T. (in press). Why isn't creativity more important to educational psychologists? Potential, pitfalls, and future directions in creativity research. *Educational Psychologist.*

Plucker, J., & Gorman, M. E. (1999). Invention is in the mind of the adolescent: Evaluation of a summer course one year later. *Creativity Research Journal, 12,* 141–150.

Plucker, J., & McIntire, J. (1996). Academic survivability in high potential, middle school students. *Gifted Child Quarterly, 40,* 7–14.

Plucker, J., & Nowak, J. (2000). Creativity in science for K-8 practitioners: Problem-based approaches to discover and invention. In M. D. Lynch & C. R. Harris (Eds.), *Fostering creativity in children, K-8* (pp. 145–158). Boston: Allyn & Bacon.

Renzulli, J. S. (1978). What makes giftedness? Reexamining a definition. *Phi Delta Kappan, 60,* 180–184, 261.

Renzulli, J. S. (1994). *Schools for talent development.* Mansfield Center, CT: Creative Learning Press.

Renzulli, J. S. (2002). Expanding the conception of giftedness to include co-cognitive traits and to promote social capital. *Phi Delta Kappan, 84*(1), 33–40, 57–58.

Renzulli, J. S., & Reis, S. M. (1985). *The schoolwide enrichment model: A comprehensive plan for educational excellence.* Mansfield Center, CT: Creative Learning Press.

Savery, J., & Duffy, T. (1996). Problem based learning. An instructional model and its constructionist framework. In B. Wilson (Ed.), *Constructivist learning environments: Case studies in instructional design* (pp. 135–148). Englewood Cliffs, NJ: Educational Technology.

Schoenfeld, A. H. (1992). On paradigms and methods: What do you do when the ones you know don't do what you want them to? Issues in the analysis of data in the form of videotapes. *The Journal of the Learning Sciences, 2*(2), 179–214.

Simonton, D. K. (1999). Talent and its development: An emergenic and epigenetic model. *Psychological Review, 106*, 435–457.

Simonton, D. K. (2001). Talent development as a multidimensional, multiplicative, and dynamic process. *Current Directions in Psychological Science, 10*, 39–43.

Snow, R. E. (1992). Aptitude theory: Yesterday, today, and tomorrow. *Educational Psychologist, 27*(1), 5–32.

Snow, R. E. (1997). Aptitudes and symbol systems in adaptive classroom teaching. *Phi Delta Kappan, 78*(5), 354–360.

Spearman, C. (1904). General intelligence, objectively determined and measured. *American Journal of Psychology, 15*, 201–293.

Stanford Aptitude Seminar. (2001). *Remaking the concept of aptitude: Extending the legacy of Richard E. Snow*, Mahwah, NJ: Lawrence Erlbaum Associates.

Stanley, J. C. (1980). On educating the gifted. *Educational Researcher, 9*(3), 8–12.

Stanley, J. C., & Benbow, C. P. (1986). Youths who reason exceptionally well mathematically. R. J. Sternberg & J. E. Davidson (Eds.), *Conceptions of giftedness* (pp. 361–387). New York: Cambridge University Press.

Sternberg, R. J. (1985). *Beyond IQ: A triarchic theory of human intelligence*. New York: Cambridge University Press.

Sternberg, R. J. (1986). A triarchic theory of intellectual giftedness. R. J. Sternberg & J. E. Davidson (Eds.), *Conceptions of giftedness* (pp. 223–243). New York: Cambridge University Press.

Sternberg, R. J., & Davidson, J. E. (Eds.). (1986). *Conceptions of giftedness*. New York: Cambridge University Press.

Stolorow, R. D., Atwood, G. E., & Orange, D. M. (2002). *Worlds of experience: Interweaving philosophical and clinical dimensions in psychoanalysis*. New York: Basic Books.

Thurstone, L. L. (1938). *Primary mental abilities*. Chicago: University of Chicago Press.

Toulmin, S. (1958). *The uses of argument*. Cambridge, England: Cambridge University Press.

Turvey, M. T. (1992). Affordances and prospective control: An outline of the ontology. *Ecological Psychology, 4*, 173–187.

Turvey, M. T., & Shaw, R. E. (1995). Toward an ecological physics and a physical psychology. In R. L. Solso & D. W. Massaro (Eds.), *The science of the mind: 2001 and beyond* (pp. 144–169). New York: Oxford University Press.

VanTassel-Baska, J. (1998). The development of academic talent. *Phi Delta Kappan, 79*(10), 760–763.

Weiner, B. (1992). *Human motivation: Metaphors, theories, and research*. Newbury Park, CA: Sage.

Whitehead, A. N. (1929). *The aims of education and other essays*. New York: MacMillan.

13

Feminist Perspectives on Talent Development

A Research-Based Conception of Giftedness in Women

Sally M. Reis

> "Tremendous amounts of talent are being lost to our society just because that talent wears a skirt."
>
> Shirley Chisolm

The stories of talented and eminent women are too seldom told. Little research has been conducted and less is known about the ways women's talents emerge and are developed, how they differ from the talents of men, and the choices some women make to construct and use their gifts and talents. The social and political movement focusing on women during the past five decades has provided an emerging understanding of their talents as well as the roles that some gifted women have played in our society and the forces that shaped those roles. Over the last two decades, I have studied talented girls and women from all domains across their life spans and have answered some questions, but introduced even more (Reis, 1987, 1995, 1998, 2001). The decision to identify this diverse group as talented or eminent rather than gifted stems from their collective preferences for these descriptors. Through these collective research experiences, a definition of talent in women has emerged that is summarized as follows. *Feminine talent development occurs when women with high intellectual, creative, artistic, or leadership ability or potential achieve in an area they choose and when they make contributions that they consider meaningful to society. These contributions are enhanced when women develop personally satisfying relationships and pursue what they believe to be important work that helps to make the world a healthier, more beautiful and peaceful place in which diverse expressions of art and humanity are celebrated.* The research reviewed in this chapter highlights the complex choices made by talented girls and women as well as the belief that the outcomes of these choices are profound, both in the women's individual lives and for society at large.

There is an absence of continuity in the recognition of women's contributions in history, resulting in the need for each generation of women to reinvent both their ideas and their collective feminist consciousness. Gerda Lerner (1993), for example, believes that throughout history, women's talents have enabled them to challenge and disregard patriarchal constraints, gender-defined roles, and the continuing barrage of discouragement they have faced. Lerner believes that the inner assurance and serenity that accompany a developed talent have enabled some women to achieve at high levels but, too often, in isolation, loneliness, and under the derision of contemporaries.

Little doubt exists that regardless of the indicator used, fewer women than men achieve at levels that would enable them to be identified as gifted. Whether we consider books written, leadership positions attained, patents granted, or awards achieved, fewer women than men are recognized as gifted, and fewer produce this type and level of seminal work. Male professors, for example, produce more creative work in research publications than do female professors (Axelrod, 1988; Ajzenberg-Selove, 1994; Bateson, 1990), and men produce more works of art and make more contributions in all professional fields (Callahan, 1979; Ochse, 1991; Piirto, 1991; Reis, 1987, 1998). As Callahan pointed out in 1979, and as is still true today, men write more books and win more prizes than do women. The September 2003 cover of *American Psychologist*, for example, lists the names of more than 30 Nobel winners in multiple areas, all of whom were male. Some of the complex reasons that fewer talented women with high potential achieve this level of eminence and the characteristics of those who do are summarized in this chapter.

NUANCES ABOUT FEMALE TALENT DEVELOPMENT

A fundamental question that underlies conceptions of giftedness and talent involves societal perceptions of, and who has the right to determine how, talents should be used. One of my closest childhood friends was a brilliant student in math and science who lived in a rather shabby second-floor apartment in the middle of the small factory city in which we grew up. Her father was a salesman and her mother stayed at home to raise my friend and her four siblings. My friend's mother was a graduate of a fine East Coast women's college and she read avidly, devouring books on philosophy, science, poetry, and fine fiction. Whenever our friends visited her apartment, she engaged us in provocative and lively discussions about some of the disciplines we later studied in college. I thought about my friend's mother often during those years and wondered how she could be content in her life, why she didn't find work that would enable her to use her considerable intellect, or what she might have become had she been born a few decades later. After college I returned to my home town to teach English and saw my friend's mother often in the city library. We continued our talks and I came to understand that she was happy in her choices to raise her children and passionately pursue lifelong learning. My friend grew up to be a scientist, one of the few women in her college class to earn a doctorate, and she told me that her mother was her greatest support system. All of her younger siblings finished their college degrees and lead success adult lives (Reis, 1998).

Some may believe that this woman's considerable intellectual talents were squandered because she failed to earn an advanced degree or work in a high-status profession. Others may believe that her talents were well used because she raised children who made positive contributions to the world. Have expectations about how a talented woman should use her potential changed in the last few decades? Many talented and highly educated women make decisions not to marry in order to pursue their talents, although that number has decreased from previous decades. For example, 75% of all women who received a Ph.D. between the years of 1877 and 1924 never married (Hutchinson, 1930). Lise Meitner, Rosalind Franklin, and Rachel Carson never married. Although Margaret Sanger and Margaret Mead married, they divorced early and lived their most productive years alone, as did Marie Curie, whose husband died only 11 years after their marriage. Margaret Bourke-White married twice for brief periods and her divorces enabled her to focus singly on her photography. Einstein's first wife, Mileva Maric, sacrificed her own career in physics to assist him in his early work and subsequently raise their children and maintain their home life, but even that sacrifice was not enough to keep the marriage intact (Gabor, 1995). Lee Krasner, married to Jackson Pollock, sacrificed years of her own productivity in art to help hold his life together, help him battle problems with alcohol and depression, and increase his productivity at a cost to hers. Although Mileva Maric never recovered her career, Lee Krasner was able to apply her talent and determination to achieve eminence later in life, although the relationship with Pollock cost her dearly. Marriage, for some of these women, caused them to sacrifice their own talent to the development of the talent of males in their family. For others who make these commitments, it is not marriage but rather other family ties that demand attention. Sir Francis Galton's older sister, Milicent Adele, devoted a good part of her formative years to tutoring and caring for her younger prodigy brother. Thomas Edison's mother spent almost two decades raising and home schooling her brilliant, unusual son. Do similarly intelligent and talented women with high levels of potential who follow paths destined to nurture the talents of others underachieve in life? Should my friend's brilliant mother be considered an underachiever? Or does the response to this question depend on the time period of the life of the person being considered?

PROFILES OF TALENTED WOMEN

Like a broken record, many of the talented women I have studied who have not achieved high levels of success tell a similar story (Reis, 1995; 1998).

They were extremely bright in school, but as they grew up, they began to feel ambivalence about their future and their responsibilities to loved ones. Their dreams for future high-profile careers and important work wavered and diminished and they began to doubt what they previously believed they could accomplish. Their beliefs about their own ability as well as their self-confidence were undermined during childhood or adolescence. They acquired some "feminine modesty," leading to changes in self-perceptions of ability and talent, which subsequently affected others' perceptions of their potential. Some fell in love in college and, suddenly and unexpectedly, the dreams of the person they loved became more important to them than their own dreams and they lowered their aspirations to pursue the relationship. Some decided to become nurses instead of doctors, and some completed a bachelor's degree instead of a Ph.D. Some accepted less challenging work that was different from what they dreamed about doing a decade earlier, but that enabled them sufficient time to raise their families and support their partner's work (Reis, 1987, 1995, 1998). Some of those talented women born after the Women's Movement were shocked to find that they were expected to make choices that benefited those they loved, after being consistently told that they could "have and do it all." They found out, often without preparation, that they could not. It was almost as if they had been told that there were no windmills on their journey and when they encountered one on the road to a successful career, they simply did not understand what to do.

This profile, however, does not describe all talented women. Some do achieve at the highest possible levels, but there are fewer of these women than men, and it is this fact that raises the most difficult question of all: Why are there so few eminent female creators and inventors (Ochse, 1991; Piirto, 1991)? As the majority of research conducted on high levels of productivity has concentrated on men (Cattell, 1903; Diamond, 1986; Lindauer, 1992; McLeish, 1976; Oden, 1968; Schneidman, 1989; Sears, 1977; Simonton, 1975, 1977, 1984, 1988, 1989), these questions are difficult to answer, but some of the reasons that have been suggested are discussed in this chapter. A case study of one of the women who participated in this research is included in the next section.

ACHIEVEMENT DIFFERENCES BETWEEN TALENTED WOMEN AND MEN

The reasons that some talented women underachieve are different from those that affect their male counterparts. Life events, especially involving relationships with partners, loved ones, and children, have the most compelling impact on decisions about whether one can develop her talents to the highest levels (Reis, 1998). As noted, in most professions and occupations, men continue to surpass women in the highest levels of professional and creative accomplishments (Arnold & Denny, 1985; Callahan,

1979; Hollinger and Fleming, 1988; Kerr, 1985; Ochse, 1991; Piirto, 1991; Reis, 1987; 1998; Subotnik & Arnold, 1995). Yet, success in our society is primarily defined by male standards, such as status, productive work accomplishments, financial benefits, fame, and levels of importance. These indicators do not adequately define accomplishment for some talented women who define success as having a positive impact on the world, making changes that benefit and improve the life of others or the health of the planet, and living a life that adheres to a system of values based on integrity, honesty, and compassion (Reis, 1987; 1998). This does not mean that all successful men eschew these values, nor does it mean that all talented women who fail to succeed in these areas of status do not have regrets about lost opportunities. Some talented women feel deep loss when they reflect on the loss of the chance to complete work that made a positive impact on the world (Reis, 1995; 1998). Some believe that they had the potential to become inventors, composers, politicians, and to achieve high levels of accomplishment. Although they understand the reasons their lives flowed in other directions, often because of those they love, they look back with regret on "what might have been," despite their pride about lives lived with dignity, integrity, and in service to others (Reis, 1995).

Many measures of success used to define accomplishment in our society are based on male indicators and, in addition, men, and primarily White men, have developed most of the conceptions of giftedness and talent that have been recognized in both contemporary psychology and educational psychology (Sternberg & Davidson, 1986). They have also developed most historical and contemporary conceptions of intelligence and most assessment instruments and tools currently used to measure general intelligence. The work of women and culturally diverse theorists has only recently begun to influence current conceptions of talents and intelligence, and when a more comprehensive body of this work is developed, beliefs and perceptions may change. This chapter summarizes my current work on feminine perspectives of giftedness and talent development, as well as some of the interactions of personal and external barriers that influence this development.

A MODEL OF TALENT REALIZATION IN WOMEN

To understand the perspectives of talent realization in women, I studied 22 American women who gained eminence in diverse fields using the case study approach discussed by Gruber (1986). Using questionnaires, in-depth interviews, and document review, I probed these women's perceptions about their work. Primary source data were used to document accomplishments, including their books, plays, articles, diaries, environmental successes, legislation, chapters, records, compact discs, as well as articles, chapters, books, dissertations, or other interviews with them or about them. Each of these women was recognized as a major contributor to her field, and several achieved the distinction of being the first or one of the first women in her respective field. In other words, all achieved eminence and some were American pioneers in theater, politics, academia, literature and poetry, science, musical composition, government, business, environmental sciences, art, education, and other fields.

Over a decade of research in this area, a preliminary conception of talent realization in women emerged, which is further refined in this chapter (Reis, 1996, 1998). The factors that contribute to this model include: abilities (intelligence and special talents), personality traits, environmental factors, and personal perceptions, such as the social importance of the use of one's talents to make a positive difference in the world. Each of these factors contributes to what Gruber called "self-mobilization" (p. 258), characterized in these women by the development of belief in self, a fervent desire to develop these talents, and a sense of destiny in women who made an active, conscious decision to develop their talents, often with little support and against many obstacles.

The talents of these eminent women evolved over many years and were constructed using varied earlier life experiences that served as valuable background and preparation for future accomplishments. The participants in this study illustrate that only some of these experiences were academic, as they often learned more from events in their lives after school ended. For example, an award-winning children's writer waited until her children were older and then began to write, weaving into her literary work both her Hispanic heritage and the insights she gained as a mother. A congresswoman credited her successful tenure in the House of Representatives more on the organizational skills gathered in local community action groups such as the Parent Teacher Association (PTA) and on local political action than on the degree she had received decades earlier from a prestigious women's college. It was, however, the career office at her college that helped her to better understand her qualifications for her campaign for Congress (Reis, 1998, p. 269).

Another interesting finding was the self-knowledge the women gained about the intensity of their lives, characterized by their need and obligation to pursue their talents in an active way. Many compared their own lives to the lives of their contemporaries – other equally talented women who appeared to live much calmer and, in some cases, happier lives. Still another finding was the diversification of talents in the majority of the women, as opposed to the single-minded focus of a few. In Isaiah Berlin's 1953 essay *The Hedgehog and the Fox,* he quotes Archilochus as saying that the fox knows many things, but the hedgehog knows one big thing. Berlin's essay explores types of intellectual thought and divides great Western thinkers into two intellectual camps, hedgehogs and foxes. Few of the talented

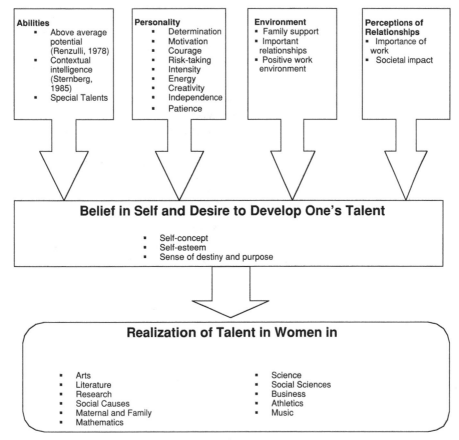

FIGURE 13.1. Reis's Model of Talent Realization in Women

women in this study were hedgehogs, as most diversify their abilities. This may be one of the reasons that some eminent women will not receive a Nobel Prize or become renowned outside of their fields, but they will contribute to, in the words of one woman, "a life well-lived, with the rich benefits of interesting relationships, meaningful work, intense interests, love, and contentment."

The common traits characterizing these eminent women are summarized in Figure 13.1 and of particular note were the women's self-perceptions, personalities, and experiences. Most made an intensely personal and conscious decision to actively nurture and develop their talents. Each of the factors in Figure 13.1 helped these women to believe in their potential to continually develop their talent and to contribute to positive changes in the world.

Abilities

Most of the women described themselves as having been well-above-average but not superior students in school; however, all but a few acknowledged having some special talents in areas such as music, writing, speech and debate, or theater. Renzulli (1978) discussed the distinction between above-average and superior abilities in giftedness in his three-ring conception of giftedness. In later work (1986), he distinguished between schoolhouse giftedness and creative–productive giftedness. He found that although both types of giftedness are important, persons who make "gifted" contributions within a particular domain of human performance are often those who display creative–productive giftedness. These women were not always superlative students, but each displayed creative and productive behaviors in their domains as adults. In every case, their abilities, interests, creativity, and motivation merged to enable them to develop their talents. Sternberg's (1985; 1986) notion of contextual intelligence was also displayed by many of these women, who had to adapt to, change, or leave their environment in order for their talents to be realized and developed. One participant in the study, Dr. Francelia Butler, was married to someone she loved deeply. During their married life, her husband, a well-known newspaper editor, had consistently downplayed her talents. When he became gravely ill, he told her that he had not given her enough credit or encouragement for her talents, and apologized. Upon his death, which she described as the saddest period of her life, she gave up her security and her home, and moved with their young child to pursue her doctorate in English, eventually emerging as eminent in her field.

Personality Traits

The personality traits of these women differed greatly, but commonalities were found, such as determination, motivation, creativity, patience, and the ability to take and in some cases thrive on risks. Every woman exhibited determination, reflected by an ability to strive for success and to continue to persevere, often under adverse conditions and sometimes without the love and support of her family and/or partner. Each explained her source of determination differently. Some were certain that it had developed from the positive role modeling of parents who demanded elevated work habits. The congresswoman believed that her work ethic came directly from her parents, who never accepted less than her best efforts. Others explained that they developed their motivation, determination, and work ethic because their perceptions of the strong purpose they had to fulfill in their lives, such as preserving the environment, emerging as a successful composer, or providing talented economically disadvantaged urban youth with quality theater experiences and training. Still others believed that their motivation came from their desire to produce, to have a positive impact on the world, and from the sheer joy of the act of creativity. An artist explained

The process of doing art is often more important than the product to me because of my feeling that I have to get something out. The act of welding, of fusing metal together, is very important to me. The passion I feel, the violence of creating something as the sparks fly everywhere...gives me feelings that are hard to describe. It's a rich feeling, one of power, I guess (Reis, 1998, p. 232–233).

Each displayed a form of creativity rooted in the love of work, interests, and the way time was found for other essential aspects of life, such as family and relationships. Their sheer volume of work and persistent evolution into higher talent forms interacted with what appeared to be "learned creativity" as well as intense love for work. They also displayed patience, as some waited years to have the opportunity to invest considerable blocks of time to their talent, whereas others worked steadily over the years. The congresswoman waited until her youngest daughter was ready for college before running for office, and the environmental ecologist continued to work in her field for five decades despite initially being denied employment based on her sex. Each woman displayed careful patience in the development of her talent. In addition, each displayed a willingness to take risks and attempt tasks that she perceived other female intellectual peers did not have the courage or the interest to pursue.

Another personality trait displayed by each of these women was an intensity about work characterized by energy, passionate interest, and enjoyment. Some of the women were outwardly enthusiastic, whereas others were intensely quiet. Some laughed frequently and moved constantly; others were still, calm, shy, and almost reserved. However, each woman exuded an intense concentration, focus, and passion about her work. Several indicated that they experienced some feelings of guilt because they would rather be doing their work than anything else, and during these periods, they attempted to do more for their partners or children, sentiments also echoed by other eminent women (Antler, 1987; Dash, 1988; Gabor, 1995; Winstone, 1978). Eventually, most gained an acceptance of their choices in life.

Environmental Factors

Environmental factors that contributed to eminence in these women were diverse. Some came from upper-middle-class families; others were born into either middle-class or poor families. Most had parents who were well educated, but a few had parents who had little or no college education. Some attended prestigious women's colleges, some went to large state universities, and still others did not graduate from college. Some environmental factors were common across the majority of the women. Most had nurturing families who supported their talents and academic promise, although a few had nonsupportive families, and two came from abusive or distant families. Almost all had siblings, and although some were the oldest child, many were not. Those who had brothers usually believed that their parents paid more attention and gave more encouragement to their brothers. Most, but not all, were married or had long-term relationships, and all but two who married had children. A few decided not to have children so that they could pursue their talents without diversifying their lives. Two had husbands who had died young and, although they acknowledged their grief about these tragedies in their lives, these women also acknowledged that their husbands' early deaths enabled them to more fully develop their own potential. Some divorced after realizing that their partners were not supportive of their talent development. Some delayed placing a primary emphasis on their career until they were able to because they believed their children needed them; others labored consistently on their journey of accomplishment.

Their home environments were quite diverse, as were their work environments. Some changed their daily work schedules often to enable their work to evolve, and several shifted paid employment often. Some accepted barriers at work and found creative options from work at home; others fought against negative work environments, eventually changing them. Some worked alone with singular concentration, whereas others needed the interaction of a group of colleagues, requiring less time for solitary work. All traveled a unique path to eminence, actively sought support for the development of their talents, continued to learn with formal or more personalized education and knowledge, and gained increasing levels of sophistication in their knowledge about both their needs for work and personal lives. Some enjoyed their personal lives, and others acknowledged that they experienced frequent periods of unhappiness, characterized by some loneliness, self-sacrifice, and a conscious decision to avoid what they considered a more conventional life. Some actively strived to separate their personal life and relationships from their work life and relationships, indicating that they needed that distance to achieve balance. Others combined work and personal lives, drawing no line whatsoever between the two, and were happy with this combination of activity in both lives.

Perceptions of the Social Importance of Their Work and a Sense of Destiny in Life

Each woman had a strong desire to use her talents in personally satisfying ways that would benefit society, and each had a sense of purpose and destiny about the importance of her work and contributions. In general, most enjoyed their lives, readily acknowledging that they would not have been content simply to raise families, have good relationships with partners and friends, and pursue interests. Their work was critical to them and, because they believed their work could make a difference, they were willing to sacrifice some, but not all, of their personal choices to achieve in their fields. Some sacrificed having children or had fewer children, some gave up friendships or leisure activities, but all had close personal relationships with partners, husbands, siblings or friends that sustained them. When a controversial college president credited with many successes in her tenure was asked about friends, she answered simply that she had none, because of the time commitment and her perception that few people understood her obsession about her work. She did, however, have an extremely close relationship with her husband and her siblings (Reis, 1998).

Belief in Self, Sense of Destiny and Purpose, and Desire to Contribute and Develop Their Talents

Each eminent woman developed over time a belief in herself and a desire to translate her potential into work that made a difference in the world or was a creative contribution in life. Each had a sense of purpose about her talents and believed her positive belief in herself had emerged from success in work, as well as the development over time of a satisfying personal life. In the later years of their lives, each was satisfied with her life. Each had wanted to contribute and *make a difference* in the world, and believed that there was no choice about this contribution. These women were not satisfied with their lives unless they could continue to actively develop their talents. Most reported that they had friends and/or siblings with similarly high potential who were content to lead very different lives, ones that did not involve the sacrifices made to expend such high levels of focused work and energy. The congresswoman explained that her friends could not understand why she could not relax and enjoy her life after she had worked so hard and spent so many terms in the House of Representatives. These women, with similar levels of ability and education, would consistently ask why she would put herself through a rigorous campaign again and why she was not ready to relax, retire, and spend time on leisure activities. One of the most consistent findings in this research was the way that each woman explained her work ethic: Each wanted to contribute in some way, and believed that she had no choice in her actions, explaining that work was essential to her well-being and that "Something inside of me had to come out." In other words, they actively constructed their giftedness.

This conception has similarities and differences to another model of talent development in women conceived by Noble, Subotnik, and Arnold (1996). In their model, the outcome's component focuses on the fulfillment of potential in gifted women across many domains or spheres, such as those for fulfilling personal and family relationships, community relationships, and the self-actualization of potential. The public sphere incorporates the fulfillment of talent by achieving leadership and eminence in professional domains, including the creation of ideas or products that change the course of a domain or a social arena (Noble, et al., 1996). In both the model I propose in this chapter and the Noble, Arnold, and Subotnik model, women can apply their talents and gifts to raising children, developing relationships, and making contributions within the community. In the public sphere of the Noble, Arnold, and Subotnik model, opportunities are provided for women to achieve high levels of accomplishment and leadership in professional areas, as well. The model for female talent development proposed in this chapter also differs from other models of giftedness in ways that are unique to women. An extended discussion of these differences is beyond the scope of this chapter, but Tannenbaum (1983, 1991), for example, proposed five factors that are essential to the fulfillment of gifted potential: superior general intellect, distinctive special aptitudes, a supportive array of nonintellectual traits, a challenging and facilitative environment, and the smile of good fortune and chance at crucial periods of life. None of the women in this study reported that they exhibited superior intellect as children, some grew up or lived as an adult in non-supportive environments, and many believed that they experienced "bad luck" at crucial periods in their lives. Most lacked high self-esteem as children, but increased their self-esteem and self-concept with age as they overcame obstacles.

Similarities also exist to earlier discussions of giftedness in the previous volume by Sternberg and Davidson (1986). In addition to findings supporting the work of Renzulli (1986) and Sternberg (1986) discussed earlier, this research supports the work of Gruber. These women lived their lives to achieve the kind of giftedness in which Gruber was interested, "the kind that can be transformed by its possessor into effective creative work for the aesthetic enrichment of human experience, for the improvement of our understanding of the world, or for the betterment of the human condition and of our prospects for survival as a species" (p. 248). This research also supports the later work of Sternberg (1999) and Sternberg and Grigorenko (2002) regarding the development of successful intelligence, as these eminent women succeeded in life on their own terms by developing their strengths, compensating for their weaknesses, and shaping their home and work environment to develop their unique gifts. To illustrate the richness of the lives of these women and some of the similarities and differences from previous work in this area, brief summaries of the lives of two women who participated in my study of eminent women are provided.

CASE STUDIES OF TWO FEMALE PIONEERS

Mary Hunter Wolf, Broadway Producer and Director, and Children's Theater Activist (1904–2002)

Mary was born in Bakersfield, California, in 1904 and her mother died two weeks later. Within two years of his wife's death, her father, a rancher, moved to Beverly Hills, an area that was at that time still rural. Her father took a job in banking and remarried when Mary was four years old. Mary remembered her stepmother as someone who was concerned about and attentive to her needs. Mary had many interests as a child but two stood out: reading and debates. By the time she reached high school she had attended several different schools and had learned to love the theater, dance, and drama. Her father died when she was 12 years old, and Mary continued to live with her stepmother, although her father's sister, Mary Austin, became more involved in her life. Mary Austin was divorced and her only child had been born with severe developmental delays and eventually died. An ardent feminist, she was the author of numerous books, articles, and plays, including a play titled *The Arrow Maker*, written in 1911, about the devaluation of women's talents. Austin also wrote a novel titled *A Woman of Genius*, which describes how traditional marriages can stifle women's creativity. In addition to this manuscript, Austin also wrote *Greatness in Women* in 1923 and *A Woman Looks at Her World* in 1924.

It is apparent that Mary Austin had a significant impact on the life of Mary Hunter Wolf, as did her childhood friend, Agnes de Mille, with whom she remained close friends all of her life. De Mille became Mary's friend when they attended the Hollywood School for Girls and they were involved in drama productions and theater games together. Agnes de Mille often asked Mary to accompany her to the theater, as her father was a producer and director of the earliest Hollywood films, including *Four Horseman* with Rudolph Valentino. During summers while she was in high school, Mary worked in a Hollywood theater where de Mille's father was producing films. After her high school graduation, Mary left California to attend Wellesley but was surprised at the prep school mentality she encountered at Wellesley and the lack of social consciousness of the student body in the 1920s. She continued to be involved in theater productions at Wellesley, but left college after her junior year because of health problems and spent the next few years with her aunt in New Mexico. There she lived, taught, and acted as a secretary for her aunt until moving to Chicago to finish college and begin her theater work. She worked temporarily as a sales clerk and a radio talk show host, and eventually landed the part of "Marge" in *Easy Aces*, a radio comedy show that was nearly as famous as the *Amos and Andy Show*.

While living in Chicago, Mary married a law student, joined the social-ist party, and subsequently moved to New York with the troupe involved in *Easy Aces*. With the Depression, many of her friends were out of work, so Mary was thrilled to have a steady income. Her husband finished law school and remained in Chicago for about a year before joining Mary in New York. Unfortunately, and because of, she believed, the rise in her in-come as compared with her husband's, the marriage began to disintegrate and eventually ended as her career began to peak. From 1938 to 1944, she directed six stage productions for the American Actors Company, which she had helped to found. From 1944 to 1955 she directed five Broadway productions and assisted with a sixth. She worked with Jerome Robbins on *Peter Pan*, and helped nurture the careers of several choreographers play-wrights, including Tennessee Williams. She was one of a group of nine female directors in the U.S. who directed but did not act, all of whom were single and childless.

At the height of her directing and theater career in New York City, two friends from her years in Chicago reentered her life. Mary had maintained a very close relationship with these friends, who were married and lived in Connecticut with their three young children. Then tragedy struck, and the husband was widowed and left with children to raise by himself. Mary recalled that considerable pressure was put on her to marry her friend and become a stepmother to the three children, who were eleven, eight and five. She left New York, moved to Connecticut, married, and became a mother to the children, who were, she recalled, in "terrible shape and needed her very much." She remembered this time as fascinating, difficult, absorbing, and creative. Although her life had changed drastically, she sought other creative challenges in the schools and the community, working with dis-advantaged youngsters in the urban areas. Mary described this period of her life as a time when she gave support and love to both her husband and the children.

Her husband decided to end the marriage after ten years, having fallen in love with someone else. Mary was initially very hurt, but what troubled her more was that he also tried to end her relationship with her children, who by then regarded Mary as their mother. By this time, she had been away from the theater for so long that she could not simply return to Broadway as a director and producer. Additionally, as she emphasized, she could not consider leaving Connecticut because her children were there and she believed that they still needed her. When asked if she had any regrets about having left Broadway at the peak of her career, she exclaimed with surprise: "Regrets? How could I have regrets? If I had not married him, I would not have had my children."

Rather than feel bitterness about what had happened with her mar-riages, Mary described these times in her life as "creative passages" af-fected positively by the impact of caring for three children and adjusting to a new husband at the age of 50, which she described as stimulating. For decades following her divorce, she remained close to her children and entered a new phase in her life, dedicating her talents and energies to urban arts education. She was active in the Connecticut Commission on the Arts, eventually serving as chair. She was a producer for the American Shakespeare Festival Theater (ASFT), for which she developed education outreach programs for schools. She started an innovative counseling program, which later became a model program in the country, using theater techniques with students who were economically disadvantaged. She also kept many of her New York connections, including her relationships with Agnes de Mille, Jerome Robbins, and many other actors, choreographers, directors, producers, and people associated with the theater. She moved to New Haven, which allowed her greater access to New York City, and she embarked on new challenges, including starting innovative theater programs that are still active today, three years after her death.

Joan Tower, American Composer (1938–)

Joan Tower, known as one of the leading American composers of the modern period, is an energetic, attractive woman with brown hair and a wide smile. She is humble, laughs quickly, and often jokes about herself. Her father was a mining engineer who played the violin, and her mother, a housewife, played the piano. Joan had a sister who was nine years older and a brother who was nine years younger. She attended public schools and began piano lessons when she was six, and when she was nine, the family moved to Bolivia, where her father had accepted a job as a mine supervisor. Joan's older sister remained in the States to attend college and her brother was a baby, so she felt somewhat alone as she adjusted to a new home, a new language, and a new environment. She interacted frequently with the native Bolivians who worked with her family and attended festivals celebrating religious holidays and other events, where she remembers hearing different types of musical instruments. She also traveled with her father on business, sometimes riding on llamas to the mines. Joan's piano teacher in Bolivia held high expectations for her, including frequent practice. She recalls that music was always a part of her life. Her family would often gather around the piano after dinner, where her father played the violin or sang, her mother played the piano, and Joan would improvise on South American percussion instruments.

She loved horses and often rode for enjoyment, convincing her father to buy her a racehorse, which was affordable in Bolivia. She admitted that she was rebellious in school and when her family returned to the United States, Joan completed her last two years in a boarding school, where she continued piano lessons and practiced for several hours each day.

She pursued her musical interests while attending Bennington College in Vermont, where she completed her first musical composition as an assigned class project. She graduated from Bennington in 1961 and moved to New York City, where she became a graduate student in composition at Columbia University. She earned a master's degree in 1964 and her doctoral degree in music in 1978. Joan supported herself by giving piano lessons and forming a chamber group, the De Capo Chamber Players, devoted to performing new pieces of music. In addition, she organized a series of contemporary music concerts and raised the money to hire the musicians. She wrote one new composition each season for the series, which provided the opportunity for her to hear her own music performed. The chamber group she started became very well known, produced several recordings, performed all over the world, and premiered over 100 new works.

By 1985, Joan had composed more than 17 pieces, including solos for clarinet, violin, and flute, and a number of pieces for multiple instruments. Her first work for orchestra, *Sequoia*, written in 1981, became extremely successful, having been played by 30 orchestras, including the New York Philharmonic. Reviews of her work have appeared in major newspapers, journals, magazines, and music periodicals, and she has received numerous awards, commissions, fellowships, and grants from the Guggenheim, Fromm, Naumburg, Kousssevitzky, and Jerome Foundations. She was profiled in an award winning PBS documentary and major symphonies continue to perform her work. Recently, one of her compositions, *Silver Ladders*, competed against 140 other new orchestral works to win the Grawemeyer Award, the largest cash prize award in music. She has had a long-term relationship with a man with whom she has lived for almost 30 years (whom she married in 2001), and has never had children. She has many commissions, and admits that on the days of the week she is not teaching, she often spends seven or eight hours a day composing. She does not like to take time off from her work and feels an obligation to be a female composer who continues to contribute. "We still have such a long way to go," she explained. "I mean, just look at the statistics. How many pieces by women composers do you know? And how many do you really know? The musicology network is still overwhelmingly a male network. I mean, the standard music history textbook – the *Grout History of Music* – listed two women. That's for the whole history of music."

In more recent years, her work has gained even more prestige. Her *Fanfare for the Uncommon Woman (No. 1)* has been played by more than 500 different ensembles since its 1987 premiere and is recorded on RCA (Saint Louis Symphony/Slatkin). The *Second, Third, Fourth*, and *Fifth Fanfares* were commissioned respectively by Absolut Vodka, Carnegie Hall, the Kansas City Symphony, and the Aspen Music Festival. She has many recent commissions and she has conducted at the White House (*Celebration from Stepping Stones*), the Scotia Festival in Canada, the Fairbanks Symphony, the Hudson Valley Philharmonic, and the American Symphony Orchestra.

Tower has been the subject of television documentaries on WGBH (Boston), CBS Sunday Morning, and MJW Productions (England). Her second and third quartets (*In Memory* and *Incandescent*) have toured throughout the world with the Tokyo and Emerson Quartets.

In 1998, she was elected to the American Academy of Arts and Letters and in 2004 to the American Academy of Arts and Sciences. She continues as the Asher Edelman Professor of Music at Bard College, where she has taught since 1972, and she has interesting views about female composers: "I think some people are not aware that there are no women composers in their concerts. So for that reason, I do like to be reminded, this is a woman composer. Other than that, music is the music and the fact that I'm a woman doesn't make a difference to the music." She also believes that it is important to remind people that there are women who can compose and that the public can buy their records. She feels strongly that she needs to help other women as a mentor and role model, and that progress is slow because "there are a lot of women out there who are very passive" and, as she explained:

they are more critical of their talent than their male counterparts. If male composers feel that way they certainly don't broadcast it. But there's a problem with that. Women don't have a lot of role models certainly, especially among dead composers, and they don't have enough of a support system within their own community. So they have to forge their way very much by themselves and some of them just don't have the strength to do this.

RESEARCH THEMES ABOUT TALENTED AND EMINENT WOMEN

In a society in which the majority of our inventors, leaders, politicians, artists, and musicians have been male, how does a woman *develop* a philosophical belief about her own potential and the support system needed for high levels of creative work? How might she overcome her upbringing, her parents' and teachers' advice and imprinting on her manners and personal characteristics, and the knowledge that high-level contributions take large blocks of time away from those she loves? When Maria Goeppart-Mayer made the discovery that later resulted in a Nobel Prize, she delayed publishing her results for months. A biographer concluded that modesty may have caused this delay (Dash, 1973, p. 322); however, Goeppart-Mayer's hesitation may also reflect a fear of failure or even the intrinsic belief imposed on highly able women by our society – that discoveries, inventions, and creations are usually the work of men. Until many more women are visible as discoverers, inventors, composers, or creators, they may be relegated to the roles they have traditionally held – implementers of others' ideas, organizers, service providers, and the painters of the backdrop of creation. Only more research about women of accomplishment and those with high potential who do not achieve work at the highest levels will enable a better understanding of these complex variables. To help frame a future direction for this research, I have classified the relatively sparse research focusing on the development of women's talents into four major themes.

Theme One: Personality Characteristics of Talented Women

The first theme relates to the identification of personality characteristics of talented women and the study of these characteristics as a means of learning what may be necessary to develop talents. Research in this area generally falls under the umbrella of historical views using retrospective analyses or contemporary research about talented women, such as the eminent women discussed earlier in this chapter. When they conduct historical research, researchers use biographical works to identify common personality factors of famous women writers, scientists, and artists (e.g. Antler, 1987; Dash, 1988; Gabor, 1995). Both retrospective and contemporary analyses generally identify personality factors such as the persistence to overcome challenges or problems, independence, and a willingness to live a life different from their peers' or counterparts'. Wallace and Wahlberg (1995), for example, attempted to identify the early conditions of successful adult females by using a historical analysis of traits. As girls, notable women were intelligent, hardworking, imaginative, and strong willed. In addition, girls who became famous writers were more apt to question assumptions and conventions than were those who became notable artists, scientists, lawyers, and politicians. Helson (1996) described the personality characteristics of creative female mathematicians as compared with males as highly flexible, original, and able to reject outside influences. She also found that they were rebellious, independent, introverted, and flexible, both in their general attitudes and in their mathematical work. A summary of pertinent research that identifies personal characteristics of gifted and talented women suggests the existence of several common personality characteristics (Wasserman, 2000; Kennedy & McConnell, 2001; Arnold, Noble & Subotnik, 1996; Linehan, 2001; Omar & Davidson, 2001; Dash, 1973; Reis, 1998; 2002; Bateson, 1990; Wallace & Wahlberg, 1995; Ajzenberg-Selove, F., 1994; Oppenheimer, 1988). These include task commitment, resilience, and determination; individualism; openness to exploration of wide range of interests; creativity and risk-taking; ability to maintain focus despite diversity of interests; and energy and excitement about work.

Theme Two: Internal and External Barriers that Impede the Development of Women's Talents and Gifts

The second research theme relates to barriers that may impede the development of women's talents. Research with high-potential women suggests that internal, personal barriers as well as external barriers hinder the completion of high-level work (Arnold & Denny, 1985; Callahan, 1979; Hollinger & Fleming, 1988; Kerr, 1985; Ochse, 1991; Piirto, 1991; Reis, 1987, 1998; Subotnik & Arnold, 1995). External barriers include the way women were raised as children and the cultural messages they encounter in life; external barriers contribute to internal barriers. These internal barriers are often deeply personal; for example, an artist explained that her children had caused her to put her sculpting talents on hold: "I have spent the last 25 years sculpting my three children. They have taken every ounce of my creativity, and there has been little left, either in talent, time, or creative energy, for my other work" (Reis, 1998). Although she had difficulty saying this, she did explain that she sometimes wondered what might have happened to her artistic talent if she had decided not to have children.

Research about these external barriers can also be historical or contemporary. Historical explanations posit that women were often underrated or ignored in history, perhaps because many girls were not encouraged or allowed to engage in intellectual pursuits. They usually received less education than boys, and were often denied access to teachers and opportunities to develop their potential. In the past, women, especially minority women, undoubtedly received little encouragement, stimulation, and access to the tools necessary for building intellectual skills and developing the ability to create something of cultural value. Women were regarded as less able than males to creatively use their intellectual skills, and if they attempted to do so, they often expressed constraints in their personal lives (Reis, 1998). Contemporary explanations raise questions about why women do not follow their interests into career preparation, or place more importance on the works they produce (Arnold, 1995; Callahan, 1979; Kerr, 1985; Reis, 1987; 1998). The problem may be further exacerbated for women who do produce original, creative work, as they are more conscious of criticism than men and find it more difficult to deal with negative perceptions of their work (Baer, 1997; Roberts, 1991; Roberts & Nolen-Hoeksema, 1994; Reis, 1998). The importance of relationships and guilt about putting work ahead of personal relationships appears to be the most compelling and frequently mentioned internal barrier (Arnold, 1995; Reis, 1998). Other external barriers include multiple demands on time, feelings of guilt when they attempt to work during time that others (mothers, sisters, friends) tell them should be spent with family, or in some cases, lack of support, negative perceptions of others, difficulty in work environments, and a lack of interest in working alone for the periods of time necessary for creative accomplishment (Callahan, 1979; Kerr, 1985; Ochse, 1991; Piirto, 1991; Reis, 1987; 1998). During the same years in which Lehman (1953) found the height of male creative productivity to occur, women's responsibilities to children increase (Reis, 1998). Some contemporary researchers have also noted that in our society, exceptionally able women experience considerable stress related to role conflict and overload, which may reduce creative urges (Ochse, 1991; Piirto, 1991; Reis, 1987; 1998).

A summary of selected research on internal and external barriers suggests that several internal and external factors commonly affect talented women (Knights & Richards, 2003; Reis, 2002; Linehan, 2001; Nelson & Burke, 2002; Wasserman, 2000; O'Donovan-Polter, 2001; Omar & Davidson, 2001; Arnold, Noble, & Subotnik, 1996; Reis, 1998; Bateson, 1990; Oppenheimer, 1988; Dash, 1973). Internal factors include: focus on the importance of relationships over achievement; internalization of external values and gender role definitions; feelings of loneliness, isolation, and lack of support; devaluing of one's own abilities and self-sabotage; and unrealistic expectations. A summary of external barriers (Wasserman, 2000; Kennedy & McConnell, 2001; O'Donovan-Polter, 2001; Burke, 2001a; Linehan, 2001; Omar & Davidson, 2001; Knights & Richards, 2003; Arnold, Noble, & Subotnik, 1996; Dash, 1973; Reis, 1998; Nelson & Burke, 2002; Reis, 2001; 2002; Oppenheimer, 1988; Bateson, 1990; Hardwick, 1990) includes the nature of choices between work and family; lack of support for achievement and ambition from family and friends; absence or negative influence of other women in the workplace; colleagues' negative perception of women in professional settings; and the negative effects of the general social perception of women's abilities and roles.

Theme Three: Factors that Enable Talented Women to Succeed

Women who achieve eminence often display single-minded purpose, make difficult choices about personal lives (including decisions to divorce or not to marry, to have fewer children or none at all, to live alone, etc.) and create support systems (including, for example, supportive spouses) to enable their creative productivity to emerge. Decisions are usually consciously made to support the adaptation of a lifestyle conducive to the production of highly challenging work. In research examining how highly creative female artists develop their talents, List and Renzulli (1991) found that they had generally supportive families, at least one influential mentor in their lives, a strong, personal drive to create, and a need to share their products with appropriate audiences. Roscher (1987) studied successful scientists who attributed part of their accomplishments to a role model, whether during high school or college, or an individual professor or family member who provided encouragement. The women who married also attributed their continued success to the encouragement of their spouse, often a scientist, who recognized the sacrifices necessary for success. In some cases, talented women such as Shirley Jackson and Maria Mayer were almost "bullied" into producing work that their husbands believed would be noteworthy.

Theme Four: Differences Between Women's and Men's Work Process and Product

The last theme relates to gender differences that exist in work products and creative work processes. Some researchers have called for changes in the paradigm of how we view women and talent development, and the need for changes in society that could facilitate the development of high potential in women (Bateson, 1990; Kirschenbaum & Reis, 1997). Women have made and continue to make many creative contributions that are different from the accomplishments made by men, yet men's creative accomplishments seem to be valued more by society (Reis, 1987; 1995; 1996; 1998). The accomplishments of women may not reflect the form of creative productivity that results in awards, prizes, books, articles, art, patents, professional stature, and financial gain. Rather, their creative efforts may differ from those of their male counterparts.

Because women's life experiences in society may be vastly different from men's, (Gilligan, 1982; Miller, 1976), it seems logical that differences in process and productivity also exist. For example, some female artists believe that the creative growth gained from both childbirth and parenting can actually contribute to creative growth in their art (Kirschenbaum & Reis, 1997). One highly productive female scientist with several patents and more than 100 scientific papers acknowledged that she did her research in addition to being the dean of science in a highly competitive university. She carried the responsibility for almost 100 faculty members, more than $20 million in budget and grants, and she ran a large lab on her own research initiatives. She was committed to having more economically disadvantaged and culturally diverse students become scientists and a critical part of her work continued to be the mentoring of young, talented African American students from urban high schools. She explained that she was very efficient and could engage in multiple tasks. On weekends, she did not continue with her academic work but rather pursued another love, gardening. She had three children who had all graduated from college and were successful in their lives, and a loving relationship with her husband, an architect, who explained that his work had always been secondary to that of his wife. They had been happily married for 30 years. She may never win a Nobel Prize, but she chose, like many other highly accomplished women, to diversify her talents, applying them to her lab, her work as an administrator and professor, her role as a mentor to economically disadvantaged students, her spouse and children, and her interests and hobbies, especially her gardening. She did this because all of these areas brought her joy, she explained, and because she felt a

sense of responsibility across all of these areas, particularly in her relationships with her family, her graduate students and faculty, and her high
school students, many of whom pursued graduate work in her area of
science.

Perhaps the most controversial issue related to women and their work
process is the claim that there may be a potential mismatch between the
single-minded devotion necessary for creative accomplishment and either
their personalities or their need and desire to balance family and career
(Piirto, 1991; Subotnik & Arnold, 1995). In fact, many women have the
potential to display single-minded devotion to their work but they choose
to diversify their creative efforts as did Mary Hunter Wolf and the scientist
described previously (Reis, 2002b).

Recent research (Reis, 1987, 1995; 1996; 1998) has demonstrated that
some women's talents are diversified across multiple areas in their lives
(foxes, rather than hedgehogs), including relationships, work related to
family and home, personal interests, aesthetic sensitivities, and appearances. This diversification of their creative talents emerges in their work
but also in other areas including relationships with family and friends, and
in the ways they decorate their homes, prepare meals, plan complicated
schedules for their families, balance time between work and personal life,
and stretch the family budget. When asked about various periods of high-
level productivity in her life shortly before she died, Mary Hunter Wolf
discussed her beliefs about the ways in which women's creative work
evolved in a different pattern than men's:

Women spend their lives moving from one creative act to another and they find
satisfaction from their creative expression in many different outlets. I have found
that men, on the other hand, see an end goal and move directly toward the pursuit
of that creative goal. That is why men are able to achieve goals and fame more
quickly than women, but I think that women have a richer creative journey, find
joy in the diversity of their creative acts, and in the end, enjoy the creative process
and their own talents so much more.

Perhaps because women have had to struggle to find a place for themselves in work situations, they have not yet had the time or experience
to be able to engage in the single-minded devotion to work that men
have had. Perhaps the barriers that they have experienced over time have
led to the need to diversify their talents (Kirschenbaum & Reis, 1997; List
and Renzulli, 1991; Ochse, 1991; Piirto, 1991; Reis, 1987; 1995; 1996; 1998;
Roscher, 1987), or it may be that they simply prefer the diverse expressions
of their creativity and talent.

The creative process in women may emerge differently than in men
and their creative work products may also differ. Female writers, artists,
scientists, and creators in all domains interact primarily with male standards of productivity that have been accepted as the standard within a

domain, but may actually only be the standard for male creators (Reis, 1998). Therefore, until more women are able to produce in more areas, their productivity may be lower. A synthesis of some research reviewed in this chapter also suggests that the work process of talented women focuses more on team building, integrating personal relationships with their careers, and understanding – without accepting – the reality of higher workloads accompanied by lower status in their work environment. These women also pursue, with intensity, the social responsibilities related to their work and the impact of this work on the betterment of society.

IDENTIFYING AND SERVING GIFTED GIRLS IN SCHOOL

It is difficult, if not impossible, to discuss gifted girls without discussing gifted women, because many young gifted girls believe that they can "do it all" or "have it all," whereas many older gifted females have learned that they cannot. Many gifted girls excelled in school, but as they grew older, ambivalence about their future caused their hopes and career dreams to waiver. As one talented woman who was a high school valedictorian explained in an interview, "I used to think I could become president. I was so supremely confident and so positive I would succeed. Now, I work part-time in a non-challenging job, take care of my three kids, go to the grocery store, and try to finish the laundry by Sunday night so they will all have clean clothes for school on Monday. I just don't know how all of this happened" (Reis, 1995). Understanding more about why hope fades is one reason that research about gifted girls and women continues; another is to add to the intriguing discussion about why early precocity often does not translate into eminence in later life.

Research indicates that both belief in ability and self-confidence of talented females is undermined or diminished during childhood or adolescence. In one qualitative study, not one gifted girl attributed her success in school to extraordinary ability (Callahan, Cunningham, & Plucker, 1994). Other research has indicated that despite a degree of "feminine modesty," some gifted females have realistic fears and diminished self-confidence about the future (Reis, Hébert, Diaz, Maxfield, & Ratley, 1995). What factors help some smart young girls become self-fulfilled, talented adults who can achieve at high levels and enjoy personal happiness? Some studies of gifted women summarized in this chapter provide suggestions about how to enhance the experiences of smart girls during childhood and adolescence to help increase the likelihood that they will achieve their dreams. First, they should be identified as having talents and encouraged to engage in as many enriching opportunities as possible to expose them to a wide a range of experiences, such as those suggested in our work on the Schoolwide Enrichment Model (Renzulli & Reis, 1985; 1997). Identification should be based on interests and on a broad range of talents, including those relating to social action. Diverse opportunities for creative–productive work should be provided, including competitions like History Day and experiences such as Girl Scouts and summer programs that expose young girls to multiple areas of interest (Reis, 1998; Rimm, 1999). In particular, younger gifted girls should have the chance to discuss what happens to older gifted women of accomplishment, to hear their stories and their ideas, and to learn from them. They should be able to read biographies and autobiographies of these women and to learn from their experiences about the windmills they saw and conquered. Suggested opportunities, resources, and encouragement for gifted girls are summarized in a book written about this topic (Reis, 1998).

CONCLUSION

The reasons for the successful accomplishments of some talented girls and women and the failure of others to realize their high potential in meaningful work are complex and depend on many factors including values, personal choices, and sociocultural forces. Today, in our current societal structure, a strong possibility exists that many talented females, especially those who are married and have children, may not produce the same level of work as their male counterparts. Therefore, the realization of women's talents may need to be redefined or expanded to include, for example, the joy of accomplishment as they pursue a career that still allows time for a satisfying personal life, the nurturing of children and family, or the success of being outstanding in an area outside of professional work (Reis, 1987). Yet, although the importance of these types of contributions cannot be underestimated and may be essential for societal well-being, they are simply not enough for many talented women who have a sense of destiny about their own potential to produce meaningful work that makes a difference (Reis, 1998). Some of these women make active choices to pursue their talents because they have a sense of destiny about the importance of their work. With societal changes in the role of men, more women may seek and find partners who are more willing to support their hopes and dreams, assuming more of the responsibilities for children, home, and community. Women, of course, will have to be willing to gracefully accept and celebrate these partnerships.

The experiences of the eminent women described in this chapter suggest that many personal choices and barriers confronted this diverse group. The development of a creatively productive life is intricate and complex, and decidedly personal. What one regarded as an obstacle, another perceived as an intriguing challenge. Some were negatively influenced by their parents' lack of support and withdrew from relationships; others used this anger and rebelled, and eventually became eminent in their selected area of endeavor. The ways in which the same barriers differentially affect talented women provides the fascination about conducting research on the individual paths they follow to achieve high levels of accomplishment. Not all gifted females experience the same barriers, but my research suggests a combination of the following that occur across the lifespan and differentially affect productivity at different ages and stages: personality characteristics such as modesty, dilemmas about abilities and talents, personal decisions about family, and decisions about duty and caring (putting the needs of others first) as opposed to nurturing personal, religious, and social issues. Some of these dilemmas cannot be resolved to the satisfaction of everyone involved. Rather, they shift or are eliminated when changes occur in a woman's life, such as when her children grow up, her marriage ends, a new relationship starts, or she changes a home or work environment.

If our society is to more actively support talented girls and adult women to realize their abilities and potential, work environments must be altered and we must support diversity of life choices. All of the eminent women that I studied were able to combine meaningful work with what they considered to be a content personal life, and most achieved some level of harmony and balance among their talents, their personal lives, and their contributions to society. Perhaps it is the importance of relationships and care that creates this balance and it may be that this same priority will eventually be as critical to men. It seems clear that it is becoming that way. But the barriers still exist for women in our society, as talented women "opt out" as they tire of the struggle between work and family in what has been called a revolution (Belkin, 2003). Virginia Woolf wrote that we must slay the angel in the house and the censor within us. Speaking out, asking why, and developing the courage to create are all essential to the emergence of feminist talents that will not be manifested in a singular voice or a similar form to men's, but rather in a multitude of voices and forms. A celebration of these and a realization of the need for meaningful work that makes a difference will help more talented women create their own unique voice and form. Although it is impossible to measure how many talented women underachieve, we can listen carefully to older women of high potential who look back at their lives with feelings of regret and say: "I might have, but..." or "I could have if..." or "I never had time to...". Our society needs this talent source today in many roles, and it is time for us to benefit more fully from the changes that may occur in the environment, politics, healthcare, technology, legislation, science, art, music, and other areas if more talented women are able to emerge as leaders and producers.

References

Ajzenberg-Selove, F. (1994). *A matter of choices: Memoirs of a female physicist.* Brunswick, NJ: Rutgers University Press.

Antler, J. (1987). *Lucy Sprague Mitchell.* New Haven: Yale University Press.

Arnold, K. D. (1995). *Lives of promise*. San Francisco: Jossey-Bass.

Arnold, K. D., & Denny, T. (1985, April). *The lives of academic achievers: The career aspiration of male and female high school valedictorians and salutatorians.* Paper presented at the annual meeting of the American Educational Research Association, Chicago, IL.

Arnold, K. D., Noble, K. D., & Subotnik, R. F. (1996). Remarkable women: Perspectives on female talent development. Cresskill, NJ: Hampton.

Axelrod, T. (1988). Patently successful. *Ms., 16*(10), 44–45.

Baer, J. (1997). Gender differences in the effects of anticipated evaluation of creativity. *Creativity Research Journal, 10*(1), 25–31.

Bateson, M. C. (1990). *Composing a life*. New York. Plume.

Belkin, L. (2003, October 23). The opt-out revolution. *New York Times Magazine*, 42–47, 58, 85–86.

Berlin, I. (1953). *The hedgehog and the fox*. New York: Simon & Schuster.

Burke, R. J. (2001a). Managerial women's career experiences, satisfaction, and well-being: A five-country study. *Cross-Cultural Management, 8*(3/4), 117–133.

Burke, R. J. (2001b). Women in management: Cross-cultural research. *Cross-Cultural Management, 8*(3/4), 3–10.

Burton, L. J. (2002). Talent development in female Olympians: A phenomenological approach. Unpublished doctoral dissertation: University of Connecticut, Storrs.

Callahan, C. M. (1979). The gifted and talented woman. In A. H. Passow (Ed.), *The gifted and talented* (pp. 401–423). Chicago: National Society for the Study of Education.

Callahan, C. M., Cunningham, C. M., & Plucker, J. A. (1994). Foundations for the future: The socio-emotional development of gifted, adolescent women. *Roeper Review, 17*(2), 99–105.

Cattell, J. M. (1903). A statistical study of eminent men. *Popular Science Monthly, 62*, 359–377.

Dash, J. (1973). A life of one's own: Three gifted women and the men they married. New York: Paragon.

Dash, J. (1988). *A life of one's own*. New York: Paragon.

Diamond, A. (1986). Guests at the table: Feminists and contracts. *Thought and Action, 2*, 123–34.

Gabor, A. (1995). *Einstein's wife: Work and marriage in the lives of five great twenty-first century women*. New York: Viking.

Gilligan, C. (1982). *In a different voice: Psychological theory and women's development*. Cambridge, MA: Harvard University Press.

Gruber, H. E. (1986). The self-construction of the extraordinary. In R. J. Sternberg & J. E. Davidson (Eds.), *Conceptions of giftedness* (pp. 247–260). New York: Cambridge University Press.

Hardwick, J. (1990). *An immodest violet*. London: Andre Deutsch.

Helson, R. (1996). In search of the creative personality. *Creativity Research Journal, 9*(4), 295–306.

Hollinger, C. L., & Fleming, E. S. (1988). Gifted and talented young women: Antecedents and correlates of life satisfaction. *Gifted Child Quarterly, 32*(2), 254–260.

Hutchinson, E. J. (1930). *Women and the Ph.D.* Greensboro, NC: College for Women.

Kennedy, C. J., & McConnell, M. (2001). *Generally speaking*. New York: Warner.

Kerr, B. A. (1985). *Smart girls, gifted women*. Columbus, OH: Ohio Psychology.

Kirschenbaum, R. J., & Reis, S. M. (1997). Conflicts in creativity: Talented female artists. *Creativity Research Journal, 10*(2&3), 251–263.

Knights, D., & Richards, W. (2003). Sex discrimination in UK academia. *Gender, Work, and Organization, 10*(2), 213–238.

Lehman, H. C. (1953). *Age and achievement*. Princeton, NJ: Princeton University Press.

Lerner, G. (1993). *The creation of feminist consciousness*. New York: Oxford University Press.

Lindauer, M. S. (1992). Creativity in aging artists. *Creativity Research Journal, 5*(3), 211–231.

Linehan, M. (2001). Women international managers: The European experience. *Cross-Cultural Management, 8*(3/4), 68–84.

List, K., & Renzulli, J. (1991). Creative women's developmental patterns through age thirty-five. *Gifted Education International, 7*(3), 114–122.

McLeish, J. A. B. (1976). *The Ulyssean adult: Creative in the middle and later years*. New York: McGraw-Hill.

Miller, J. B. (1976). *Toward a new psychology of women*. Boston: Beacon.

Nelson, D. L., & Burke, R. J. (Eds.). (2002). Gender, work stress, and health. Washington, DC: American Psychological Association.

Noble, K., Subotnik, R., & Arnold, K. (1996). A new model for adult female talent development: A synthesis of perspectives from remarkable women. In K. Arnold, K. Noble, & R. Subotnik (Eds.), *Remarkable women: Perspectives on female talent development*. Cresskill, NJ: Hampton.

Ochse, R. (1991). Why there were relatively few eminent women creators. *Journal of Creative Behavior, 25*(4), 334–343.

O'Connell, A. N., & Russo, N. F. (1983). Models of achievement: Reflections of eminent women in psychology. New York: Columbia University Press.

Oden, M. H. (1968). The fulfillment of promise. *Genetic Psychology Monographs, 77*(1), 3–93.

O'Donovan-Polter, S. (2001). The scales of success: Constructions of life-career success of eminent men and women lawyers. Toronto, Canada: University of Toronto Press.

Omar, A., & Davidson, M. J. (2001). Women in management: A comparative cross-cultural overview. *Cross-Cultural Management, 8*(3/4), 35–67.

Oppenheimer, J. (1988). Private demons: The life of Shirley Jackson. New York: Ballantine.

Piirto, J. (1991). Why are there so few? (creative women: visual artists, mathematicians, musicians). *Roeper Review, 13*(3), 142–147.

Reis, S. M. (1987). We can't change what we don't recognize: Understanding the special needs of gifted females. *Gifted Child Quarterly, 31*, 83–88.

Reis, S. M. (1995). Talent ignored, talent diverted: The cultural context underlying giftedness in females. *Gifted Child Quarterly, 39*, 162–170.

Reis, S. M. (1996). Older women's reflections on eminence: Obstacles and opportunities. In K. D. Arnold, K. D. Noble, & R. F. Subotnik (Eds.), *Remarkable women: Perspectives on female talent development* (pp. 149–168). Cresskill, NJ: Hampton.

Reis, S. M. (1998). *Work left undone*. Mansfield Center, CT: Creative Learning Press.

Reis, S. M. (2001). External barriers experienced by gifted and talented girls and women. *Gifted Child Today, 24*(4), 26–35, 65.

Reis, S. M. (2002a). Internal barriers, personal issues, and decisions faced by gifted and talented females. *Gifted Child Today, 25*(1), 14–28.

Reis, S. M. (2002b). Toward a theory of creativity in diverse creative women. *Creativity Research Journal, 14*(3–4), 305–316.

Reis, S. M., Hébert, T. P., Diaz, E. I., Maxfield, L. R., & Ratley, M. E. (1995). *Case studies of talented students who achieve and underachieve in an urban high school* (Research Monograph 95114). Storrs, CT: University of Connecticut, The National Research Center for the Gifted and Talented.

Renzulli, J. S. (1978). What makes giftedness? Re-examining a definition. *Phi Delta Kappan, 60*, 180–184, 261.

Renzulli, J. S. (1986). The three-ring conception of giftedness: A developmental model for creative productivity. In R. J. Sternberg & J. E. Davidson (Eds.), *Conceptions of giftedness* (pp. 53–92). New York: Cambridge University Press.

Renzulli, J. S. (1991). The national research center on the gifted and talented: The dream, the design, and the destination. *Gifted Child Quarterly, 35*(2), 73–80.

Renzulli, J. S., & Reis, S. M. (1985). *The schoolwide enrichment model: A comprehensive plan for educational excellence*. Mansfield Center, CT: Creative Learning Press.

Renzulli, J. S., & Reis, S. M. (1997). *The schoolwide enrichment model: A how-to guide for educational excellence*. Mansfield Center, CT: Creative Learning Press.

Rimm, S., Rimm-Kaufman, S., & Rimm, I. (1999). See Jane win. New York: Crown.

Roberts, T. (1991). Gender and the influence of evaluations on self-assessments in achievement settings. *Psychological Bulletin, 109*(2), 297–308.

Roberts, T., & Nolen-Hoeksema, S. (1994). Gender comparisons in responsiveness to others' evaluations in achievement settings. *Psychology of Women Quarterly, 18*, 221–240.

Roscher, N. (1987). Chemistry's creative women. *Journal of Chemical Education, 56*(4), 748–752.

Schneidman, E. (1989). The Indian summer of life: A preliminary study of septuagenarians. *American Psychologist, 44*, 684–694.

Sears, R. (1977). Sources of satisfactions of Terman's gifted men. *American Psychologist, 32*, 119–128.

Simonton, D. K. (1975). Sociocultural context of individual creativity: A transhistorical time-series analysis. *Journal of Personality and Social Psychology, 32*, 1119–1133.

Simonton, D. K. (1977). Creative productivity, age, and stress: A biographical time-series analysis of 10 classical composers. *Journal of Personality and Social Psychology, 35*, 791–804.

Simonton, D. K. (1984). Artistic creativity and interpersonal relations across and within generations. *Journal of Personality and Social Psychology, 46*, 1273–1286.

Simonton, D. K. (1988). Age and outstanding achievement: What do we know after a century of research? *Psychological Bulletin, 104*, 251–267.

Simonton, D. K. (1989). The swan-song phenomenon: Last-work effects for 172 classical composers. *Psychology and Aging, 4*, 42–47.

Sternberg, R. J. (1985). Beyond IQ: A triarchic theory of human intelligence. New York: Cambridge University Press.

Sternberg, R. J. (1986). A triarchic theory of intellectual giftedness. In R. J. Sternberg & J. E. Davidson (Eds.), *Conceptions of giftedness* (pp. 233–243). New York: Cambridge University Press.

Sternberg, R. J. (1999). The theory of successful intelligence. *Review of General Psychology, 3,* 292–316.

Sternberg, R. J., & Davidson, J. E. (Eds.). (1986). *Conceptions of giftedness.* New York: Cambridge University Press.

Sternberg, R. J., & Gregorenko, E. L. (2002). The theory of successful intelligence as a basis for gifted education. *Gifted Child Quarterly, 46*(4), 265–277.

Subotnik, R., & Arnold, K. (1995). Passing through the gates: Career establishment of talented women scientists. *Roeper Review, 13*(3), 55–61.

Tannenbaum, A. J. (1983). *Gifted children: Psychological and educational perspectives.* New York: Macmillan.

Tannenbaum, A. J. (1991). The social psychology of giftedness. In N. Colangelo & G. A. Davis (Eds.), *Handbook of gifted education* (pp. 27–44). Boston: Allyn & Bacon.

Vance, C. M., & Paik, Y. (2001). Where do American women face their biggest obstacle to expatriate success? Back in their own backyard. *Cross-Cultural Management, 8*(3/4), 98–116.

Varma, A., & Stroh, L. K. (2001). Different perspectives on selection for international assignments: The impact of LMX and gender. *Cross-Cultural Management, 8*(3/4), 85–97.

Wallace, T., & Walberg, H. (1995). Girls who became famous literalists of the imagination. *Roeper Review, 13*(3), 24–27.

Wasserman, E. (2000). The door in the dream: Conversations with eminent women in science. Washington, DC: Joseph Henry.

Winstone, H. V. F. (1978). *Gertrude Bell.* New York: Quartet.

Woolf, V. (1957). *A room of one's own.* New York: Harcourt Brace.

14

The Three-Ring Conception of Giftedness

A Developmental Model for Promoting
Creative Productivity

Joseph S. Renzulli

> Outwitted
> He drew a circle to shut us out
> Heretic, rebel, a thing to flout.
> But love and I had the wit to win
> We drew a circle that took him in.
>   Edwin Markham, *Quatrains*

The record of human accomplishments and the progress of civilization can, in many ways, be charted by the actions of history's most gifted and talented contributors to the arts, sciences, and all other areas of human performance. As early as 2200 B.C., the Chinese had developed an elaborate system of competitive examinations to select outstanding persons for government positions (DuBois, 1970), and down through the ages almost every culture has had a special fascination for persons who have made notable contributions to their respective areas of interest and involvement. The areas of performance in which one might be recognized as a "gifted" person are determined by the needs and values of the prevailing culture, and scholars and laypersons alike have debated (and continue to debate) the age-old issues of how certain human abilities, personalities, and environmental conditions contribute to what we call giftedness.

A fascination with persons of unusual ability and potential for extraordinary expertise in any and all fields of human performance has given rise to an area of study in psychology and education called gifted education. In a very general sense, this field focuses on two major questions:

1. What makes giftedness?
2. How can we develop giftedness in young people and adults?

These two questions are the focus of the conception of giftedness described in this chapter, which has evolved over a period of more than

30 years. Because this theory views giftedness as something we develop in certain people, at certain times, and under certain circumstances, a program development plan called the Enrichment Triad Model paralleled work on the conception of giftedness. This plan for the delivery of services describes how we can go about promoting creative–productive giftedness and how various types of general enrichment for larger groups of students can serve as "identification situations" for more focused and advanced-level experiences designed to develop gifted behaviors in smaller numbers of students (Renzulli, 1977, 1982, 1992). This approach is a high-end learning example of what is popularly called performance-based or dynamic assessment. Both the conception of giftedness and program development theories have been paralleled by the creation of a wide array of practical instruments and procedures designed to implement the theories in a variety of learning environments (Reis, Burns, & Renzulli, 1992; Renzulli, 1997a, 1997b; Renzulli & Reis, 1997; Renzulli, Rizza, & Smith, 2002; Renzulli, Smith, White, Callahan, Hartman, Westberg, 2002). I have always believed that, in an applied field of study, theory is not of much value unless it can give relatively specific direction to the persons ultimately responsible for putting the theory into practice. Most theorists leave practical applications to others; however, one of the characteristics of my work is that it has proceeded simultaneously along both theoretical and practical lines. For better or worse, I have never been content with developing theoretical concepts without devoting equal or even greater attention to creating instruments, procedures, and materials for implementing the various concepts. And theory in an applied field does not have much value if it is not compatible with practical realities, such as policies, personalities, governance, finances, how schools work, teachers' ways of knowing, and practices that can reasonably be expected to endure *beyond* the support usually accorded to pilot projects or experimental research studies. This approach has both advantages and disadvantages. An eye toward implementation allows for theory testing in practical settings and the opportunity to generate research data that can lend credence to the theory and/or point out directions where additional work needs to be done.

The research supporting the theory described in this chapter, as well as reactions to commentary by other writers, has been updated in a number of publications over the years (Renzulli, 1986, 1988, 1999). Because of space limitations, the majority of this research is referenced rather than described in detail. I do, however, refer to some of the modern theories of intelligence that have emerged since the original publication of this work because they have implications for the role that various kinds of intelligences play in the development of giftedness. In this chapter, I provide a description of the major theoretical issues underlying various conceptions of giftedness, an overview of the three-ring conception of giftedness, some of the research that led to the initial development of the theory, and a brief description of research carried out in places that have used this model. Also included are a new dimension of the overall theory that deals with co-cognitive characteristics and a brief description of a plan for identifying students for special programs and services based on this conception of giftedness.

I would like to point out at the outset that I use the G-word as an adjective rather than a noun. So rather than writing about "the gifted," my preference is to discuss the development of gifted behaviors or giftedness. This use of terminology is in no way intended to negate the existence of persons who are at the high end of a continuum in any domain – general intelligence, mathematics, swimming, piano playing – but my preference is to write about a gifted mathematician, a gifted swimmer, or a gifted piano player. I also make a distinction between potential and performance. Persons can have remarkable potentials for mathematics, swimming, or piano playing, but until that potential is manifested in some type of superior performance, I am reluctant to say they have displayed gifted behaviors. And, of course, our main challenge as educators is to create the conditions that convert potential into performance.

ISSUES IN THE STUDY OF CONCEPTIONS OF GIFTEDNESS

Relationships Among Purpose, Conceptions, and Programming

One of the first and most important issues that should be dealt with in a search for the meaning of giftedness is that there must be a purpose for defining this concept. In view of the practical applications for which a definition might be used, it is necessary to consider any definition in the larger context of overall programming for the target population we are attempting to serve. In other words, the way in which one views giftedness will be a primary factor in both constructing a plan for identification and in providing services that are relevant to the characteristics that brought certain youngsters to our attention in the first place. If, for example, one identifies giftedness as extremely high mathematical aptitude, then it would seem nothing short of common sense to use assessment procedures that readily identify potential for superior performance in this particular domain. And it would be equally reasonable to assume that a program based on this definition and identification procedure should devote major emphasis to the enhancement of performance in mathematics and related areas. Similarly, a definition that emphasizes artistic abilities should point the way toward relatively specific identification and programming practices. As long as there are differences of opinion among reasonable scholars, there will never be a single definition of giftedness, and this is probably the way that it should be. But one requirement for which all writers of definitions should be accountable is the necessity of showing a logical relationship between definitions on the one hand and recommended identification and programming practices on the other.

Implicit in any efforts to define and identify the potential for gifted behaviors in young people is the assumption that we will "do something" to provide various types of specialized learning experiences that show promise of promoting the development of characteristics implicit in the definition. In other words, the *why* question supersedes the *who* and *how* questions. Although there are two generally accepted purposes for providing special education for young people with high potential, I believe that these two purposes in combination give rise to a third purpose that is intimately related to the definition question.

The first purpose of gifted education is to provide young people with maximum opportunities for self-fulfillment through the development and expression of one or a combination of performance areas in which superior potential may be present. The second purpose is to increase society's supply of persons who will help to solve the problems of contemporary civilization by becoming producers of knowledge and art rather than mere consumers of existing information. Although there may be some arguments for and against both of these purposes, most people would agree that goals related to self-fulfillment and/or societal contributions are generally consistent with democratic philosophies of education. What is even more important is that the two goals are highly interactive and mutually supportive of each other. In other words, the self-satisfying work of scientists, artists, and leaders in all walks of life has the potential to produce results that might be valuable contributions to society. If, as Gowan (1978) has pointed out, the purpose of gifted programs is to increase the size of society's reservoir of potentially creative and productive adults, then the argument for gifted-education programs that focus on creative productivity (rather than lesson-learning giftedness) is a very simple one. If we agree with the goals of gifted education set forth earlier in the chapter, and if we believe that our programs should produce the next generation of leaders, problem solvers, and persons who will make important contributions to the arts and sciences, then does it not make good sense to model special programs and services after the *modus operandi* of these persons rather than after those of the lesson learner? This is especially true because research (as described later in the chapter) tells us that the most efficient lesson learners are not necessarily those persons who go on to make important contributions in the realm of creative productivity. And in this day and age, when knowledge is expanding at almost geometric proportions, it would seem wise to consider a model that focuses on how our most able students access and make use of information rather than merely on how they accumulate and store it.

Giftedness and Intelligence

A major issue that must be dealt with is that our present efforts to define giftedness are based on a long history of previous studies dealing with human abilities. Most of these studies focused mainly on the concept of intelligence and are briefly discussed here to establish an important point about the process of defining concepts rather than any attempt to equate intelligence with giftedness. Although a detailed review of these studies is beyond the scope of the present chapter, a few of the general conclusions from earlier research are necessary to set the stage for this analysis.[1]

The first conclusion is that intelligence is not a unitary concept but rather, there are many kinds of intelligence and therefore single definitions cannot be used to explain this complicated concept. The confusion and inconclusiveness about present theories of intelligence has led Sternberg (1984), Gardner (1983), and others to develop new models for explaining this complicated concept. After having studied the three aspects of intelligence for some years, Sternberg (1996, 2001) concluded that the answer to the question of intelligence is even more than just *the amount* of a person's analytical, creative, and practical abilities. A person may be gifted with respect to any one of these abilities or with respect to the way she or he *balances the abilities* to succeed (Sternberg & Grigorenko, 2002). "The notion of someone's being 'gifted' or not is a relic of an antiquated, test-based way of thinking" (Sternberg, 1996, p. 197). Intelligence, according to Sternberg and Grigorenko (2002), is not a fixed entity, but a flexible and dynamic one (i.e., it is a form of developing expertise). Developing expertise is "the ongoing process of the acquisition and consolidation of a set of skills needed for a high level of mastery in one or more domains of life performance" (Sternberg & Grigorenko, 2002, p. 267). Thus, someone can be gifted in one domain but not in another. Further, according to Sternberg and colleagues (Sternberg & Lubart, 1995; Sternberg & O'Hara, 1999), intelligence is just one of six forces that generate creative thought and behavior. It is the confluence of intelligence, knowledge, thinking styles, personality, motivation, and the environment that forms gifted behavior as viewed from a creative–productive perspective.

Howard Gardner (1983) initially formulated a list of seven domain-specific intelligences and added an eighth one several years later. The first two intelligences – *linguistic* and *logical–mathematical* – are ones that have been typically valued in schools; *musical, bodily–kinesthetic*, and *spacial* are usually associated with the arts; and another two – *interpersonal* and *intrapersonal* – are what Gardner called "personal intelligences." After considering a few additional intelligences, including spiritual, moral, and

---

[1] Persons interested in a succinct examination of problems associated with defining intelligence are advised to review "The Concept of Intelligence" (Neisser, 1979).

existential intelligences, Gardner concluded that only the *naturalist* intelligence qualifies as intelligence in his Multiple Intelligences theory (Gardner, 1999). Linguistic intelligence, which involves sensitivity to spoken and written language, the ability to learn languages, and the capacity to use language to accomplish certain goals, is required of people such as writers, lawyers, and speakers. Scientific and mathematical thinking – required of mathematicians and physicists – on the other hand requires logical–mathematical intelligence, which includes the ability to analyze problems logically (i.e., detect patterns, reason deductively, and think logically). Musical intelligence includes the capacity to recognize and compose musical pitches, tones, and rhythms, skills necessary for performance, composition, and appreciation of musical patterns. Dancers, athletes, and mimes use their whole body or parts of the body to solve problems. Gardner calls the mental ability necessary to coordinate bodily movements bodily–kinesthetic intelligence. Spatial intelligence, the ability to represent and manipulate three-dimensional configurations, is needed by architects, engineers, sculptors, and chess players. The capacity to understand the intentions, motivations, desires, and actions of others and to act sensibly and productively based on that knowledge – interpersonal intelligence – is needed by counselors, teachers, political leaders, and evangelists. A good understanding of one's own cognitive strengths and weaknesses, thinking styles, feelings, and emotions is based on intrapersonal intelligence. Biologists need high levels of naturalist intelligence, which includes extensive knowledge of the living world and its taxonomies, and high capability in recognizing and classifying plants and animals.

In view of this recent work and numerous earlier cautions about the dangers of trying to describe intelligence through the use of single scores, it seems safe to conclude that this practice has been and always will be questionable. At the very least, attributes of intelligent behavior must be considered within the context of cultural and situational factors. Indeed, some of the most extensive examinations have concluded that "[t]he concept of intelligence *cannot* be explicitly defined, not only because of the nature of intelligence but also because of the nature of concepts" (Neisser, 1979, p. 179). Psychologists in the 1990s pointed out the existence of a wide range of contemporary conceptions of intelligence and how it should be measured. Although the psychometric approach is the oldest and best established, it is limited in its ability to explain intelligence. Multiple forms of intelligence such as Sternberg's and Gardner's theories, theories of developmental progression, and biological approaches have much to contribute to a better understanding of intelligence. Thus, some contemporary psychologists suggest that "we should be open to the possibility that our understanding of intelligence in the future will be rather different from what it is today" (Neisser et al., 1996, p. 80).

A second conclusion is that there is no ideal way to measure intelligence and therefore we must avoid the typical practice of believing that if we know a person's IQ score, we also know his or her intelligence. Even Terman warned against total reliance on tests: "We must guard against defining intelligence solely in terms of ability to pass the tests of a given intelligence scale" (1926, p. 131). E. L. Thorndike echoed Terman's concern by stating, "To assume that we have measured some general power which resides in [the person being tested] and determines his ability in every variety of intellectual task in its entirety is to fly directly in the face of all that is known about the organization of the intellect" (Thorndike, 1921, p. 126).

Although to date the heritability of cognitive ability in childhood seemed to be well established (McGue, Bouchard, Iacono, & Lykken, 1993; Plomin, 1999; as cited in Turkheimer, Haley, Waldron, D'Onofrio, & Gottesman, 2003), recent research adds a new dimension to the relationship between intelligence and measured IQ. Studies among twins or adoptees and their biological and adoptive parents typically yield large genetic effects and relatively smaller effects of family environments. However, most of these studies include children from middle-class and affluent families. Turkheimer et al. (2003) conducted a study that included a substantial proportion of minority twins raised in families living near or below the poverty level. Their study showed that, in the most impoverished families, the modeled heritability of full-scale IQ was essentially zero, and shared environment accounted for almost 60 percent of the variability; whereas in the most affluent families, virtually all of the modeled variability in IQ was attributable to heritability. In other words, whereas genetic makeup explains most of the differences in IQ for children in adequate environments (middle and high socioeconomic status), *environment* – not genes – makes a bigger difference for minority children in low-income homes. The use of IQ scores as a measure of intelligence, therefore, may be even more questionable for children from impoverished families than they are for the general population. Sternberg cautioned that even if heritability is fairly high for a certain population, it does not mean that intelligence cannot be modified (Miele, 1995).

Two Kinds of Giftedness

The reason I have cited these concerns about the historical difficulty of defining and measuring intelligence is to highlight the even larger problem of isolating a unitary definition of giftedness. At the very least, we will always have several conceptions (and therefore definitions) of giftedness; but it will help in this analysis to begin by examining two broad categories that have been dealt with in the research literature. The distinction between these two categories is the foundation for the theory presented in this chapter and, in many ways, it represents the theme of my overall approach to both the identification and development of gifted behaviors. I refer to the first category as "schoolhouse giftedness" and to the second as "creative–productive giftedness." Before going on to describe each type, I want to emphasize that:

1. Both types are important.
2. There is usually an interaction between the two types.
3. Special programs should make appropriate provisions for encouraging both types of giftedness as well as the numerous occasions when the two types interact with each other.

Schoolhouse Giftedness. Schoolhouse giftedness might also be called test-taking or lesson-learning giftedness. It is the kind most easily measured by IQ or other cognitive ability tests and, for this reason, it is also the type most often used for selecting students for entrance into special programs. The abilities people display on IQ and aptitude tests are exactly the kinds of abilities most valued in traditional school learning situations. In other words, the games people play on ability tests are similar to games that teachers require in most lesson-learning situations. Research tells us that students who score high on IQ tests are also likely to get high grades in school. Research also has shown that these test-taking and lesson-learning abilities generally remain stable over time. The results of this research should lead us to some very obvious conclusions about schoolhouse giftedness: It exists in varying degrees, it can be identified through standardized assessment techniques, and we should therefore do everything in our power to make appropriate modifications for students who have the ability to cover regular curricular material at advanced rates and levels of understanding. Curriculum compacting (Renzulli, Smith, & Reis, 1992), a procedure used for modifying curricular content to accommodate advanced learners, and other acceleration techniques should represent an essential part of any school program that strives to respect the individual differences that are clearly evident from scores yielded by cognitive ability tests.

Although there is a generally positive correlation between IQ scores and school grades, we should not conclude that test scores are the only factors that contribute to success in school. Because IQ scores correlate only from 0.40 to 0.60 with school grades, they account for only 16 to 36 percent of the variance in these indicators of potential. Many youngsters who are moderately below the traditional 3 to 5 percent test score cut-off levels for entrance into gifted programs clearly have shown that they can do advanced-level work. Indeed, most of the students in the nation's major universities and four-year colleges come from the top 20 percent of the general population (rather than just the top 3 to 5 percent), and Jones (1982) reported that a majority of college graduates in every scientific field of study had IQs between 110 and 120. Are we "making sense" when we exclude such students from access to special services? To deny them this opportunity would be analogous to *forbidding* a youngster from trying out for the basketball team because he or she missed a predetermined "cut-off height" by a few inches! Basketball coaches are not foolish enough to establish *inflexible* cut-off heights because they know that such an arbitrary practice would cause them to overlook the talents of youngsters who may overcome slight limitations in inches with other abilities such as drive, speed, teamwork, ball-handling skills, and perhaps even the ability and motivation to outjump taller persons who are trying out for the team. As educators of gifted and talented youth, we can undoubtedly take a few lessons about flexibility from coaches!

Creative–Productive Giftedness. If scores on IQ tests and other measures of cognitive ability only account for a limited proportion of the common variance with school grades, we can be equally certain that these measures do not tell the whole story when it comes to making predictions about creative–productive giftedness. Before defending this assertion with some research findings, let us briefly review what is meant by this second type of giftedness, the important role it should play in programming, and, therefore, the reasons we should attempt to assess it in our identification procedures – even if such assessment causes us to look below the top 3 to 5 percent on the normal curve of IQ scores.

Some phenomena are called by the name "creativity" and are qualitatively different from creative–productive giftedness. For purposes of clarification, I will briefly discuss Csikszentmihalyi's (1996) distinction between three phenomena. The first phenomenon refers to unusual and stimulating thoughts. People who express this kind of thinking may be referred to as *brilliant* rather than creative, unless they also contribute something of permanent significance. Second, the term *creativity* is used for people who experience the world in novel and original ways. Their perceptions are fresh and their judgments insightful. Csikszentmihalyi likes to call them *personally creative*. They may make important discoveries that are very important to themselves, but others do not know about those discoveries. Third, people who have changed our culture in some important respect can, according to Csikszentmihalyi (1996), be called *creative* without qualifications. He further emphasized:

The difference among these three meanings is not just a matter of degree. The last kind of creativity is not simply a more developed form of the two. These are actually different ways of being creative, each to a large measure unrelated to the others. (pp. 25–26)

The development of creative–productive giftedness aims to increase the chances that more students will become creative in the third way described, that is, their ideas and work will actually have an impact on others and cause change. This product-oriented view is in line with most current Western definitions of creativity. The most often mentioned features of the end product are novelty and appropriateness. Programming that addresses this kind of creativity must be qualitatively different from regular schooling. It should primarily focus on students who fall into the following two categories of talent, proposed by Tannenbaum (Sternberg & Davidson, 1986): scarcity and surplus talents. For purposes of preservation and advancement, the world needs inventive people like Jonas Salk, Martin Luther King, Jr., Marie Curie, and Sigmund Freud. Such *scarcity* talents are forever in short supply. Society also seeks beauty, which can be provided by people who possess what Tannenbaum called *surplus* talent. These people (e.g., Picasso, Mozart, and C. S. Lewis) have the rare ability to elevate people's sensibility and sensitivities to new heights through the production of great art, literature, music, and philosophy.

Psychologists who studied motivated behavior (e.g., Deci & Ryan, 1985) found that people have a desire for self-determination and competence. The need for self-determination or a sense of autonomy is satisfied when one is free to behave of one's own volition, rather than being forced to behave according to the desires of another. One also strives to feel proficient and capable of performing the task in which they choose to engage. These needs for self-determination and competence motivate people to seek and conquer optimal challenges that stretch their abilities when trying something *new* (Deci & Ryan, 1985; Deci, Vallerand, Pelletier, & Ryan, 1991). The challenge of a situation depends on the degree of match between a person's internal structures and the demands of the environment. Creative–productive giftedness, therefore, describes those aspects of human activity and involvement in which a premium is placed on the development of original thought, solutions, material, and products that are purposefully designed to have an impact on one or more target audiences. Learning situations that are designed to promote creative–productive giftedness emphasize the use and application of information (content) and thinking processes in an integrated, inductive, and real-problem-oriented manner, which allows students to be self-determined first hand inquirers. Creative–productive giftedness also implies acting on what one knows and believes rather than merely acquiring and storing knowledge for its own sake.

The role of the student is transformed from that of a learner of prescribed lessons to one in which she or he uses the *modus operandi* of a firsthand inquirer. This approach is quite different from the development of lesson-learning giftedness, which tends to emphasize deductive learning, structured training in the development of thinking processes, and the acquisition, storage, and retrieval of information. In other words, creative–productive giftedness is simply putting one's abilities to work on problems and areas of study that have personal relevance to oneself and that can be escalated to appropriately challenging levels of investigative activity.

The roles that both students and teachers should play in the pursuit of these problems have been described elsewhere (Renzulli, 1982, 1983).

Why is creative–productive giftedness important enough for us to question the "tidy" and relatively easy approach that traditionally has been used to select students on the basis of test scores? Why do some people want to rock the boat by challenging a conception of giftedness that can be numerically defined by simply giving a test? The answers to these questions are simple and yet very compelling. The research reviewed in the second section of this chapter tells us that there is much more to the development of gifted behaviors than the abilities revealed on traditional tests of intelligence, aptitude, and achievement. Furthermore, history tells us it has been the creative and productive people of the world, the producers rather than consumers of knowledge, the reconstructionists of thought in all areas of human endeavor, who have become recognized as "truly gifted" individuals. History does not remember persons who merely scored well on IQ tests or those who learned their lessons well but did not apply their knowledge in innovative and action-oriented ways.

It is important to mention once again that high levels of traditional achievement are necessary for all students. The breadth and depth of one's declarative knowledge base improves the foundation on which creative–productive behaviors can be based and, coupled with advanced training in procedural knowledge (thinking skills, research methods, various forms of expression), combined to form the necessary ingredients for the type of giftedness described here.

THE THREE-RING CONCEPTION OF GIFTEDNESS

The three-ring conception of giftedness is a theory that attempts to portray the main dimensions of human potential for creative productivity. The name derives from the conceptual framework of the theory – namely, three interacting clusters of traits (above average ability, task commitment, and creativity) and their relationship with general and specific areas of human performance (see Figure 14.1). The three rings are embedded in a Houndstooth background that represents the interaction between personality and environmental factors that give rise to the three rings.

Research Underlying the Three-Ring Conception of Giftedness

One way of analyzing the research underlying conceptions of giftedness is to review existing definitions along a continuum ranging from *conservative* to *liberal*. Conservative and liberal are used here not in their political connotations, but rather according to the degree of restrictiveness that is used in determining who is eligible for special programs and services.

General Performance Area

Mathematics	Visual Arts	Physical Sciences
Philosophy	Social Sciences	Law
Religion	Language Arts	Music
Life Sciences		Movement Arts

Specific Performance Areas

Cartooning	Demography	Electronic Music
Astronomy	Microphotography	Child Care
Public Opinion Polling	City Planning	Consumer Protection
Jewelry Design	Pollution Control	Cooking
Map Making	Poetry	Ornithology
Choreography	Fashion Design	Furniture Design
Biography	Weaving	Navigation
Film Making	Play Writing	Genealogy
Statistics	Advertising	Sculpture
Local History	Costume Design	Wildlife Management
Electronics	Meteorology	Set Design
Musical Composition	Puppetry	Agricultural
Landscape	Marketing	Research
Architecture	Game Design	Animal Learning
Chemistry	Journalism	Film Criticism
etc.	etc.	etc.

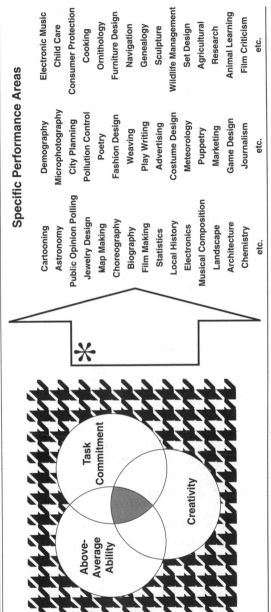

*This arrow should read as "... brought to bear upon ..."

FIGURE 14.1. Graphic Representation of the Three-Ring Definition of Giftedness.

257

Restrictiveness can be expressed in two ways. First, a definition can limit the number of specific performance areas that are considered in determining eligibility for special programs. A conservative definition, for example, might limit eligibility to academic performance only and exclude other areas such as music, art, drama, leadership, public speaking, social service, and creative writing. Second, a definition can limit the degree or level of excellence that one must attain by establishing extremely high cut-off points. At the conservative end of the continuum is Terman's (1926) definition of giftedness as "the top 1 percent level in general intellectual ability as measured by the Stanford–Binet Intelligence Scale or a comparable instrument" (p. 43). In this definition, restrictiveness is present in terms of both the type of performance specified (i.e., how well one scores on an intelligence test) and the level of performance one must attain to be considered gifted (top 1 percent). At the other end of the continuum can be found more liberal definitions, such as the following one by Witty (1958):

There are children whose outstanding potentialities in art, in writing, or in social leadership can be recognized largely by their performance. Hence, we have recommended that the definition of giftedness be expanded and that we consider any child gifted whose performance, in a potentially valuable line of human activity, is consistently remarkable. (p. 62)

Although liberal definitions have the obvious advantage of expanding the conception of giftedness, they also open up two "cans of worms" by introducing a values issue (what are the potentially valuable lines of human activity?) and the age-old problem of subjectivity in measurement. In recent years, the values issue has been largely resolved. There are very few educators who cling tenaciously to a "straight IQ" or purely academic definition of giftedness. "Multiple talent" and "multiple criteria" are almost the bywords of the present-day gifted student movement, and most persons would have little difficulty in accepting a definition that includes almost every area of human activity that manifests itself in a socially useful form of expression.

The problem of subjectivity in measurement is not as easily resolved. As the definition of giftedness is extended beyond those abilities that are clearly reflected in tests of intelligence, achievement, and academic aptitude, it becomes necessary to put less emphasis on precise estimates of performance and potential and more emphasis on the opinions of qualified human judges in making decisions about admission to special programs. The crux of the issue boils down to a simple and yet very important question: How much of a trade-off are we willing to make on the objective–subjective continuum to allow recognition of a broader spectrum of human abilities? If some degree of subjectivity cannot be tolerated, then our definition of giftedness and the resulting programs will logically be limited to abilities that can be measured only by objective tests.

Research on creative–productive people has consistently shown that, although no single criterion can be used to determine giftedness, persons who have achieved recognition because of their unique accomplishments and creative contributions possess a relatively well-defined set of three interlocking clusters of traits. These clusters consist of (a) above average, although not necessarily superior ability, (b) creativity, and (c) task commitment. It is important to point out that no single cluster "makes giftedness" (in the sense of "gifted behavior" or creative productivity). Rather, it is the *interaction* among the three clusters that research has shown to be the necessary ingredient for creative–productive accomplishment (Renzulli, 1978). The shaded portion of Figure 14.1 represents this interaction. It is also important to point out that each cluster plays an important role in contributing to the development of gifted behaviors. This point is emphasized because one of the major errors that continues to be made in identification procedures is to overemphasize superior abilities at the expense of the other two clusters of traits.

Amabile's (1983, 1996) Componential Theory of Creativity comprises three components that are very similar to the three clusters I proposed in the original article on the three-ring conception (Renzulli, 1978). Her essential three components for creative performance are: (a) domain-relevant skills (knowledge, talents, and technical skills in the domain), (b) creativity-relevant skills (cognitive styles, working styles, and creativity heuristics), and (c) task motivation (motivational variables that determine an individual's approach to a given task). Amabile (1996) emphasized that each of the model's three components – domain-relevant skills, creativity-relevant skills, and task motivation – is necessary, and none is sufficient for creativity in and of itself. She also proposed that the level of creativity of a product or response varies as a function of the levels of each of the three components.

Well-Above-Average Ability

Well-above-average ability can be defined in two ways. *General ability* consists of traits that can be applied across all domains (e.g., general intelligence) or broad domains (e.g., general verbal ability applied to several dimensions of the language arts). These abilities consist of the capacity to process information, to integrate experiences that result in appropriate and adaptive responses to new situations, and the capacity to engage in abstract thinking. Examples of general ability are verbal and numerical reasoning, spatial relations, memory, and word fluency. These abilities are usually measured by tests of general aptitude or intelligence and are broadly applicable to a variety of traditional learning situations.

Specific abilities consist of the capacity to acquire knowledge, skill, or the ability to perform in one or more activities of a specialized kind and within a restricted range. These abilities are defined in a manner that represents the ways in which human beings express themselves in real-life (i.e., nontest) situations. Examples of specific abilities are chemistry, ballet, mathematics, musical composition, sculpture, and photography. Each specific ability can be further subdivided into even more specific areas (e.g., portrait photography, astrophotography, photojournalism). Specific abilities in certain areas such as mathematics and chemistry have a strong relationship with general ability and, therefore, some indication of potential in these areas can be determined from tests of general aptitude and intelligence. They can also be measured by achievement tests and tests of specific aptitude. Many specific abilities, however, cannot be easily measured by tests, and, therefore, areas such as the the fine and applied arts, athletics, leadership, planning, and human relations skills must be evaluated through observation by skilled observers or other performance-based assessment techniques.

Within this model, the term *above average ability* is used to describe both general and specific abilities. *Above average* should also be interpreted to mean the upper range of potential within any given area. Although it is difficult to assign numerical values to many specific areas of ability, when I refer to "well above average ability," I clearly have in mind persons who are capable of performance or *possess the potential for performance* that is representative of the top 15 to 20 percent of any given area of human endeavor. One of the criticisms of this work has been that one must "perform" or produce a product to be "gifted." This is clearly not the intention, and I have responded to these criticisms in detail elsewhere (Renzulli, 1999). I also want to emphasize once again that when I refer to above average abilities that I am not restricting my use of percentages to only those things that can be measured by tests.

Although the influence of intelligence, as traditionally measured, quite obviously varies with specific areas of performance, many researchers have found that creative accomplishment is not necessarily a function of measured intelligence. In a review of several research studies dealing with the relationship between academic aptitude tests and professional achievement, Wallach (1976) has concluded that "above intermediate score levels, academic skills assessments are found to show so little criterion validity as to be a questionable basis on which to make consequential decisions about students' futures. What the academic tests do predict are the results a person will obtain on other tests of the same kind" (p. 57). Wallach goes on to point out that academic test scores at the upper ranges – precisely the score levels that are most often used for selecting persons for entrance into special programs – do not necessarily reflect the potential for creative–productive accomplishment. He suggests that test scores be used to screen out persons who score in the lower ranges and that, beyond this point, decisions should be based on other indicators of potential for superior performance.

Numerous research studies support Wallach's findings that there is a limited relationship between test scores and school grades on the one hand and real-world accomplishments on the other (Bloom, 1963; Harmon, 1963; Helson & Crutchfield, 1970; Hudson, 1960; Mednick, 1963; Parloff, Datta, Kleman, & Handlon, 1968; Richards, Holland, & Lutz, 1967; Wallach & Wing, 1969). In fact, in a study dealing with the prediction of various dimensions of achievement among college students, Holland and Astin (1962) found that "getting good grades in college has little connection with more remote and more socially relevant kinds of achievement; indeed, in some colleges, the higher the student's grades, the less likely it is that he is a person with creative potential. So it seems desirable to extend our criteria of talented performance" (pp. 132–133). A study by the American College Testing Program (Munday & Davis, 1974) titled "Varieties of Accomplishment After College: Perspectives on the Meaning of Academic Talent," concluded that

the adult accomplishments were found to be uncorrelated with academic talent, including test scores, high school grades, and college grades. However, the adult accomplishments were related to comparable high school nonacademic (extracurricular) accomplishments. This suggests that there are many kinds of talents related to later success which might be identified and nurtured by educational institutions. (p. 2)

Sternberg (1997) reported that tested differences in ability account for approximately "10% of the variation among workers in job performance" (p. 9). However, based on correlations between intelligence tests and various measures of job performance, Neisser et al. (1996) concluded that "across a wide range of occupations, intelligence test performance accounts for some 29% of the variance in job performance" (p. 83), which leaves 71 percent of variation in job performance unexplained. The pervasiveness of this general finding was demonstrated as early as 1965 by Hoyt (1965), who reviewed 46 studies dealing with the relationship between traditional indications of academic success and postcollege performance in the fields of business, teaching, engineering, medicine, scientific research, and other areas such as the ministry, journalism, government, and miscellaneous professions. From this extensive review, Hoyt concluded that traditional indications of academic success have no more than a very modest correlation with various indicators of success in the adult world and that "there is good reason to believe that academic achievement (knowledge) and other types of educational growth and development are relatively independent of each other" (p. 73).

The experimental studies conducted by Sternberg (1981) and Sternberg and Davidson (1982) have added a new dimension to our understanding about the role that intelligence tests should play in making identification decisions. After numerous investigations into the relationship between traditionally measured intelligence and other factors, such as problem solving and insightful solutions to complex problems, Sternberg (1982) concluded that

> tests only work for some of the people some of the time – not for all of the people all of the time – and that some of the assumptions we make in our use of tests are, at best, correct only for a segment of the tested population, and at worst, correct for none of it. As a result we fail to identify many gifted individuals for whom the assumptions underlying our use of tests are particularly inadequate. The problem, then, is not only that tests are of limited validity for everyone but that their validity varies across individuals. For some people, tests scores may be quite informative, for others such scores may be worse than useless. Use of test score cutoffs and formulas results in a serious problem of underidentification of gifted children. (p. 157)

These studies raise some basic questions about the use of tests as a major criterion for making selection decisions. The research reported above clearly indicates that vast numbers *and* proportions of our most productive persons are *not* those who scored at the 95th percentile or above on standardized tests of intelligence, nor were they necessarily straight-A students who discovered early how to play the lesson-learning game. In other words, more creative–productive persons came from below the 95th percentile than above it, and if such cut-off scores are needed to determine entrance into special programs, we may be guilty of actually discriminating against persons who have the greatest potential for high levels of accomplishment.

The most defensible conclusion about the use of intelligence tests that can be put forward at this time is based on research findings dealing with the "threshold effect." Reviews by Chambers (1969) and Stein (1968) and research by Walberg (1969, 1971) indicate that accomplishments in various fields require minimal levels of intelligence, but that beyond these levels, degrees of attainment are weakly associated with intelligence. In studies of creativity, it is generally acknowledged that a fairly high although not exceptional level of intelligence is necessary for high degrees of creative achievement (Barron, 1969; Campbell, 1960; Guilford, 1964, 1967; McNemar, 1964; Vernon, 1967).

Research on the threshold effect indicates that different fields and subject-matter areas require varying degrees of intelligence for high-level accomplishment. In mathematics and physics, the correlation of measured intelligence with originality in problem solving tends to be positive but quite low. Correlations between intelligence and the rated quality of work by painters, sculptors, and designers is zero or slightly negative (Barron, 1968). Although it is difficult to determine exactly how much measured intelligence is necessary for high levels of creative and productive accomplishment within any given field, there is a consensus among many researchers (Barron, 1969; Bloom, 1963; Cox, 1926; Harmon, 1963; Helson & Crutchfield, 1970; MacKinnon, 1964, 1965; Oden, 1968; Roe, 1952; Terman, 1954) that once the IQ is 120 or higher, other variables become increasingly important. These variables are discussed in the following sections.

Task Commitment

A second cluster of traits that consistently has been found in creative–productive persons is a refined or focused form of motivation that I have called task commitment. Whereas motivation is usually defined in terms of a general energizing process that triggers responses in organisms, task commitment represents energy brought to bear on a particular problem (task) or specific performance area. The terms that are most frequently used to describe task commitment are perseverance, endurance, hard work, dedicated practice, self-confidence, a belief in one's ability to carry out important work, and action applied to one's area(s) of interest. In addition to perceptiveness (Albert, 1975) and a better sense for identifying significant problems (Zuckerman, 1979), research on persons of unusual accomplishment has consistently shown that a special fascination for and involvement with the subject matter of one's chosen field "are the almost invariable precursors of original and distinctive work" (Barron, 1969, p. 3). This motivation to engage in an activity primarily for its own sake is often called intrinsic motivation. When one feels both self-determined and competent in pursuing a certain task, intrinsic motivation arises and leads to action. According to Deci and Ryan (1985), intrinsic motivation is innate to the human organism and is ever present as a motivator. It is a "natural ongoing state of the organism unless it is interrupted" (Deci & Ryan, 1985, p. 234) because intrinsically motivated behaviors satisfy a person's need to feel both competent and autonomous. Extrinsic motivation, often caused by factors such as money or rewards, on the other hand, can undermine one's sense of autonomy if they are perceived as externally controlling (Amabile, Hill, Hennessey, & Tighe, 1994). The identification of these two types of motivation – intrinsic and extrinsic motivation – was, according to Collins and Amabile (1999), a breakthrough in research on the forces driving creativity. It seems, however, that any extrinsic factors that support one's sense of competence or enable one's deeper involvement with the task itself (without undermining one's sense of self-determination) may have a reinforcing effect on intrinsic motivation. This positive combination of seemingly opposite types of motivation can be called "extrinsics in service of intrinsics" (Collins & Amabile, 1999). More research on motivation and especially on the synergistic effect of extrinsic motivators on intrinsic motivation is necessary. A person's high commitment toward a task seems to be the result of this synergistic effect.

Even in young people whom Bloom and Sosniak (1981) identified as extreme cases of talent development, early evidence of task commitment was present. Bloom and Sosniak report that "after age 12 our talented individuals spent as much time on their talent field each week as their average peer spent watching television" (p. 94). The argument for including this nonintellective cluster of traits in a definition of giftedness is nothing short of overwhelming. From popular maxims and autobiographical accounts to hard-core research findings, one of the key ingredients that has characterized the work of gifted contributors is their ability to involve themselves totally in a specific problem or area for an extended period of time.

The legacy of both Sir Francis Galton and Lewis Terman clearly indicates that task commitment is an important part of the making of a gifted person. Although Galton was a strong proponent of the hereditary basis for what he called "natural ability," he nevertheless subscribed heavily to the belief that hard work was part and parcel of giftedness:

By natural ability, I mean those qualities of intellect and disposition, which urge and qualify a man to perform acts that lead to reputation. I do not mean capacity without zeal, nor zeal without capacity, nor even a combination of both of them, without an adequate power of doing a great deal of very laborious work. But I mean a nature which, when left to itself, will, urged by an inherent stimulus, climb the path that leads to eminence and has strength to reach the summit – on which, if hindered or thwarted, will fret and strive until the hindrance is overcome, and it is again free to follow its laboring instinct (Galton, 1869, p. 33, as cited in Albert, 1975, p. 142).

The monumental studies of Lewis Terman undoubtedly represent the most widely recognized and frequently quoted research on the characteristics of gifted persons. Terman's studies, however, have unintentionally left a mixed legacy because most persons have dwelt (and continue to dwell) on "early Terman" rather than the conclusions he reached *after* several decades of intensive research. As such, it is important to consider the following conclusion that he reached as a result of 30 years of follow-up studies on his initial population:

A detailed analysis was made of the 150 most successful and 150 least successful men among the gifted subjects in an attempt to identify some of the nonintellectual factors that affect life success.... Since the less successful subjects do not differ to any extent in intelligence as measured by tests, it is clear that notable achievement calls for more than a high order of intelligence. The results [of the follow-up] indicated that personality factors are extremely important determiners of achievement.... The four traits on which [the most and least successful groups] differed most widely were *persistence in the accomplishment of ends, integration toward goals, self-confidence, and freedom from inferiority feelings.* In the total picture the greatest contrast between the two groups was in all-round emotional and social adjustment, and in *drive to achieve.* (Terman & Oden, 1959, p. 148; italics added)

Although Terman never suggested that task commitment should replace intelligence in our conception of giftedness, he did state that "intellect and achievement are far from perfectly correlated" p. 146.

Several more recent research studies support the findings of Galton and Terman and have shown that creative–productive persons are far more task-oriented and involved in their work than are people in the general population. Perhaps the best known of these studies is the work of Roe (1952) and MacKinnon (1964, 1965). Roe conducted an intensive study of the characteristics of 64 eminent scientists and found that *all* of her subjects had a high level of commitment to their work. MacKinnon pointed out traits that were important in creative accomplishments: "It is clear that creative architects more often stress their inventiveness, independence and individuality, their *enthusiasm, determination,* and *industry*" (1964, p. 365; italics added).

Extensive reviews of research carried out by Nicholls (1972) and Mc-Curdy (1960) found patterns of characteristics that were consistently similar to the findings reported by Roe and MacKinnon. Although the studies cited thus far used different research procedures and dealt with a variety of populations, there is a striking similarity in their major conclusions. First, academic ability (as traditionally measured by tests or grade-point averages) showed limited relationships to creative–productive accomplishment. Second, nonintellectual factors, and especially those related to task commitment, consistently played an important part in the cluster of traits that characterized highly productive people. Although this second cluster of traits is not as easily and objectively identifiable as are general cognitive abilities, they are nevertheless a major component of giftedness and should, therefore, be reflected in our definition.

Creativity

The third cluster of traits that characterizes gifted persons consists of factors usually lumped together under the general heading of "creativity." As one reviews the literature in this area, it becomes readily apparent that the words *gifted, genius,* and *eminent creators* or *highly creative persons* are used synonymously. In many of the research projects discussed previously, the persons ultimately selected for intensive study were, in fact, recognized *because* of their creative accomplishments. In MacKinnon's (1964) study, for example, panels of qualified judges (professors of architecture and editors of major American architectural journals) were asked first to nominate and later to rate an initial pool of nominees, using the following dimensions of creativity:

1. Originality of thinking and freshness of approaches to architectural problems.

2. Constructive ingenuity.
3. Ability to set aside established conventions and procedures when appropriate.
4. A flair for devising effective and original fulfillments of the major demands of architecture, namely, technology (firmness), visual form (delight), planning (commodity), and human awareness and social purpose. (p. 360)

When discussing creativity, it is important to consider the problems researchers have encountered in establishing relationships between creativity tests and other more substantial accomplishments. A major issue that has been raised by several investigators deals with whether or not tests of divergent thinking actually measure "true" creativity. Although some validation studies have reported limited relationships between measures of divergent thinking and creative performance criteria (Dellas & Gaier, 1970; Guilford, 1967; Shapiro, 1968; Torrance, 1969), the research evidence for the predictive validity of such tests has been limited. Unfortunately, very few tests have been validated against real-life criteria of creative accomplishment; however, future longitudinal studies using these relatively new instruments might show promise of establishing higher levels of predictive validity. Thus, although divergent thinking is indeed a characteristic of highly creative persons, caution should be exercised in the use and interpretation of tests designed to measure this capacity.

Given the inherent limitations of creativity tests, a number of writers have focused attention on alternative methods for assessing creativity. Among others, Nicholls (1972) suggested that an analysis of creative products is preferable to the trait-based approach in making predictions about creative potential (p. 721), and Wallach (1976) proposes that student self-reports about creative accomplishment are sufficiently accurate to provide a usable source of data.

Although few persons would argue against the importance of including creativity in a definition of giftedness, the conclusions and recommendations discussed previously raise the haunting issue of subjectivity in measurement. In view of what the research suggests about the questionable value of more objective measures of divergent thinking, perhaps the time has come for persons in all areas of endeavor to develop more careful procedures for evaluating the products of candidates for special programs.

A DEFINITION OF GIFTED BEHAVIOR

Although no single statement can effectively integrate the many ramifications of the research studies I have described, the following definition of gifted behavior attempts to summarize the major conclusions and generalizations resulting from this review of research.

Gifted behavior consists of thought and action resulting from an inter-action among three basic clusters of human traits, above average general and/or specific abilities, high levels of task commitment, and high levels of creativity. Children who manifest *or are capable of developing* an interaction among the three clusters require a wide variety of educational opportunities, resources, and encouragement above and beyond those ordinarily provided through regular instructional programs.

RESEARCH ON THE THREE-RING CONCEPTION OF GIFTEDNESS

The definition of gifted behavior reported previously has served as the basis for a large number of research studies designed to examine the effectiveness of identification practices based on the three-ring conception and programmatic interventions that focus on promoting creative–productive giftedness. Using a population of 1,162 students in grades one through six in 11 school districts, Reis and Renzulli (1982) examined several variables related to an identification process based on the three-ring conception and the Enrichment Triad programming model. Talent pools consisting of above average ability students in each district and at each grade level were divided into two groups. Group A consisted of students who scored in the top 5 percent on standardized tests of intelligence and achievement. Group B consisted of students who scored from 10 to 15 percentile points below the top 5 percent. Both groups participated equally in all program activities.

An instrument called the Student Product Assessment Form (SPAF) was used to compare the quality of products from each group. This instrument provides individual ratings for eight specific qualitative characteristics of products and seven factors related to overall product quality. The validity and reliability of the SPAF were established through a year-long series of studies (Reis, 1981) that yielded reliability coefficients as high as 0.98. A double-blind method of product coding was used so that the expert judges did not know group membership (i.e., A or B) when evaluating individual products. A two-way analysis of variance indicated that there were no significant differences between Group A and Group B with respect to the quality of students' products. These findings are offered as a verification of the three-ring conception of giftedness and as support for the effectiveness of the model in serving a group somewhat larger than the traditional top 5 percent. Questionnaires and interviews were used to examine several other factors related to overall program effectiveness. Data obtained from classroom and special program teachers, parents, and talent pool students indicated that attitudes toward this identification system were highly positive. Many classroom teachers reported that their high level of involvement in the program had favorably influenced their teaching practices and promoted more favorable attitudes toward special programs. Parents whose children had been placed previously in traditional programs for the gifted did not differ in their opinions from parents whose children had been identified as gifted under the expanded criteria. Resource teachers – many of whom had previously been involved in traditional programs for the gifted – overwhelmingly preferred the expanded identification procedure to the traditional reliance on test scores alone. In fact, several resource teachers said they would resign or request transfers to regular classrooms if their school systems did not continue to use this more flexible approach!

Additional research examined academic self-concept, locus of control, correlates of creative productivity, and administrators' attitudes toward programs based on the three-ring conception of giftedness. A summary of these and other studies about this combined identification and programming approach can be found in Renzulli and Reis (1994), and updates are included on our web site (www.gifted.uconn.edu).

NEW DIMENSIONS TO THE THREE-RING CONCEPTION OF GIFTEDNESS

In the early 1970s, when I began work on a conception of giftedness that challenged the traditional view of this concept, I embedded the rings in a Houndstooth background that represented the interaction between personality and environment. In recent years, further research and theory development has led to a new dimension of the model that calls attention to a series of six co-cognitive factors. A comprehensive review of the literature and a series of Delphi technique studies led to the development of an organizational plan for studying the 6 components and 13 subcomponents presented in Figure 14.2. I refer to these traits as co-cognitive factors because they interact with and enhance the cognitive traits that we ordinarily associate with the development of human abilities. Moon (2000) suggests that constructs of this type, including social, emotional, interpersonal, and intrapersonal intelligence, are related to each other and are independent from traditional measures of ability. The two-directional arrows in this diagram are intended to point out the many interactions that take place between and among the Houndstooth components.

This new initiative was prompted by a longstanding concern about the role that gifted education should play in preparing persons with high potential for ethical and responsible leadership in all walks of life and a concern for the well-documented decline of social capital in modern societies (Putnam, 1993, 1995; Portes, 1998). Social capital differs from economic and intellectual capital in that it focuses on a set of intangible assets that address the collective needs and problems of other individuals and our communities at large. Although social capital cannot be defined as precisely as corporate earnings or gross domestic product, Labonte (1999) eloquently defined it as: "something going on 'out there' in peoples' day-to-day relationships that is an important determinant to the quality of their lives, if not society's healthy functioning" (p. 430). This kind of capital generally enhances

OPERATION HOUNDSTOOTH

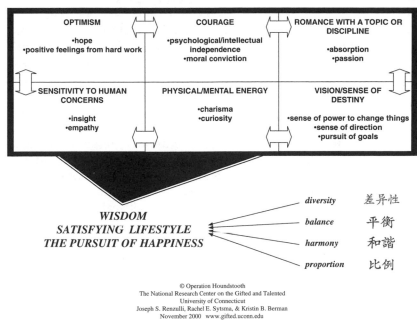

OPTIMISM	COURAGE	ROMANCE WITH A TOPIC OR DISCIPLINE
•hope •positive feelings from hard work	•psychological/intellectual independence •moral conviction	•absorption •passion
SENSITIVITY TO HUMAN CONCERNS	PHYSICAL/MENTAL ENERGY	VISION/SENSE OF DESTINY
•insight •empathy	•charisma •curiosity	•sense of power to change things •sense of direction •pursuit of goals

WISDOM
SATISFYING LIFESTYLE
THE PURSUIT OF HAPPINESS

diversity 差异性
balance 平衡
harmony 和谐
proportion 比例

© Operation Houndstooth
The National Research Center on the Gifted and Talented
University of Connecticut
Joseph S. Renzulli, Rachel E. Sytsma, & Kristin B. Berman
November 2000 www.gifted.uconn.edu

FIGURE 14.2. Operation Houndstooth.

community life and the network of obligations we have to one another. Investments in social capital benefit society as a whole because they help to create the values, norms, networks, and social trust that facilitate coordination and cooperation geared toward the greater public good. Striking evidence indicates a marked decline in American social capital over the latter half of the last century. National surveys show declines over the last few decades in voter turnout and political participation and membership in service clubs, church-related groups, parent–teacher associations, unions, and fraternal groups. These declines in civic and social participation have been paralleled by an increasing tendency for young people to focus on materialism, self-indulgence, narrow professional success, and individual economic gain (Ahuvia, 2002; Huer, 1991; Kasser, 2002; Myers, 1993; Netemeyer, Burton, & Lichtenstein, 1995; Shrader, 1992; Tatzel, 2002).

Researchers who have studied social capital have examined it mainly in terms of its impact on communities at large, but they also point out that it is created largely by the actions of individuals. They also have reported that leadership is a necessary condition for the creation of social capital. Although numerous studies and a great deal of commentary about leadership have been discussed in the gifted education literature, no one has yet examined the relationship between the characteristics of gifted leaders and their motivation to use their gifts to advance the greater public good. A scientific examination of a more focused set of background components is necessary for us to understand the sources of gifted behaviors and, more importantly, the ways in which people transform their gifted assets into constructive action. What causes people like Martin Luther King Jr., Mother Teresa, Nelson Mandela, and Rachel Carson to devote their time and energy to socially responsible endeavors that improve the lives of so many people? And can a better understanding of people who use their gifts in socially constructive ways help us create conditions that expand the number of young people who may make commitments to the growth of social as well as economic capital? Can our gifted education programs produce future corporate leaders who are as sensitive to aesthetic and environmental concerns as they are to the corporate bottom line? Can we influence the ethics and morality of future industrial and political leaders so that they place gross national happiness on an equal or higher scale of values than gross national product? These are some of the questions we are attempting to address in an ongoing series of research studies that examine the relationship between noncognitive personal characteristics and the role that these characteristics play in the development of giftedness.

A detailed discussion of the Houndstooth factors, the research that led to their development, and an intervention theory that promotes them is beyond the scope of this chapter; however, a description of the rationale for including them in an expanded conception of giftedness and the research that led to the identification of the factors can be found in a recent article devoted entirely to this topic (Renzulli, 2002). We are only in the early stages of examining these admittedly imprecise factors and developing strategies for promoting them, but I believe that if the gifted education community is sincere about its frequent claims of producing the next generation of leaders, our conception of giftedness and the services we provide should place some emphasis on leaders who are committed to making the world a better place. As Nelson Mandela said, "A good head and a good heart are always a formidable combination."

A Practical Plan for Identification

Translating theory into practice is always a challenging task! Although my work on a conception of giftedness has dealt with theory development, equal attention has been given to how the theory can guide practical strategies for the identification of *all* students who can benefit from special services. And therein lies one of the greatest challenges because a more flexible approach to identification often is at odds with traditional state or local regulations that require precision, names on lists signifying who is "gifted," and resource allocations that make sharp distinctions between the work of special program personnel and other teachers who may be able to contribute to a school's total talent development mission. These practical realities have led to an identification plan that is a compromise between a totally performance-based system and one that targets certain students while still maintaining a degree of flexibility. An overview of the plan follows, and a more detailed description titled *A Practical Plan for Identifying Gifted and Talented Students* can be found in Renzulli (1990) and on our Web site (www.gifted.uconn.edu).

The essence of this plan is to form a talent pool of students who are targeted because of strengths in particular areas that will serve as a primary (but not total) rationale for the services that the special program will provide. Before listing the steps involved in this identification system, three important considerations are discussed. First, talent pool size will vary in any given school depending on the general nature of the total student body. In schools with unusually large numbers of high achieving students, it is conceivable that talent pools will be larger than in lower-scoring schools. But even in schools where achievement levels are below national norms, there still exists an upper-level group of students who need services above and beyond those that are provided for the majority of the school population. Some of our most successful programs have been in inner-city schools that serve disadvantaged and bilingual youth; and even though these schools were below national norms, talent pools of approximately 15 percent of students needing supplementary services were still identified. Talent pool size is also a function of the availability of resources (both human and material) and the extent to which the general faculty is willing to (a) make modifications in the regular curriculum for above-average-ability students, (b) participate in various kinds of enrichment and mentoring activities, and (c) work cooperatively with any and all personnel who may have special program assignments. It is very important to determine beforehand the number of students who can be served in ways that "show up" when program accountability is considered.

Because teacher nomination plays an important role in this identification system, a second consideration is the extent of orientation and training that teachers have had about both the program and procedures for nominating students. In this regard, we recommend the use of a training activity that is designed to orient teachers to the behavioral characteristics of superior students (Renzulli et al., 2002, pp. 24–28).

A third consideration is, of course, the type of program for which students are being identified. The identification system is based on models that combine both enrichment and acceleration, whether or not they are carried out in self-contained programs, inclusion programs, pull-out programs, or any other organizational arrangement. Regardless of the type of

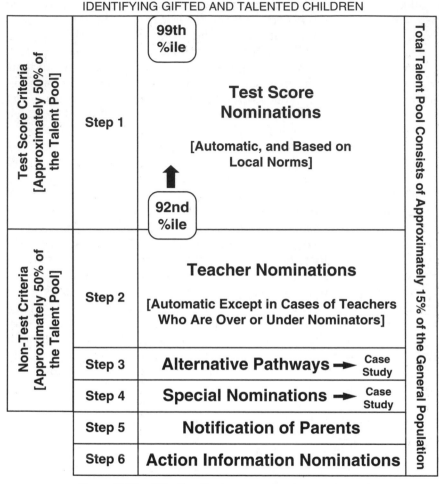

FIGURE 14.3. Renzulli Identification System.

organizational model used, it is also recommended that a strong component of curriculum compacting (Reis et al., 1992) be a part of the services offered to high-achieving talent pool students.

Once a target number or percent of the school population is established, that number should be divided in half. In the 15 percent talent pool depicted in Figure 14.3, approximately half the students will be selected on the basis of test scores, thus guaranteeing that the process will not discriminate against traditionally high-scoring students. Step 2 uses a research-based teacher nomination scale (Renzulli et al., 2002) for students not included in Step 1. Again, the previously mentioned training helps to improve the reliability of ratings. With the exception of teachers who are habitually under- or over-nominators, these ratings are treated on a par value with test scores. Our experience has shown that the vast majority of talent pool nominees result from Steps 1 and 2.

Steps 3 allows for the use of other criteria (e.g., parent, peer, or self-nomination; previous product assessment) that a school may or may not want to consider but, in this case, the information is reviewed in a case-study fashion by a selection committee. Step 4 allows previous-year teachers to recommend students who were not nominated in the first three steps. This "safety valve" guards against bias or incompatibility on the part of the nominator in Step 2, and it allows for consideration of student potential that may be presently unrecognized because of personal or family issues or a turn-off to school. Step 5 provides parents with information about why their son or daughter was nominated for the talent pool, the goals and nature of the program as it relates to their child's strength areas, and how a program based on the three-ring conception of giftedness differs from other types of programs. Step 6 is a second safety valve. Action information nomination allows for consideration of targeted services for a young person who may show a remarkable display of creativity, task commitment, or a previously unrecognized need for highly challenging opportunities.

SUMMARY: WHAT MAKES GIFTEDNESS?

In recent years, we have seen a resurgence of interest in all aspects of the study of giftedness and related efforts to provide services for at-risk youth and young people who may show their potential in ways that are not always challenged in traditional school programs. A healthy aspect of this renewed interest has been the emergence of new and innovative theories to explain the concept and a greater variety of research studies that show promise of giving us better insights and more defensible approaches to both identification and programming. Conflicting theoretical explanations abound, and various interpretations of research findings add an element of excitement and challenge that can only result in greater understanding of the concept in the years ahead. As long as the concept itself is viewed from the vantage points of different subcultures within the general population and differing societal values, we can be assured that there will always be a wholesome variety of answers to the age-old question: What makes giftedness? These differences in interpretation are indeed a salient and positive characteristic of any field that attempts to further our understanding of the human condition.

In this chapter, I have attempted to provide a framework that draws on the best available research about creative and productive individuals. I have also referenced research in support of the validity of the three-ring conception of giftedness. The conception and definition presented in this chapter have been developed from a decidedly educational perspective because I believe that efforts to define this concept must be relevant to the people in schools who may be most influenced by this work. I also believe that conceptual explanations and definitions must point the way toward practices that are economical, realistic, and defensible in terms of an organized body of underlying research and follow-up validation studies. This kind of technical information should be presented to decision makers who raise questions about *why* particular identification and programming models are being suggested by persons who are interested in serving gifted youth.

The task of providing better services to our most promising young people cannot wait until theorists and researchers produce an unassailable ultimate truth, because such truths probably do not exist. But the needs and opportunities to improve educational services for these young people exist in countless classrooms every day of the week. The best conclusions I can reach at the present time are presented previously, although I also believe that we must continue the search for greater understanding of this concept, which is so crucial to the further advancement of civilization. In the meantime, we should follow the advice in the poem by Edward Markham at the beginning of this chapter – we must draw our circles larger so that we do not overlook any young person who has the potential for high levels of creative productivity.

References

Ahuvia, A. C. (2002). Individualism/collectivism and cultures of happiness: A theoretical conjecture on the relationship between consumption, culture and subjective well-being at the national level. *Journal of Happiness Studies, 3*, 23–36.

Albert, R. S. (1975). Toward a behavioral definition of genius. *American Psychologist, 30*, 140–151.

Amabile, T. M. (1983). *The social psychology of creativity.* New York: Springer-Verlag.

Amabile, T. M. (1996). *Creativity in context.* Boulder, CO: Westview Press.

Amabile, T. M., Hill, K. G., Hennessey, B. A., & Tighe, E. M. (1994). The work preference inventory: Assessing intrinsic and extrinsic motivational orientations. *Journal of Personality and Social Psychology, 66*, 950–967.

Barron, F. (1968). *Creativity and personal freedom.* New York: Van Nostrand.

Barron, F. (1969). *Creative person and creative process.* New York: Holt, Rinehart & Winston. Bloom, B. S. (Ed.). (1956). *Taxonomy of educational objectives: Handbook 1. Cognitive domain.* New York: McKay.

Bloom, B. S. (1963). Report on creativity research by the examiner's office of the University of Chicago. In C. W. Taylor & F. Barron (Eds.), *Scientific creativity: Its recognition and development* (pp. 263–315). New York: Wiley.

Bloom, B. S., & Sosniak, L. A. (1981). Talent development vs. schooling. *Educational Leadership, 38*, 86–94.

Campbell, D. T. (1960). Blind variation and selective retention in creative thought as in other knowledge processes. *Psychological Review, 67*, 380–400.

Chambers, J. A. (1969). A multidimensional theory of creativity. *Psychological Reports, 25*, 779–799.

Collins, M. A., & Amabile, T. M. (1999). Motivation and creativity. In R. J. Sternberg (Ed.), *Handbook of creativity* (pp. 297–312). New York: Cambridge University Press.

Cox, C. M. (1926). *Genetic studies of genius: Vol. 2. The early mental traits of three hundred geniuses.* Stanford, CA: Stanford University Press.

Csikszentmihalyi, M. (1996). *Creativity: Flow and the psychology of discovery and invention.* New York: HarperCollins.

Deci, E. L., & Ryan, R. M. (1985). *Intrinsic motivation and self-determination in human behavior.* New York: Plenum.

Deci, E. L., Vallerand, R. J., Pelletier, L. G., & Ryan, R. M. (1991). Motivation and education: The self-determination perspective. *Educational Psychologist, 26*, 325–346.

Dellas, M., & Gaier, E. L. (1970). Identification of creativity: The individual. *Psychological Bulletin, 73*, 55–73.

DuBois, P. H. (1970). *A history of psychological testing.* Boston: Allyn & Bacon.

Gardner, H. (1983). *Frames of mind: The theory of multiple intelligences.* New York: Basic Books.

Gardner, H. (1999). *Intelligence reframed: Multiple intelligences for the 21st century.* New York: Basic Books.

Gowan, J. C. (1978, July 25). New directions for gifted education. Paper presented at the University of Connecticut, Storrs.

Guilford, J. P. (1964). Some new looks at the nature of creative processes. In M. Fredrickson & H. Gilliksen (Eds.), *Contributions to mathematical psychology* (pp. 42–66). New York: Holt, Rinehart & Winston.

Guilford, J. P. (1967). *The nature of human intelligence.* New York: McGraw-Hill.

Harmon, L. R. (1963). The development of a criterion of scientific competence. In C. W. Taylor & F. Barron (Eds.), *Scientific creativity: Its recognition and development* (pp. 147–165). New York: Wiley.

Helson, R., & Crutchfield, R. S. (1970). Mathematicians: The creative researcher and the average Ph.D. *Journal of Consulting and Clinical Psychology, 34*, 250–257.

Holland, J. L., & Astin, A. W. (1962). The prediction of the academic, artistic, scientific and social achievement of undergraduates of superior scholastic aptitude. *Journal of Educational Psychology, 53*, 182–183.

Hoyt, D. P. (1965). *The relationship between college grades and adult achievement: A review of the literature* (Research Report No. 7). Iowa City: American College Testing Program.

Hudson, L. (1960). Degree class and attainment in scientific research. *British Journal of Psychology, 51*, 67–73.

Huer, J. (1991). *The wages of sin: America's dilemma of profit against humanity.* New York: Praeger.

Jones, J. (1982). The gifted student at university. *Gifted International, 1*, 49–65.

Kasser, T. (2002). *The high price of materialism.* Cambridge, MA: MIT Press.

LaBonte, R. (1999). Social capital and community development: Practitioner emptor. *Australian and New Zealand Journal of Public Health, 23*(4), 430–433.

MacKinnon, D. W. (1962). The nature and nurture of creative talent. *American Psychologist, 17*, 484–495.

MacKinnon, D. W. (1964). The creativity of architects. In C. W. Taylor (Ed.), *Widening horizons in creativity.* New York: Wiley.

MacKinnon, D. W. (1965). Personality and the realization of creative potential. *American Psychologist, 20,* 273–281.

Mandela, N. www.thinkexist.com/English/Author/x/Author_3761_1.htm. Retreieved February 12, 2004.

McCurdy, H. G. (1960). The childhood pattern of genius. *Horizon, 2,* 33–38.

McGue, M., Bouchard, T. J., Jr., Iacono, W. G., & Lykken, D. T. (1993). Behavioral genetics of cognitive ability: A life-span perspective. In R. Plomin & G. E. McClearn (Eds.), *Nature, nurture and psychology,* pp. 59–76. Washington, DC: American Psychology Association.

McNemar, Q. (1964). Lost: Our intelligence? Why? *American Psychologist, 19,* 871–882.

Mednick, M. T. (1963). Research creativity in psychology graduate students. *Journal of Consulting Psychology, 27,* 265–266.

Miele, F. (1995). Magazine interview with Robert Sternberg on *The bell curve. Skeptic, 3* (3), 72–80.

Moon, S. M. (2000, May). Personal talent: What is it and how can we study it? Paper presented at the Fifth Biennial Henry B. and Joycelyn Wallace National Research Symposium on Talent Development, Iowa City, IA.

Munday, L. A., & Davis, J. C. (1974). *Varieties of accomplishment after college: Perspectives on the meaning of academic talent* (Research Report No. 62). Iowa City: American College Testing Program.

Myers, D. G. (1993). *Authentic happiness: Using the new positive psychology to realize your potential for lasting fulfillment.* New York: Avon Books.

Neisser, U. (1979). The concept of intelligence. In R. J. Sternberg & D. K. Detterman (Eds.), *Human Intelligence* (pp. 179–189). Norwood, NJ.: Ablex.

Neisser, U., Boodoo, G., Bouchard, T. J., Jr., Boykin, A. W., Brody, N., Ceci, S. J., et al. (1996). Intelligence: Knowns and unknowns. *American Psychologist, 51,* 77–101.

Netemeyer, R. G., Burton, S., & Lichtenstein, D. R. (1995). Trait aspects of vanity: Measurement and relevance to consumer behavior. *The Journal of Consumer Research, 21*(4), 612–626.

Nicholls, J. C. (1972). Creativity in the person who will never produce anything original and useful: The concept of creativity as a normally distributed trait. *American Psychologist, 27,* 717–727.

Oden, M. H. (1968). The fulfillment of promise: 40-year follow-up of the Terman gifted group. *Genetic Psychology Monograph, 77,* 3–93.

Parloff, M. B., Datta, L., Kleman, M., & Handlon, J. H. (1968). Personality characteristics which differentiate creative male adolescents and adults. *Journal of Personality, 36,* 528–552.

Portes, A. (1998). Social capital: Its origins and applications in modern sociology. *Annual Review of Sociology, 24,* 1–24.

Putnam, R. (1993). *Making democracy work: Civic traditions in modern Italy.* Princeton, NJ: Princeton University Press.

Putnam, R. (1995). Bowling alone: America's declining social capital. *Journal Of Democracy, 6*(January 1995), 65–78.

Reis, S. M. (1981). *An analysis of the productivity of gifted students participating in programs using the revolving door identification model.* Unpublished doctoral dissertation, University of Connecticut, Storrs.

Reis, S. M., Burns, D. E., & Renzulli, J. S. (1992). *Curriculum compacting: The complete guide to modifying the regular curriculum for high ability students.* Mansfield Center, CT: Creative Learning Press.

Reis, S. M., & Renzulli, J. S. (1982). A research report on the revolving door identification model: A case for the broadened conception of giftedness. *Phi Delta Kappan, 63,* 619–620.

Renzulli, J. S. (1977). *The enrichment triad model: A guide for developing defensible programs for the gifted and talented.* Mansfield Center, CT: Creative Learning Press.

Renzulli, J. S. (1978). What makes giftedness? Reexamining a definition. *Phi Delta Kappan, 60,* 180–184, 261.

Renzulli, J. S. (1982). What makes a problem real: Stalking the illusive meaning of qualitative differences in gifted education. *Gifted Child Quarterly, 26*(4), 148–156.

Renzulli, J. S. (1983). Guiding the gifted in the pursuit of real problems: The transformed role of the teacher. *The Journal of Creative Behavior, 17*(1), 49–59.

Renzulli, J. S. (1986). The three-ring conception of giftedness: A developmental model for creative productivity. In R. J. Sternberg & J. E. Davidson (Eds.), *Conceptions of giftedness* (pp. 53–92). New York: Cambridge University Press.

Renzulli, J. S. (1988). A decade of dialogue on the three-ring conception of giftedness. *Roeper Review, 11,* 18–25.

Renzulli, J. S. (1990). A practical system for identifying gifted and talented students. *Early Childhood Development, 63,* 9–18.

Renzulli, J. S. (1992). A general theory for the development of creative productivity in young people. In F. J. Mönks & W. A. M. Peters (Eds.), *Talent for the future* (pp. 51–72). Assen, The Netherlands: Van Gorcum.

Renzulli, J. S. (1997a). *Interest-A-Lyzer: Family of instruments. A manual for teachers.* Mansfield, CT: Creative Learning Press.

Renzulli, J. S. (1997b). *The Total Talent Portfolio: Looking at the best in every student.* Mansfield, CT: Creative Learning Press.

Renzulli, J. S. (1999). What is this thing called giftedness, and how do we develop it? A twenty-five year perspective. *Journal for the education of the gifted, 23,* 3–54.

Renzulli, J. S. (2002). Expanding the conception of giftedness to include co-cognitive traits and to promote social capital. *Phi Delta Kappan, 84,* 33–40, 57–58.

Renzulli, J. S., & Reis, S. M. (1994). Research related to the Schoolwide Enrichment Triad Model. *Gifted Child Quarterly, 38*(1), 7–20.

Renzulli, J. S., & Reis, S. M. (1997). *The schoolwide enrichment model: A how-to guide for educational excellence.* Mansfield Center, CT: Creative Learning Press.

Renzulli, J. S., Rizza, M. G., & Smith, L. H. (2002). *Learning styles inventory-version III: A measure of student preferences for instructional techniques. Technical and administration manual.* Mansfield Center, CT: Creative Learning Press.

Renzulli, J. S., Smith, L. H., & Reis, S. M. (1992). *Curriculum compacting: The complete guide to modifying the regular curriculum for high ability students.* Mansfield Center, CT: Creative Learning Press.

Renzulli, J. S., Smith, L. H., White, A. J., Callahan, C. M., Hartman, R. K., & Westberg, K. L. (2002). *Scales for rating the behavioral characteristics of superior students – revised edition.* Mansfield Center, CT: Creative Learning Press.

Richards, J. M, Jr., Holland, J. L., & Lutz, S. W. (1967). Prediction of student accomplishment in college. *Journal of Educational Psychology, 58,* 343–355.

Roe, A. (1952). *The making of a scientist.* New York: Dodd, Mead.

Shapiro, R. J. (1968). Creative research scientists. *Psychologia Africana*. Monograph supplement 4.

Shrader, W. K. (1992). *Media blight and the dehumanizing of America*. New York: Praeger.

Stein, M. I. (1968). Creativity. In E. Borgalta & W. W. Lambert (Eds.), *Handbook of personality theory and research*. Chicago: Rand McNally.

Sternberg, R. J. (1981). Intelligence and nonentrenchment. *Journal of Educational Psychology, 73*, 1–16.

Sternberg, R. J. (1982). Lies we live by: Misapplication of tests in identifying the gifted. *Gifted Child Quarterly, 26*(4), 157–161.

Sternberg, R. J. (1984). Toward a triarchic theory of human intelligence. *Behavioral and Brain Sciences, 7*(2), 269–316.

Sternberg, R. J. (1995). Interview with Robert Sternberg on The Bell Curve. *Skeptic, 3*(5), 72–80.

Sternberg, R. J. (1996). *Successful intelligence: How practical and creative intelligence determine success in life*. New York: Simon & Schuster.

Sternberg, R. J. (1997). *Thinking styles*. New York: Cambridge University Press.

Sternberg, R. J. (1998). A balance theory of wisdom. *Review of General Psychology, 2*(4), 347–365.

Sternberg, R. J. (2001, November). The theory of wisdom. Talk given at the 48th annual conference of the National Association for Gifted Children, Cincinnati, OH.

Sternberg, R. J., & Davidson, J. E. (1982, June). The mind of the puzzler. *Psychology Today, 16*, 37–44.

Sternberg, R. J., & Grigorenko, E. L. (2002). The theory of successful intelligence as a basis for gifted education. *Gifted Child Quarterly, 46*, 265–277.

Sternberg, R. J., & Lubart, T. I. (1995). An investment perspective on creative insight. In R. J. Sternberg & J. E. Davidson (Eds.), *The nature of insight* (pp. 535–558). Cambridge, MA: Bradford.

Sternberg, R. J., & O'Hara, L. A. (1999). Creativity and intelligence. In R. J. Sternberg (Ed.), *Handbook of creativity* (pp. 251–272). New York: Cambridge University Press.

Tatzel, M. (2002). "Money worlds" and well-being: An integration of money dispositions, materialism and price-related behavior. *Journal of Economic Psychology, 23*, 103–126.

Terman, L. M. (1954). The discovery and encouragement of exceptional talent. *American Psychologist, 9*, 221–230.

Terman, L. M., Baldwin, B. T., Bronson, E., DeVoss, J. C., Fuller, F., Goodenough, F. L., Kelley, T. L., et al. (1926). *Genetic studies of genius: Mental and physical traits of a thousand gifted children* (2nd ed.) Stanford, CA: Stanford University Press.

Terman, L. M., & Oden, M. H. (1959). *Genetic studies of genius: The gifted group at mid-life*. Stanford, CA: Stanford University Press.

Thorndike, E. L. (1921). Intelligence and its measurement. *Journal of Educational Psychology, 12*, 124–127.

Torrance, E. P. (1969). Prediction of adult creative achievement among high school seniors. *Gifted Child Quarterly, 13*, 223–229.

Turkheimer, E., Haley, A., Waldron, M., D'Onofrio, B., & Gottesman, I. I. (2003). Socioeconomic status modifies heratibility of IQ in young children. *Psychological Science, 14*, 623–628.

Vernon, P. E. (1967). Psychological studies of creativity. *Journal of Child Psychology and Psychiatry, 8*, 153–164.

Walberg, H. J. (1969). A portrait of the artist and scientist as young men. *Exceptional Children, 35*, 5–12.

Walberg, H. J. (1971). Varieties of adolescent creativity and the high school environment. *Exceptional Children, 38*, 111–116.

Wallach, M. A. (1976). Tests tell us little about talent. *American Scientist, 64*, 57–63.

Wallach, M. A., & Wing, C. W., Jr. (1969). *The talented students: A validation of the creativity–intelligence distinction.* New York: Holt, Rinehart & Winston.

Witty, P. A. (1958). Who are the gifted? In N. B. Henry (Ed.), *Education of the gifted. Fifty-seventh Yearbook of the National Society for the Study of Education, Part 2* (pp. 41–63). Chicago: University of Chicago Press.

Zuckerman, H. (1979). The scientific elite: Nobel laureates' mutual influences. In R. S. Albert (Ed.), *Genius and eminence* (pp. 241–252). Elmsford, NY: Pergamon.

15

In Defense of a Psychometric Approach to the Definition of Academic Giftedness

A Conservative View from a Die-Hard Liberal

Nancy M. Robinson

A DEVELOPMENTALIST'S VIEW OF GIFTEDNESS

Orienting a definition to educational issues limits one view of the field in ways that a developmental psychologist actually finds quite comfortable. Aside from simplifying matters by centering on academic domains that constitute the agenda we set for young people, one can *focus on childhood,* during which *developmental trajectories* can be described and mapped; one can define giftedness as *precocity,* or a *rapid pace* of development; and one need not worry so much about the future as the *present,* or worry about productivity to the exclusion of *promise.* Furthermore, because of near-universal schooling, it is feasible to use *cross-age* methods to describe the *maturity* of children we define as gifted. (Not that we do this very often.) None of these aspects makes much sense if we are talking about gifted adults.

Factor-Analytic Hierarchy of Abilities

I am content to borrow John Carroll's (1993) factor-analytic conception of *g,* or general intelligence, as a basic guide. This is where a bit of autobiography may be relevant. All my post-secondary degrees, and my late husband's, are from Stanford University, that bastion of *g*-dom. Maud Merrill, coauthor of the 1937 and 1960 Stanford–Binet scales, was our mentor. The next 10 years (1959–1969) we spent at a bastion of factor analysis, the University of North Carolina. Although L. L. Thurstone (1938) died a few years before we arrived and Carroll arrived at Chapel Hill a few years after we left, it is not surprising that I should choose this view of abilities.

Carroll's work consisted of a labor of love – a painstaking analysis of literally hundreds of empirical sets of test scores on the broadest possible variety of tests of mental abilities. From the work, he derived a broad array of abilities at three levels. At the top of the pyramid is the most general factor, or *g*, and at the bottom, numerous fairly specific abilities. Most interesting is the middle level, those we often call *group factors*; moreover, within this middle set of factors, some are "more equal" than others. Carroll found a fluid-intelligence factor and a crystallized-intelligence factor most closely related to *g*, followed by a factor of general memory and learning. More distal are the factors of visual perception, auditory perception, retrieval ability, cognitive speediness, and decision speed. For my purposes, the first three suffice. Carroll subsumed significant components of quantitative reasoning under fluid intelligence, much of language and verbal reasoning under crystallized intelligence, and what we now call working memory span under the third. Thus, we have the underpinnings of contemporary measures of intelligence in children – or close enough.

Assessment of Ability and Achievement

Within this context, my view is old-fashioned and pragmatic – a definition of academic giftedness that has as its bedrock *measurable* attainment of excellence in the domains under question (Jackson & Butterfield, 1986). The opportunity for assessment rests on the existence of tests standardized on representative populations within national boundaries or some other defined group, such as college applicants or military enlistees. In young children, we cannot expect giftedness to show itself in polished form, but precocious toddlers and preschoolers can demonstrate advanced language, math, and reasoning on measures appropriate to their stage of development. Tests of emerging abilities are pretty accurate reflections of those abilities as seen in real-life, as I later discuss. As children enter school, we acquire evidence of attainment from standardized achievement tests in reading, math, and writing, and, secondarily, portfolios and projects that are evaluated according to objective rubrics. Subjective, informal modes of assessment are, we should remember, not as predictive as formal, objective approaches (Grove & Meehl, 1996), however appealing they may be.

Is this all there is to giftedness? No, of course not. Eventual accomplishment by children with the potential to succeed will depend much more on motivation, creativity, and luck than ability tests can suggest. But the primary prerequisites for development as an academically gifted person are a rapid pace of cognitive development (i.e., to think like older persons and therefore more efficiently and abstractly), the power to reason well, and facility in learning and problem solving – all aspects of development that several existing tests measure rather effectively and efficiently.

"Bias" in Testing

Those who blame ethnic imbalances in special classrooms on the selection instruments assume that the tests must be biased against groups of children whose scores are not as high as others. Group differences do not by themselves demonstrate test bias. Bias in measurement exists when given scores have different implications depending on one's group membership (Jensen, 1979). We have no evidence that this is the case with commonly used measures of academic ability and achievement – indeed, the test producers have made every effort to eliminate items that increase group differences. Tests used inappropriately (e.g., a verbal reasoning test given to a child who is new to English or a written test given to a child who struggles to read) can of course be meaningless for prediction. But such situations are not what is ordinarily referred to by the uninformed. It is life, not the tests, that is unfair to many children in our communities (Robinson, 2003). But more of this later.

NOMENCLATURE

Please permit a short digression. I believe that the term *gifted* and the term *talented* have outlived their usefulness. We have little to no consensus about what constitutes these concepts, despite the fact that each of us is willing to write so authoritatively about them. Some authors, such as Gagné (1999), use the former term to refer to natural, untrained abilities that depend largely on one's "given" biological equipment and the latter to refer to developed abilities manifested in skills and attainments. Others, of whom I am one, use the term *giftedness* as implying more generalized abilities and *talents* to refer to abilities in more specific areas (such as a talent for music or mathematics). There have been previous attempts to clarify terms (e.g., Feldhusen, 1998; Gagné, 1985, 1995; Tannenbaum, 1983), but no consensus has emerged. The National Association for Gifted Children (NAGC) once established a task force to consider standardizing terminology or creating a whole new set, but members eventually concluded that the terms were so deeply entrenched in legislation and common usage that the task was infeasible. I believe the decision should be reconsidered.

Again, some autobiography. I spent 30 professional years at the other end of the normal curve of intelligence, during which a number of terms came and went. In the 1950s, the term *feebleminded* was laid to rest, and with it the subcategories *moron, imbecile,* and *idiot,* which once were as nonpejorative as the modern-day terms *mild, moderate,* and *severe.* Next came *mental deficiency* and, after it, *mental retardation.* Today, we use the somewhat broader term *developmental disability* but eventually it, too, shall pass. Why have the original terms been discarded? Primarily because, like used-up flypaper, they have a tendency to collect unwanted connotations. Some unfortunate connotations of giftedness are privilege, elitism, exclusivity, arrogance, and social ineptitude. Without really confronting or solving the issues, some groups have adopted terms like *highly capable, high-ability* or *high-performance* students. We need occasionally to throw away outworn terms, reach a consensus about new nomenclature, and expect to repeat the cycle when the new terms in their turn become old.

Even thoughtful discourse, such as that in which we are now engaged, will not suffice to reach agreement. Professionals and governmental agencies will need to surrender some autonomy by authorizing a body to act on their behalf. Since 1959, the American Association on Mental Retardation has taken on such a role. Because of the diversity of the gifted population, the situation with giftedness is more complex, but perhaps it is time for NAGC to revisit the question.

DESCRIPTION VERSUS DEFINITION

Some definitions of giftedness have incorporated descriptors rather than critical defining qualities. I suggest that we not mix the two. As Winner (2000) pointed out, "Our understanding of giftedness is most likely to advance if we define giftedness simply as unusually high ability in any area (including domain-specific ability as well as high global IQ) and then proceed to investigate the correlates (e.g., drive, creativity) and developmental path of each type of high ability" (p. 153).

One descriptive definition is that proposed by the Columbus Group (Morelock, 1996), defining giftedness essentially as asynchrony of development. Gifted children are typically more advanced in mental than in physical or emotional development and more uneven in their mental abilities than typically developing individuals (Achter, Lubinski, & Benbow, 1996; Detterman & Daniel, 1989), but other groups, such as those with specific disabilities, show asynchrony as well. Renzulli's (1986) definition that incorporates above average mental ability, creativity, and task commitment, is similarly descriptive. Persons of high ability (I wouldn't settle for "above average") may or may not show creativity and/or high motivation – indeed, under many of the circumstances into which we thrust them will *not* show such behaviors. For high creative productivity and ultimate adult accomplishment, these assets are essential, but they are highly dependent on environment and opportunity. Similarly, Tannenbaum's (1983) psychosocial definition of giftedness states:

There are five factors that have to mesh in order for a child to become truly gifted: (a) superior general intellect, (b) distinctive special aptitudes, (c) the right blending of nonintellective traits, (d) a challenging environment, and (e) the smile of good fortune at crucial periods of life. (p. 49)

Tannenbaum proceeds to say that creativity is a component of each. "The five factors interact in different ways for separate talent domains, but they are *all* represented in some way in *every* form of giftedness" (p. 49, emphasis Tannenbaum's).

We need not belabor the point. A categorical definition is most useful when pruned to the fewest possible dimensions. Reasoning ability is the foundation on which academically gifted behaviors and fulfillment of promise are built – not "innate ability" or that fictional "potential" that was present at conception. What is critical are children's abilities as they have developed to any given point in time – the product of a lived life, even if that life has so far been short. Some abilities will have been encouraged and promoted, some discouraged, some even destroyed. A child's giftedness represents a current possibility, the aptitude to respond to educational challenge and the expectations and support of family, school, and community – from this point on.

ADVANTAGES OF USING A PSYCHOMETRIC APPROACH

Among the advantages of using a psychometric approach to defining academic giftedness are (1) its compatibility with a developmental view of individual differences, (2) its flexibility (choice of instruments), (3) its effectiveness, and (4) the fact that errors tend to occur in one direction.

Psychometric Developmental Viewpoints: Age-Oriented Origins

The scientific study of giftedness can be traced to the work of Francis Galton (1869) and Lewis Terman (1916, 1921, 1925). Galton tried his hand at psychometrics, but what he tried to measure were largely anthropometric characteristics with little relationship to cognitive abilities. It was not until Binet and Simon (1905) created a test designed to assess children's mental development that a psychometric concept of giftedness could emerge. Following a sensible suggestion by Stern (1914) that one could derive a simple quotient from the ratio of mental to chronological age, Terman (1916) was able to give us a quantitative handle on a child's intellectual development, a notion of intellectual maturity (MA) as well as rate of growth ($IQ = MA \div CA$ [chronological age] $\times 100$). With Terman, the notions of giftedness and measurement began to go hand in hand. IQ became an index by which to define giftedness as *rapid rate of cognitive development*.

The concept of mental age has fallen out of favor in the last few decades for a number of practical reasons. Mental age is specified by the average performance attained on a cognitive measure by a representative population of children of a given age. Note that this concept works only during childhood, begins to break down during the teenage years, and is useless in describing adult performance.

Think how difficult it was to construct tests like the 1916 and 1937 Stanford–Binet scales. First, to emphasize general intelligence, items were selected on the basis of their correlation with age. Preliminary age groupings of diverse items were created. Then, the mean points earned, expressed in months of credit, by children in each age group in the standardization sample (unfortunately, English-speaking White children only) had to be juggled to equal their chronological age. This was accomplished by meticulous balancing of the criteria for passing an item. The distribution of scores had to correspond to something like a normal curve, with equal variance at every age. Terman and Merrill (1937) were not as successful with the variance side of things as with the means. Furthermore, to restandardize the test, one had to start all over. Keep in mind that this work was accomplished before the days of computers, and then consider the profound tediousness of it all. Forms L and M were equivalent, so the work was double in scope. It was a monumental undertaking, an approach doomed to suffocate of its own weight.

In creating Form L-M for the 1960 revision (Terman & Merrill, 1960), Merrill retained the mental age scores but not the Ratio IQ, adopting the Deviation IQ approach already introduced by Wechsler (1939). Because he started with adults, Wechsler had already seen the need to use artificially constructed normal distributions. The concept of mental age was eventually abandoned altogether for Stanford–Binet IV (Thorndike, Hagen, & Sattler, 1986) and Stanford–Binet V (Roid, 2003), so out went the notion of IQ as rate of growth and out went the MA as a way of expressing mental maturity.

Giving up the MA concept is a loss in selecting educational options matched to a child's academic maturity. Developmental research has also lost a valuable tool, the CA–MA match, in which children with high or low ability can be compared not only with normative chronological-age peers, but with normative mental-age peers. This method has the potential to clarify one of the burning questions in the field of giftedness: Are what seem to be qualitative differences in, for example, executive function, when gifted children are compared with CA-mates anything more than maturity differences? In contrast with the field of mental retardation, we have very few such studies, Kanevsky's (1992) and Johnson, Im-Bolter, and Pascual-Leone's (2003) being exceptions. Without such research, we may well be misled.

Even so, the developmental phenomena revealed by mental tests have not evaporated. Tests that span several ages still describe underlying age patterns of growth, and children still develop at varying rates of speed. Age-equivalents for subtests (only) are furnished by most publishers, and one can still estimate mental age either by taking the median subtest age-equivalent or by multiplying the IQ by CA and dividing by 100 (e.g., a child with a CA of 6 and an IQ of 150 has an estimated MA of 9). Mental age was always a ballpark estimate. Mental maturity is a concept we should not lose.

Giftedness in Terms of Readiness

Assessment of ability and achievement is useful in estimating children's readiness for next steps. Such knowledge facilitates an optimal educational match (Robinson & Robinson, 1982), an appropriate degree of challenge. Is acceleration an option for this child and, if so, how much? The Iowa Acceleration Scale (Assouline, 2003) is one example of using ability testing results as part of decision making about grade placement.

This approach has proven effective in a variety of settings. The regional talent searches typically use test scores alone to select highly able adolescents for rigorous summer courses, with very few problems. One program of very early admission to college that initially ignored psychometric evidence that the students were not ready for college suffered a wobble (Cornell, Callahan, & Loyd, 1991) before modifying its procedures. The Early Entrance Program at the University of Washington, which admits students aged 12–14 years, uses out-of-level ability testing as a first screen. When the program has not proved to be a good fit, the problems have almost invariably stemmed from motivational issues, undiagnosed learning or attention problems, or conflicted family dynamics. At this transitional age, however, occasional students persist for a time in concrete thinking and struggle with highly verbal courses.

Assessment: Choosing One's Weapons

Some measures are more useful than others at predicting outstanding academic attainment. It is axiomatic *that tests must match the programs* for which they are being used. Because school achievement is so closely related to verbal and quantitative reasoning, as well as working memory span in those domains, appropriate tests will target the abilities specific to the program being contemplated (e.g., quantitative reasoning for a math–science program).

Contrary to popular opinion and some authors (e.g., Naglieri & Ford, 2003), tests of spatial reasoning should have a limited place in a battery of measures to identify academically gifted students. Lohman (in press), Gohm, Humphreys, and Yao (1998), and others have demonstrated that high spatial reasoning in the absence of high verbal reasoning is, surprisingly, a *negative* predictor of school achievement and has little value for our purposes except for fields such as engineering or architecture (Shea, Lubinski, & Benbow, 2001). As a last resort, spatial reasoning tests are also used in special situations, such as assessing children with limited English proficiency or language delays. Spatial and figural reasoning tests are favored by many school districts because they are thought to reduce racial/ethnic differences, but often do not (Lohman, in press). Even if they did, it would be a mistake to use measures that are, in fact, mildly predictive in the wrong direction of success in rigorous school programs.

Tests as a Reflection of Real-Life Development

We have conducted several short-term longitudinal studies of precocity in very young children, in each case asking parents to nominate their children. The first study enrolled 550 children ages 2 to 5 years who were thought to be advanced in any of a number of domains, including general mental ability. More than half the children attained IQs of 132 or higher on a brief form of the then-new 1972 Stanford–Binet (Robinson & Robinson, 1992). Another study enlisted 18-month-olds who were highly verbal and followed them to age 6 (Dale, Crain-Thoreson, & Robinson, 1995; Robinson, Dale, & Landesman, 1990). Mothers' initial reports of toddlers' language at home correlated 0.63 with verbal items of the Bayley Mental Scale and 0.37 with a 50-utterance sample of language during free play (Robinson et al., 1990), despite an attenuated range of scores. Still another study enrolled math-precocious children at the end of preschool or kindergarten (Robinson, Abbott, Berninger, & Busse, 1996; Robinson, Abbott, Berninger, Busse, & Mukhopadhyay, 1997). A factor derived from parental descriptions of their kindergartners' advanced math abilities correlated 0.48 and 0.41 with two math-screening measures (Pletan, Robinson, Berninger, & Abbott, 1995).

These observations all confirm the accuracy of parental observations and make it clear that educators ought to listen to parents who see their children as more gifted than they seem in school. But the reverse is equally true: The confirmatory findings in each of these studies also show that *test results correspond to the children's actual behavior at home – they are not artifacts of the laboratory*.

Large-scale studies of the correspondence of test scores and vocational and economic achievement in adult groups also confirm the meaningfulness of test findings (e.g., Gottfredson, 1997). Adolescents with exceptionally high Scholastic Aptitude Test (SAT) scores have been shown to pursue doctoral degrees at rates more than 50 times base-rate expectations, sometimes creating noteworthy literary, scientific, or technical products by their early 20s (Lubinski, Webb, Morelock, & Benbow, 2001). Although prediction for individuals (as opposed to groups) needs to take into account interests, values, and lifestyle preferences (Webb, Lubinski, & Benbow, 2002), clearly the abilities revealed by measures like these make a difference in the real world.

Predictive Usefulness of Psychometric Information

Because ability test scores tend to be relatively stable over time, even when the first test is given at a preschool age and the last in middle age (Kangas & Bradway, 1971), they are useful as predictors of development. Although scores are somewhat less stable at the high end than at the low end (McNemar, 1942), even quite young, gifted children show considerable stability on both general (Robinson & Robinson, 1992) and domain-specific tests (Robinson et al., 1997).

The precise data we would wish to have do not seem to exist: Is there a satisfactory correlation between initial assessments and performance in academically rigorous programs for gifted students? Informal data from years of providing programs for gifted students, both in school and in summer programs, suggest that the approach works. There exist analogous findings for prediction of college grades on the basis of the SAT-I and SAT-II that demonstrate a substantial correlation, albeit an imperfect one (e.g., Bridgeman, Burton, & Cline, 2001).

In other words, students seldom make scores that are "too high," although they can make scores that are too low. When errors occur, test performance fails to reveal actual talent. This fact has energized the movement to find unidentified academically gifted children in underserved minority groups, but as we have seen, there is as yet no evidence that such groups harbor more than their share of unidentified gifted children.

EDUCATIONAL ISSUES

Achieving an Optimal Match

Surveying the research literature on social–emotional factors in giftedness, a task force of the National Association for Gifted Children highlighted the needs of gifted children for both academic challenge and the company of peers who share their interests and advancement (Neihart, Reis, Robinson, & Moon, 2002). To create such settings, educators need to understand gifted students' pace of development (IQ) and their readiness for new challenges (achievement grade levels). Other information is of course helpful, such as the specific curricula completed, students' interests, social–emotional maturity, and alternative options – but test scores are a solid place to start.

Motivation and Creativity

For the eventual flowering of giftedness, high ability and achievement alone are not enough. What Renzulli and Reis (2000) term "creative productivity" requires a high degree of energy, motivation to succeed, perseverance in the face of frustration, and the flexibility, ingenuity, and courage to take intellectual risks. Opportunity and pure luck also play their roles (Tannenbaum, 1983). Winner (1996) refered to the "rage to master" as a characteristic of successful gifted children and adults, and of course she is right. These are not characteristics easily picked up by test scores, although they will make themselves known to alert testers in one-to-one situations.

Even with early and intensive programs, achieving stable increases in IQ and learning in at-risk children is not easy (Campbell & Ramey, 1994;

Gross, Spiker, & Hughes, 1997). On the other hand, motivation and creativity are probably more readily malleable. Creative behaviors can certainly be squelched and can probably be increased, at least in a given context (Torrance, 1965), with family characteristics such as some family turbulence and respect for individuality (Olszewski-Kubilius, 2002) being important as well. Children's motivation to succeed also depends both on parental expectations and encouragement of independence (Csikszentmihalyi, Rathunde, & Whalen, 1993), and on opportunities to pursue interests (Siegle & McCoach, 2002). Under these circumstances, it makes even more sense to select students on the basis of cognitive abilities and skills, as I have suggested, and then to afford them academic programs that invite and reward creativity. Appropriate teaching will enhance curiosity, a sense of wonder, skills in thinking flexibly and insightfully, and the ability to follow hunches, to generate multiple hypotheses, and, ultimately, to pick productive ones. In addition, programs must generate strong engagement that energizes the commitment to practice, practice, practice to achieve expertise (Ericsson, 2001). To define giftedness and thereby to limit programs to students who already show these characteristics is, I believe, short-sighted.

CRITICISMS OF A PSYCHOMETRIC APPROACH TO DEFINITION

A definition of academic giftedness that relies as heavily as this one on measured abilities and achievement is of course imperfect. Some of its problems:

- Tests don't tell us what proportion of the population should be considered gifted. Unlike the community concerned with mental retardation, we have no consensus, but at least tests – based on a normal curve – give us grounds for discussion.
- A psychometric definition is at the mercy of test developers. Even when authors use compatible theories of intelligence, they may not do a good job of tapping into the highest levels of ability.
- Children, especially young children, will not always demonstrate the best of their reasoning abilities. They may feel threatened for any of a number of reasons: they may be hungry or not feeling well; they may be inexperienced test-takers; or they may not take the situation seriously. These risks are reduced in one-to-one testing.
- Tests may miss talents not represented in the assessment. We have yet to see evidence that this situation really exists with respect to academic talents required by core curricula, but of course if tests are used improperly – if, for example, a math test is used to identify students for a high-verbal class – this can happen.

- Too much weight is placed on single-episode testing. To the extent that this is true, tests are being misused. Test results should always be taken in the context of a child's history of school achievement and any other evidence (such as portfolios or prior tests) that can reveal talents. When these are at variance, further evaluation of the situation is necessary. Frequently, this will require individual assessment.

- Using tests for selection, enrollment in classes for gifted children will seldom be racially or ethnically proportional to the presence of those groups in the school or district. The problem here is more socioeconomic than racial or ethnic, but the facts are true: Children growing up in circumstances that are unfavorable to optimal child development are seriously affected (Robinson, 2003). Parents under stress; parents with limited economic, educational, and personal resources; parents who are discouraged by unemployment, marginalization, and racism; parents who fail to converse with, read to, and otherwise support the intellectual development of their children; and parents who themselves feel alienated from the educational system will seldom produce gifted children. Everything we have learned about optimal child development is true. It is also true that some families living in or near poverty, by virtue of their personal resources, positive child-rearing practices, and school involvement, will be able to raise high-achieving children (Robinson, Lanzi, Weinberg, Ramey, & Ramey, 2002). The fault that produces imbalance does not lie in the tests, Horatio, but in life itself.

"CHILDREN OF PROMISE"

Much of the objection to the use of psychometric instruments in identifying gifted children stems from a political agenda (Benbow & Stanley, 1996). We all regret the imbalance in the representation of racial, ethnic, and socioeconomic groups in special classrooms, but the solution requires the involvement of the whole society.

Giftedness is not a dichotomy but a dimension. Where we draw the line is too often based on budgets for special services. Gifted children are distinctly advanced, although not rare; how we decide to meet their needs – in regular or special classrooms – is a separate question.

I propose that we think about at least two steps on the scale of advanced ability. First, we define as gifted those with rapidly developing talents who are markedly different from their age-peers – perhaps the top 1 to 3 percent of their age cohort. In most regular classrooms, to thrive they need special curricular adaptations as well as the company of others of similar advancement. Second, however, we must remain on the lookout for what I term "children of promise," children whose talents are well above average (perhaps in the top 10 percent) *and* who come from backgrounds that have not afforded them the resources that might have optimized their development (Turkheimer, Haley, Waldron, Onofrio, & Gottesman, 2003). These children deserve special watching and energetic programs designed to help them bring out their best, beginning as early as possible. Psychometric assessment can help us to identify these children, although we should cast our nets wide to find them.

Some programs reaching out to "promising" young students already exist. Rather than placing these students in advanced classes for which they are not yet prepared, these programs are expected to pay off at the secondary and post-secondary level. In Seattle, for example, the Rainier Scholars program identifies promising children of color during their fifth-grade year and offers intensive summer programs, winter-long after-school programs, mentorships, and so on. I would like to see programs starting much earlier, embedded in Project Head Start. My belief is that such intervention is our best hope.

CONCLUSION

A psychometric definition of giftedness leaves a good many questions unanswered, to be sure. But such an approach is at risk of being discarded because, I believe, of irrelevant agenda. I plead here for us to keep the proverbial baby even if the bathwater is turbulent. Those who are born with the potential for high academic attainment will reach those heights only if they are nourished, challenged, supported, and believed in. Those properly described as academically gifted need and deserve rigorous, challenging, engaging learning opportunities with others who are similarly able, motivated, and mature. We owe them our best.

References

Achter, J. A., Lubinski, D., & Benbow, C. P. (1996). Multipotentiality among the intellectually gifted: "It never was there and already it's vanishing." *Journal of Counseling Psychology, 43*, 65–76.

Assouline, S. (2003). *The Iowa Acceleration Scale* (2nd ed.). Scottsdale, AZ: Great Potential Press.

Benbow, C. P., & Stanley, J. C. (1996). Inequity in equity: How "equity" can lead to inequity for high-potential students. *Psychology, Public Policy, and Law, 22,* 49–292.

Binet, A., & Simon, T. (1905). Méthodes nouvelles pour le diagnostic du niveau intellectuel des anormaux. *Année Psychologique, 11,* 191–244.

Bridgeman, B., Burton, N., & Cline, F. (2001). Substituting SAT-II: Subjects test for SAT-I: Reasoning Tests: Impact on admitted class composition and quality. *College Board Report 2001–3, ETS RR-01–07.*

Campbell, F. A., & Ramey, C. T. (1994). Effects of early intervention on intellectual and academic achievement: A follow-up study of children from low-income families. *Child Development, 65,* 684–698.

Carroll, J. B. (1993). *Human cognitive abilities: A survey of factor-analytic studies.* New York: Cambridge University Press.

Cornell, D. G., Callahan, C. M., & Loyd, B. H. (1991). Socioemotional adjustment of adolescent girls enrolled in a residential acceleration program. *Gifted Child Quarterly, 35*, 58–66.

Csikszentmihalyi, M., Rathunde, K., & Whalen, S. (1993). *Talented teenagers: The roots of success and failure.* Cambridge, England: Cambridge University Press.

Dale, P. S., Crain-Thoreson, C., & Robinson, N. M. (1995). Linguistic precocity and the development of reading: The role of extra-linguistic factors. *Applied Psycholinguistics, 16*, 173–187.

Detterman, D. K., & Daniel, M. H. (1989). Correlations of mental tests with each other and with cognitive variables are highest for low IQ groups. *Intelligence, 13*, 349–359.

Ericsson, A. (2001). The acquired nature of expert performance: Implications for conceptions of giftedness and innate talent? In N. Colangelo & S. G. Assouline (Eds.), *Talent Development IV: Proceedings from the 1998 Henry B. and Jocelyn Wallace National Research Symposium on Talent Development* (pp. 11–26). Scottsdale, AZ: Great Potential Press.

Feldhusen, J. F. (1998). A conception of talent and talent development. In R. C. Friedman & K. B. Rogers (Eds.), *Talent in context: Historical and social perspectives on giftedness* (pp. 193–209). Washington, DC: American Psychological Association.

Gagné, F. (1985). Giftedness and talent: Reexamining a reexamination of the definitions. *Gifted Child Quarterly, 29*, 103–112.

Gagné, F. (1995). From giftedness to talent: A developmental model and its impact on the language of the field. *Roeper Review, 18*, 103–111.

Gagné, F. (1999). My convictions about the nature of abilities, gifts, and talents. *Journal for the Education of the Gifted, 22*, 109–136.

Galton, F. (1869). *Hereditary genius: An inquiry into its causes and consequences.* New York: Macmillan.

Gohm, C. L., Humphreys, L. G., & Yao, G. (1998). Underachievement among spatially gifted students. *American Educational Research Journal, 35*, 515–531.

Gottfredson, L. S. (1997). Why *g* matters: The complexity of everyday life. *Intelligence, 24*, 79–132.

Gross, R. T., Spiker, D., & Hayes, C. (Eds.). (1997). *Helping low birth weight premature babies: The Infant Health and Development Program.* Stanford, CA: Stanford University Press.

Grove, W. M., & Meehl, P. E. (1996). Comparative efficiency of informal (subjective, impressionistic) and formal (mechanical, algorithmic) prediction procedures: The clinical-statistical controversy. *Psychology, Public Policy, and Law, 2*, 293–323.

Jackson, N. E., & Butterfield, E. C. (1986). A conception of giftedness designed to promote research. In R. J. Sternberg & J. E. Davidson (Eds.), *Conceptions of giftedness* (pp. 151–181). Cambridge, England: Cambridge University Press.

Jensen, A. R. (1979). *Bias in mental testing.* New York: Free Press.

Johnson, J., Im-Bolter, N., & Pascual-Leone, J. (2003). Development of mental attention in gifted and mainstream children: The role of mental capacity, inhibition, and speed of processing. *Child Development, 74*, 1594–1614.

Kanevsky, L. (1992). The learning game. In P. S. Klein & A. J. Tannenbaum (Eds.), *To be young and gifted* (pp. 204–241). Norwood, NJ: Ablex.

Kangas, J., & Bradway, K. (1971). Intelligence at middle age: A thirty-eight-year follow-up. *Developmental Psychology, 5*, 333–337.

Lohman, D. F. (in press). The role of nonverbal ability tests in identifying academically gifted students: An aptitude perspective. *Gifted Child Quarterly*.

Lubinski, D., Webb, R. M., Morelock, M. J., & Benbow, C. P. (2001). Top 1 in 10,000: A 10-year follow-up of the profoundly gifted. *Journal of Applied Psychology, 86*, 718–729.

McNemar, Q. (1942). *The revision of the Stanford–Binet scale*. Boston: Houghton-Mifflin.

Morelock, M. J. (1996). On the nature of giftedness and talent: Imposing order on chaos. *Roeper Review, 19*, 4–12.

Naglieri, J. A., & Ford, D. Y. (2003). Addressing underrepresentation of gifted minority children using the Naglieri Nonverbal Ability Test (NNAT). *Gifted Child Quarterly, 47*, 155–160.

Neihart, M., Reis, S. M., Robinson, N. M., & Moon, S. M. (Eds.). (2002). *The social and emotional development of gifted children: What do we know?* Waco, TX: Prufrock Press.

Olszewski-Kubilius, P. (2002). Parenting practices that promote talent development, creativity, and optimal adjustment. In M. Neihart, S. M. Reis, N. M. Robinson, & S. M. Moon (Eds.). (2002), *The social and emotional development of gifted children: What do we know?* (pp. 205–212). Waco, TX: Prufrock Press.

Pletan, M. D., Robinson, N. M., Berninger, V. W., & Abbott, R. D. (1995). Parents' observations of kindergartners who are advanced in mathematical reasoning. *Journal for the Education of the Gifted, 19*, 30–44.

Renzulli, J. S. (1986). The three-ring conception of giftedness: A developmental model for creative productivity. In R. J. Sternberg & J. E. Davidson (Eds.), *Conceptions of giftedness* (pp. 53–92). Cambridge, England: Cambridge University Press.

Renzulli, J. S., & Reis, S. M. (2000). The schoolwide enrichment model. In K. A. Heller, F. J. Mönks, R. J. Sternberg, & R. F. Subotnik (Eds.), *International handbook of giftedness and talent* (pp. 367–382). New York: Elsevier.

Robinson, N. M. (2003). Two wrongs do not make a right: Sacrificing the needs of academically talented students does not solve society's unsolved problems. *Journal for the Education of the Gifted, 26*, 321–328.

Robinson, N. M., Abbott, R. D., Berninger, V. W., & Busse, J. (1996). The structure of abilities in young, math-precocious children: Gender similarities and differences. *Journal of Educational Psychology, 88*, 341–352.

Robinson, N. M., Abbott, R. D., Berninger, V. W., Busse, J., & Mukhopadhyay, S. (1997). Developmental changes in mathematically precocious young children: Matthew and gender effects. *Gifted Child Quarterly, 41*, 145–159.

Robinson, N. M., Dale, P. S., & Landesman, S. J. (1990). Validity of Stanford–Binet IV with young children exhibiting precocious language. *Intelligence, 14*, 173–186.

Robinson, N. M., Lanzi, R. G., Weinberg, R. A., Ramey, S. L., & Ramey, C. T. (2002). Factors associated with high academic competence in former Head Start children at third grade. *Gifted Child Quarterly, 46*, 281–294.

Robinson, N. M., & Robinson, H. B. (1982). The optimal match: Devising the best compromise for the highly gifted student. In D. Feldman (Ed.), *Developmental approaches to giftedness and creativity* (pp. 79–94). San Francisco: Jossey-Bass.

Robinson, N. M., & Robinson, H. (1992). The use of standardized tests with young gifted children. In P. S. Klein & A. J. Tannenbaum (Eds.), *To be young and gifted* (pp. 141–170). Norwood, NJ: Ablex.

Roid, G. (2003). *The Stanford–Binet Intelligence Scales* (5th ed.). Chicago: Riverside.

Shea, D. L., Lubinski, D., & Benbow, C. P. (2001). Importance of assessing spatial ability in intellectually talented young adolescents: A 20-year longitudinal study. *Journal of Educational Psychology, 93,* 604–614.

Siegle, D., & McCoach, D. B. (2002). Promoting a positive achievement attitude with gifted and talented students. In M. Neihart, S. M. Reis, N. M. Robinson, & S. M. Moon (Eds.), *The social and emotional development of gifted children: What do we know?* (pp. 237–249). Waco, TX: Prufrock Press.

Stern, W. (1914). The psychological methods of testing intelligence. *Educational Psychology Monographs, 13* (G. M. Whipple, Trans.). Baltimore: Warwick & York.

Tannenbaum, A. J. (1983). *Gifted children: Psychological and educational perspectives.* New York: Macmillan.

Terman, L. M. (1916). *The measurement of intelligence: An explanation of and a complete guide for the use of the Stanford revision and extension of the Binet-Simon intelligence scale.* Boston: Houghton Mifflin.

Terman, L. M. (1921). Intelligence and its measurement: A symposium. *Journal of Educational Psychology, 12,* 127–133.

Terman, L. M. (1925). *Genetic studies of genius: Vol. I. Mental and physical traits of a thousand gifted children.* Stanford, CA: Stanford University Press.

Terman, L. M., & Merrill, M. A. (1937). *Measuring intelligence.* Boston: Houghton Mifflin.

Terman, L. M., & Merrill, M. A. (1960). *Stanford–Binet Intelligence Scale, Form L-M* (Revised 1972). Boston: Houghton Mifflin.

Thorndike, R. L., Hagen, E. P., & Sattler, J. M. (1986). *Guide for administering and scoring the Stanford–Binet Intelligence Scale* (4th ed.). Chicago: Riverside.

Thurstone, L. L. (1938). Primary mental abilities. *Psychometric Monographs, 1.*

Torrance, E. P. (1965). *Rewarding creative behavior: Experiments in classroom activity.* Englewood Cliffs, NJ: Prentice Hall.

Turkheimer, E., Halen, A., Waldron, M., Onofrio, B., & Gottesman, I. I. (2003). Socioeconomic status modifies heritability of IQ in young children. *Psychological Science, 14,* 623–628.

Webb, R. M., Lubinski, D., & Benbow, C. P. (2002). Mathematically facile adolescents with math-science aspirations: New perspectives on their educational and vocational development. *Journal of Educational Psychology, 94,* 785–794.

Wechsler, D. (1939). *The measurement of adult intelligence.* Baltimore: Williams & Wilkins.

Winner, E. (1996). *Gifted children: Myths and realities.* New York: Basic Books.

Winner, E. (2000). Giftedness: Current theory and research. *Current Directions in Psychological Science, 9,* 153–156.

16

Creative Giftedness

Mark A. Runco

An ideal definition of giftedness should be optimally specific and operational. It should be optimal in the sense that it is not too general or too specific. It should not be too general because there are differences between mathematical giftedness and musical giftedness, and further differences between those two and verbal giftedness. There are, in short, clear-cut domain differences. The mathematical, musical, and verbal domains are just examples; there are numerous others in which an individual can excel. Yet a useful definition of giftedness should be general enough to capture critical commonalities. There must be commonality or else we should probably not refer to these individuals all the same way, as "gifted." The theory described in this chapter suggests that all expressions of giftedness share the potential for creative work. The gifted child may have domain-specific knowledge and be motivated to invest in only one particular domain; but whichever domain it is, the gifted individual will have the capacity for original work. Creative potential is one of the most critical commonalities among the various domains of giftedness.

The other requirement for the ideal definition – that it is operational – implies that reliable judgments can be made about gifted individuals. It implies that giftedness can be measured, quantified, and predicted. Without this requirement, a definition would be untenable and potentially unfair. One objective of this chapter is to demonstrate how creative giftedness can be operationalized such that it can be reliably assessed. This may sound like a psychometric focus for this chapter, but actually the theory presented herein offers a moderate number of suggestions for educators and anyone else who wishes to identify, understand, or enhance creative potential.

CREATIVE GIFTEDNESS

The specificity mentioned in the first paragraph of this chapter applies to definitions of giftedness in the sense of *domains* (e.g., verbal versus mathematical or musical) but also in the sense of explanatory power. Such explanatory power requires that we pinpoint what Jay and Perkins (1998) described as the *mechanism* underlying creative behavior and creative action. Mere indicators, correlates, and descriptions of creativity and giftedness are not enough. Educators will only be able to fulfill creative behavior if the underlying mechanism is identified and carefully targeted. The mechanism underlying creative efforts should allow for development, at least in the sense that it can describe how a child can become an adult who applies his or her creative talents in a mature and productive fashion. It is not tenable to view the creative activities of children as resulting from a process that is different from that used by a creative adult. If the creative child and the creative adult use different processes, it is probably best to view one as creative and one as something other than creative.

Consider divergent thinking in this regard. Tests of divergent thinking are highly reliable and correlated with certain forms of creative performance (Hocevar, 1981; Milgram, 1976; Runco, 1986; Runco et al., 2000). Yet, it is often difficult or even impossible to find how the ideational skills that are used by the young participants in this research have been employed by Picasso, Einstein, or Mozart. In fact, even though tests of divergent thinking are reliable indicators of originality on presented tasks (i.e., those presented in a controlled setting), there is no guarantee that persons who earn high scores on a paper-and-pencil test of divergent thinking will use those exact same skills in the natural environment. Divergent thinking is one example of a skill we have identified but that is associated with only certain forms of original behavior. It may help us to understand children's potential for creative problem solving, but to date, it has done little if anything to forward our understanding of mature creative accomplishment.

This chapter outlines a view of creativity that pinpoints a mechanism that underlies all creative work, including that of children and adults, and that allows objective study and assessment. It is grounded in existing theories of lifespan development, and it translates easily to practice. Examples of such practices are discussed throughout this chapter. This chapter also compares this theory of creative giftedness with other existing theories. We will see that there are both points of agreement and points of disagreement. First, the mechanism underlying original and creative activity is described.

PERSONAL CREATIVITY

The theory of creative giftedness described here was constructed in response to (a) theories of development that indicated that children have what it takes to be truly creative, and (b) theories that confuse creativity with fame and other social expressions of talent. The former includes Piaget's (1970, 1976) theory of development through adaptation. Piaget described how a child's adaption is a result of the processes of *assimilation* and *accommodation*. Assimilation is the cognitive process that allows the child to bring new information into his or her cognitive system – even though the child does not yet understand that new information. The only way to accomplish this is to assimilate, meaning that the information is altered or transformed. Once transformed, the information can fit into existing cognitive structures and be considered, even if not fully understood. A child may see a cloud with five extremities and label the cloud "doggie." The extremities could in some way resemble a mammal's arms, legs, and a head, but for the child to think that the cloud is a doggie, he or she needs to ignore the fact that the cloud is all white, floating, and lacks vital body parts (e.g., ears, mouth, and tail). This is a part of assimilation and transformation: The child ignores certain things (e.g., the fact that the cloud is all white and floating), selects certain things (e.g., the extremities), and may even misinterpret certain things (e.g., the head).

Very importantly, the child does not see the cloud as "a cloud that looks like a doggie." The child imagines the cloud to *be* a doggie – not a cloud that looks like a doggie, but an actual doggie. This is most likely at about 4 years of age (Piaget, 1970, 1976), when the child's imaginary world is his or her reality. At this point, the child's assimilatory power is at its peak; the child will pretend regularly and often not distinguish between pretending and reality. For Piaget, pretending is the epitome of assimilation. In the theory of personal creativity outlined here, assimilation gives the child the cognitive potential to construct meaningful and original interpretations of his or her experience. That is one important part of creativity – and one that is used by all creative persons of all ages. It is also one that is easy to encourage. Children do need to learn the difference between fantasy and reality, but they also benefit to the extreme when they are allowed to pretend and play in an imaginary world. It may be difficult to entirely understand how a child equates a cloud with a doggie, but clearly parents and teachers should support rather than discourage imaginary play. It might be best to say "Yes, that does look like a doggie" instead of "But doggies don't float." It would even make sense to direct children to clouds and ask what they see in them.

The mechanism mentioned previously is, then, assimilation – the construction of original and meaningful interpretations. This is the process that produces the originality that is necessary for creative thinking. Interestingly, there are theories of creativity that emphasize accommodation rather than assimilation. These tend to focus on insightful thinking, however, like that which occurs when an individual has a sudden "aha!" experience. Such sudden insights are apparently not really all that sudden, but are instead protracted – they are developed over time (Gruber, 1981, 1988). They do, however, feel sudden. The insight itself may reflect accommodation in the sense that the individual finds a solution – the insight – by changing his or her understanding of the problem or situation. This is accommodation precisely because it is the individual (or more precisely, his or her cognitive structures) that change. Assimilation, in contrast, occurs when the individual changes experience by altering or reinterpreting it. The individual does not change when assimilating, only the information does. The emphasis in the theory presented herein is assimilation, but insightful problem solving also seems to be involved in some creative problem solving (Gruber, 1985). Gifted children often excel at insightful problem solving, but apparently there are several things adults can do to facilitate insight (Davidson & Sternberg, 1986).

Assimilation and interpretation are virtually universal. The implication is that the capacity for creative performance is widely distributed – as widely as assimilatory processes, which for Piaget (1970, 1976) meant just about everyone had them. This claim about the wide distribution of creative potential may be controversial. Sometimes creativity is reserved for those who achieve great things. It could be that assimilatory efficiency is not universal in the sense of being equal in everyone; it could be normally distributed instead. In that light, everyone would have the capacity, just as they have vision or some other basic capacity, but people would have it in varying degrees. This idea of a normal distribution is important for a theory of creative giftedness because it implies that creatively gifted persons may have a kind of assimilatory efficiency. They may be inordinately and exceptionally capable of constructing original interpretations of experience. Then again, they may have a normal level of assimilatory capacity but use it more frequently than others. That possibility is addressed when the other features of personal creativity are described below. These other features are probably not normally distributed, and that may help us to understand exceptionality and therefore giftedness.

TO UNDERSTAND IS TO INVENT

Before turning to the other two features of the creative process, something more should be said about assimilation. You might have noticed that when assimilation was defined previously it was described using the terms *interpretation* and *transformation*. Think about what occurs when someone forms an interpretation: They are constructing a personal understanding. Piaget (1976) said, "To understand is to invent," and he emphasized that the individual must invent the understanding for himself or herself. That is why assimilation leads to originality. This is also one reason I refer to the capacity discussed in this chapter as "personal creativity" (Runco, 1996). The other reason I do that is because, as noted previously, this theory was developed in response to theories that define creativity in social (rather than personal) ways. More on that follows.

The originality of interpretations is obvious when you think about how they differ from one person to another. Two people can have the exact same experience and yet walk away with different interpretations. This occurs because the meaning each person finds in the experience is not really found *in* the experience but is instead assigned to it. So again, each individual has his or her own unique interpretation, and that means each is constructing an original understanding. This is a crucial point because originality is a prerequisite for creativity. Creativity always involves originality. Originality does not guarantee creativity, but it is necessary for it. Note also the implications: If we realize that interpretations of experience are always personally constructed, we might better understand why people do not always agree. They have constructed different interpretations. This may help you understand other adults, but it is especially useful to keep this in mind when you are around children. They are "cognitive aliens" and will very frequently have different interpretations. Beause those are indicative of the assimilatory process, which underlies their capacity for original and creative thought, parents and teachers should at least some of the time appreciate the unique interpretations offered by their students or their own children.

It is also useful to view assimilation as transformation. Piaget (1976) described why "thinking cannot be reduced to speaking, to classifying objects into categories, nor even to abstracting. To think is to act on the object and to transform it" (p. 90). Guilford (1983) underscored the role of transformations in his last publication before his death. He stated, "From an exploratory study . . . it could be concluded that transformation abilities are more important than divergent-production abilities in creative thinking" (p. 75). Hofstadter (1985), O'Quin and Besemer (1989), Bachelor and Michael (1991), Jackson and Messick (1967), and Puccio, Treffinger, and Talbot (1995) all included some sort of transformational index in their empirical work on creativity. Each of these can be viewed as assimilatory.

Parents and teachers should encourage assimilation and transformations, as well as the obvious manifestations of them such as imaginary play, pretending, and personal interpretations. They should keep in mind that these things are each related to one another and each related to the potential for creative thinking. But although there is value in personally constructed interpretations of experience, conventional interpretations should also be considered. Again, originality is necessary but not sufficient for creativity. That is why discretion is important for creativity.

DISCRETION FOR PERSONAL CREATIVITY

Creativity involves the construction of original and meaningful interpretations of experience, as well as the discretion to know when it is useful to be original and when it is not wise to be original. Discretion in this context is much like the discretion that "is the better part of valor"; it is a kind of decision making, a judgment. Without this kind of discretion, the individual might live entirely in a fantasy world! Indeed, it is discretion and the control over one's original interpretations that separates creative talent from psychosis. That may sound like a huge claim, but psychotic persons have been found to earn high scores on tests of originality (Eysenck, 1993). Apparently, they share with creative persons a tendency to construct original meanings and idiosyncratic interpretations. Sadly, the psychotic individual does not know when to rely on those and when to conform to rote or conventional interpretations. They lack discretion and control.

Most likely, the discretion that plays a role in creative thinking falls along a continuum, with some people exercising too much control and rarely risking an original interpretation and others (the psychotics) treating all of their original interpretations as reality. Somewhere in between those extremes are people who most of the time control their interpretative processes and their originality, but sometimes surprise their peers or family with bizarre, child like, or eccentric behavior (Weeks & James, 1995). Most of the time, they may fit in just fine, but once in a while they are notably unconventional. This may be because they misjudge the opportunity for originality or at least misjudge it according to conventional standards. Of course, eccentrics can be quite creative. Many other unconventional tendencies of creative persons can be explained in the same fashion: The creative person once in a while, perhaps out of excitement over a topic or problem, relies a bit too heavily on an original interpretation instead of a conventional one. It is for precisely this reason that they may be labeled eccentric, unconventional, child like, contrarian, or nonconformist.

Actually, this part of personal creativity is quite amenable. There is much that can be done to help children exercise their discretion and thereby fulfill their creative potentials. There are, for example, many educational programs already in place that focus on children's decision making. The DARE program and school slogan "just say no" assume that children can exercise discretion and "make good choices." Other existent programs are designed to help children make moral and ethical decisions (Kohlberg, 1987), and because their focus is decision making, they too might be adapted to enhance the kind of discretion that should monitor and direct originality. Just as children might sometimes need to "just say no" to peer pressure to experiment with alcohol or cigarettes, so too might they learn to resist peer pressure and think for themselves and follow an original line of thought. Langer's (1999) work on mindfulness would also be useful in this regard, for it forces individuals to think for themselves rather than relying on rote "mindless" thinking.

MOTIVATION AND INTENTIONS

Granted, a child will not choose to put the effort into constructing an original interpretation unless he or she is motivated to do so. This is why Piaget's theory is often described as a theory of capacity or potential. He described what children are capable of doing, but that does not guarantee that children will actually do it. There is a big difference between capacity and actual performance. This difference characterizes the cognitive skills Piaget described (e.g., conservation, seriation, hypothetico-deductive thinking) and the discretionary and original interpretations that are central to personal creativity. In both cases, individuals must be motivated to use their skills.

Many theories of creativity and giftedness include motivation (Amabile, 1990; Eisenberger, 2003; Renzulli, 1978; Runco, 1993); typically, it is intrinsic motivation rather than extrinsic, although realistically both may be involved (Rubenson & Runco, 1992, 1995). The intriguing thing is that motivation may depend on cognition, and in particular on *cognitive appraisals*. There is some controversy here, but it does make a great deal of sense that individuals are not motivated about things they do not understand and that understanding therefore requires a cognitive appraisal (Lazarus, 1991; Zajonc, 1980). Piaget's (1970, 1976) view can again be cited; he felt that children will adapt because they are intrinsically motivated to understand. In that case, the motivation precedes and initiates the cognitive effort. Applying this to the role of assimilation in creative work outlined previously, it may be that certain situations attract the attention of the creative person and, as a result he or she thinks about it and perhaps continues to explore it and put effort into constructing meaningful interpretations and reinterpretations. This perspective is entirely consistent with the research showing that creatively gifted children often appear to be "on fire" and hugely interested in the domain that has attracted their attention. Creatively gifted children tend to be highly persistent, and sometimes they are so interested in a domain or problem that they invest all of their discretionary time into it. The result: a huge knowledge base and the domain-specific skills that may allow them to become productive and creative adults.

PERSONAL CREATIVITY VERSUS SOCIAL IMPACT

How does the theory of personal creativity fit with existing theories? As noted previously, the theory of personal creativity was in part developed in response to social theories of creativity. These defined creativity in terms of some product or social recognition. Goleman, Kaufman, and Ray (1992), for example, claimed that "an important dimension of creativity . . . is the audience. There is a crucial social dimension to the creative act" (p. 25). Houtz (2003) defined creativity as "a person's capacity to produce new or original ideas, insights, restructuring, inventions, or artistic objects, which are accepted by experts as being of scientific, aesthetic, social, or technological value" (p. 136). Both of these definitions require a "social dimension" or expert judgment. Simonton (1995, p. 4) put it this way: "A leader or creator is a Person to whom Others attribute leadership or creativity. The

greater the intensity, frequency, duration, and universality of this attribution, the more exceptional the influence exhibited." Given the need for
an attribution, Simonton seems to have been discussing "influence." He
mentions creativity, but it depends on other people and their attributions.
Amabile (1995) added this: "It is trivially obvious that there would be *no*
creativity whatsoever without the person and his or her cognitive abilities,
personality dispositions, and other personal resources, *nor* would there be
any creativity whatsoever without a context in which to create – a context of resources, education, exposure, encouragement, stimulation, and
appreciation (pp. 423–426)." My only concern here is with "appreciation,"
for that assumes expression and social acknowledgment.

Sometimes this troubling social requirement is tied to a second concern,
namely, a requirement of productivity. Kasof (1995), for instance, claimed
that "the creative product must be unusually original, rare, novel, statistically infrequent, and . . . it must be approved, accepted, valued, considered
'appropriate' or 'good' (pp. 311–366)." Perhaps it is now obvious why I
prefer the term *personal creativity*: It relegates social judgments. (Earlier I
considered the terms *inherent creativity* and *attributed creativity*, as well as
options in the literature. Stein [1953] previously distinguished between
subjective and *objective creativity*, for example, and Maslow [1971] differentiated *primary* from *secondary creativity*. The term *personal* seems to keep the
focus where it belongs, especially if we are interested in encouraging children with creative potential. The best labels, it seems to me, are personal
creativity and social creativity.)

It is possible to distinguish personal from social (and productive) processes by standing back and considering stages of creativity and influence. In this light, personal creativity comes first and social attributions
later. Consider Csikszentmihalyi's (in press) description of the creative
process:

In my opinion, it is impossible to understand creativity focusing on the person
alone. Every creative process or product is co-constituted by a matrix of information
(or domain), a group of experts (or field), and a person who produces a novel change
in the domain's structure of information, which the field accepts as viable, and adds
to the domain (pp. 60–61).

The theory of personal creativity suggests that individuals sometimes –
but not always – fulfill their potentials. They may also develop expertise
within a domain. They may even produce something that changes a field.
But it starts with the individual, and it would seem to be the most par-
simonious to describe "changing a field" as impact, fame, or reputation
rather than creativity. Separating creative insight from impact also makes
sense because fame and the like may result from creative work, but they
sometimes result from noncreative activity. Obnoxious people sometimes
attract attention, as do the infamous.

The definitions of creativity that look to products rather than individuals have their advantages. Products are, for example, certainly easy to study, for they can be counted, stored, and reexamined. It is easy to quantify products and thus easy to defend judgments or decisions (e.g., inclusion in a gifted educational program) when we have quantities and numbers to cite. Yet, that would leave us in a position in which we must infer what kind of person created the product. Counting products tells us mostly about products. Another concern with product views of creativity and giftedness is that they assume that a domain has useful products, and this assumption may not apply well to *everyday creativity* (Richards, 1998; Runco & Richards, 1998). Along the same lines, children may be creative in their play and self-expression, and neither of these can be easily treated as a product. Even more problematic is the failure of product views of creativity to recognize creative potential and inchoate forms of talent.

Ignoring creative potential – and children's creative skills – is a bit like claiming that the destination is all-important when traveling and that the route and steps along the way are unimportant. If educators were to define creativity only in terms of products, they would not recognize the child who has great talent but needs a bit of encouragement or needs to develop a tactic for finalizing his or her work. Educators looking only to productive children will not see the potential (e.g., interpretive or assimilatory efficiency) in nonproductive children. With a focus on products, educators will not be able to help the children who need help the most – those with potential who could be productive but are not yet quite ready.

DEFINING CREATIVE GIFTEDNESS AND WHAT CAN BE DONE ABOUT IT

Now it can be simply stated: Giftedness can be defined as (a) an exceptional level of interpretive capacity; (b) the discretion to use that capacity to construct meaningful and original ideas, options, and solutions; and (c) the motivation to apply, maintain, and develop the interpretive capacity and discretion. Giftedness, in this light, requires creativity, but it does not require that the child have all of the skills that would allow him or her to produce socially impressive artifacts. If the creatively gifted child develops those skills, we can view him or her as creatively gifted *and* productive.

A number of things can be done to support personal creativity. Because interest, intentions, and motivation are important, parents and educators can do their best to ensure that children are exposed to different domains and perspectives. If children do not know about a domain, they may not know what is available to them. Without broad exposure, they may not find the one domain that grabs them. Exposure to diverse domains and experiences increases the likelihood that a child will find something that is

intrinsically motivating. Children can also be protected from overjustifica-
tion, which is the loss of intrinsic motivation. Amabile (1990) demonstrated
how this kind of *immunization* can be accomplished via role playing and
modeling.

The discretionary part of personal creativity can also be exercised. It
would be important for children to recognize that they can make choices
and that their choices are important and under their control. As previously
mentioned, there are programs to help children with moral decisions (e.g.,
Kohlberg, 1987), and these might be adapted to the kind of discretion that
is vital for personal creativity. The difference would be in the values or
criteria targeted by the exercise. If the focus is on moral reasoning, cultural values might be underscored when the children are allowed to make
ethical decisions for themselves. For creativity, the emphasis should be
on originality, self-expression, and creativity. The children could use their
decision-making skills not to find a morally correct answer but one that
allows them to express themselves and show their uniqueness.

Actually, it is possible that programs like Kohlberg's will help children to
be creative, even if morality is emphasized instead of originality. This is because children may develop *postconventional thinking* skills when practicing
moral reasoning, and these thinking skills are defined as taking conventions into account but making a decision for one's self. Postconventional
thinking is, then, a kind of independent thought, and independent thinking will often lead to the expression of one's own ideas. In other words,
postconventional thinking will very likely support originality and thereby
creativity (Runco, 1996). Gruber (1993), Runco (1993), and McLaren (1993)
each explored other parallels between moral reasoning and creative
behavior.

Intrinsic motivation can be encouraged and protected, and discretion
exercised, but what about the third part of personal creativity? What about
assimilation? Earlier I offered suggestions about allowing pretending, but
actually assimilation may require less from parents and teachers than motivation and discretion. That is because all children assimilate. It may be
universal. All parents and teachers need to do is ensure that children maintain their tendency to control their interpretations and construct their own
understandings. Parents and teachers should recognize that as children
get older they will tend toward more conventional thinking. This is why
there is a fourth-grade slump in originality (Runco, 1999b; Torrance, 1968).
Many children at that age apparently realize that there are advantages to
fitting in, going along with peer pressure, and conforming. When they
do, their originality suffers. What parents and teachers should do is help
children avoid the slump. This might be accomplished by protecting children from conformity. Indeed, creative potential will definitely benefit if
we implement educational programs that allow children to stand up for
themselves and resist conforming. Perhaps most important would be to

ensure that children have the ego strength and confidence they need to withstand pressures to conform. Ego strength should also be modeled, practiced, and reinforced.

Some conformity should be expected. In fact, we do not want complete rebels; some conformity is good! Children should conform if they receive a test in school that asks them to name the first president of the United States: That is not a good time to be original. Children need to conform when it is appropriate, but should express their own uniqueness when they can. This is why discretion is included in the theory of personal creativity. Recall here also the definition of postconventional thinking: taking conventions into account but thinking for oneself. It is not just a matter of thinking for oneself; the individual does consider conventional options.

Late in childhood and during preadolescence, the individual will acquire the capacity to benefit from tactical thinking. Tactics are techniques that can be used to find original ideas. Young children may not need them, and in fact they probably are incapable of using them, but anyone who has developed a respect for conventionality, who conforms some of the time, or who has acquired inhibitions or makes assumptions based on past experience (i.e., adolescents and adults) will benefit from tactical creativity. Tactical creativity may compensate for the loss of spontaneity and the reliance on routine and assumption that go along with aging. Tactics are often quite simple (e.g., "change your perspective," "question your assumptions"). The literature contains many examples showing how tactics can be communicated to children even as young as 8 or 9 years of age (Runco, 1986, 1999; Davidson & Sternberg, 1983).

Something can also be said about what parents and teachers should not encourage. If creative talent is defined in terms of socially acknowledged products, it would be tempting to target social judgment as part of a program to encourage creative work. This is no straw argument: Kasof (1995) suggested precisely this in his attributional theory of creativity. He concluded that creativity is dependent on social judgments (see previous quotation) and concluded that creative individuals would benefit from *impression management*. This would allow the individual to ensure that his or her work is socially acknowledged and appreciated. The problems with this perspective are numerous. A concern for social judgment could, for example, suggest that the individual conform to expectations rather than express himself or herself in an original fashion. Additionally, any time invested in impression management is time taken away from practice developing ego strength, tactics, and the decision making that will support creativity. Runco (1992) concluded that parents and teachers need to both (a) encourage certain behaviors, such as pretending, and (b) avoid certain things, such as conformity and impression management. He suggested (a) creating *opportunities* for children to pretend and be original, (b) *modeling* original behavior for children, and (c) *rewarding* authentic self-expressions and spontaneous original actions. Much can be done to encourage children's creativity.

CONCLUSIONS

One premise in the theory of personal creativity (Runco, 1995, 1996) is that children have the capacity for personal creativity, and it is the same capacity that might be used by creative adults. The eminent creative genius uses his or her personal creativity just as the average child does. Obviously, they use personal creative talents to different ends, the adult often producing something tangible and perhaps socially impressive (e.g., a work of art, an invention) and the child often just creating a useful and original interpretation of his or her experience. There are differences between the adult and the child, of course, but not in their creative potential. These differences reflect knowledge, or even expertise, which the adult has accumulated and applied to his or her work.

The definition of creative giftedness used here may differ from most other conceptions of giftedness or creativity. There certainly is a difference between what I called the social and product views and my conception of personal creativity. The product view is apparent in the research on eminent adults, but also in the gifted literature, when assessments target products, achievements, and accomplishments. The conception of creative giftedness outlined here also differs from views that emphasize domain-specific skills. Actually, personal creativity is compatible with the idea of domain specificity – domain-specific skills may, for example, work with the interpretive skills reviewed previously and help an individual with potential to achieve his or her goals – but one premise of personal creativity is that the cognitive mechanism is nearly universally distributed. Personal creativity is a general tendency, and this is somewhat at odds with the trend toward domain specificity.

Personal creativity is more clearly compatible with theories that emphasize motivation. Intrinsic motivation in particular is an important part of personal creativity and important in numerous other definitions of talent. I actually prefer the term *intentions* over motivation. Intentions seem to mesh better with discretion and the pertinent decision making (Runco, 1993, 1996; Runco et al., 1999). Sometimes people do things without much thought (Langer, 1999). They may even be original without much effort! Originality can be an accident, or it can be serendipitous. What is most informative (and predictive of achievement) is originality that is intended. If we know what a person intends to do, we know they were motivated to do it and chose to do it. They have exercised their discretion and are likely to bring their talents to bear on the problem or topic.

The need to take motivation and intentions into account is not unique to the theory of personal creativity. As a matter of fact, there is one clear parallel between this theory and just about every other view of giftedness, creativity, or talent of any sort, namely, the assumption about the use of potentials. Any time a paper-and-pencil test is used, it is assumed that the resulting test score predicts something important. There is no guarantee that the individual who scores well on the test will be interested in using his or her talents in the natural environment. The test is, in that sense, an estimate of potential. Predictions might be the safest when tests are avoided and indices of actual performance are used. That is one assumption of the product view of talent, the other assumption being that products are easy to measure in an objective fashion. These assumptions are held by various psychometricians who have suggested that portfolios and measures of extracurricular activity and achievement be used (e.g., Hocever, 1981; Holland, 1961; Milgram, 1976; Wallach & Wing, 1969). But even here there is uncertainty. Just because someone applied himself or herself in the past, there is no guarantee that he or she will continue to use those same talents in the future. Even indices of past performance, such as the activity and achievement measures, assume that the individual will be motivated and interested in the future, and this not so different from the assumption of personal creativity: The individual has the capacity (potential) to construct original interpretations, but he or she must be motivated to do so or that potential will not be fulfilled and it is unlikely that any notably creative behavior will be expressed. The point is that the assumption of potential found in the theory of personal creativity is not too different from the assumptions about the predictiveness of creative achievement that characterize other competing theories.

The next important assumption of this theory of personal creativity is that originality is the key to creative work. Assimilation, for instance, allows the individual to construct spontaneous and meaningful interpretations of experience, which are relevant because those will be original for the individual. But, again, the assumption is that this originality is a part of creativity. This assumption is a tenable one. After all, originality is the only aspect of creative persons or products on which everyone agrees – even those definitions cited previously to exemplify the product view recognize originality. This is in part because originality is easier to operationalize (and study and identify) than creativity per se. Originality is a statistical characteristic. Original ideas and solutions are unusual or even unique. They are statistically infrequent. Unlike creativity per se, we can measure originality in a fairly simple and highly reliable manner. This is exemplified in the research on musical compositions (Simonton, 1988), solutions and ideas (Runco, 1991), and inventions (Weber, 1996).

Admittedly, we cannot rely on originality as an index of creativity. This is because bizarre behaviors, including psychotic behaviors, are often original, although not at all creative (Eysenck, 2003). They are original in the sense of being highly unusual, but they lack the effectiveness (Bruner, 1970), appropriateness (Runco & Charles, 1993), or aesthetic appeal (Csikszent-mihalyi & Getzels, 1971) of truly creative things. It is in that sense that originality is necessary but not sufficient for creativity. Effectiveness and appropriateness are satisfied in the personal creative process in that the interpretations constructed are meaningful. They are constructed precisely because they allow the individual to deal with an experience. In a sense, they are solutions, at least if we view experience as open-ended and filled with workaday hurdles. Recall that assimilation plays a role in the Piagetian (1970, 1976) view of cognitive development, and interpretations are constructed to allow the individual to adapt to experience.

This brings us to the last assumption. This is the assumption that personal creativity is tied to genius, eminence, achievement, and outstanding accomplishment, as well as giftedness. Personal creativity does rely on assimilative and interpretive processes, and these are involved in everyday adaptations. Yet they also play a role in exceptional performances in that those exceptional performances are often solutions to important problems. Surely, gifted children often do remarkable things, but those things must begin somewhere. The assumption is that they begin with the construction of a meaningful interpretation. An exceptional performance may very well involve much more than just an original interpretation. It may require elaboration or validation. The writer, for example, may construct an interpretation of perspective (see Wallace, 1991) and then explore that in a novel or other literary work. That literary work may require persistence and special knowledge for it to come to fruition, but it all begins with the original insight provided by the interpretive (cognitive) capacity of personal creativity.

Exceptional performances do often lead to socially acknowledged achievement, and it will only be socially acknowledged if it impresses other people. But it can be creative even if it does not impress an audience. If it impresses other people, it is "impressive," and it may have impact, but the creative part of the performance is a function of the originality and discretion of the individual.

References

Amabile, T. M. (1990). Within you, without you: Toward a social psychology of creativity and beyond. In M. A. Runco & R. S. Albert (Eds.), *Theories of creativity* (pp. 61–91). Newbury Park, CA: Sage.

Amabile, T. M. (1995). Attributions of creativity: What are the consequences? *Creativity Research Journal, 8,* 423–426.

Bachelor, P., & Michael, W. B. (1991). Higher-order factors of creativity within Guilford's structure-of-intellect model: A re-analysis of a 53 variable data base. *Creativity Research Journal, 4,* 157–175.

Bruner, J. (1970). *Essays for the left hand*. New York: Norton.

Csikszentmihalyi, M., & Getzels, J. W. (1971). Discovery-oriented behavior and the originality of creative products: A study with artists. *Journal of Personality and Social Psychology, 19*, 47–52.

Csikszentmihalyi, M. (in press). The domain of creativity. In M. A. Runco & R. S. Albert (Eds.), *Theories of creativity* (rev. ed.). Cresskill, NJ: Hampton.

Davidson, J. E., & Sternberg, R. J. (1983). The role of insight in intellectual giftedness. *Gifted Child Quarterly, 28*, 58–64.

Eisenberger, R., & Shanock, L. (2003). Rewards, Intrinsic Motivation, and Creativity: A Case Study of Conceptual and Methodological Isolation. *Creativity Research Journal, 15*, 121–130.

Eysenck, H. J. (2003). Creativity, personality, and the convergent-divergent continuum. In M. A. Runco (Ed.), *Critical creative processes* (pp. 195–214). Cresskill, NJ: Hampton.

Goleman, D., Kaufman, P., & Ray, M. (1992). *The creative spirit*. New York: Penguin.

Gruber, H. E. (1981). On the relation between "aha" experiences and the construction of ideas. *History of Science, 19*, 41–59.

Gruber, H. E. (1988). The evolving systems approach to creative work. *Creativity Research Journal, 1*, 27–51.

Gruber, H. E. (1993). Creativity in the moral domain: Ought implies can implies create. *Creativity Research Journal, 6*, 3–15.

Guilford, J. P. (1983). Transformation abilities or functions. *Journal of Creative Behavior, 17*, 75–83.

Hocevar, D. (1981). Measurement of creativity: Review and critique. *Journal of Personality Assessment, 45*, 450–464.

Hofstadter, D. (1985). *Metamagical themas: Questing for the essence of mind and patterns*. New York: Bantam.

Holland, J. L. (1961). Creative and academic achievement among talented adolescents. *Journal of Educational Psychology, 52*, 136–147.

Houtz, J. (Ed.). (2003). *An educational psychology of creativity*. Cresskill, NJ: Hampton Press.

Jackson, P. W., & Messick, S. (1967). The person, the product, and the response: Conceptual problems in the assessment of creativity. In J. Kagan (Ed.), *Creativity and learning* (pp. 1–19). Boston, MA: Beacon.

Jay, E., & Perkins, D. (1998). Problem finding: The search for mechanism. In M. A. Runco (Ed.), *Creativity research handbook* (pp. 257–293). Cresskill, NJ: Hampton.

Kasof, J. (1995). Explaining creativity: The attributional perspective. *Creativity Research Journal, 8*, 311–366.

Kohlberg, L. (1987). The development of moral judgment and moral action. In L. Kohlberg (Ed.), *Child psychology and childhood education: A cognitive developmental view*. New York: Longman.

Lazarus, R. S. (1991). Cognition and motivation in emotion. *American Psychologist, 46*, 352–367.

Maslow, A. H. (1971). *The farther reaches of human nature*. New York: Viking.

McLaren, R. (1993). The dark side of creativity. *Creativity Research Journal, 6*, 137–144.

Milgram, R. M., & Milgram, N. (1976). Creative thinking and creative performance in Israeli students. *Journal of Educational Psychology, 68*, 255–258.

Moldoveanu, M. C., & Langer, E. (1999). Mindfulness. In M. A. Runco & S. Pritzker (Eds.), *Encyclopedia of creativity*, pp. 221–234. New York: Academic.

O'Quin, K., Bessemer, S. (1989). The development, reliability, and validity of the revised creative product semantic scale. *Creativity Research Journal, 2*, 268–278.

Piaget, J. (1970). Piaget's theory. In P. H. Mussen (Ed.), *Carmichael's handbook of child psychology* (3rd ed., pp. 703–732). New York: Wiley.

Piaget, J. (1976). *To understand is to invent*. New York: Penguin.

Puccio, G. J., Treffinger, D. J., & Talbot, R. (1995). Exploratory examination of relations between creative styles and creative products. *Creativity Research Journal, 8*(2), 157–172.

Renzulli, J. (1978). What makes giftedness? Re-examining a defintion. *Phi Delta Kappan, 60*, 180–184.

Richards, R. (1990). Everyday creativity, eminent creativity, and health. *Creativity Research Journal, 3*, 300–326.

Rogers, C. R. (1961). *On becoming a person*. Boston, MA: Houghton Mifflin.

Rubenson, D. L., & Runco, M. A. (1992). The psychoeconomic approach to creativity. *New Ideas in Psychology, 10*, 131–147.

Rubenson, D. L., & Runco, M. A. (1995). The psychoeconomic view of creative work in groups and organizations. *Creativity and Innovation Management, 4*, 232–241.

Runco, M. A. (1986). Divergent thinking and creative performance in gifted and nongifted children. *Educational and Psychological Measurement, 46*, 375–384.

Runco, M. A. (Ed.). (1991). *Divergent thinking*. Norwood, NJ: Ablex Publishing Corporation.

Runco, M. A. (1992). *Creativity as an educational objective for disadvantaged students*. Storrs, CT: National Research Center on the Gifted and Talented.

Runco, M. A. (1993). Creative morality: Intentional and unconventional. *Creativity Research Journal, 6*, 17–28.

Runco, M. A. (1995). Insight for creativity, expression for impact. *Creativity Research Journal, 8*, 377–390.

Runco, M. A. (1996, Summer). Personal creativity: Definition and developmental issues. *New Directions for Child Development, 72*, 3–30.

Runco, M. A. (1999a). Tactics and strategies for creativity. In M. A. Runco & Steven Pritzker (Eds.), *Encyclopedia of creativity* (pp. 611–615). New York: Academic.

Runco, M. A. (1999b). The fourth-grade slump. In M. A. Runco & Steven Pritzker (Eds.), *Encyclopedia of creativity* (pp. 743–744). New York: Academic Press.

Runco, M. A., & Charles, R. (1993). Judgments of originality and appropriateness as predictors of creativity. *Personality and Individual Differences, 15*, 537–546.

Runco, M. A., & Richards, R. (Eds.). (1998). *Eminent creativity, everyday creativity, and health*. Norwood, NJ: Ablex.

Runco, M. A., Johnson, D., & Gaynor, J. R. (1999). The judgmental bases of creativity and implications for the study of gifted youth. In A. Fishkin, B. Cramond, & P. Olszewski-Kubilius (Eds.), *Creativity in youth: Research and methods* (pp. 113–141). Cresskill, NJ: Hampton.

Runco, M. A., Plucker, J. A., & Lim, W. (2000). Development and psychometric integrity of a measure of ideational behavior. *Creativity Research Journal, 13*, 393–400.

Simonton, D. K. (1988). *Scientific genius*. New York: Cambridge University Press.

Simonton, D. K. (1995). Exceptional personal influence: An integrative paradigm. *Creativity Research Journal, 8*, 371–376.

Stein, M. I. (1953). Creativity and culture. *Journal of Psychology, 36*, 311–322.

Torrance, E. P. (1968). A longitudinal examination of the fourth-grade slump in creativity. *Gifted Child Quarterly, 12*, 195–199.

Wallace, D. B. (1991). The genesis and microgenesis of sudden insight in the creation of literature. *Creativity Research Journal, 4*, 41–50.

Wallach, M. A., & Wing, C. (1969). *The talented student*. New York: Holt, Rinehart & Winston.

Weber R. (1996). Toward a language of invention and synthetic thinking. Creativity Research Journal.

Weeks, D., & James, J. (1995). *Eccentrics*. London: Weidenfeld & Nicolson.

Zajonc, R. B. (1980). Feeling and thinking: Preferences need no inferences. *American Psychologist, 35*, 151–175.

17

Genetics of Giftedness

The Implications of an Emergenic–Epigenetic Model

Dean Keith Simonton

THE IMPLICATIONS OF AN EMERGENIC–EPIGENETIC MODEL

According to the dictionary definition, the concept of giftedness is closely tied to talent, so much so that the terms are sometimes used interchangeably. Thus, on the one hand, to be gifted means to be "endowed with great natural ability, intelligence, or talent: *a gifted child; a gifted pianist*" (*American Heritage Dictionary*, 1992). On the other hand, a talent is "a marked innate ability, as for artistic accomplishment" or a "natural endowment or ability of a superior quality" (*American Heritage Dictionary*, 1992). From these definitions, it would seem either that the two terms are synonymous or that one can be considered a special case of the other (viz., talent may be viewed as a specific form of giftedness). Whatever their proper semantic significance, the terms agree on two explicit claims. First, both maintain that some individuals can be distinguished by exceptional abilities or capacities that set them well above normal expectation. Second, both terms affirm that these extraordinary qualities are in some way *innate*, the literal *gift* of some unspecified *natural endowment*. Most commonly, this innateness is conceived in terms of genetic inheritance.

Aside from these two explicit features of talent and giftedness, there are two other features implied by the definitions that are far more implicit and yet no less important. First, both talent and giftedness seem to represent a static quality of the person – somewhat like the color of a person's eyes. At some point relatively early in life, a child or adolescent is seen as having a gift or talent, and then that attribute, in line with other natural or endowed individual characteristics, simply exists as a stable aspect of the talented or gifted person. Second, a talent or gift appears to represent a single coherent ability rather than a collection of abilities. Thus, we speak of having the gift for perfect pitch as if it were a unified skill, like being able to wiggle one's ears. Although perfect pitch might be this simple, other forms of giftedness or talent may actually consist of multiple abilities and may even encompass interests and values in the mix. In brief, giftedness may be multidimensional rather than unidimensional. Once we allow for the potential multidimensionality of giftedness, then a new question emerges: How are those diverse components combined to produce the overall natural endowment?

In a nutshell, giftedness and talent may be far more complex than the dictionary definitions might suggest. In this chapter, I outline some of these potential complexities. My initial focus is on the innate, particularly genetic, features of giftedness. After scrutinizing the intricacies of genetic endowment, I turn briefly to the role of the environment in converting potential giftedness into actual outstanding achievement. The chapter closes with a discussion of the more practical implications of this more complicated view of giftedness.

ENDOWMENT AND GIFTEDNESS

Because giftedness and talent are so intimately related, I base the treatment of the genetics of giftedness on a theoretical model that was previously designed to explicate talent development (Simonton, 1999, 2001). In fact, the changes that must be made to advance this application are actually quite minimal. Although the model was originally expressed in mathematical terms, I concentrate here on its conceptual assumptions and their implications. In any case, according to this model, giftedness must be examined from two interrelated perspectives: emergenic inheritance and epigenetic development.

Emergenic Inheritance

Let us begin by assuming that most forms of giftedness are not contingent on the inheritance of a single trait. On the contrary, most are assumed to be complex enough to require the simultaneous inheritance of several traits. In other words, endowed capacity usually consists of multiple components. These components include all physical, physiological, cognitive, and dispositional traits that facilitate the manifestation of superior achievement in the domain in which giftedness is displayed. Some of these component traits may concern mostly the acquisition of the necessary expertise, whereas other components may largely affect the performance of whatever expertise has already been acquired. To simplify discussion, let it be supposed that each of these genetic traits varies along a ratio scale with a true zero point, which represents the total absence of the corresponding characteristic from the genotype. This would reflect the situation in which each component consists of numerous genes that may be inherited in any combination (i.e., polygenic with the possibility that none of the genes are inherited).

In the more complex forms of giftedness, these multiple components are presumed to operate in a multiplicative rather than additive manner. That is, the hypothetical scores of the component traits are multiplied rather than added together. This means that if any of the essential components is absent (or at least fails to meet a certain minimum "threshold" value),[1] the corresponding form of giftedness is absent, too. In other words, if a trait is truly required for the acquisition or performance of an exceptional skill, then its absence exerts veto power over the manifestation of that skill. To illustrate, if someone is born with an exceptional athletic ability in terms of innate physique, but without any inherent kinesthetic intelligence, the talent would remain nil. Another way of stating this requirement is that many types of giftedness may demand a specific weighted combination of traits, all of which must be present for the capacity to exist at all. This configurational type of genetic inheritance has been called *emergenic* by Lykken (1982, 1998) and colleagues (Lykken, McGue, Tellegen, & Bouchard, 1992).

Giftedness inherited according to this multidimensional and multiplicative process would operate in a fashion rather more complicated than is commonly assumed. The following four consequences are worth special attention:

1. Although it is often assumed that various forms of giftedness are domain-specific (e.g., giftedness in mathematics is not the same as giftedness in music), it is not necessary to assume that all of the genetic components that contribute to an individual's giftedness are themselves domain-specific. Although some of these components might be somewhat domain-specific (e.g., height for basketball players), some undetermined number may instead be rather generic (e.g., general intelligence, or "Spearman's *g*"). As a consequence, the domain specificity of many types of giftedness may actually reside in the distinctive configuration of essential traits, not in the traits themselves. The genes that provide the basis for one form of giftedness may actually contribute to the emergence of other forms of giftedness but in different combinations. Moreover, two kinds of giftedness might even exist that require the same components, but assign those components different weights (e.g., kindred gifts like music performance versus music composition). There already exists ample evidence that inheritable traits can contribute to more than one domain in which giftedness is displayed, but with

---

[1] Many genetic components may only exert influence if they surpass a level that represents the norm in either the general population or some subpopulation (e.g., competitors in the same achievement domain). For instance, intelligence may operate this way in the case of leadership (Simonton, 1985). Below that threshold, the component in effect has a zero value. For a more formal presentation of this possibility, see Simonton (1999).

distinctive emphases according to the specific demands of each domain (Simonton, 1999).

2. Two individuals in the same domain do not have to inherit the same traits to the same degree to display the same level of genetic endowment underlying their giftedness. It is the total product of the components that determines the degree of giftedness. So long as no component is zero, the two individuals can possess extremely heterogeneous profiles and still exhibit the same overall level of giftedness. For example, two painters could have the same overall innate gifts, but one inherits superior color discrimination whereas the other inherits superior sensitivity to form. Hence, the genetic endowments underlying a given domain-specific achievement do not have to be uniform. By the same token, two individuals may both lack any giftedness for a particular domain but exhibit extremely divergent genetic profiles because it only takes one missing component to veto the manifestation of the corresponding capacity, and the missing component need not be identical for the two persons. Neither the gifted nor the ungifted form genetically homogeneous groups.

3. It is often assumed that most human characteristics are normally distributed in the general population. Presumably, the genetic components underlying a given form of giftedness would also be described by the same bell-shaped curve. The sum of these would then be normally distributed. Yet under the nonadditive or emergenic model, the product of these components would not fit a normal distribution. Instead, any multidimensional and multiplicative type of giftedness would exhibit an extremely skewed (loglinear) distribution (Simonton, 1999; see also Burt, 1943; Shockley, 1957). At one extreme, a large proportion of the population would have no giftedness at all because they lack one or more essential components. At the other extreme would be those few individuals who are several standard deviations above the mean. Exceptional giftedness would be extremely rare in any complex domain. There exists a considerable amount of empirical data showing that the cross-sectional distribution of performance is most accurately described by curves that have a strong positive skew rather than a symmetric distribution (Walberg, Strykowski, Rovai, & Hung, 1984). For example, creative productivity is characterized by such a distinctive distribution (Lotka, 1926; Price, 1963; Simonton, 1997).

4. Giftedness according to the proposed model would be much more difficult to predict than would be the case were giftedness defined as a simple homogeneous construct. Most researchers attempt to predict exceptional performance according to the usual linear and additive models (e.g., Cattell & Butcher, 1968). To the extent that a

specific form of giftedness is actually multidimensional and multiplicative, the validity coefficients will be attenuated – even when
all the components have been reliably assessed. More remarkably,
such giftedness cannot even be predicted according to family pedi-
grees. Emergenic giftedness necessarily exhibits low familial heri-
tabilities. A child cannot inherit a gift from his or her parents unless
the whole configuration of component traits is inherited, and the
odds of that happening are extremely small. Indeed, only identical
(monozygotic) twins would receive equivalent forms of giftedness.
This feature provides a useful technique for determining whether a
given type of giftedness is emergenic. Giftedness that exhibits zero
heritability for fraternal twins but high heritability for identical twins
would best fit the emergenic model. Empirical evidence for such
emergenesis has already been found for creativity, leadership, and
other ways of being gifted (Lykken et al., 1992; Waller, Bouchard,
Lykken, Tellegen, & Blacker, 1993).

The foregoing implications depend on the assumption that a particular
type of giftedness is multidimensional. Yet it is probably the case that
types of giftedness may differ greatly in their complexity, that is, they may
vary in the number of essential components. Some types may demand
only one or two genetic components, whereas others may require a dozen
or so. This means that the previously mentioned consequences become
all the more paramount to the extent that a given form of giftedness is
multidimensional. Most significantly, the more complex types of giftedness
should exhibit more heterogeneous trait profiles, more extremely skewed
cross-sectional distributions, and reduced familial inheritance.

Epigenetic Development

Although giftedness becomes a much more complex behavioral phenomenon under the emergenic model, the model needs to incorporate
another critical complication: Genetic traits do not manifest themselves
all at once at birth but, rather, they must develop according to inherited
epigenetic trajectories. By epigenesis I mean that innate characteristics do
not appear all at once but rather develop gradually through some process
of growth and differentiation. It is partly for this reason that identical twins
reared apart will tend to become increasingly similar with age rather than
more dissimilar, as one would expect if the environment exerted increasing influence with maturation (Simonton, 1999). Accordingly, each of the
components making up a particular emergenic gift should possess its own
distinctive growth pattern. This epigenetic pattern will determine when
the trait's development begins to "kick in," the speed that it grows, and
the point at which growth levels off and terminates. This means that the

development of giftedness must be a dynamic process such that the very composition of a youth's gifts transforms over the course of childhood, adolescence, and early adulthood. Such an epigenetic–emergenic model has the following four repercussions:

1. Although many researchers have looked for early indicators of specific forms of giftedness (e.g., perfect pitch for music), such indicators or "early signs" are not required for any form of giftedness that is emergenic and epigenetic. The first component to begin growth for one individual might be among the last to develop for another individual. In fact, at least in theory, there are as many ways to initiate the development of giftedness as there are components contributing to acquisition and performance in a given domain of achievement.

2. The model provides a genetic basis for understanding the distinction between early- versus late-bloomers. Under an additive model, a gifted individual begins development when the *first* genetic component first emerges, whereas under a multiplicative model, the giftedness does not begin to grow until the *last* component begins development. A late-bloomer, in contrast to an early-bloomer, is a youth who has at least one component that displays a retarded epigenetic trajectory. Because the component does not initiate growth until later than normal, the composite giftedness must wait longer to materialize.

3. If the innate capacity for exceptional performance in a particular domain is multidimensional, and if each component has its own distinctive growth trajectory, then a youth's optimal form of giftedness will not be stable over time but rather will dynamically change. As new components begin to initiate their development, the youth may discover a greater proclivity for some related domain of achievement. For instance, a child might start out playing piano, transfer to composition, and end up becoming a conductor.

4. Because giftedness is not stable over time, it is possible for certain individuals to lose their gifts with age. The promising child may become a mediocre adolescent. According to the epigenetic model, there are two types of loss in giftedness: relative and absolute (Simonton, 1999). In relative loss, an individual's magnitude of giftedness changes its ordinal position compared with others in the same cohort. This can occur because others may have epigenetic trajectories with later onsets but more rapid growth rates. Hence, a late-bloomer might overtake an early-bloomer. In absolute loss in giftedness, certain genetic traits begin to develop that are detrimental to the further growth of the overall potential (e.g., increased weight for gymnasts or the onset of mental illness for scientists). Ultimately, the initial gift may vanish altogether.

Taken together, these implications suggest that the development of giftedness can occur in very different ways for genotypically distinct individuals. Two adults with the same form and level of giftedness may have gotten there via contrary epigenetic routes, whereas two adults with totally different forms of giftedness may have had very similar childhood beginnings. Moreover, even individuals who more or less stayed with the same type of giftedness throughout their youth may have displayed contrasting spurt and lull periods, so that their relative level of giftedness may have constantly transformed with age. Making matters all the more intricate is the previously mentioned possibility that various types of giftedness may vary greatly in the number of essential components. Playing master-level chess may require far fewer genetic traits than composing operas, for instance. The more components there are that participate in the constitution of a given gift, the greater the heterogeneity of available epigenetic profiles. In addition, for highly complex manifestations of giftedness, it becomes more likely that much more time will be required before all the requisite components initiate and complete their growth trajectories. Hence, although simple forms of giftedness might appear in childhood or early adolescence, complex forms of giftedness may not emerge until late adolescence or early adulthood.

Environment and Giftedness

The discussion thus far has focused exclusively on the genetic foundations of giftedness. In a sense, I have been following a tradition that goes back to Galton's (1869) *Hereditary Genius*, which argued that genius was born, not made. Yet Galton's biological determinism was quickly challenged by his contemporaries who demonstrated the influence of environmental factors (e.g., Candolle, 1873). Galton (1874) soon retreated from his extremist position and, in doing so, introduced the terms *nature* and *nurture* to describe the two main forces that shape human development. Nonetheless, some psychologists have advocated an extreme stance in the opposite direction, arguing that giftedness and talent are nothing more than the effects of acquired expertise (Ericsson, 1996; Howe, Davidson, & Sloboda, 1998). With sufficient study and practice, practically anyone can become gifted, even a world-class genius.

Even so, this alternative perspective has run into numerous empirical and theoretical problems (Simonton, 2000). For instance, the extreme environmentalist position fails to account for the exceptional rates at which highly gifted individuals can acquire mastery of a chosen domain (Lubinski, Webb, Morelock, & Benbow, 2001; Simonton, 1991). Nevertheless, it remains true that the environment plays a critical part in the development of giftedness (Simonton, 1987; Winner, 1996). Numerous investigations have documented the extent to which giftedness is encouraged or discouraged by family background, educational experiences, role models and mentors, and even larger sociocultural forces, such as the political and economic context. Moreover, many of these environmental factors are probably linked in intimate ways with the epigenetic realization of genetic potential. These environmental–genetic linkages can include interaction effects such that the impact of nature is moderated by nurture or vice versa. For instance, the consequences of birth order are partly contingent on such genetically influenced traits as shyness (Sulloway, 1996). Specifically, first-borns who are innately shy are less able to assume the characteristics associated with that birth order and will have their personality development altered accordingly.

Indeed, just as we have assumed that genetic traits enter into multidimensional and multiplicative relations, so may we conjecture that environmental factors enter into the developmental process via similarly complex relations both with each other and with the genetic factors (Eysenck, 1995). As a result, giftedness must emerge out of a highly distinctive configuration of developmental influences. The repercussion of this configurational development would be to accentuate all the more the inferences drawn earlier from the purely genetic model. For instance, notable giftedness would become all the more rare and the cross-sectional distribution of giftedness even more skewed. In addition, the number of alternative developmental trajectories would immensely multiply. Particularly crucial would be the multitude of trajectories in which environmental factors lead epigenetic development astray and thereby guide the young talent down the wrong pathway, leading them to a cul-de-sac. For instance, at a critical moment, the gifted child might identify with the wrong peer group (Csikszentmihalyi, Rathunde, & Whalen, 1993; Harris, 1998). This identification can divert their efforts toward their weaknesses rather than toward their strengths (e.g., switching from classical piano to rock guitar). The result is a once-gifted child who failed to realize his or her potential.

Implications: Consolidation and Extension

Although the environment has a critical part to play in the realization of giftedness, it must be emphasized that the concept of giftedness, like that of talent, has a more fundamental link with natural endowment. Therefore, although acknowledging the impact of nurture, I now consolidate and extend the crucial implications that can be derived from the manner in which nature is presumed to influence giftedness. More specifically, the implications originate in the possibility that many forms of giftedness may be inherited according to the emergenic and epigenetic processes treated earlier. Yet it must also be recognized that some types of giftedness might not operate in such a fashion. Accordingly, genetic inheritance or natural

TABLE 17.1. *Fourfold Typology of Giftedness: Simple versus Complex and Additive versus Multiplicative Giftedness*

	Additive		Multiplicative	
Consequences	Simple	Complex	Simple	Complex
Trait profiles	Uniform	Diverse	Uniform	Diverse
Cross-sectional distribution	Normal	Normal	Skewed	Extremely Skewed
Proportion ungifted	Small	Extremely Small	Large	Extremely Large
Familial inheritance	Highest	High	Low	Lowest
Developmental trajectories	Few	Numerous	Few	Numerous
Developmental onset	Early	Earliest	Later	Latest
Identifiability	Highest	High	Low	Lowest
Instruction/training strategies	Few	Numerous	Few	Numerous

Note: Simple types of giftedness are those in which the number of genetic components is small, perhaps even unidimensional, whereas complex types are those in which the number of components is large and hence highly multidimensional.

endowment may participate in quite contrary ways in different varieties of giftedness. These contrasts can be pinpointed by developing a fourfold typology of giftedness, as shown in Table 17.1. This typology begins with the assumption that various forms of giftedness may vary in two major ways.

First, some types are simple and others complex. Simple types of giftedness require relatively few genetic traits and in the extreme case could involve only one trait and thus be unidimensional. An example of extremely simple "gifts" would be visual acuity and physical height – attributes that are polygenic but homogeneous. Complex types, in contrast, presuppose a large number of distinctly different endowed attributes and are therefore multidimensional. Examples might include political and entrepreneurial leadership, as well as cinematic and choreographic creativity. Political leadership, for instance, is contingent on a diversity of traits, both physical (e.g., height, energy) and psychological (e.g., intelligence, extraversion, power motivation).

Second, forms of giftedness may vary according to how these traits are combined. On the one hand, the traits might operate according to an additive model. This means that no trait has veto power over the appearance of the gift. A potential example might be scholastic aptitude, as gauged by a student's performance on psychometric measures. On the other hand, the traits might be combined according to a multiplicative model, that is, the particular guise of giftedness may be emergent. It is conceivable that most forms of giftedness that result in genuine achievements are of this nature, including most types of creativity and leadership.

We thus obtain four broad classes of giftedness: simple additive, complex additive, simple multiplicative, and complex multiplicative. As summarized in the table, these four types may then differ along the following eight criteria:

1. *Trait profiles* – Simple types of giftedness, whether additive or multiplicative, will be relatively uniform regarding their trait profiles. That is, individuals displaying that particular gift will be very homogeneous in makeup regarding the component traits – the degree of similarity becoming especially pronounced for unidimensional types. In stark contrast, complex or multidimensional types of giftedness, again whether additive or multiplicative, would encompass a wide diversity of trait profiles. For instance, there may not be very many genetic underpinnings to exceptional visual acuity, but there are certainly a large number of possible genetic foundations of extraordinary leadership as president of the United States, as the rather divergent personalities of George Washington, Abraham Lincoln, and Franklin Roosevelt amply demonstrate (Simonton, 1986, 1988).

2. *Cross-sectional distribution* – If it is assumed that all component genetic traits are normally distributed in the population, then the distribution of the corresponding giftedness will also be normally distributed in the population under both additive models. In fact, if the form of giftedness is multidimensional but still additive, it will still have a roughly normal distribution, even if the underlying traits are not always normally distributed. By comparison, the cross-sectional distribution for multiplicative (emergenic) types will always be skewed, with most of the gifts being concentrated in an elite few. The greater the complexity of the giftedness type, the more skewed the distribution and more exceptional the resulting elite become. An illustration might be the capacity to compose classical music in a variety of genre because nearly one fifth of all music in the regular repertoire can be attributed to just three composers, namely, Mozart, Beethoven, and Bach (Moles, 1958/1968).

3. *Proportion ungifted* – Under an additive model, no component trait can exert veto power, and thus the odds of exhibiting zero talent would be relatively small. This is particularly true for complex forms of giftedness because it only takes one nonzero component to produce a nonzero level of giftedness. The greater the number of required traits, the higher the probability that at least one trait will be present. The outcome is dramatically different for multiplicative forms of giftedness. In the first place, even for simple forms, only one component needs to be absent for giftedness to be absent. That

necessarily lowers the likelihood that anyone would display giftedness relative to an additive form with an equal number of essential
components. In addition, as the complexity of the type increases,
the probability of exhibiting giftedness decreases because the odds
of obtaining nonzero values on all traits also decrease. To put it in
concrete terms, the number of persons who show no innate capacity
whatsoever in architecture or choreography should be far greater
than the number of persons showing none at all in chess or javelin
throwing.

4. *Familial inheritance* – The pattern seen in this criterion is distinct from
any of the preceding three. Children are most likely to inherit giftedness from their parents if the type is simple and additive. In the
extreme case, if a type of giftedness requires only one trait, so that
the additive–multiplicative distinction becomes irrelevant, then the
odds of inheriting the trait from the parent who possesses that trait
are extremely high. However, as the number of required components
increases, the likelihood of inheriting some or all declines proportionately. Matters get much worse in the case of multiplicative types
of giftedness. In that situation, if one trait fails to become part of
the person's genetic constitution, then the specific form of giftedness will fail to manifest itself. Worse still, as the complexity of the
form increases, the likelihood of failing to inherit the entire collection of components decreases proportionately. Hence, complex and
multiplicative manifestations of giftedness are very unlikely to exhibit familial inheritance, such as that documented in Galton's (1869)
Hereditary Genius. For example, gifted choreographers are very unlikely to be the sons or daughters of gifted choreographers.

5. *Developmental trajectories* – Up to this point, the implications ensue from the possibility that some types of giftedness might be
emergenic – particularly multidimensional (complex) and multiplicative. Yet the phenomenon of epigenesis is no less crucial to a full
appreciation of the nature of giftedness. Because each genetic trait
is characterized by a specific developmental path within a particular individual, it is necessary to ask how these separate components
combine to produce the overall growth trajectory for a given type
of giftedness. In this case, it should be clear that the crucial parame-
ter is the complexity of the gift – where it stands on the continuum
connecting unidimensional and highly multidimensional guises of
giftedness. If a type is simple, then the number of potential developmental patterns is relatively small. Indeed, in the simplest case of
a gift with only a single component, there can be only one possible
trajectory, namely that of the essential trait. Yet as the number of
genetic ingredients increases, so does the number of potential trajectories, depending on which component exhibits an accelerated

growth curve compared with the other components constituting the gift. More specifically, a type of giftedness with, say, a dozen distinct components will have at least 12 different developmental pathways. Notice that according to this criterion, the additive or multiplicative status of the gift is irrelevant.

6. *Developmental onset* – The irrelevance of the additive–multiplicative distinction does not apply to the fifth criterion, namely, the age at which a person begins to manifest a type of giftedness. If a particular form is additive, then giftedness begins to develop at the moment the first component begins to develop. This onset will be earliest for the complex additive forms because there are more available components on which the individual can display precocity compared with the simple additive forms. This differential reverses for the multiplicative types of giftedness. For one thing, the development of giftedness does not become apparent until all of the components begin development. That happens because giftedness is absent so long as a single essential component is absent. It should be evident, furthermore, that as the number of required genetic traits increases, the probability that all will have initiated growth at a given time will decrease. Consequently, for complex, multiplicative manifestations of giftedness, the onset of the gift's development will be extremely retarded. In support of this anticipation, I might cite the fact that within classical music, achievement in more complex genre, such as opera, arrives at a much later age than achievement in more simple genre, such as the art song, whereas genre like the symphony have onsets somewhere in between (Lehman, 1953).

7. *Identifiability* – The final two implications deal with the more practical ramifications of the emergenic–epigenetic perspective. The first concerns the ability to identify early and accurately those youths who display potential signs of giftedness. As is evident from Table 17.1, the four types of giftedness exhibit a distinct pattern by this criterion. Identification is highest for simple and additive gifts because they only require a few traits, and the form of giftedness begins to manifest itself as soon as the first component begins development. Identification becomes more difficult for complex types because more traits have to appear before the specific developmental trajectory can be easily anticipated. For multiplicative forms of giftedness, in contrast, identification becomes much more insecure. Because all components must begin growth before the gift's development properly begins, the specific form of giftedness cannot be identified until the full set of components is developmentally in place. If identification is based on a subset of the components, with no assurance that the full set will appear, then a predictive error will have been committed. Naturally, as a given guise of giftedness becomes ever more complex, this

identification problem is all the more aggravated. Hence, a multidimensional gift such as architecture will be more difficult to discern than a simpler gift such as chess.

8. *Instruction/training strategies* – The second, more practical implication concerns the best approach to the nurture of a given form of giftedness. That is, if we can assume that we have correctly identified individuals with a potential gift, what can be done to foster that gift? The fundamental principle here is that nurture must conform to nature. More specifically, instruction, training, coaching, education, and other interventions must not only fit a particular type of giftedness, but also fit an individual's distinctive trait profile allowable within that type. This principle implies that the number of possible strategies should closely parallel the number of permissible profiles. It is for this reason that the pattern of results follows that for the trait profiles criterion. Whether multiplicative or additive, simple gifts with relatively few possible profiles will require a smaller repertoire of interventions than will complex gifts with a great many potential profiles. Hence, instruction or training strategies will be more numerous for highly multidimensional forms of giftedness than for those with much fewer dimensions. One way of looking at this difference is to think in terms of the need to aim the intervention at potential weaknesses. The more complex the manifestation of giftedness, the greater is the potential variety of weakness patterns and thus the larger is the number of strategies that must be available to cultivate successfully those weaknesses until they become strengths.

Taken altogether, the implications summarized in Table 17.1 suggest that giftedness is by no means a straightforward phenomenon. According to the emergenic–epigenetic model, the first task must be to determine whether a given form of giftedness is additive or multiplicative, simple or complex. That decision then has critical consequences regarding the number of possible trait profiles, the skewness of the cross-sectional distribution, the proportion of individuals that can be considered to lack the gift, the degree of familial inheritance, the number of developmental trajectories, the age of onset for the gift's development, the ease of identifying the specific form of giftedness, and the number of instruction or training strategies that must be available. Needless to say, these complications actually understate the full intricacies inherent in the phenomenon. After all, the emphasis has been on the genetics of giftedness – on the niceties of natural development. The situation would become all the more involved once environmental factors were incorporated explicitly into the model. Even so, it should be apparent that, to the extent that a form of giftedness displays emergenic inheritance and epigenetic development, the complexities are already far more impressive than the dictionary definitions tend to imply.

References

American Heritage Electronic Dictionary (3rd ed.). (1992). Boston: Houghton Mifflin.

Burt, C. (1943). Ability and income. *British Journal of Educational Psychology, 12,* 83–98.

Candolle, A. de (1873). *Histoire des sciences et des savants depuis deux siècles.* Geneva, Switzerland: Georg.

Cattell, R. B., & Butcher, H. J. (1968). *The prediction of achievement and creativity.* Indianapolis, IN: Bobbs-Merrill.

Csikszentmihalyi, M., Rathunde, K., & Whalen, S. (1993). *Talented teenagers: The roots of success and failure.* Cambridge, England: Cambridge University Press.

Ericsson, K. A. (Ed.). (1996). *The road to expert performance: Empirical evidence from the arts and sciences, sports, and games.* Mahwah, NJ: Lawrence Erlbaum Associates.

Eysenck, H. J. (1995). *Genius: The natural history of creativity.* Cambridge, England: Cambridge University Press.

Galton, F. (1869). *Hereditary genius: An inquiry into its laws and consequences.* New York: Macmillan.

Galton, F. (1874). *English men of science: Their nature and nurture.* New York: Macmillan.

Harris, J. R. (1998). *The nurture assumption: Why children turn out the way they do.* New York: Free Press.

Howe, M. J. A., Davidson, J. W., & Sloboda, J. A. (1998). Innate talents: Reality or myth? *Behavioral and Brain Sciences, 21,* 399–442.

Lehman, H. C. (1953). *Age and achievement.* Princeton, NJ: Princeton University Press.

Lotka, A. J. (1926). The frequency distribution of scientific productivity. *Journal of the Washington Academy of Sciences, 16,* 317–323.

Lubinski, D., Webb, R. M., Morelock, M. J., & Benbow, C. P. (2001). Top 1 in 10,000: A 10-year follow-up of the profoundly gifted. *Journal of Applied Psychology, 86,* 718–729.

Lykken, D. T. (1982). Research with twins: The concept of emergenesis. *Psychophysiology, 19,* 361–373.

Lykken, D. T. (1998). The genetics of genius. In A. Steptoe (Ed.), *Genius and the mind: Studies of creativity and temperament in the historical record* (pp. 15–37). New York: Oxford University Press.

Lykken, D. T., McGue, M., Tellegen, A., & Bouchard, T. J., Jr. (1992). Emergenesis: Genetic traits that may not run in families. *American Psychologist, 47,* 1565–1577.

Moles, A. (1968). *Information theory and esthetic perception* (J. E. Cohen, Trans.). Urbana: University of Illinois Press. (Original work published 1958.)

Price, D. (1963). *Little science, big science.* New York: Columbia University Press.

Shockley, W. (1957). On the statistics of individual variations of productivity in research laboratories. *Proceedings of the Institute of Radio Engineers, 45,* 279–290.

Simonton, D. K. (1985). Intelligence and personal influence in groups: Four nonlinear models. *Psychological Review, 92,* 532–547.

Simonton, D. K. (1986). Presidential personality: Biographical use of the Gough Adjective Check List. *Journal of Personality and Social Psychology, 51,* 149–160.

Simonton, D. K. (1987). Developmental antecedents of achieved eminence. *Annals of Child Development, 5,* 131–169.

Simonton, D. K. (1988). Presidential style: Personality, biography, and performance. *Journal of Personality and Social Psychology, 55,* 928–936.

Simonton, D. K. (1991). Emergence and realization of genius: The lives and works of 120 classical composers. *Journal of Personality and Social Psychology, 61,* 829–840.

Simonton, D. K. (1997). Creative productivity: A predictive and explanatory model of career trajectories and landmarks. *Psychological Review, 104,* 66–89.

Simonton, D. K. (1999). Talent and its development: An emergenic and epigenetic model. *Psychological Review, 106,* 435–457.

Simonton, D. K. (2000). Creative development as acquired expertise: Theoretical issues and an empirical test. *Developmental Review, 20,* 283–318.

Simonton, D. K. (2001). Talent development as a multidimensional, multiplicative, and dynamic process. *Current Directions in Psychological Science, 10,* 39–43.

Sulloway, F. J. (1996). *Born to rebel: Birth order, family dynamics, and creative lives.* New York: Pantheon.

Walberg, H. J., Strykowski, B. F., Rovai, E., & Hung, S. S. (1984). Exceptional performance. *Review of Educational Research, 54,* 87–112.

Waller, N. G., Bouchard, T. J., Jr., Lykken, D. T., Tellegen, A., & Blacker, D. M. (1993). Creativity, heritability, familiality: Which word does not belong? *Psychological Inquiry, 4,* 235–237.

Winner, E. (1996). *Gifted children: Myths and realities.* New York: Basic Books.

18

The WICS Model of Giftedness

Robert J. Sternberg

What happened to Denny (Trillin, 1994)? Roger "Denny" Hansen was a classmate of author Calvin Trillin. He was a Rhodes Scholar who had all the markings of early success. But life did not prove kind to him, and after a series of failures, Denny committed suicide at the age of 55. Of course there are other examples of spectacular failures, such as William James Sidis, who never lived up to the potential he had shown as an intellectual child prodigy.

The WICS model is a possible common basis for identifying gifted individuals (Sternberg, 2003c). WICS is an acronym standing for Wisdom, Intelligence, Creativity, Synthesized. According to this model, wisdom, intelligence, and creativity are sine qua nons for the gifted leaders of the future. Without a synthesis of these three attributes, someone can be a decent contributor to society, and perhaps even a good one, but never a great one.

In the remainder of this chapter, each of these attributes is discussed, although for didactic purposes, they are not discussed in the order in which they are stated in the acronym. The discussion starts with intelligence, which is a basis for creativity and wisdom and so should be discussed first. Then, creativity is discussed, which is essential in wisdom, as well. Finally, wisdom is discussed, which builds on but goes beyond intelligence and creativity. Then, methods are described for measuring the attributes. Finally, some general conclusions are drawn.

Intelligence

There are many definitions of intelligence, although intelligence is typically defined in terms of a person's ability to adapt to the environment and to learn from experience (Sternberg & Detterman, 1986). The definition of intelligence here is somewhat more elaborate and is based on Sternberg's (1997, 1999) theory of successful intelligence. According to this definition, (successful) intelligence is (1) the ability to achieve one's goals in life, given one's sociocultural context, (2) by capitalizing on strengths and correcting or compensating for weaknesses (3) in order to adapt to, shape, and select environments (4) through a combination of analytical, creative, and practical abilities.

The first item recognizes that "intelligence" means something somewhat different to each individual. The student who wishes to become a Supreme Court judge will be taking a different path from the student who wishes to become a distinguished novelist – but both will have formulated a set of coherent goals toward which to work. A program for identifying the gifted should care less what goal is chosen than that the individual has chosen a worthwhile set of goals and shown the ability to achieve them.

The second item recognizes that, although psychologists sometimes talk of a "general" factor of intelligence (Jensen, 1998; Spearman, 1927; see Sternberg & Grigorenko, 2002), virtually no one is good at everything or bad at everything. People who are the future leaders of society are people who have identified their strengths and weaknesses, and found ways to work within that pattern of abilities.

The third item recognizes that intelligence broadly defined refers to more than just "adapting to the environment," which is the mainstay of conventional definitions of intelligence. The theory of successful intelligence distinguishes among adapting, shaping, and selecting. In adaptation to the environment, one modifies oneself to fit an environment. In life, adaptation is not enough, however. Adaptation needs to be balanced with shaping. In shaping, one modifies the environment to fit what one seeks of it, rather than modifying oneself to fit the environment. Truly great people in any field are not just adaptors, they are also shapers. They recognize that they cannot change everything, but that if they want to have an impact on the world, they have to change some things. Part of successful intelligence is deciding what to change and then how to change it. Sometimes, one attempts unsuccessfully to adapt to an environment and then also fails in shaping that environment. No matter what one does to try to make the environment work out, nothing in fact seems to work. In such cases, the appropriate action may be to select another environment.

The fourth item points out that successful intelligence involves a broader range of abilities than is typically measured by tests of intellectual and academic skills. Most of these tests measure primarily or exclusively memory and analytical abilities. With regard to memory, they assess the abilities to recall and recognize information. With regard to analytical abilities, they measure the skills involved when one analyzes, compares and contrasts, evaluates, critiques, and judges. These are important skills during the school years and in later life. But they are not the only skills that matter for school and life success. One needs not only to remember and analyze concepts, one needs to be able to generate and apply them.

Intelligence is not, as Edwin Boring (1923) once suggested, merely what intelligence tests test. Intelligence tests and other tests of cognitive and academic skills measure part of the range of intellectual skills. They do not measure the whole range. One should not conclude that a person who does not test well is not smart. Rather, one should merely look at test scores as one indicator among many of a person's intellectual skills.

Creativity

Creativity is not an attribute limited to the historic "greats" – the Darwins, the Picassos, the Hemingways. Rather, it is something anyone can use. To a large extent, creativity is a decision.

According to the investment theory of creativity, creative thinkers are like good investors: They buy low and sell high (Sternberg, 2003b; Sternberg & Lubart, 1995, 1996). Whereas investors do so in the world of finance, creative people do so in the world of ideas. Creative people generate ideas that are like undervalued stocks (stocks with a low price-to-earnings ratio), and both the stocks and the ideas are generally rejected by the public. When creative ideas are proposed, they often are viewed as bizarre, useless, and even foolish, and are summarily rejected. The person proposing them often is regarded with suspicion and perhaps even with disdain and derision.

Creative ideas are both novel and valuable. They potentially have impact (Sternberg, 2003a). But they are often rejected because the creative innovator stands up to vested interests and defies the crowd. The crowd does not maliciously or willfully reject creative notions. Rather, it does not realize, and often does not want to realize, that the proposed idea represents a valid and advanced way of thinking. Society generally perceives opposition to the status quo as annoying, offensive, and reason enough to ignore innovative ideas.

Evidence abounds that creative ideas are often rejected (Sternberg, 2003b; Sternberg & Lubart, 1995). Initial reviews of major works of literature and art are often negative. Toni Morrison's *Tar Baby* received negative reviews when it was first published, as did Sylvia Plath's *The Bell Jar*. The first exhibition in Munich of the work of Norwegian painter Edvard Munch opened and closed the same day because of the strong negative response from the critics. Some of the greatest scientific papers have been rejected not just by one journal, but even by several journals before being published. For example, John Garcia, a distinguished biopsychologist, was immediately denounced when he first proposed that a form of learning called classical conditioning could be produced in a single trial of learning (Garcia & Koelling, 1966).

From the investment view, then, the creative person buys low by presenting a unique idea and then attempting to convince other people of its value. After convincing others that the idea is valuable, which increases the perceived value of the investment, the creative person sells high by leaving the idea to others and moving on to another idea. People typically want others to love their ideas, but immediate universal applause for an idea usually indicates that it is not particularly creative.

Creativity is as much a decision about and an attitude toward life as it is a matter of ability. Creativity is often obvious in young children, but it is harder to find in older children and adults because their creative potential has been suppressed by a society that encourages intellectual conformity.

Creative work requires applying and balancing the three intellectual abilities – creative, analytic, and practical – all of which can be developed (Sternberg, 1985; Sternberg & Lubart, 1995; Sternberg & O'Hara, 1999; Sternberg & Williams, 1996). Creative ability is used to generate ideas. Everyone, even the most creative person, has better and worse ideas. Without well-developed analytic ability, the creative thinker is as likely to pursue bad ideas as to pursue good ones. The creative individual uses analytic ability to work out the implications of a creative idea and to test it. Practical ability is the ability to translate theory into practice and abstract ideas into practical accomplishments. An implication of the investment theory of creativity is that good ideas do not sell themselves. The creative person uses practical ability to convince other people that an idea is valuable. For example, every organization has a set of ideas that dictates how things, or at least some things, should be done. When individuals propose new procedures, they must sell them by convincing others that they are better than the old ones. Practical ability is also used to recognize ideas that have a potential audience.

Creativity requires these three skills. The person who is only synthetic may come up with innovative ideas, but cannot recognize or sell them. The person who is only analytic may be an excellent critic of other people's ideas, but is not likely to generate creative ideas. The person who is only practical may be an excellent salesperson, but is as likely to promote ideas or products of little or no value as to promote genuinely creative ideas.

What are some particular characteristics one can seek to determine whether an individual decides for creativity? Put another way, what kinds of attributes should one look for in individuals in order to assess their creativity?

1. *Redefining problems.* Redefining a problem means taking a problem and turning it on its head. Many times in life, individuals have a problem and they just do not see how to solve it. They are stuck in a box. Redefining

a problem essentially means extricating oneself from the box. This process is the synthetic part of creative thinking.

The gifted individual will encounter many kinds of novel situations that resist easy definition in terms of past experience. The more flexible the individual is in redefining these situations so that they make sense to him or her, the more likely the gifted individual is to succeed.

2. *Questioning and analyzing assumptions.* Everyone has assumptions. Often one does not know he or she has these assumptions because they are widely shared. Creative people question assumptions and eventually lead others to do the same. Questioning assumptions is part of the analytical thinking involved in creativity. When Copernicus suggested that Earth revolves around the sun, the suggestion was viewed as preposterous because everyone could see that the sun revolves around Earth. Galileo's ideas, including the relative rates of falling objects, caused him to be banned as a heretic.

3. *Realizing that creative ideas do not sell themselves.* Everyone would like to assume that their wonderful, creative ideas will sell themselves. But as Galileo, Edvard Munch, Toni Morrison, Sylvia Plath, and millions of others have discovered, they do not. On the contrary, creative ideas are usually viewed with suspicion and distrust. Moreover, those who propose such ideas may be viewed with suspicion and distrust as well. Because people are comfortable with the ways they already think, and because they probably have a vested interest in their existing way of thinking, it can be extremely difficult to dislodge them from their current way of thinking. Scholarship winners need to be people who are not only highly creatively competent, but ones who have convinced others of their creative competence.

4. *Recognizing that knowledge is a double-edged sword.* On the one hand, one cannot be creative without knowledge. Quite simply, one cannot go beyond the existing state of knowledge if one does not know what that state is. Many students have ideas that are creative with respect to themselves, but not with respect to the field because others have had the same ideas before. Those with a greater knowledge base can be creative in ways that those who are still learning the basics of the field cannot be.

At the same time, those who have an expert level of knowledge can experience tunnel vision, narrow thinking, and entrenchment. Experts can become so stuck in a way of thinking that they become unable to extricate themselves from it (Frensch & Sternberg, 1989). Learning must be a lifelong process, not one that terminates when a person achieves some measure of recognition. When a person believes that he or she knows everything there is to know, he or she is unlikely to ever show truly meaningful creativity again.

5. *Willingness to surmount obstacles.* Buying low and selling high means defying the crowd. And people who defy the crowd – people who think

creatively – almost inevitably encounter resistance. The question is not whether one will encounter obstacles; that obstacles will be encountered is a fact. The question is whether the creative thinker has the fortitude to persevere. I have often wondered why so many people start off their careers doing creative work and then vanish from the radar screen. Here is at least one reason why: Sooner or later, they decide that being creative is not worth the resistance and punishment. The truly creative thinkers pay the short-term price because they recognize that they can make a difference in the long term. But often it is a long while before the value of creative ideas is recognized and appreciated.

Gifted individuals will encounter many obstacles in their lives. Some of them have led "charmed" lives, as did Trilling's Denny. But sooner or later, the obstacles start to present themselves. The ones who go on to greatness will be those who are prepared to surmount rather than succumb to these obstacles.

5. *Willingness to take sensible risks.* When creative people defy the crowd by buying low and selling high, they take risks in much the same way as do people who invest. Some such investments simply may not pan out. Moreover, defying the crowd means risking the crowd's wrath. But there are levels of sensibility to keep in mind when defying the crowd. Creative people take sensible risks and produce ideas that others ultimately admire and respect as trend-setting. In taking these risks, creative people sometimes make mistakes, fail, and fall flat on their faces.

Nearly every major discovery or invention entailed some risk. When a movie theater was the only place to see a movie, someone created the idea of the home video machine. Skeptics questioned if anyone would want to see videos on a small screen. Another initially risky idea was the home computer. Many wondered if anyone would have enough use for a home computer to justify the cost. These ideas were once risks that are now ingrained in our society.

6. *Tolerance of ambiguity.* People like things to be in black and white. They like to think that a country is good or bad (ally or enemy) or that a given idea in education works or does not work. The problem is that there are a lot of grey areas in creative work. Artists working on new paintings and writers working on new books often report feeling scattered and unsure in their thoughts. They often need to figure out whether they are even on the right track. Scientists often are not sure whether the theory they have developed is exactly correct. These creative thinkers need to tolerate the ambiguity and uncertainty until they get the idea just right.

A creative idea tends to come in bits and pieces and develops over time. However, the period in which the idea is developing tends to be uncomfortable. Without time or the ability to tolerate ambiguity, many may jump to a less than optimal solution. Gifted individuals often will be undertaking major projects in their graduate years. They should be individuals who are willing to tolerate ambiguity long enough to make these projects not just good, but great.

7. *Self-efficacy.* People often reach a point when they feel as if no one believes in them. We reach this point frequently, feeling that no one values or even appreciates what we are doing. Because creative work often does not get a warm reception, it is extremely important that the creative people believe in the value of what they are doing. This is not to say that individuals should believe that every idea they have is a good idea. Rather, individuals need to believe that, ultimately, they have the ability to make a difference. In the course of their studies, there will come times when gifted individuals will doubt themselves. That is what happened to Trillin's Denny. He seemingly lost confidence in himself at Oxford, which he never was able to gain back. To succeed in life, one has to believe not in each and everything one does, but in one's ability to get done what needs to be done and to recover from the inevitable setbacks that life throws at one.

8. *Finding what one loves to do.* Teachers must help students find what excites them to unleash their students' best creative performances. Teachers need to remember that this may not be what really excites them. People who truly excel creatively in a pursuit, whether vocational or avocational, almost always genuinely love what they do. Certainly, the most creative people are intrinsically motivated in their work (Amabile, 1996). Less creative people often pick a career for the money or prestige and are bored with or loathe their career. Most often, these people do not do work that makes a difference in their field.

9. *Willingness to delay gratification.* Part of being creative means being able to work on a project or task for a long time without immediate or interim rewards. Students must learn that rewards are not always immediate and that there are benefits to delaying gratification. The fact of the matter is that, in the short term, people are often ignored when they do creative work or even punished for doing it.

Hard work often does not bring immediate rewards. Students do not immediately become expert baseball players, dancers, musicians, or sculptors. And the reward of becoming an expert can seem very far away. Students often succumb to the temptations of the moment, such as watching television or playing video games. The people who make the most of their abilities are those who wait for a reward and recognize that few serious challenges can be met in a moment.

10. *Courage.* Defying the crowd takes, above all, courage. Those who do not have courage may be many things, but they will not be creative. A gifted individual can be many things. If he or she is not courageous, the other things may not matter.

Wisdom

Wisdom may be the most important attribute to seek in gifted individuals. People can be intelligent or creative but not wise. People who use their cognitive skills for evil or even selfish purposes, or who ignore the well-being of others, may be smart, but they are also foolish.

According to Sternberg's balance theory of wisdom (Sternberg, 1998, 2001), wisdom is defined as the application of intelligence and creativity as mediated by values toward the achievement of a common good through a balance among (a) intrapersonal, (b) interpersonal, and (c) extrapersonal interests, over the (a) short- and (b) long-terms to achieve a balance among (a) adaptation to existing environments, (b) shaping of existing environments, and (c) selection of new environments.

Wisdom is not just about maximizing one's own or someone else's self-interest, but about balancing various self-interests (intrapersonal) with the interests of others (interpersonal) and of other aspects of the context in which one lives (extrapersonal), such as one's city, country, environment, or even God.

A person could be practically intelligent, but use his or her practical intelligence toward bad or selfish ends. In wisdom, one certainly may seek good ends for oneself, but one also seeks common good outcomes for others. If one's motivations are to maximize certain people's interests and minimize other people's, wisdom is not involved. In wisdom, one seeks a common good, realizing that this common good may be better for some than for others.

Problems requiring wisdom always involve at least some element of each of intrapersonal, interpersonal, and extrapersonal interests. For example, one might decide that it is wise to take advantage of a particular opportunity, a decision that seemingly involves only one person. But many people are typically affected by, for example, an individual's decision to go away to study – significant others, perhaps children, perhaps parents and friends. And the decision always has to be made in the context of what the whole range of available options is.

What kinds of considerations might be included under each of the three kinds of interests? Intrapersonal interests might include the desire to enhance one's popularity or prestige, to make more money, to learn more, to increase one's spiritual well-being, to increase one's power, and so forth. Interpersonal interests might be quite similar, except they apply to other people rather than oneself. Extrapersonal interests might include contributing to the welfare of one's school, helping one's community, contributing to the well-being of one's country, or serving God, and so forth. Different people balance these interests in different ways. At one extreme, a malevolent dictator might emphasize his or her own personal power and wealth; at the other extreme, a saint might emphasize only serving others and God.

Wisdom involves a balancing not only of the three kinds of interests, but also of three possible courses of action in response to this balancing: adaptation of oneself or others to existing environments; shaping of environments to render them more compatible with oneself or others; and selection of new environments.

Some people are intelligent and creative, but foolish. They lack wisdom. What are the characteristics of people who are smart, but foolish? Consider five characteristics, based on Sternberg (2002).

The first is *insouciance* with respect to the long-term consequences of what they do. They may believe themselves to be so smart that they believe that, whatever they do, it will work out all right. They may overly trust their own intuitions, believing that their brilliance means that they can do no wrong.

The second is *egocentrism*. Many smart people have been so highly rewarded in their lives that they lose sight of the interests of others. They start to act as though the whole world revolves around them. In doing so, they often set themselves up for downfalls, as happened to both Presidents Nixon and Clinton, the former in the case of Watergate, the latter in the case of "Monicagate."

The third characteristic is a sense of *omniscience*. Smart people typically know a lot. They get in trouble, however, when they start to think they "know it all." They may have expertise in one area, but then start to fancy themselves experts in practically everything. At that point, they become susceptible to remarkable downfalls, because they act as experts in areas where they are not and can make disastrous mistakes in doing so.

The fourth characteristic is a sense of *omnipotence*. Many smart people find themselves in positions of substantial power. Sometimes they lose sight of the limitations of their power and start to act as though they are omnipotent. Several U.S. presidents as well as presidents of other countries have had this problem, leading their countries to disasters on the basis of personal whims. Many corporate chieftains have also started to think of themselves as omnipotent, unfortunately, cooking the books of their corporations at will.

The fifth characteristic is a sense of *invulnerability*. Not only do the individuals think they can do anything, they also believe they can get away with it. They believe that either they are too smart to be found out or, even if found out, they will escape any punishment for misdeeds. The result is the kind of disasters the United States has seen in the recent Enron, Worldcom, and Arthur Andersen debacles.

Measurement of Intelligence, Creativity, and Wisdom

There is no one magic-bullet method for measuring intelligence, creativity, and wisdom. Rather, there are a number of techniques that can be used:

application forms, interviews, letters of recommendation, grades, and assessment scores. We at the PACE Center at Yale have tried to develop assessments of many of the various skills described in this chapter. Consider some examples of assessments we have used.

(Successful) Intelligence. In one study (Sternberg, Grigorenko, Ferrari, & Clinkenbeard, 1999), Sternberg and colleagues used the so-called Sternberg Triarchic Abilities Test (STAT; Sternberg, 1993) to investigate the internal validity of the theory of successful intelligence. Three hundred twenty-six high school students, primarily from diverse parts of the United States, took the test, which comprised 12 subtests in all. There were four subtests, each measuring analytical, creative, and practical abilities. For each type of ability, there were three multiple-choice tests and one essay test. The multiple-choice tests, in turn, involved, respectively, verbal, quantitative, and figural content.

Confirmatory factor analysis on the data was supportive of the triarchic theory of human intelligence, yielding separate and uncorrelated analytical, creative, and practical factors. The lack of correlation was due to the inclusion of essay as well as multiple-choice subtests. Although multiple-choice tests tended to correlate substantially with multiple-choice tests, their correlations with essay tests were much weaker. The multiple-choice analytical subtest loaded most highly on the analytical factor, but the essay creative and practical subtests loaded most highly on their respective factors. Thus, measurement of creative and practical abilities probably ideally should be accomplished with other kinds of testing instruments that complement multiple-choice instruments.

In a second study, conducted with 3,252 students in the United States, Finland, and Spain, Sternberg and colleagues used the multiple-choice section of the STAT to compare five alternative models of intelligence, again via confirmatory factor analysis. A model featuring a general factor of intelligence fit the data relatively poorly. The triarchic model, allowing for intercorrelation among the analytic, creative, and practical factors, provided the best fit to the data (Sternberg, Castejón, Prieto, Hautamäki, & Grigorenko, 2001).

In a very recent study supported by the College Board (Sternberg & the Rainbow Project Team, 2002), we used an expanded set of tests on 1,015 students at 15 different institutions (13 colleges and 2 high schools). Our goal was not to replace the Scholastic Aptitude Test (SAT), but to devise tests that would supplement the SAT, measuring skills that this test does not measure. In addition to the multiple-choice tests described previously, we used three additional measures of creative skills and three of practical skills. The three creative tests required captioning of cartoons, writing creative stories, and telling creative stories. The three practical tests involved solving problems presented in movie form, solving school-based practical problems presented in written form, and solving workplace-based practical problems presented in written form.

We found that our tests significantly and substantially improved on the validity of the SAT for predicting first-year college grades (Sternberg & the Rainbow Project Team, in press). The test also improved equity: Using the test to admit a class would result in greater ethnic diversity than would using just the SAT or just the SAT and grade-point average. This test is now going into Phase-2 piloting, where it will be tried out on a larger sample of individuals.

Creativity. In work with divergent-thinking problems having no one best answer, we asked 63 people to create various kinds of products (Lubart & Sternberg, 1995; Sternberg & Lubart, 1991, 1995, 1996). An infinite variety of responses was possible. Individuals were asked to create products in the realms of writing, art, advertising, and science. In writing, they would be asked to write very short stories for which the investigators would give them a choice of titles, such as "Beyond the Edge" or "The Octopus's Sneakers" (as in our Rainbow Project). In art, the participants were asked to produce art compositions with titles such as "The Beginning of Time" or "Earth from an Insect's Point of View." In advertising, they were asked to produce advertisements for products such as a brand of bow tie or a brand of doorknob. In science, they were asked to solve problems such as one asking them how people might detect extraterrestrial aliens among us who are seeking to escape detection. Participants created two products in each domain.

Sternberg and Lubart (1991, 1995, 1996) found, first, that creativity comprises the components proposed by their investment model of creativity: intelligence, knowledge, thinking styles, personality, and motivation. Second, they found that creativity is relatively, although not wholly, domain-specific. Correlations of ratings of the creative quality of the products across domains were lower than correlations of ratings and generally were at about the 0.4 level. Thus, there was some degree of relation across domains, at the same time that there was plenty of room for someone to be strong in one or more domains but not in others. Third, Sternberg and Lubart found a range of correlations of measures of creative performance with conventional tests of abilities. As was the case for the correlations obtained with convergent problems, correlations were higher to the extent that problems on the conventional tests were nonentrenched. For example, correlations were higher with fluid than with crystallized ability tests, and correlations were higher the more novel the fluid test was. These results show that tests of creative intelligence have some overlap with conventional tests (e.g., in requiring verbal skills or the ability to analyze one's own ideas) (Sternberg & Lubart, 1995) but also tap skills beyond those measured even by relatively novel kinds of items on the conventional tests of intelligence.

We have also used convergent problems that have a single answer. In this work, Sternberg (1982) presented 80 individuals with novel kinds of reasoning problems that had a single best answer. For example, they might be told, based on Goodman's (1955) new riddle of induction, that some objects are green and others blue, but still other objects might be grue, meaning green until the year 3000 and blue thereafter, or bleen, meaning blue until the year 3000 and green thereafter. Or they might be told of four kinds of people on the planet Kyron: blens, who are born young and die young; kwefs, who are born old and die old; balts, who are born young and die old; and prosses, who are born old and die young (Sternberg, 1982; Tetewsky & Sternberg, 1986). Their task was to predict future states from past states, given incomplete information. In another set of studies, 60 people were given more conventional kinds of inductive reasoning problems, such as analogies, series completions, and classifications, and were told to solve them. But the problems had premises preceding them that were either conventional (dancers wear shoes) or novel (dancers eat shoes). The participants had to solve the problems as though the counterfactuals were true (Sternberg & Gastel, 1989a, 1989b).

In these studies, Sternberg and colleagues found that correlations with conventional kinds of tests depended on how novel or nonentrenched the conventional tests were. The more novel the items, the higher the correlations of our tests with scores on successively more novel conventional tests. Sternberg and colleagues also found that some components better measured the creative aspect of intelligence than did others. For example, in the "grue–bleen" task mentioned previously, the information-processing component requiring people to switch from conventional green–blue thinking to grue–bleen thinking and then back to green–blue thinking again was a particularly good measure of the ability to cope with novelty. Creative people, in other words, are those who think flexibly – who can easily move back and forth between conceptual systems.

Wisdom. Our work on wisdom is relatively recent (Sternberg, 1998, 2002) and is very much "work-in-progress"; we are currently developing and validating various assessments of wisdom. Because both wisdom and practical intelligence are measured through scenario-based measures, it might be useful to review results we have obtained for practical intelligence (Sternberg et al., 2000). Keep in mind that practical intelligence is related to wisdom but is not the same as wisdom. A person could be practically intelligent and look out only for his or her own interests. A wise person never could look out only for himself or herself.

In scenario-based studies, in which individuals are presented with real-life scenarios depicting problems to be solved, Sternberg and colleagues (2000) found, first, that practical intelligence as embodied in tacit knowledge increases with experience, but it is profiting from experience, rather than experience per se, that results in increases in scores. Some people have been in school or in a job for years and still have acquired relatively little tacit knowledge. Second, they also found that subscores on tests of tacit knowledge – such as for managing oneself, managing others, and managing tasks – correlate significantly with each other. Third, scores on various tests of tacit knowledge, such as for academics and managers, are also correlated fairly substantially (at about the 0.5 level) with each other. Thus, fourth, tests of tacit knowledge may yield a general factor across these tests. However, fifth, scores on tacit-knowledge tests do not correlate with scores on conventional tests of intelligence, whether the measures used are single-score measures of multiple-ability batteries. Thus, any general factor from the tacit-knowledge tests is not the same as any general factor from tests of academic abilities (suggesting that neither kind of g factor is truly general, but rather, general only across a limited range of measuring instruments). Sixth, despite the lack of correlation of practical-intellectual with conventional measures, the scores on tacit-knowledge tests predict performance on the job as well as or better than do conventional psychometric intelligence tests. In one study done at the Center for Creative Leadership, my colleagues and I further found, seventh, that scores on our tests of tacit knowledge for management were the best single predictor of performance on a managerial simulation. In a hierarchical regression, scores on conventional tests of intelligence, personality, styles, and interpersonal orientation were entered first and scores on the test of tacit knowledge were entered last. Scores on the test of tacit knowledge were the single best predictor of managerial simulation score. Moreover, these scores also contributed significantly to the prediction even after everything else was entered first into the equation. In recent work on military leadership (Sternberg et al., 2000), it was found, eighth, that scores of 562 participants on tests of tacit knowledge for military leadership predicted ratings of leadership effectiveness, whereas scores on a conventional test of intelligence and on a tacit-knowledge test for managers did not significantly predict the ratings of effectiveness.

Wisdom scenarios differ from practical-intelligence scenarios in that they more involve balancing of interests toward a common good. Here is an example of a scenario we are using in our current research:

Felicia and Alexander have been in an intimate relationship for their entire four years of college. Felicia has now been accepted for graduate school in French by a prestigious graduate program in northern California. Alexander was not admitted to the law school in this university, nor to any other law school in the northern California area. Alexander was admitted to a good although not outstanding law school in southern California, but he was also admitted to an outstanding law school in Massachusetts. Felicia has no viable opportunities for graduate study on the East Coast, at least at this time. Alexander is trying to decide whether to attend the less prestigious law school in southern California or the more prestigious one in Massachusetts. He would like to continue the relationship, as would Felicia, and both ultimately hope to get married to each other. A complicating factor is that the law school in Massachusetts has offered Alexander a half-scholarship, whereas the law school in southern California has not offered financial aid for the first year, although it has indicated that there is a possibility of financial aid in subsequent years. Alexander's parents have indicated that, although they would be willing to pay his half-tuition for the more prestigious law school, they do not believe it is fair to ask them to pay full tuition for the less prestigious one. They also believe his going to the less prestigious law school will only hurt Alexander's career advancement. Felicia is torn and is leaving it to Alexander to decide what to do. What should Alexander do and why?

We do not yet have data on these problems, but shall have them soon.

So where does our consideration of the WICS framework leave us? What conclusions can we draw?

CONCLUSIONS

In identifying gifted individuals, three very important factors to consider are intelligence, creativity, and wisdom – synthesized so that they work together effectively. These are not the only attributes that matter. For example, motivation and energy are extremely important as well. However, motivation is partly (although not exclusively) situational. With the proper environment, anyone can be motivated to achieve.

This chapter has concentrated on "tests" as measures of intelligence, creativity, and wisdom, but they represent only one of many ways of assessing these attributes. Interviews, questionnaires, letters of recommendation, and project work all can help in assessing these attributes. The important thing is to provide the best possible assessments, regardless of the form they take. One also must remember that tests can only identify present functioning. They cannot tell us a person's future potential functioning.

ACKNOWLEDGMENT

Preparation of this chapter was supported by the Rockefeller Foundation.

References

Amabile, T. M. (1996). *Creativity in context*. Boulder, CO: Westview.

Boring, E. G. (1923, June 6). Intelligence as the tests test it. *New Republic*, 35–37.

Frensch, P. A., & Sternberg, R. J. (1989). Expertise and intelligent thinking: When is it worse to know better? In R. J. Sternberg (Ed.), *Advances in the psychology of human intelligence* (Vol. 5, pp. 157–188). Hillsdale, NJ: Lawrence Erlbaum Associates.

Garcia, J., & Koelling, R. A. (1966). The relation of cue to consequence in avoidance learning. *Psychonomic Science, 4*, 123–124.

Goodman, N. (1955). *Fact, fiction, and forecast*. Cambridge, MA: Harvard University Press.

Jensen, A. R. (1998). *The g factor: The science of mental ability*. Westport, CT: Praeger.

Lubart, T. I., & Sternberg, R. J. (1995). An investment approach to creativity: Theory and data. In S. M. Smith, T. B. Ward, & R. A. Finke (Eds.), *The creative cognition approach* (pp. 271–302). Cambridge, MA: MIT Press.

Spearman, C. (1927). *The abilities of man*. New York: Macmillan.

Sternberg, R. J. (1982). Natural, unnatural, and supernatural concepts. *Cognitive Psychology, 14*, 451–488.

Sternberg, R. J. (1985). *Beyond IQ: A triarchic theory of human intelligence*. New York: Cambridge University Press.

Sternberg, R. J. (1993). *Sternberg Triarchic Abilities Test*. Unpublished test.

Sternberg, R. J. (1997). *Successful intelligence*. New York: Plume.

Sternberg, R. J. (1998). A balance theory of wisdom. *Review of General Psychology, 2*, 347–365.

Sternberg, R. J. (1999). The theory of successful intelligence. *Review of General Psychology, 3*, 292–316.

Sternberg, R. J. (2001). How wise is it to teach for wisdom? A reply to five critiques. *Educational Psychologist, 36*(4), 269–272.

Sternberg, R. J. (2002). Smart people are not stupid, but they sure can be foolish: The imbalance theory of foolishness. In R. J. Sternberg (Ed.), *Why smart people can be so stupid*. New Haven: Yale University Press.

Sternberg, R. J. (Ed.). (2003a). *The anatomy of impact: What has made the great works of psychology great?* Washington, DC: American Psychological Association.

Sternberg, R. J. (Ed.). (2003b). *Psychologists defying the crowd: Stories of those who battled the establishment and won*. Washington, DC: American Psychological Association.

Sternberg, R. J. (2003c). *Wisdom, intelligence, and creativity, synthesized*. New York: Cambridge University Press.

Sternberg, R. J., Castejón, J. L., Prieto, M. D., Hautamäki, J., & Grigorenko, E. L. (2001). Confirmatory factor analysis of the Sternberg triarchic abilities test in three international samples: An empirical test of the triarchic theory of intelligence. *European Journal of Psychological Assessment, 17*(1), 1–16.

Sternberg, R. J., & Detterman, D. K. (1986). *What is intelligence?* Norwood, NJ: Ablex.

Sternberg, R. J., Forsythe, G. B., Hedlund, J., Horvath, J., Snook, S., Williams, W. M., et al. (2000). *Practical intelligence in everyday life*. New York: Cambridge University Press.

Sternberg, R. J., & Gastel, J. (1989a). Coping with novelty in human intelligence: An empirical investigation. *Intelligence, 13*, 187–197.

Sternberg, R. J., & Gastel, J. (1989b). If dancers ate their shoes: Inductive reasoning with factual and counterfactual premises. *Memory and Cognition, 17*, 1–10.

Sternberg, R. J., & Grigorenko, E. L. (Eds.). (2002). *The general factor of intelligence: How general is it?* Mahwah, NJ: Lawrence Erlbaum Associates.

Sternberg, R. J., Grigorenko, E. L., Ferrari, M., & Clinkenbeard, P. (1999). A triarchic analysis of an aptitude–treatment interaction. *European Journal of Psychological Assessment, 15*(1), 1–11.

Sternberg, R. J., & Lubart, T. I. (1991). An investment theory of creativity and its development. *Human Development, 34*(1), 1–31.

Sternberg, R. J., & Lubart, T. I. (1995). *Defying the crowd: Cultivating creativity in a culture of conformity.* New York: Free Press.

Sternberg, R. J., & Lubart, T. I. (1996). Investing in creativity. *American Psychologist, 51*(7), 677–688.

Sternberg, R. J., & O'Hara, L. (1999). Creativity and intelligence. In R. J. Sternberg (Ed.), *Handbook of creativity* (pp. 251–272). New York: Cambridge University Press.

Sternberg, R. J., & the Rainbow Project Team. (2002, February 16). *The Rainbow Project: Augmenting the validity of the SAT.* Paper presented at American Academy of Arts and Sciences, Boston, MA.

Sternberg, R. J., & the Rainbow Project Team. (in press). *The Rainbow Project: Enhancing the SAT through assessments of analytical, creative, and practical skills.* New York: The College Board.

Sternberg, R. J., & Williams, W. M. (1996). *How to develop student creativity.* Alexandria, VA: Association for Supervision and Curriculum Development.

Tetewsky, S. J., & Sternberg, R. J. (1986). Conceptual and lexical determinants of nonentrenched thinking. *Journal of Memory and Language, 25*, 202–225.

Trillin, C. (1994). *Remembering Denny.* New York: Warner Books.

19

Beyond Expertise

Conceptions of Giftedness as Great Performance

Rena F. Subotnik and Linda Jarvin

WHAT IS GIFTEDNESS?

Our conception of giftedness rests on three theoretical premises. The first is that abilities are forms of developing expertise (Sternberg, 1998). Second, beyond the level of expertise exists the realm of elite talent (Subotnik, 2000; 2004a), or what we call scholarly productivity or artistry (SP/A). Finally, in the course of transition from novice to expert and beyond, key personality, ability, and skill factors become increasingly or decreasingly important (Subotnik, Jarvin, Moga, & Sternberg, 2003). In accordance with these premises, we believe that abilities have interactive genetic and environmental components, yet are modifiable and capable of being flexibly deployed. We view abilities as necessary but not sufficient for generating expertise or SP/A. From our perspective, giftedness in its early stages is defined as the efficient yet comprehensive development of ability into competence in a domain. During the middle stage, giftedness becomes associated with precocious achievement of expertise. Finally, we view giftedness in adulthood as SP/A, taking the form of unique contributions to a field or domain. In the course of offering details on the transformation of abilities into competencies, expertise, and, in some cases, SP/A, we focus on examples from the domain of music.

Substantial evidence exists that abilities can be enhanced, at least to some degree (see Feuerstein, 1980; Herrnstein, Nickerson, deSanchez, & Swets, 1986; Nickerson, 1986; Nickerson, Perkins, & Smith, 1985; Perkins, 1995; Perkins & Grotzer, 1997; Ramey, 1994; Sternberg, 1988, 1994, 1997; Sternberg & Spear-Swerling, 1996). The best evidence favors a complex mix of genetic and environmental origins of abilities, interacting in ways that are not as yet fully known (see Sternberg & Grigorenko, 1997). The question we explore here is how abilities are developed to elicit elite performance.

The foundations of elite talent can be found in an individual's abilities, competencies, and expertise. Extraordinary *abilities* tend to be manifested in one or two domains, and not across the board. Without opportunities to learn from skilled instructors, such abilities may develop too slowly or even counterproductively. Incorrect fingering on an instrument or poor handling of athletic equipment can lead to injury. Insufficiently challenging instruction can also hamper opportunities available to a youngster with high abilities. For example, introducing classic dance instruction to a 16-year-old would most likely preclude career advancement, since by that point, peers would have benefited physically, cognitively, and aesthetically from at least four years of instruction and practice. Notably, the age at which the different stages of the transformation process from ability to SP/A take place will vary, even within a domain. In music, for example, a singer will develop much later than a violinist.

A high-quality teacher channels abilities into _competencies_ by introducing a series of sufficiently challenging experiences that can be practiced and mastered. With each level of mastery, the student becomes increasingly competent. True competency, in contrast with false praise for meeting mediocre standards, cannot be achieved without student motivation. Some levels of drive are derived from temperament, but can also be elicited from challenging peers and engaging curriculum. Great teachers encourage their students to embrace rather than fear adversity, as mastery over such fear allows for persistence through practice, disappointment, and even failure.

Expertise is derived from using one's abilities to acquire, store, and utilize at least two kinds of knowledge: explicit knowledge of a domain and implicit or tacit knowledge of a field (see Sternberg, Wagner, Williams, & Horvath, 1995). We define _domain_ as a knowledge base, and _field_ as the social organization of that knowledge base (Csikszentmihalyi, 1988, 1996). Explicit knowledge is the kind most frequently studied in the literature on expertise (see Chi, Glaser, & Farr, 1988; Ericsson & Smith, 1991). It is knowledge of the facts, formulas, principles, and major ideas of a domain of inquiry. Implicit or tacit knowledge of a field is the informally taught knowledge one needs to attain success in a field. For example, in music, the composition of a diminished seventh chord would constitute explicit knowledge, whereas how to get a gig would constitute informal or tacit knowledge. Although it represents the pinnacle of acquired wisdom, skill, and knowledge, expertise is a passive enterprise. It does not incorporate the addition of new ideas or levels of performance to a field, discipline, or domain. In order to describe the genesis of groundbreaking performance or transformational ideas, another category is needed. Such a category can be labeled as _SP/A (Scholarly Productivity/Artistry)._

Through our investigations of giftedness in the domain of music, we have developed a model for the development of abilities into competencies, expertise, and SP/A. The model was developed on the basis of interviews (more than 80 to date) conducted with students at different stages of their musical training at three elite American conservatories; the music faculty at these institutions, most of whom are working performers themselves; and "gatekeepers," or those who exercise influence over musicians' opportunities to perform and make a living, for example, music critics for national newspapers, artistic directors for prestigious concert halls, and the agents that act as intermediaries between artists and artistic directors. Although this model was developed to describe the development of elite talent in music, we propose that the model also describes the path to eminence in most domains. Figure 19.1 summarizes this model of giftedness.

Abilities

Initial abilities with interactive genetic and environmental components in our model include intrinsic motivation, charisma, and musicality. Although we have argued for the plasticity of abilities, according to our study outcomes (Subotnik, 2004a, 2000; Subotnik, Jarvin, Moga, & Sternberg, 2003) these three abilities are not teachable.

Intrinsic motivation is associated with the love of communicating through music, in spite of how difficult it is to make a living solely through performance or composition. Charisma, which plays a significant role later in the talent development process, refers to the ability to draw listeners to a performer, either through his or her music or through the force of his personality. Musicality is the capability to communicate effectively through music.

From Abilities to Competencies

With high-quality instruction, a child can develop these abilities into competencies. The instruction should emphasize exposure to and guided practice of the skills and knowledge of the domain. The effectiveness of this instruction is mediated by:

- how fast students can learn,
- technical proficiency the child can attain,
- parental support or pressure,
- the child's "teachability" (i.e., the willingness and openness to being taught),
- the quality of the student–teacher experience,
- the availability of external rewards such as praise and recognition, and
- persistence through good and bad times.

The more quickly a student can move through the repertoire, the more the student can benefit from exposure to musical ideas, and the more a teacher can provide in terms of guidance. According to our interviewees – students at different stages in their musical training, faculty members, and gatekeepers – *speed of learning* is helpful but not essential to success in the

Ability	Competence	Expertise	SP/A
Opportunity for instruction with emphasis on exposure, and guided practice. *Mediating variables:*	*Opportunity for instruction with emphasis on moving beyond technical proficiency.* *Mediating variables:*	*Opportunity for socialization into the field and networking guided by master teachers, agents, and other gatekeepers.* *Mediating variables:*	
Learn fast, analyze patterns & structures			
Technical proficiency	Technical proficiency		
Parental support or pressure	Parental support		
Teachability	Teachability (beginning of differentiation)		
Quality of student-teacher experience	Quality of student-teacher experience		
External rewards: recognition	External rewards: Recognition, opportunity to perform, and financial independence	External rewards: Recognition, opportunity to perform, and financial independence	
Persistence in good and bad times	Persistence in good and bad times	Persistence in good and bad times	
Intrinsic motivation	Intrinsic motivation	Intrinsic motivation	
Musicality	Musicality	Musicality	
	Knowing your weaknesses and strengths	Capitalizing on strengths	
	Self-promotion	Promotion of self through an agent	
	Learning how to play the game	Mastering the game	
	Social skills: collegiality	Social skills: collegiality and engaging patrons	
	Restoring self-confidence	Exuding self-confidence	
		Risk taking	
		Charisma	

FIGURE 19.1. Domain affects the age at which each stage of the process takes place.

early stages of talent development, and does not increase in importance over time. The one clear advantage of learning quickly at the expert level lies in the possibility of standing in for an absent colleague at short notice, which has been known historically to lead to a career-making performance.

The level of *technical proficiency* a child can attain will depend a great deal on the skill of the teacher and the child's commitment to practice. A hand injury derived from faulty technique can lead to constant muscle strain and inflammation that will impede development. *Parental involvement* can be either negative (nagging, restricting freedom of choice, turning an initially pleasurable experience into a constraint) or positive. Positive parental involvement can take the form of initial pressure or of support, and many of the musicians we interviewed who started very young indicated that without their parents' insistence on a consistent practice schedule, they would not have transformed their abilities into competencies. Negative parental involvement can also take the form of mixed messages: On the one hand, the parent likes the idea that their child is learning music, considering it a form of refinement. On the other hand, the parent may not want the child to invest in music completely and consider a career as a musical artist.

The child's "teachability," in other words, his or her willingness and openness to being taught, is considered by most highly expert teachers we interviewed to be a very attractive quality in a new student. If a student seems resistant to instruction in a conservatory audition, he or she will not be viewed as a good investment for the teacher's studio.

The quality of *the student–teacher relationship* defines the likelihood that musicality and intrinsic motivation will be directed productively. Talented young musicians and their families choose their teachers carefully based on the teacher's ability to maintain a rigorous curriculum and high expectations.

Although much of the pleasure a child derives from music making is intrinsic, practice and persistence are buttressed by positive reinforcement from parents and especially teachers. Recognition for one's exceptional talent is an important *external reward* for young musicians. *Persistence through good and bad times*, assisted by positive reinforcement and parental pressure, prepares young musicians for the inevitable rejections or failures that are part of the growth process in talent development.

At this stage and throughout the process of elite talent development, intrinsic motivation and musicality remain important factors.

From Competency to Expertise

Most young musicians enter conservatory highly competent. To move from competence to expertise, they need continued opportunity for instruction with an emphasis on technical proficiency. The ability to learn quickly diminishes in importance.

Mediating variables at this transitional stage remain *technical proficiency, parental support, teachability, quality of the student–teacher experience, availability of external rewards, persistence through good and bad times, intrinsic motivation, and musicality.* Many of our interviewees pointed out that, past a certain threshold of *technical proficiency,* a (relative) technical flaw can be interesting. According to one gatekeeper, "somewhat flawed" is better than "push the play button," especially for vocalists who can make up for less than perfect technique with their stage presence or the loveliness of their sound more so than can instrumentalists. In regard to teachability, over time during the conservatory years, teachers expect their best students to "bite back" and insist on cultivating their own style, voice, or message.

Although recognition remains an important external reward, two others play a growing role in reinforcement: financial independence and opportunities to perform. With advancing age and responsibility, conservatory students know that they will need to support themselves. If they are not successful in acquiring gigs, then they'll have to drain their time and energy with unrelated employment. Also, opportunities for performance during the conservatory years are constrained by the institutions' responsibility to provide equitable display of all students' talent. Competitions, both internal and external, therefore take on more importance. The thrill of performance at such a high level becomes the central expressive outlet for the musician's life.

On the path to competence, studio teachers a*nalyze students' strengths and weaknesses* and focus mostly on ameliorating weaknesses. During the transition from competence to expertise, however, teachers expect students to analyze and appreciate their own profiles of strengths and weaknesses and approach their practice and choice of repertoire, accordingly.

New mediating variables include:

- Knowing your strengths and weaknesses
- Self-promotion
- Learning how to play the game
- Social skills
- Restoring self-confidence.

The gatekeepers we interviewed recognized that *self-promotion* is necessary for success as a performer, and that knowing when and how to promote oneself is part of being effective at securing jobs. Concurrently, they disdained efforts at channeling creativity into playing the game instead of into one's music. Teachers provide the tacit knowledge needed to prepare their students to *play the game* by modeling how to be graceful in success and failure, and engender a reputation as a professional. Most students we interviewed recognized the role played by self-promotion but found the notion repulsive. With reluctance, young musicians learn from their peers and teachers that there are "games to be played" beyond the acquisition of exquisite performance skills – for example, a notable resumé, a good headshot, an agent, patrons.

Teachers at this stage also play an important role in promoting *social skills* such as arriving on time and well prepared, being courteous, and learning to accept success gracefully and failure with resilience. The conservatories with which we worked acknowledged the need for this socialization and have started offering classes addressing the details associated with becoming a professional musician.

Most students enter conservatory confident in their abilities. As in all transitions to more competitive environments, many will temporarily question their abilities as they witness the competence of their new peers Students need the resources (both internal and external) to work through this challenge and *restore* their *self-confidence.*

From Expertise to SP/A

The last transition in our model is from expertise to scholarly productivity or artistry (SP/A), and relies on the opportunity for master teachers, agents, and other gatekeepers to impart their tacit knowledge and networking for their protégées. The transition from expert to SP/A tends to take place for string and piano players during their conservatory years. Those conservatory students who are not identified as stars begin to self-select into other aspects of the music business. Vocalists, whose training begins in early adulthood, experience the transition from expertise to possible SP/A after completing conservatory training.

Mediating variables at this transition include the availability of *external rewards, persistence through good and bad times, intrinsic motivation, musicality, capitalizing on strengths, promotion through an agent, mastering the game, social skills, and exuding self-confidence. Technical proficiency, parental support, teachability, and the quality of the student–teacher experience* no longer play an influential role in the talent development process.

Even if one is highly successful, *persistence through good and bad times* and intrinsic motivation remain crucial variables. The bad times may change in nature, but persistence and resiliency remain crucial as outstanding success and recognition may elicit jealousy and ungrounded or excessive criticism.

In the course of achieving competence, young musicians' teachers identified weaknesses and focused guided practice on ameliorating them. During the transition to expertise, musicians are expected to monitor their technical proficiency, focusing on both strengths and weaknesses. In the final stage, an artist will capitalize on strengths and shy away from performance situations where one would display weaknesses. More productively, an artist would use his or her weaknesses to advantage, such as a singer using a technical flaw to display added charm.

An artist at this stage would be expected to have solicited the support of an agent to perform most of the legwork in acquiring performance opportunities and ensuring financial stability. Many agents also play the important role of financial advisor and life coach. The agent also ensures that the artist *masters the game*, which at this stage becomes part of the professional career in music.

Social skills remain important to success in musical careers. In addition to exhibiting excellent professionalism, an artist needs to engage and maintain the interest of patrons. Our gatekeeper interviewees stressed the fact that the music world was so competitive that diva behavior was less tolerated and that talent is less likely than ever to neutralize shortcomings in the nonmusical variables we have identified.

Self-confidence, whether it is deeply felt or not, must be displayed for the audience. According to our gatekeepers, the most exciting performers keep their audiences on edge through their control of the instrument and the music.

Additional characteristics at this stage include:

- risk-taking and
- charisma.

The most interesting artists are those who control audiences' engagement in anticipation of the unexpected based on creative *risk taking*.

Charisma also emerges as a key to success at the highest levels of artistry. According to our study participants, there are two kinds of charisma: one centered on the artist and one centered on the music. Artists of the first kind draw people to them because their presence is larger than life. Another kind arises from the power of their performance.

How Does This Conception of Giftedness Compare to Other Conceptions of Giftedness?

Let us compare this conception of giftedness with those of three other scholars whose theories or models have influenced our SP/A model most: Bloom, Tannenbaum (who contributed to the 1986 edition of this volume), and Gagné, whose work appears in this volume as well. Bloom provides us with developmental stages of instruction and support on the part of parents and expert teachers. Tannenbaum provides us with the key variables that enhance or impede talent development, and Gagné highlights how key variables transform gifts into talents.

Bloom and his colleagues (1985) conducted a seminal retrospective study of eminence or elite talent in six fields: two in sports, two in the arts, and two in academics. He sought to uncover the unique components of talent development in each field, while concurrently seeking cross-disciplinary generalizations. The generalized model includes three stages that, according to Bloom, describe the talent development process in each field.

The first stage of the Bloom model is characterized by recreational involvement with a domain. Often the family or community values this domain, even if they are not active participants in that arena. Teachers convey the romance of the domain and view those with ability as fast learners. They offer praise and opportunities for successful competition as incentives. The middle stage of the model is characterized by a special teacher's focus on technique, skill, and learning the rules and mores of the domain. Concurrently, parents continue to provide support financially and emotionally. As the learner progresses, he or she identifies him or herself as a swimmer, scientist, musician, and so on. The talented individual becomes his or her own critic, which can lead to first-time feelings of self-doubt.

Should a learner overcome self-doubt and become sufficiently expert to pursue the third stage of Bloom's talent development model, he or she would be guided by a teacher who would focus on the learner's unique qualities as scholar or performer. Opportunities to demonstrate one's special expertise are sought and capitalized upon.

Bloom's model is developmental, and addresses elite talent, with various factors playing a more important role at different points in time. Although the model addresses catalysts such as good teaching and peer and family support, it downplays the role of personality or social interaction factors in achieving SP/A. Also, the model is based on retrospective rather than current data, and diminishes the role of abilities as a source of elite talent.

In 1983, Abraham Tannenbaum proposed that giftedness (defined as high levels of g) in childhood would translate into critically acclaimed performance or production of great ideas (corresponding to SP/A) in adulthood under the following conditions: g is channeled into a specific talent domain, personality characteristics such as motivation and persistence are developed, recognition and support are received from some important stakeholder(s), and the individual capitalizes on being in the right place at the right time. As a further elaboration of the theory, Tannenbaum explains that g need not be equally high in every domain to achieve greatness. According to Tannenbaum, an outstanding physicist needs a higher IQ than an outstanding teacher. Similarly, personality variables may be more or less conducive to fulfilling potential depending on the domain at hand. Although a teacher and a physicist both need motivation and persistence to achieve excellence, a teacher may need to be more extroverted and gregarious than a physicist.

Tannenbaum's theory views fulfillment of potential as domain specific, identifies outstanding performance or the generation of great ideas as a desired outcome, and highlights the importance of supportive teachers, family, and peers. He also stresses the roles played by personality and capitalizing on opportunity. In these ways, the theory is consistent with the model we propose in this chapter.

Our view differs from Tannenbaum's in that we substitute *abilities* for *g* because in the case of many important domains outside the intellectual and academic realm, general intelligence does not describe the foundational *ability* associated with great performance or idea generation. Sensitivity to sound and touch is more central to musical ability than IQ, and the spatial awareness and coordination required of a dancer or athlete trump *g* in those domains. Second, Tannenbaum does not frame his model in developmental terms. Tannenbaum identifies those variables that enhance or impede the transformation of *g* to outstanding performance or great ideas, but leaves the path from abilities to SP/A undocumented.

Gagné's theory (2003) is also multifaceted and domain specific, and we therefore especially value its elegance. The model begins with abilities (which he calls *giftedness* or *aptitude domains*). Four catalysts transform those abilities either positively or negatively:

(1) intrapersonal variables such as motivation and personality,
(2) environmental conditions (surroundings, people, activities, and events),
(3) developmental processes (learning, training, and practicing), and
(4) chance factors.

Our research supports the key roles of the four catalysts described by Gagné. However, unlike Gagné, we assign weights to each variable in terms of importance at each developmental level. Finally, we pursue eminence or SP/A as our outcome, whereas Gagné's model focuses on the transformation of giftedness or abilities into high-level expertise.

How Should Gifted Individuals Be Identified?

Most school districts use standardized ability and achievement test scores as the primary identifiers for inclusion in gifted programming (Feldhusen, Jarwan, Kanevsky, et al., 2000) because such measures are relatively inexpensive, easy to administer, and usually well normed. Yet, a quick review of the literature (see Kwiatkowski & Sternberg, in press) on gifted education reveals that new theories of gifted identification comprise a potential goldmine of new identification procedures.

We argue that the use of standardized ability and achievement test scores as the primary identifiers for inclusion in secondary-level gifted programming is both too narrow and too broad (Sternberg & Subotnik, 2000). Employing standardized test scores of ability is too narrow a standard because intrinsic motivation and a domain-relevant ability are key variables for real-life success, the ultimate criterion for adult giftedness (Subotnik, 2004). Concurrently, we argue against the use of standardized criteria for program admission that include both quantitative and verbal excellence as this approach tends to deny opportunity to those with specific talents in one of those domains.

Abilities in all domains are too often assessed serendipitously. The two environments of greatest importance in assessing abilities are home (which includes realms of extended family as well as local cultural and religious organizations that are part of the family routine) and school. If the family culture values such abilities in any way, it is likely that the abilities may be noticed by a relative, clergyperson, neighbor, or coach. If an ability is not particularly valued by the family or community, unusual sensitivities may go unnoticed or be misinterpreted as strange or inappropriate behavior.

School is another place where abilities can be displayed. If a child expresses great interest in rhyming words, for example, her teacher may notice and praise her, even if her peers may ridicule her. More commonly, if there are no available opportunities to demonstrate unusual responses to enriching stimuli, an ability will likely stagnate. If there is no well-designed physical education or writing program available, for example, then it is not likely that any child with such proclivities will be noticed, especially if the family culture does not support or encourage athletics or writing.

Although schools and homes are petri dishes for talent identification, abilities can be assessed most effectively by artists/scholars. Renowned choreographer Eliot Feld and his colleagues visit hundreds of New York City third-grade classrooms to hold 10-minute auditions (Subotnik, 2002). Children are assessed on their visual memory for movement, their flexibility, their physical proportions, and their response to the music or task at hand. From these thousands of mini-auditions, Feld and his colleagues identify 800 to 1,000 students who receive free dance instruction. Approximately 10 percent of the students persist for more than a year or two. Eventually, 20 to 25 committed and clearly talented students are invited to attend his special school and highly regarded professional performance group, Feld's wide-net assessment and nurturing of raw, untrained ability is an excellent model for all domains but requires the exquisite judgment of an experienced master.

Selective academic high school programs assess abilities with words or numbers by way of standardized tests. Teacher recommendations tend to be viewed with suspicion of bias or general distrust of their judgment. Relying on standardized tests rather than a form of audition, however, makes the process of identifying abilities less content-valid, especially during the transition from competence to expertise of adolescents and young adults. Giftedness in adolescence is better identified through samples of poetry, creative stories, quantitative musings, or scientific reasoning revealed after exposure to excellent teaching and demonstrated receptivity to advanced instruction (Subotnik, 2004b).

Let us consider a specific example in the domain of music. The audition committee at The Juilliard School is regularly confronted with a number of highly competent young musicians vying for a small number of places in their departments. Maintaining a regime of disciplined practice serves to transform an individual's competence into expertise. Further, managing adversity requires great personal strength to persist through the good and bad times of the talent development process.

Under those circumstances, the committee values those who appear to be ready to maximize opportunities for education in the conservatory. According to the Juilliard faculty, some candidates are clearly receptive to instruction and are "teachable," whereas others are resistant to technical or aesthetic suggestions for change. Although great performers and creators are known for their unique ideas or techniques, there is a delicate balance between receptivity to ideas and confidence in one's own judgment that emerges in the talent development process. When ensconced in the transition from expertise to artistry or scholarship, reliance on one's own judgment, even stubbornly, may be essential and appropriate.

By the time candidates audition for conservatory in violin, they will have been playing for at least 10 years. The level of skill that is evidenced at the top music schools is tremendous, making selection for performance opportunities based simply on technique or even teachability virtually impossible. Other characteristics, such as practical and creative skills, and traits such as charisma, differentiate those who are given opportunities to perform or take on exciting jobs. Artistic directors look for a deep connection with the music and an ability to communicate it with zeal. This passion is magnetic, drawing audiences into the performer's spell.

How Should Gifted Individuals Be Instructed in School and Elsewhere?

The methods used to identify students for special programming and the methods used to deliver such programming must match. If there is no match, then the children who are supposed to benefit from the programming may not be served appropriately. We promote instruction that develops students' abilities into competencies, expertise, and finally into SP/A by balancing analytical, creative, and practical skills. Throughout the process of instruction, the teacher or mentor also capitalizes on key personality factors that with guidance will elicit the greatest potential for success in life, whether inside or outside the classroom.

Providers of high-quality instruction are deeply familiar with the acquired knowledge of a domain, including its criteria for excellence. They are able to design a clearly articulated set of problems and assignments that lead to mastery of increasingly challenging material. Highly competent students need to work in specialized environments, whether full-time, after school, or during summers.

Without the chance to learn from skilled instructors, abilities may develop too slowly or even counterproductively. In addition, when a domain is highly competitive, insufficiently challenging instruction can hamper the schooling, training, or performance opportunities available to youngsters with high abilities. Special instruction should socialize pupils into the values of the domain, and provide peers that reinforce and challenge one another's progress. In other words, a high-quality teacher, coach, or trainer channels abilities into *competencies* and competencies into expertise by introducing a series of sufficiently challenging experiences that can be practiced and mastered.

How Should the Achievement of Gifted Individuals be Assessed?

We believe that the development of giftedness follows the three stages we have outlined above: *Abilities* transform into *competencies*, which in turn can develop into *expertise* and finally into *SP/A*. Though the sequence of these stages is consistent across domains, the age at which an individual is expected to reach a given stage is domain specific, and therefore the assessment of giftedness should also be domain specific. For example, giftedness as a musician is assessed differently from giftedness as a poet. Even within a domain such as music, performance expectations for a 15-year-old violinist are much higher than for a 15-year-old vocalist.

In its early to middle stages, giftedness can be defined as a high level of competence in the domain of choice. For a violinist, for example, this would be reflected in solid technique. We propose that secondary programs for gifted students be domain specific and focus on developing expertise in those domains. The passage into the expert level of giftedness is defined by mastery of the field, encompassing a thorough knowledge of past trends, ideas, and occurrences. For a violinist, this would be, for example, the ability to interpret a piece of music in different styles that have been performed by earlier masters. Finally, SP/A is achieved when a musician employs his or her musical ability and expertise to engage a present-day audience in an emotionally moving or intellectually powerful experience.

In conclusion, we have presented here a model of giftedness by referring to the specific domain of music. The model defines giftedness as a transitional process in which different characteristics contribute to the transformation of abilities into competencies and expertise and, in exceptional cases, into scholarly productivity or artistry. This transformation is made possible through the interaction of innate abilities and context, as specified at each stage. We have also outlined how we believe education can best facilitate the passage from abilities to competencies to expertise and scholarly productivity or artistry. We offer this model, based on research in the domain of music in the United States, as a useful framework for understanding, comparing, and nurturing talent development in other domains and other countries.

ACKNOWLEDGMENT

Preparation of this chapter was supported by a grant under the Javits Act Program (Grant No. R206R000001) as administered by the Institute of Educational Sciences, formerly the Office of Educational Research and Improvement, U.S. Department of Education. Grantees undertaking such projects are encouraged to express freely their professional judgment. This article, therefore, does not necessarily represent the position or policies of the Institute of Educational Sciences or the U.S. Department of Education, and no official endorsement should be inferred.

References

Bloom, B. (1985). *Developing talent in young people*. New York: Ballantine.
Chi, M. T. H., Glaser, R., & Farr, M. J. (Eds.). (1988). *The nature of expertise*. Hillsdale, NJ: Lawrence Erlbaum Associates.
Csikszentmihalyi, M. (1988). Society, culture, and person: A systems view of creativity. In R. J. Sternberg (Ed.), *The nature of creativity* (pp. 325–339). New York: Cambridge University Press.
Csikszentmihalyi, M. (1996). *Creativity: Flow and the psychology of discovery and invention*. New York: HarperCollins.
Ericsson, K. A., & Smith, J. (1991). Prospects and limits in the empirical study of expertise: An introduction. In K. A. Ericsson & J. Smith (Eds.). *Toward a general theory of expertise: Prospects and limits* (pp. 19–38). Cambridge, UK: Cambridge University Press.
Feldhusen, J. F., Jarwan, F. A., Kanevsky, L., Perleth, C., Schatz, T., Moenks, F. J., Trost, G. (2000). Part III: Identification of giftedness and talent. In K. A. Heller, F. J. Moenks, et al. (Eds.), *International handbook of giftedness and talent* (2nd ed., pp. 271–327).
Feuerstein, R. (1980). Instrumental enrichment: *An intervention program for cognitive modifiability*. Baltimore, MD: University Park Press.
Gagné, F. (2003). Transforming gifts into talents: The DMGT as a developmental theory. In N. Colangelo & G. A. Davis (Eds.), *Handbook of gifted education* (3rd ed., pp. 60–74). Boston: Allyn and Bacon.
Herrnstein, R., Nickerson, R. S., deSanchez, M., & Swets, J. A. (1986). Teaching thinking skills. *American Psychologist, 41*, 1279–1289.
Kwiatkowski, J., & Sternberg, R. J. (in press). Getting practical about gifted education. In D. Boothe & J. C. Stanley (Eds.) *In the eyes of the beholder: Critical issues for diversity in gifted education*. Waco, TX: Prufrock Press, Inc.
Nickerson, R. S. (1986). *Reflections on reasoning*. Hillsdale, NJ: Lawrence Erlbaum Associates.
Nickerson, R. S., Perkins, D. N., & Smith, E. E. (1985). *The teaching of thinking*. Hillsdale, NJ: Lawrence Erlbaum Associates.
Perkins, D. N. (1995). *Outsmarting IQ: The emerging science of learnable intelligence*. New York: Free Press.
Perkins, D. N., & Grotzer, T. A. (1997). Teaching intelligence. *American Psychologist, 52*, 1125–1133.

Ramey, C. T. (1994). Abecedarian project. In R. J. Sternberg (Ed.), *Encyclopedia of human intelligence* (Vol. 1, pp. 1–3). New York: Macmillan.

Sternberg, R. J. (1988). Intellectual development: Psychometric and information-processing approaches. In M. Bornstein & M. Lamb (Eds.), *Developmental psychology: An advanced textbook* (2nd ed., pp. 261–295). Hillsdale, NJ: Lawrence Erlbaum Associates.

Sternberg, R. J. (1994). Changing conceptions of intelligence and their impact upon the concept of giftedness: The Triarchic theory of intelligence. In J. L. Genshaft, M. Bireley, & C. L. Hollinger (Eds.), *Serving gifted and talented students* (pp. 33–47). Austin, TX: PRO-ED.

Sternberg, R. J. (1997). *Successful intelligence.* New York: Plume.

Sternberg, R. J. (1998). Abilities are forms of developing expertise. *Educational Researcher, 27*, 11–20.

Sternberg, R. J., & Grigorenko, E. L. (Eds.) (1997). *Intelligence, heredity, and environment.* New York: Cambridge University Press.

Sternberg, R. J., & Spear-Swerling, L. (1996). *Teaching for thinking.* Washington, DC: American Psychological Association.

Sternberg, R. J., & Subotnik, R. F. (2000). A Multidimensional Framework for Synthesizing Disparate Issues in Identifying, Selecting, and Serving Gifted Children. In Heller, K. A., Mönks, F. J., Sternberg, R. J., & Subotnik, R. F. (Eds.) *International handbook of giftedness and talent* (pp. 831–838). Oxford, UK: Elsevier.

Sternberg, R. J., Wagner, R. K., Williams, W. M., & Horvath, J. A. (1995). Testing common sense. *American Psychologist, 50*(11), 912–927.

Subotnik, R. F. (2000). Developing young adolescent performers at Juilliard: An educational prototype for elite level talent development in the arts and sciences. In C. F. Van Lieshout & P. G. Heymans (Eds.) *Talent, resilience, and wisdom across the lifespan* (pp. 249–276). Hove, UK: Psychology Press.

Subotnik, R. F. (2002). Talent developed: Conversations with masters in the arts and sciences – Eliot Feld. *Journal for the Education of the Gifted, 25*, 290–302.

Subotnik, R. F. (2004a). Transforming elite musicians into professional artists: A view of the talent development process at the Juilliard School. In L.V. Shavinina and M. Ferrari (Eds.) *Beyond knowledge: Extra cognitive aspects of developing high ability.* Mahwah, NJ: Lawrence Erlbaum Associates.

Subotnik, R. F. (2004b). A developmental view of giftedness: From being to doing. *Roeper Review.*

Subotnik, R. F., Jarvin, L., Moga, E., & Sternberg, R. J. (2003). Wisdom from gatekeepers: Secrets of success in music performance. *Bulletin of Psychology and the Arts: 4*(1), 5–9.

Tannenbaum, A. J. (1983). *Gifted children: Psychological and educational perspectives.* New York: Macmillan.

20

Domain-Specific Giftedness

Applications in School and Life

Joyce VanTassel-Baska

Our conceptions of giftedness vary greatly based on cultural and genetic assumptions about intelligence – what it is and what it is not. Whether we ascribe to a view of *g*-factor intelligence, which is well supported in the literature (Jensen, 1998; Carroll, 1993), or a more domain-specific orientation to intelligence (Gardner, 1983; Benbow & Stanley, 1996), which also has a substantial literature base, it affects our conception of giftedness in important ways that in turn affect our ways of interpreting it in school for identification and programming purposes and in life for purposes of college and career planning and development.

Conceptions of giftedness that focus on domain-specific considerations hold the most promise for promoting talent development in individuals at all stages of development because of the capacity to make appropriate correspondences between aptitudes and interventions, between predispositions and interests, and between the life of the mind and creating a life in the real world. Although general intelligence thresholds matter in real-world and school-based problem-solving situations, the level of *g* necessary to function at very high levels in specific domains remains debatable (Tannenbaum, 1996) and may depend greatly on a particular discipline or field (Jensen, 1998).

This chapter explores the theories and applications of domain-specific giftedness as they have been articulated to date and analyzes how they differ from other conceptions of giftedness. The chapter concludes with applications of a domain-specific conception of giftedness to practice in the areas of identification, curriculum and instruction, and assessment in school and beyond.

WHAT IS GIFTEDNESS?

In a domain-specific conception of intelligence, giftedness becomes the manifestation of intelligence within specific domains at very high levels.

Research on prodigies fits nicely into this orientation, as they are individuals with extraordinary abilities in a specific area at a young age (Feldman, 1991). So, too, does research on eminence suggesting that individuals across cultures and time periods create products in specific domains (Simonton, 1994, 1999; Piirto, 2004).

Yet, giftedness is about potential for creation as much as it is about the actual creation itself. Thus, a definition of domain-specific giftedness must retain an appreciation for evidence of potential as well as performance. To say that Mozart's sister or Schumann's wife had domain-specific ability in music and demonstrated it in several ways and on various occasions in their contexts is an important acknowledgment of their abilities, even though such promise was not fulfilled at the level of Mozart or Schumann as eminent musicians. In other words, giftedness is recognized in a temporal and spatial context that does not necessarily transcend across contexts to become universal for a variety of reasons that may include social, political, and/or individual circumstances.

There is also a need to acknowledge that giftedness is culturally bound and field-dependent (Csikszentmihalyi, 2000). In a world that is more and more specialized, the issue of the conversion of giftedness to eminence today is quite different from what it was 50 years ago. Today, discoveries or contributions are being accomplished in more specialized fields and many times by teams rather than just individuals. Nobel laureates in science, for example, typically have been awarded to two or more persons for a single contribution, the most famous example being Watson and Crick for their unraveling of DNA. This greater specialization within disciplines and the creation of new fields of knowledge renders the connection between giftedness and eminence all the more complex in that the possibilities in actual number for contributors increases as fields proliferate and resources follow to create systematic programs of research, yet diminish as the labyrinthine processes to secure credentials to such specialized fields increase. Ability without considerable preparation and experience in a specialized area stands little chance of making a societal contribution. How different from 18th-century England, when interdisciplinary enlightenment could emerge from individuals with high ability and modest formal preparation!

Giftedness then might be defined as follows:

Giftedness is the manifestation of general intelligence in a specific domain of human functioning at a level significantly beyond the norm such as to show promise for original contributions to a field of endeavor.

Thus, a conception of giftedness must entertain the idea of aptitude in domain-specific areas such as verbal, mathematical, scientific, artistic, and social, given a superior level of general ability. At the same time, it must embrace an understanding of "degrees of difference," recognizing an individual who is capable of performing at levels atypical within the domain based on age or years in training, factors related to skill development, or an actual performance or set of products completed that demonstrate extraordinary ability. Finally, a conception of giftedness must presage the potential for actual creative and/or productive performance in a given area recognized as culturally valuable. This definition of giftedness then creates a strong basis for the application of a talent development paradigm in the realms of identification, instruction, and assessment.

HOW DOES THE DOMAIN-SPECIFIC CONCEPTION OF INTELLIGENCE COMPARE WITH OTHERS?

As one considers the relationship among various conceptions of giftedness, key factors appear to separate them. These factors include:

- multidimensional versus unidimensional perspectives
- the importance of intellective abilities versus nonintellective abilities
- global versus specific views of giftedness
- the role of creativity in giftedness
- the relationship of speed and complexity in judging giftedness

A domain-specific model of giftedness that focuses strongly on evidence of advanced ability and performance represents a more unidimensional view of giftedness in some respects than do many other models, for it is doubly bounded. First, it is bounded by the specific domain within which evidence of giftedness has been displayed, and, secondly, it is bounded by a strong fusion of ability and aptitude for specialized work within that domain that may narrow the conception even further. A linguist, for example, may have strong domain-specific verbal skills, but has chosen to develop particularized verbal skills as they relate to language learning as opposed to literature, writing, or communication skills. Thus, the manifestation of giftedness in the verbal area by necessity has narrowed in order to go deeper into a specialty within the domain. This, it seems, is how giftedness works in the real world. Depth of focus in complex specialty areas prevents the likelihood of "renaissance people" except in cases of very high general intelligence. Although high g can and does affect real world problem solving, making connections, and performing at high levels within chosen domains, it does not dominate the picture of domain-specific talent development.

This domain-specific view is antithetical to several existing conceptions of giftedness and more compatible with others. It is perhaps most antithetical to conceptions of giftedness that proclaim nonintellective traits to be at the same level of importance as intellective ones in defining giftedness (Renzulli, 2002). It is my contention that constructs such as motivation, task commitment, and even creativity are born of the talent development process itself and not part of giftedness per se. Hence, they are secondary considerations in thinking about the conception of giftedness, rather providing the fuel for the development of aptitude. Moreover, for purposes of identifying students in schools or selecting candidates for a job, evidence of these nonintellective traits is elusive, best seen over time as they emerge in performance.

The view is also antithetical to a pure or global g factor model of intelligence. Although the evidence for the presence of g is somewhat irrefutable (Jensen, 1998; Carroll, 1993), its utility in the real world of talent development is not. High g-factor intelligence that is not linked well to a specific domain of functioning in the modern world may bring great satisfaction to the individual but make little impression on the society that has spawned it. Practice and hard work appear to be the strongest nonintellective traits displayed by those who reach the heights of eminent performance (Ochse, 1990; Ericsson, 1996). Real-world productive and creative giftedness requires applications to fields and years spent in a career honing specific skills for particularized work. It is in this focusing over time that motivation, commitment, and creativity are built.

The conception is most compatible with Gruber's (1981) evolving systems model of giftedness, which acknowledges strongly the domain-specific view nested in a set of evolving systems of personal motivation, a set of relevant skills, and connection to an evolving field of study. His in-depth case study of Darwin still stands as a prototype of understanding the processes at work in talent development. It also is compatible with Csikszentmihalyi's (1996) idea of the role of context in conceptions of giftedness suggesting that cultural influences, including the field of interest to study, impacts strongly on the nature and direction that giftedness takes over a period of time. Studying creative success among older people reminds us of the importance of the connection to their area of expertise.

Gardner's (1983) multiple intelligences model also has many commonalities with this view, especially in respect to domain specificity and the matching of intelligences to how disciplines of thought are organized. This idea is also reminiscent of the work of Phenix (1964), who posited "realms of meaning" within which human beings were able to manifest their abilities. Yet, the Gardner model does not acknowledge the role of general ability in its favoring of a more specific conception. In the conception offered here, levels of general intelligence tend to "broker" the manifestation of specific aptitude in an area.

Sternberg's information-processing model of giftedness is highly complex and models well on our current level of understanding about how the mind works at a mechanistic level. His applied intelligence areas of analytic, synthetic, and practical mirror some aspects of real-world domain applications, yet they remain at a more abstract level where the integration of skills to create different patterns of organization in respect to them accounts for giftedness displayed in various specific areas of human activity. The beauty of his conception of giftedness lies not so much in its separate features but its capacity to explain quite different real prototypes of performance at a complex level by focusing on preferred thinking styles employed. Yet a pure domain-specific conception of giftedness puts the same emphasis on the demands of disciplines and fields as on the abilities and aptitudes of individuals, a key facet of the Csikszentmihalyi (1996) view and that of Amabile (1996) as well. The transformation of giftedness from "in the mind" to "out in the world" requires the rigor of an organized body of learning to provide the grist for development. Sternberg's model treats the importance of a knowledge base as a part of the system of intelligence, but assigns it a smaller role than most domain-specific models.

A domain-specific model of giftedness also is tilted equally in the direction of honoring complexity and speed in developing abilities and aptitudes. Clearly, prodigies reflect a strong emphasis on speed, yet even prodigies must overcome key transition periods in their areas of performance that require more complexity in their thinking and execution (Bamberger, 1975). Applications of giftedness almost always call for this same ordering – speed followed by complexity as the demands of performance areas become more advanced and rigorous to master, a model illustrated well in the longitudinal study of domain-specific abilities identified by talent searches over the past 20 years (Benbow & Lubinski, 1996).

Another difference in a domain-specific model of giftedness from ones that are more pure g or multidimensional is the role of creativity in the process. Recent studies have clearly demonstrated that creativity itself is domain-specific (Simonton, 1999; Amabile, 1996; Piirto, 2004). Thus, a view of giftedness that is domain specific is highly compatible with current conceptions of creativity as well. Creativity research suggests that the construct is an emergent quality based on a strong knowledge base, motivation, and creative skills relevant to a given domain. Such a viewpoint is consistent with considering creative production as an output, not an input, in respect to giftedness.

If intelligence involves the capacity to solve problems at higher levels, to develop high-level expertise in a discrete area, and to plan, monitor, and assess one's work in a reflective manner, then giftedness must be an appellation reserved for those students who perform these feats at very high levels compared with same-age peers. At a simplistic level, then, giftedness may be considered evidence of advanced development across intellectual areas, advanced development within a specific academic or arts-related area, or unusual organizational power for bringing about desired results. Functionally, schools assess such development through the tools available to them, namely, tests, inventories, checklists, and student performance.

TABLE 20.1. *Overview of Commonly Used Identification Tools*

Traditional	Nontraditional
Intelligence tests	Nonverbal ability tests
Achievement tests	Creativity tests
Aptitude tests (domain-specific)	Student portfolios and performance by audition
Grades	Performance-based assessment
Teacher recommendations	Parent, peer, and community recommendations

THE IDENTIFICATION OF GIFTEDNESS IN SCHOOLS

In school-based settings, giftedness is most frequently identified by a combination of criteria. The tools most commonly employed are listed in Table 20.1. The increasing use of nontraditional tools demonstrates how dissatisfied the field of gifted education has become with using only traditional tools, which have not yielded enough students of color, students of low socioeconomic levels or students with uneven profiles. In recent years, both performance-based and portfolio approaches have gained favor and are included in several states' identification guidelines (Karnes, 2000).

Issues surrounding the identification of gifted children have long been debated in the field of gifted education. In the gifted education literature, more citations exist on identification than on any other topic. Yet, identification remains one of the most common program development problems cited by school district personnel and state department coordinators administering programs and services to gifted children (VanTassel-Baska & Feng, 2004).

The difficult problems associated with identification of the gifted stem from a number of issues. One relates to whether giftedness should be thought of as absolute or relative. Because newer definitional structures are attuned to the idea of relativity, gifted educators today generally consider the context of the school, the nature of the student's background, and the demands of the program as they make decisions about individual learners. A second issue relates to the range of individual differences within the group of learners who might be designated gifted. Gifted educators often tend to spend a great deal of time deciding who will be the last student in the program. However, cutting on a continuum of human ability is a risky venture that often is difficult to justify. And at the same time that such debates on identification rage, highly gifted students frequently lack extensive and intensive enough services because programs are far more likely to focus resources on the mildly gifted group, which may be larger and require attention based on parent demands for service. A third issue is the nagging concern that underrepresented groups are not adequately being assessed for inclusion in gifted programs. Thus, testing becomes the proverbial messenger to be attacked, and the search goes on for a better instrument that may reveal greater parity in performance between under-represented and mainstreamed groups.

Any one of these issues would put identification high on the list of concerns for local school districts' planning and implementing gifted programs. The three taken together guarantee that identification will always be a controversial topic.

Until beliefs about identification change, little progress can occur in developing a system that resolves all of the issues noted. The task is not to identify only the highly gifted but also to locate students who demonstrate undeveloped intellectual potential in specific areas, including academic, artistic, and leadership domains. Moreover, the task is not to select students for all time but to select them for enhanced instructional opportunities that may benefit them at a given stage of development. Students in all gifted programs should be regularly reassessed for new opportunities and dropped from those that are not meeting their needs. Finally, the task is not to be gatekeepers to exclude students but rather to be custodians of student growth by recognizing discernible strengths and working with the school community to enhance them, whether that is done through the gifted program or another medium. Establishing numerical cut-offs on relevant criteria may be less useful than gaining a holistic assessment of the students being considered and matching programs to the strengths of that particular population.

Understanding current ideas about the act of identification may help deal with the difficulties inherent in the process, especially as educators move toward a paradigm of talent development:

1. *Giftedness is multidimensional.* Many studies and authors favoring newer conceptual definitions of giftedness acknowledge the multi-dimensionality of the phenomenon (Gardner, 1999; Sternberg, 1996). Some students are omnibus gifted, highly capable across many do-mains and areas. Yet the majority of gifted students have distinct profiles of strengths and relative weaknesses. Their abilities may be discerned by performance and not by paper-and-pencil tests. Their giftedness may not be evoked by the school environment but may shine in the context of community. Some may experience develop-mental spurts at key stages of development, revealing abilities that could not be discerned earlier. The interests of a student may be piqued at some stage, motivating him or her to develop abilities in relevant areas. All of these examples show that giftedness may be elusive in its manner and context of manifestation.

2. *Both genetic and environmental factors influence the manifestation of gift-edness.* Individuals vary considerably in their ability to function

effectively in various domains. Attention must be paid to the "rubber band" effect of human potential: Our genetic markers allow for expansive growth and development but not to an unlimited extent. We can stretch ourselves within a range that is based on the genetic potential we possess. The role of education is to provide the experiences that may stretch an individual's potential in his or her areas of greatest flexibility for learning. This recognition of preexisting individual differences should help educators realize the folly of trying to find a "one size fits all" program of study or curriculum. As long as differentiated practices are reserved for labeled special populations, the spirit of individualized learning will be in jeopardy. Giftedness does not guarantee entitlement to educational privilege, but it does call for a flexible response by schools and other agencies to higher levels of functioning that is based on the individual, not just age.

3. *The concept of degree or extent of giftedness should be considered in developing identification processes and curriculum.* When I directed the talent search program at Northwestern University, teachers would tell me that seventh-grade students who were scoring at the 600 level in mathematics on the Scholastic Aptitude Test were not truly precocious in mathematics, even though their scores placed them in the top 2 percent of the age population. Only students scoring at the 700 level met that criterion. These teachers were noting the wide band of difference that exists within any gifted population, such that students at the bottom of a particular group may function very differently from those at the top. In psychometric language, this means that gifted students may vary among themselves by as much as three standard deviations in respect to mental functioning in one or more areas. Reading level in a fifth-grade gifted program, for example, could range from seventh-grade to college level. Thus, gifted educators must decide how broad a group might benefit from a particular intervention and then ensure differentiation of instruction in the delivery of that intervention such that students at the top of the group are adequately challenged and those at the bottom are not made unduly anxious. Wide ranges of abilities have to be tolerated in most gifted programs, because the context of delivery frequently requires sufficient numbers of students to justify the special intervention.

4. *The recognition of advanced behavior is the most critical variable in determining who can best profit from advanced work and instruction.* To deny services to students who clearly are advanced in reading, mathematics, the arts, or other domains because they have not been formally assessed calls into question a school system's capacity to respond to individual differences. Responding to advanced student behaviors is facilitated by the inclusion of teacher, parent, and community

input in the identification process. Domain-specific checklists can be used to assess such behavior in context. Such checklists also contribute important insights into effective programming for individual children.

5. *Ability must be coupled with focused effort for success to ensue.* Work in talent development (e.g., Csikszentmihalyi, 1996; Simonton, 1999) has convinced most people in the gifted education field that ability alone may be insufficient to predict success in gifted programs, let alone in life endeavors. Nonintellectual factors, such as motivation, personality, persistence, and concentration, greatly influence creative productivity at particular stages of development and over the life span. Thus, identification processes should be sensitive to students whose ability threshold is slightly lower than established cut-off scores but whose capacity and zeal to do work in a given domain are very high.

Currently, there is a call for a new paradigm for identification that takes into account the constructs of giftedness just described (Passow & Frasier, 1996). This new paradigm would recognize the different ways in which students display giftedness and would call for more varied and authentic assessment. Instead of relying solely on intelligence and achievement scores for identification, multiple criteria would be used, including more nontraditional measures, such as observing students interacting with a variety of learning opportunities (Passow & Frasier, 1996). Many gifted educators believe that new conceptions of giftedness and a new paradigm for identifying and selecting students will help minority and disadvantaged students become more represented in gifted programs (Ford, 1996; VanTassel-Baska, Patton, & Prillaman, 1991).

Part of the process of nontraditional assessment involves trying to tap into fluid rather than crystallized abilities. The approaches assess cognitive abilities that often are not apparent when most forms of standardized tests are employed. One such approach, dynamic assessment, usually consists of a test–intervention–retest format, with the focus being on the improvement students make after an intervention as a result of learning cognitive strategies related to mastery of the tested task (Kirschenbaum, 1998).

Supporting the use of nontraditional assessment is research evidence suggesting that disadvantaged learners perform better on tasks that emphasize fluid over crystallized intelligence (Mills & Tissot, 1995) and spatial over verbal and mathematical reasoning (Naglieri, 1999). Employing an assessment approach that contains a strong spatial component may reduce disparities between scores for different socioeconomic status levels or ethnic groups (Bracken, 2000). Thus, assessment using such instruments as the Matrix Analysis Test and the Ravens Progressive Matrices may yield somewhat different populations of students than assessment with traditional intelligence tests that emphasize verbal tasks. The new Universal Nonverbal Intelligence Test (UNIT) also offers promise in this regard as a full-scale measure.

In addition, a two-stage process of screening and identification would help to ensure that appropriate measures are used in the selection of students for a gifted program. Simply using group achievement and intelligence test score data as the final arbiters for selection – say, by putting the cut-off at 98 percent – is not defensible. Many times, large numbers of students would qualify at 95 percent. When norm-referenced tests that are grade-level calibrated are used to make judgments about students at the top end, problems of ceiling effect occur. A better and more defensible strategy is to use off-level aptitude and achievement measures – such as the PLUS test; the School, College, and Ability Test (SCAT); and the Scholastic Aptitude Test (SAT) – to ascertain a true dispersion of the student scores in order to select the most able. Over the past 25 years, these instruments have demonstrated effectiveness and efficiency in discerning able students' range of functioning in critical domains (Benbow & Stanley, 1996).

The measures used must also be relevant to a program's emphasis. This is especially true for the identification stage of the process. Using verbal measures to decide who should be in a math program makes no sense. If a program's emphasis is writing, a writing sample should be included at the identification stage; if a program's emphasis is science, a performance-based science assessment or science project portfolio should be included. Such authentic assessment data help gifted educators select the most apt students for participation in carefully defined program areas (VanTassel-Baska, 1998).

Further, best practice calls for the use of identification protocols that are appropriate for the students' stage of development. Early childhood identification procedures, because of the children's age and lack of contact with the school, have to consider parental feedback more carefully, use testing data more judiciously, and consider advanced performance tasks more heavily. Identification procedures at the secondary level, dependent on the organizational contest, have to focus on finding students in a broader range of talent areas. Domain-specific approaches based on departmental courses of study must also be considered.

Making placement decisions based on individual profile data is also considered best practice. This practice allows professional judgment to be exercised rather than simply relying on a numerical cut-off score on a matrix model to determine placement (Borland & Wright, 1994). Finally, the identification process must be equitable with respect to the selection, validation, and placement of students. Such fairness can only be obtained

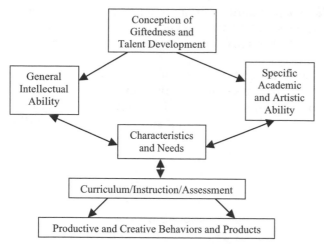

FIGURE 20.1. Context for Designing Differentiated Curricula.

through the careful delineation and implementation of well-understood procedures by conscientious educators.

Curriculum and Instruction for Gifted Students

When considering the concept of giftedness through a curriculum lens, curriculum planners must analyze the characteristics and needs of gifted children and organize curricula that are responsive to them. Once a program is in place, teachers must be cognizant of the identification data on each gifted child and tailor the curriculum to ensure that student profiles are used in the classroom. Figure 20.1 illustrates the relationship between conceptions of giftedness and curriculum planning. Inputs to curriculum planning are derived from the conception of giftedness employed in a school district and the interplay of that conception with group and individual student characteristics and needs. Outputs from an appropriately tailored curriculum, instruction, and assessment system are gifted student creativity and productivity.

Curricula for gifted learners should be based on several assumptions that are critical to ensuring that gifted students receive appropriate services:

1. *All children can learn, but they do so in different ways at different times in different contexts.* Educators of the gifted support this fundamental principle of the standards-based reform movement and applaud it as a necessary belief for improving schooling. Yet educators, in implementing the common standards, must recognize individual differences and accommodate them through flexible means.

2. *Some children learn more quickly than others.* This assumption has been demonstrated over and over again in research studies, yet the power of this difference in learning rate is obscured by age-grade notions of curriculum readiness. Gifted students can learn new material at least twice as fast as typical learners can. If the curriculum is reorganized into "larger chunks," learning rates often can increase exponentially.

3. *Gifted children find different curriculum areas easy to learn and therefore learn them at different rates.* Gifted learners vary as much from one another as they do from the nongifted population both in rate of learning and areas in which they may be ready for advanced learning.

4. *Intrinsic motivation for cognitive learning varies considerably among gifted learners.* The individual differences in motivation for learning, which may be related to cognitive capacity, tend to show up in critical ways as students attempt schoolwork.

5. *Not every student (or every gifted student) will attain a useful mastery of concepts and skills beyond a certain level of complexity and abstraction.* Many students, including some of the gifted, cannot handle advanced mathematics and science, both of which are highly abstract subject areas. Other gifted students encounter difficulty in interpreting complex passages of written text. Students who experience these difficulties may be encountering the maximal degree of abstraction they can handle at their stage of development.

6. *Learning should provide "a basic diet but also favorite foods."* One of the current assumptions of curricula for the gifted is that both specialization and opportunities for other modes of learning are important. Self-selected subjects, special project work, mentorships, and other activities provide opportunities for strong growth in specialized areas.

7. *Intra- and inter-individual variability is the rule in development.* For neither gifted students nor any other group of learners can learning be viewed as a group phenomenon. Rather, individual differences coupled with the subtle dynamics of group classroom interactions determine the nature and extent of understanding at any given moment. As Dimitriou and Valanides (1998) observed, "Classrooms are developmental mixers in which each student's developmental dynamics constrain and are constrained by the developmental dynamics of every other student and of the classroom as a whole" (p. 195).

Thus, the beginning point for all meaningful curricula for the gifted must be the individual and group characteristics and needs of these students. Existing curricula found to be effective with the gifted have evolved primarily from this understanding (Maker, Nielson, & Rogers, 1994; VanTassel-Baska, 2003).

The cognitive and affective characteristics of the gifted form the basis for the three major curriculum approaches used in developing programs for gifted learners.

1. *Content-based instruction* at advanced levels has been a staple of gifted curricula since the early years and has gained in popularity, particularly with middle-school and secondary-level students, through the national network of talent searches (Benbow & Stanley, 1996; VanTassel-Baska, 1998).

2. *Process skills as a basis for curriculum-making* for the gifted has been popularized through model curricula developed around higher-level thinking skills, creative thinking, and problem solving (Maker & Nielson, 1996). An emphasis on product development has emerged with curriculum models that stress independent learning for the gifted, the gifted as practicing investigators of real-world problems, and generative learning practices resulting in creative products (Renzulli, 2002; Treffinger, 1998).

3. *Concept- or theme-based curricula* for the gifted are derived from early work on the importance of students' understanding of the disciplines (Phenix, 1964; Schwab, 1964) and the later translation of these ideas to the field of gifted education (Ward, 1980). Theme-based curricula for the gifted also receive support from general education ranks through the ideas engendered in Adler's *Paidaeia Proposal* (1984).

In designing an integrated interdisciplinary curriculum for gifted learners, gifted educators must have a good understanding of the nature of the effort. Unfortunately, understanding has been hindered by the use of ambiguous terminology and a lack of helpful models to guide the development process (Davison, Miller, & Methany, 1995), despite the plethora of articles, workshops, and symposia devoted to the topic (Berlin, 1991). Moreover, evidence for the effectiveness of this type of curriculum is scant (VanTassel-Baska, 2000). An "interdisciplinary" curriculum may be defined as one that links two or more disciplines through a major theme or concept as well as the language and methodology of each discipline. An integrated curriculum, as explicated in the Integrated Curriculum Model (VanTassel-Baska, 1998), refers to an inclusive curriculum with respect to approaches employed, models used, assessment techniques, and the blend of general reform principles with gifted education pedagogy. Table 20.2 displays this integration pattern.

The success of domain-specific curriculum work is difficult to dispute, given a 25-year history of effectiveness. The talent searches have systematically demonstrated the student growth possible in specific domains of study after compressed but limited contact time (Olszewski-Kubilius, 2003). Moreover, evidence of contributing growth in these areas of learning has been documented longitudinally (Swiatek & Benbow, 1991). At the level of curriculum units of study, domain-specific student growth in

TABLE 20.2. *Integration in a Curriculum for Gifted Learners*

Dimensions of Connectivity	Features of Curriculum
Organization	Employs content, process, product, and concept opportunities
Models	Uses concept development, reasoning skills, and research models that transcend curriculum areas studied
Assessments	Performance-based and portfolio assessment are integrated into regular use
Reform elements and gifted education	Emphasis is on meaning-making through student-centered challenging activities

higher-level content skills has also been well documented over the past 10 years (VanTassel-Baska, Bass, Avery, Ries, & Poland, 1998; VanTassel-Baska, Zuo, Avery, & Little, 2002).

THE ASSESSMENT OF GIFTED ACHIEVEMENT

Because traditional assessments are problematic in assessing the learning of gifted students due to ceiling effect and lack of consonance with gifted program objectives, off-level standardized instruments and nontraditional approaches must be employed. Off-level instrument use has proven difficult in school district settings but quite effective in the larger talent search venues (Assouline, 1997). Portfolio and performance-based assessments assess high-level performance authentically (i.e., in realistic contexts) and provide teachers and other decision makers with credible evidence of student potential and growth (VanTassel-Baska, Johnson, & Avery, 2002).

A frequently employed evaluation tool to assist in these types of authentic assessments is the use of rubrics to judge the quality of a product or performance. A rubric gives a more descriptive, holistic characterization of the quality of students' work than a conventional rating scale does. In designing and using a rubric, the concern is less with assigning a number to indicate quality than with selecting a verbal description that clearly communicates, based on the performance or product exhibited, what the student knows and is able to do. Thus, rubrics can be highly informative and useful for feedback purposes (Anderson, 2003). However, developing distinct categories and meaningful verbal descriptions and scoring them reliably can be difficult. Rubrics are much more informative about student skill levels than letter grades or numerical scores. They are also a helpful tool for enhancing gifted learners' understanding of expectations for specific assignments and the criteria by which they will be assessed. Many programs for the gifted engage students in the development of rubrics and in peer assessment processes for using them.

Portfolios

Portfolios represent an important form of authentic assessment for the gifted. Tierney, Carter, and Desi (1991, p. 41) defined portfolios as "systematic collection by both students and teachers [that] can serve as the basis to examine effort, improvement, processes, and achievement as well as to meet accountability demands usually achieved by more formal testing procedures." Portfolios can illuminate strengths and needs in the instructional process. Teachers who use portfolio assessment often involve students in selecting samples of their work for their portfolios and have them update the portfolios over time so that improvements or changes in the quality of work may be noted.

Based on their instructional objectives, teachers must identify criteria for judging the work. Criteria for evaluating a portfolio of writing samples, for example, might include organization, elaboration of ideas, clarity, and correct mechanics. Teachers also must determine a mode for evaluating each piece in a student's portfolio. Rating scales (e.g., poor, average, superior) and comments (e.g., "shows good effort but lacks fundamentals") are the most frequently employed methods. Often, these ratings are converted to a numerical scale at the end of an instructional segment to facilitate the assessment of patterns of growth in key areas. Portfolios can also take varied forms, including the following:

- *showcase portfolio* – presents the student's "best" work while emphasizing self-assessment, reflection, and ownership.
- *evaluation portfolio* – presents representative work to be evaluated on the basis of showing movement toward a specific academic goal.
- *process portfolio* – presents student reflections on work produced over time for the purpose of helping them develop points of view on their long-term learning process and subject synthesis.

Performance Assessment

Performance assessment requires students to construct a response, create a product, or perform a demonstration. Because performance assessments generally do not yield a single correct answer or solution method, evaluations are based on judgments guided by criteria. Teachers and other educators who design these assessments must be creative, making decisions about content and scope, processes to be employed, and overall effect with respect to coherence. Important considerations in the design process have been outlined by Wiggins (1992). When the designers move to task development, they need to contextualize the tasks so that the situations are authentic to the field being studied and ensure that the tasks represent tests of knowledge in use, not drills made up of unrelated items.

Schulman (1996) noted the following key questions that developers of performance-based assessments must ask themselves to ensure appropriate task demands:

- What important concepts does this assessment task address?
- How can responses to this task inform instruction?
- How does the task allow for a variety of responses and modes of response?
- What references do students have for knowing what is expected of them in this task?
- What other sources of evidence exist to support inferences made from the assessment?
- How does this task fit with learning goals and procedures?

Performance-based assessment protocols demonstrate the capacity for gifted students to grow and develop skills in a specific area of a domain. They also highlight the striking truth that many students come into a gifted curriculum with relatively low-level skills that need bolstering. The use of pre-assessment helps the teacher pinpoint such areas of instructional need.

Use of performance-based assessment with gifted students has yielded strong evidence of learning gains in specific areas within curriculum domains, including scientific research skills (VanTassel-Baska et al., 1998), literary analysis and interpretation, and persuasive writing (VanTassel-Baska et al., 2002). Care must be taken to ensure that tasks are sufficiently challenging to engage gifted learners to a high degree.

The true authentic achievement of gifted students necessitates the use of tools that require higher-order thinking and problem solving, the use of advanced skills in a domain, and open-endedness in response. Performance and portfolio models are important approaches to realize this goal and enhance the credibility of gifted programs.

CONCLUSION

The importance of having a coherent and cohesive conception of giftedness for purposes of running school-based programs and services cannot be overestimated. Using the organizational structures of society for knowledge production and utilization as a foundation for instruction and assessment of learning is an essential cornerstone for talent development. Coupled with the importance of such an emphasis is a need to identify at key points in time students for whom such instruction may be most propitious in specific areas. Thus, conceptions of giftedness can and should translate effectively into definitions, identification protocols, and service delivery models if they are to be viable in the world of school and life.

References

Adler, M. J. (1984). *The Paideia program: An educational syllabus*. New York: Macmillan.

Amabile, T. (1996). *Creativity in context*. Boulder, CO: Westview Press.

Anderson, L. W. (2003). *Classroom assessment*. Mahwah, NJ: Lawrence Erlbaum Associates.

Assouline, S. (1997). Performance on specific tests. *Vision (Spring)*. Iowa City, IA: Belin-Blank Center for Gifted and Talent Development.

Bamberger, J. (1975). The development of musical intelligence: Strategies for representing simple rhythms. Cambridge, MA: MIT Press.

Benbow, C. P., & Lubinski, D. (1996). *Intellectual talent*. Baltimore: John's Hopkins Press.

Benbow, C. P., & Stanley, J. C. (1996). Inequity in equity: How "equity" can lead to inequity for high-potential students. *Psychology, Public Policy, and Law, 2,* 249–292.

Berlin, D. F. (1991). *A bibliography of integrated science and mathematics teaching and learning literature. School Science and Mathematics Association topics for teachers series, no. 6*. Bowling Green, OH: School Science and Mathematics Association.

Borland, J. H., & Wright, L. (1994). Identifying young, potentially gifted, economically disadvantaged students. *Gifted Child Quarterly, 38,* 164–171.

Bracken, B. A. (2000, April). *An approach for identifying under-represented populations for G/T programs: The UNIT Test*. Paper presented at graduate seminar, College of William and Mary, Williamsburg, VA.

Carroll, J. B. (1993). *Human cognitive abilities: A survey of factor-analytic studies*. New York: Cambridge University Press.

Csikszentmihalyi, M. (1996). *Creativity: Flow and the psychology of discovery and invention*. New York: HarperCollins.

Csikszentmihalyi, M. (2000). *Becoming adult: How teenagers prepare for the world of work*. New York: Basic Books.

Davison, D. M., Miller, K. W., & Methany, D. L. (1995). What does integration of science and mathematics really mean? *School Science and Mathematics, 95,* 226–230.

Dimitriou, A., & Valanides, N. (1998). A three-level theory of the developing mind: Basic principles and implications for instruction and assessment. In R. Sternberg & W. Williams (Eds.), *Intelligence, instruction and assessment* (pp. 149–199). Mahwah, NJ: Lawrence Erlbaum Associates.

Ericsson, K. A. (1996). *The road to excellence: The acquisition of expert performance in the arts and sciences, sports, and games*. Mahwah, NJ: Lawrence Erlbaum Associates.

Feldman, D. H., & Goldsmith, L. T. (1991). *Nature's gambit: Child prodigies and the development of human potential*. New York: Teachers College Press.

Ford, D. Y. (1996). *Reversing underachievement among gifted black students: Promising programs and practices*. New York: Teachers College Press.

Gardner, H. (1983). *Frames of mind: The theory of multiple intelligences*. London: Paladin.

Gardner, H. (1991). *Creating minds*. New York: Basic Books.

Gardner, H. (1999). *Intelligence reframed*. New York: Basic Books.

Gruber, H. (1981). *Darwin on man: A psychological study of scientific creativity*. Chicago: University of Chicago Press.

Jensen, A. R. (1998). *The g factor: The science of mental ability.* Westport, CT: Greenwood.

Karnes, F. A. (2000). State definitions for the gifted and talented revisited. *Exceptional Children, 66,* 219–238.

Kirschenbaum, R. J. (1998). Dynamic assessment and its use with underserved gifted and talented. *Gifted Child Quarterly, 42,* 140–147.

Maker, C. J., & Nielson, A. B. (1996). *Curriculum development and teaching strategies for gifted learners.* Austin, TX: PRO-ED.

Maker, C. J., Nielson, A. B., & Rogers, J. A. (1994). Multiple intelligences: Giftedness, diversity, and problem-solving. *Teaching Exceptional Children, 27*(1), 4–19.

Mills, C., & Tissot, S. (1995). Identifying academic potential in students from under-represented populations: Is using the Ravens Progressive Matrices a good idea? *Gifted Child Quarterly, 39,* 209–217.

Naglieri, J. A. (1999). *The essentials of CAS assessment.* New York: Wiley.

Ochse, R. (1990). *Before the gates of excellence: Determinants of creative genius.* Cambridge, England: Cambridge University Press.

Olszewski-Kubilius, P. (2003). Special summer and Saturday programs for gifted students. In N. Colangelo & G. A. Davis (Eds.), *Handbook of gifted education* (3rd ed.) (pp. 219–228). Boston: Allyn & Bacon.

Passow, A. H., & Frasier, M. M. (1996). Toward improving identification of talent potential among minority and disadvantaged students. *Roeper Review, 18,* 198–202.

Phenix, P. (1964). *Realms of meaning.* New York: McGraw-Hill.

Piirto, J. (2004). *Understanding creativity.* Scottsdale, AZ: Arizona Great Potential Press.

Renzulli, J. S. (2002). Emerging conceptions of giftedness: Building a bridge to the new century. *Exceptionality, 10*(2), 67–75.

Schulman, L. (1996). New assessment practices in mathematics. *Journal of Education, 178,* 61–71.

Schwab, J. (Ed.). (1964). *Education and the structure of knowledge.* Chicago: Rand McNally.

Simonton, D. K. (1994). *Greatness: Who makes history and why.* New York: Guilford.

Simonton, D. K. (1999). *Origins of genius: Darwinian perspectives on creativity.* New York: Oxford University Press.

Sternberg, R. J. (1996). *Successful intelligence: How practical and creative intelligence determine success in life.* New York: Simon & Schuster.

Sternberg, R. J. (1985). *Beyond I.Q.* New York: Basic Books.

Swiatek, M. A., & Benbow, C. P. (1991). A ten-year longitudinal follow-up of ability-matched accelerated and unaccelerated gifted students. *Journal of Educational Psychology, 83,* 528–538.

Tannenbaum, A. (1996). The IQ controversy and the gifted. In Benbow & Lubinski's (Eds.) *Intellectual talent* (pp. 44–77). Baltimore: Johns Hopkins University Press.

Tierney, R. J., Carter, M. A., & Desi, L. E. (1991). *Portfolio assessment in the reading-writing classroom.* Norwood, MA: Christopher Gordon.

Treffinger, D. J. (1998). From gifted education to programming for talent development. *Phi Delta Kappan, 79*(10), 752–755.

VanTassel-Baska, J. (1995). *Comprehensive curriculum for gifted learners* (2nd ed.). Boston: Allyn & Bacon.

VanTassel-Baska, J. (1998). *Excellence in educating the gifted* (3rd ed.). Denver: Love.

VanTassel-Baska, J. (2000). Curriculum policy development for secondary gifted programs: A prescription for reform coverage. *NASSP Bulletin*, 14–29.

VanTassel-Baska, J. (2003). *Curriculum planning and instructional design for gifted learners.* Denver: Love.

VanTassel-Baska, J., Bass, G., Avery, L., Ries, R., & Poland, D. (1998). A national pilot study of science curriculum effectiveness for high-ability students. *Gifted Child Quarterly, 42*, 200–211.

VanTassel-Baska, J., & Feng, A. (2004). *Designing and utilizing evaluation for gifted program improvement.* Waco, TX: Prufrock Press.

VanTassel-Baska, J., Patton, J., & Prillaman, D. (1991). *Gifted youth at risk: A report of a national study.* Reston, VA: Council for Exceptional Children.

VanTassel-Baska, J., Zuo, L., Avery, L., & Little, C. (2002). A curriculum study of gifted student learning in the language arts. *Gifted Child Quarterly, 46*, 30–44.

Ward, V. (1980). *Differential education for the gifted.* Ventura, CA: Office of Ventura County Superintendent of Schools.

Wiggins, G. (1992). Creating tests worth taking. *Educational Leadership, 49*(8), 26–33.

21

Extreme Giftedness

Catya von Károlyi and Ellen Winner

GIFTEDNESS AS HIGH ABILITY OR POTENTIAL

Giftedness, as we conceive it, is unusually high ability or potential in any domain. Giftedness at its core is difference in the direction of advantage. We believe that giftedness exists even when unrecognized by society and that it exists even when the gift has not been actualized through achievements. Further, giftedness exists when the domain of the gift is not valued by society. For example, Ramanujan, a mathematical prodigy, was born in India in 1887, where his gifts were not recognized. He failed his school examinations and was employed as a clerk (Weisstein, n.d.). Unless a gift is recognized and nurtured, it may die, undeveloped, on the vine.

Giftedness is not always revealed in high achievement, but it may also be defined by high potential in the absence of unusual achievement. The determination of giftedness through assessment of ability or potential is more difficult than the determination of giftedness through recognition of achievement. Unusual potential in the absence of high achievement can often be seen in children's passions and interests outside of school.

There are a variety of reasons why children may have unusually high aptitude without showing high achievement. High achievement can only emerge after a child has experience in the domain in which there is high potential to achieve. Given a disadvantaged background or a learning disorder, children with high potential in a given domain may well never develop the knowledge base in that domain that would make high achievement possible. Another reason for lack of achievement despite high ability is boredom and insufficient challenge in the classroom. However, if one looks closely at how such children process information (as well as at their passions and interests), one may be able to recognize the unusual aptitude of such children.

We focus here on *extreme giftedness* – individuals whose potential and/or achievement are several standard deviations above the norm. We focus our attention on children because we are interested in early signs of giftedness and in how such atypical children are best identified, assessed, and educated. Where one draws the line between moderate and extreme giftedness is arbitrary. When we use the term *gifted* in this chapter, we are referring to a fairly rare group of individuals who are at the extreme in their area of ability.

Gifted children stand out in four striking ways. They are precocious in their domain of ability; they are passionate about and have a rage to master that domain; they think, learn, and solve problems in ways that are qualitatively different from typical children; and they are aware of being different from others.

A Different Timetable: Precocity

The most obvious way in which gifted children are different is that they are precocious. They are ahead of schedule in their interest in and mastery of a particular domain or domains. They grasp and apply underlying principles of a body of knowledge much more quickly than do their peers. This rapid progress can manifest itself either in breadth or depth of understanding, or both.

It has been argued by some that precocious achievement is entirely explainable in terms of practice: The higher the level of expertise reached by adults in particular domains, the more hours of practice they have put in over their lifetime (Ericsson, Krampe, & Tesch-Roemer, 1993). However, in our view, the conclusion that deliberate practice is *solely* responsible for extraordinary performance is flawed because it is based entirely on correlational evidence and thus cannot tell us whether practice causes high achievement or innate ability leads to extensive practice. Hard work is certainly necessary for extraordinary performance, but the correlational data do not show that hard work is sufficient.

There are at least two empirical reasons to reject this practice-only learning perspective (Winner, 1996a). The first reason is that extreme precocity makes its appearance prior to practice or training. Consider the following examples of prodigious behavior: Peter, who began to draw at 10 months, a behavior that typically emerges around 2 years of age, and drew representationally by age 2, a behavior that typically does not emerge until age 3 (Winner, 1996a); Garett, who read at 18 months (von Karolyi, 1995), a skill typically learned in school at age 6; Adam, who spoke two-word sentences at 3 months, a behavior that typically emerges at 18 months (Feldman & Goldsmith, 1986); and Amy, who did algebra for fun at age 4 (von Károlyi, 1995), a subject not typically learned until junior high school. These startling accomplishments suggest that extremely gifted children come "hard-wired" with both interest and ability in particular domains. The second reason to reject the practice-only learning perspective is that it is impossible to force typical children to spend time attending to something that does not hold their interest. Any parent knows this. Some passion, some rage to master, must drive children to devote uncounted hours to understanding a domain. A rage to master typically accompanies high ability, and both rage to master and high ability must have an inborn, biological component.

A Different Drive

Extremely gifted children are driven by *a rage to master* material in their domain(s) of giftedness, and this rage typically makes itself known in the first few years of life (Winner, 1996a). Peter's drive to draw bordered on obsession: He drew when he awoke, as he ate, as soon as he got home from school, and as often as he could until he went to bed (Winner, 1996a). Such children push themselves and create stimulation for themselves by posing challenging problems to solve. Peter, for example, chose to draw foreshortened forms and figures in motion, and he mixed up the pieces from three different jigsaw puzzles to increase the difficulty of completing the puzzles. KyLee was a self-described "number boy" (Winner, 1996a, p. 39). He had a precocious interest in numbers, evident at age 2, and spent hours using a calculator and memorizing the numbers he read in his environment, such as hotel room doors and license plate numbers. By the age of 5, he had mastered the basics of calculation and spent hours at a time involved in math-related activities. Stephen was a child who read complex musical scores and computer programming manuals for hours at a time when he was in elementary school (Winner, 1996a).

Although it is commonly assumed that parents are pushing these children, just the opposite is usually the case: The parent is running along behind the child trying desperately to keep up. Just as a family's response to a child with mental retardation is molded by the nature of a child's exceptionality (Turnbull & Turnbull, 1990), so, too, is a family's response to a gifted child. Families are profoundly affected (and frequently stressed) by having a child who does things "at the wrong age" and who shows the kind of determination and focus one expects in a highly accomplished adult. The stress is caused not only by having an atypical child but also by having a kind of child for whom our schools are not designed, as we discuss later in this chapter.

A Different Drummer

There is consensus that gifted children do things early and are both better and faster at certain cognitive tasks (Rogers, 1986). Whether they are atypical in how they think, however, is less clear. Based on a review of the extant evidence, Rogers (1986) concluded that gifted students (not specifically extremely gifted) are quantitatively but not qualitatively different from typical students in their thinking. She asserts that they do things earlier and faster, but not in a different way.

Although there are few studies reporting a qualitative difference in the thinking of gifted children, there is some evidence that extremely gifted children are not only faster to develop, but that they develop in atypical ways. First, gifted children have been found to process information in qualitatively distinct ways. For example, compared with typical children, gifted children take *longer* to encode new information (Sternberg & Rifkin, 1979), are more focused on relevant information (Marr & Sternberg, 1986), and develop elaborate associations and representations of new information (Butterfield & Feretti, 1987).

Second, gifted children appear to solve problems in qualitatively distinct ways. They use divergent approaches to problems solving, consider more options when selecting their problem-solving strategies, and are less rigid in their thinking compared with typical students (Jausovec, 1991; Shore, 2000) (for more on the inverse relationship between rigidity and intelligence, see also Schultz & Searleman, 2002). They are also more likely to employ metacognitive strategies than are typical children when solving problems as well as when learning new information (Alexander, Carr, & Schwanenflugel, 1995; Bamberger, 1982; Carr, Alexander, & Schwanenflugel, 1996; Shore, 2000; Swanson, 1992).

Third, gifted children differ qualitatively from typical children in their variable and unpredictable need for adult scaffolding. Some gifted children need almost no adult assistance when learning in their domain. Winner (1996a) described David, a child who learned to read with almost no assistance. By the time he entered kindergarten at the age of five, he was reading at the sixth-grade level.

There are also situations, however, in which gifted children need more adult scaffolding than do typical children. They sometimes need help when school requires them to think and perform like typical children. Amy, a mathematically gifted 8-year-old who learned algebra at home "for fun," was unable to get through her school worksheets because she could not "show her work" and had not memorized her multiplication tables (and seemed to have an aversion to doing so) (von Károlyi, 1995). This child needed and requested adult help with arithmetic but not with algebra. According to her perceptive explanation for this juxtaposition of mathematical strength and arithmetic weakness, "What is hard is easy and what is easy is hard" (Winner & von Károlyi, 1998).

When teachers are unwilling to allow gifted children to process information in their own way, such children may also need adult support. For example, one profoundly gifted 6-year-old spent six hours a day reading and became a natural speed reader. Her fifth-grade teacher read stories aloud to his class and then gave quizzes on the stories. She performed poorly on the quizzes until a creative and counterintuitive solution was found. After consultation with the mother, the teacher determined that this child could not attend to the story because it was being read too slowly and she could not stay focused at such a slow rate. The solution was to allow the child to engage in another activity as she listened to the story. The child chose to read another story *at the same time* as she listened to her teacher reading an entirely different story aloud to the class (C. Morgan-Janes, personal communication, October 1990). To learn effectively, this child needed the extra stimulation of doing two things at once.

These examples support the position that gifted children think in an atypical manner that cannot simply be mapped on to how older, typical children think. Although there is a considerable amount of systematic research documenting precocity in gifted children, much of the evidence describing qualitative differences associated with giftedness is anecdotal. There is, thus, a need for more systematic investigation into qualitative differences in gifted children's thinking in particular domains. Based on what we now know, however, it is reasonable to conclude that extremely gifted children think in ways that are both qualitatively and quantitatively distinct – they march to a different drummer.

Feeling Different

At all levels of giftedness, gifted children are well aware that they are different. They perceive themselves as different from others and feel that others see and treat them differently (Cross, Coleman, & Stewart, 1993; Freeman, 1994; Janos & Robinson, 1985; Janos, Fung, & Robinson, 1985; Robinson, 1990; Subotnik, Kassan, Summers, & Wasser, 1993). Even those gifted students who are exceedingly comfortable with being labeled as gifted report that their parents and close friends treated them differently because of their giftedness (Robinson, 1990).

Feeling different can mean feeling different in a positive way – feeling curious and capable, feeling in command of additional resources, and feeling proud (Subotnik et al., 1993; also see Freeman, 1994). But feeling different from others has been associated in gifted children with reduced self-concept, feeling unpopular, feeling isolated, believing that being smart makes friendships harder, and feeling that one makes others uncomfortable (Cross et al., 1993; Freeman, 1994; Janos et al., 1974; Subotnik et al., 1993). And some gifted children deny their giftedness so as to reduce the feeling of being different (Cross et al., 1993; Kerr, Colangelo, & Gaeth, 1988).

HOW OUR CONCEPTION OF GIFTEDNESS DIVERGES
FROM EXISTING THEORIES

Giftedness traditionally has been construed as exceptional intellectual ability of the sort measured by intelligence tests. Although we include intellectual giftedness in our conception, we see this as just one area in which giftedness can be observed. We are not alone in this perspective: Numerous theorists have proposed broader conceptions of intelligence than that identified by intelligence tests (i.e., Gardner, 1983/1994; Renzulli, 1977; Sternberg, 1986). However, our conception differs from these broader conceptions in its inclusiveness. We do not specify the specific domains in which giftedness can be observed. Instead, we hold that giftedness can occur in *any* domain.

Many contemporary theorists assert that giftedness exists *only* in a social context (i.e., Csikszentmihalyi & Robinson, 1986; Feldman, 1980; Gardner, 1999). In other words, an individual is considered gifted only when society recognizes the individual's high achievements, values achievement of the sort displayed by the individual, and thereby deems him or her gifted. From our perspective, giftedness can exist in spheres that are unrecognized and not valued by society. Although the *operational definition* of giftedness is inextricably bound to and delineated by the social context, we view giftedness as any higher than average ability. Our conception of giftedness can also be applied to other species: Gifted gorillas or racehorses, thus, have a place (Helton, 2003).

IDENTIFYING GIFTED STUDENTS AND ASSESSING THEIR ACHIEVEMENTS

We began this chapter with an assertion that giftedness is not merely a social construct, but also a biological potential. The social context determines whether giftedness is recognized, how it is identified, and how it is educated. In spite of efforts to broaden our conception of intelligence (i.e., Gardner, 1983/1994; Renzulli, 1977; Sternberg, 1986), most schools rely heavily on IQ tests to identify students for gifted programs. If giftedness can exist in any domain, then schools should have ways to identify a range of kinds of giftedness. We do not argue that it is the responsibility of schools to identify all forms of giftedness. But schools should identify those forms of giftedness that are considered to be of value to society. Schools should also then be able to educate these gifted children, including those who are gifted in the extreme.

Currently, there are a number of ways to identify and evaluate giftedness. However, these approaches characteristically assess only intellectual giftedness. Typically, schools employ some combination of IQ tests, achievement tests, and recommendations by teachers, parents, and peers. Out-of-level testing (i.e., taking Scholastic Aptitude Tests [SATs], typically administered to high school seniors, in sixth or seventh grade) has recently gained favor as a means of identifying students for talent searches, and many schools accept extremely high performance on such out-of-level tests as indicators of giftedness. IQ tests remain the most common method of identifying students for gifted programs.

IQ Tests

Traditionally, giftedness is a psychometric term indicating performance at 2+ SDs from the mean on a standardized IQ test (Clark, 1988, 1992; Silverman, 1993). In addition to assessing (culturally embedded) general knowledge, intelligence tests primarily assess verbal–abstract, logical, mathematical, and in some cases, visual spatial reasoning and social cognition (Gardner, 1983/1994, 1999; Kaufman, 1984; Terman, 1925). These tests also measure how well students respond to taking tests (for more on the effect of testing situations on IQ scores, see Steele, 1997; Spencer, Steele, & Quinn, 1999; Steele & Aronson, 1995).

Many theorists hold that the concept of intelligence that is measured by IQ tests is too narrowly defined and fails to value important and relevant human capacities (Ceci, 1990; Feldman, 1980; Gardner, 1983/1994; Getzels & Jackson, 1961, 1962; Guilford, 1967; Renzulli & Smith, 1980; Sternberg 1986; Thurstone, 1938; Torrance, 1981). In addition, there are many limitations and problems associated with the use of IQ tests for identifying gifted children. IQ tests may fail to reflect the intelligence of students with learning, developmental, emotional, and behavioral disorders, as well as students for whom English is a second language or students whose cultural or environmental background deviates substantially from that represented in the test questions. These students are unlikely, for example, to share the body of general knowledge held by children from middle-class suburban backgrounds. As has often been noted, the overreliance on IQ tests to identify gifted students may be responsible, in part, for the underrepresentation of certain minority groups for gifted programming (for a review, see Frasier, García, & Passow, 1995). In spite of serious limitations, IQ tests provide valuable information for many students and are effective at identifying a substantial portion of children who are intellectually gifted. IQ tests may be most valuable for identifying intellectually gifted children who have not achieved at a high level, but who nonetheless have gifted potential.

Promising Solutions

Recently, alternative approaches to these assessment approaches, which target a broader range of abilities, have emerged. For example, Gardner (1991, 2000) proposes that we assess students through *performances of understanding*. According to Gardner, the goal of education is deep understanding of culturally meaningful domains. Surface understanding, he argues, should never be the goal of education. Real understanding of a discipline means grasping its core ideas and being able to apply these to new situations (for more on Gardner's concept of real versus surface understanding, see Gardner, 1991, 2000; see also von

Károlyi, Ford-Ramos, & Gardner, 2003). Performances of understanding allow teachers the opportunity to observe students' progress toward mastery and can also be employed in the assessment and identification of giftedness (von Károlyi, Ford-Ramos, & Gardner, 2003). Student performance of understanding assessments can take a variety of forms and assess a wide range of abilities. They might be productions, demonstrations or exhibitions, debates, models, journals, inventions, or accounts of the processes involved in accomplishing large-scale projects. A portfolio can also be the medium for a performance of understanding.

Portfolios

Portfolios have long been used as a means of assessing ability and achievement in the visual arts. Typically, a portfolio shows a student's progress and achievement through a collection of the student's best work over time. Portfolios can be used to identify giftedness (Kingore, 1993) in any domain (von Károlyi, Ford-Ramos, & Gardner, 2003).

One expanded approach to the use of portfolios is to include student work that illustrates their exploration and progress, in addition to showing examples of best work. Such portfolios have been termed *process-folios* (Wolf, Bixby, Glenn, & Gardner, 1991). Identifying giftedness in multiple domains as well as using an expanded conception of intelligence(s) should increase minority representation in gifted programs.

Kingore (1993) recommends using portfolios to assess complexity, depth, abstraction, and rate of new learning. Student portfolios can also be used to identify creatively gifted students. Using this approach substantially increased the proportion of Hispanic students of low socioeconomic status who were identified for the gifted program of a Texas elementary school (Midkif et al., 2002). Portfolios as an identification tool should be further investigated and embraced by the field.

Dynamic Assessment

Dynamic assessment (Feuerstein, Rand, & Hoffman, 1979) has been used successfully for the identification of gifted students and has been shown to increase the identification of disadvantaged and minority populations (Borland & Wright, 1994; Lidz, 2002). Dynamic assessment is rooted in Vygotsky's (1935/1978) concept of the *zone of proximal development*, which distinguishes between what children can accomplish independently (what traditional tests measure) and what they can accomplish with the scaffolding of more advanced others. Dynamic assessment evaluates students' ability to solve novel problems with assistance. Because dynamic assessment emphasizes the *process* of student leaning, it is a means of evaluating potential rather than achievement.

Recommendations for Assessment

We suggest that schools continue to employ a range of traditional assessment approaches and tools (including IQ testing) for the identification of intellectually gifted children to identify children who are gifted but underachieving or not producing in school. However, we believe that these tests should be supplemented both by portfolio assessment and by dynamic assessment. The use of these two alternative means of assessment would allow us to broaden the domains in which we can assess giftedness and should also identify those who are underrepresented in gifted programs today.

In addition, we speculate that a hybrid of these two approaches, where the new learning occurring during dynamic assessment is evaluated in terms of its extent but also in terms of its rate, depth, complexity, and level of abstraction, could provide another useful identification strategy. Our goal ought to be to identify as many gifted students as possible in those domains deemed by society to be of importance. Of course, once we locate these students, we must provide them with suitable educational opportunities.

EDUCATING EXTREMELY GIFTED STUDENTS

Few disagree that some students are gifted in athletics, music, or art and that such students need advanced training in these fields. Because advanced training in these domains is provided primarily after school or outside of school, provision of such training remains uncontroversial. In contrast, providing a differentiated education to intellectually gifted students invariably elicits objections about elitism and the violation of egalitarianism (e.g., Oakes, 1985). But the cost of failing to provide extremely intellectually gifted children suitable challenges is often ignored. When such children are not challenged, and when they find themselves more advanced than all of the others in the classroom, they may adopt an outcast role, hide their giftedness and underachieve (Whitmore, 1980), or direct their achievement away from academics and toward more socially acceptable activities, such as sports or extracurricular activities.

All children deserve an "equal opportunity to struggle" to learn (Morealle, 1995, p. 4). It is a great disservice to gifted children to allow them to coast, and it sets them up to turn away from challenges. Practicing coping with the feelings of not knowing how to do something, of having to struggle, is an important skill for anyone to develop. This notion is consistent with Vygotsky's (1935/1978) concept of the zone of proximal development. All too often, extremely gifted children's coursework falls below the base of this zone (what a child can already accomplish independently) and precludes new learning. When every student is working within his or her zone of proximal development, every student must stretch intellectually and will thus be engaged in new learning.

In principle, then, schools should provide every child with an individualized education appropriate to his or her zone of proximal development. Providing a differentiated education for each child, however, is not feasible. Schools should at the very least provide an individualized education for each student whose needs vary substantially from those of the majority of students.

Differences in Educational Needs

Extremely gifted children have two pressing needs – to be challenged and to be around like-minded peers (Colangelo & Peterson, 1993; Elkind, 1988; Gross, 1989; Silverman, 1993; Stanley, 1978; Terman, 1925; Webb, Meckstroth, & Tolan, 1982; Winner & von Karolyi, 1998). Actually, these needs are no different from those of all children. The problem is that when the extremely gifted are not given any kind of differentiated education, which is typically the case in the regular classroom (Archambault et al., 1993), neither of these needs are met. A differentiated education for the intellectually gifted can be accomplished in many ways: flexible ability grouping within the classroom for particular subject matters, grade skipping, advanced classes in particular subject matters, advanced classes in all subject matters, and special schools for the gifted. When none of these are feasible, as in rural districts where there may be very few such children, educational plans can be designed so that these children can be challenged individually. This solution, however, only serves the goal of challenging, but leaves untouched the social goal. Alternatively, extremely gifted students can come together for weekly or monthly meetings, but this solution only serves the social goal and does not meet the need for such children to be challenged in school. Interactive televised courses or online courses, commonly used at the college level, can also be employed across grade levels to provide *virtual* grouping of extremely gifted students. Whatever methods are employed, it is critical for such children to be challenged and to share time with one another. Without suitable opportunities to learn new things and interact with like-minded peers, extremely gifted children feel isolated, bored, and unhappy.

Addressing Differences in Educational Need

Because extremely gifted students are so atypical, what they need to learn and possibly how they need to learn will also be atypical. If, as we assert, gifted children's thinking differs both quantitatively and qualitatively from that of typical children, the education of gifted children should be both quantitatively and qualitatively differentiated. We know that acceleration and compacting curriculum (removing previously learned and redundant material and allowing the student to proceed through the coursework at an accelerated rate) benefits gifted children (Rogers, 1998), but we also need to develop and evaluate programs designed specifically to address qualitative differences in gifted children's processing. We need to compare the effects of grouping gifted children and providing them with qualitatively differentiated educational experiences versus accelerating them and thereby grouping them with older but typical students. It is likely that a gifted 6-year-old and a typical 12-year-old who perform equally on a math achievement test may, nevertheless, think sufficiently differently about the mathematics that they would benefit from separate classes employing qualitatively different instructional approaches. Parents and teachers of extremely gifted children should pay attention to the atypical timetables and processing of these children and follow these children's lead as they march to a very different drummer.

According to many gifted children and their parents, complexity is a delight and fundamentals are torture. Schools often deny extremely gifted children suitable educational experiences because their learning is so out of sync with educators' expectations. A child who has not yet mastered arithmetic facts is typically not allowed to learn algebra or geometry. The child who has such a rage to master advanced skills might be allowed to learn fundamentals in an advanced context.

Even if all schools were to implement exemplary gifted programs, there would remain some extremely gifted students whose needs cannot be met in school. Tutors and mentors can help educate extremely gifted children. And some parents choose to teach their children at home all or part of the time. In the current educational environment, many families of gifted students must resort to homeschooling (Feldman & Goldsmith, 1986; Hollingworth, 1942; Brangham & Hughes, 1995) in response to their dissatisfaction with how our schools currently educate gifted students. Although homeschooling can be an effective solution for some families of extremely gifted students, it is not a solution for all. Not all families have the skills or resources needed for homeschooling.

Equity demands that we challenge *all* children to reach somewhat beyond what they can do on their own. Given that we mandate education for all students, schools should provide all students suitable education. Following, we propose two school-based, individualized approaches to educating extremely gifted students.

A Two-Pronged Approach

Winner (1996a) recommended implementing a two-pronged approach to the challenge of educating gifted children. First, educational standards and expectations should be raised for *all* students. Schools in East Asia and Western Europe hold standards that far exceed those of schools in the United States (Riley, 1993). There is evidence that when the bar is raised, many will rise to meet the challenge, including those at the bottom (Knight & Stallings, 1995; Peterson, 1989). Raising standards will not only improve the educational attainments of our typical students, but will also mean that most moderately gifted children will be appropriately challenged and therefore will not need gifted programming.

The second prong of the solution is to identify those children who still need additional challenges even when schools are more challenging. These will be the extremely gifted students, those who perform several years ahead of their peers in one or more subject areas. Once these students have been identified, they should be provided suitably challenging advanced coursework. Why not bring the high school model of advanced classes down to the elementary school level? Our schools could provide advanced instruction in basic academic subjects beginning in first grade. These classes need not be labeled as classes for the gifted, but simply as classes for students who want and need advanced instruction in a particular subject.

We suggest that, on a trial basis, students have the opportunity to self-select into advanced classes whose pace and level are genuinely advanced and not watered down. If suitably taught, these classes should draw in some gifted students who have not been otherwise identified as gifted. They will also draw in students who are not gifted but who are high achievers or extremely motivated. An IQ score should be irrelevant for entry: If a student can do the work, that student should be let in; if a student is let in and proves unable, that student should be counseled out with no shame.

Adult guidance should be available to assist students to make appropriate decisions about whether to take this sort of advanced course and to encourage students who would benefit from such classes, but who might not self-select such classes for social reasons or because of a lack of self-efficacy, and so on. In addition, disadvantaged children with high potential should be offered extra support, such as after-school tutoring, Saturday classes, or summer programs to prepare them for such advanced coursework.

An advanced coursework approach can be used as a screening tool to identify students who should be referred for further assessment. It is important to distinguish between those who do poorly in such advanced classes because they are in over their heads and those who do poorly because they still are underchallenged. Extremely gifted students should be allowed to select from advanced coursework offered at all grade levels.

The Case-Manager Model

As alternative to Winner's (1996a) two-pronged approach is an approach developed by von Károlyi and Wilson (1997). In this model, educational plans for each gifted child are developed and implemented by a team. The team is led by a case manager who is a specialist in gifted education. As is typical in team meetings for students with other sorts of special educational needs, the team is made up of the student, the parents, the teacher, the school psychologist, an administrator, and the guidance counselor. Ideally, a mentor or an advocate who works with the student over a number of years would also be part of this team. The team goal is to develop, implement, and regularly update a suitable educational plan for each extremely gifted student. The personalized educational plan (PEP) provides the framework for differentiation. Such a plan could include any number of approaches, including advanced classes, ability grouping, independent work, work with mentors or tutors, apprenticeships, multidisciplinary projects (e.g., Hollingworth's [1926] *evolution of common things* curriculum), enrollment in a magnet school or in special programs for gifted students (e.g., those provided by many talent-search programs), or even, when appropriate, curriculum differentiation within the traditional classroom.

Each member of the team has a well-defined role in the development of the gifted student's PEP. The age, needs, motivation, and temperament of the extremely gifted student will affect the roles that the other team members play. The student would be involved in planning, implementing, and evaluating the PEP; would participate in at least one team meeting a year; would communicate regularly with the case manager; and would agree to periodically reevaluate the plan.

The teacher's responsibility is to follow the PEP for each extremely gifted student in his or her charge and to provide feedback to the student, parents, and case manager about the student's progress and the effectiveness of the PEP. The teacher must learn about the characteristics of this population and the specific characteristics of each gifted student in his or her charge by becoming familiar with the student's record and consulting with the case manager. The teacher must create a classroom atmosphere that welcomes diversity and individual differences and must refuse to tolerate stereotyping and the use of demeaning terms or name-calling in the classroom. He or she must also create an environment of safety to express unusual opinions. Finally, the teacher must be flexible and willing to adapt to the changing needs of the gifted student.

A gifted-education specialist acts as a case manager for the gifted student to ensure that the PEP is suitable and suitably implemented. The case manager helps the student to work on developing his or her input for the PEP, acts as a liaison and consultant for the team members, and chairs the team meetings. The case manager seeks resources for the student and provides in-service training to teachers. The guidance counselor's role is to provide early career guidance, monitor the student for risk of dropping out of school, and help the student deal with social or emotional issues that arise in response to being gifted.

The case manager model of gifted education draws heavily on the model employed for students with other sorts of special educational needs and thus could be implemented in a variety of settings, ranging from public schools to special schools for the gifted. A modified version of the case manager model could also be employed by partial homeschoolers (families whose children attend school part-time) who wish to draw on some of the resources available in their local school system.

A well-designed PEP provides the sort of individualization needed by extremely gifted children. Using a team approach ensures that a variety of ideas contribute to the development of such a plan. It also ensures that each team member is informed about the characteristics, needs, and interests of each gifted child and is invested in meeting those needs.

Winner's (1996a) two-pronged approach urges higher expectations and standards for all students and individualized opportunities for students who remain underchallenged in spite of such improvements. The case manager model (von Károlyi et al., 1997) provides a framework for creating personalized plans using a team approach. Although both approaches are based on what we know about extremely gifted children, research is needed to determine whether these particular approaches are the best ones possible for educating extremely gifted children. There is little doubt, however, that either of these approaches would be considerably more effective than what most schools currently do (or fail to do) for these children.

CONCLUSIONS AND RECOMMENDATIONS

Extremely gifted children are different. They develop on a different time-table, their drive is different, they march to a different drummer, and they feel different from others. They are very different from one another as well. As a society, we must pinpoint those areas of giftedness that we value and wish to develop. Then, we must develop and test new approaches to identifying giftedness (such as Gardner's [1991; 2000] performances of understanding; Borland & Wright's [1994] and Lidz' [2002] approaches to dynamic assessment; and Kingore's [1993] or Wolf et al.'s [1991] approaches to portfolio assessment). Individualization and differentiation are essential if we are to educate extremely gifted children, and we must develop and test new approaches to educating these students (such as Winner's [1996a] two-pronged approach and von Károlyi et al.'s [1997] case manager model). Finally, we must train educators not only about the nature, identification, and education of extreme giftedness, but also about how to address the educational needs of the specific gifted children in their charge.

References

Alexander, J., Carr, M., & Schwanenflugel, P. (1995). Development of metacognition in gifted children: Directions for future research. *Developmental Review, 15*, 1–37.

Archambault, F. X., Westberg, K. L., Brown, S. W., Hallmark, B. W., Zhang, W., & Emmons, C. L. (1993). Classroom practices used with gifted third- and fourth-grade students. *Journal for the Education of the Gifted, 16*(2), 103–119.

Bamberger, J. (1982). Growing up prodigies: The midlife crisis. *New Directions for Child Development, 16*, 62–77.

Borland, J. H., & Wright, L. (1994). Identifying young, potentially gifted, economically disadvantaged students. *Gifted Child Quarterly, 38*(4), 164–171.

Brangham, W., & Hughes, K. (Producers). (1995, May). *Turning point: Whiz kids.* [Television broadcast]. New York: American Broadcasting Company.

Butterfield, E. C., & Feretti, R. P. (1987). Toward a theoretical integration of cognitive hypotheses about intellectual differences among children. In J. G. Borkowski & J. D. Day (Eds.), *Cognition in special children: Comparative approaches to retardation, learning disabilities, and giftedness* (pp. 195–233). Norwood, NJ: Ablex.

Carr, M., Alexander, J., & Schwanenflugel, P. (1996). Where gifted children do and do not excel on metacognitive tasks. *Roeper Review, 18*, 212–17.

Ceci, S. J. (1990). *On intelligence–more or less: A bio-ecological treatise on intellectual development.* Englewood Cliffs, NJ: Prentice Hall.

Clark, B. (1988). *Growing up gifted: Developing the potential of children at home and at school* (3rd ed.). Columbus, OH: Merrill.

Clark, B. (1992). *Growing up gifted: Developing the potential of children at home and at school* (4th ed.). New York: Macmillan.

Colangelo, N., & Peterson, J. S. (1993). Group counseling with gifted students. In L. K. Silverman (Ed.), *Counseling the gifted and talented* (pp. 111–129). Denver: Love.

Cross, T. L., Coleman, L. J., & Stewart, R. A. (1993). The social cognition of gifted adolescents: An exploration of the stigma of giftedness paradigm. *Roeper Review, 16*(1), 37–40.

Csikszentmihalyi, M., & Robinson, R. E. (1986). Culture, time and the development of talent. In R. J. Sternberg & J. E. Davidson (Eds.), *Conceptions of giftedness* (pp. 264–284). New York: Cambridge University Press.

Delisle, J. R. (1992). Guiding the social and emotional development of gifted youth: A practical guide for educators and counselors. New York: Longman.

Elkind, D. (1988). Acceleration. *Young Children, 43*(4), 2.

Ericsson, K. A., Krampe, R. T., & Tesch-Roemer, C. (1993). The role of deliberate practice in the acquisition of expert performance. *Psychological Review, 100*(3), 363–406.

Feldman, D. H. (1980). *Beyond universals in cognitive development.* New York: Ablex.

Feldman, D. H., & Goldsmith, L. T. (1986). *Nature's gambit.* New York: Basic Books.

Feuerstein, R., Rand, Y., & Hoffman, M. B. (1979). *The dynamic assessment of retarded performers: The Learning Potential Assessment Device theory, instruments, and techniques.* Baltimore: University Park Press.

Frasier, M. M., García, J. H., & Passow, A. H. (1995). *A review of assessment issues in gifted education and their implications for identifying gifted minority students* (Research Monograph 95204). Storrs, CT: The National Research Center on the Gifted and Talented, University of Connecticut.

Freeman, J. (1994). Some emotional aspects of being gifted. *Journal for the Education of the Gifted, 17*(2), 180–197.

Gardner, H. (1983/1994). *Frames of mind: The Theory of Multiple Intelligences.* New York: Basic Books.

Gardner, H. (1991). *The unschooled mind: How children think & how schools should teach.* New York: Basic Books.

Gardner, H. (1999). *Intelligence reframed: Multiple Intelligences for the 21st century.* New York: Basic Books.

Gardner, H. (2000). *The disciplined mind: Beyond facts and standardized tests, the K-12 education that every child deserves.* New York: Penguin.

Getzels, J. W., & Jackson, P. W. (1961). Family environment and cognitive style: A study of the sources of highly intelligent and of highly creative adolescents. *American Sociological Review, 26*(3), 351–359.

Getzels, J. W., & Jackson, P. W. (1962). *Creativity and intelligence: Explorations with gifted students.* New York: Wiley.

Gross, M. U. M. (1989). The pursuit of excellence or the search for intimacy? The forced-choice dilemma of gifted youth. *Roeper Review, 11*(4), 189–194.

Guilford, J. P. (1967). *The nature of human intelligence.* New York: McGraw-Hill.

Helton, W. W. (2003). *The development of expertise: Animal models?* Unpublished manuscript, Wilmington College.

Hollingworth, L. S. (1926). *Gifted children: Their nature and nurture.* New York: Macmillan.

Hollingworth, L. S. (1942). *Children above 180 IQ. Stanford–Binet: Origin and development.* New York: World Book.

Janos, P. M., Fung, H. C., & Robinson, N. M. (1974). Self-concept, self-esteem, and peer relations among gifted children who feel different. *Gifted Child Quarterly, 29*(2), 78–82.

Janos, P. M., & Robinson, N. M. (1985). Psychosocial development in intellectually gifted children. In F. D. Horowitz & M. O'Brien (Eds.), *The gifted and talented: Developmental perspectives* (pp. 149–195). Washington, DC: American Psychological Association.

Jausovec, N. (1991). Flexible strategy use: A characteristic of gifted problem solving. *Creativity Research Journal, 4,* 349–366.

Kaufman, A. S. (1984). K-ABC and giftedness. *Roeper Review, 7*(2), 84–86.

Kerr, B., Colangelo, N., & Gaeth, J. (1988). Gifted adolescents' attitudes toward their giftedness. *Gifted Child Quarterly, 32*(2), 245–247.

Kingore, B. W. (1993). *Portfolios: Enriching and assessing all students, identifying the gifted grades K-6.* Des Moines, IA: Leadership.

Knight, S., & Stallings, J. (1995). The implementation of the Accelerated School Model in an urban elementary school. In R. Allington & S. Walmsley (Eds.), *No quick fix: Rethinking literacy programs in American elementary schools.* New York: Teachers College Press.

Lidz, C. S. (2002). Mediated Learning Experience (MLE) as a basis for an alternative approach to assessment *School Psychology International, 23*(1), 68–84.

Marr, D. B., & Sternberg, R. J. (1986). Analogical reasoning with novel concepts: Differential attention of intellectually gifted and nongifted children to relevant and irrelevant novel stimuli. *Cognitive Development, 1,* 73–78.

Midkif, D., Shaver, C. M., Murry, V., Flowers, B., Chastain, S., & Kingore, B. (2002, November). *The challenge of change: Identifying underrepresented populations.* Paper presented at the 49th Annual Convention of the National Association for Gifted Children (NAGC). Denver, CO.

Morealle, C. J. (1995). Rights of students. *Highly Gifted Children, 10*(4), 4.

Oakes, J. (1985). *Keeping track: How schools structure inequality*. New Haven, CT: Yale University Press.

Peterson, J. M. (1989). Remediation is no remedy. *Educational Leadership, 49*(6), 24–25.

Renzulli, J. S. (1977). *The enrichment triad model: A guide for developing defensible programs for the gifted and talented*. Mansfield Center, CT: Creative Learning Press.

Renzulli, J. S., & Smith, L. H. (1980). An alternative approach to identifying and programming for gifted and talented students. *Gifted Child Today, 15*, 4–11.

Riley, (1993). *National excellence: A case for developing America's talent*. Washington, DC: U.S. Department of Education.

Robinson, A. (1990). Cooperation or exploitation? The argument against cooperative learning for talented students. *Journal for the Education of the Gifted, 14*, 9–27.

Rogers, K. B. (1986). Do the gifted think and learn differently? A review of recent research and its implications for instruction. *Journal for the Education of the Gifted, 10*, 17–39.

Rogers, K. B. (1998). Using current research to make "good" decisions about grouping. *National Association of Secondary School Principals Bulletin, 82*(595), 38–46.

Schultz, P. W., & Searleman, A. (2002). Rigidity of thought and behavior: 100 years of research. *Genetic, Social & General Psychology Monographs, 128*(2), 165–209.

Shore, B. M. (2000). Metacognition and flexibility: Qualitative differences in how gifted children think. In R. C. Friedman (Ed.). *Talents unfolding: Cognition and development* (pp. 167–187). Washington, DC: American Psychological Association.

Silverman, L. K. (Ed.). (1993). *Counseling the gifted and talented*. Denver: Love.

Spencer, S. J., Steele, C. M., & Quinn, D. M. (1999). Stereotype threat and women's math performance. *Journal of Experimental Social Psychology, 35*(1), 4–28.

Stanley, J. S. (1978). Educational non-acceleration: An international tragedy. *Gifted Child Today, 1*(3), 2–5, 53–57, 60–63.

Steele, C. M. (1997). A threat in the air: How stereotypes shape intellectual identity and performance. *American Psychologist, 52*(6), 613–629.

Steele, C. M., & Aronson, J. (1995). Stereotype threat and the intellectual test performance of African Americans. *Journal of Personality & Social Psychology, 69*(5), 797–811.

Sternberg, R. J. (1986). A triarchic theory of intellectual giftedness. In R. J. Sternberg & J. E. Davidson (Eds.), *Conceptions of Giftedness* (pp. 223–243). New York: Cambridge University Press.

Sternberg, R. J., & Rifkin, B. (1979). The development of analogical reasoning processes. *Journal of Experimental Child Psychology, 27*, 195–232.

Subotnik, R., Kassan, L., Summers, E., & Wasser, A. (1993). *Genius revisited: High IQ children grow up*. Norwood, NJ: Ablex.

Swanson, H. L. (1992). The relationship between metacognition and problem solving in gifted children. *Roeper Review, 15*(1), 43–48.

Terman, L. M. (1925). *Genetic studies of genius*. (Vol. 1). Stanford, CA: Stanford University Press.

Thurstone, L. (1938). *Primary mental abilities*. Chicago: Chicago University Press.

Torrance, E. P. (1981). Emerging conceptions of giftedness. In Walter B. Barbe & J. S. Renzulli (Eds.), *Psychology and the education of the gifted* (3rd ed., pp. 47–54). New York: Irvington.

Turnbull, A. P., & Turnbull, H. R. (1990). *Families, professionals and exceptionality* (2nd ed., pp. 114). Columbus: Merrill.

von Károlyi, C. (1995). How weird and how unbelievable, how strange this child is. *Highly Gifted Children 10*(4), 1, 17–18.

von Károlyi, C., Ford-Ramos, V., & Gardner, H. (2003). Giftedness from a Multiple Intelligences perspective (pp. 100–112). In N. Colangelo & G. A. Davis (Eds.), *Handbook of gifted education.* (3rd ed.), Needham Heights, MA: Allyn & Bacon.

von Károlyi, C., & Wilson, G. (Eds.) (1997). The gifted and talented program team. *Gifted and talented education: Report of recommendations from the Advisory Committee to the SAD 35 School Board.* (Available from Maine School Administrative District 35, Eliot, Maine 03903).

Vygotsky, L. S. (1935/1978). Interaction between learning and development. In L. S. Vygotsky (Ed.), *Mind in society: The development of higher psychological processes* (M. Cole, V. John-Steiner, S. Scribner, & E. Souberman, Eds. and Trans., pp. 79–91). Cambridge, MA: Harvard University Press. (Original work published 1935.)

Webb, J. T., Meckstroth, E. A., & Tolan, S. S. (1982). *Guiding the gifted child: A practical source for parents and teachers.* Ohio Psychological Press.

Weisstein, E. W. (n.d.). *Ramanujan, Srinivasa (1887–1920). Eric Weisstein's World of Science.* Retrieved November 22, 2003, from http://scienceworld.wolfram.com/biography/Ramanujan.html.

Whitmore, J. R. (1980). *Giftedness, conflict and underachievement.* Needham Heights, MA: Allyn & Bacon.

Winner, E. (1996a). *Gifted children: Myths and realities.* New York: Basic Books.

Winner, E. (1996b). The rage to master: The decisive case for talent in the visual arts. In K. A. Ericsson (Ed.), *The road to excellence: The acquisition of expert performance in the arts and sciences, sports and games* (p. 271–301). Hillsdale, NJ: Lawrence Erlbaum Associates.

Winner, E., & von Károlyi, C. (1998). Giftedness and egalitarianism in education: A zero sum? *National Association of Secondary School Principals Bulletin 82*(595), 47–60.

Wolf, D. P., Bixby, J., Glenn, J., & Gardner, H. (1991). To use their minds well: Investigating new forms of student assessment. In G. Grant (Ed.), *Review of research in education* (Vol. 17, pp. 31–74). Washington, DC: American Educational Research Association.

22

Making Giftedness Productive

Herbert J. Walberg and Susan J. Paik

What may best distinguish our approach from that of others is its emphasis on accomplishment in the case of children and youth, and eminence in the case of adults. For us, accomplishment rather than potential is the best indication of giftedness. Giftedness is only one of several factors that may affect how much a person attains over the course of childhood, youth, or a lifetime. For example, without large amounts of intensive practice, parental support, and expert instruction, giftedness rarely comes to full fruition.

Though fundamentally psychological and educational, our approach is derivative of the "new economics" that broadly applies well-established economic principles to explain human behavior outside its traditional monetary purview, including learning, human and social capital, marriage, divorce, crime, addictions, suicide, and other phenomena (Becker, 1976). This economic approach employs only a few central ideas to parsimoniously explain and predict a wide variety of human behavior.

Provocative and productive, new applications of economics echo the original Greek meaning of the term – the management of household affairs. Though founded in agreed-on theory, the economic principles accord well with common sense and have many practical applications. For example, dealing with scarcity – not just of money, but of time, energy, and attention – is a classic problem not only of economics but of human life. Economists also influence policy makers because they explicitly quantify the benefits, costs, and risks that should weigh heavily in rational decision making.

Can economic ideas help us think more clearly about making giftedness fruitful or, in the language of economics, "productive"? The "opportunity costs" of notable accomplishment or eminence in violin playing preclude top ballet performance and world-class chess. To reach a field's pinnacle may require a decade of a child or youth's intense concentration and, as a consequence, the sacrifice of other valuable pursuits. The highest accomplishments require not only such "foregone opportunities," but also the effortful "investments" of dedicated parents, expert teachers, eminent practitioners, and peers competing for the highest standards. Though difficult to impute, value of the "social capital," attention, and time invested may far outweigh the monetary costs.

Should investments be broad or concentrated? Though general knowledge and skills in language and mathematics are foundations of many pursuits, deep knowledge and exemplary mastery of a special, even a very narrow, field is often most prized. In our modern "division of labor," such special expertise enables eminent individuals to provide the breakthroughs and otherwise missing ingredients for solving problems and achieving great feats. Modern technology and communications, moreover, increasingly make for a "winner takes all" phenomenon. Why listen to a second-rate hometown cellist or read less than top-ranked writing when the world's best are now readily available in convenient modern media, particularly the Internet?

Thus, goals and costs should weigh heavily for youngsters who may have potential for making their giftedness productive. Much psychological research shows that setting specific, challenging goals leads to higher performance than setting easy goals, "do your best" goals, or no goals. "Goals," it has been concluded, "affect performance by directing attention, mobilizing effort, increasing persistence, and motivating strategy development. Goal setting is most likely to improve task performance when the goals are specific and sufficiently challenging ... feedback is provided ... the experimenter or manager is supportive, and assigned goals are accepted by the individual" (Lock, Shaw, Saari, & Latham, 1981, p. 125).

Time costs should also be a crucial consideration. East Asian K–12 students generally achieve the highest test scores in the world in mathematics and science. Asian countries have challenging, nationally uniform school achievement goals, and students spend from 80 to 100 percent more total hours in regular and tutoring schools and in homework during the first 18 years of life (Paik, Wang, & Walberg, 2002).

"Scarcity," a fundamental idea in economics, suggests how productive giftedness might be realistically considered. Out of 1 million piano, chess, or basketball players, perhaps 1, 10, or 100 can make a living in one of these fields. Perhaps 1, 2, or none are truly world class. Such scarce fruition of giftedness is likely to be generously rewarded in prestige, honor, and compensation – but perhaps not in happiness.

For these reasons, "modern portfolio theory of investment" should loom large in the thinking of parents, teachers, coaches, policy makers, and the gifted themselves. Financial investment of all assets in one stock may result in high gain at high risk but may also result in catastrophic loss. Investing all of a child's attention and time, and parents' money, in support of chess or one of the performing arts is highly unlikely to yield monetary returns or even much recognition. Yet, it might. And the pursuit may be more satisfying than any result, even though such calculations of the future are subject to great risk, uncertainty, and subjectivity.

The conventional solution to the risk problem in financial investment is "diversification" in a portfolio of items preferably unrelated to one another so that even if one does not prove fruitful, another might. Thus, by analogy, the aspiring violinist takes Advanced Placement biology in case a medical career later seems practical. Yet, a "trade-off" is implied: The time taken from the violin for science may mean second-rate violin playing and the possible disappointment or delight of finding one calling or another. Had Isaac Newton and Albert Einstein been more scientifically encouraged as youngsters, would they have contributed even more to physics instead of engaging in public affairs?

Neither economics nor psychology can answer the vexing value questions raised by such career possibilities. But, along with wise parents and expert teachers and coaches, both disciplines can help illuminate what is required for accomplishments and even eminence in various fields so that parents and youngsters can make informed decisions. Toward that end, this chapter explains the findings of our research program and sets forth what makes for exceptional performance in school and in nonacademic pursuits. It summarizes our studies of the childhood traits and environments of eminent men of Western history and of 20th-century American women, as well as the family and school environments of 20th-century gifted adolescents.

CONCEPTIONS OF PRODUCTIVE GIFTEDNESS

More than two centuries ago, Adam Smith (1776) declared that the wealth of nations depends not only on financial and physical capital such as money, land, buildings, and machines but also the "complementary" abilities of people. As interpreted in this century, "human capital" refers to workers' knowledge and skills – assets that are by far the most valuable to themselves and society. Because our attention and time are severely limited, allocating them efficiently to developing human capital is the key to creativity, prosperity, and the quality of life. Parents' and educators' efforts to develop youths' portfolio of knowledge and skills are perhaps the best of all long-term investments.

PORTFOLIO THEORY

Productive giftedness may be better understood if costs and benefits are better understood or even imputed and analyzed. Childrearing costs, for example, may be thought of as foregone earnings of parents; increased adult earnings of the child may be viewed as a primary benefit. Investments to make giftedness productive, however, may be motivated by nonmonetary benefits: Productive giftedness may bring not only honor and prestige to the individual but also great benefits to society, such as a medical breakthrough or artistic insight.

The nonmonetary rewards may include altruistic satisfaction in seeing others benefit from one's work and the joy of creative accomplishment – subjective but real incentives for accomplishment and eminence. The productively gifted may also be paid more, but the work of outstanding writers and artists might be recognized as outstanding long after its production or even after their demise. Clear examples are James Joyce (1882–1941), perhaps the greatest novelist of the 20th century, and Paul Gauguin (1848–1903), now recognized as one of the greatest Postimpressionists.

And what drives such people to give so much to their chosen endeavors? Some would argue it is the intrinsic satisfaction of their work or the pursuit of truth or beauty. The new economics would suggest that incentives matter and assume that we do better under explicit or implicit compensation that rewards merit or results. In addition to money, the broader new economic view of incentives may include honor, obligation, reciprocity, religion, family, friendship, altruism, teamwork, and other motivators.

Such a variety of intrinsic and extrinsic motivators may apply in various intensities, depending on the person and setting. Though plausible, such motivators seem poorly understood and unreliably measured because investigators must usually rely on self-reports of people who may not assuredly know what really drives them.

Motivators and incentives, moreover, may change unpredictably. As in financial investments, which bear risks of unpredictable changes in preferences, styles in fields of accomplishment may change, which affects the value of social and human capital invested in them. Skilled trial advocacy today is as valuable as it was a century ago, but the styles of contemporary music change rapidly. The classic profession of law appears more stable than artistic pursuits. For these reasons, pursuing productive giftedness in various fields may vary from a wild speculation to a blue chip investment.

VALUE OF LONG-TERM INVESTMENT

Some children begin school with a "comparative advantage." Their parents may transfer to them not only the advantages of wealth, but of genes and stimulating environments. Musically talented parents, for example, may transfer genetic potential, provide models, and enrich the child's musical environment. Children with greater endowments, advantages, and acquired skills may have much greater continuing opportunities during childhood and over a lifetime than others, even from the same school and neighborhood.

Such "Matthew effects" are cumulative advantages that characterize human capital investments throughout a period of time (Walberg & Tsai,

1983). The amount invested in a person in a given period is statistically proportional to that already invested: "To him that hath," according to Matthew in the Bible, "shall be given, and he shall have abundance." In productive giftedness, precociousness naturally draws parental encouragement and attracts superior coaches and teachers. The early years may be critical, not only in initially developing giftedness, but in allowing more time for giftedness to bear fruit, which is analogous to the principle of compound interest that means that even small annual returns over a long period yield a huge future value.

Studies of Nobel laureates in science suggest that "the rich getting richer" theory also may apply throughout life (Merton, 1968). There are, for example, huge advantages to starting a scientific career early. The benefits of rigorous high school and university study, early undergraduate or perhaps even high school exposure and work with eminent scientists, publishing early, and initial job placement multiply over time to produce highly skewed productivity in scientific work. A combination of such rare circumstances and individual giftedness results in as few as a tenth of scientists producing nine-tenths of the important, highly cited work. Similarly, distinguished faculty and students, grants, intellectual contacts, and other factors lead to continuing and often increasing distinction of institutions over long periods of time.

What Matthew effects accomplish in essence may be an early investment from sustained, concentrated efforts. In the following sections, the research of Simon, Campbell, Sternberg, Bloom, and Walberg is cited to explain the psychology of such sustained efforts and their consequences.

PSYCHOLOGICAL EXPLANATIONS OF PRODUCTIVE GIFTEDNESS

Human Information Processing

Simon's (1954) "Berlitz model" is an example of acquiring and processing special knowledge over time. The model involves learning a second language, one of the more difficult adult tasks that demand considerable time, effort, and concentrated attention involved in practice. More practice, however, makes the language easier. Ease increases pleasantness and pleasantness increases practice. Excessive difficulty may slow practice because it is unpleasant; but if learners persevere through difficulty, learning is likely to again become pleasant, and further practice leads to mastery.

Simon (1981), Sternberg and Davidson (1985), and others have shown the same fundamental thought processes appear to be required in both elementary and advanced learning, although their stores of knowledge and the speeds of problem solving differ. The major constraints on acquiring knowledge and skill are the few items of information that can be processed and the 5 to 10 seconds it may require to store an item in long-term memory.

Experts have stored huge amounts of information in permanent memory for ready access and efficient processing. They have indexed information in many ways and can bring it rapidly to conscious memory, even if some of the index links are broken.

Even children differ greatly in their stores of information and rates of accessing it, which enables some children to acquire and process new information more quickly than others. As Sternberg and Davidson (1985) report, "Precocious children form connections at a much more rapid rate than ordinary children, and exceptional adults have formed exceptionally large numbers of variegated stimulus–response connections" (p. 44).

The greatest advantage of the expert and obstacle for the novice is chunking – clustering abstract elements of knowledge. Simon (1981) estimates that 50,000 chunks may be required for the expert mastery of a special field (i.e., about the same magnitude as the recognition vocabulary of college-educated readers). The highest achievements in various disciplines may require a memory of 1 million chunks, which may take even the talented about 70 hours of concentrated effort per week for a decade, although Mozart and Bobbie Fisher were seven- to nine-year exceptions.

Even so, even the most eminent masters might have been able to acquire and process much more had circumstances been ideally productive, for example, all the youngster's attention and time were concentrated on one endeavor. According to Simon (1981), about 200 million items could be stored in a lifetime. "Hence, the problem for the human being is to allocate his very limited processing capacity among several functions of noticing, storing, and indexing on the input side, and retrieving, reorganizing, and controlling . . . on the output side" (p. 167).

Problem Solving

Sir Isaac Newton (1777–1855) was once asked how he managed to surpass the discoveries of his predecessors; he replied, "By always thinking about them" (Fenn, N.R. [Ct]). Gauss (1643–1727) said, "If others would but reflect on mathematical truths as deeply and continuously as I have, they would make my discoveries" (http://en.thinkexist.com/quotation/if_others_would_but_reflect_on_mathematical/181371.html). Both Newton and Gauss knew what it would take to discover profound truths – practice, persistence, and thoughtful perseverance. Although discovery may occur in a split second, it usually requires a decade of preparation and commitment in a specialized field. Newton and Gauss are examples of gifted individuals who, through opportunity, concentrated efforts, and perseverance became eminent in their fields. Claude Monet (1840–1926) and Pablo Picasso (1891–1973) may have surpassed nearly all modern visual artists in the totality and versatility of their work, partly because they continued painting throughout their long lives.

Concentrated efforts involve creative problem finding and solving – the trial and error search for innovative and practical solutions of stored and externally found elements. For experts, items are elaborately associated with one another to facilitate in trial-and-error problem solving. According to Campbell (1960), trial and error suffices to explain creative thought as well as other mental processes. Blind-variation-and-selective-retention processes are "fundamental to all inductive achievements, to all genuine increases in knowledge, to all increases in fit of system to environment" (p. 380). "For this reason, three conditions for creativity are necessary: a mechanism for introducing variation, a consistent selection process, and a mechanism for preserving and reproducing the selected variations" (p. 381).

Similarly, according to Sternberg and Davidson (1985), "individuals may be gifted in cognitive functioning of the kinds measured by conventional tests; contextual fitting that requires adaptation to, selection of, or shaping of environments; and the ability to deal with novelty or to automatize information processing effectively" (p. 42). Our point about these psychological conceptions is that notable accomplishments require large investments of the individual's time and concentration. Also crucial is the "social capital" of parents, coaches, and teachers as well as the means and media that may be required in various fields.

WHAT MAKES GIFTEDNESS PRODUCTIVE?

Productive giftedness implies both value and scarcity. To bear maximum fruit, a child's or an adult's giftedness must be nurtured by multiple causes over multiple time periods. Any one of these causes and time periods may be necessary but insufficient by itself. Rather, it seems that sustained application of the necessary causes seems crucial for eminence or the highest levels of accomplishment.

Loehle (1994) suggests that individual scientific discoveries are multiplicative products of cumulative events. For example, suppose a scientific discovery requires 20 necessary steps, such as asking the right question, setting forth a researchable hypothesis, gaining financial support for the research, developing a detailed research plan, hiring capable assistants, supervising them, collecting data, analyzing it, drawing graphs, drafting a paper, submitting it to a scientific journal, and so on. Even if each step has an easy 90 percent probability of success, the multiplicative product $(0.9 \times 0.9 \times 0.9 \ldots)$ or probability of project completion is only 12 percent. This poor overall success rate explains why many scientists rarely or never publish articles and why productive giftedness or eminence is rare.

As applied to childhood development of eminence, the causes appear more general, but no less crucial. Bloom (1985) conducted research on how giftedness or extraordinary talent is developed among concert pianists, sculptors, research mathematicians, research neurologists, Olympic swimmers, and tennis champions. His study examined the roles of teachers, parents, and out-of-school personnel in the developmental process. One of the findings of these studies was that once parents became aware of their child's exceptional talent, they took a more active role in developing that talent. In many cases, parents employed special out-of-school coaches, teachers, programs, and institutions to maximize their children's early giftedness. Of course, the specific means vary from field to field, but the general factors – discussed in a subsequent section – such as parental encouragement, appear similar.

Those who excel earlier tend to excel later because their earlier and later social environments tend to give them similar advantages. A child musically stimulated at age 2 is more likely than others to be further stimulated as an adolescent. Early environments, particularly parental stimulation, predict later environments, and both have an impact on learning and the degree of later accomplishment. Early influences provide a background of early achievement, which increases the rate of progress. With some exceptions, eminent adults tend to work diligently, choose their goals carefully, and once committed, complete difficult tasks.

The word "workaholic," with its pejorative overtones, is only a recent invention. Accomplished individuals, in any case, are exceedingly well organized – hard workers who often routinize or leave to others time-consuming tasks that contribute little to their accomplishment. One clear example is Thomas Jefferson, who, along with scientist/inventor/artist Leonardo da Vinci, was one of the few people in history who was eminent and highly accomplished in more than one field. An active plantation farmer, architect, ambassador to France, and president of the United States two-time, he conducted world-class research on agronomy and botany and wrote books, pamphlets, and tens of thousands of letters on a variety of subjects.

At his Monticello home, Jefferson set his bed in an alcove between two rooms, which enabled him to rise in either room. "A typical day for Jefferson started early, because, in his own words, 'Whether I retire to bed early or late, I rise with the sun.' He told of a 50-year period in which the sun had never caught him in bed; he rose as soon as he could read the hands of the clock kept directly opposite his bed."

In his pockets, Jefferson carried scales, drawing instruments, a thermometer, a surveying compass, and a level. To record his observations, he carried a forerunner of today's personal digital assistant, a bound set of small, reusable ivory note pages for penciling observations that could later be transferred to permanent ink records.

Jefferson invented ingenious time-savers, such as a manuscript copying mechanism, a desk stand that could rotate any one of several projects to his attention, and the equivalent of a modern database of letters organized by correspondent and date, any one of which could be sent

TABLE 22.1. *Three Sets of Nine Productivity Factors*

Aptitude includes:
(1) ability or prior achievement, as measured on the usual standardized tests;
(2) development, as indexed by age or stage of development; and
(3) motivation or self-concept, as indexed by personality tests or willingness to persevere on learning tasks.

Instruction includes:
(4) the amount of time students engage in classroom learning and
(5) the quality of the instructional experience including both its psychological and curricular aspects.

The aspects of the psychological environment that bear on learning are:
(6) the curriculum or academic environment of the home;
(7) the social climate of the classroom group;
(8) the peer group outside school; and
(9) (negative) exposure to mass media, notably, television.

---

for while abroad. For other instances of Jefferson's concentration, habits, and work aids see, for example, http://www.monticello.org/jefferson/dayinlife/sunrise/home.html. Wouldn't it be fascinating to find out and compile such personal predilections of Aristotle, Mother Teresa, and other productively gifted people of ancient and modern times?

Enhancing Educational Productivity

Though a necessary determinant of productive giftedness, hard work alone can hardly be the only cause. Psychologists have long been interested in identifying the factors that promote academic and other learning in general and among gifted students in particular. The following paragraphs explain a nine-factor theory of educational productivity and review research that indicates how academic learning can be enhanced and giftedness can be made productive by educational and psychological means. Several thousand comparisons show that the amount and quality of instruction and stimulation in classrooms, homes, peer groups, and mass media have consistent and powerful effects on learning (Walberg, 1984a). When taken as a whole, the factors that promote learning can be increased, which promotes a disciplined mastery of a general or specialized field. Research syntheses (or "meta-analyses") of many studies of the nine factors show that learning can be made far more productive. Quantitative estimates of the effects show the factors to be potent, consistent, and widely generalizable. These nine factors fall into three groups shown in Table 22.1. Specific aspects of the factors and the magnitude of their effects are specified elsewhere (Walberg, 1984a) and are illustrated in a subsequent section of this chapter.

Research consistently shows that the home and school can serve as places of continual stimulation and encouragement for a child. For reasons of first learning and quantity of time alone, the home is foundational and of continuous importance; about 92 percent of children's time in the first 18 years of life is under the responsibility of parents, and only 8 percent is spent in school (Walberg, 1984a). Home influences include informed parent–child conversations about school and everyday events; encouragement and discussion of leisure reading; monitoring and talking about television and peer activities; deferral of immediate gratifications to accomplish long-term human capital goals; and providing a warm, nurturing environment where the child's basic needs are met and ideas and habits may be constructively challenged.

The nine-factor productivity model posits that factors can be adjusted and, when optimized, can be powerful. For example, in the classroom, specific methods of teaching and certain new programs in schools may be more effective than others (i.e., mastery learning, cooperative learning, and adaptive education). To teach habits associated with hard work, parents and teachers can provide supportive environments. Parents should be invested in their child's education, and teachers can offer demanding courses, assign reasonable amounts of well-designed homework, and provide incentives to stimulate and reward hard work.

PRODUCTIVE GIFTEDNESS AMONG HISTORICAL FIGURES

The nine factors found to promote academic learning have also proven helpful in studying the lives of accomplished adolescents and the childhoods of eminent men and women of history. This section provides an overview of common childhood traits and learning environments, which may be useful in designing experiences and programs for all students, including the gifted.

Eminent Men

Walberg (1981) and 76 other scholars studied the leading biographies of more than 200 eminent men born between the 14th and 20th centuries, including Bacon, Beethoven, da Vinci, Darwin, Dickens, Goethe, Lincoln, Milton, Napoleon, Newton, Rembrandt, Voltaire, and Washington. We rated their childhood characteristics and environments through age 13. The sample traces back to the turn-of-the-century work of James McKean Cattell, founder of the biographical volumes called *American Men and Women of Science*. In 1903, Cattell listed in rank order 1,000 eminent men according to the number of words that had been written about each in American, English, French, and German biographical dictionaries.

Statistical analysis of our ratings revealed the prevalence of intellectual competence and motivation, social and communication skills, general psychological wholesomeness, and both versatility and perseverance during childhood. Cultural stimuli, materials related to their field of eminence, teachers, parents, and other adults were clearly indicated for most eminent individuals. Most of the men had clear parental expectations for their conduct, but they also had the opportunity for exploration on their own.

The most distinctive rating of all the childhood traits was estimated intelligence, which was rated superior for 97 percent of the sampled men. The brightest, however, were not necessarily the most eminent. Character traits and early environments also counted. Research on contemporary adolescents and adults suggests that only a minimal level of measured intelligence may be necessary as one of the several factors predictive of success. Without sufficient opportunities, intelligence and motivation may count for little.

Stimulating family, educational, and cultural conditions during childhood were strong indicators of later eminence. Seventy percent of the men had clear parental expectations; but nearly 9 out of 10 were permitted to explore their environments on their own. A little more than half were encouraged by parents, and the majority was encouraged by teachers and other adults. Many were exposed to eminent adults at an early age. More than a majority were successful in school and liked it, and less than a quarter had school problems. The majority of men also showed a large number of distinctive affective traits that collectively suggest psychological wholesomeness. Being ethical, sensitive, solid, magnetic, optimistic, and popular were common traits. About a quarter to a third of the sample, however, showed introversion, neuroses, and physical sickliness. Only 38 percent were rated tall, but the majority were handsome and possessed vitality.

As we pointed out in our initial studies, the biographical accounts undoubtedly contained cultural and historical bias, and our ratings may have been additionally prejudiced by our own times and predilections. What may have been conducive for eminence in past centuries may no longer apply.

Even in the sample, there were outstanding exceptions to what may seem inevitable causes of eminence: Consider Lincoln, perhaps one of our two or three greatest presidents. He had to help his illiterate parents in Illinois fields and had little time for his tiny, one-room school. Still, his family moved from Kentucky to Illinois because of his father's ardent abolitionist beliefs, which may have given Lincoln the will to face the Civil War. In any case, whatever biases and exceptions in drawing inferences from biographies, it is fascinating to read about the traits and early environments of unquestionably eminent contributors to Western civilization and to reflect on what may have been the reasons for their accomplishments. (Hearing stories and reading about them may serve to inspire gifted children and adolescents; it may also inform them of sacrifices others have made to achieve productive giftedness.)

Eminent Women

Sicherman and Green's (1980) careful and exhaustive work with many scholars to objectively identify eminent American women of the 20th century made it possible for us to extend our work with a similar biographical rating form. The women included skater Sonja Henie, actress Ethel Barrymore, singer Mahalia Jackson, athlete Babe Didrikson Zaharias, businesswoman Helena Rubinstein, blind and deaf leader Helen Keller, poet Marianne Moore, painter Grandma Moses, reformer Margaret Sanger, educator and civil rights leader Mary McLeod Bethune, scientist Rachel Carson, suffragist Jeannette Rankin, and political leader Eleanor Roosevelt. Referencing from one to six biographies, we rated the early traits, conditions, and experiences through age 13 of each of the 256 eminent women.

The most common psychological trait of eminent women during childhood was the same as the previous study on men – intelligence. More than half of the women showed high intelligence in their early years. The other top-ranking traits for both men and women were perseverance and hard work, especially in music and the visual arts.

The eminent women shared a number of traits in their childhoods that can be divided into four categories:

1. force of character – strong willed, vital, confident, adventurous, single-minded, challenging, emotionally secure, energetic, and joyful in work;
2. independence – imaginative, creative, original, well traveled, alert to novelty, inquisitive, and questioning of conventions;
3. intellectual competence – precocious, knowledgeable, well informed, versatile, and broad interests; and
4. academic propensity – bookish, well read, scholarly, skillful in writing, and positive school attitudes.

One third to half of the women were directly taught or strongly encouraged by fathers, mothers, or other adults. Three in 10 girls had clear parental expectations, yet nearly a fourth were allowed to explore on their own. Forty-six percent came from financially advantaged families, though more than half came from culturally advantaged families. More than a third were exposed to cultural materials and stimulation, which may or may not have been related to their current fields.

PRODUCTIVE GIFTEDNESS AMONG ADOLESCENTS

Are such early traits and conditions also associated with productive giftedness of 20th century adolescents? We carried out two studies to answer this question.

Artists and Scientists

From a large, random national sample of high school youngsters, we identified those gifted in science and the arts (Walberg, 1969a). Those defined as gifted in science had won science contests. Artistic accomplishment was similarly identified; writers, for example, had their work published in a newspaper or magazine. We asked gifted and other students 300 questions about their motives, abilities, circumstances, and attitudes toward school and life. We analyzed their answers to find out how the scientifically and artistically accomplished adolescents differed from one another and from other students in their classes.

Both scientists and artists described themselves as friendly, outgoing, and self-confident, but they were more likely to find books more interesting than people. Both groups were interested in mechanical and scientific objects and the arts. Bookish, they liked to read outside of school, especially professional and technical books. They enjoyed visiting libraries and had numerous books at home. They liked school and worked harder and faster than their peers. They were also interested in finely detailed work and were persistent in finishing their tasks.

Both groups were interested in and confident of their own creativity and intelligence. Both groups were also ambitious and set high values on their future education and salary. Even so, the scientists and artists chose creativity more often than did others in identifying the best characteristic to develop in life and less often chose wealth and power.

How did the groups differ from one another? Scientists seemed preoccupied with things and ideas rather than people and feelings. They had more difficulty relating to others and may have avoided intense emotional closeness. Scientists were task-oriented and persisted through difficult tasks, and were attracted to academic work and detail. Scientists were more interested in presenting truth than portraying the aesthetic value of the project. Scientists dated less and were more bookish.

Scientists expressed more confidence in their own intelligence, whereas the artists felt this way about their creativity. More than artists, scientists tended to favor "security" as the best characteristic of a job. Artists were preoccupied with communication of inner feelings, whereas scientists were more singleminded and determined in conceptualizing external reality. In contrast to the group winning no awards in science or the arts, artists and scientists appeared wholesome and ambitious.

Gifted Adolescents

As a follow-up to the previous study, we drew another national random sample to study the traits and conditions of gifted adolescents, including school leaders who had held a significant class office or other position in the school or community (Walberg, 1971). Corroborating others' previous studies, the study showed conventional intelligence measures were very weakly related to giftedness. The gifted students in science, artistic fields, and leadership, nonetheless, were different from those who did not achieve distinction. The gifted groups thought they were more creative and imaginative. Most liked school and received good grades, but questioned their teachers more often than others. They thought that it was important to be intelligent, studied and read outside of school, had numerous books at home, and inquired of adults about occupations. They were also able to persist through difficult tasks.

In contrast to scientists, artists characteristically had more diversified, less concentrated interests and opportunities. Artists, particularly musicians and theatrical performers, had more opportunities outside of school than in school and were less persistent in their studies. In summary, though all gifted groups were more actively involved in school than other students, scientists and group leaders tended to be more involved in academic life than did performers and musicians. The findings show that accomplished groups in different fields resemble one another more than they resemble students who are not as accomplished or have not won any awards or distinction.

CONCLUSION

Our studies lead us to think that productive giftedness is best indicated by present accomplishment, sometimes even in childhood. Though exceptions can be noted, excellent second-grade readers are more likely than others to become editors of a school or college newspaper and possibly even eminent writers in adulthood. A high school student who completes Advanced Placement courses in calculus, biology, chemistry, and physics is far more likely than others to become an outstanding physician or scientist. Even the visual and performing arts have very few eminent "late bloomers." American folk artist Grandma Moses (1860–1961), who began painting in her 70s, is such an exception (perhaps in part because of her three-decade career).

Economic theory, research on the nine factors shown in Table 22.1, the biographies of eminent men and women, and studies of outstanding adolescents suggest to us that early childhood and adolescent traits and psychological conditions are far more important than conventionally measured intelligence in productive giftedness. The traits include will power, perseverance through difficulties, sufficient independence to originate and sustain new ideas despite others' objections, and deep knowledge and mastery of a specialized field. Gifted students, particularly in science and other academic subjects, tend to be bookish and successful in school.

Of course, many exceptions can be noted. Usually focused on the arts and sciences, for example, few studies have been made of the childhoods of attorneys, business people, and politicians – even though they are no less important in American society. Sayings about their preparation, however, offer telling caveats about what might be concluded about the possible linkages of preparatory academic success and adult success. In business, it is said with a grain of insight – or salt – that the "A" students become professors, and "B" students work for "C" students.

Finally, as illustrated in our previous works and better in the biographies we relied on, we point with respect to the huge importance of parents, teachers, coaches, and others who encourage productive giftedness. They encourage. They inform. And they provide resources, advantages, and opportunities.

References

Becker, G. S. (1976). *The economic approach to human behavior*. Chicago: The University of Chicago Press.

Bloom, B. S. (1985). Generalizations about talent development. In B. S. Bloom (Ed.), *Developing talent in young people*, pp. 507–549. New York: Ballantine.

Campbell, D. T. (1960). Blind variation and selective retention in creative thought as in other knowledge processes. *Psychological Review, 67*, 380–400.

Cattell, J. M. (1903, February). A statistical study of eminent men. *Popular Science Monthly*, 359–377.

Fenn, N. R. (Ct). Sir Isaac Newton and his diamond in the ruff (n.d). Retrieved November 1, 2004, from www. Selfgrowth.com/articles/Fenn28.html.

Lock, E. A., Shaw, K. N., L. Saari, M., & Latham, G. P. (1981). Goal setting and task performance. *Psychological Bulletin, 90*, 125–152.

Loehle, C. (1994). A critical path analysis of scientific productivity. *Journal of Creative Behavior, 18*, 33–47.

Merton, R. K. (1968). The Matthew effect in science, *Science, 159*, 56–63.

Monticello: The Home of Thomas Jefferson. A Day in the Life of Thomas Jefferson: "I rise with the sun." Retrieved November 1, 2004, from www.monticello. org/jefferson/dayinlife/sunrise/home.html.

Paik, S., Wang, D., & Walberg, H. (2002). Timely improvements in learning. *Educational Horizons, 80*(2), 69–71.

Sicherman, B., & Green, C. H. (Eds.) (1980). Notable American women: The modern period. Cambridge, MA: Harvard University Press.

Simon, H. A. (1954). Some strategic considerations in the construction of social science models. In P. Lazarsfeld (Ed.), *Mathematical thinking in the social sciences* (pp. 123–142). Glencoe, IL: Free Press.

Simon, H. A. (1981). *Sciences of the artificial*. Cambridge, MA: MIT Press.

Smith, Adam. (1937/1776). *Wealth of nations*. New York: Random House.

Sternberg, R. J., & Davidson, J. E. (1985). Cognitive development in gifted and talented. In F. D. Horowitz & M. O'Brien (Eds.), *The gifted and talented* (pp. 156–178). Washington, DC: American Psychological Association.

Thinkexist.com. My quotation book. Retrieved November 1, 2004, from http://en.thinkexist.com/quotation/if_others_would_but_reflect_on_mathematical/181371.html.

Walberg, H. J. (1969a). A portrait of the artist and scientist as young men. *Exceptional Children, 36,* 5–11.

Walberg, H. J. (1969b). Physics, femininity, and creativity. *Developmental Psychology, 1,* 45–54.

Walberg, H. J. (1971). Varieties of creativity and the high school environment. *Exceptional Children, 38,* 111–116.

Walberg, H. J. (1981, Summer). Childhood traits and environmental conditions of highly eminent adults. *Gifted Child Quarterly, 25,* 103–107.

Walberg, H. J. (1984a). Improving the productivity of America's schools. *Educational Leadership, 41,* 19–27.

Walberg, H. J. (1984b, May). *National abilities and economic growth.* Paper presented at the American Association for the Advancement of Science, New York.

Walberg, H. J., & Tsai, S. L. (1983). Matthew effects in education. *American Educational Research Journal, 20,* 359–374.

23

The Actiotope Model of Giftedness

Albert Ziegler

Every empirical science must first determine its object of investigation. In most cases, this is predetermined by a cultural imprint. In the case of empirical giftedness research, the roots reach back to the beginning of the last century. Many scholars were fascinated by the phenomenon that some persons act much more efficiently in particular fields than others. It seemed to be completely out of the question that a normal person would be able to attain this same level of efficiency, even through extensive learning and with the best means of support. However, terms such as *gifts*, *talents*, or *genius* were suggested as causal explanations – regardless of the fact that they originated from mythological, theological, and metaphysical traditions (Ziegler & Heller, 2002).

No science can be content with nonscientific concepts in the long run. Consequently, the theoretical development in the last century was marked by the longing to determine what these terms "really" meant and to supply them with an empirical substance. Obviously, this attempt only makes sense if there are entities within the human psyche that correspond to these terms. Unfortunately, this has only rarely, with a few notable exceptions (e.g., Margolin, 1994; Tannenbaum, 1983), been subjected to serious scrutiny. Fascinating terms such as *genius* or *talent* were bandied about, and a spectacular quest for the psychic entities with which these names could be christened was inaugurated.

The first momentous attempt to replace talent with a psychological construct was made by Terman (1925). In his empirical work, gifts were synonymous with high intelligence. His research program, which indisputably led to valuable results for scholars interested in intelligence, turned out to be of less importance for conceptions of giftedness. The first reason was the lack of explanatory power intelligence has for excellence in the academic domain and in the career area (e.g., Simonton, 2000; Trost, 2000).

The second reason can be traced to the great demands that were placed on the explanatory power of gifts and talents. For example, DeHaan and Havighurst (1957) defined talents as extraordinary achievements in one of the following areas: intellectual abilities, creative thinking, scientific abilities, social leadership qualities, mechanical abilities, and artistic abilities. This wide-ranging abundance of phenomena exceeded the explanatory power of one psychological construct by far.

A logical consequence was to eliminate the limitation of gifts and talents to one psychological construct. One alternative was to subclassify intelligence into *several intelligences* (e.g., Gardner, 1983/1994). A further alternative was to assign gifts to an *ensemble* of several psychological variables as suggested by Sternberg (2003) or Renzulli (1986). However, neither the multiplication of intelligence nor its enhancement through additional psychological variables was able to procure more than a partial clarification of what gifts or talents really were and what role they played in the emergence of achievement excellence.

Observations of current developments in this field reveal an improvement in the so far unsatisfactory prognostic ability and explanatory power of the preceding trait models through the integration of various environmental variables. For example, Mönks (1992) expanded the three-ring conception of giftedness developed by Renzulli (1986) by including the influences exerted by peers, parents, and teachers. A further attempt was the Differentiated Model of Giftedness and Talent (DMGT) developed by Gagné (2000, 2003), in which the environment acts as a catalyst of talents. Gagné's model is fascinating and a substantial advancement because, by including intrapersonal catalysts, he also postulates an environment of talents and gifts *within* the individual himself. However, models that actively take the environment into consideration are also, as was the case with their predecessors, subject to several fundamental objections:

(1) The individual is still conceptualized as being the "owner" of gifts and the question is one of drawing a connection between the gifts and the appropriate psychological concepts. The possibility that these mystic entities do not exist and that there is nothing to map onto the psychological concepts is still largely underestimated. (2) Although the environment is assimilated into these models, it is only of interest with respect to the unidirectional influence it has on gifts. Gifts remain the focus of such models, and gifts (sometimes talents) explain excellence as proximal variables – a perfect example of the powerful attraction of centralized explanations (Kelly, 1994). (3) Unfortunately, there are currently no empirical studies that make a critical comparison of the explanatory power of different conceptions of giftedness. Which conception of giftedness one tends to favor is a question of taste, not a question of the thorough consideration of empirical findings.

ANCHORING THE STATE OF GIFTEDNESS RESEARCH

In my opinion, the situation portrayed demands a "conceptual reboot." First, the central assumptions of giftedness research should be thoroughly scrutinized. Second, a theoretical regeneration of the actual object of giftedness research should be undertaken, that of excellence in various areas.

The Sleep Argument: Gifts are Not Personal Attributes!

With a few notable exceptions (e.g., Margolin, 1994), gifts have been conceptualized as the properties of an individual. However, such approaches would be caught in a predicament if it could be shown that talents or gifts emerge and disappear with changes in environmental factors. Such a case would clearly demonstrate that giftedness and talent must be something more than mere personal attributes and that at least the environment in which an individual is acting must be integrated into the construct.

Let us assume that the rules for the game of basketball were altered so that the basket now hangs 20 cm lower than previously dictated. This would seriously reduce the significance of height for success in this game. Let us consider the point in time where this rule comes into effect. All of a sudden, many players who were considered to be gifted in this domain would "lose" their gift, and many for whom nobody had seriously prophesied a big future in this game would now experience a "gain" in their talent. This situation is not different from the position many theoretical physicists found themselves in as the computer revolution came into full gear. Suddenly, success in this domain was more or less bound to the ability to be able to generate computer-based simulations of complex physical processes.

I now imagine two young basketball players and two young theoretical physicists. I differentiate the first two on the basis of height, the second two on the basis of computer skills. They are both at home asleep at that moment in time when, respectively, the rule change in basketball becomes valid, and the computer revolution takes place. Even with the most sensitive of measuring instruments, we would not be able to confirm any type of change in the personality characteristics of the basketball players or the theoretical physicists at this point in time!

The only thing that has changed, other than the basketball rules and the start of a new computer generation, has happened in our own heads. *We* as researchers no longer see plausible opportunities for the tall basketball player and the theoretical physicist with insufficient computer skills to attain excellence in their domains. *We* as researchers no longer consider them to be talented. *We* as researchers can now, however, recognize the possibility that the shorter basketball player and the theoretical physicist with good computer skills can attain excellence in their domains. *We* as researchers now consider them to be talented.

Let us make clear: Talents and gifts are not personal attributes, but attributions made by scientists. These are based on our assumptions that a person is in the position to carry out specific *actions* in the future (e.g., great shots in basketball, discoveries in theoretical physics). To keep these assumptions substantiated, we have to renounce a rather convenient approach: norm orientation. The reward here is that we will be better situated to understand two stubborn problems facing gifted researchers: the domain problem and the Aldrin effect.

Norm Orientation and Its Disagreeable Consequences

Giftedness research attempts to explain efficient actions in specific domains that other persons are apparently not able to realize. In our reading of the last sentence, we can put more emphasis on either the phrase "other persons" or "apparently not able to realize." Focusing on the latter phenomenon would have opened a productive path for empirical research; unfortunately, the other path was preferred in giftedness research. Through social norms, the meaning of the phrase "apparently not able to realize" was provided by a statistical trick. Let us assume that, for example, the top 10 percent of performers in a specific domain are defined as gifted. Whether this domain is particularly supported or whether those active in this domain work harder than persons active in other domains does not contribute to the psychological meaning of "apparently not able to realize." At any random point in time, this 10 percent will be guaranteed – regardless of the domain we are talking about.

The Domain Problem. The rigorous orientation on norms creates the problem that we are no longer able to make comparisons of excellence from different domains. How many people have learned how to play the violin; how many have learned the contrabass? How many people have run the 100-meter sprint; how many have experience in synchronized swimming? How many people have had their skills in mathematics placed under analysis; how many in archaeology? Aren't the demands placed on violinists, sprinters, and mathematicians much higher with respect to achievement prerequisites, necessary learning practice, and the achievement levels they have actually attained when they aspire to attain excellence in these areas? Don't contrabass players, synchronized swimmers, and archaeologists profit somewhat from the "Big Fish–Little Pond effect" (Marsh, 1987)?

Investigations of excellence in the areas of music, sports, and academics must take such differences into consideration. In athletics, for example, it has long been decided that a thorough specification analysis of the actions required for the individual types of sports should be undertaken. These supply a starting point on which one can assess whether a person is in the position to eventually perform these actions after extended learning.

A conception of giftedness cannot effectively operate as a scientific theory as long as it objectifies a random percentage of persons. More appropriate objects of investigation are specific *actions*. However, one must also be more precise here, because we customarily focus on the product of actions, not on the actions themselves, which in itself leads to problems.

The Aldrin Effect. A few moments after Neil A. Armstrong made history as the first human being to set foot on the moon, the action was "copied" by Edwin "Buzz" Aldrin. Armstrong has been celebrated as a hero; Aldrin has been just about forgotten. Similar effects have been reported on actions in giftedness research. A spectacular example can be found in the work of Qin and Simon (1990). They provided college sophomores with the data set used by Kepler. Some of the students were actually capable of recognizing, in less than an hour, the mathematical relationships in this data set, which Kepler needed 10 years to verify. Were these university students just as gifted as Kepler, who many consider to be a genius? Is this measurement of excellence comparable?

An orientation on norms is neither capable of providing the motivation nor is it the means to be able to accurately investigate the qualitative similarities or differences between the actions taken by Kepler, who surmounted the physicists of his time, and the randomly chosen and otherwise not particularly conspicuous students. However, the caveat made in the last section, that we should focus on actions in giftedness research, must also be specified at this point. Obviously, it would not suffice to merely consider the *product* of actions. One would also want to include the means (e.g., pocket calculator) or prior knowledge (e.g., socialization in an antiempirical era versus an era marked by an express awareness of technology and the natural sciences) in the analyses, because they obviously exercise an important influence on the actions one is in the position to engage in.

Although products of actions are definitely of interest from an analytical perspective, they are not, however, the actual object of the analysis. But if not the products of actions, what is it about actions that we need to focus on if we intend to use them as the manifestation of excellence? Intuitively, we incline to refer to the genesis of these actions in our answer. A brief glance herein, however, completely disrupts our traditional approaches to the phenomenon of excellence, because it brings up aspects that we cannot analyze within our models.

A Look at the Entire Complexity: The Curie Problem

One can safely assume that Marie Curie would never have been in the position to experience her extraordinary career if she had not made the decision to leave her homeland of Poland. In the year 1891, she sent a gripping letter to her sister Bonia, who was living in Paris at the time. She related that she had decided to pursue an academic career in Paris and asked for support. Bonia agreed to this. One can single out several further crucial stations in Curie's life, such as the matriculation at the Sorbonne or the fact that no one had discovered the existence of polonium and radium before she did, and that this offered her the opportunity to work in a field ideally suited to her specific talents. If we want to include the genesis of the excellence of Marie Curie in our analyses, then don't we also need to consider the chain of decisions, "random" events, and particular circumstances that were necessary for a woman to be able to sustain the most brilliant of scientific careers at that point in time?

Gagné (2003) recognized the necessity of incorporating such occurrences into the explanation of excellence. However, his concept of "chance" seems at present to be rather unspecific and operates rather as a "miscellaneous" category. The question is whether a better, more systematic possibility can be found to embrace such critical life events into a scientific model of giftedness. However, it is questionable whether such complex processes can be portrayed in linear causal models. In fact, a system theoretic approach is much more suitable in this case. However, before we venture to take the first steps into this new area, we need to first take a step back to the phenomenon itself, that is, to excellence in different domains and its development.

Back to the Phenomenon: A Few Consequences Taken from Biographies of Persons Demonstrating Excellence

Despite the existence of literally thousands of biographies on eminent persons (e.g., Simonton, 1994) and an immense number of participants in empirical investigations on expertise and talent (e.g., Ericsson, 1996), we are still not yet in possession of a reliable outline of the prototypical course of the development of excellence. From what we have been able to learn so far, I hold the following points to be instructive with respect to the direction in which a model of giftedness should be developed. In this listing, I introduce a few new terms, which will be explained in greater detail in later passages of this text.

(1) From a descriptive perspective, it becomes obvious that the development of excellence ensues over a long period of time, which, as a rule of thumb, takes about 10 years (Ericsson, Krampe, & Tesch-Römer, 1993). Although reports abound that some persons are able to attain exceptional

achievements before this period of time has elapsed, the fascination here seems to be rather more a result of the seemingly young age of so-called prodigies and less so in the achievements themselves, which seldom reach the level of an adult deemed to have attained excellence (Howe, Davidson, & Sloboda, 1998). These long periods of time necessitate the establishment of a *developmental perspective* in the explanation of excellence (Mönks & Mason, 2000).

(2) Characteristic of the developmental process of excellence is the execution of an extremely large number of *actions* in a specific domain. According to various estimations (e.g., Ericsson, 1998), these add up over time to a total of about 10,000 hours of intensive learning practice.

(3) Actions in a specific domain are governed by various *goals*. During the first phase, the pleasure derived from playing the game itself is the principal factor. The next phase is dominated by consequential improvement in performance. When a specific achievement level has been reached, under certain circumstances, the opportunity is then open to speak of the utilization of excellence. The predominant objective is now a faultless execution of skills by the person in question, for example the performance of a violinist during a concert. However, goals can also be identified on further, much more specific levels.

(4) The development of excellence can be described as a successive and continual expansion of *action repertoires*. A person who is at first only able to solve simple arithmetic problems will later be able to solve algebra problems or problems that necessitate the mastery of infinitesimal calculus. The intrapersonal factors that are involved in bringing about interindividual differences in attainment of action repertoires has yet to be clarified. In my opinion, learning theories (e.g., Ericsson et al., 1993), cognitive theories (e.g., Sternberg, 1986), sophisticated syntheses of learning and trait approaches (e.g., Gagné, 2003; Schneider, 2000), and genetic approaches (e.g., Thompson & Plomin, 2000) can all make valuable contributions.

(5) An individual can, at any random point in time, be characterized as a source of effervescent wishes (Gollwitzer, Heckhausen, & Steller, 1990; Heckhausen, 1991). Usually, a wide array of alternative actions that could be taken to realize one of these wishes is continuously at his or her disposal. When acting, an individual has already chosen specific actions out of the universe of those that were subjectively available, which we might term a *subjective action space*.

The courses of action that are available in the subjective action space are not only a necessary precondition for acting, they define the action limits as well. Writers, for example, report that they suddenly suffer from a lack of confidence, experience periods of self-doubt, and may wind up with writer's block. In other words, no potential action course could be represented in their subjective action space that would allow them to continue their artistic accomplishment.

(6) The enormous degree of organization inherent in the learning process, wherein the *environment* plays an immense role, is impressive. For example, the attainment of academic excellence is utterly impossible without the support of professional instruction. In the school, situations are staged in such a manner that those actions taken best enable optimal learning. Trained pedagogic personnel keep track of the learning progress; learning times, learning locations, learning material, and learning content are determined. Similar conditions can be identified for other known areas of excellence, including athletics, music, and chess. In these fields, excellence would also be far out of reach without competent and meticulous planning. In general, one observes that with the increasing degree of expertise in the learner, the environment becomes increasingly more professional and more tailored to his or her specific learning needs.

(7) The concepts addressed – development, action, goals, action repertoire, subjective action space, and environment – are components of a *network*. Network means that these areas overlap. For example, goals are the objective of every action, which had been represented in the subjective action space and which must also be available in the action repertoire. Network also means that these areas interact in many manners. Alterations in one of the components always implicate alterations for the other components. For example, new goals will result in other actions or a change in the intensity of the present action. Actions also always effect a change in the environment, and so on.

(8) The interactions and reciprocal influences of the components are not random events; they can rather be described as functioning in the form of feedback loops. For example, a good tennis coach who discovers a weakness in the backhand of his protégé during a training session would not merely try to work out this flaw in the current session. In contrast, he would create a learning situation in which an opponent would pointedly and repeatedly focus play on the weaker backhand of the protégé. Within a short period of time, several dozen learning opportunities could be applied to improve the backhand. In this case, a good trainer would offer competent feedback in that comments would be repeatedly given in a feed-forward loop until he was satisfied with the resulting change in behavior.

A First Summary

The intent of the previous passages was to make the following points clear:

- Gifts and talents are *not* personal attributes.
- An orientation on social norms proves to be ill-suited for the concept of excellence. The focus of the analysis should be on actions and their determinants, rather than on persons and their characteristics.

- In answering the question of whether a person will ever attain excellence, social norms are not very helpful. Instead, one should refer to a specification analysis of the actions we expect to find among persons who demonstrate excellence. This examination will provide us with information needed to concretely address the question of whether this person, through learning, will eventually be in the position to acquire the competencies required to act out these actions.
- One must take a large number of variables into consideration in this assessment, which not only deal with the current action repertoire and its determinants, but also goals, subjective action space, and in particular environmental aspects.
- In making this analysis, we must also be prepared to incorporate interactions among the components as well as feedback loops into the process.
- The results of previous analyses lead me to question whether excellence can adequately be investigated within the framework of causal linear models. Instead, it appears to me as though a theoretical approach must be taken which demonstrates the following properties. It must be:
  - *action-oriented*, instead of trait-oriented;
  - *individualistic*, because the constellations of conditions and learning processes that lead to excellence are always unique;
  - *holistic*, in the sense that it permits the analysis of disparate entities and processes within a single theoretical frame;
  - *systemic*, because the entities and processes are related to one another in that they have the common goal of the optimization of excellence; and
  - *attachable* to existing and not yet advanced theories of the conditions and the development of excellence.

AN OVERVIEW OF THE ACTIOTOPE MODEL OF GIFTEDNESS

According to an observation made by Kauffman (1995), science in the 18th century, following the Newtonian revolution, was for the most part the science of organized simplicity. The science of the 19th century focused, via statistical mechanics, on disorganized complexity. Only in the 20th and 21st centuries did one start to come to terms with organized complexity. In the Actiotope Model of Giftedness, excellence is also considered a result of self-organization and the adaptation of a highly complex system. The focus is no longer on personal attributes, but on actions and their development within a complex system. Theoretical access is enabled by system theory, in particular, the complexity theory.

System theories constitute a wide-ranging and multifaceted area; their overviews now fill volumes. Even a brief account of the area would be neither necessary nor meaningful. I am content here to describe the application of the system theory in the Actiotope Model of Giftedness and to point out the fundamental processes involved.

Let us begin with a very basic principle, which most researchers would undoubtedly agree on, to serve as a starting point for further considerations. One characteristic of living systems is that they develop *and* evolve. In the short run – according to general consensus – the sustainment of a system always has priority; in the long run, it is in jeopardy of extinction if it fails to evolve. Indeed, the concept of the evolution of dynamic systems is not limited to species, but can also be transferred to social groups[1] (e.g., von Cranach & Bangerter, 2000) and individuals.

Living systems maintain themselves and evolve both within and alongside the exchange with their environments and the systems contained therein (coevolution). They are simultaneously interacting with several systems, which are also simultaneously evolving. When, for example, a boy develops a new basketball skill, he not only expands his own action repertoire and can therefore pursue new goals. His newly won ability is also now available to his basketball team. The integration into various systems contributes thereby to the network as a whole.

The comprehensive potential of system theory enables an exploratory transfer of this heuristic analogy of evolving living systems to individual development and the phenomenon of excellence. Admittedly, our context is bound to a few important deferrals. In contrast to the development of a species, we are no longer interested in (1a) the maintenance and evolution of a (2a) species in a (3a) habitat, but rather efficient (1b) actions and their evolution for an (2b) individual in a (3b) specific talent domain. In an analogy to the system of environment and species, which is referred to as a *biotope*, the action system that encompasses the environment and the individual is referred to as an *Actiotope*.

The Components of an Actiotope

Figure 23.1 illustrates the components of the Actiotope Model of Giftedness. To keep the figure intelligible, their interactions and functions were limited to a noteworthy subset. Detailed specifications can be found in the corresponding text.

---

[1] It is remarkable that investigations have almost exclusively concentrated on gifted individuals, but no gifted groups have been subjected to investigation. This appears to be overdue in a time in which we are just as familiar with the excellence of teams (e.g., research teams, sport teams, orchestras) as we are with the excellence of individuals. In my opinion, this unwillingness to confront the excellence of social groups is tightly bound to the trait orientation of conceptions of giftedness. The composition of groups is often subjected to rapid modification and is thereby ill suited to the search for explanations that are based on stable factors.

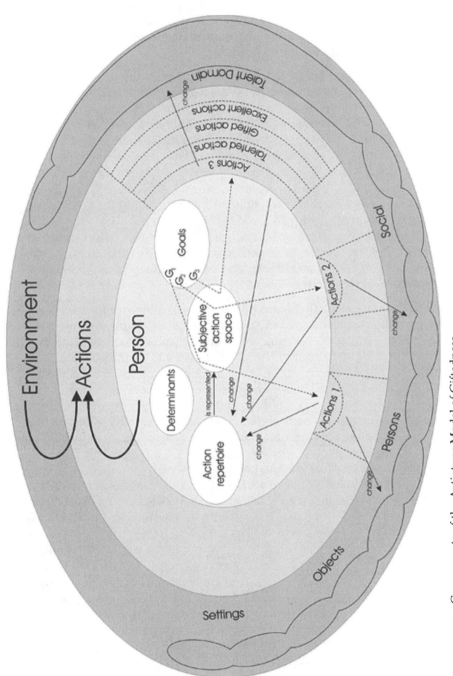

FIGURE 23.1. Components of the Actiotope Model of Giftedness.
Note: Interactions and functions were limited to a subset.

Actions. Excellence refers to a specific quality of actions. For this reason, we need to take a closer look at some important attributes of actions. The three-dimensional organization is striking:

- They have a *phase structure*, that is, they consist of a sequence of partial actions. From the perspective of the observing scientist, this is expressed as the well-known accordion effect (Davidson, 1990). The action in question can be described in either wide terms or tight terms, similar to how an accordion can either be pulled wide apart or squeezed tightly together.
- They are actually a composition of *parallel or multiple actions*. A simple example of this is found in the feat of playing the piano, which we often describe as a single action. Actually, several actions are occurring in parallel: the movements of the fingers, a monitoring of the notes being played, enjoying the self-produced music, and so on.
- They require *regulations on several levels* (e.g., the correct execution of motor, cognitive, auditory, and other activities; effort and intensity; the capacity to cope with negative effects; and examination of whether the desired effect was attained).

The three-dimensionality has a phenomenal significance for the *specification analysis* of efficient actions. An example: Let us assume that we want to determine which actions a later world master in chess will need to have. Trivially, he or she will need to win more chess matches than the toughest challengers. Do we hence want to consider a chess match itself as the action element to be placed under analysis? Or do we need to deconstruct a chess match into an opening, middle, and end game? Or are we interested in the individual moves themselves? Obviously, the quality of our results is dependent on the specification analysis and a functional subdivision of the phase structure.

Which actions are to be executed in parallel; which should never be executed in parallel? What abilities does the execution of these actions require? In a game of chess, one must be able to mentally foresee a relatively long series of moves and also have the capability to compare and evaluate individual moves with the consequences with which they are associated. In all probability, a preeminent chess player is not in the position to simultaneously enjoy any form of aesthetic pleasure because it may well reduce the player's level of concentration. And concentration is one of the most important factors a chess player must be able to regulate during a match.

In summary, the specification analysis of efficient actions requires, first, the selection of a functional description of the phase structure of the actions; second, a specification of the action to be executed; and, third, a specification of the regulations of the actions at hand. Only then can an adequate appraisal be made of whether a person will ever be in the position to execute these actions.

Action Repertoire. What we understand by action repertoire are the objectively sustainable *possibilities* for action persons have at their disposal, in other words, all the actions persons are capable of executing when (a) they consider engaging in this possible action in a subjective action space (see the Subjective Action Space section), (b) they formulate a corresponding goal (see the Goals section) and (c) the composition of the environment permits the execution of this action (see the Environment section).

Of extraordinarily high scientific interest are the intrapersonal determinants of the action repertoire. In fact, the greater part of the conceptions of giftedness is almost exclusively concerned with these factors, for example genetic factors (Thompson & Plomin, 2000) or cognitive abilities (Sternberg, 1986). If one takes further areas of excellence into consideration, such as artistic abilities, then determinants such as perceptual abilities and motor skills win a high level of significance. In general, most models of giftedness can be integrated into the Actiotope Model of Giftedness at this point as *subtheories.*

However, one must be well aware of the hazard that these subtheories usually are, at best, very general theories about the conditions of excellent actions. In some cases, this may suffice, and a limitation in the number of variables is of course simpler and more convenient when one can be content with rough prognoses or has other practical grounds. However, the call for detailed scientific consideration of excellence in a specific domain requires a fundamental specification analysis of the abilities considered to be excellent. This is the only basis on which the determinants of the required actions can be soundly specified.

Subjective Action Space. To be able to deliberate actions, generate meaningful intentions, execute actions, and so forth there must be a psychological entity that represents the action opportunities available to a person. This point of view is not new to psychology. Expectancy value models of motivation (Heckhausen, 1991), for example, assume that prior to the development of an intention, possible actions are subjected to assessment. Meanwhile, elaborate models have also been published on anticipative action control (Hoffmann & Sebald, 2000). This psychological entity is designated as the *subjective action space* in the Actiotope Model of Giftedness. Important here is that we are not speaking of an entity that corresponds to a material substrate of the human brain. The subjective action space is much better understood as a functional unit with a system character, whereby these functions are to be seen as real.

The conceptual roots of the subjective action space can be traced back to the construct of problem space. This can be seen as the universe of all possible steps to solve a problem that an individual can theoretically navigate. The subjective action space of a person can also be seen as the universe of possible action steps and actions a person can anticipate traversing in the planning and regulation of an action.

This action space is termed *subjective* because it is a personal construct that doesn't necessarily have to be in agreement with reality. In a specific situation, individuals may either overestimate or underestimate their action repertoire. When we look, for example, to studies of girls gifted in mathematics, science, and technology, we find that they perceive a limited subjective action space, despite having demonstrated similar achievement levels (Zorman & David, 2000). Girls underestimate their competencies and are of the opinion that they have to apply more effort to attain the same degree of success as boys. They have lower control convictions and describe themselves, even at this early point in time, as being more helpless than their fellow students (Schober, 2002).

Goals. Human behavior is always engaged in the intention of attaining a specific goal (of course not always consciously), whereby several goals can be pursued with the same action. Goals have three main functions: They are involved in the selection of action alternatives, they energize actions, and they provide direction to the action being engaged prior to and during its execution as an orientation for regulation, for example, in the comparison of the action results attained so far with the result envisioned for the current action.

There have been numerous attempts to classify human goals. However, current research in this area is probably still rather far removed from a final classification system. For giftedness research, however, two clusters of goals seem to be of central importance. They are directed to:

- the development of excellence and
- the employment of an excellent action repertoire.

Ericsson (1998) assumes that only goals that aim to improve the current state of performance encourage the development of excellence. Our investigations have indeed demonstrated that, for example, musicians and chess players had accumulated a large amount of practice time without being able to demonstrate an improvement in their performances (Gruber, Weber, & Ziegler, 1996). They had been primarily pursuing the goal of using their abilities to generate the highest degree of pleasure possible from their activities.

In the utilization of an excellent action repertoire, goals may come into conflict with one another. When, for example, a violinist is pursuing the goal of leaving his audience with a good impression of himself over the course of a concert, he will apply less concentration to the musical expression of his craft.

Besides these two clusters of goals, numerous other approaches seem to be relevant for giftedness research and deserve much more attention. One example is theories on motivational orientations. Persons who are goal oriented with regard to learning attempt to expand on their competencies, to learn new things, and to understand new concepts. Persons who are goal oriented with regard to performance, in contrast, want to make a display of their successes and to conceal their failures. There are notable indications that a goal orientation toward learning is more advantageous to the learning process. On the other hand, one must keep in mind that goals also have an energizing component. From the perspective of endurance, when confronted with rather protracted learning processes, it may be beneficial to be able to demonstrate both orientations. More on this can be found in Ziegler, Heller, and Stachl (1998).

Environment. In Figure 23.1, the environment is represented by the designation of several of its central components, such as social actors, resources, and settings, the significance of which has already been indicated in the discussion of the development of excellence.[2] They can and should also be considered from the perspective of a system theory. Of particular importance for giftedness research is the section pertaining to the system environment, which constitutes the talent domain in Figure 23.1.

In the literature, a talent domain is usually seen as an action field, which, first, can be contrasted with other action fields; second, offers a standard of excellence; and third, must be "socially valuable" in some form or another (Ziegler & Heller, 2002). As much sense as these criteria must make from the perspective of a sociologist, from the perspective of a psychologist they are far from reasonable. What is, for example, the psychological definition of the concept of "socially valuable," or how can a psychologist who is interested in excellence distinguish between outstanding actions in socially valuable and less valuable action fields?

If one wants to approach a more meaningful definition of a talent domain, then the system character must be brought to light. Furthermore, it must be demonstrated that this system interacts with the Actiotope of an individual; this means the action repertoire, the subjective action space, the goals, and finally the actions *in* this domain. Only the area in which these interactions occur can define the action field in which a person may possibly have attained excellence, and this is designated the talent domain. For example, in most cases, it is rather easy to just say that someone

---

[2] Because of space limitations, suggestions on possible environmental structures are not discussed here. These explanations would have required a transdisciplinary discussion of the topic, which would have necessitated the introduction of additional concepts. The goal of this contribution is, however, to provide a wide range of readers with a discernible overview of the Actiotope Model of Giftedness, whereby formal abstract representations are avoided and the application of system-theory–based terminology will be accordingly limited.

has attained a level of excellence in physics. Although she may really be a brilliant theoretical physicist, she may just be an average experimental physicist. If we want to be able to scientifically describe the excellence of such a person, we need to pay attention to such details. Important indicators of the individual talent domain of a person can be found in their learning or the successive enhancements of their Actiotope.

The definition of a talent domain from individual and system-based perspectives does not, however, mean that its objective structure can be neglected. This borders on the success and efficiency of human behavior. This objective structure is of extraordinary significance from the perspective of giftedness research. It permits (1) an at least rudimentary analysis of the universe of possible actions contained in an environmental system, and (2) the establishment of a relationship between the current action competencies of individuals and their developmental potential. Well-known examples can be found in the world of athletics (cf. Ericsson et al., 1993), where analyses have been able to reveal which physical body measurements would be ideal for the optimal execution of important movements for sports such as cycling or rowing.

The rapid alteration of domains is another reason why the analysis of the objective structure of a talent domain and the postulation of the characteristics of efficient action are so important. One can, for example, well imagine that a grand master in the game of chess, who is a specialist at a specific opening, is capable of finding a way to refute this very same opening. In an extreme case, he may well lose his claim to excellence because he is inferior to his opponents in the other opening systems, which he now must draw on. This example is also a good illustration of the systemic networking and the diverse kinds of feedback that are prominent in the area of excellence.

Interactions Among the Components of the Actiotope

The components of an Actiotope compose a system that is distinguished by manifold interactions among these components. For example, alterations in the goals being pursued sometimes have very reticulate effects on the other components, and the resulting reactions in turn have an effect on the development of goals. One might easily be prone to assume that the Actiotope as a system is primarily in a constant quest for *equilibrium*. This is, in fact, the case in many areas, but *not* in the development of excellence in a talent domain.

Individuals attempt – as do all living systems – in the process of preservation and maintenance of well-being to keep several types of equilibriums in balance; for example, in the procurement of nutrition or the contentment of social relationships and their emotional states. However, individuals who attain excellence effectively adapt their Actiotope to the talent domain. The achievement level that they want to attain is always higher than that which has just been reached. The Actiotope of an individual who is pursuing excellence is a dynamic, ceaselessly evolving system. Therefore, it is permanently being *removed* from its state of equilibrium. In this process, the Actiotope must, on the one hand, demonstrate enough flexibility to enable change, but also retain enough stability to be in the position to successfully implement these modifications and transformations. The development of an Actiotope can therefore be described as a type of a complex adaptive system, whereby the development of excellence represents "the product of progressive adaptations" (Holland, 1995, p. 29).

A progressive adaptation is based on five points, which play a particularly central role for promotion of excellence:

(1) The individual must realize when an action has been successful for the attainment of a goal. Young violinists who have never been told that they are playing cleanly will probably never be able to recognize this themselves and will have little chance of being able to attain excellence in this domain.

(2) Many studies show that knowledge remains inert. Although declarative (knowledge of facts) and procedural (knowledge of how to act) knowledge can be acquired, this is not necessarily the case for conditional knowledge (Mandl & Gerstenmaier, 2000). Individuals must also be able to recognize situations in which the implementation of this action will generate success.

(3) Individuals must be able to generate variations of actions within their subjective action space and be able to make explicit selections from their action repertoire. In the first place, this is necessary to be able to act successfully in altered environments. In the second place, the generation of action variants is also of extreme importance for the development of excellence, because they compete with one another in an evolutionary process governed by the survival of the fittest action. This is of particular importance when our instructional knowledge is insufficient and we leave the learners to find out on their own which of their action variants is the most successful.

(4) To remain adaptive, the Actiotope must not only be reactive, but also anticipative. If specific actions were successful in previous environments, there is no guarantee that this will also be the case in future environments. In our educational institutions, curricula support individuals in the acquisition of anticipative competencies. For example, psychology students attend courses to acquire statistical skills long before they are in the position to conduct their first investigative studies.

(5) Individuals must have effective feedback and feed-forward loops (in some instances, also recursive) at their disposal in the talent domain,

so that adaptations are just as feasible as reorganizations. It has already been mentioned how important adequate feedback is and how feedback loops are employed to bring forward the acquisition of competence for the execution of an action. This can also – at least in part – be attained by the individual himself in the form of self-regulated learning processes (Stoeger & Ziegler, in press). In many cases, however, the assistance of competent persons is needed, such as teachers, parents, and coaches, who meticulously work on weaknesses and faults with their protégés, often over a period of several years (Ericsson et al., 1993).

An important characteristic of the interactions within complex adaptive systems is the coevolution and coadaptation of their components. In older conceptions of giftedness, the development of excellence was understood by and large as being autocatalytic. If the environment (and to some degree also traits such as motivation) does not stand in the way of the gifts, excellence will somehow find a way to develop (e.g., Terman, 1925). Gagné (2003), in contrast, accords a more active role to the environment and various intrapersonal catalytic factors for the development of excellence. His concept of catalysts, borrowed from the field of chemistry, assumes that catalysts can either stimulate or inhibit processes, but cannot be changed by these processes themselves. In the Actiotope Model of Giftedness, in contrast, it is explicitly assumed that the individual components of the Actiotope must coevolve. During the learning process, individuals explore a huge space of possibilities in their subjective action space. Some of these possibilities are selected for execution. These can also effect changes in the action repertoire if the action permits learning. The subjective action space and the goals must now be coadapted so that new actions can be executed. If a learning goal has been reached, the action repertoire has evolved. More challenging learning goals must now be developed to spur on the learning process. To attain these new goals, new possibilities for action must be generated in the subjective action space or through instruction. In this manner, new openings to higher levels of complexity of actions are made accessible. However, the learning environment itself must also evolve. Sometimes, a complete change of the environment is necessary when an environmental system can no longer respond to the expanding action repertoire of an individual and the interactions are no longer conducive to learning. Familiar examples from everyday life include the movement from high school to university, the change of coaches of a professional sport team, or skipping a grade in school.

The break-off of interactions within a specific environmental system leads to nonlinear changes in the Actiotope. However, nonlinear changes can also be the result of increasing complexity. By way of illustration, learning experiences are processed and filtered at different levels and proceed, for example, from sensation and perception through cognition and conception to reflection. Complex adaptive systems can therefore also be described as "adaptive nonlinear networks" (Holland, 1995), in that several systems interact with one another and produce sudden, emergent changes in the Actiotope.

EDUCATION

It must first be maintained that, although excellence can represent an important goal in the upbringing of an individual, above and beyond this there are more momentous goals one can pursue, such as autonomy, tolerance, or the capacity to assume social responsibility. Excellence can exist as one goal among many, and other goals should not suffer under the promotion of excellence, but rather should also be advanced through this encouragement. Regrettably, because of space limitations I cannot present a model of integrated, systemic education at this time. Instead, I concentrate on some of the important specifics inherent in an educational process focused on excellence.

In the Actiotope Model of Giftedness, 11 clusters of educational goals are postulated, of which 4 are related to the components of the Actiotope, 5 to the advancement of the adaptability of the Actiotope, and 2 to the Actiotope as a system. To make these goals more concrete, educators need to be in the possession of specific knowledge that enables them to make optional adjustments with respect to the Actiotope of the individual. To simplify matters, we will assume that this knowledge (e.g., specification analysis of excellent actions, awareness of educational methods conducive to an effective action repertoire) is manifest. In the enumeration of these points, we limit ourselves to short comments that should make the core ideas of these points discernible.

(1) Among the methods with which the *action repertoire and its determinants* can be advanced, one includes the techniques already known to support the competencies needed in the execution of actions (e.g., motor actions, cognitive operations, socially competent behavior, knowledge access), such as instruction and modeling. In addition, one needs to include promotional methods that can encourage the potential determinants of the action repertoire, such as intelligence, concentration, or creativity.

(2) In the first place, the subjective *action space* must be a representation of effective action alternatives, and ineffective alternatives must be weeded out. In the second place, realistic assessments of the action alternatives must be enabled. In particular, goals such as the improvement of self-efficacy must be pursued. In the third place, because actions are also coordinated and directed in the subjective action space, the regulation of actions – such as an improvement in self-regulated learning – are further meaningful facets of this goal cluster.

(3) Each and every *goal* should be mediated, which enables an optimal evolution of the Actiotope with respect to excellence. Furthermore, should

such dysfunctional goals surface, as, for example, those demonstrated by the phenomenon of perfectionism, they should be eliminated.

(4) A learning *environment* must be prepared, which enables an optimal development of the Actiotope with respect to excellence. Repressive influences exerted by the environment (such as noise when one desires to study) must be disabled.

(5) A standard must be mediated with which the individual will be able to *identify efficient and inefficient actions* (violinists must be able to sense when they are playing cleanly or not). Professional feedback must be made available when the individual is not able to do this for himself or herself.

(6) To enable the *identification of situations for the execution of efficient actions*, conditional knowledge must be meditated (Mandl & Gerstenmaier, 2000).

(7) To be able to *generate action variants*, the individual must be able to apply his knowledge in the most diverse of situations. Possible methods of encouraging this have been developed by proponents of the cognitive flexibility approach (Spiro, Feltovich, Jacobson, & Coulson, 1991).

(8) The advancement of an *anticipative Actiotope* has many facets, which can best be depicted through three examples: (i) An individual must be prepared to execute an action under new circumstances. Here, the storage of signals that give rise to specific actions on a conceptual instead of perceptual level can be helpful. (ii) Individuals may find themselves in situations in which they cannot effectively process new information, a function that is vital for the evolution of their Actiotope. Here, the mediation of learning strategies could be of service. (iii) An individual must also be able to cope with learning setbacks. To maintain the pursuit of goals and to avoid the surfacing of resignation, the mediation of coping strategies is a sensible strategy.

(9) *Effective feedback and feed-forward loops in the talent domain* can be attained through learning sequences that consist of cycles of instruction, actions, and feedback.

(10) A chess player who has been playing in the same class for several years, who is satisfied with the level of performance he has attained, who really just wants to enjoy playing his game and for this reason no longer expands his Actiotope is a prime example of the equilibrium-like state of an Actiotope. The expansion of an Actiotope, in contrast, is a process that always brings about a *disruption in the state of equilibrium*. Often, impulses must be given to activate these developments and to assist in their maintenance. One must, however, keep in mind that permanent adaptations could lead to the destabilization of an individual's Actiotope (see following discussion). Consequently, there seem to be limitations on the amount of effective daily learning an individual can endure. Furthermore, an

individual may very well need assistance in managing the tempo with which an Actiotope is expanded, or else the individual may suffer the consequences of excessive demand or fatigue.

(11) An adaptive system that is as complex as a developing Actiotope necessitates sufficient *stability* to be able to successfully execute modifications and transformations. In addition to the previously mentioned temporal management of development, one needs to pay attention to the *coadaptation* of the individual components. My personal hypothesis is that such a-synchronies in the development of the components of an Actiotope provide far better explanations as to why many talents never reach excellence than what is offered by personality traits such as intelligence. The following are all examples that corroborate the necessity of systemic encouragement: peers who develop feelings of envy, teachers who experience threats to their self-esteem, a subjective action space in which the required learning actions are not adequately represented, and the failure of the goals to adjust to the improved action repertoire.

IDENTIFICATION

The Actiotope Model of Giftedness refutes the dominating view that gifts or talents are attributes of a person. For this reason, and in direct contrast to alternative approaches to the identification of giftedness, the goal is not to categorize *persons* as gifted, but rather to identify a *learning path* for an individual that leads to excellence. Two points are taken under closer inspection. First, analog to the normally posed question of whether individuals can be differentiated qualitatively (talents, gifted persons), the question of whether one can identify meaningful phases in the development of an Actiotope is discussed. Second, some criteria that are important for identification in a practical setting are depicted.

What Is Meant by Excellent, Talented, and Gifted?

We define excellence as the state of an Actiotope that is characterized by particularly effective actions.[3] Excellence is thereby a term that refers inherently to performances, rather than to the potential for astounding learning. Therefore, excellence is identified by outstanding actions. This is no trivial task, as seen, for example, in the difficulties experienced by talent scouts who look for and identify the proper players for professional sports leagues around the world.

---

[3] I am concerned here with individuals. In an analog characterization of the excellence of groups, the term *Actiotope* would have to have been replaced by the term *Sociotope* in this passage.

In their meta-theory of giftedness, Ziegler and Heller (2002) examine two earlier phases that are more important for identification in practice. The first phase encompasses the prenatal and early-childhood developmental phase through to the attainment of a critical state, a point from which one can expect an evolution of the Actiotope to excellence to be plausible. During the period of time prior to the attainment of the critical state, individuals could become conspicuous by exhibiting particularly quick learning progress or precocious achievement. Their actions can be labeled as being *talented*. The actions of a person whose Actiotope has reached a critical state are described as being *gifted*. Although we are talking about persons when we assess if someone is in the talented, gifted, or excellent phase, as a matter of fact we are describing *our* subjective assessment as diagnosticians of whether a person can *possibly* realize excellence (talented), will *probably* realize excellence (gifted), or has *already* realized excellence (excellent).

The assessment of which phase the Actiotope of a person is currently in can only be made on the basis of current knowledge concerning the level of achievement development in a specific talent domain. Even among persons who are outstanding, an appraisal needs to be conducted to determine whether normal persons would be capable of attaining the same high level of achievement under optimal training conditions. It may very well be the case that no persons can be found to be in the excellent phase in a specific domain because the performance level in this domain is rather low and just about every person who is active in the domain is capable of attaining this level of performance. It may, however, also be true that despite incredibly impressive achievements in a domain, actions will not be recognized as excellent, as exemplified by the competence of being able to use correct grammar when speaking. All persons are capable of attaining this impressive accomplishment within the framework of a normal development. In this case, the concept of excellence must be transferred to a species. Consequently, a figure as to how many persons attain or are capable of attaining excellence in a specific domain – 1:100, 1:1,000, 1:10,000 – is not one that can be rigidly fixed a priori for all domains.

A related question of considerable practical importance is that of who, with the best promotional support, we can expect to find among the group of the best achievers in a specific area, that is, who the experts will be. To answer this question, one can obviously use the Actiotope Model of Giftedness and the identification processes that are founded on its principles. However, it makes no sense at all that a conception of giftedness should be able to answer questions like, "What is the percentage of gifted mathematicians?" or, "What is the percentage of gifted cooks?" in a population. Rather, the giftedness researcher who wants to help should reply, "How many cooks do you need?"

Central Criteria for Practical Identification

Ziegler and Stoeger (in press) have presented a method of identification in their ENTER Model, which permits diagnoses on the basis of the Actiotope Model of Giftedness. The methodological process is constructed in a manner that assesses not only the actual state (e.g., momentary IQ score), but also examines the dynamic of the development of the entire Actiotope. This includes the components of the Actiotope and opportunities to increase the adaptability of the Actiotope, as well as the Actiotope as a system. This information is considered in relation to the goal of the identification at hand. A few examples may be:

- The attainment of excellence; here, one needs to make use of a specification analysis and, on the basis of existing theoretical knowledge, make an assessment on whether an individual will ever be in the position to execute these tasks.
- Skipping a grade; here, one needs to assess whether the Actiotope is already developed enough, or will be sufficiently developed, so that the action demands that will be made in the class that the student will now enter can be properly fulfilled.

In the ENTER Model, five steps are suggested for the identification process. The name of the model is an acronym made up of the first letters of the terms *explore, narrow, test, evaluate,* and *review.* In the first step, explore, the Actiotope is examined. The second step, narrow, concentrates on the Actiotope in the talent domain. In the third step, test, identification is concerned with the learning path that leads to the goal of the identification at hand. In the fourth step, evaluate, an evaluation is made to determine whether the aim of the identification has been attained, and in the fifth step, review, the significance of the aim of the identification is analyzed within the entire adaptation of the Actiotope, whereby the psychological theories applied in the prognosis are also placed under examination (for details and specific application, see Ziegler & Stoeger, in press).

CONCLUSIONS

At the outset of the chapter, it was pointed out that the concepts of *gifts* and *talents* have their origins in mythology, theology, and metaphysics. The main reason for their adoption into science was the compulsion to find explanatory concepts for the phenomenon that some persons attain a level of efficiency in a specific domain that normally cannot be achieved, even with extreme learning efforts and the best of support. To explain this phenomenon, the Actiotope Model of Giftedness places the focus on the actions of an individual and their evolution. The development of excellence is understood as an adaptation of a dynamic system, which intensifies in complexity through interactions with the objective structure of a domain, whereby with increasing excellence, the individual will also increasingly effect changes in the objective structure of the domain itself. This chapter considered the coadaptation and coevolution of the components of the Actiotope, such as the action repertoire and its determinants, goals, subjective action space, and environment, as well as the interaction of these components within a network. Gifts and talents, which are traditionally understood as attributes of an individual, therefore, have several mothers and fathers. It is now time to recognize them by their true names. It is also time to give their talented children the chance to attain excellence by providing them with an individually tailored promotion of their *entire* Actiotope.

References

Davidson, D. (1990). *Handlung und Ereignis* [Action and event]. Frankfurt, Germany: Suhrkamp.

DeHaan, R. G., & Havighurst, R. J. (1957). *Educating the gifted*. Chicago: University of Chicago Press.

Ericsson, K. A. (Ed.). (1996). *The road to excellence: The acquisition of expert performance in the arts and sciences, sports, and games*. Mahwah, NJ: Lawrence Erlbaum Associates.

Ericsson, K. A. (1998). The scientific study of expert levels of performance: General implications for optimal learning and creativity. *High Ability Studies, 9*, 75–100.

Ericsson, K. A., Krampe, R. T., & Tesch-Römer, C. (1993). The role of deliberate practice in the acquisition of expert performance. *Psychological Review, 100*, 363–406.

Gagné, F. (2000). Understanding the complex choreography of talent development through DMGT-based analysis. In K. A. Heller, F. J. Mönks, R. J. Sternberg, & R. Subotnik (Eds.), *International handbook for research on giftedness and talent* (2nd ed., pp. 67–79). Oxford, England: Pergamon.

Gagné, F. (2003). Transforming gifts into talents: The DMGT as a developmental theory. In N. Colangelo & G. A. Davis (Eds.), *Handbook of gifted education* (3rd ed., pp. 60–74). Boston: Allyn & Bacon.

Gardner, H. (1983/1994). *Frames of mind: The theory of multiple intelligences*. New York: Basic Books.

Gollwitzer, P., Heckhausen, H., & Steller, B. (1990). Deliberative and implemental mind-sets: Cognitive tuning toward congruous thoughts and information. *Journal of Personality and Social Psychology, 59*, 1119–1127.

Gruber, H., Weber, A., & Ziegler, A. (Eds.). (1996). *Expertiseforschung* [Expertise research]. Opladen, Germany: Westdeutscher Verlag.

Heckhausen, H. (1991). *Motivation and action*. New York: Springer.

Hoffmann, J., & Sebald, A. (2000) Antizipative Verhaltenskontrolle [Anticipative behavior control]. In J. Moeller, B. Strauss, S. Juergensen (Eds.), *Psychologie und Zukunft. Prognosen, Prophezeiungen, Plaene* (pp. 125–147). Goetttingen, Germany, Hogrefe.

Holland, J. H. (1995). *Hidden order*. Reading, MA: Helix.

Howe, M. J. A., Davidson, J. W., & Sloboda, J. A. (1998). Innate talents: Reality or myth? *Behavioral and Brain Sciences, 21*, 399–442.

Kauffman, S. (1995). *At home in the universe: The search for the laws of self-organization and complexity*. Oxford, England: Oxford University Press.

Kelly, K. (1994). *Out of control*. New York: Addison-Wesley.

Mandl, H. & Gerstenmaier, J. (Eds.). (2000). *Die Kluft zwischen Wissen und Handeln. Empirische und theoretische Loesungsansaetze* [The gap between knowledge and action. Empirical and theoretical approaches]. Goettingen, Germany: Hogrefe.

Margolin, L. (1994). *Goodness personified. The emergence of gifted children*. New York: Aldine de Gruyter.

Marsh, H. W. (1987). The big-fish-little-pond effect on academic self-concept. *Journal of Educational Psychology, 79*, 280–295.

Mönks, F. J. (1992). Development of gifted children: The issue of identification and programming. In F. J. Mönks, & W. A. M. Peters (Eds.), *Talent for the future* (pp. 191–202). Assen, The Netherlands: Van Gorcum.

Mönks, F. J., & Mason, E. J. (2000). Developmental psychology and giftedness: Theories and research. In K. A. Heller, F. J. Mönks, R. Sternberg, & R. Subotnik (Eds.), *International handbook of research and development of giftedness and talent* (2nd ed., pp. 141–156). Oxford, England: Pergamon.

Qin, Y., & Simon, H. A. (1990) Laboratory replication of scientific discovery processes. *Cognitive Science, 14*, 281–312.

Renzulli, J. S. (1986). The three-ring conception of giftedness: A developmental model for creative productivity. In R. J. Sternberg & J. E. Davidson (Eds.), *Conceptions of giftedness* (pp. 53–92). New York: Cambridge University Press.

Schneider, W. (2000). Giftedness, expertise, and (exceptional) performance: A developmental perspective. In K. A. Heller, F. J. Mönks, R. J. Sternberg, & R. Subotnik (Eds.), *International handbook for research on giftedness and talent* (2nd ed., pp. 165–177). Oxford, England: Pergamon.

Schober, B. (2002). *Entwicklung und Evaluation des Münchner Motivationstrainings* [Development and evaluation of the Munich Motivational Training]. Regensburg, Germany: Roderer.

Simonton, D. K. (1994). *Greatness: Who makes history and why*. New York: Guilford.

Simonton, D. K. (2000). Genius and giftedness: Same or different? In K. A. Heller, F. J. Mönks, R. Sternberg, & R. Subotnik (Eds.), *International handbook of research and development of giftedness and talent* (2nd ed., pp. 111–122). Oxford, England: Pergamon.

Spiro, R. J., Feltovich, P. J., Jacobson, M. J., & Coulson, R. L. (1991). Cognitive flexibility, constructivism, and hypertext: Random access instruction for advanced knowledge acquisition in ill-structured domains. *Educational Technology, 31*, 24–33.

Sternberg, R. J. (1986). A triarchic theory of intellectual giftedness. In R. J. Sternberg & J. E. Davidson (Eds.), *Conceptions of giftedness* (pp. 223–243). New York: Cambridge University Press.

Sternberg, R. J. (2003). WICS as a model of giftedness. *High Ability Studies, 14*, 109–138.

Stoeger, H., & Ziegler, A. (in press). Evaluation of an elementary classroom self-regulated learning program for gifted math underachievers. *International Education Journal*.

Tannenbaum, A. (1983). Giftedness: A psychosocial approach. In Sternberg, R. J., & Davidson, J. E. (Eds.), *Conceptions of giftedness* (pp. 21–52). Cambridge, England: Cambridge University Press.

Terman, L. M. (1925). *Genetic studies of genius: Vol. 1. Mental and physical traits of a thousand gifted children.* Stanford, CA: Stanford University Press.

Thompson, L. A., & Plomin, R. (2000). Gentic tools for exploring individual differences in intelligence. In K. A. Heller, F. J. Mönks, R. Sternberg, & R. Subotnik (Eds.), *International handbook of research and development of giftedness and talent* (2nd ed., pp. 157–164). Oxford, England: Pergamon.

Trost, G. (2000). Prediction of excellence in school, university, and work. In K. A. Heller, F. J. Mönks, R. Sternberg, & R. Subotnik (Eds.), *International handbook of research and development of giftedness and talent* (2nd ed., pp. 317–330). Oxford, England: Pergamon.

Von Cranach, M., & Bangerter, A. (2000). Wissen und Handeln in systemischer Perspektive: Ein komplexes Problem [Knowledge and action from a systemic view: A complex problem]. In H. Mandl & Gerstenmaier, J. (Eds.), *Die Kluft zwischen Wissen und Handeln. Empirische und theoretische Loesungsansaetze* (pp. 221–252). Goettingen, Germany: Hogrefe.

Ziegler, A., & Heller, K. A. (2000). Conceptions of giftedness: A meta-theoretical perspective. In K. A. Heller, F. J. Mönks, R. Sternberg, & R. Subotnik (Eds.), *International handbook of research and development of giftedness and talent* (2nd ed., pp. 3–22). Oxford, England: Pergamon.

Ziegler, A., Heller, K. A., & Stachl, S. (1998). Comparison of the general school related motivational set of average, gifted and highly gifted boys or girls. *Gifted and Talented International, 13,* 58–65.

Ziegler, A., & Stoeger, H. (in press). The ENTER Model for the Identification of Talented Persons. *Psychology Science*.

Zorman, R., & David, H. (2000). *Female achievement and challenges toward the third millennium.* Jerusalem, Israel: Henrietta Szold Institute.

24

The Scientific Study of Giftedness

Richard E. Mayer

As you look at the crisp night sky, you see that one star stands out — brighter than all others. Perhaps, so it is with giftedness: As you look into a classroom, you see that one student stands out – brighter than all others. Although astrophysicists can explain the nature of an extraordinary star, psychologists continue to struggle with how to conceptualize giftedness. *Conceptions of Giftedness* provides an up-to-date and diverse collection of ideas about what giftedness is and how gifted students should be educated.

There are many ways to conceptualize giftedness, ranging from practical conceptualizations based on years of experience in working with gifted students to political conceptualizations based on moral principles. However, the distinguishing feature of the scientific study of giftedness is that theories are tested against evidence that has been collected using sound methodologies. The theme of this chapter is that there is value in the scientific study of giftedness, that is, in using an evidence-based approach to assessing the usefulness of various theories of giftedness and in assessing the effects of various academic programs for gifted students.

FIVE QUESTIONS ABOUT GIFTEDNESS

In the book's introduction, the editors – Robert J. Sternberg and Janet E. Davidson – begin by listing five questions about giftedness that each author was asked to answer. I attempt to answer the five questions – which are listed in Table 24.1 – based on work presented in these chapters. Then, I briefly offer my opinion concerning future directions for the field.

What Is Giftedness?

Although the authors differ on how to define giftedness, they often agree on the dimensions along which the definition must fit. The top portion

TABLE 24.1. *Five Questions About Giftedness*

Question	Tentative (Short) Answer
1. What is giftedness?	Extraordinary achievement in a field
Is giftedness general or specific?	Specific
Is giftedness potential or achieved?	Achieved
Is giftedness learned or innate?	Both
Are noncognitive factors involved in giftedness?	Yes, such as determination and commitment
Is giftedness based on racism, sexism, or elitism?	No
2. How do conceptions of giftedness differ from one another?	On each of the points listed above (in Question 1)
3. How should gifted individuals be identified?	Accomplishment in the upper 5 percent of peers
4. How should gifted individuals be instructed in school and elsewhere?	Acceleration
5. How should the achievement of gifted individuals be assessed?	Compare programs' effects on student performance in randomized experiments

of Table 24.1 lists some questions for framing the debate concerning the definition of giftedness.

Is Giftedness General or Specific? First, is giftedness general or specific, that is, are people gifted in general or only with respect to a specific domain? The consensus among the contributors is that giftedness is specific. For example, Cross and Coleman state that "to be gifted means gifted at something"; Feldhusen notes that giftedness "must be in a particular domain"; Robinson calls for viewing giftedness with respect to what is "required by essential core curriculum"; Plucker and Barab define giftedness as extraordinary achievement "within a specific context"; Monks and Katzko define giftedness as exceptional achievements "in one or more domains"; von Karolyi and Winner define giftedness as exceptional ability "in any domain"; and Brody and Stanley define giftedness as "advanced mental age in specific areas." In particular, many contributors focus on giftedness within academic domains, which Cross and Coleman call "school-based conceptions of giftedness"; Renzulli calls "schoolhouse giftedness," and Robinson calls "academic giftedness."

Although many contributors focus on giftedness in specific school subjects, some offer a broader vision that includes creative production as either a complement or alternative to academic giftedness. For example, Renzulli distinguishes between two types of giftedness – "schoolhouse giftedness" and "creative–productive giftedness," whereas Callahan and Miller make a similar distinction between "academic activism and problem-solving innovators." Going somewhat further, Runco argues that creativity and originality are the defining features of a gifted person, and Cross and Coleman state that "giftedness is a combination of advanced development and creativity." In spite of these more inclusive conceptions, the dominant conception of giftedness presented in this collection is that giftedness should be defined with respect to specific domains, particularly school subjects. Given that the field of giftedness research is still striving to emerge as a scientifically rigorous field of study, I agree that it makes sense to focus initially on the study of giftedness in specific academic disciplines.

Is Giftedness Potential or Achieved? Perhaps the most contentious definitional issue concerns whether giftedness refers to potential – the ability to attain high achievement in the future – or achievement – demonstrated high performance in the present. On the side of potential, Monks and Katzko define giftedness as "an individual's potential for exceptional or outstanding achievement . . . " and VanTassel-Baska's definition includes the "promise for original contributions to a field." On the side of achievement, Plucker and Barab define giftedness as "extraordinary achievement," Ziegler defines giftedness in terms of "particularly effective actions," and Walberg and Paik argue that "accomplishment rather than potential is the best indication of giftedness."

Is there a compromise in which the definition of giftedness includes "evidence of potential as well as performance" (as suggested by VanTassel-Baska)? Cross and Coleman offer a compromise in which giftedness is "an age-specific term" that refers to potential for younger students and performance for older students. Similarly, Subotnik and Jarvin suggest three age-based stages of giftedness – an early stage in which ability develops into competence in a domain, a middle stage in which students demonstrate precocious achievement of expertise, and an adult stage marked by eminence in performance, such as scholarly productivity or artistic contribution. Thus, an interesting compromise that makes sense to me is to view giftedness as an age-specific term that refers to potential for the beginning stage, achievement for the intermediate stage, and eminence for the advanced stage.

The potential-versus-achieved debate is also reflected in the way that some scholars use "ability" or "talent" in their definitions of giftedness. For Robinson, giftedness involves "unusually high ability"; for Simonton, giftedness involves "exceptional abilities or capabilities"; and for Brody and Stanley, giftedness involves "exceptional ability." Such definitions appear to favor the potential view of giftedness because ability refers to the potential to learn and develop; however, in some cases, the scholars propose using achievement tests to measure these abilities, an approach that seems to favor the achieved view. A compromise is that giftedness is reflected in precocity – developing or learning at a faster rate than one's cohort. For example, Feldhusen notes that gifted students "learn rapidly and get far ahead of age mates," Cross and Coleman state that gifted students "have demonstrated rapid learning in comparison to peers," and von Karolyi and Winner observe that gifted students are "ahead of schedule in their interest and mastery of a particular domain." In my view, including precocity in the definition of giftedness – at least in the first stage – makes sense and offers a way of using observations of achievement as indications of gifted potential.

Is Giftedness Innate or Learned? A long-standing debate among gifted-ness researchers concerns whether gifted individuals are born or made. On the side of the innate view, from the very beginning in the 1800s, Galton (1869) argued that giftedness was inherited. Current proponents of the innate view include Simonton's claim that giftedness involves "natural endowment" that is "in some way innate." Similarly, von Karolyi and Winner reject the idea that giftedness depends mainly on sustained practice because precocity appears prior to practice. Robinson reports a study in which infants who were assessed to have high intelligence tended to achieve extremely high IQs as adults. On the side of the learned view, all of the authors recognize that people's experiences are crucial for their development as gifted individuals. For example, in Reis's case studies of 22 gifted American women, the distinguishing characteristics included nurturing families and childhood experiences that did not undermine self-confidence. Feldhusen notes that giftedness requires a large knowledge base that is achieved through sustained practice, and Walberg and Paik report on case studies of eminent people that show "huge advantages to starting a scientific career early."

A reasonable compromise is to acknowledge that giftedness depends on both natural endowment and life experiences – that is, giftedness is both innate and learned. The development of giftedness depends on appropriate experiences – including social support and a rich learning environment – as well as above average natural ability.

Are Noncognitive Factors Involved in Giftedness? Mainly on the basis of case studies of gifted people, many of the authors point to the role of noncognitive factors in fostering the development of giftedness. Reis notes that in a biographical study of 22 gifted American women, noncognitive factors such as intensity about one's work, belief in one's self, determination, and motivation were common themes. In a study of the biographies of eminent people, Walberg and Paik found that common traits were force of character, independence, and a tendency to "find books more interesting than people." Renzulli makes the case that task commitment (or diligence) is as important as intellectual ability and creativity in determining giftedness. von Karolyi and Winner claim that gifted students have a "rage to master" in their domain. In summary, there is ample reason to further investigate the idea that noncognitive factors – such as determination – play an important role in giftedness.

Is Giftedness Based on Racism, Sexism, and Elitism? Some of the authors raise the specter that racism, sexism, or elitism may be tied to the concept of giftedness. Borland argues that the fact that minority students are underrepresented in gifted programs is evidence that "the practice of gifted education is rife with inequities that have been extremely difficult to eliminate." According to Borland, the underrepresentation of poor children and children of color in gifted programs "perpetuates vicious inequities in our society." Gordon and Bridglall similarly call attention to the "under representation of students of color among populations of gifted students," but they also point to a gifted program that has been successful in recruiting such students. Reis observes that "fewer women than men achieve at levels that would enable them to be identified as gifted" and notes that the reasons for the discrepancy include "life events especially involving relationships with partners, loved ones, and children."

In contrast, Robinson argues that the underrepresentation problem reflects a larger social problem that is not unique to gifted programs: "We all regret the imbalance of racial, ethnic, and socioeconomic groups in special classrooms, but the solution requires the involvement of the whole society." In short, the fact that students show different levels of accomplishment does not in itself constitute evidence that gifted programs are inherently racist, sexist, or elitist. Instead, the guiding principle is that all students deserve the opportunity to develop to their full potential. Brody and Stanley note that all students do not achieve equally in all areas, even when they are given equal opportunities. Thus, the goal of gifted instruction as well as all education should be to help students develop as fully as they can.

Overall, giftedness can be defined as extraordinary achievement in a field. This definition is consistent with the idea that giftedness is specific rather than general, achieved rather than potential, both learned and innate, related to noncognitive factors such as determination, and not based on racism or sexism.

How Do Conceptions of Giftedness Differ from One Another?

The second section of Table 24.1 concerns differences among conceptions of giftedness. All authors point to difficulties in conceptualizing giftedness, but there appear to be three approaches to how to deal with the difficulties. In one camp, for example, are those who claim that the concept should be dropped altogether. Borland takes the hard stand that "the concept of the gifted child is logically, pragmatically, and morally untenable" and "the concept of giftedness has outlived whatever usefulness it once may have had." Robinson states that "the term *gifted* and the term *talented* have outlived their usefulness" and that "we have little consensus about what constitutes these concepts."

In another camp are those who note the overwhelming conflicts in conceptualizing giftedness. Freeman observes that "there are perhaps 100 definitions of giftedness around," whereas Monks and Katzko state that "a concise definition is almost impossible." Gagné adds that "conceptions abound and often contradict one another." In a particularly blatant example, Gagné points out that talent sometimes is used to mean the potential to become gifted, whereas at other times it is used to mean a gifted level of achievement or performance.

Finally, in a third camp are those who, although cognizant that the field is emerging, have attempted to offer useful conceptualizations. Renzulli, for example, recognizes that "we will always have several conceptualizations . . . of giftedness" but goes on to offer a "three-ring" conceptualization based on "above average mental ability, creativity, and task commitment."

I find myself in the third camp. In response to the first camp, I do not think it makes sense to ignore individual differences and especially to ignore the overwhelming evidence that people learn at different rates and to different levels of mastery. However, a careful reading of the critiques of the concept of giftedness suggests that the main criticism is not that people are all the same, but rather that there is not a hard-and-fast dividing line between the "gifted" and the "nongifted." In response to the second camp, I do not think it makes sense to give up on trying to understand giftedness just because it is a difficult task. Again, a careful reading of these critiques is not that we should give up, but rather that we should acknowledge the complexity of the issue. The third camp makes the most sense to me, and many of the authors have made progress in defining giftedness – as I document in the foregoing section.

How Should Gifted Individuals Be Identified?

Potential or Accomplishment. The third portion of Table 24.1 concerns how to identify gifted people. Monks and Katzko offer an important justification for finding an appropriate identification method: "If we follow the principle that everyone is to be given the opportunity to develop his/her full potential and talent, then identification is essential." In seeking to accomplish this goal, the authors tend to focus on two methods for identifying gifted individuals – potential and accomplishment. For example, Jeltova and Grigorenko distinguish between potential giftedness (i.e., potential) and actual giftedness (i.e., accomplishment).

On the one side are those who favor identifying gifted people on the basis of ability or achievement test scores. Potential (sometimes called talent) involves possessing outstanding natural abilities as measured by standardized test scores that place a student among the top of age-peers in a field. Cognitive ability tests – including intelligence tests – have been widely used to identify gifted individuals, including Terman's (1925) famous studies of gifted individuals. Robinson calls for "selecting students on the basis of cognitive abilities and skills" as measured by "traditional psychometric ability and achievement measures and other observations that are codified by objective criteria." Sternberg describes tests that measure cognitive abilities related to giftedness – namely, the Sternberg Triarchic Abilities Test. Similarly, Brody and Stanley identified gifted mathematics students on the basis of exceptionally high performance on mathematics and verbal achievement tests. Gagné noted that gifted individuals can be identified on the basis of talent, which can be defined as outstanding mastery of knowledge and skills that place a student among the top of age-peers in a field. Feldhusen notes that "high IQ" was one of the original measures of potential giftedness.

In contrast, on the other side are those who favor identifying gifted people on the basis of extraordinary performance. Accomplishment refers to the idea that gifted individuals exhibit extraordinary performance on some objective measure. In their youth, gifted people are precocious – showing extraordinary speed and commitment in mastering a domain – and, in adulthood, they are high achievers – showing extraordinary levels of productivity. For example, Jeltova and Grigorenko favor identifying gifted individuals based on performance on academic tasks compared with other students. An example of such an approach involves Olympiads – academic contests similar to spelling bees – in various scholarly disciplines, which are widely used in Russia. Heller, Perleth, and Lim explore the use of talent searches. Walberg and Paik call for objective measures of accomplishment in children (such as winning a science fair) and objective measures of eminence in adults (such as exceptional productivity in one's field). VanTassel-Baska calls for assessing performance using portfolio assessment or performance assessment, but others have criticized such measures for not being sufficiently reliable.

Several authors explicitly criticize standardized ability tests. Plucker and Barab argue that such tests "tell us very little about giftedness...because they examine behavior out of context." Cross and Coleman argue that "performance is the key" and state that they "would abandon the widespread use of ability measures in the identification of children who are gifted."

Is there a resolution to the apparent disagreement between assessment based on potential versus assessment based on accomplishment? In my opinion, the most convincing elements in both views are performance, domain specificity, and objectivity. The most useful measures of accomplishment focus on objective performance within a specific field – such as a high school student winning a science fair or an adult winning a Nobel Prize. The most useful measures of potential also focus on object performance within a specific domain – such as a middle school student scoring at the 98th percentile on a mathematics achievement test intended as a college entrance exam. In short, gifted individuals should be identified on the basis of extraordinary performance on authentic tasks. For children, extraordinary performance can be manifested as precocity in a field, and for adults, extraordinary performance can be manifested as productivity in a field.

How Should "Extraordinary" Be Operationalized? If giftedness is defined as extraordinary achievement in a field, then it is important to specify what level of achievement constitutes an extraordinary level. Most often, giftedness is defined as achievement in the upper 5 percent of one's cohort, although the percentage ranged from 1 to 20 percent among the chapter authors. On the conservative side, Robinson focuses on students whose scores are in the upper 1 percent to 3 percent in relation to peers, and Brody and Stanley focus on the upper 3 percent. On the liberal side, Gagné chooses to focus on the upper 10 percent and Gordon and Bridglall select the upper 15 percent. In between, Freeman defines "extraordinary" achievement as performing in the upper 5 to 10 percent in relation to one's peers, and Renzulli notes that the percentage used to characterize gifted achievement ranges from 1 to 20 percent in the literature. Thus, a reasonable compromise is to identify gifted students as those performing in the upper 5 percent of their cohort.

How Should Gifted Individuals Be Instructed in School and Elsewhere?

Acceleration versus Enrichment. The fourth section of Table 24.1 concerns gifted instruction. There is overwhelming consensus among the authors that gifted students need instruction that is accelerated and differentiated, that is, instruction at a faster rate and at a higher level than standard instruction. In contrast, the authors offer little support for instructional programs based on enrichment – in which gifted instruction is at the same rate as regular instruction, but offers extra activities. Cross and Coleman observe that "acceleration has been shown to be a stronger intervention for advanced development than enrichment." Based on their well-known program to teach "mathematically precocious youth," which serves thousands of students in 23 sites around the nation, Brody and Stanley rely on acceleration because "children learn at different rates" and "effective teaching involves a match between the child's readiness to learn and the level of content presented."

Gordon and Bridglall describe the Meyerhoff Scholars Program for gifted students, which includes acceleration as a key ingredient. VanTassel-Baska notes that gifted instruction should differ from regular instruction with respect to rate of instruction and complexity of the material.

Gifted instruction needs to be differentiated even among gifted students. Callahan and Miller propose that academic activists – extremely high-achieving students – need acceleration, whereas problem-solving innovators – extremely creative students – need highly challenging environments. Importantly, gifted instruction can help students who might not be labeled as gifted. Renzulli reports a study in which students in the upper 20 percent benefited just as much from gifted instruction as did those in the upper 5 percent.

In summary, the consensus is that gifted individuals should receive differentiated curriculum and instruction, relying on acceleration.

How Should the Achievement of Gifted Individuals Be Assessed?

The final section of Table 24.1 concerns how to assess the success of gifted students. Although many authors do not directly address this question, the responding authors seem to have reached consensus that the effectiveness of gifted programs should be assessed by measuring the learning outcomes of students who have been instructed in various programs. This answer has two important elements: (a) The independent variable should be the type of instructional method; and (b) the dependent measure should be objective measures of learning outcomes, such as performance on authentic tasks.

However, in spite of some agreement about the need for experimental assessments of gifted programs, there is also criticism that this need is not being adequately met. Freeman states that she "has not yet found a single scientific comparison between specified gifted programs." Borland claims that "there is little evidence that [gifted] programs are effective." Robinson notes: "There do not seem to exist the precise data we would wish" concerning "performance in academically rigorous programs for gifted students."

In short, gifted programs should be compared with each other using randomized experimental designs, with student performance on academic tasks as a major dependent measure.

WHERE DO WE GO FROM HERE?

I have been given the assignment of reviewing the chapters in this volume, with a goal of offering suggestions for how to move this field forward. On the positive side, the contributing authors of *Conceptions of Giftedness* offer important insights into the nature of giftedness and offer many recommendations for how to educate gifted students. The chapters in *Conceptions of*

TABLE 24.2. *What Is Needed and Not Needed in the Scientific Study of Giftedness*

Need Less Like This	Need More Like This
Vague and conflicting definitions	Consensus definitions
Unspecified measures	Straightforward objective measures
Broad, untestable models	Clear testable theories
Sweeping speculations	Conclusions based directly on evidence
Anecdotes	Valid scientific data
Descriptions of programs	Controlled evaluations of programs

Giftedness provide an overview of the state of research and theory on giftedness. The book shows that the study of giftedness is an old research area dating back to Galton's (1869) pioneering work in the 1800s, but that today, those studying giftedness are grappling to build a new research area that is coherent and sound. In my opinion, a major potential contribution of this book is to stimulate thinking and discussion about the nature of giftedness and how it can be studied scientifically.

On the negative side, the inconsistencies among the contributing authors highlight just how much work remains to be done. In my opinion, this book helps demonstrate the need for giftedness to continue to develop into a scientific field of study in which practical issues are addressed in the context of scientific evidence and testable theories. It is clear that everyone has opinions about giftedness and how it should be addressed in schools; however, for the field to continue to move forward, what is needed is to move from the realm of opinions and speculations to the realm of the scientific study of giftedness. My reading of the book indicates that there is much to be done in six major areas: creating consensus definitions, devising objective measures of giftedness, generating testable theories, drawing evidence-based conclusions, gathering scientifically reliable data, and conducting scientifically valid evaluations. Table 24.2 lists what is needed and what is not needed in the scientific study of giftedness.

First, what exactly do we mean by terms such as *gifted* and *talented*? Instead of generating definitions based on various philosophical perspectives, we need consensus definitions based on objective evidence and reasoned argument. In the foregoing section titled "What is giftedness?" I tried to make progress toward a consensus definition based on the idea that giftedness is exceptional performance in a particular domain. Such a definition may be useful because it can lead to objective measurements that have validity, particularly within authentic academic disciplines.

Second, how should we measure giftedness? Instead of unspecified measures of giftedness, we need straightforward measures of giftedness that are objective, valid, and reliable. In the foregoing section on how gifted individuals should be identified, I offered suggestions for how to create such measures of accomplishment based on the existing work in the field.

Third, how does giftedness happen? Instead of generating broad conceptual models that do not lead to testable predictions, what is needed are clear, testable theories of giftedness. Renzulli's three-ring model is an example of a long-term effort to achieve this goal, although more work is needed to clarify the underlying cognitive mechanisms.

Fourth, what do we know about giftedness? Instead of offering sweeping speculations and unsupported claims, we need conclusions based directly on scientific evidence. Many of the authors noted the need for basing educational practice on research evidence.

Fifth, how should giftedness be studied? Instead of anecdotes about gifted people, what is needed is valid scientific evidence. Carefully conducted case studies certainly have much to contribute, and several such studies are presented in this volume. However, hypothesis-based experimental tests based on relevant empirical data are hard to find.

Sixth, how should gifted students be taught? Instead of descriptions of gifted programs, what is needed is a commitment to conduct controlled evaluations of programs in which gifted programs are compared with each other and to conventional instruction. Several authors point out that the literature currently does not contain many such studies.

In summary, research on giftedness will advance to the degree that it matures as a scientific field of study. The characteristics of the scientific study of giftedness are that giftedness be clearly defined and measured, that theories of giftedness be clear and testable, that conclusions about how to identify and teach gifted students are based on evidence, that research methods that generate valid and reliable data are used, and that gifted programs are evaluated in controlled experimental trials.

References

Galton, F. (1869). *Hereditary genius*. London: Macmillan.

Terman, L. M. (1925). *Genetic studies of genius*. Stanford, CA: Stanford University Press.

Author Index

Subject Index

Figures are indicated by f, tables by t, and footnotes by n following page number.